The Law of Watercourses

VOLUME I

A Treatise on the Law of Watercourses

with

An Appendix

containing

Statutes of Flowing

and

Forms of Declarations

By

JOSEPH K. ANGELL

Seventh Edition

VOLUME I

BeardBooks
Washington, D.C.

Reprinted 2000 by Beard Books, Washington, D.C.

ISBN 1-893122-92-1

Printed in the United States of America

PREFACE

TO THE SEVENTH EDITION.

In the preparation of this, the seventh edition of "Angell on Watercourses," the editor has carefully examined and cited, and, where required, stated all the important and leading cases on the subject that have been published since the sixth edition was issued, in 1869. There have also been added in the Appendix various concise and convenient forms adapted to proceedings to obtain redress for injuries done to and by water and watercourses, — both proceedings at Common Law, and for damages under the Mill Acts. These forms have been collected from authentic and approved sources; and it is confidently believed they will prove useful to the profession in this department of the law. It has been deemed expedient and just towards the parties whose labors are embodied in this work as now published, that there should be some mark of distinction between the different parts of the volume which have been contributed by the author and by the editor. To this end, the additions made to the work by the editor, both in the text and notes, in this and the sixth edition, have been designated by being enclosed in brackets.

For other matters, reference is made to the preface to the sixth edition.

PREFACE

TO THE SIXTH EDITION.

It is now nearly fifteen years since the last edition of this work was published by Mr. Angell, in 1854. It has been for several years out of print. This delay in the issue of a new edition has been caused, in a great measure, by the death of Mr. Angell, which occurred several years since. It is much to be regretted that the work, by his decease, necessarily falls into other hands to be adapted to the vastly important developments in the Law of Watercourses which have taken place since Mr. Angell's last publication.

The work has been very much enlarged, both in text and notes, by the editor. He has examined and cited over eight hundred cases which did not appear in the previous edition. He has added nearly a hundred and fifty new sections, and made constant and numerous additions to the former sections. The subject of "Surface Water and Drainage" is entirely new to this edition; most of the law upon it has been decided and settled since Mr. Angell wrote.

The whole subject of "Eaves Drip," and much of that part of the work relating to "Subterranean Diversion" of underground streams and percolations of water, as well as of that relating to implied easements, connected with water, are additions of new matter to the volume.

Nearly all of the notes, which do not consist of mere citations of cases, are additions by the editor. The above statements have been made because the book nowhere exhibits any marks of distinction between the labors of the author and those of the editor.

In making additions to the text, the editor, as far as he has been able, has pursued the author's plan, which appears to have been received with favor, of stating cases and decisions with considerable fulness where the opinions of different courts have not been harmonious, in order that the reader may, as far as practicable and useful, have the benefit of the entire discussion of the subject-matter, and of the reasons given for different results.

In preparing the Index of Cases, the whole of them, both English and American, have been mingled together, without the distinction between them made in previous editions.

An entirely new, more full, and complete index of subjects, has been prepared for this edition.

The latest Mill Acts of Massachusetts, Maine, and Rhode Island, have been substituted for the earlier ones, which appeared in previous editions.

In all the labor of preparing this edition, the editor has endeavored to make the work exhibit the present condition of the law of watercourses in such form as to render it instructive to the student, and useful and convenient to the professional reader.

The book is now submitted, in its renewed condition, to the continued indulgence of the profession,

By the editor,

J. C. P.

PREFACE

TO THE FOURTH EDITION.

SUCH were the author's engagements, that a considerable period elapsed, after the final disposition of the preceding edition of the following work, before he was able to undertake the one here presented to the public. The ultimate result of this last enterprise, is something far different from a mere revision of the former editions. The arrangement of the subject-matter, it will at once be perceived, is essentially new, while in bulk it is vastly increased. The very material change in the arrangement was suggested by a renewed and further consideration of the subject, and it is designed to render it more deductive, and, therefore, more advantageous, and better entitled to public favor.

The author has been led also to perceive, while engaged in the revision of the authorities contained in the preceding edition, that they may be treated in the present work, in a manner more circumstantial, and more explanatory of the facts and principles to which they relate. What, however, has contributed still more to the enlargement of the work, is the copious accumulation of judicial authorities, in further and important illustration of those which had previously been cited. But, beyond this explanation of its great increase in size, the addition which has been made to the use of water, as a motive power, has thrown open new sources of litigation, and has thus associated the subject more largely with the rudiments of general jurisprudence. This extended use has required a judicial construction of particular grants, and of written and unwritten contracts, of legislative acts and of constitutional law, which, while it has much enlarged the volume, has vindicated the soundness of the assertion of Lord Mansfield, that the predominating characteristic of the Common Law is, that it is a *science of principles.*

Actuated by a strong disposition to afford an entire, correct, and comprehensible view of the Law of Watercourses, as it has thus been elaborated and expanded, the author has been indefatigable in research, to collect it, and studious in exertion, to present it with accuracy and perspicuity.

In the Appendix will be found the statutes of Massachusetts, Maine, and Rhode Island, authorizing the owners and occupants of mills to overflow, subject to certain liabilities, the lands of other persons. The statute of Virginia, in relation to the same subject, which is substantially different in its provisions from those just named, is also given. That of Kentucky, and those of other western and southern States, are modelled so much after the law of Virginia, that it has been deemed inexpedient to swell the size of the volume by inserting them. The Appendix also contains forms of declarations, to be used in actions for injuries done to, or by means of, watercourses.

Following the Appendix is an Index, though this has been rendered almost superfluous, as so much attention and care have been bestowed on the arrangement and fulness of the Table of Contents.

PROVIDENCE, June 25, 1850.

TABLE OF CONTENTS.

CHAPTER I.

MEANING OF WATERCOURSE, AND OF THE GENERAL RIGHT OF PROPERTY THEREIN.

CHAPTER II.

OF INSULAR AND ALLUVIAL RIGHTS, AND OF RIGHT TO SOIL RELICTED, AS INCIDENT TO THE RIGHT OF PROPERTY IN A WATERCOURSE.

CHAPTER III.

OF THE RIGHT OF FISHERY AS INCIDENT TO THE RIGHT OF PROPERTY IN A WATERCOURSE.

CHAPTER IV.

OF THE RIGHT OF USE OF THE WATER AS A CORPOREAL HEREDITAMENT.

CHAPTER V.

OF THE RIGHT TO THE USE OF WATER AS DERIVED FROM SPECIAL GRANTS AND RESERVATIONS.

CHAPTER VI.

OF THE RIGHT TO THE USE OF WATER AS DERIVED FROM PRESCRIPTION, OR FROM PRESUMED GRANT.

CHAPTER VII.

OF THE RIGHT TO THE USE OF THE WATER AS DEPENDING UPON CONTRACTS AND AGREEMENTS IN WRITING.

CHAPTER VIII.

OF THE RIGHT TO THE USE OF THE WATER AS DEPENDING UPON PAROL AND VERBAL LICENSE.

CHAPTER IX.

OF INUNDATION AND BACKWATER, CAUSED BY THE USE OF THE WATER.

CHAPTER X.

OF THE NATURE OF THE INJURIES DONE TO, AND BY MEANS OF, A WATERCOURSE; THE REMEDIES; AND OF THE PARTIES, PLEADINGS, AND EVIDENCE.

CHAPTER XI.

OF THE RIGHT OF EMINENT DOMAIN AS APPLIED TO PRIVATE PROPERTY IN WATERCOURSES.

CHAPTER XII.

STATUTES FOR THE ENCOURAGEMENT AND SUPPORT OF MILLS, BY AUTHORIZING THE OWNERS AND OCCUPANTS THEREOF TO OVERFLOW THE LAND OF OTHER PERSONS.

CHAPTER XIII.

OF SUCH WATERCOURSES AS ARE SUBJECTED TO PUBLIC USE.

APPENDIX.

INDEX TO CASES CITED.

THE FIGURES REFER TO THE SECTIONS.

A.

B.

I.

J.

M.

N.

O.

P.

V.

W.

Y.

Z.

LAW OF WATERCOURSES.

CHAPTER I.

MEANING OF WATERCOURSE, AND OF THE GENERAL RIGHT OF PROPERTY THEREIN.

1. *Meaning of Watercourse.*

§ 1. In considering movable and running water in reference to the right of property therein, and as something subservient to rules of jurisprudence, it may be distinguished as *tide* or *inland.* With the former the present work has nothing to do, further than to explain, before its conclusion and when it becomes more demanded, the legal distinction between them.

§ 2. Of bodies of water issuing *ex jure naturæ* from the earth, and by the same law pursuing a certain direction until they form a confluence with *tide-water*, there are known in the law two kinds; viz., those in which the proprietary interest is altogether private, and those in which it is both private and public; or those in which the private right of property is subservient to the right of public use.[1] No proprietary interest in streams of inland water so diminutive in their natural state, that they cannot be used as *boatable*, or for the transportation of property (even though by artificial means, at the expense of the owner,

[1] It will be shown, in a subsequent portion of the work, that all flowing water is by the law regarded in three distinct points of view; namely, 1. Where it is altogether private. 2. Where it is private, and at the same time subject to public use. 3. Where the use and property are both public.

they may be made of such public use), becomes vested in the public.[1]

§ 3. Of the two descriptions of running water (not tide-water) mentioned in the preceding section, it is proposed to treat under the name of "Watercourses;"[2] though very commonly they are denominated "rivers" or "rivulets," according to their magnitude.[3]

§ 4. A watercourse consists of *bed*, *banks*, and *water*;[4] yet the water need not flow continually; and there are many water-

[1] Wadsworth *v.* Smith, 11 Maine, 278; post, §§ 539, 553 *a*.

[2] "And they shall spring up as among the grass, as willows by the water-courses." Isaiah xliv. 4.

[3] The word "streams," in the English statute of sewers, is said not to apply to rivers, pools, ponds &c., because those waters have their peculiar banks, bounds, and channels; but streams are currents of water flowing independently over the land, and they are placed under the control of the commissioners of sewers. But *rivers*, although not expressly mentioned, are yet within the survey. A river is defined to be "a running stream pent in on either side, with walls and banks." Woolrych on Sewers, 51. And it bears that name as well where the waters flow and reflow, as where they have their current one way. Woolrych, Law of Waters, 40. Mr. Sergeant Callis lays it down broadly that rivers, and their channels, waters, and banks, are all fully within the laws of sewers. Callis on Sewers, 77. This must, however, be understood of such rivers as are immediately beneficial to navigation, or to the public. Springs make rivers, and these united form brooks, which, coming forward in streams, compose great rivers that run into the sea. Locke, cited in Johns. Dict. 4to ed. "River."

[4] Hale's Treatise, De Jure Maris &c. (As to the authorship of this treatise, see post, § 54, note); Starr *v.* Child, 20 Wend. 149; Gavit *v.* Chambers, 3 Ohio, 495. [It is said by Mr. Phear, in his work on Rights of Water, p. 31, that the definition which probably may best serve to separate a flow of water having a public character, from water in any other condition, is the interpretation which Lord Tenterden, in Rex *v.* Oxfordshire, 1 B. & Ad. 301, judicially gave to the words *flumen vel cursus aquæ;* namely, "water flowing in a channel between banks more or less defined."] A bank of a river is that space of rising ground above low-water mark which is usually covered by high water; and the term, when used to designate a precise line, may be somewhat vague and indefinite. Howard *v.* Ingersoll, 17 Ala. N.S. 780. Bouvier (1 Law Dict.) says, "Banks of rivers contain the river in its natural channel, when there is the greatest flow of water." The Supreme Court of Louisiana have held, "that the vendee of a riparious estate acquires a qualified property in the bank of a river, and, consequently, the *batture*, which may thereafter arise before the estate; and that the intervention of a highway does not prevent this, where the owner of the estate is bound to repair it, and the soil of it is at his risk." Morgan *v.* Livingston, 6 Mart. (La.) 19. Curtis J. in Howard *v.* Ingersoll, 13 How. (U.S.) 426, says, "The banks of a river are those elevations of land which confine the waters, when they rise out of the bed; and the bed is that soil so usually covered by water as to be distinguishable from the banks, by the character of the soil or vegetation, or both, produced by the common presence and action of flowing water. But neither the line of ordinary high-water mark, nor of ordinary low-water mark, nor of a middle stage of the water, can be assumed as the line dividing the bed from the banks. The line is to be found by examining the bed and banks, and ascertaining where the presence and action of water are so common and usual, and so long

courses which are *sometimes* dry.[1] There is, however, a distinction to be taken in law between a regular flowing stream of water, which at certain seasons is dried up, and those occasional bursts of water, which, in times of freshet, or melting of ice and snow, descend from the hills and inundate the country.[2] [To

continued in all ordinary years, as to mark upon the soil of the bed a character distinct from that of the banks, in respect to vegetation, as well as in respect to the nature of the soil itself. Whether this line between the bed and the banks will be found above or below, or at a middle stage of water, must depend on the character of the stream. The height of a stream, during much the larger part of the year, may be above or below a middle point between its highest and least flow. Something must depend also upon the rapidity of the stream, and other circumstances. But, in all cases, the bed of a river is a natural object, and is to be sought for, not merely by the application of any abstract rules, but as other natural objects are sought for and found, by the distinctive appearances they present; the banks being fast land, on which vegetation, appropriate to such land in the particular locality, grows, wherever the bank is not too steep to permit such growth, and the bed being soil of a different character, and having no vegetation or only such as exists when commonly submerged in water." The question, in this case, was as to the jurisdiction of Georgia over the Chattahoochee River; and see the learned and ingenious argument of Mr. Berrien, on p. 391 of ib., et seq.

1 [Shields *v.* Arndt, 3 Green Ch. (N.J.) 246, 247; Wagner *v.* Long Island R.R. Co., 5 N.Y. Sup. Ct. 163; 2 Hun, 633. A spring on the defendant's land, sixteen rods from the land of the plaintiff, supplied a small stream of water that ran to the plaintiff's land; the water, as it came from the spring, being sufficient to fill a half-inch pipe, and the flow being constant and nearly uniform, except in very dry times, when it failed to run. For seven rods the stream descended rapidly, in a well-defined course, to a piece of marshy ground, where it spread so that its flow was slight, and not sufficient to break the turf, but was generally sufficient to form a continuous sluggish current along the surface in a natural depression, to a watering place within the plaintiff's line. This was adjudged to be a watercourse within the meaning attached in law to that term. Gillett *v.* Johnson, 30 Conn. 180; Macomber *v.* Godfrey, 108 Mass. 219. So in Reynolds *v.* M'Arthur, 2 Peters (U.S.) 417, 438, Marshall C.J. said, "A stream may acquire the name of a river, in the channel of which, at some seasons of extreme drought, no water flows. It would be against all usage to say that the general source of the river was at that point in its channel from which the water always flows." — "The accustomed, though not continuous, flowage of waters is a stream in the eye of the law, and its channel is no more to be obstructed than if it was the channel of a stream that never failed." Kauffman *v.* Griesemer, 20 Penn. St. 407.]

2 Reynolds *v.* M'Arthur, 2 Peters (U.S.) 417; and opinion of Pennington Ch. in Shields *v.* Arndt, 3 Green (N.J.) Ch. 234; [Luther *v.* Winnisimmet Co., 9 Cush. 171; Ashley *v.* Wolcott, 11 Cush. 192, 195; Flagg *v.* Worcester, 13 Gray, 601, 607; Parks *v.* Newburyport, 10 Gray, 28; Dickinson *v.* Worcester, 7 Allen, 19, 21, 22; Gannon *v.* Hargadon, 10 Allen, 106, 109; Rawstron *v.* Taylor, 11 Exch. 369; Broadbent *v.* Ramsbotham, 11 Exch. 602; Bangor *v.* Lansil, 51 Maine, 521, 525. In Earle *v.* DeHart, 1 Beasley Ch. (N.J.) 283, 284, Williamson Ch. said, "A watercourse is defined to be 'a channel or canal for the conveyance of water, particularly in draining lands.' It may be natural, as where it is made by the natural flow of the water, caused by the general superficies of the surrounding land from which the water is collected into one channel; or it may be artificial, as in case of a ditch, or other artificial means, used to divert the water from its natural channel, or to carry it from low lands,

maintain the right to a watercourse or brook, it must be made to appear that the water usually flows in a certain direction, and by a regular channel, with banks or sides. It need not be shown to flow continually, as stated above, and it may at times be dry; but it must have a well-defined and substantial existence. A mere right of drainage over the general surface of land is very different from the right to the flow of a stream or brook across the premises of another.[1] "It is not essential to a watercourse that the banks should be absolutely unchangeable, the flow constant, the size uniform, or the waters entirely unmixed with earth, or flowing with any fixed velocity; but the law does not and cannot fix the limits of variation in these particulars."[2]

§ 4 *a*. Substantially in accordance with the description of a watercourse as given in the preceding section, Mr. Justice Bigelow, in a late case in Massachusetts,[3] defined a watercourse as a stream of water, usually flowing in a definite channel, having a bed and sides or banks, and usually discharging itself into some other stream or body of water. "To constitute a watercourse," he says, "the size of the stream is not important; it may be very small, and the flow of water need not be constant, but it must be something more than a mere surface drainage over the entire face of a tract of land occasioned by unusual freshets or other extraordinary causes."

§ 4 *b*. A river or stream begins at its source, when it comes to

from which it will not flow, in consequence of the natural formation of the surface of the surrounding land. It is an ancient watercourse, if the channel through which it naturally runs has existed from time immemorial. Whether it is entitled to be called an ancient watercourse, and, as such, legal rights can be acquired and lost in it, does not depend upon the quantity of water it discharges. Many ancient streams of water, which, if dammed up, would inundate a large region of country, are dry for a great portion of the year. If the face of the country is such, that it necessarily collects in one body so large a quantity of water, after heavy rains and the melting of large bodies of snow, as to require an outlet to some common reservoir, and if such water is regularly discharged through a well-defined channel, which the force of the water has made for itself, and which is the accustomed channel through which it flows, and has flowed from time immemorial, such channel is an ancient natural watercourse." See Arnold *v.* Foot, 12 Wend. 330; Wood *v.* Waud, 3 Exch. 748, 779.]

[1] [Ashley *v.* Wolcott, 11 Cush. 195; Shields *v.* Arndt, 3 Green (N.J.) Ch. 234, 246; Bangor *v.* Lansil, 51 Maine, 521, 525; Kauffman *v.* Griesemer, 26 Penn. St. 407; Earle *v.* DeHart, 1 Beasley Ch. (N.J.) 280, 283; Conhocton Stone Road Co. *v.* Buffalo, New York and Erie R.R. Co., 5 N.Y. Sup. Ct. 651; Wagner *v.* Long Island R.R. Co., 5 N.Y. Sup. Ct. Rep. 163.]

[2] [Bartlett J., in Bassett *v.* Salisbury Manuf. Co., 43 N.H. 569, 578.]

[3] [Luther *v.* Winnisimmet Co., 9 Cush. 174.]

the surface; and the owners of lands adjoining upon it have a natural right to the use of the water of it from its source to its termination. In a late case, in the Exchequer,[1] it appeared that the water from a spring flowed in a gully or natural channel to a stream on which was a mill. The spring was cut off at its source, and the water was received into a tank as it rose from the earth, by the license of the owner of the soil on which the spring rose. The action was for diversion, by the mill-owner. The Judge, at the trial, told the jury that the questions for them were, whether there was a *natural or defined watercourse* from the spring head to the stream, and, if so, whether the defendant had diverted the water from this watercourse. Pollock C.B. said, "The real question is, whether there is a natural watercourse which, but for the acts done by the defendant, would have conveyed water to the stream, and from thence to the mill of the plaintiff. If there is a natural spring, the water from which flows in a natural channel, it cannot be lawfully diverted by any one to the injury of the riparian proprietors. When the stream is above ground, a grant must be presumed, not only of the thing itself, but of all things necessary to the complete enjoyment of it. If the channel or course under ground is known, as in the case of the river Mole, it cannot be interfered with. It is otherwise when nothing is known, as to the sources of supply; in that case, as no right can be acquired against the owner of the land under which the spring exists, he may do as he pleases with it, and if in mining or draining his land he taps a spring, he cannot be made responsible. . . . The law of the case is clear and undoubted. This was a natural spring, the waters of which had acquired a natural channel from its source to the river. It is absurd to say that a man might take the water of such a stream four feet from the surface." Martin B.: "A river begins at its source, when it comes to the surface, and the owner of the land on which it rises cannot monopolize all the water at the source so as to prevent its reaching the lands of other proprietors lower down." Watson B.: "The stoppage at the spring head is just as much a diversion as if the water had been taken lower down."[2]

§ 4 *c*. The principle of the law as to water flowing in a certain

[1] [Dudden *v.* The Guardians of the Poor of the Clutton Union, 11 Exch. 627.]

[2] [See Rawstron *v.* Taylor, 11 Exch. 369; Broadbent *v.* Ramsbotham, 11 Exch. 602; Wood *v.* Waud, 3 Exch. 748, 779;

and definite channel seems to be applicable to all water known to be so flowing, whether under ground or upon its surface. In Dickinson *v.* Canal Co.,[1] Pollock C.B. said, "If the course of a subterranean stream were well known, as is the case with many which sink under ground, pursue for a short space a subterraneous course, and then emerge again, it could never be contended that the owner of the soil under which the stream flowed could not maintain an action for the diversion of it, if it took place under such circumstances as would have enabled him to recover if the stream had been wholly above ground." The remarks of the same learned Judge quoted in the preceding section are to the same effect. Lord Chelmsford expresses his concurrence with this statement of the law in Chasemore *v.* Richards,[2] when that case came before the House of Lords.

§ 4 *d.* But waters, whether under or above ground, having no certain course or defined limits, such as those merely percolating through the strata of the earth, and those diffused over its surface, are not watercourses, nor are they subject to the rules of law applicable to watercourses.[3] Water flowing through a hollow or ravine only in times of rain, or melting of snow, is not, in contemplation of law, a watercourse.[4] This subject will be discussed more fully hereafter.

§ 4 *e.* Where an island is formed in the middle of a river, two streams are necessarily formed by the original river, dividing it into two branches; the island itself, having become solid land, forms itself a bank of the new stream on the one side, and the old bank on the main shore forms the other. And the same rule applies to the other side of the island. There must, then, be a *filum aquæ* to each of these streams, whilst the old *filum aquæ* is obliterated to the extent to which land has taken the place of water. If another island is formed in one of these branches,

Wheatley *v.* Baugh, 25 Penn. St. 528; Eddy *v.* Simpson, 3 Cal. 249; Macomber *v.* Godfrey, 108 Mass. 219. Every owner of land has the right to clean out and tube or wall up a natural spring upon his own land, for his own use and convenience, when he does not thereby change the natural course of the flow of the water therefrom, and makes no change to the injury of another except what may result from an increased flow of water in the natural channel or outlet of the spring. Waffle *v.* Porter, 61 Barb. 130.]

[1] [7 Exch. 300, 301. See post, § 112 *b*, et seq.; Bassett *v.* Salisbury Manuf. Co., 43 N.H. 578.]

[2] [5 H. & N. 982, 986, 987. See post, § 112 *b*.]

[3] [Chasemore *v.* Richards, 7 H. L. Cas. 349; 5 H. & N. 982, 986, 987; s.c. 2 H. & N. 168.]

[4] [Shields *v.* Arndt, 3 Green Ch. (N.J.) 234.]

between the first island and the original main shore, it seems that it must be divided upon the same principle as the first; but, in doing it, it will be necessary to assume as the *filum aquæ* the middle line between the first island and the original river bank on that side.[1]]

§ 4*f*. A portion of a river may be designated as a *bay*,[2] but it is not the less a river on account of such name.[3] And, on the other hand, bays may be connected with rivers in such a way as to form a body of waters extending inland, and not be considered part of the river.[4] [A sheet of water in which there is a current from its head towards its outlet, is not, therefore, a river. The outlet of a lake may be a river, but the lake does not lose its distinctive character, because there is a current in it for a certain distance tending towards the outlet. As the fact that there is a current from a higher to a lower level does not make that a river which would otherwise be a lake, so the fact that a river swells out into broad, pond-like sheets, with a current, does not make that a lake which would otherwise be a river. But when it appears that the water is not a lake, nor a pond, — the material difference between which is in size, — the only criterion by which to determine whether it is a river, is the existence of a current.[5]]

2. *How the Private Right of Property in a Watercourse is derived.*

§ 5. The right of private property in a watercourse is derived,

[1] [Per Shaw C.J., in Trustees &c. *v.* Dickinson, 9 Cush. 548, 549.]

[2] [A bay is a bending or curving of the shore of the sea or of a lake, and is derived from an Anglo-Saxon word signifying to *bow* or *bend*. For a similar reason the word bay is, in Latin, termed *sinus*, which expresses a curvature or recess in the coast. State *v.* Gilmanton, 14 N.H. 477.]

[3] [State *v.* Gilmanton, 9 N.H. 461; s.c. 14 N.H. 477.]

[4] Per Parker C.J., in State *v.* Gilmanton, 9 N.H. 461; s.c. 14 N.H. 467. For the difference, in the eye of the law, between a watercourse and a *lake* see post, § 41.

[5] [State *v.* Gilmanton, 14 N.H. 476, 477; s.c. 9 N.H. 461. In Bassett *v.* Salisbury Manuf. Co., 43 N.H. 569, 578, Bartlett J. said, "It is by no means certain that the entire absence of current in a lake would prevent the application of the general principles that protect the rights of land owners on running streams; for perhaps it will be found that owners of land upon such lakes have similar qualified rights to the enjoyment of these waters in their natural condition, and to the reasonable use of them, and may claim that the water shall not be unreasonably raised, lowered, or polluted, to their injury. Where a watercourse originates, and is supplied from a natural lake, the current in the latter may be hardly perceptible, yet it may be doubted if any one could justify the entire withholding of its waters from the stream it should feed."]

as a *corporeal right* or *hereditament*,[1] from, or is embraced by, the ownership of the soil over which it naturally passes. The well-known maxim, *cujus est solum, ejus est usque ad cœlum*, inculcates, that land, in its legal signification, has an indefinite extent upwards;[2] and therefore it is that a grant of it conveys to the grantee not only the "field" or the "meadow," but all growing timber and *water* standing and being thereupon;[3] and a *stream of water* is, therefore, as much the property of the owner of the soil over which it passes, as the stones scattered over it.[4] Where the lines given in a grant of land include a

[1] *Land* means the whole surface of the earth; *tenement* is a word of still greater extent, signifying every thing that may be holden by tenure; but *hereditament* is the largest and most comprehensive word, including not only lands and tenements, but whatever may be inherited. 1 Greenleaf's Ed. Cruise's Dig. 39; Sacket *v.* Wheaton, 17 Pick. 105.

[2] 3 Bla. Com. 18; Co. Litt. 4; 2 Brownl. 142; [post § 90; Woolrych, Law of Waters, 146; Brace *v.* Yale, 10 Allen, 443].

[3] Real property is corporeal or incorporeal. Corporeal property consists wholly of substantial and permanent subjects, all of which may be comprehended under the general denomination of land; which Lord Coke says, in its legal signification, comprehends any ground, soil, or earth whatsoever; as meadows, pastures, woods, *waters*, marshes, furzes, and heath. It has, also, in its legal signification, an indefinite extent upwards as well as downwards; for it is a maxim of law, *cujus est solum, ejus est usque ad cœlum*. 1 Greenleaf's Ed. Cruise's Dig. 37.

[4] By the Court, in Buckingham *v.* Smith, 10 Ohio, 288. See, also, Bullen *v.* Runnels, 2 N.H. 255; Canal Commissioners *v.* The People, 5 Wend. 423; Newson *v.* Pryor, 7 Wheat. 7; Den *v.* Wright, 1 Peters, C.C. 64; Winthrop *v.* Curtis, 3 Greenl. 110; Williams *v.* Jackson, 5 John. 489; Van Gorden *v.* Jackson, 5 John. 440; Pejepscot Proprietors *v.* Cushman, 2 Greenl. 94. [The general rule, as a rule of the Common Law of England, was long since laid down as unquestionable by Lord Holt, who says, in the case of Rex *v.* Wharton, Holt, 499, that a river, of common right, belongs to the proprietors of the land between which it runs, to each that part nearest his land. This has been frequently, if not uniformly, adopted as the established rule. It is derived mainly from the rule that the riparian proprietor is owner of the soil under the water, and by the general law of property becomes entitled as of right to all accessions. Shaw C.J., in Trustees &c. *v.* Dickinson, 9 Cush. 547. "The right to flowing water is now well settled to be a right incident to property in the land." Shaw C.J., in Elliott *v.* Fitchburg R.R. Co., 10 Cush. 193. "This right or corporeal hereditament, which is embraced within or appertains to the ownership of the land over and through which a watercourse runs, is subject to the same incidents as all other interests in real property. It may be conveyed absolutely, or its use may be modified or restricted by grant; so, too, it may be lost, or acquired either wholly or in part by an adverse user sufficiently long, exclusive, and notorious to furnish adequate grounds for the presumption of a grant." Bigelow C.J., in Brace *v.* Yale, 10 Allen, 443. But it was maintained in Lyon *v.* Fishmongers' Company, 1 App. Cas. 662, that the right of a riparian owner to the use of the stream does not depend on the ownership of the soil of the stream. As to this, Lord Selborne said: "With respect to the ownership of the bed of the river, this cannot be the foundation of riparian rights, properly so called, because the word 'riparian' is rela-

stream of water, the soil covered by the water, and, consequently, the water itself, will pass, although the land is not described as *aqua co-operta*.[1] [The words "a natural spring of water" import that the water of the spring was a part of the land, and susceptible of absolute ownership.[2]] The proprietor of adjoining lands, who is also the proprietor of the bed of a river, may grant and convey the bed of the river separate from the land which bounds it;[3] [he may convey his estate in the bed of the river without his upland, or his upland without the bed of the river; and such conveyance will be good and available; or he may convey a part of his estate in the bed of the river, and may divide it in any form, or by any lines, which he may think proper[4]]; but a grant of a stream of water or watercourse, *eo nomine*, will not pass the land over which the water runs.[5] [In Egremont *v.* Williams,[6] Coleridge J. said, "Now, without saying that a watercourse may never mean the channel in which water flows, it certainly may mean also the stream or flow of the water itself; and whether it means the one or the other in any instrument, will very materially depend on the context. And in the case before us, it appears to us that that which flows through lands named, for the purpose of watering

tive to the banks, and not the bed, of the stream; and the connection, where it exists, of property on the bank with property in the bed of the stream depends, not upon nature, but on grant or presumption of law. . . . The title to the soil constituting the bed of the river, does not carry with it any exclusive right of property in the running water of the stream, which can only be appropriated by severance, and which may be lawfully so appropriated by every one having a right of access to it. It is, of course, necessary for the existence of a riparian right, that the land should be in contact with the flow of the stream; but lateral contact is as good, *jure naturæ*, as vertical. . . . It is true that the bank of a tidal river, of which the foreshore is left bare at low water, is not always in contact with the flow of the stream; but it is in such contact for a great part of every day, in the ordinary and regular course of nature, which is an amply sufficient foundation for a natural riparian right." 1 App. Cas. 683; s.c. L.R. 10 Ch. Ap. 679.]

[1] Browne *v.* Kennedy, 5 H. & John. 195; Clark *v.* Conroe, 38 Vt. 469.

[2] [Per Wilson J., in Clark *v.* Conroe, 38 Vt. 474. Where a spring had been set out and separated from other lands by the owner, so as to extend three rods each way from the central portion covered by the water, it was held that the land, so set out and separated to be used with the spring, would be conveyed by a deed of the same under the term "spring." Woodcock *v.* Estey, 43 Vt. 515; Mixer *v.* Reed, 25 Vt. 254.]

[3] Den *v.* Wright, 1 Peters C.C. 64. And see Ashley *v.* Pease, 18 Pick. 268.

[4] [Per Shaw C.J., in Knight *v.* Wilder, 2 Cush. 209. See 3 Kent, 428.]

[5] Jackson *v.* Halstead, 5 Cowen, 216.

[6] [11 Ad. & Ell. N.S. 707. See Woolrych, Law of Waters, 146; post, § 90, and note.]

them and other specified lands, must be taken to be the water itself, and not the channel through which it flows." [1]]

§ 6. In this country, a grant by a State conveying a tract of territory, carries with it a right of property in all the watercourses within the boundaries of the grant.[2] A patent from the State of New York conveying territory twenty-four miles in width on the river Hudson, above tide-water, with the territory described as "lying and being in and upon the banks of Hudson River," includes the soil under the river, as far as the patent extends up and down the river.[3] In Pennsylvania, all rivers and streams of water are comprehended within the charter bounds of the Province, and passed to William Penn, in the same manner as the soil; and in grants of vacant land by him and his successors, during the proprietary times, and by the Commonwealth since, streams of water not navigable, falling within the lines of a survey, were covered by them, and belonged to the owner of the tract; and such owner might convey the body of the stream to one person, and the adjoining land to another, or he might convey the adjoining land only to one, who would then be riparian proprietor to the middle of the stream.[4]

§ 7. In a case in the State of New York, it appeared that a valuable waterfall in the middle sprout of the Mohawk River, which falls into the river Hudson, had been destroyed by a dam erected for the use of the canals. This fall was granted in terms, as so much land covered with water, 1752, by Stephen Van Renssellaer, and had come by mesne conveyances to the relator; there being an actual individual seisin of the fall *eo nomine* for upwards of thirty years. It was well known that the land on both sides of the fall was granted away at a very early period by the State, which had not afterwards asserted the least claim. The canal appraisers refused to allow the relator any damages, on the *sole ground* that the land under water belonged to the

[1] [The words of exception, on which this decision was founded, were in a lease, and followed after a grant of all waters and watercourses belonging &c. These words were, "except a certain watercourse *flowing* through Little Moor Mead, and thence into another mead named, for watering it and other lands of Sir C. Wyndham." 11 Ad. & Ell. 700.]

[2] Lunt *v.* Holland, 14 Mass. 149; Middleton *v.* Pritchard, 3 Scam. (Ill.) 520.

[3] Canal Commissioners *v.* The People, 5 Wend. 423; and see People *v.* Canal Appraisers, 13 Wend. 355; Rogers *v.* Jones, 1 Wend. 255.

[4] Coovert *v.* O'Connor, 8 Watts, 470.

State; but the Supreme Court granted a mandamus against the appraisers.[1]

§ 8. It has, therefore, as a matter of course, been held, that the right to a watercourse is a part of the *freehold*, of which no man can be disseised but by lawful judgment of his peers, or by due process of law.[2] Still, no action will lie to recover possession of a watercourse, by that name; either by estimating the capacity of the water, as for so many cubical yards, or by superficial measure, for "twenty acres of water;" or by a more general description, as for "a river" or "stream of water." The action must be for the *land* at the bottom, calling it "twenty acres of land covered by water."[3] To give execution of that

[1] Tobias, *ex parte*, referred to in note to 6 Cowen, 551; and see Jennings, *ex parte*, Cowen, 518.

[2] Gardner *v.* Newburgh, 2 John. Ch. 162. And see Beidelman *v.* Foulk, 5 Watts, 308. [In Cary *v.* Daniels, 5 Met. 238, Wilde J. said, "The right which a party has to the use of water flowing over his own land is undoubtedly identified with the realty, and is a real or corporeal hereditament, and not an easement, but the right of a party to have the water of a stream or watercourse flow to or from his lands or mill, over the land of another, is an incorporeal hereditament, and an easement, or a predial service, as defined by the civil law. And it is immaterial whether the watercourse be natural or artificial; or whether the right is derived *ex jure naturæ*, or by grant or prescription." And in Crittenton *v.* Alger, 11 Met. 284, Hubbard J., referring to the above statements of the law, said, "We entertain no doubt of the correctness of this position." See post, §§ 90, 123 and note, 141. But, strictly speaking, the riparian proprietor has no property in the water itself; but a simple use of it while it passes along. Story J., in Tyler *v.* Wilkinson, 4 Mason, 400. See Stein *v.* Burden, 29 Ala. N.S. 127; S.C. 24 Ala. N.S. 130; Burden *v.* Stein, 27 Ala. N.S. 104.]

[3] 2 Bla. Com. 18; Runnington on Eject. 131. [In Race *v.* Ward, 4 El. & Bl., 708, Lord Campbell C.J., said, that an action for taking water, the property of the plaintiff, could not be supported unless the water were contained in a cistern or some vessel in which he had placed it for his private use. The defendant claimed, in the above case, a right by immemorial custom, in all the inhabitants of the township, to take water from a spring issuing from the plaintiff's close, and to carry it to their dwelling-houses for domestic purposes. Lord Campbell said, "The water which they claim a right to take is not the produce of the plaintiff's close; it is not the subject of property. Blackstone, following other elementary writers, classes water with the elements of light and air. 2 Bl. 14. Afterwards, having stated that a man cannot bring an action to recover possession of a pool or other piece of water, either calculating its capacity, as for so many cubical yards, or by superficial measure for twenty acres of water, he gives the reason: 'For water is a movable, wandering thing, and must of necessity continue common by the law of nature' (p. 18). It is not disputed that this would be so with respect to the water of a river or any open running stream. We think it equally true as to the water of a spring, when it first issues from the ground. This is no part of the soil, like sand, or clay, or stones; nor the produce of the soil, like grass, or turves, or trees. A right to take these by custom, claimed by all the inhabitants of a district, would clearly be bad; for they all come under the category of *profit à prendre*, being part of the soil or the produce of the soil; and such a claim, which might leave nothing for the owner of the soil, is wholly inconsistent with the right of

which is so wandering and fugitive as running water, is indeed impracticable.[1]

§ 9. The only mode by which a right of property in a watercourse, above tide-water, can be withheld from a person who receives a grant of the land, is by a reservation directly expressed or clearly implied to such effect. If the intention of the grantor is not to convey any interest in the water, or any portion of it,

property in the soil. But the spring of water is supplied and renewed by nature; it must have flowed from a distance by an underground channel; and, when it issues from the ground, till appropriated for use, it flows onward by the law of gravitation. While it remains in the field where it issues forth, in the absence of any servitude or custom giving a right to others, the owner of the field, and he only, has a right to appropriate it; for no one else can do so without committing a trespass upon the field; but, when it has left his field, he has no more power over it, or interest in it, than any other stranger." See Year Book, Trin. 15 Ed. 4, fol. 29 A. pl. 7; Weekly *v.* Wildman, 1 Ld. Ray. 407; Manning *v.* Wasdale, 5 Ad. & El. 758; Blewett *v.* Tregonning, 3 Ad & El. 554.]

[1] In Challenor *v.* Thomas, Yelv. (Metcalf's ed.) 143, error was brought on a judgment given in ejectment in *Com. Carmarthen.* And Yelverton assigned the error, because the ejectment was brought *de aquæ cursu,* called Lochar in Llandeby, and declared on the lease of David Rees ap Thomas *de quodam rivulo et aquæ cursu ut supra.* And, *per totam curiam,* the judgment was reversed; for *rivulus seu aquæ cursus* doth not lie in demand, neither doth a *præcipe* lie of it, nor can livery of seisin be made of it; for *non moratur,* but is ever flowing; nor can execution by *habere fac. seisinam* be made of it; for it is not constant to be put in possession of it. And it is like a protection *quia moratur super mare,* which is not allowable by 35 *H.* 6, for *mare non moratur;* but as 12 *H.* 7, 4, is, the action ought to be for so many acres of land *aqua co-operta;* and ejectment well lies of a gorce or pool, for a *præcipe* lies for them, and a wife shall be endowed of the third part of the gorce, as 11 *E.* 3 is. But if the land under the river or water does not belong to the plaintiff, but the river only, then on a disturbance his remedy is only by action on the case on any diversion of it. In Godbolt, 157, pl. 213, it is said, "It was adjudged in this court (B.R.) that an *ejectione firmæ* doth lie *de aquæ cursu.*" That, probably, is a wrong report of the case in the text, as it appears to have been of the same Term, — Mich. 6 Jac. Bacon, Espinasse, and Selwyn state that ejectment will not lie for a watercourse or stream of water; on the authority of Yelverton and Brownlow's report of this case. So do Runnington and Adams, in their respective treatises on the action of ejectment. See Woolrych, Law of Waters, 276, 295. An ejectment has, however, been sustained for a *boilery* of salt, i.e., where there is a well of salt water, and a man has no inheritance in the soil, but only a grant of so many buckets of the water as will arise, which are called *boileries.* Any one who withholds the buckets of water from the grantee is liable to an action of ejectment for the injury. Cro. Jac. 150, 1 Lev. 44, Reg. 227. But this is obviously different from a river which is always running; for here the water is fixed in a certain place, and within the bounds and compass of the well, and is considered as a part of the soil. So an ejectment lies *pro stagno,* for in law the word *stagnum* comprehends both land and water. Co. Litt. 5. [" In the same manner, *gurges,* a deep pit of water, consisteth of water and land; and therefore by the grant thereof by that name the soil doth pass, and a *præcipe* doth lie thereof." Co. Litt. 5; Johnson *v.* Rayner, 6 Gray, 110. So the term "well," aptly designates the soil covered by and used with it; and a grant thereof passes the fee in the premises occupied by the well. Johnson *v.* Rayner, supra; Owen *v.* Field, 102 Mass. 104. See post, § 41.]

he can exclude it by the insertion in the instrument of conveyance of proper words for the purpose of doing so; but in the absence of such words, the bed, and consequently the stream itself, passes by the conveyance.[1] In a case in the Supreme Court of the State of New York,[2] it appeared, that in 1784, the country through which a river called the "Saranac" runs, was wild and uninhabited; and that a patent for a tract of land was in that year granted, bounding on the east by Lake Champlain, and extending west on both sides of said river, and being seven miles square. The patent contained no other reservation than of "all mines of gold and silver,[3] salt springs, lakes, and mines of

[1] Claremont *v.* Carlton, 2 N.H. 371; Hay *v.* Bowman, 1 Rand. (Va.) 420; Waterman *v.* Johnson, 13 Pick. 261; Brown *v.* Kennedy, 5 H. & John. 195; Gavit *v.* Chambers, 3 Ohio, 495; 3 Kent, 427, 428; Knight *v.* Wilder, 2 Cush. 199, 209; and see post, ch. V. A deed conveying to the grantee fifty acres of land, being half of a certain hundred-acre lot described as bounded by a river, "said half to be taken off the width of said lot on said river" (which was at the south end), "and so far back as to make the half of said lot, quantity and quality, as it now stands," does not convey any interest in the north end of the lot, so as to constitute the grantor and grantee tenants in common of the whole lot. If, however, such deed were construed as constituting a tenancy in common, the fact that the north and south portion of the lot had been long possessed in severalty, each party claiming a dividing line between them, with an agreed boundary on the west line of the lot, would be conclusive evidence of partition, notwithstanding the monuments to which they claimed on the east side were different. Smith *v.* Powers, 15 N.H. 546.

[2] People *v.* Platt, 17 John. 195; and see Colvin *v.* Burnet, 2 Hill, 620.

[3] Not only has land, in its legal signification, an indefinite extent upwards, but, in contemplation of law, it extends also downwards, so that whatever is in a direct line beneath the surface of any land and the centre of the earth, belongs to the owner of the surface; and, therefore, if a man grants all his lands, he grants thereby all his *mines*. 2 Bla. Com. 18. See Acton *v.* Blundell, 12 M. & W. 324; Doe *v.* Freeland, 1 T. R. 701. See ante, § 5, as to the maxim *cujus est solum* &c. When the surface of land belongs to one man, and the minerals belong to another, no evidence of title appearing to regulate or qualify their rights of enjoyment, the owners of the minerals cannot remove them without leaving support sufficient to maintain the surface in its natural state. The owner of the surface close, while unincumbered with buildings, and in its natural state, is entitled to have it supported by the subjacent mineral strata; and if the surface subsides and is injured by the removal of these strata, although the operation of removal may not have been conducted negligently, nor contrary to the custom of the country, the owner of the surface may maintain an action against the owner of the minerals for the damage sustained by the subsidence. Humphries *v.* Brogden, 12 Q.B. 739; [Rowbotham *v.* Wilson, 8 El. & Bl. 123; s.c. 6 El. & Bl. 693; s.c. 8 H. L. Cas. 348; Harris *v.* Ryding, 5 M. & W. 60; Smart *v.* Morton, 5 El. & Bl. 30; Haines *v.* Roberts, 7 El. & Bl. 625; s.c. 6 El. & Bl. 643; Bonomi *v.* Backhouse, El. Bl. & El. 622; Rogers *v.* Taylor, 2 H. & N. 828; Partridge *v.* Scott, 3 M. & W. 220; Strogan *v.* Knowles, 6 H. & N. 454, 465; Brown *v.* Robins, 4 H. & N. 186; North Eastern Railway Co. *v.* Elliot, 1 John. & H. 145. The same rules apply to cases of lateral support of land. Foley *v.* Wyeth, 2 Allen, 131; Solomon *v.* The Vintners' Co., 4 H. & N. 585; The Caledonian Railway Co. *v.* Sprot, 2 Macq. H. L. Cas. 449; Richardson *v.* Vermont Central

salt, and carrying places upon any water communication which may be found or contained within the limits of the said land." The Court held, that, as there was no other reservation of the river, nor any restriction imposed in the use of the water expressed in the grant, the whole river within the bounds of the patent passed to the patentee as his exclusive property.

3. *How the Private Right of Property in a Watercourse is apportioned between Opposite Riparian Owners.*

§ 10. The owners of watercourses are denominated by the civilians *riparian* proprietors,[1] and the use of the same significant and convenient term is now fully introduced into the common law. The soil of the bed itself, and consequently the water, may be, and most often is, divided between two opposite riparian owners; that is, the land on one side may be owned by one person, and the land on the opposite side by another. When such is the case, each proprietor owns to the middle, or what is called the *thread* of the river, or, as it is expressed in Latin, *usque ad filum aquæ*.[2] There is but one difference between a

R.R., 25 Vt. 465; Radcliff *v.* Mayor &c., of Brooklyn, 4 Comst. 195; Thurston *v.* Hancock, 12 Mass. 220; Lasala *v.* Holbrook, 4 Paige, 169; Beard *v.* Murphy, 37 Vt. 101. "This doctrine," said Lord Campbell C.J., in Humphries *v.* Brogden, 12 Q.B. 739, "stands on natural justice, and is essential to the protection and enjoyment of property in the soil." The legal remedy for an invasion of the right of horizontal or vertical support of land "does not depend upon any rule of negligence or unskilfulness, but upon the violation of a right of property which has been invaded and disturbed. This unqualified rule is limited to injuries caused to the land itself, and does not afford relief for damages by the same means to artificial structures. For an injury to buildings, which is unavoidably incident to the depression or slide of the soil on which they stand, caused by the excavation of a pit on adjoining land, an action can only be maintained when a want of due care or skill, or positive negligence, has contributed to produce it." Merrick J., in Foley *v.* Wyeth, 2 Allen, 133].

[1] [In Bardwell *v.* Ames, 22 Pick. 333, 335, Shaw C.J. said, "By this designation — riparian proprietor — I understand, an owner of land, bounded generally upon a stream of water, and, as such, having a qualified property in the soil to the thread of the stream, with the privileges annexed thereto by law." In the note to Commonwealth *v.* Roxbury, 9 Gray, 521, Mr. Gray says: "The words 'riparian proprietor' have been heedlessly extended from rivers and streams to the shores of the sea. If it is necessary to express it by a single adjective, the term 'littoral proprietor,' as used by the plaintiff's counsel in Commonwealth *v.* Roxbury, 9 Gray, 472, and by the Supreme Court of the United States in Boston *v.* Lecraw, 17 How. 432, 433, is more accurate."]

[2] See Lord Hale's Treatise, *De Jure Maris* &c., Harg. Tracts, 5 (see post, § 54, note); Holt, 499; Tyler *v.* Wilkinson, 4 Mason, 397; [Bardwell *v.* Ames, 22 Pick. 354; Fletcher *v.* Phelps, 28 Vt. 257, 262, per Isham J.; Claremont *v.* Carlton, 2 N.H. 369]; and the authorities cited, ante, § 5, et seq. ["This is the legal effect of the conveyance, and it cannot be varied or

stream running through a man's land, and one which runs by the side of it; in the former case he owns the whole, and in the latter but half.[1]

§ 11. A watercourse is considered the safest boundary of real estate, as it is a natural boundary;[2] and the invariable construction in this country has been, as it has been for centuries in England, that, whenever land or a mill site is sold and conveyed as being bounded by a watercourse, the watercourse *usque ad filum aquæ* is included.[3] In numerous cases of much importance in

controlled by parol testimony." Per Isham J., in Fletcher *v.* Phelps, 28 Vt. 257, 262.] The word "thread" is defined by Johnson "a small line," "any thing continued in a course." Johns. Dict. A party having made a ditch six feet wide through his land, and conveyed a part of it bounding the grantee on the ditch, it was held, that the grant extended to the middle of the ditch. Warner *v.* Southworth, 6 Conn. 471; [Agawam Canal Co. *v.* Edwards, 36 Conn. 476, 501, 502. In Trustees &c. *v.* Dickinson, 9 Cush. 544, 552, Shaw C.J. said, "In ascertaining the thread of the river, it will be proper to take the middle line between the shores upon each side, without regard to the channel, or lowest and deepest part of the stream. And in ascertaining the shores or water-lines on each side, to measure, it will be proper to find what those lines are when the water is in its natural and ordinary stage at a medium height, neither swollen by freshets nor shrunk by drought." Pratt *v.* Lamson, 2 Allen, 275, stated post, § 101 *a*].

[1] Starr *v.* Child, 20 Wend. 149. ["If the same person be the owner of the lands on both sides of the river, he owns the whole river to the extent of the length of his lands upon it." 3 Kent, 428; Jones *v.* Pettibone, 2 Wis. 308. See Granger *v.* Avery, 64 Maine, 292.]

[2] Per Washington J., in Den *v.* Wright, 1 Peters C.C. 64. [In Dunklee *v.* The Wilton R.R. Co., 24 N.H. 489, 507, 508, where the land conveyed was bounded on the "Saw-mill Brook," which was admitted to be an artificial raceway into which the water of the brook had been turned, and, "on the Bridge Meadow Brook," which was the original channel of the brook; and the deed contained no reservation or stipulation looking to any change proposed or feared of these watercourses, — the Court said, "Now, we think the mention of this raceway as *the saw-mill brook*, is a recognition of it as being, as between these parties, the brook, the natural channel; since that is the force and significance of the word *brook*, and is entirely equivalent to an agreement that, as between these parties, this raceway is to be regarded as the natural stream."]

[3] Mayo *v.* Quimby (1799), cited in 3 Dane Abr. 4; Hatch *v.* Dwight, 17 Mass. 289; [Cold Spring Iron Works *v.* Tolland, 9 Cush. 492, 495. When the boundary of two properties passes along or over a stream or piece of water, it is taken *primâ facie* to coincide with the *medium filum* of the stream, or the diameter of the pool; although, of course, it may be proved expressly to have some other direction. In moving that the decision appealed from, in Wishart *v.* Wyllie, 1 Macq. H.L. Cas. 389, should be affirmed, the Lord Chancellor (Lord Cranworth) said, "If a stream separates properties A. and B., *primâ facie*, the owner of the land A., as to his land on one side, and the owner of the land B., as to his land on the other, are each entitled to the soil of the stream, *usque ad medium aquæ*; that is, *primâ facie* so. It may be rebutted; but, generally speaking, an imaginary line, running through the middle of the stream, is the boundary; just as, if a road separates two properties, the ownership of the road belongs half-way to one and half-way to the other. It may be rebutted by circumstances; but, if not rebutted, that is the legal presumption. Then, if two

this country, it has been declared, that the common law on this subject prevailed here, and that conveyances of land bounded on rivers and streams of water (above tide-water) extend *usque ad filum aquæ*.[1] A grant of all the land situated east and north of a certain stream was held to extend to the middle of the stream.[2] Each riparian proprietor owns an equal share of the bed of the stream in proportion to his line on the margin of the stream, together with that portion of the bed of the stream which lies opposite, in front of, or adjacent to, his upland; and this, in the absence of any controlling grant, will be effected by the straight lines, at right angles, which will in general be the shortest and most direct lines to the thread of the river. And it cannot well be perceived how this consideration can be influenced by the shape of the upland lot, or by the direction of its side lines back from the river.[3]

§ 12. The same rule holds, whether a grant of land is made

properties are divided by a river, the boundary is an imaginary line in the middle of that river; but to say that the whole of the river is a sort of common property, which belongs to no one, is not a correct view of the case." See 3 Kent, 427, 428. Chancellor Kent says, "Where a stream is used in a grant as a boundary or monument, it is used as an entirety to the centre of it, and to that extent the fee passes. *Primâ facie*, said the Vice-Chancellor of England, in Wright *v.* Howard, 1 Sim. & Stu. 190, the proprietor of each bank of a stream is the proprietor of half the land covered by the stream." 3 Kent, 428; Pratt *v.* Lamson, 2 Allen, 284. In Pratt *v.* Lamson, it was held, that if a natural stream of water flows and forms the boundary between the lands of different proprietors, the fee of each owner includes one-half of the bed of the stream; but each is entitled to use one-half of the water which flows in the stream, without regard to the position and course of its principal channel and current. This case is more fully stated on this last point, post, § 101 *a*. But deeds of land bounding on a stream do not affect previous independent conveyances of all the water power therein. Crittenden *v.* Field, 8 Gray, 621].

[1] Palmer *v.* Mulligan, 3 Caines, 319; Canal Commissioners *v.* The People, 5 Wend. 423; Tyler *v.* Wilkinson, 4 Mason, 397; Claremont *v.* Carlton, 2 N.H. 369; Ingraham *v.* Wilkinson, 4 Pick. 468; People *v.* Seymour, 6 Cowen, 579; Hooker *v.* Cummings, 20 John. 91; Arnold *v.* Munday, 1 Halst. (N.J.) 1; Adams *v.* Pease, 2 Conn. 481; Mead *v.* Haynes, 3 Rand. (Va.) 33; Blanchard *v.* Baker, 8 Greenl. 253; Bliss *v.* Rice, 17 Pick. 23; Waterman *v.* Johnson, 13 Pick. 261; Williams *v.* Buchanan, 1 Ire. 535; Canal Appraisers *v.* People, 17 Wend. 590; Commissioners of Canal Fund *v.* Kempshall, 26 Wend. 404; Child *v.* Starr, 4 Hill, 369; [Brown *v.* Chadbourne, 31 Maine, 9; Pike *v.* Munroe, 36 Maine, 309; Trustees &c. *v.* Dickinson, 9 Cush. 546, 547; State *v.* Gilmanton, 9 N.H. 463; though the courses and distances do not agree with the actual course of the stream. Browne *v.* Kennedy, 5 H. & John. 195, 205, 207. This doctrine applies to the great rivers in this country, like the Mississippi, subject to the public right of passing over them as highways. 3 Kent, 427; Morgan *v.* Reading, 3 S. & Marsh. 366, 403; Jones *v.* Soulard, 24 How. (U.S.) 41].

[2] Morrison *v.* Keen, 3 Greenl. 474.

[3] Per Shaw C.J., in Knight *v.* Wilder, 2 Cush. 199; and see post, §§ 55, 56.

by a State or an individual.[1] In Maryland, the State is entitled to certain unnavigable rivers, and to the soil they occupy; and it is held by the courts there, that, if the State grants land on one of such rivers, and the grant calls for the river as a boundary, the grantee becomes riparian proprietor, and is entitled to the land the river covers *ad filum medium aquæ;* and that any subsequent grantee, under the same description, is alike entitled.[2] Grants by the legislature of New York of islands in rivers and streams of water, where the tide does not ebb and flow, although made during a long series of years, do not justify the conclusion that the principle of the common law has not been adopted, that grants of land bounded on such waters carry the exclusive right of the grantees to the middle thereof.[3]

§ 13. Lots bounding on the Oswego River, and immediately below a dam belonging to the State of New York, erected for canal uses, were sold by the commissioners of the land-office as water lots bounding on the river. It was held, that the purchaser of such water lots was entitled to the water privileges connected with such lots at the time of the sale, by the natural flow of the surplus water over the State dam, so far as such waters could be used, to the middle of the stream, provided the public right of navigation was not molested; and that State officers could not afterwards lease such surplus waters, and authorize the lessee to prevent them from flowing over the dam, to the injury of the water privileges connected with the water lots thus sold.[4]

§ 14. So, grants by the general government of the United States are construed by the Common-Law rule, unless there is something to exclude or qualify that construction. A grant by the United States of land lying upon the river Mississippi,

[1] Hayes *v.* Bowman, 1 Rand. (Va.) 420; and ante, § 6 et seq.; Jennings *ex parte*, 6 Cowen, 518; and see the note of the reporter in the same volume, p. 536; Arthur *v.* Case, 1 Paige, 447.

[2] Brown *v.* Kennedy, 5 H. & John. 195. A grantee from the State is entitled to whatever falls within the tract described in his patent; and, therefore, is entitled to alluvian accretions, and insular formations. Ridgeley *v.* Johnson, 1 Bland Ch. 316; and see Baltimore *v.* McKim, 3 Bland Ch. 453. [As the boundary of the State of Georgia is the western bank of the Chattahoochee River, the rights of riparian proprietors therein extend beyond the middle of the stream to that bank. Jones *v.* Water Lot Co., 18 Geo. 539.]

[3] People *v.* Canal Appraisers, 13 Wend. 355; s.c. 17 Wend. 571; *Ex parte* Jennings, 6 Cowen, 548; Commissioners *v.* Kempshall, 26 Wend. 404.

[4] Varick *v.* Smith, 9 Paige, 547; and see 5 Paige, 138.

without reservation, was held to pass to the grantee a title to the middle of the river.[1] So the act of Congress establishing the Mississippi River as the western boundary of the Mississippi Territory, and adopting the Common Law for the government of that territory, fixed the middle of the river as the boundary line; and the rights of the riparian proprietors on the east shore of that river must be determined by the Common Law.[2] In Gavit *v.* Chambers, in Ohio,[3] the Court say, "If it be assumed that the United States retain the fee-simple in the beds of our rivers, who is to preserve them from individual trespasses, or determine matters of wrong between the trespassers and themselves? It cannot be reasonably doubted that if all the beds of our rivers supposed to be navigable, and treated as such by the United States in selling lands, are to be regarded as unappropriated territory, a door is opened for incalculable mischiefs. Intruders upon the common waste would fall into endless broils amongst themselves, and involve the owners of adjacent lands in controversies innumerable. Stones, soil, gravel, the right to fish, would all be subjects of individual scramble, necessarily leading to violence and outrage." The United States have no other rights within the several States than as a landholder, and when they grant a portion of their domain, such rights and such only as are incident to the land, pass to the purchaser.[4]

§ 15. It is, therefore, obvious, that, in respect to tenants in common whenever they make partition, by assigning the land on one side of a watercourse to one of the co-tenants, and the land on the opposite side to the other, the two tracts are separated by the *thread* of the river.[5]

[1] Middleton *v.* Pritchard, 3 Scam. (Ill.) 510.

[2] Morgan *v.* Reading, 3 S. & Marsh. 366. [So in Cold Spring Iron Works *v.* Tolland, 9 Cush. 492, it was held that under a statute by which a stream not navigable is made the boundary of an incorporated territory, the centre of the stream, and not the edge or margin, is the true boundary line; and this is so, although the monuments were described as standing on the margin or bank of the stream.]

[3] Gavit *v.* Chambers, 3 Ohio, 495.

[4] Hendricks *v.* Johnson, 6 Port. (Ala.) 472.

[5] King *v.* King, 7 Mass. 496. [Where parties own in common a water power, and mills, machinery, dam, and other appurtenances, a partition of the whole property may be made; such partition, if insisted upon, must be made regardless of the inconvenience or hardship thereby occasioned. Hanson *v.* Willard, 12 Maine, 142; Smith *v.* Smith, 10 Paige, 470; Cooper *v.* Cedar Rapids Water Power Co., 42 Iowa, 398.]

§ 16. Proprietors of islands own to the thread of each branch of the river, which, in its natural course divides it from the main land.[1] And, where a watercourse is divided by an island, and the smaller portion of the stream dividing it descends on one side of it, and the residue on the other, the riparian proprietor of the main land by which the smallest quantity flows, is entitled to the use of no more of the water than naturally runs between his bank and the island.[2]

4. *When Persons become Riparian Owners.*

§ 17. It matters not what may be the intention of the grantor of land described as being bounded by a watercourse, or by words as comprehensive or in law equivalent; the grantee in such case will hold to the thread of the river, even if such was not the grantor's intention.[3] As a reservation of a right of way in a grant of land so bounded, upon the bank of the stream, does not prevent the fee in the land from vesting in the grantee, it does not limit his riparian rights.[4]

§ 18. What words employed in a grant of land bounded by a watercourse, will exclude the bed of the stream, and consequently all aquatic right, has, in this country, been a fertile subject-matter of litigation. It has been settled that territory described as "lying between" two rivers, is the whole country from their sources to their mouths; and if no fork of either of them has acquired the name, in exclusion of another, the *main* branch, to its source, must be considered as the true river.[5] In South Carolina it has been held, that where a certain survey called "Dean's Swamp" as a boundary, the creek or main stream of the swamp was intended, and not the outer edge or margin of low marshy land that frequently bounds the main stream.[6]

[1] People *v.* Canal Appraisers, ubi sup.

[2] Crooker *v.* Bragg, 10 Wend. 260 [3 Kent, 428. "If a river be divided into two courses by an island in its middle, the *medium filum* for boundary purposes is that which bisects the island, but if the island be nearer one side than the other, no account is taken of the smaller branch; the other alone represents the whole river, and its *medium filum* constitutes the *primâ facie* line of proprietary division." Phear Rights of Water, 11, 12].

[3] See ante, § 9; Waterman *v.* Johnson, 13 Pick. 261; Nickerson *v.* Crawford, 16 Maine, 245.

[4] Hagan *v.* Campbell, 8 Port. (Ala.) 9.

[5] Doddridge *v.* Thompson, 9 Wheat. 470; Beuner *v.* Platter, 6 Ham. (Ohio) 504.

[6] Felder *v.* Bonnet, 2 M'Mull. (S.C.) 44.

§ 19. A description in a grant calling for the mouth of "Lodge's Run" as the place of beginning, thence by several courses and distances to a *stone bridge* over the run, it being in the main road, at twelve perches north-east of a certain corner, mentioned in a deed, &c., thence down along the said run on the southwardly side thereof to the place of beginning, the said described run to be the boundary, was held proper to be applied by the Jury, and not, the Court, to evidence that there was, at the date of the deed, a *wooden* bridge, and *not* a *stone* one, over the main branch, which was usually called "Lodge's Run;" and that there was a stone bridge over a gut or small branch of it, at the specified distance from the particular corner tree.[1]

§ 20. A patent in North Carolina described the land as lying on the north side of a river, and the line in dispute called for "a pine on the marsh branch, then along the said branch 320 poles thence to the beginning," and the branch meets the river at a shorter distance. It was held that the branch was the boundary, and the mouth the corner of the land covered by the patent, and that the distance was to be disregarded.[2]

§ 21. It has been held in Maine, that if a tract of land is granted, fronting on and bounded by a river, the side lines are to be continued to the main stream, though they thereby cross a point formed by the junction of one of its branches with the principal river. Trespass was brought for entry upon land, which was the point of land made by the junction of a creek, called "Molasses Creek," with a river, called "Cathance" River, in Maine; and the plaintiff claimed the land in question as a part of a lot called "letter A." The question was at first, by rule of Court, referred to arbitrators; and upon the coming in of their report, which was in favor of the plaintiff, it was contested by the defendant, and on his motion recommitted. After a second hearing, a report was again returned for the plaintiff and again contested by the defendant. It appeared from examination of the referees, that the principal controversy was whether the *locus in quo* was part of the lot called A., belonging to the plaintiff, or of B., belonging to the defendant. These lots in point of

[1] Nourse *v.* Lloyd, 1 Penn. St. 220.

[2] Carraway *v.* Witherington, N. Carolina Term R. 275; 1 Ired. (N.C.) Dig. 107.

fact, upon actual survey, were situated as thus described by the continued lines: —

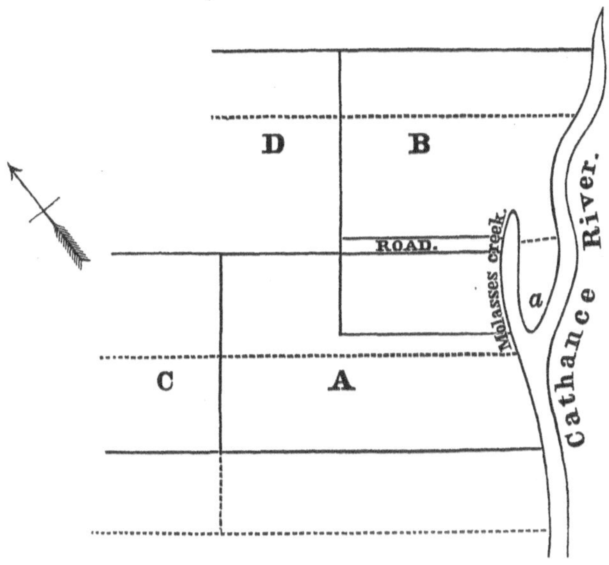

A. Plaintiff's Lot. B. Defendant's Lot. *a.* The *locus in quo.*

It appeared further before the referees, that a plan of these lots, with others, was made by John Merrill, in 1772; the part representing these lots purporting to be copied from McKenzie's plan, by which the lots were represented as lying farther down the river, and the road between the two lots as touching the river below the *locus in quo*, as appears by the dotted lines in the above diagram. The plaintiff hereupon contended that the lot A. extended across the creek to Cathance River, on which it was bounded by the deed; and further proved, that in low tides the water wholly flowed out of the creek at low water, in the part contiguous to his lot. But the defendants insisted that no more land would pass by the grant of lot A. than was delineated on the plan; by which the flats in question were evidently a part of lot B. But the referees, intending, as they said, to decide according to law as well as equity, were of opinion that as the side lines of the lots and of the road, as far as the creek, were undisputed and unquestionable, the division line must be taken to extend by the same course to the river, the creek not being mentioned as a boundary in the deed, and thereupon decided for the plaintiff. The exceptions to the report were overruled by the Court;

Weston J., who delivered their opinion, observing, "There being no question about the side lines of the lots A. or B., the flats in controversy belong to the plaintiff, as the owner of A., if that lot extends to the river. The title of both the parties to their respective lots is derived from a conveyance by James Bowdoin of lot A. to Abraham Preble, Jr., and of lot B. to Abraham Preble. By that conveyance, lot A. is bounded easterly on Cathance River. Lot A. then very clearly embraced these flats. It is contended, however, that this plain and necessary result is to be controlled and modified by a certain plan, made by John Merrill, in 1772, upon which these lots were delineated. No plan is referred to or mentioned in Bowdoin's deed; but it is urged, that the designation of the lots by letters implies and supposes a plan. This does not necessarily follow. A survey might be made, and the lots now owned by the parties, and the rear lots upon which they were bounded, might receive the names of A., B., C., and D., without making a plan. And if a plan was made, and A. did not, as laid down upon it, go to the river; if the owner did not refer to the plan, and thought proper distinctly and expressly to extend it to the river, in his conveyance, he had a perfect right so to do; and the grantee would hold accordingly. But if the plan exhibited to the referees and now produced to the Court had been referred to, the limits of A. would not thereby be curtailed. By that plan, the whole easterly line of A. is bounded on Cathance River. It is true, Molasses Creek is there represented as entering upon the south side of B. and extending northerly thereon; whereas, in fact, it enters upon A. But this mistake in the location of the creek does not change the rights of the parties. The creek is not given as a boundary in the deed, but each lot is expressly bounded on the river, both in the deed and on the plan. When the survey was made, the waters of the river might have been so high that the mouth of the creek might appear to the eye to be on B., and this may account for its having been thus delineated; but, however occasioned, this error in a part of the plan, altogether immaterial in fixing the location of the lots, can have no legal influence in the decision of the cause."[1]

§ 22. In North Carolina it is a principle clearly settled, that a

[1] Graves *v.* Fisher, 5 Greenl. 69.

natural and permanent object shall be deemed the boundary in preference to the line designated by course and distance. It is true that the call for a natural boundary may be, itself, vague or imperfect, or even contradictory ; as in the case of a stream of water where there are two of the same name ; or, if it be uncertain which of the two bears the name, then, necessarily, the case is open for evidence to the jury, as to which was the object meant, and by which the survey was actually made.[1] In Hurley *v.* Morgan, in North Carolina,[2] it was held, that, as a general rule, in questions of boundary, a natural object has a preference over marked lines or corners, and will control them when the natural object is of such a nature as cannot easily be mistaken by the parties either in name or situation, as in the case of a *river*. But the reason of this rule does not apply to very *small streams* which either have no names, or have formerly had a different name from that which they now bear. With respect to these, it is open to evidence *which stream* the parties meant by a particular name ; and the jury, if satisfied of the fact, from proof of possession or the like, may find a stream to be the one meant, although not the one bearing the name mentioned in the deed.

§ 23. It appears to be generally understood, that, where general terms are used in a description in a deed, the Court will put a construction upon those terms where any definite rule has been established. Thus, premises conveyed and described as being bounded by a watercourse, extend by legal operation to the thread of the river ; yet in this case the grant *may* be limited by language sufficiently strong and definite to give a different operation and exclude the watercourse ; for, where parties make any definite agreement in their deed, such agreement will control any legal implication.[3] The cases, on the whole, may be said to demonstrate the existence of the rule, that a grantee bounded on a river (and it is almost immaterial by what mode of expression) goes *ad medium filum aquæ*, unless there be decided language

[1] Becton *v.* Chestnut, 4 Dev. & Bat. (N.C.) 335.

[2] Hurley *v.* Morgan, 1 Dev. & Bat. (N.C.) 425; and see Lynch *v.* Allen, 4 Dev. & Bat. (N.C.) 62.

[3] Waterman *v.* Johnson, 13 Pick. 261; Hammond *v.* Ridgely, 5 H. & John. 215. The owner of land on each side of a road or stream of water not navigable, is *primâ facie* presumed to own to the centre ; and in the construction of deeds, the general rule is, that when a grant of land is bounded on a highway, it conveys the land to the centre of the road, *unless there be decided and controlling words or specific descriptions to show a contrary intent.* Herring *v.* Fisher, 1 Sandf. 344; Hammond *v.* McLachan, 1 Sandf. 323.

showing a *manifest intent* to stop at the water's edge;[1] and there seems a distinct and strong tendency in the cases to turn every doubt upon expressions which fix the boundary next the river, in favor of a contact with the water.[2] The words which create

[1] 3 Kent, 429 [post, § 29, note; Walker *v.* Shepardson, 4 Wis. 486].

[2] [This tendency was not followed in the case of Chapman *v.* Edmands, 3 Allen, 512, in which it was held, that flats are not included in a description of land bounding on a salt-water "creek betwixt said land and land of J. L." But if it were not for the eminent source from which this decision emanated, the remark would be adventured, that the expression quoted was merely a description of the creek, and not an exclusion of it. If, however, it did exclude it, the question would arise, at what state of the tide? The remark made in the decision of the above case, that the above expression "shows that the creek was regarded as separate and distinct from the adjoining land, and was not intended by the parties as an abuttal by which the extent of the proprietary right in the premises described in the indenture was defined and limited," seems to be hardly an obvious conclusion from the premises. The case of Harlow *v.* Fisk, 12 Cush. 302, more clearly expresses the law of boundary on a creek or watercourse according to the tendency of the later cases. In this case it was held that a deed of all the land on "the easterly side of a creek, meaning to convey all the land between" certain other specified bounds and said creek, conveys the flats adjoining, to the centre of the creek. Shaw C.J. said, "It is, therefore, the ordinary case of land bounding on a creek or watercourse, where neither of the side lines nor the middle line is expressed. The conclusion of law is, that the channel or middle line, or *filum aquæ*, is intended." The case of Lord *v.* The Comms. for the City of Sidney, 12 Moore P.C. 473, in which a boundary on a creek was under consideration, strongly exhibits the same tendency. See Berridge *v.* Ward, 10 C.B. N.S. 400, 411. A township bounded "easterly and northerly on Schoodiac River" carries the grant to the middle thread of the river above tide-waters. Granger *v.* Avery, 64 Maine, 292. A patent describing land as bounded by a line commencing at a point on the river, then running outward and returning to a point on the same, and thence by the river to the place of beginning, conveys title to low-water mark, with a frontage at low-water mark equal to the distance between the termini. Wood *v.* Appal, 63 Penn. St. 210. In Watson *v.* Peters, 26 Mich. 508, it was decided that the grant of a city lot bounded on a navigable stream, with the water as a boundary, in the absence of any express reservation, conveys to the grantee the land under the water to the centre of the stream; and the fact that the grantor, before conveying, platted the land into lots and blocks, with distinct lines and distances marking the boundaries of each lot, and with the water boundary of the river lots indicated by a line representing the shore line, and conveyed by such plat, will not limit the grant to such shore line, or operate to reserve to him proprietary rights in front of the lots conveyed. Cooley J. said: "The owner of city lots bounded on navigable streams, like the owner of any other lands thus bounded, may limit his conveyance thereof within specific limits, if he shall so choose; but where he conveys with the water as a boundary, it will never be presumed that he reserves to himself proprietary rights in front of the land conveyed, which he may grant to others for private occupation, or so occupy himself as to cut off his grantee from the privileges and conveniences which appertain to the shore of navigable water. Such privileges and conveniences constitute a part, and in many cases the principal part, of the value of the grant; and it is precisely in these cases of city lots that they are of most value, and generally constitute the chief inducement to the purchase, and the chief, or at least a very important, element in determining the

the most difficulties are where the *termini* of the river line stand on the bank at some distance from the stream, and the line is prescribed to run between them "along the river," or "up the river," or "down the river," or the like.[1] The description of "margin" of a river was used in a grant of land made by the State of New York; and it was contended that the State, by such description, had *reserved* the bed of the river, and of course the right to the river itself. The Court, however, decided, that such a construction was a misapprehension of the legal meaning and extent of the grant; and they held, that though land, nominally and in terms, is bounded on the "margin" of a river, it extends, by construction of law, to the centre or thread of the river.[2]

§ 24. The word "bank"[3] of the river, may be used as synonymous with the river, carrying the boundary line *to* the bank, and then along the river, and not along the "bank of the river."[4]

price. These cases, therefore, of all others, are those in which the reason of the rule which infers an intent to convey the land under the water, is most apparent and forcible. And the rule itself is too valuable, and too important, to be varied by so immaterial a circumstance as that the boundary on the water is defined by a line, instead of by making use of words which to the common understanding would convey the same meaning. And what we have said of navigable waters is equally applicable to all natural watercourses. If, on the face of the plat by reference to which the defendant bought, there was any thing which distinctly indicated an intent on the part of the proprietors to make this case exceptional, and to reserve to themselves any rights in front of the water lots marked on it, after they should have been sold, the case would have been different." See Child *v.* Starr, 4 Hill, 369; Trustees of Illinois and Michigan Canal *v.* Haven, 11 Ill. 554; Ryan *v.* Brown, 18 Mich. 196; Yates *v.* Milwaukee, 10 Wallace, 497. Such riparian rights will not be affected or limited by a mere sand bar or place of shallow water, exposed only when the wind is favorable or the water low. Watson *v.* Peters, supra.]

[1] The opinion of Cowen J., in Starr *v.* Child, 20 Wend. 149; [Pike *v.* Munroe, 36 Maine, 309].

[2] Jennings, *ex parte*, 6 Cowen, 518.

[3] [Various legal definitions, generally agreeing in substance, have been given of this word; such as, "The *bank* is the outermost part of the bed in which the river naturally flows." Grotius de Jur. B. et P. 2, 8, 9. In the words of the Digest, "that is considered the bank which contains the river when *fullest.*" Digest, 43, 12, 3. It is that line or ridge of earth which ordinarily holds or contains the river. The banks of a river are not changed because in times of freshets, heavy rains, or other extraordinary causes, they may be overflowed. The bank is "the fast land which confines the water of the river in its channel or bed in its whole width." Wayne J., in Howard *v.* Ingersoll, 13 How. (U.S.) 417. "The banks of a river are those elevations of land which confine the waters when they rise out of the bed." Curtis J., 13 How. (U.S.) 427. "Land usually of some elevation, along the side of a river or stream, confining the water in its channel or bed." Burrill Law Dict. verb. "Bank." See Stone *v.* Augusta, 46 Maine, 127, 137.]

[4] Per Gridley V.C., in Varick *v.* Smith, 9 Paige, 547; Lamb *v.* Rickets, 11 Ohio, 311.

The Supreme Court of Massachusetts say, that, without doubt, the owner of land extending to the "bank" of a river, will own to the middle of the river; but that the owner "may sell the land without the privilege of the stream, as he will if he *bounds his grant by the bank*."[1] The Court, it appears, admit that an owner to the "bank" of the river owns the river; but they immediately say that he *may* bound his grant by the "bank," and the stream will not pass. This has been considered as evidently meaning a bounding by a reservation, or plain exclusion; or, otherwise, the expression would be inconsistent in itself and incompatible with principle and all the cases; and that it is plain that the naked circumstance of bounding a grant *on*, *to*, or *by* a "bank," cannot exclude the stream any more than bounding on the "margin" of the stream.[2] The remark of the Court in the case in Massachusetts, that where land is bounded by the "bank" of a stream, such description excludes the bed of the stream, it

[1] Hatch *v.* Dwight, 17 Mass. 289; [Bradford *v.* Cressey, 45 Maine, 13. In Stone *v.* Augusta, 46 Maine, 127, it was held, that, where the boundaries of land conveyed by a deed were, "thence to mill-brook; thence *by the bank* of said brook, to" &c., the grantee's land is bounded by ordinary high-water mark; and this principle is not changed by the fact, that the land continues to rise more or less precipitously above that point. His land is not limited to the top of the hill or bank beside the stream, but extends to the margin of the stream, to that point where the bank comes in contact with the stream. The land which was the subject of controversy in this case was upon the margin of a stream in which, according to the testimony, the tide ebbed and flowed, though the water was fresh. See Lapish *v.* Bangor, 8 Maine, 85].

[2] See the note of the Reporter to the case of Jennings, *ex parte*, 6 Cowen, 549, and ubi sup. In the case of Hatch *v.* Dwight, 17 Mass. 289, E., in 1807, mortgaged a strip of land including mills, and running a considerable distance along the river; but, in 1810, having sold a small piece of the mortgaged premises for a hide mill and lime vats, he obtained a grant, or rather *release*, from the mortgage, for a nominal consideration of what he (E.) had sold, described thus: Beginning at the *end of a dam*, running up the river two rods, and so round *to the bank of the river*. The mortgagee afterwards having foreclosed, one question was, whether the release gave a right to the centre of the river; and it appeared that if it was to have this effect, it would destroy the value of the mortgagee's mill privileges. For this and other reasons, it was held that it should not extend beyond the bank. The various reasons assigned by the Court were, that the release was limited to the bank; that there were no general words showing that a right to keep up a dam was intended to pass; that the consideration was nominal; and that it was not to be inferred that the mortgagee intended to release every thing valuable in the mortgaged premises, for which he had given a large consideration. The Court considered the release, under these circumstances, as being no more than a mere *exception* to the mortgage; and there were various other special circumstances in the case which led the Court to infer that the *intention* of the parties was to limit the grant or release to the bank. See the note of the Reporter to Jennings, *ex parte*, 6 Cowen, 636, et seq.

was held by the Vice-Chancellor of New York (Gridley) to be clearly founded in truth, *as applied to the facts of that case;*[1] and the facts of the case, he held to be such as to indicate, with great certainty, that, by the use of the phraseology employed, the parties intended to exclude from the operation of the release the bed of the stream. But he was at the same time of opinion that this was not the necessary construction of such descriptive words in a grant. The popular understanding of them, he considered, would doubtless limit the grant of the land adjacent to the stream; and so would the popular understanding of a description which bounded the premises upon the "margin" of a stream, or on the stream itself; but the legal construction of such words contained in the description of premises in a grant, had, by repeated adjudications, been established otherwise.[2]

§ 25. In an important case in Ohio, it appeared that the plaintiff had taken possession of the *bed* of the river Sandusky, and had built a mill; and he sued the defendants for building below and flowing back water upon the mill. The defendants denied that the plaintiffs owned the bed of the stream; for they claimed under a conveyance from the United States, bounding them on the "bank;" and, indeed, the area of the river was deducted by the United States, and only lands on the shores paid for. Yet the bed of the stream was held to pass, though there was every thing but an express exception by the United States. They had included the river in their surveys, but deducted the bed from the price, and bounded the patentee on the banks. The Court ask, "At what point does the right of the owner of the adjoining lands terminate? on the top or at the bottom of the bank? at high or low water mark? does his boundary recede or advance with the water, or is it stationary at some point? and where is that point?" The Court then say, "No satisfactory rules can be laid down in answer to these questions, if the Common-Law doctrines be departed from."[3]

§ 26. It thus appears to be well established that the *bank* and the *water* are correlative, and that one cannot be owned without

[1] Which are stated in the preceding note.

[2] Varick *v.* Smith, 9 Paige, 547. A line called for "171 poles to Roanoke River," the call to the river terminates, when the line reaches the "margin" or "bank" of the river, without regard to distance; and the intersection of the lines with the river is the point from which the next line commences. Haughton *v.* Rascoe, 3 Hawks (N.C.) 21.

[3] Gavit *v.* Chambers, 3 Ohio, 495.

touching the other; that the *bank* is the principal object; so that when the law once fixes the proprietorship of *that*, the soil of the river follows as an incident; or rather (as it has been said), "as part of the subject-matter, *usque ad filum aquæ*."[1] If a boundary is described as running to a monument standing on the bank, and from thence running "by the river" or "along the river," it does not restrict the grant to the bank of the stream; for the monument in such case is only referred to as giving the directions of the line *to the river*, and not as restricting the boundary *on the river*. If, however, the grantor, after giving the line to the river, restricts his land to the *bank* of the river, or describes the line as running *along the bank* of the river, his intention is manifested not to consider the whole *alveus* of the stream a mere mathematical line, so as to carry his grant to the middle of the river.[2] [And in all cases where the language used clearly shows such to be the intention of the grantor, the bank, side, margin, or shore become themselves monuments, and are to be treated as such.[3] By a deed of a parcel of land, the east line of which is described, "thence east until it strikes the creek on which the mill stands, thence south-westerly on the west bank of said creek" (which is a small, unnavigable, fresh-water stream), the grantee is restricted to the *bank* of the creek. And such grant does not extend to the centre or thread of the stream, unless there are, in the deed, other words indicating that such was the grantor's intention.[4]]

§ 26 *a*. There is obviously an essential difference between "fronting *to*," and "fronting *upon*," and it has thus been illustrated by Mr. Livingston, counsel for the defendants in Morgan *v*. Livingston, in Louisiana:[5] "The cathedral (New Orleans) fronts the public square and the river; but it fronts upon

[1] By Cowen J., in Starr *v*. Child, 20 Wend. 149. [But adverse possession of the bank is not by construction of law possession to the centre of the stream. Corning *v*. Troy &c. Factory, 34 Barb. 529.]

[2] Per Walworth Ch., in Child *v*. Starr, 4 Hill, 369; Lamb *v*. Ricketts, 11 Ohio, 311. In Tennessee, where the grant called for a "tree" and the "river bank," thence *down the river* to another "tree" on the "bank of the river;" it was held, that the meanders of the river must be the boundary, and not a straight line. Weakley *v*. Legrand, 1 Tenn. 269.

[3] [Bradford *v*. Cressey, 45 Maine, 13; Starr *v*. Child, 5 Denio, 599; Sizer *v*. Devereux, 16 Barb. 160; Hatch *v*. Dwight, 17 Mass. 289; Halsey *v*. McCormick, 13 N. Y. (3 Kernan) 296; Bradley *v*. Rice, 13 Maine, 198; Dunlap *v*. Stetson, 4 Mason, 349; 3 Kent, 434; Hathorn *v*. Stinson, 10 Maine, 224.]

[4] [Bradford *v*. Cressey, 45 Maine, 9.]

[5] Morgan *v*. Livingston, 6 Mart. (La.) 19.

Chatres Street. The expression, then, *front*, or *front to*, only means the exposure, the direction of that boundary of a house or lot, in which is the principal entrance. How many houses, lots, and farms, on the heights about New York and Naples, front those bays, which are yet miles distant from the water!"

§ 27. In a conveyance of a lot of land situate in Rochester, in the State of New York, the lot was described as a "mill lot," "beginning, &c., and running eastwardly to the Genesee River; thence northwardly along the *shore* of said river to Buffalo Street." It was held, by the Supreme Court of that State, that the grantee took *usque ad filum aquæ*.[1] But Bronson J. dissented; and on appeal to a Court of Errors, the decision was reversed. By that Court it was held, that no part of the bed of the river passed under the conveyance, and that the grantee took only to low-water mark. And the fact, that the premises conveyed in this case were described in the deeds as "mill lots," could not operate to extend the grant into the *alveus* or bed of the river, for the deeds also showed, that *the contemplated mills were to be supplied with water from the mill-race already constructed;* and not by water to be taken from the Genesee River opposite the lots granted; and the right to discharge the water into the river after it had been used to propel the machinery on the mill lot, was at most but an easement, and did not require for its ownership any part of the bed of the stream by the grantees. It was, moreover, considered that a river in which the tide does not ebb and flow, has, properly speaking, no *shore;* that it has *ripam*, but not *littus;*[2] that when the term *shore* is applied to such a river, it means the river's banks above the low-water mark, rather than those portions of the banks of the river which touch the margin or edges of the water; so that a grant of land which is bounded by the *shore* of a fresh-water river conveys only the land to the water's edge, at low water.[3]

[1] Starr *v.* Child, 20 Wend. 149.

[2] See Hall on Rights to the Sea; and Angell on Tide-Waters.

[3] Child *v.* Starr, 4 Hill, 369. In the case in the Supreme Court (Starr *v.* Child, ubi sup.), Cowen J., in giving the opinion of the Court, thus criticises the word *shore:* "I admit that it is not critically correct to say the *shore* of a river; the term belongs, in its strict sense, to the ocean. Dr. Johnson says it applies to a river only in a secondary, or, as he calls it, a *licentious* sense. 'Beside the fruitful *shore* of muddy Nile.' Johns. Dic. 4to. 'Shore.' Yet it is sometimes so applied in legal proceedings. The compact between Virginia and Kentucky speaks of the *shores* of the Ohio; which word *shores* was treated by C.J. Marshall as the same with *side* or *bank*. Handly *v.* An-

§ 28. Where a line is described as running in a certain direction to a river, thence "up the same," or "down the same," or "with the river," those words necessarily imply that the line is to follow the river, according to its meanderings or turnings; and that, of course, must be the middle of the river.[1]

§ 29. Where land adjoining a river is described as bounded by a *monument* standing on the bank of the river, and a course is given as running from it down the river as it turns, to another monument, the grantee takes to the middle of the river.[2] So where land is bounded by a line commencing at a *stake* "by the side of the river or mill-pond," and running "by the side of said pond" to another *stake* "by the side of said pond," the grant extends to the thread of the river.[3] The decision in Lunt *v.* Holland, in Massachusetts,[4] is, that a line running between two trees, one standing "by the side of," and the other "by the river," is a bounding on the river; and that the grantee is,

thony, 5 Wheat. 385." . . . "It is conceded," says the learned Judge, "that the words *to and along the river* would include the stream. What difference between that and *to and along the shore?* A difference in words signifying the same thing. In either case, taken literally or according to common understanding, they carry you to a line immediate the water and the land, and touching both. How do they take more? Upon construction of law, which does not require express words for the grant of every part, as houses, fences, mines, or the elements of water or air, which all pass by the word *land;* and as a grant of land by certain boundaries, *primâ facie* passes all such parts to the grantee, *usque ad cœlum et ad infernos;* so within the same principle it passes the adjoining fresh-water stream *usque ad filum aquæ.*"

[1] Jackson *v.* Snow, 12 John. 252; Johnson *v.* Pannel, 2 Wheat. 206. A call in a grant from a bound on a river, "*west* up the river to a *stake,*" is in law equivalent to "*with* the river," and the line must pursue the course of the stream. Denn *v.* Mabe, 4 Dev. (N.C.) 180. "Thence 50° east, down the creek," the creek is the boundary. Smith *v.* Auldridge, 2 Hay. (N.C.) 382.

[2] Luce *v.* Carley, 24 Wend. 451. [A grant of land, bounded on a stream not navigable, carries the exclusive right and title of the grantee to the centre of the stream, unless the terms of the grant clearly denote the intention to stop at the edge or margin. And this is so, although the monuments are described as standing on the margin or bank of the stream. Cold Spring Iron Works *v.* Tolland, 9 Cush. 495, 496; Robinson *v.* White, 42 Maine, 209, 217, 218; Child *v.* Starr, 4 Hill, 375, per Walworth Ch.; Coovert *v.* O'Conner, 8 Watts, 470; Knight *v.* Wilder, 2 Cush. 199; Inhab. of Ipswich, Pet'rs, 13 Pick. 431; Bradford *v.* Cressey, 45 Maine, 13; Beahan *v.* Stapleton, 13 Gray, 427; 3 Kent, 427; Gray J., in Paine *v.* Woods, 108 Mass. 169; Agawam Canal Co. *v.* Edwards, 36 Conn. 476, 501; Bishop *v.* Seeley, 18 Conn. 393; Martin *v.* Nance, 8 Head (Tenn.) 649. It would require an express exception in the grant, or some clear and unequivocal declaration, or certain and immemorial usage, to limit the title of the owner, in such cases, to the edge of the river. 3 Kent, 428; Walker *v.* Shepardson, 4 Wis. 486. But the owner in fee of the land under an unnavigable river, may sell such land separate from the upland to which it is attached. Knight *v.* Wilder, 2 Cush. 199.]

[3] Lowell *v.* Robinson, 16 Maine, 357. Running to a *stake* on the Ohio River, held to be a boundary on the river. 1 Pirt. (Ken.) Dig. 130.

[4] Lunt *v.* Holland, 14 Mass. 149.

therefore, a riparian proprietor, and his land extends *usque ad filum aquæ.* The line around a tract of land was described in a deed as "running to a stake at the river, thence on the river north 6° 40′ west, 23 perches; thence north 39° 50′ west, 33 perches; thence north 20° 20′ west, 35 perches and 3 links, to a stake by the river." This description, it was held, made the river the boundary.[1]

§ 30. It is considered to be settled in North Carolina, that "up the river," is the same as "along the river," unless there be something else besides course and distance to control it. Thus a call in a grant from a river "*west up* the river to a *stake*," was held in law to be equivalent to "*with* the river," and the line must pursue the course of the stream; but this sense of the words might *possibly* be controlled by a call for a line of marked trees, or a visible permanent corner, and a meaning thereby given them equivalent to "*up*," not "*with*, the river;" but by no call less certain can they be controlled.[2] The last line given in

[1] Rix *v.* Johnson, 5 N.H. 520. Richardson C.J., in this case, said, "We were at first inclined to think that the return had not made the river a boundary. For, although the stakes are described as *at* and *by* the river, and the line is said to run on the river, yet, taking the whole return together, we thought it not improbable that the words, *at*, *by*, and *near*, the river might be intended to express nothing more than 'near the river.' And the circumstance that the line along the river is so particularly described by courses and distances, seemed to us to countenance such a construction of the return.

"But there are circumstances and arguments which, upon a more attentive consideration of the case, seem to us much more decisive, to show that the river must have been intended as a boundary.

"In the first place, there are no monuments mentioned in the return, at the river, except in the lines that run to and from the river. In the description of the lines along the river, although the course changes twice, no bound is mentioned. If the intention was to make the river the boundary, this is all natural. But if the intention was to have the line upon the bank, it would have been according to the usual practice to have mentioned a monument at each change of the course.

"In stating the course of the line along the river, from the 'stake at the river,' it is expressly said to be 'on the river;' and although the words 'on the river' are not repeated at each change of the course of the line, yet, as the line ends at a stake by the river, and, in fact, nearly coincides through the whole extent with the ridge of the bank, the words '*on the river*' may perhaps be fairly enough considered as intended to apply to the line in its whole extent. If this be so, it is a strong argument to show that the river was intended as a boundary. And this argument is greatly strengthened by the consideration, that, if the river had not been intended as the boundary, it would have been natural to use the words '*on the bank*,' instead of '*on the river*,' in this place, which would have removed all doubt. If the line had been stated as running to a stake at the river, thence on the bank of the river, the courses and distances mentioned in the return, there would have been no pretence for saying that the river was a boundary. 4 Mason, 365, 366; 17 Mass. 298."

[2] Rogers *v.* Nabe, 4 Dev. (N.C.) 180; and see Slade *v.* Neal, 2 Dev. (N.C.) 61; and ante, § 22.

a deed of land in North Carolina, was thence "along the river to the beginning," and the river was held to be the boundary, although the line coming towards the river called for a *white oak* as its termination, which was half a mile distant from the river.[1] In another case in the same State, the lines called for were "east 177 poles to an oak, thence southwardly along the various courses of the river." There was a marked oak at the end of the distance; and the river, from whence the point where a direct line from the oak would intersect it, ran southwardly. The east or third line called for, it was contended, extended to the river, because the river was the boundary called for between the corner of the third line and the beginning. This, as an abstract proposition, the Court said, was true, but then there was evidence that an oak actually stood at the spot where the 177 poles end; and a southwardly course from thence would strike the river at a small distance, and the river from the point where it is intersected by a line from the oak to the nearest part of the river runs southwardly to the beginning. If, said the Court, the line be not stopped at the oak, but is extended to the river, the course of the river from thence would not be in a southwardly but in a westwardly course till we got opposite the oak, and then southwardly. It was left to the jury with the instruction, that, if they believed the oak to have been made the point of termination when the *original survey* was made, they should make it now the boundary.[2]

§ 31. A grant of land in Maryland described the land as lying on the west side of N. branch of P. River, beginning at a bounded oak standing by the said branch, and running, &c., &c., to a bounded white oak standing by the said river, then bounding on the said river running S. 50 E. 270 perches, then by a straight line to the first bounded tree. It was held to be uncertain whether the last line bounded on and followed the meanders of the river, or whether it ran in a straight line to the boundary; and that the question was to be decided by the jury.[3] But where, in a grant of a tract of land, it is described as "lying on the west side of the N. branch of Patuxent River, beginning at a bounded red oak, standing by the said river, and running [three

[1] Sundifer *v.* Foster, 1 Hay. (N.C.) 237.

[2] Conder *v.* Coor, 2 Hay. (N.C.) 183.

[3] Corsey *v.* Hammond, 1 H. & John. 190.

courses] to a bounded white oak, standing by the said river, and then bounding on the said river, running S. 50 E. 270 perches, then by a straight line to the first bounded tree; it was held, that the construction of that grant was for the Court, and that the imperative construction was, that the fifth or last line could only be located by beginning at the end of the fourth line, wherever that was, and running a straight course to the beginning, without regard to the meanders of the Patuxent River.[1] In Hammond *v.* Ridgely, in Maryland,[2] it was held, that where a grant of a tract of land is described as "beginning at three bounded white oaks standing by Patuxent River, and *running* and *bounding* on the said river N. 4 E. 87 perches; then N. [sundry courses]; then N. 1 W. 48 perches, to a bound white oak, by the river; then S. 47 E. 388 perches, to a bound white oak; then by a straight line to the first-mentioned white oaks;" the first course is to be run N. 4 E. 87 perches, bounding the same on the River Patuxent, and all the subsequent courses were to be run according to the course and distance, until the course N. 1 W. 48 perches.

§ 32. When a grant of land refers to a *map*, upon which the land is laid down as bounded on a watercourse, the grantee is entitled to hold *usque ad filum aquæ*.[3] In a sale of land in the village of Oswego, in the State of New York (by virtue of which the grantee claimed the use of the water to the thread of the river), the lots were not very particularly described in the certificate of sale; but a map of the village in the office of the Secretary of State was referred to, and the lots were sold as laid down on that map. In a bill in Chancery by the grantee for a diversion of the water by canal commissioners, it was stated that the map designated the lots as being mill and water lots; and that the surveyor-general, at the sale, represented the lots as such, and that the purchaser would have the right to use them as such. The construction given by the Court was, that the grant of the lots under the above description and circumstances included a right to the watercourse.[4]

§ 33. In Kentucky, the *plat* of public lands is, by law, a necessary part of the surveyor's report, and it is, therefore, proper evidence in ascertaining the position of the land, and what it

[1] Hammond *v.* Ridgely, 5 H. & John. 245.

[2] 5 H. & John. 245.

[3] Newson *v.* Pryor, 7 Wheat. 7.

[4] Varick *v.* Smith, 5 Paige, 137; ib. 547.

includes. It has often happened in that State, that surveyors have one or more lines, bounded by streams of water, calling for divers courses, as meanders thereof, and the plat itself exhibits the stream as composing such lines; but whenever there is an attempt to run their courses and distances contained in a certificate and patent, they will not follow the stream at all, but widely depart from it; and, in such cases, it is held, that the stream must control the courses and distances called for, because *the plat makes the stream the boundary.*[1]

§ 34. Where a verdict in an action of ejectment called to run from one fixed object to another, with the meanders of the stream, *not located upon the plats;* it was considered by the Court so entirely uncertain, whether it was within the lines of the tract claimed and defended, or not, that no judgment could be entered upon it, nor writ of possession executed under it.[2]

§ 35. In a case decided by the Supreme Court of Maine, it appeared that a lot of land, being one of several fronting on the river, was sold by reference to a plan, without other description; and it also appeared that the surveyor, in laying out a large number of river lots, measured the front lines and marked the corners of the river, but never surveyed the sides nor the rear lines; nor did he correctly lay down the course of the river, but represented the place in question as a regular curve, and laid down the rear lines of the lots from corner to corner, as part of a larger concentric circle, when in fact the course of the river at that place was irregularly serpentine. It was held that the lots were to be located by laying off the side lines by the courses and distances from the river, according to the plan, and then drawing the rear lines from one corner to another, thus making them conform to the true course of the river, as originally designed, though not so delineated by the surveyor.[3]

§ 36. Whenever the beginning of a tract of land is ascertained, and the lines from thence are to terminate at a watercourse, if the course and distance given will not extend the line to the watercourse, the course and distance must be disregarded; and the line, notwithstanding these, must be extended to the

[1] Reid *v.* Langford, 3 J. J. Marsh. 420.

[2] Miles *v.* Knott, 12 Gill & J. 442.

[3] Loring *v.* Norton, 8 Greenl. 61. The Court cited as authority, Bowman *v.* White, decided in Maine in 1861; and Proprietors of Ken. Purchase *v.* Tiffany, 1 Greenl. 210.

watercourse, that being a natural boundary.[1] Where a line was described as running S.W. by S., to the head of "Howard's Branch," it was held, that it must run in a straight line from its beginning to that boundary.[2]

§ 37. In Harramond *v.* McGlaughan, in North Carolina,[3] it appeared that about fifty years before the year 1798, the State had granted to the defendant a tract of land beginning at a hickory, standing *not far* from a river, and running thence *down the river* a certain course and distance; but the course ran *obliquely* from the river, leaving between it and the river a triangular piece of land. The State claimed this triangle, and in 1787 granted it to the plaintiff, who sued in ejectment. The Court held, that the river was the boundary of the first grant, and decided against the claim of the State; and they used the following language: "When a deed, patent, or grant describes a boundary from a certain point *down a river*, mentioning also courses and distances, should the latter be found not to agree with the course of the river, it ought to be disregarded, and the river considered the true boundary."

§ 38. One of the lines in a deed of conveyance was thus described: "Beginning at the mouth of Black Brook, on the south side of the brook, and running from thence up said brook, due west, until it strikes the common land." The brook was very crooked, running sometimes on one side and sometimes on the other side of a due west line. It was held, that the brook was not designated as a monument with sufficient certainty to control the point of compass.[4]

§ 39. A grant of land extending to a certain distance on each side of a river (and no courses are given) is to be located in such a manner that every point in the exterior line shall be exactly that distance from the *nearest* point of the river. The words of the grant in Winthrop *v.* Curtis, in Maine,[5] were "the space of fifteen miles on each side of the Kennebec River; and it was held by the Court, that the location of the land was to be made in the mode just mentioned. The same is the established rule in New York, and prevailed in the Court of Errors in that State, in the location of the Catskill patent, which was to extend

[1] Pollock *v.* Harris, 1 Hay. (N.C.) 252; and see cases referred to in 1 Ire. (N.C.) Dig. 107, and ante § 22.

[2] Howard *v.* Moale, 2 H. & John. 249.

[3] Harramond *v.* McGlaughan, Taylor (N.C.) 196.

[4] Bowman *v.* Farmer, 8 N.H. 402.

[5] Winthrop *v.* Curtis, 3 Greenl. 110.

four English miles "from five great plains." That Court held the true construction of the patent to be, that its boundaries were to be ascertained by lines four miles distant, in every direction from the five plains mentioned in the patent, so as to make the exterior lines correspond as far as possible with the sinuosities of the plains.[1] The location of the Hoosack patent, which extended for two miles on each side of the river by that name, was the subject of controversy in the same Court; and DeWitt Clinton, Senator, in delivering his opinion, in which a majority of the Court concurred, states, that "the mode now adopted by the State, and considered the only practicable one in cases like the present, is to run the bounds so that every point in them shall be exactly the given distance from the point nearest to it in the creek or river."[2] In the case of Jackson *v.* Lunt, in New York,[3] Staat's patent was under consideration. This patent was to run up the river Hudson as that river runs, from a certain point, two hundred chains; thence up into the woods, north-west twenty chains, to the mountain; thence along said mountain, parallel with the Hudson River, to a certain rivulet; thence down that rivulet to the place of beginning. Spencer J., in delivering the opinion of the Court, observed, that in running a line parallel with a river, it is only requisite that the distance, where that is to control, should be such that the river in some one point is not further off than is required. In other words, the west line of Staat's patent, without reference to the mountain, if run parallel with the general course of the river, might in some places be at a greater distance than twenty chains, and yet be correctly run. But if *particular courses* are given in a grant of a tract of land bounding on a river, to the exterior side lines, the location must be determined accordingly. Thus, where a tract of land was granted *fronting on a brook*, and extending back *by a given course*, two miles; it was held, that by this description each side line should be two miles in length, and that the rear line must be parallel with the front.[4]

§ 40. An entry of Virginia military lands, in Ohio, read as follows: "Churchill Jones enters 1,000 acres of land, part of a military warrant, 2,311, on the north-west side of the Ohio, beginning at the mouth of Brush or Eighteen Mile Creek, run-

1 Van Gorden *v.* Jackson, 5 John. 440.
2 Williams *v.* Jackson, 5 John. 489.
3 Jackson *v.* Lunt, 2 Caines, 363.
4 Keith *v.* Reynolds, 3 Greenl. 393.

ning up the river 50 poles, thence from the beginning down the river 500 poles when reduced to a straight line, thence at right angles from the general course of the river, for quantity." The true construction of this entry, it was held, was to give a base on the Ohio River of 500 poles, including the 50 poles above the creek.[1] Another entry of the same kind called for 1,000 acres on the lower side of Brush Creek, "beginning at a marked cherry-tree, supposed about ten miles above Tod's Road, running thence west 400 poles, and from each end of this line for quantity." The distance was understood to be in a direct line, and not by the meanders of the creek, it being a small stream, and the usual line of travel not upon its banks.[2]

5. *Difference between a Boundary on a Watercourse, and a Boundary on a Lake or Pond.*

§ 41. When land is conveyed bounding upon a *lake* or *pond*, if it is a *natural* pond, the grant extends only to the water's edge;[3] but if it is an *artificial* pond, like a mill-pond, caused by the flowing back of the water of a river, the grant extends to the middle of the stream, in its natural state.[4] [A deed described the boundary of certain land as running "to the pond to a stake and stones," and it was held, in Robinson *v.* White,[5] that this restricted the grantee to the "stake and stones," if they, or their original location, could be ascertained; if not, then

[1] Hastings *v.* Stevenson, 2 Ohio, 8.

[2] Buckley *v.* Gilmore, 12 Ohio, 63.

[3] [The boundary on a natural pond extends only to low-water mark. Per Hoar J., in West Roxbury *v.* Stoddard, 7 Allen, 167; Wheeler *v.* Spinola, 54 N.Y. 377. In Marshall *v.* Steam Nav. Co., 3 B. & S. 732, it is queried, whether the soil of lakes, like that of fresh-water rivers, *primâ facie* belongs to the owner of the land on either side, *ad medium filum aquæ*, or whether it belongs to the king in right of his prerogative. Riparian owners on Lake Michigan own to the line where the water usually stands, when unaffected by any disturbing cause. Seaman *v.* Smith, 24 Ill. 521.]

[4] State *v.* Gilmanton, 9 N.H. 461; Hathorn *v.* Stinson, 1 Fairf. 238. See also Smith *v.* Miller, 5 Mason, 196; [Robinson *v.* White, 42 Maine, 209, 218; Lowell *v.* Robinson, 16 Maine, 357; Mansur *v.* Blake, 62 Maine, 38; Wheeler *v.* Spinola, 54 N.Y. 377].

[5] [Robinson *v.* White, 42 Maine, 209, 218. Where the boundary line along a pond commenced at "a stake near the high-water mark of the pond," running thence, "along the high-water mark of said pond, to the upper end of said pond," it was held that the line thus given was a fixed and permanent one, and did not follow the changes in the high-water mark of the pond, and that the defendant, who owned the bank bounded by said line, could not claim any accretions or land left dry in consequence of the water of the pond receding, although the gradual and imperceptible result of natural causes. Cook *v.* McClure, 58 N.Y. 437.]

his grant extended "to the pond."] In Bradley *v.* Rice, in Maine,[1] it was contended, that a certain lot which was conveyed bounding on a natural pond raised by artificial means, was not limited by the margin of the pond, and that, by construction of law, it extended to the centre. But the Court held otherwise, and made a distinction between such a pond and a stream of water. No case, they observed, had been cited, nor had any been found by them, where the rule of construction had been extended to a natural pond; and they then proceeded to say, "The proprietors of the pond and of the contiguous land, when they sold to the pond, must have intended to reserve that as a reservoir for the purpose to which it had been appropriated." And they add, "Had the land been bounded by a river or stream, or upon an artificial pond created by expanding a stream, by means of a dam, the riparian proprietor would go to the thread of the stream."[2] But this, though they conceived it to be law well settled and understood, did not, in their opinion, apply generally to ponds and lakes. They cite the similar case of Waterman *v.* Johnson, in Massachusetts,[3] as being one strictly in point. In that case the land conveyed was a farm, the bounds of which were described in the deed as beginning at "Jones's River Pond," and, after several courses, running to the "Ferse Pond," thence up stream by said pond to the canal that leads from "Jones's River Pond," thence by said canal to "Jones's River Pond," thence by said pond to the first-mentioned bound. It was in evidence that "Jones's River Pond" was a natural pond, and that ever since the memory of man, it had at times been flowed beyond its natural dimensions, by artificial means. Parol evidence was held to be competent to prove, that a certain line was agreed on and understood at the time of the conveyance, as the boundary. Shaw C.J., in giving the opinion of the Court, said, "Now the word 'pond' is indefinite. It may mean a natural pond, or an artificial pond raised for mill purposes, either permanent or temporary, and in both cases the limits of such body of water may vary at different times and seasons, by use,

1 Bradley *v.* Rice, 13 Maine, 198.

2 Phinney *v.* Watts, 9 Gray, 269; [Mansur *v.* Blake, 62 Maine, 38. It was held in this last case that when the lines of a deed, beginning at a road, run thence to an artificial pond, thence by the side of the same a specified distance, thence by a line parallel with the first line to the road, thence to the place of beginning; the grant runs to the centre of the pond].

3 Waterman *v.* Johnson, 13 Pick. 261.

or by natural causes; and where the one or the other is adopted as a descriptive limit or boundary, a different rule of construction may apply. A large natural pond may have a definite low-water line; and then it would seem to be the most natural construction, and one which would be most likely to carry into effect the intent of the parties, to hold, that land bounded upon such a pond would extend to low-water line; it being presumed that it is intended to give to the grantee the benefit of the water, whatever it may be, which he could not have upon any other construction.[1] Where an artificial pond is raised by a dam, swelling a stream over its banks, it would be natural to presume, that a grant of land bounding upon such a pond would extend to the thread of the stream upon which it is raised, unless the pond had been so long kept up as to become permanent, and to have acquired another well-defined boundary.[2] But it is difficult to apply either of these rules to the present case, which is that of a pond originally natural, but which has been raised more or less by artificial means. The discovery of this fact, upon applying the deed to the local objects embraced within its descriptive terms, discloses a latent ambiguity. According to a well-established rule of evidence, therefore, it is competent to resort to parol proof, showing all the circumstances from which a legal inference can be drawn, that one or another line was intended by the ambiguous description used in the deed. And this is, in truth, what both parties have done in the present case."

[§ 41 *a*. It was decided in Phinney *v.* Watts,[3] that a deed bounded "westerly by P.'s Mill Pond," which has been artificially created by erecting a dam across a stream, and through which the thread of the stream has always been apparent, passes the land to the thread of the stream. Metcalf J. said, "By the deed under which the plaintiff claims title to the *locus in quo*, he is bounded 'westerly by Phinney's Mill Pond,' which, according to the agreed facts, is sometimes called by that name, and sometimes by the name of 'Trout Brook,' and which is

[1] [Fletcher *v.* Phelps, 28 Vt. 257, 262. In Wood *v.* Kelley, 30 Maine, 55, Shepley C.J., having quoted this passage from the opinion in Waterman *v.* Johnson, said, "It is not perceived, why the same presumption respecting the intention does not arise, when the land is bounded upon a natural pond after it has been for a long time enlarged by artificial means, and thereby determine, that the line of boundary is to be found at low-water mark."]

[2] [Phinney *v.* Watts, 9 Gray, 269.]

[3] [Phinney *v.* Watts, 9 Gray, 269, 270.]

about thirty rods long, and through which the thread of the stream has always been apparent. On this state of facts, the Court are of opinion that the western boundary of the plaintiff's land is the centre or thread of the stream; as it unquestionably would have been, if the deed had bounded him on Trout Brook, the other name by which the water was known and called."[1]

§ 41 *b*. In Wood *v.* Kelley,[2] it was held that where there is a conveyance of land bounded on a fresh-water pond, which had been permanently enlarged by means of a dam at its mouth, the title extends to low-water mark of the pond in its enlarged state. In vindication of this rule the Court say, "The use of the waters of such ponds at all seasons is of great importance to the owners of the adjoining lands. When the water is low, its use becomes more desirable and valuable. Such waters are most valuable to the owners of land adjoining them for purposes for which tide-waters cannot be used. Unless rebutted by some proof, the presumption is, that it was the intention of the parties to a conveyance of land bounded by a pond, that the land should be bounded upon it at all seasons of the year, and not while the pond remained only at the level existing at the time of the conveyance. If the contrary doctrine were adopted, a person who received a conveyance of land adjoining on a pond, when the water was quite low, might convey it to another at a more elevated and yet not high state of the water with a like boundary, and retain a small strip of land between those two water lines; and there might, under the application of the doctrine, be several strips of land thus owned by different persons, when conveyances were made at several different states of the water. No grantor or grantee can be supposed to have intended to produce such results."[3] This case is distinguished from Bradley *v.* Rice.[4]]

[1] [Fletcher *v.* Phelps, 28 Vt. 257, 262; Gray J., in Paine *v.* Woods, 108 Mass. 169, 170; Hathorn *v.* Stinson, 1 Fairf. 238; s.c. 3 Fairf. 183.]

[2] [Wood *v.* Kelley, 30 Maine, 47.]

[3] [In Paine *v.* Woods, 108 Mass. 160, it was decided that a deed of land bounded "on" a pond which was used to be raised to an artificial height in the winter, and allowed in summer to remain at its natural level, conveys to low-water mark of the pond in its natural state; and it is immaterial that it was executed in the winter.]

[4] [Stated in § 41, ante. Vattel, when speaking of lakes, observes, "If some of the lands bordering on the lake are only overflowed at high water, this transient accident cannot produce any change in their dependence. The reason why the soil which the lake invades by little and little, belongs to the master of the lake, and perishes with respect to the ancient proprietor, is, because the proprietor has

§ 42. The law of boundary, as applied to rivers, is, without doubt, inapplicable to the *lakes* and other large natural collections of fresh water in this country.[1] The ordinary Common-Law rule of extending the right of soil in running fresh-water streams, to riparian grantees, Chancellor Walworth considered was not sufficiently broad to embrace the large fresh-water lakes, or "inland seas," in the State of New York; and that they were wholly unprovided for by the Common Law of England. As to these, said he, there is neither flow of the tide nor thread of the river; and it appeared that the local law of the State had assigned the shores down to the ordinary low-water mark to the riparian owners, and the beds of the lakes with the islands therein, to the public.[2] Such is the judicial construction in

no other limits besides the lake, nor any other mark besides its bank, to ascertain how far his possession extends. If the water advances insensibly, he loses; if it retires in like manner, he gains. Such must have been the intention of the people who have respectively appropriated the lake and the neighboring territories to each other; it can scarcely be supposed, that they had any other intention. But a territory overflowed for a time, is not confounded with the rest of the lake; it is still to be known, and the master may preserve his right as proprietor." B. I., ch. 22, § 275. "This doctrine," Shepley C.J. remarks in Wood *v.* Kelley, 30 Maine, 56, "is alike applicable to large ponds; and if a line as permanently existing could be established at the margin of the waters at the time of the conveyance, its application to them would be excluded. Such line could not be varied by a permanent encroachment of the pond." In Paine *v.* Woods, 108 Mass. 169, 170, Gray J. said, "A grant of land bounded by a river or stream above the ebb and flow of the tide, carries the grantor's title to the thread of the stream. Boston *v.* Richardson, 13 Allen, 146, 154; s.c. 105 Mass. 351, 352, and cases cited. And this, even if at the time of the grant the water of the stream has been permanently raised by artificial means so as to create a pond, and the grant is bounded generally by that pond. Phinney *v.* Watts, 9 Gray, 269, and cases cited. In like manner, a grant bounded by a great pond or lake, which is public property, extends to low-water mark. Walworth C., in Canal Commissioners *v.* People, 5 Wend. 423, 447; Shaw C.J., in Waterman *v.* Johnson, 13 Pick. 261, 265; Hoar J., in West Roxbury *v.* Stoddard, 7 Allen, 158, 167; Wood *v.* Kelley, 30 Maine, 47, 57; Fletcher *v.* Phelps, 28 Vt. 275." The learned Judge, in the above case of Paine *v.* Woods, reviewed and distinguished the case of Waterman *v.* Johnson, 13 Pick. 261, and also noticed the difference between the decision in Bradley *v.* Rice, 13 Maine, 198, and the decision in Wood *v.* Kelley, supra.]

[1] State *v.* Gilmanton, ubi sup.; Hathorn *v.* Stinson, ubi sup.; [Fletcher *v.* Phelps, 28 Vt. 257, 262. But in Bassett *v.* Salisbury Manuf. Co., 43 N.H. 578, Bartlett J. said, "It is by no means certain that the entire absence of current in a lake would prevent the application of the general principles that protect the rights of land-owners on running streams"].

[2] Canal Commissioners *v.* People, 5 Wend. 423. [But, in a recent case in the Supreme Court of New York, it was held that a lake measuring less than a mile in width by five miles in length, and having no navigable outlet, would pass under a grant of a large tract of land which included it in its boundaries. Ledyard *v.* Ten Eyck, 36 Barb. 102. The rule that the proprietors of lands, bordering upon streams and waters in which the tide ebbs and flows, own only to high-water mark, is not applicable to a case where, by the cutting of a

New Hampshire; and it seems to have been the construction of the legislature of that State, as appears from the annexation of islands in Winnipiseogee Lake, to the towns adjacent.[1] If a town in that State strikes any large body of water, by whatever name it may be called, it will go only to the water's edge, and be there bounded; that is, if there is nothing in the terms of the grant to show that it was to be extended further.[2] [It has been held in Vermont, that lands bounded on Lake Champlain extend to the edge of the water at low-water mark. And the same rule was applied to lands near the lake, bounded on a creek emptying into it, the waters of which ordinarily maintain the same level, and rise and fall with those of the lake; there being no claim made in the case that the boundary should extend to the centre of the creek.[3]]

§ 43. If a lot of land is conveyed agreeably to a plan, and is described as bounding one end on a pond, and there is a narrow arm of the pond extending from the pond across the lot, and if the land conveyed is to be limited by this arm, the lines will not correspond with those of the adjoining lots, and there would remain a portion of land not conveyed between the arm and the pond; the land granted extends across the arm to the main body of water called the pond.[4]

channel between a fresh-water pond and some body of salt-water, the water of the former becomes salt, and the tide ebbs and flows therein. In such case the rights of the riparian proprietors are not affected thereby. Wheeler *v.* Spinola, 54 N.Y. 377.]

[1] State *v.* Gilmanton, 9 N.H. 461.

[2] State *v.* Gilmanton, 9 N.H. 461.

[3] [Fletcher *v.* Phelps, 28 Vt. 257. In Austin *v.* Rutland R.R. Co., 45 Vt. 215, it was decided that owners of land bordering on the waters of Lake Champlain, have no title to the soil beyond low-water mark, nor right appurtenant, but only a statutory right to build wharves and storehouses into the lake, in front of their land. Therefore, if land is made by a stranger by filling in earth in front of their land from the line of low-water mark into the lake, and wharves and docks are built thereon, they cannot maintain ejectment therefor. Austin *v.* Rutland R.R. Co., 45 Vt. 215.]

[4] Nelson *v.* Butterfield, 21 Maine, 220.

CHAPTER II.

OF INSULAR AND ALLUVIAL RIGHTS, AND OF RIGHT TO SOIL RELICTED, &C., AS INCIDENT TO THE RIGHT OF PROPERTY IN A WATERCOURSE.

1. *Islands.*

§ 44. In treating, in the preceding chapter, of the apportionment of a watercourse between opposite riparian proprietors, it has appeared that the estate of each proprietor extends to the middle of the stream. Now, according to this rule, if there be a newly formed island exactly in the middle of the stream, it is equally divided between the two proprietors;[1] and so it is laid down both by ancient and modern writers.[2] But if one portion of the island approaches nearer to one side of a stream than it does to the other, the greater part belongs to the owner of the nearer estate, according to its approximation thereto. To establish, therefore, how great an extent of property in an island is annexed to the adjoining estates, the vicinity and remoteness of the island from the shore is to be taken into

[1] [In Trustees &c. *v.* Dickinson, 9 Cush. 548, Shaw C.J. stated the rule to be, that if an island gradually arises above the surface in a river, and becomes valuable for use as land, and it is so situated that it is partly on one side and partly on the other of the thread of the river, it shall be divided by that line which was the thread of the river immediately before the rise of the island, and in that manner be held in severalty by the adjacent proprietors.]

[2] Fleta, lib. 3, ch. ii. § 6; Bracton, lib. 2, ch. ii.; 2 Bla. Com. 261; 1 Swift's Dig. 111; Schultes on Aquatic Rights, 117; Woolrych Law of Waters &c. 38; Ingraham *v.* Wilkinson, 4 Pick. 268; 3 Kent, 428; Phear Rights of Water, 11, 12; Shaw C J., in Trustees &c. *v.* Dickinson, 9 Cush. 548. And see Giraud *v.* Hughes, 1 Gill & J. 249; People *v.* Canal Appraisers, 13 Wend. 355; Deerfield *v.* Arms, 17 Pick. 41. [If the same person owns the land on both sides of a stream, above tide waters, he owns the islands therein, to the extent of the length of his lands opposite to them. Granger *v.* Avery, 64 Maine, 292; ante, § 10 note.]

consideration.[1] This doctrine is agreeable to, and is unquestionably copied from, the Civil Law,[2] which says, "If an island rises in a river, and is placed exactly in the middle of it, such island shall be in common to them who possess the land near the banks. But if the island is nearer to one side than to the other, it belongs to them only who possess the land next to the banks on that side to which the island is nearest."[3]

§ 45. The rules on this subject are very definitely laid down in the code of Louisiana,[4] as follows: "Islands and sandbars, which are formed in streams not navigable, belong to the riparian proprietors, and are divided among them according to the rules prescibed in the following articles: If the island be formed in the middle of the stream, it belongs to the riparian proprietors whose lands are situated opposite the island. If they wish to divide it, it must be divided by a line supposed to be drawn along the middle of the river. The riparian proprietors then severally take the portion of the island which is opposite their land, in proportion to the front they respectively have on the stream, opposite the island. If, on the contrary, the island lie on one of the sides of the line thus supposed to be drawn, it belongs to the riparian proprietors on the side on which the island is, and must be divided among them, in proportion to the front they respectively have on the stream, opposite the island."[5]

§ 46. Supposing that another island should arise between an island already risen, on one side of the stream, and which

[1] Ibid. [3 Kent, 428; Phear Rights of Water, 11, 12. The rule of the Common Law assigns the whole island, or bare ground formed in the bed of the river, if it be wholly on one side of the bed of the river, to the owner on that side. Shaw C.J., in Trustees &c. *v.* Dickinson, 9 Cush. 548. In the Earl of Zetland *v.* The Glover Incorporation of Perth, L. R. H. L. 2 Sc. 70, a question arose as to the right of fishing in the Tay, the usage being the same as the rule, that each should fish *ad medium filum*. A drifting island had sprung up which gradually increased from the operation of currents, tides, and floods. It was contended by the Earl of Zetland, that, as it was nearer his side of the river, the measurement should be from the outer side of the island; but it was held that the island was to be reckoned as part of the bed of the river. Lord Westbury said, that if the island had become annexed to the bank, so as to become a permanent accretion, he should have been of opinion that the appellant would have had the right to have the river measured from the north side of this permanent accretion.]

[2] 2 Bla. Com. 261.

[3] Coop. Just. lib. 2, t. 3; [Shaw C.J., in Trustees &c. *v.* Dickinson, 9 Cush. 548].

[4] Civil Code of Louisiana, art. 505, 506, 507.

[5] [These substantially are laid down, as rules of the Common Law, in Trustees &c. *v.* Dickinson, 9 Cush. 548, 549. See post, § 59 *a*.]

belongs wholly to the estate which it adjoins, and the opposite banks; it is declared by Fleta, that the admeasurement of property in the new island shall be made from the first, and not from the shore to which it belongs.[1]

§ 47. These provisions, though they appear to be confined to the case of islands recently formed, the same reason will extend to the case of islands the origin of which cannot be traced, unless the property in them has been *otherwise appropriated*, according to the rules of law; for whether originally formed by deposits from the water, or by a sudden division of the river, would seem to be immaterial, unless the owner of one side should be able to show it was created by a disruption of his land.[2]

§ 48. In a case in Massachusetts, the above rules were applied to the following facts: The island that was in dispute is situated in Pawtucket River, above tide-water. The plaintiff was owner of a tract of land on the east side of the river, extending up and down the river, beyond the island; and the defendant was owner of a similar tract on the west side of the river. The island was not held by any separate grant, by either; nor did any other person claim it by virtue of any grant, or by possession. Both plaintiff and defendant, and those under whom they severally claimed and held their farms on the main land, had occasionally cut trees on the island; but no agricultural improvement had been made thereon. In partition of the estate among the heirs of E. B., father of the grantor of the plaintiff, this island was set off to those heirs, in 1756; but it did not appear that any possession was taken under the partition, except the occasional cutting of wood, for forty or fifty years past. It appeared, also, that the defendant, or those under whom he claimed, had cut wood on the island, for thirty years past, at pleasure, without any objection having been made by those who held under E. B. Upon these facts, the Court considered it obvious, that neither the plaintiff nor the defendant had obtained such exclusive possession of the island, or any part of it, as would enable either to maintain trespass against the other, without referring their possession to some title. And the Court thought it equally obvious, that no title appeared in either,

[1] Fleta, lib. 3, c. ii. § 8.

[2] Per Parker C.J., in Ingraham *v.* Wilkinson, 4 Pick. 268.

except what may be derived from their property in the land on either side of the stream of the river, opposite the island. Thus were the Court obliged to consider the principles of law, as above laid down, and the result to which they came was in favor of the plaintiff.[1]

[§ 48 *a*. In a later case[2] in Massachusetts, this subject was again discussed with great fulness of statement and illustration of the law, by Mr. Chief-Justice Shaw. Referring to the case cited in the last preceding section, he says, "It recognizes the rule of the Common Law, that the property in the soil of rivers not navigable, subject to public easements, belongs to those whose lands border upon them; and from this right of property in the soil in the bed of the river the Court deduce the right of property in an island which gradually arises above the surface and becomes valuable for use as land. Assuming the thread of the stream as it was immediately before such land made its appearance, this rule assigns the whole island, or bare ground formed in the bed of the river, if it be wholly on one side of the thread of the river, to the owner on that side; but if it be so situated that it is partly on one side and partly on the other of the thread of the river, it shall be divided by such line, — *i.e.*, that line which was the thread of the river immediately before the rise of the island, — and held in severalty by the adjacent proprietors. But that line must thenceforth cease to be the thread of the river, or *filum aquæ*, because the space it occupied has ceased to be covered with water. But, by the fact of an island being formed in the middle of the river, two streams are necessarily formed by the original river, dividing it into two branches. The island itself, having become solid land, forms itself a bank of the new stream on the one side, and the old bank on the main shore forms the other. And the same rule applies on the other side of the island. There must, then, be a *filum aquæ* to each of these streams, whilst the old *filum aquæ* is obliterated to the extent to which land has taken the place of water. But this island, having all the characteristics of land, may soon be divided and subdivided, by conveyances and descents, and all the modes of transmission of property known

[1] Per Parker C.J., in Ingraham *v.* Wilkinson, 4 Pick. 268.

[2] [Trustees of Hopkins Academy *v.* Dickinson, 9 Cush. 544, 547–550.]

to the law, and thus become the property of different owners. Now suppose another island formed in one of these branches, between the first island and the original main shore. It seems to us that it must be divided upon the same principle as the first; but, in doing it, it will be necessary to assume as the *filum aquæ* the middle line between the first island and the original river bank on that side. If this is a correct view of the practical consequences flowing from the adoption of the principle stated, — and it appears to us that it is, — an obvious difficulty presents itself, in making that line a fixed standard for the demarcation of the boundaries of real estate between conterminous proprietors, which is itself fluctuating and changeable. Perhaps a satisfactory answer to this may be found in the suggestion, that the rule is equitable, and as certain as the proverbially variable nature of the subject-matter will admit; and, in adapting it to the varying circumstances of different cases, a steady regard must be had to the great principle of equity, — that of equality. This changing of the *filum aquæ* seems not to be distinctly treated in any case; but it seems that it must necessarily occur in many cases. In addition to those already mentioned, suppose a river, by slow accretions or washing away, widens or narrows on both sides as it may, but unequally, the *filum aquæ* must change its actual line. Supposing an island dividing a river for some distance shall be wholly washed away, the *filum aquæ* must shift and pass along a line which was formerly solid land." [1]]

§ 49. Where the stream is divided by an island, so that only

[1] [In a passage cited by Chief-Justice Parker, in Ingraham *v.* Wilkinson, 4 Pick. 268, from Lord Hale, such a shifting of the *filum aquæ* in one case is alluded to. The passage is this: "If the *filum aquæ* divide itself, and one part take the east and the other the west, and leave an island in the middle between both *fila*, the one half will belong to the one land, and the other to the other." And Lord Hale adds further, in the same connection, "that this is to be understood of islands newly made; for if a part of an arm of the sea—and the same thing is true of a river, which is material to the present case—by a new recess from his ancient channel, encompass the land of another man, his propriety continues unaltered." Hargrave's Law Tracts, 37. It may be added here, on the authority of Lord Hale, that he derives the title to islands, in creeks or havens or arms of the sea, from the right of property in the soil under the water, stating that this is *primâ facie* and of common right in the king; yet if, in point of propriety, it doth belong to a subject by grant or prescription, the islands that happen within the precincts of such private propriety of a subject will belong to the subject. This is applicable, by strict analogy, to the case of a river not navigable, when the right of property is admitted to be in the riparian proprietor, *ad filum aquæ*. Shaw C.J., in Trustees &c. *v.* Dickinson, 9 Cush. 549, 550.]

one-fourth of the stream descends on one side of the island, and the residue on the other, the owner of the shore where the largest quantity of water flows is entitled to the use of the whole quantity flowing there, and the owner of the other shore has no right to place obstructions at the head of the island, to cause one-half of the stream to descend on his side of the river.[1]

§ 50. In a case decided by the Supreme Court of the United States, it was determined, that the boundary of the State of Kentucky extends only to low-water mark, on the Ohio River, and therefore did not include an island separated from the main land by a channel, or bayou, filled with water only when the river rises above its banks, and is dry at other times.[2]

§ 51. If a watercourse divides itself, and encircles a field, and thereby forms an island, the property of the field is unaltered, and continues in him to whom it before appertained.[3]

§ 52. A grant of a river, *eo nomine*, as it will have no effect upon the property in the soil, can convey no property in an island.[4] But all islands situated within the limits of a patent, or grant of land, are, of course, included.[5]

[1] Crooker *v.* Bragg, 10 Wend. 260.

[2] Handly *v.* Anthony, 5 Wheat. 374. When a river is the boundary line between two nations or States, if the original property be in neither, and there be no convention respecting it, each holds to the middle of the stream. But when, as in this case, one State (Virginia) is the original proprietor, and grants the territory on one side only, it retains the river within its domain, and the newly erected State extends to the river only, and the low-water mark is its boundary. Ibid. In 1802, when Georgia ceded her back lands to the United States, she had jurisdiction over the whole of Chattahoochee River from its source to the 31st degree of north latitude. The Supreme Court of the United States held the rule to be, that where a power possesses a river, and cedes the territory on the other side of it, making the river the boundary, that power retains the river, unless there be an express stipulation for the relinquishment of the rights of soil and jurisdiction over the bed of such river. Howard *v.* Ingersoll, 13 How. (U.S.) 381. And see Missouri (State of) *v.* Iowa (State of), 7 How. (U.S.) 660.

[3] 1 Swift's Dig. 112.

[4] Jackson *v.* Halstead, 5 Cowen, 216.

[5] Lunt *v.* Holland, 14 Mass. 149. The boundaries of Mifflin County, in Pennsylvania, were fixed by an act of the legislature, of Sept. 19, 1789; and the fact that an island, evidently included by the act within the limits of that county, had been assessed for twenty-eight years in Huntingdon County, in the same State, will not avail to disturb the boundary fixed by the act. If the boundary fixed by the act were *uncertain*, such assessments, for a long period, might be admissible to show where the line was fixed by the act; but are not admissible where the line fixed by the act, viz., the Juniata River, is known. Where the two counties join at Juniata River, at their southern point of junction, their respective boundaries do not extend *usque ad filum aquæ;* but the *whole bed* of the Juniata River, from that point up to "Jack's Narrows," is in Mifflin County, and the islands in the river belong to the latter county. Johns *v.* Davidson, 16 Penn. St. 512.

2. *Alluvion.*

§ 53. Alluvion is the addition made to land by the washing of the sea or rivers; and the characteristic of alluvion is its *imperceptible* increase, so that it cannot be perceived how much is added in each moment of time.[1] The gradual alteration of a stream will of course add to one and diminish the opposite bank. In all cases where the change is so gradual as not to be perceived in any one moment of time, the proprietor, whose bank on the river is increased, is entitled to the addition.[2] The rule of the

[1] ["By alluvion here we mean," says Shaw C.J., in Trustees of Hopkins Academy *v.* Dickinson, 9 Cush. 551, "such slow, gradual, and insensible accretion, that it cannot be shown at what time it occurred."]

[2] 2 Bla. Com. 262; 1 Swift's Dig. 111; Adams *v.* Frothingham, 3 Mass. 352; Schultes, 116; Morgan *v.* Livingston, 6 Martin (La.) 19; [Halsey *v.* McCormick, 13 N.Y. 296; s.c. 18 N.Y. 147; 3 Kent, 428; Chapman *v.* Hoskins, 2 Md. Ch. 485; New Orleans *v.* United States, 10 Peters, 662; Atty.-Genl. *v.* Chambers, 4 De Gex & J. 55; Emans *v.* Turnbull, 2 John. 313; Ford *v.* Lacy, 7 H. & N. 151; Gerrish *v.* Clough, 48 N.H. 9; Lovingston *v.* St. Clair County, 64 Ill. 56; Nichaus *v.* Shepherd, 26 Ohio St. 40 Goodsell *v.* Lawson, 42 Md. 348, 362, 363; Baltimore & Ohio R.R. Co. *v.* Chase, 43 Md. 23, 34, 35; Cook *v.* McClure, 58 N.Y. 437; Kraut *v.* Crawford, 18 Iowa, 549. In County of St. Clair *v.* Lovingston, 23 Wallace, 46, 62, Mr. Justice Swayne said, "In the light of the authorities, alluvion may be defined as an addition to riparian land, gradually and imperceptibly made by the water to which the land is contiguous. It is different from reliction, and is the opposite of avulsion. The test as to what is gradual and imperceptible in the sense of the rule is, that, though the witnesses may see from time to time that progress has been made, they could not perceive it while the process was going on. Whether it is the effect of natural or artificial causes makes no difference. The result as to the ownership in either case is the same. The riparian right to future alluvion is a vested right. It is an inherent and essential attribute of the original property. The title to the increment rests in the law of nature. It is the same with that of the owner of a tree to its fruits, and of the owners of flocks and herds to their natural increase. The right is a natural, not a civil one. The maxim, *Qui sentit onus debet sentire commodum*, lies at its foundation. The owner takes the chances of injury and of benefit arising from the situation of the property. If there be a gradual loss, he must bear it; if a gradual gain, it is his. The principle applies alike to streams that do, and to those that do not, overflow their banks, and where dykes and other defences are, and where they are not, necessary to keep the water within its proper limits." Municipality No. 2 *v.* Orleans Cotton Press, 18 La. Rep. 122; Kennedy *v.* Municipality No. 2, 10 La. Ann. 54; Barrett *v.* New Orleans, 13 La. Ann. 105; Saulet *v.* Shepherd, 4 Wallace, 502; Smith *v.* St. Louis, 30 Mo. 290; Chapman *v.* Hoskins, 2 Md. Ch. 485. Sea-weed thrown upon the beach belongs to the owner of the beach. Phillips *v.* Rhodes, 7 Met. 523; Emans *v.* Turnbull, 2 John. 322]. The reader is also referred to the learned and elaborate discussion in relation to the claim to the *batture* in the city of New Orleans, 2 Am. Law Journal, 282, 393. And see Giraud *v.* Huges, 1 Gill & John. 249. Lands were thus described in a deed: "Beginning at the south bank of the Tuscarawas River, where the line between the first and second quarter of the fifth township intersects the same, where there is an old dogwood, with a notch and blaze in it, and a number of shoots springing from the roots,

Common Law, on the subject of alluvion, also, is the same as that of the Civil Law. The latter is thus translated: "That ground which a river has added to your estate by alluvion, becomes your own, by the law of nations; and that is said to be alluvion which is added so gradually that no one can judge how much is added in each moment of time." [1]

from which a white oak, fifteen inches in diameter, bears south twenty-eight degrees, west fifteen links; thence south with the division line; thence east &c.; thence north &c., seventy-two chains and ten links, to the south bank of the Tuscarawas River, from whence a maple, four inches in diameter, bears south, thirty-six degrees east, eleven links; a forked maple bears south, &c., thence with the course of the south bank of the Tuscarawas River, to the place of beginning." Before that deed was made, about ten acres of *alluvion* had been formed on the southern bank of the river, along the line between the old dogwood and the corner at the maple. It was held, that the alluvion passed by the deed. Lamb *v.* Rickets, 11 Ohio, 311; [Nichaus *v.* Shepherd, 26 Ohio St. 40, 44, 45]. And in this case it was considered a well-established principle, that formations by *slow and gradual accretion*, belong to the owner of the land, when made by *a stream forming his boundary*, and opposite thereto. [St.Louis Public Schools *v.*Risley, 40 Mo. 356; Cook *v.* Burlington, 30 Iowa, 94; Mather *v.* Chapman, 40 Conn. 382. Where the channel of a river has been gradually changing for years, by wearing away the bank on the defendant's side, and by adding and forming accretions upon the opposite shore owned by the plaintiff, by slow and imperceptible degrees, the channel, as so changed, must be regarded as the rightful and accustomed channel for the time being as between the different parties. Gerrish *v.* Clough, 48 N.H. 9. Sargent J., in this case, said, "It is very well settled that land formed on one side of a stream of water by the variations in the channel caused by the natural flowing of the water therein, belongs to the owner of the land on that side of the stream. These natural accretions are entitled to the same protection, when once acquired, that the original enclosure would have been. Either party may protect himself against any anticipated change of that kind by rubbling or securing his bank in any way that shall keep the channel in its present location, if he do not thereby injure or raise the water upon his neighbor's land, either above or opposite to him." 48 N.H. 11, and cases cited. See Pierce *v.* Kinney, 59 Barb. 56; Slater *v.* Fox, 5 Hun (N.Y.) 544.]

[1] Coop. Just. lib. 2, t. 1. ["Where a stream changes its course by slow and imperceptible steps, the riparian proprietors are obliged to accept the consequent alteration in their boundaries; but when the shifting is sudden and well marked, the original *medium filum* continues to be the border line, and the stream, so far, passes entirely within the land of the one proprietor. Harg. Tracts, De Jure Maris, cap. 1; 2 Bla. Com. 262. If an island is formed by natural causes, the property in it remains apportioned in the same manner as was, before its appearance, the property in the soil on which it stands. 2 Bract. lib. 2, cap. 2, ¶ 2; 2 Bla. Com. 261; Schultes, 118." Phear Rights of Water, 12. "The large size of the rivers in America," he adds, "and their enormous powers of denudation and deposition, have given this point a pre-eminence in that country which it does not possess here; and, accordingly, it will be found to have received in the American text-books much more elaborate treatment than it requires in England." Phear, 12. See Trustees of Hopkins Academy *v.* Dickinson, 9 Cush. 544, 547. The owner of land which is being inundated by a stream breaking away from its channel, may legally turn it back to its old channel. But he would have no right, in preventing the inundation of his own land, to cause it to flow on to the land of another except in its old channel. Tuthill *v.* Scott, 43 Vt. 525.]

§ 54. The case of the King *v.* Lord Yarborough involved the right of soil connected with *tide-water;* but the case is important as connected with the subject of this work, inasmuch as the argument in it was upon the word "*imperceptible.*" In behalf of the Crown two passages were cited from Hale's[1] *De Jure Maris*, wherein that writer speaks of land gained by alluvion as belonging generally to the Crown, unless the gain be so insensible that it cannot *by any means*, according to the words of one of the passages, or *by* any *limits or marks*, according to the words of the other passage, be found, that the sea was there; *idem est non esse et non apparere.* This led to the following interpretation of the legal meaning of the word "imperceptible" by the Court, the opinion being delivered by Abbott C.J., as follows: "In these passages, Sir Matthew Hale is speaking of the legal consequence of such an accretion, and does not explain what ought to be considered as accretion insensible or imperceptible in itself, but considers that as being insensible, of which it cannot be said, with certainty, that the sea ever was there. An accretion extremely minute, so minute as to be imperceptible even by known antecedent marks or limits at the end of four or five years, may become, by gradual increase, perceptible by such marks or limits at the end of a century, or even of forty or fifty years. For it is to be remembered, that if the limit on one side be land, or something growing or placed thereon, as a tree, a house, or a bank, the limit on the other side will be the sea, which rises to a height varying almost at every tide, and of which the variations do not depend merely upon the ordinary course of nature at fixed and ascertained periods, but in part also upon the strength and direction of the wind, which are different almost from day to day. And, therefore, these passages from the work of Sir Matthew Hale are not properly applicable to this question. And, considering the word 'imperceptible' in this issue, as connected with the words 'slow and gradual,' we

[[1] Mr. Phear, in his book on Rights of Water, p. 47, note, referring to the "valuable treatise entitled De Jure Maris, and ascribed to Lord Hale," says, "The authenticity of this work is at least doubtful, and its style of expression is so little precise, that it ought scarcely to be considered an infallible authority in its most dogmatic portions." Sergeant Mereweather says of it, "It is a treatise familiarly called Lord Hale's, but I have every reason for thinking, as far as regards the book published by Mr. Hargrave, that it is not Lord Hale's; at least, I would venture so far as to say that there is no sound reason for assuming that it is so." Mereweather on the Seashore, p. 11.]

think it must be understood as expressive only of the manner of the accretion, as the other words undoubtedly are, and as meaning imperceptible in its progress, not imperceptible after a long lapse of time. And taking this to be the meaning of the word 'imperceptible,' the only remaining point is, whether the accretion of this land might properly, upon the evidence, be considered by the jury as imperceptible. No one witness has said that it could be perceived, either in its progress, or at the end of a week or a month. One witness, who appears twice to have measured the land, says, 'that within the last four years, he could see that the sea had receded,' but he could not say how much; the same witness said, 'that it certainly had receded since he measured it last year,' but he did not say how much; and, according to his evidence, the gain in a period of twenty-six or twenty-seven years was, on the average, about five yards and a half in a year. Another witness speaks of a gain of one hundred to one hundred and fifty yards in fifteen years; a much greater increase than that mentioned by the first witness; and this second witness adds, that during the last five years there had been a visible increase in some parts of from thirty to fifty yards. Upon the evidence of this witness, it is to be observed, that he speaks very loosely, the difference between one hundred and one hundred and fifty in fifteen years, and between thirty and fifty in five years, being very great. The third witness said there had been some small increase in every year. The fourth witness said, 'the swarth increases every year gradually, and *perhaps* it had gathered a quarter of a mile in breadth in some places within his recollection, or during the last fifty-four or fifty-five years, and in some places it had gathered nothing.' And this was the whole evidence on the subject. We think the jury might, from this evidence, very reasonably find that the increase had not only been slow and gradual, but also 'imperceptible,' according to the sense in which, as I have before said, we think that word ought to be understood."[1]

[1] The King *v.* Lord Yarborough, 3 B. & C. 91; s.c. affirmed in the House of Lords, 2 Bligh, N.S. 147; 1 Dow, N.S. 176. In the controversy respecting the *batture* at New Orleans, when it was urged that it was not alluvion, because its increase *was perceptible*, after every swell of the Mississippi, it elicited from Mr. Livingston the following reply: "When the ingenious counsel can analyze the different deposits, separate the sands of the Red River, the rich mould of the Missouri from the clay and other various soils which the Mississippi receives from a thousand tributary streams; when he can dive into its turbid eddies, watch the moment of the precious

[§ 54 *a*. Where the water is diverted, by artificial means, and not imperceptibly, from the land of a proprietor bounded by

deposit, and date the existence of each stratum of its increase; then this first branch of the authority he has cited (*quantum quoque temporis momento adjiciatur*) may be applicable to his cause." 2 Hall's Law Journ. 307. "Alluvium, or alluvial deposits, a name given to those accumulations of sand, earth, and loose stones or gravel brought down by rivers, which, when spread out to any extent, form what is called *alluvial land*.

"There are three successive stages in the formation of alluvium; viz., the crumbling of the mineral crust of the earth, by the action of tides, currents, streams, and atmospheric agency; the transportation of the loosened fragments; and their deposition in the form of alluvium at the bottom of rivers, lakes, æstuaries, and the ocean.

"The mineral substances of most rocks have a tendency to combine with the oxygen of the atmosphere, under particular conditions of heat, moisture, and electricity; carbonic acid and water are absorbed by many rocks; vicissitudes of temperature tend to expand, contract, split, and disintegrate rocks; lightning often shivers a rock into innumerable fragments; every shower of hail or rain washes off fragments more or less numerous from the surface of rocks; so that by these combined agencies of air, moisture, carbonic acid, heat, electricity, hail, and rain, there is a constant wearing away of the substance of solid rocks. It is true that these agencies work very slowly, when the bulk of the rock is considered; but as time, in geological phenomena, is reckoned by ages or centuries instead of by years, this slowness does not throw any improbability over the alleged action of meteoric forces on solid rocks.

"Another kind of agency is the power of a running stream to wear away the banks and rocks against which it rubs. The force of water, when directed against any obstacle in its course, is very considerable, even by its own weight alone, especially if it be flowing over a highly inclined surface; but its destructive power is greatly augmented if it be loaded with sand and gravel. In floods, very considerable blocks are carried by the stream to great distances; for it must be remembered that these are much more easily moved in water than on land, in consequence of the law in hydrostatics, that a solid body fully immersed in water weighs so much less than it does in air by a sum equal to the weight of the mass of water which it displaces. If the water flows with a velocity of three inches per second, its force, when free from suspended matter, is sufficient to tear up fine clay; six inches per second, fine sand; twelve inches per second, fine gravel; and three feet per second, will tear up beds of loose stones of the size of an egg. Instances have been recorded in most countries of masses of stone, weighing from a hundred to a thousand pounds each, having been transported many miles by the force of a current.

"The formation of *valleys* by the erosive power of running water is another cause of the accumulation of alluvium. The explanation of this subject more fittingly belongs to another article [VALLEYS]; but it may here be observed that there is abundant proof of the power of water to cut a passage through solid rock. In Sicily, the river Simeto has cut a passage for itself through a bed of very hard rock, fifty feet deep, and several hundred feet wide. The river Nerbudda, in India, has worn away a rock to the depth of one hundred feet. Among the Alps, gorges have been scooped out to the depth of six hundred or seven hundred feet, by the action of running water alone. Such facts as these are sufficient to show that a rapidly flowing river exerts a powerful disintegrating force.

"The wearing and transporting powers of rivers depend upon the volume of water, the quantity and size of the solid matter suspended, and the velocity with which it moves. A river generally runs with greatest rapidity in the higher parts of its course, where indeed it often consists of a succession of torrents and cataracts for many miles; but it has not yet acquired its full destructive force, because

low-water mark, he acquires no title to the derelict bed of the stream.[1] But in Halsey *v.* McCormick, Pratt J. said, "I find

the mass of water is still comparatively small; nor has it yet become loaded with solid matter. In the lower part of its course, long before it joins the sea, it has usually reached a level country, and there its velocity becomes greatly retarded. The loss of destructive power, by diminished velocity in the level country, is sometimes compensated, in a considerable degree, by the effects produced by the weight of the great volume of water impinging upon certain parts.

"The tortuous courses of rivers when they are cut through solid rock, as in the case of the Moselle, whose banks are sometimes six hundred feet high, are among the strongest proofs of the destructive power of running water; for no sudden deluge, however powerful, could have scooped out such a trough; and that a cleft of such a nature should be occasioned by any disruption of the earth's crust, is not less improbable. More sudden, and therefore more striking, instances of the waste of the land occur where a river flows through a lake, and by its wasting action causes a breaking down of the barrier.

"The distance to which the detached fragments are carried depends upon the volume of water, and the nature of the ground over which it flows. The torrents from the south-western Alps, rushing over a steep uninterrupted slope, transport large blocks to the sea; but a river that runs through a long stretch of level country deposits the grosser matter in the upper part of its course, and carries to its mouth only that which is more easily held in suspension. The larger stones, after being detached from their parent rock, have therefore to undergo an immediate process of abrasion, by being rubbed against each other in the bed of the stream, before their particles are finally committed to the deep. If a river pass through a lake in its course, the solid matter will be deposited in that trough until it has filled it up; and if the lake be very large, even the lighter particles will have time to fall, and the water will flow out clear from the other extremity. Such processes are now going on, by the gradual filling up of the Lake of Geneva by the Rhone, of the Lake of Constance by the Rhine, of the Lake of Wallerstadt by the Linth, and of many other lakes which have rivers flowing through them. In other cases, the bed of the river itself is gradually being raised by the deposition of this alluvium, and the river is often turned out of its course. This process has gone on at such a rate in Lombardy, that the inhabitants are obliged to make artificial banks to confine the river Po within its proper limits.

"In a mountainous country, where the land rises rapidly from the shore, the rivers descending over a steep bed sweep all the contents into the sea. If the neighboring sea be deep, and the tides be strong, an æstuary or inlet is formed at the mouth of the river; that is, the sea forms a deep indentation into the land, of a triangular shape. If, on the other hand, a low shelving shore, and the absence of strong tidal currents, favor the gradual and tranquil deposit of the solid matter brought down by the river, an extensive level of alluvial land is formed. In this case the main river, at a distant point inland, often divides itself into two streams, which gradually diverging until they reach the sea, inclose a triangular space of land having the form of the fourth letter of the Greek Alphabet, Δ, and hence called a *delta*. The mass of water does not, however, long continue divided into two streams only; the process of separation is repeated several times, and thus the delta is traversed by several channels, and the great river empties itself into the sea by many mouths. Such a delta is formed at the mouths of the Nile, Ganges, Rhine, Rhone, Po, Danube, Wolga, Indus, Orinoco, and many other rivers. Great as is the amount of new land thus formed, it is but insignificant in comparison with the quantity of solid

[1] [Halsey *v.* McCormick, 18 N.Y. 147; s.c. 13 N.Y. 296.]

no distinction in the books between the case of alluvion formed by natural or artificial means. If, by some artificial structure or impediment in the stream, the current should be made to impinge more strongly against one bank, causing it *imperceptibly* to wear away, and causing a corresponding accretion on the opposite bank, I am not prepared to say that the riparian

matter carried down by rivers and deposited in the depths of the sea. The quantity of mud and sand poured by the Ganges into the Bay of Bengal is so great, in the flood season, that the sea recovers its transparency only at the distance of sixty miles from the coast. Mr. Lyell shows that supposing the water to contain one hundredth part of solid matter, a mass equal in bulk to the greatest of the Pyramids of Egypt is brought down by the Ganges every day. If a current runs across the mouth of such a river, it gives rise to the formation of a sand-bank, and greatly accelerates the accumulation of the delta.

"Such, then, are the numerous modes in which alluvium is formed, and fitted to become the basis of a rich vegetable soil, by converting into dry land tracts which were before covered with water.

"Besides this erosive action of rivers, there is an enormous power due to the sea itself. An extensive waste of the land is in constant progress along every line of coast which presents an abrupt face to the sea. The amount and rapidity of that waste depend upon a variety of circumstances; the nature of the rocks of which the cliffs are composed, according as they are capable of long resistance, or are easily acted upon by the weather and the sea; the force of the tides and currents; the greater or less frequency of storms, — all these accelerate or retard the destructive force of the ocean. In this case also, as well as in the action of running water on the land, the force is greatly augmented when the water is charged with solid matter. The violent surge of a tempest dashing against a cliff, detaches large blocks, and sweeps them away; but the next returning wave hurls them back again against the cliff, and thus a powerful artillery is supplied by the land for its own destruction. The east and south coasts of Great Britain, the Shetland and Orkney Islands, the shores of Denmark, and many other sea coasts of Europe, show evident signs of the power of the sea to encroach upon and wash away the cliffs; thereby adding to the quantity of alluvium brought down by the rivers.

"The instances of this destructive power are numerous, and are made evident by the circumstance that buildings which once stood far inland are now close to the cliffs, the sea having gradually washed away the intervening rock. At Sherringham on the Norfolk coast, at Reculver in Kent, and at many other places, this is observable. Geologists are of opinion that England once formed a part of France; the cliffs on the opposite side of the Channel are identical at the Straits of Dover; and between Folkestone and Boulogne a submarine chain of hills is in some places only fourteen feet below the surface at low water. From the German Ocean to the Straits the water becomes gradually more shallow, diminishing in a distance of two hundred leagues from one hundred and twenty to eighteen fathoms; and in the same manner from the Straits to the mouth of the English Channel there is a gradual increase of the depth of the water, so that at the Strait there is a ridge with a fall to the west and to the east. In the wearing of the sides, and consequent widening of the Straits, which is now going on, we see only an advanced stage of a work of destruction which has been many thousand years in operation. That Sicily was at one time united to Italy, Ceylon to Hindostan, and the West-India Islands to the Continent of America, are in like manner deemed very probable hypotheses, the destructive power having in each case been the same; viz., the sea." Nat. Cyclopædia, Vol. I. tit. Alluvium, pp. 510–513.

owner would not be entitled to the alluvion thus formed, especially as against the party who caused it."]

§ 55. Land formed by alluvion in a river is, in general, to be divided among the several riparian proprietors entitled to it, according to the following rule: Measure the whole extent of their ancient line on the river, and ascertain how many feet each proprietor owned on this line; divide the newly formed river-line into equal parts, and appropriate to each proprietor as many of these parts as he owned feet on the old line; and then draw lines from the points at which the proprietors respectively bounded on the old, to the points thus determined as the points of division on the newly formed shore. This rule is to be modified under particular circumstances; for instance, if the ancient margin has deep indentations or sharp projections, the general available line on the river ought to be taken, and not the actual length of the margin, as thus elongated by the indentations or projections.[1] [" The effect of this rule is, to give to each proprietor a length on the new water-line proportioned to his length on the old water-line, whether the one be longer or shorter than the other." [2]]

[1] Deerfield *v.* Arms, 17 Pick. 41. The Court, in this case, adopted the rule found in a work of the Civil Law, entitled, " A Collection of New Decisions," by Denisart, published in France in 1783, and is found under the title *Attérissement*. See Kennebec Ferry Company *v.* Bradstreet, 28 Maine, 374; [Trustees of Hopkins Academy *v.* Dickinson, 9 Cush. 544; 3 Kent, 428. The rule established in Deerfield *v.* Arms, supra, was followed in Batchelder *v.* Keniston, 51 N.H. 496. See Miller *v.* Hepburn, 8 Bush, 326; Thornton *v.* Grant, 10 R.I. 477; Jones *v.* Johnston, 18 How. (U.S.) 150; Delord *v.* New Orleans, 11 La. Ann. 699; O'Donnell *v.* Kelsey, 10 N.Y. 412; Attorney-General *v.* Boston Wharf Co., 12 Gray, 553. As to New Jersey, see Stockham *v.* Browning, 18 N.J. Eq. 390].

[2] [Per Shaw C.J., in Trustees &c. *v.* Dickinson, 9 Cush. 544, 552, 553. See Gray *v.* Deluce, 5 Cush. 9; Thornton *v.* Grant, 10 R.I. 477. In Clark *v.* Campau, 19 Mich. 325, it was held that the boundary line between adjoining riparian owners is to be determined by extending a line from the boundary at the shore, perpendicularly to the general course of the stream opposite that point. In this case, Campbell J. said, "The right to land under water, extending from the shore toward the centre or thread of a stream, has always been deemed as appurtenant to the shore itself. It has no reference whatever to the extent of the riparian owner's possessions back from the shore, and is the same whether those possessions consist of a deep parcel or a mere strip of shore. And this right to the covered lands in front has always been held to exclude any adjacent claimant from intercepting in any way the full extent indicated by the width at the shore, without reference to whether the track approaches the shore at right angles or diagonally. Where the stream is straight, the water front will be bounded by lines drawn at right angles with the thread of the stream, protracted until they reach the ends of the shore line. Where the stream curves, the same principle applies, and the lines running from the shore would converge or separate, according as the land lay within or without the curve.

§ 56. Analogous to the decision in the case cited in the preceding section, is the rule as to the apportionment of *flats-ground* in Massachusetts and Maine.[1] In Emerson *v.* Taylor, in the lat-

In all cases where ownership of the submerged land or of alluvial increments, appurtenant to riparian ownership, has come in question, the only elements which have ever been considered by the courts have been the shore lines and the central line or thread of the stream, and the partition among adjoining owners has been made with reference to these, but never with any reference whatever to the direction of the boundaries or the extent of the domain on the uplands. The aim in every instance has been to secure to each owner such share as was indicated by his shore line, and not by his lands back of it." Emerson *v.* Taylor, 9 Greenl. 42; Deerfield *v.* Arms, supra; Rust *v.* Boston Mill Corp., 6 Pick. 158; Sparhawk *v.* Bullard, 1 Met. 95; Knight *v.* Wilder, 2 Cush, 199; Ipswich Pet'rs, 13 Pick. 431; Jones *v.* Johnston, 18 How. (U.S.) 150; Johnston *v.* Jones, 1 Black, 209; Banks *v.* Ogden, 2 Wallace, 57; O'Donnell *v.* Kelsey, 10 N.Y. 412; Lorman *v.* Benson, 8 Mich. 18; Rice *v.* Ruddiman, 10 Mich. 125; Saulet *v.* Shepherd, 4 Wallace, 502; Jones *v.* Soulard, 24 How. (U.S.) 41; Seneca Nation *v.* Knight, 23 N.Y. 489; Steamer Magnolia *v.* Marshall, 39 Miss. 109; Stone *v.* Boston Steel & Iron Co., 14 Allen, 230. And in The Bay City Gas-Light Co. *v.* The Industrial Works, 28 Mich. 182, the same learned judge, discussing the same point, said, "There is no distinction in this regard between streams which are subject to easements of passage, and those which are not. Even the beds of navigable tide-waters are subject to the disposal of State laws, saving always any public rights that may exist in them; and it is the settled law of this State (Michigan) that any use of lands under rivers, which is compatible with the full enjoyment of the public easement, belongs with the upland to which it was originally appurtenant, unless sold or granted separately so as to sever it. Even in streams not susceptible of any public use, it can seldom happen that any riparian proprietor can occupy by erections any large portion of its bed, except where it is dammed. He cannot so use it as to destroy the benefits of the water to his neighbors. In each case the right of every owner is subject to some limitations; and he is compelled to use his own property so as not to injure the rights of others, whether public or individual." "The controversies arising concerning riparian rights upon waters having no middle thread, properly so called, can have no bearing on rivers. Whether the proprietary right is confined by high or low water mark, or extends further, it is manifest that upon the open sea or on a bay or other body of water having no defined stream running in a confined and continuous bed, the shore may be the only tangible element of computation or measurement, and it has very properly in such cases been regarded as the most important. But even there some regard has usually been paid to the common-sense rules which would prevent inequalities from being created by any blind adhesion to the accidental conformation of the shore line at the extremity of any riparian property; and regard is paid to extent, as well as to other considerations."]

[1] [In Thornton *v.* Grant, 10 R.I. 477, 488, 489, Durfee J., referring to the law of Massachusetts on this point, said, "The rule is this: Where the flats lie in a cove or recess, a front line is to be drawn from headland to headland, and from the front line so drawn division lines are to be drawn through the flats to meet the division lines of the upland at their intersection with the shore, and are to be so drawn as to give each proprietor a length of the front line proportionate to the length of his shore line at ordinary high-water mark. Rust *v.* Boston Mill Corporation, 6 Pick. 158; Deerfield *v.* Arms, 17 Pick. 41; Hopkins Academy *v.* Dickinson, 9 Cush. 544; Wonson *v.* Wonson, 14 Allen, 71; Delaware, Lackawanna, and Western R.R. Co. *v.* Hannon, 37 N.J. Law (8 Vroom) 276. This rule has been approved in other States,

ter State,[1] the question was in respect to the side lines of water-lots, from the upland to low-water mark, under the colonial ordinance of 1641 [1647.] The language of the ordinance referred to is, that "in all creeks, coves, and other places about and upon

and in the Supreme Court of the United States. O'Donnell *v.* Kelsey, 10 N.Y. 415; Miller *v.* Hepburn, 8 Barb. 332; Johnston *v.* Jones, 1 Black, 209. The rule, when applied to a cove or inlet of regular outline, is probably as just as any which can be devised. But it is easy to conceive a shore so irregular in its outline that the rule, if applied without modification, would be very unsatisfactory in its results. Indeed, Chief-Justice Shaw admits, in Deerfield *v.* Arms, that where the shore line is elongated by deep indentations or sharp projections, its length should be reduced by equitable and judicious estimate, before it is employed in making the apportionment. In Maine, a rule has been devised which is quite different from the Massachusetts rule, but which has not been so favorably regarded, because it is too complicated for every application. Emerson *v.* Taylor, 9 Greenl. 44; and see Nott *v.* Thayer, 2 Bosw. 10. Even in Massachusetts, the rule has not been invariably applied. In Gray *v.* Deluce, 5 Cush. 9, flats lying on a curving shore were divided by drawing parallel lines from the ends of the division lines of the upland to low-water mark, in such a manner that they would intersect a line drawn from headland to headland of the shore at right angles. And this rule seems to have met the approval of Chancellor Zabriskie, in Stockham *v.* Browning, 18 N.J. Eq. 391. In the case before us we are not called upon to partition alluvion or flats, but to determine the extent of the plaintiff's water front. The principle involved, however, is very much the same in the one case as in the other; and we are therefore not insensible to the guidance to be derived from the decisions cited. But those decisions do not establish any one invariable rule, and it is quite evident that no one of the several rules which they do suggest could be applied in all cases without sometimes working serious injustice. In the case at bar, a solid rock projecting out to the main channel has preserved the shore of the plaintiffs from detrition at that point, but has allowed quite a deep inward curve beyond that point, while the shore of the defendants, having no such protection, has conformed more to the course of the river. The consequence is, that if we draw a front line from headland to headland, and then draw the division line so as to give to each set of proprietors a length of front line proportionate to the length of their original shore, the division line will pass diagonally across what would ordinarily be regarded as the water in front of the defendant's land. This is a result which does not commend itself to us as either reasonable or just. We have decided upon another rule, which to us seems equitable, and which for our present purpose, in the circumstances of this case, leads to a pretty satisfactory result. The rule is this: Draw a line along the main channel, in the direction of the general course of the current in front of the two estates, and from the line so drawn, and at right angles with it, draw a line to meet the original division line on the shore. This rule is not unlike the rule adopted in Gray *v.* Deluce. It will give the plaintiffs as large an extent of water front as we are disposed to allow them; and upon the front so defined we will grant them an injunction to prevent the defendants from encroachment." See, for other modifications of the Massachusetts rule, the plans filed in the clerk's office, and recorded in the Registry of Deeds, for Essex County, in the cases of Breed *v.* Breed, 110 Mass. 532; s.c. 117 Mass. 593; and in Parkhurst *v.* Todd, Supreme Judicial Court, Essex County, Mass., April Term, 1877. In neither of these cases, however, was the attention of the Court called to the correctness of the mode of division, as there was no opposition to the mode reported. See Commonwealth *v.* Roxbury, 9 Gray, 451, 521–523; and post, § 543, note.]

[1] Emerson *v.* Taylor, 9 Greenl. 44.

salt water, where the sea ebbs and flows, the proprietor of the land adjoining shall have propriety to low-water mark, where the sea doth not ebb, above a hundred rods, and not more, wheresoever it ebbs and flows." The expression, "to low-water mark," seemed to the Court to imply to the low-water mark in the nearest direction, and without any regard to the course of the side lines of the upland to which the flats are adjoining and appurtenant.[1] Such a construction appeared to the Court more consistent than any other with the respective rights of contiguous owners of upland; and in some cases the Court considered, where the upland adjoins a cove, and the contiguous lots are so laid out or bounded, as that their side lines strike the cove (as some of them necessarily must) obliquely, the above rule must be applied as the general rule of construction; otherwise, the extension of the side lines and one of the upland lots in a straight direction, might, in some cases, deprive an adjoining lot of all benefit of the flats; and according to the plan on the following page, marked A, it would cut off from lot No. 6 most of the benefit of the flats adjoining it.

The Court, in giving their opinion, say, "After a careful examination of the subject, we perceive but one construction or application of the principle of the ordinance which will do justice to all concerned. The mode of applying the principle is this: Draw a base line from the two corners of each lot, where they strike the shore; and from those two corners, extend parallel lines to low-water mark, at right angles with the base line. If the line of the shore be straight, as in the case before us, there will be no interference in running the parallel lines.[2] If the flats lie in a cove of a regular or irregular curvature, there will be an interference in running such lines, and the loss occasioned by it must be equally borne, or gain enjoyed equally by the contiguous owners, as appears by the following plan, marked B. By the foregoing plan it will be noticed that the parallel lines, running at right angles with the base lines, are merely dotted; while the base lines and the true division lines between the flats,

[1] And the Court appear to have adopted this construction in Rust *v.* Boston Mill Corporation, 6 Pick. 158, and Knight *v.* Wilder, 2 Cush. 199; Sparhawk *v.* Bullard, 1 Met. 95, 106.

[2] [See Delaware &c. R.R. Co. *v.* Hannon, 37 N.J. Law, 276; Stone *v.* Boston Steel and Iron Co., 14 Allen, 230, 233; Gray *v.* Deluce, 5 Cush. 12; Porter *v.* Sullivan, 7 Gray, 443.]

belonging to the respective upland lots, are distinctly drawn. It will also be seen that each of the lots, 1, 2, 5, 6, have their appurtenant flats converging from the upland to low-water mark, in consequence of the recess and curvature of its margin; while the lots 3 and 4 have their appurtenant flats wider at low-water mark than where they join the upland, in consequence of the projection of each lot into the stream. On the same principle, where there is an extended projection of upland of any form, or an island, belonging to different owners, each one's lot being

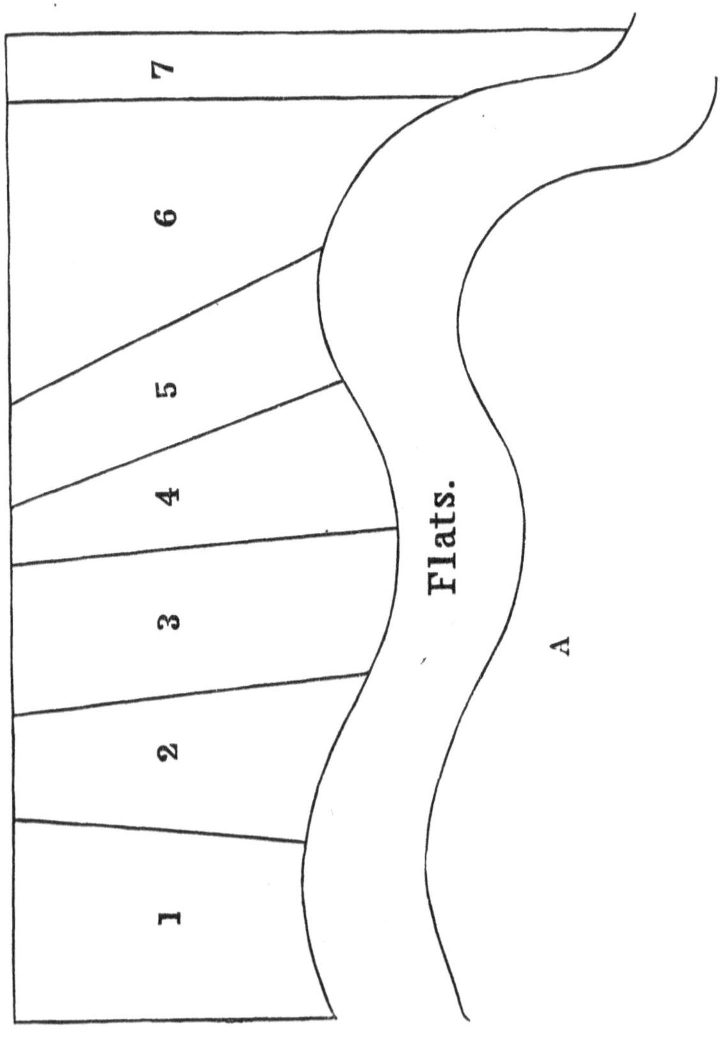

bounded on the sea, or the tide-water in which the island is situated, the surplus width of the flats at low-water mark, arising from the form of the upland, must be divided among the contiguous owners of such upland, and the mode of division and the result are to be ascertained by drawing base and parallel lines in the manner before mentioned, and then making an equal division

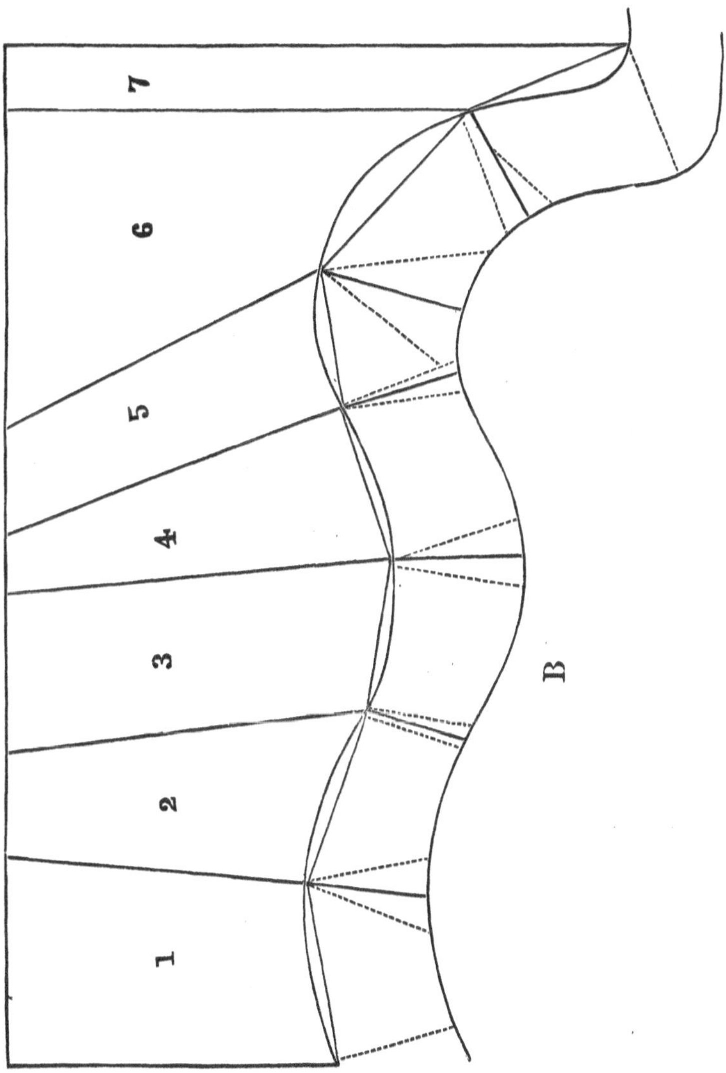

of the surplus.[1] By this process, justice will be done, and all interference of lines and titles prevented. We are not aware of any cases, where, in apportioning appurtenant flats among contiguous owners of upland, the foregoing principles and mode of proceeding would not be properly applicable as the rule of decision. Still we do not undertake to affirm that there may not be some peculiarity in the form of the upland to which flats are appurtenant, and some peculiarity of manner in which the upland may be divided among contiguous owners, the effect of which we have not anticipated, which would vary the principle. Should any such cases hereafter present themselves, requiring the application of a different principle, such new principle must of course be applied."[2]

[[1] See Treat *v.* Chipman, 35 Maine, 36; Call *v.* Carroll, 40 Maine, 31; Wonson *v.* Wonson, 14 Allen, 71, 82, 83.]

[[2] See the remarks of Wilde J., in Gray *v.* Deluce, 5 Cush. 13, 14, as to the rule laid down in Emerson *v.* Taylor, supra. In Stone *v.* Boston Steel & Iron Co., 14 Allen, 230, it appeared that upon a tide-water cove, in which the legal dividing lines of the flats were at right angles with the base line of the cove, three lots of the upland were conveyed by parallel side lines which struck the shore obliquely, the deed of each lot describing it as having a boundary line of a certain number of feet on the shore, together with flats of that number of feet in width to low-water mark. The side lines, if extended over the flats at right angles with the base line of the cove, would give substantially the specified width of flats; but if extended in the same direction as the side lines of the upland, would give a less width, and would, by means of intersecting the legal boundary of the flats belonging to a neighboring estate, afford to one of the lots granted no access to low water; and it was decided that the side lines of the flats were not to be extended in the same direction as those of the upland. Gray J., in this case, said, "Although the proprietor of land bounding on the sea-shore may sell it with or without the adjoining flats, or with such portion as he pleases of the flats which he owns, the presumption is that any deed of a lot of land with the flats adjoining is intended to pass the grantor's actual right and legal title in the flats appurtenant to, or parcel of, the lot granted; and it is well settled that the side lines of the upland have no influence in deciding the direction of the dividing lines of the flats, unless referred to as guides in particular grants; as, for instance, in Dawes *v.* Prentice, 16 Pick. 435, in which the side line of a parcel of flats granted was described in the deed as running parallel with the side of a certain wharf; and in Winnisimmet Co. *v.* Wyman, 11 Allen, 432, in which the legislature had granted rights to extend beyond low-water mark wharves already built, and there was no evidence that the form of the shore was such as to control the reasonable inference that these wharves should be extended in straight lines. Piper *v.* Richardson, 9 Met. 158; Curtis *v.* Francis, 9 Cush. 442." And with reference to the case before him the learned judge said: "It is as plain as any proposition of geometry, that the only way of making each parcel of flats equal in width to the boundary at high-water mark, is to draw the side lines of the flats at right angles with that line. Kennebec Ferry Co. *v.* Bradstreet, 28 Maine, 374. And side lines thus drawn substantially correspond with dividing lines at right angles with the base line of the cove, and are perhaps a little more favorable to the demandant than such dividing lines, or than he asks for." The rules for the division and apportionment of flats in various forms, shapes,

§ 56 *a*. In Newton *v*. Eddy, in Vermont,[1] it appeared that the corner named in certain deeds was a tree on the west bank of the stream, and the point in the centre of the stream nearest to the tree, at the date of the deeds, was easterly from the tree, and in the continuation of the line between the proprietors extending from the west to the tree, — the stream then running by the tree from the south northerly; but by the changes in the course of the stream *alluvion was formed* upon its west bank, and the direction of the stream was changed, so that it flowed by the tree from the east towards the west, and the point in the centre of the stream nearest to the tree became north of the tree, so

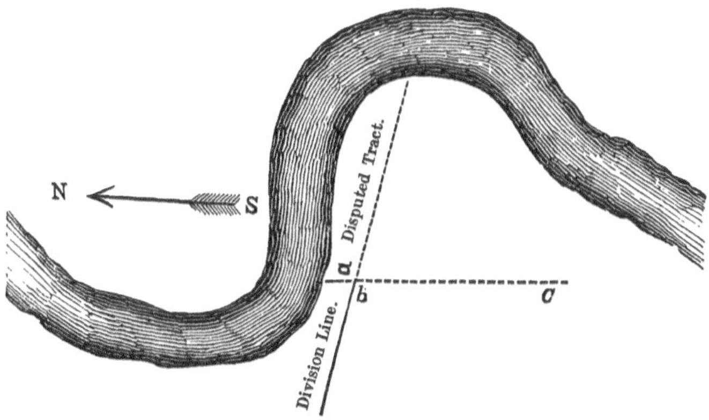

that a line extending from the tree to that point was nearly at right angles with the line extending from the west to the tree; and it was held, that the location of the true corner was thus changed to the point in the centre north of the tree, and that all the alluvion, formed upon the west bank of the stream above that point, belonged to the party who owned the land above the tree; Redfield J. dissenting.

3. *Reliction.*

§ 57. If the course of a river is *suddenly* changed, the relicted soil remains according to the former bounds. A watercourse, therefore, running between the lands of A. and B., which leaves

and conditions of the line of the shore, are stated by Gray J., in Wonson *v*. Wonson, 14 Allen, 71. See also the remarks of Campbell J., in Clark *v*. Campau, 19 Mich. 325, quoted ante, § 55 in note.]

[1] Newton *v*. Eddy, 23 Vt. 319. Plan of the premises. From *a* to *c*, original bank of Otter Creek. *b*, Butternut tree. From *a* to *b*, old fence.

its course, and suddenly and sensibly makes its channel entirely on the land of A., wholly belongs to A.[1] Where a deed calls for a line along the bank of a river, and, after the date of the deed, the bank of the river is changed by excessive floods producing violent and visible alterations, the boundary will not shift with the change of the river, but will be where the bank was at the time of the date of the deed.[2] But if a river, *by degrees*, says Blackstone, gains upon the land of a person on one side, and thereby leaves the other dry, the owner who loses his ground thus imperceptibly has no remedy.[3] A river ran between two lordships, and the soil of one side, together with the river, entirely belonged to one of the lordships; and the river, by very slow degrees, did encroach upon the soil of the opposite lordship; but so very deliberately, that it was impossible to perceive an immediate alteration; therefore, by this imperceptible increase, the land relicted became the property of the first lord. But if the river, by a sudden and unusual flood, had gained hastily a great parcel of the other lord's ground, he should still be entitled to the same.[4]

§ 58. When we treat of such watercourses as are public highways, it will appear that a river of this description, by constituting to itself a new channel, may convert a private field into public property; that is, the new channel becomes public for use and accommodation, and cannot be impeded or obstructed.[5] So

[1] Harg. Tracts, De Jure Maris &c.; Woodbury *v.* Short, 17 Vt. 387. See Trustees &c. *v.* Dickinson, 9 Cush. 454.

[2] Lynch *v.* Allen, 4 Dev. & Bat. (N.C.) 62. But the Court in this case took occasion to say that if the alteration had been by small and almost imperceptible gradations, it might have been otherwise.

[3] 2 Bla. Com. 262. And see Brown *v.* Kennedy, 5 H. & John. 195; Lynch *v.* Allen, ubi supra; [Nichaus *v.* Shepherd, 26 Ohio St. 40, 45; Goodsell *v.* Lawson, 42 Md. 348].

[4] 22 Lib. Ass. pl. 93. The changing of the bed of the river Connecticut, in the town of Wethersfield, has been the occasion of much litigation in that town, respecting the title to the soil. Mr. Butler, who owned a tract upon which the river was encroaching, found, after a while, some of his land appearing on the opposite side of the river, and accordingly laid claim to it. This claim was disputed, as he never owned land on *that* side of the river. It was a long while before this case was decided. There appeared some difficulty in making the jury who sat on the case to understand the merits of the question. Mr. Ingersoll, a member of the Ingersoll family of New Haven, was the counsel employed by Mr. Butler. He illustrated the case by supposing that Mr. B. had built a castle on the land in question. Although the ground on which it stood might be overflowed, it was still his castle, and the ground also was his on which it stood, and he had a right to his property wherever he could find it. The case was finally determined in accordance with these views. [From Hayward's New-England Gazetteer.]

[[5] "Should a person obstruct the flow

on the other hand, a river, by changing its course, may cause the channel, which was before subject to the right of the public, to vest entirely and exclusively in the owners of the banks. The law of England, in relation to this subject, also appears to have been copied from the Roman law.[1]

§ 59. If a navigable *lake* recede gradually and insensibly, the derelict land belongs to the adjacent riparian proprietors. In a case in North Carolina, the defendant claimed title to the land which was the subject of the suit under a patent, in which the boundaries were described as follows: "Beginning at a poplar *on the south side of Mattamuskeet Lake;* thence running west with the lake, to a corner; thence different courses and distances to a corner *on the lake* again; and thence *with the lake* to the beginning." The lessor of the plaintiff had obtained a grant of late date, covering lands, as he alleged, between defendant's lines and the lake, which had *become dry* by the *recession* of the lake since the patent to the defendant was issued, as stated by the plaintiff. Both sides gave evidence of what had been actually run for the lines of the defendant's land; and it was proved that the lake was a navigable water. By Hall J., in delivering the opinion of the Court: "If the recession of the lake was sudden and sensible, the land which it had covered, and which, by its dereliction, became dry, would not be, and ought not to be, included in the defendant's grant. But, if the water receded gradually and insensibly, the lake ought to be considered one of the defendant's boundaries. It is, therefore, necessary that the fact be found, whether the waters of the lake receded imper-

of the waters of a river or stream over their accustomed bed, so that they could not be used as formerly, for the purpose of boating or of floating rafts or logs, and should turn them into a new channel, he would thereby authorize the public to make use of them in the new channel, as they had been accustomed to use them in their former channel." Per Shepley J., in Dwinel *v.* Barnard, 28 Maine, 562.]

[1] [Wells J., delivering a dissenting opinion in Dwinel *v.* Barnard, 28 Maine, 469, says, "This principle is derived from the Civil Law. 'If a river, entirely forsaking its natural channel, hath begun to flow elsewhere, the first channel appertains to those who possess the lands close to the banks of it, in proportion to the extent of each man's estate next to such banks; and the new channel partakes of the nature of the river, and becomes public. And if, after some time, the river returns to its former channel, the new channel again becomes the property of those who possess the lands contiguous to its banks.' Just. Inst. lib. 2, t. 1, § 23. And this doctrine does not appear to be at variance with that of the Common Law, but it is believed that it can be clearly inferred from the principles of that law, applicable to public rivers." pp. 469, 470.]

ceptibly, or not, from the land in dispute; because on that question the rights of the parties depend."[1]

[§ 59 *a*. In Trustees of Hopkins Academy *v*. Dickinson,[2] a question recently arose respecting the right of the riparian proprietors to certain land formed in the bed of Connecticut River, between Hadley and Hatfield. It appeared by the case, that this land was formed on a part of the soil which formerly constituted the deep bed and channel of the river, where the main current of water formerly flowed, in consequence of the river having changed its course, and taken a new channel on the Hadley side. The effect of this has been, that the main body of the water has for some years flowed in a new channel, by means of which the water on the old bed of the river became stagnant, deposits of earth and sand were formed in various parts of it, which have gradually risen above the surface, and united with each other so as to become valuable land. The Court decided that where the course of a river not navigable[3] changes, and cuts off a point of land on one side, forming an island, such island still belongs to the original owner. In such case, if the old bed of the river, being gradually deserted by the current, fills up, and new land is formed, such newly formed land belongs to the opposite riparian proprietors, respectively, to the thread of the old river. And if new land be formed in the river above such island independent of the island, and not by a slow, gradual, and insensible accretion to it, such new land above belongs to the opposite riparian proprietors, respectively, to the *filum aquæ*, or thread of the river. The thread of the river in such case, would be the medium line between the shores or natural water-lines on each side at the time the new land was formed, without regard to the channel or deepest parts of the stream.[4]]

1 Murry *v*. Sermon, 1 Hawks (N.C.) 56; [Warren *v*. Chambers, 25 Ark. 120].

2 [9 Cush. 544.]

3 [The Court said, "It has been repeatedly settled, both in this State and in Connecticut, that the Connecticut River, though valuable for the purposes of boating and rafting, yet, so far as riparian proprietorship is concerned, is considered a river not navigable, as that term is used in the Common Law. Adams *v*. Pease, 2 Conn. 281; Bardwell *v*. Ames, 22 Pick. 333." 9 Cush. 547.]

4 [The opinion in the above case of Trustees of Hopkins Academy *v*. Dickinson, 9 Cush. 544, was given by Chief-Justice Shaw, who said, among other things, "The general rule, as a rule of the Common Law of England, was long since laid down as unquestionable by Lord Holt, who says, in the case of Rex *v*. Wharton, Holt, 499, that a river, of common right, belongs to the proprietors of the land between which it runs, to each that part nearest his land. This has been frequently, if not uniformly, adopted

4. *Avulsion.*

§ 60. Avulsion is where, by the immediate and manifest power of the stream, the soil is taken suddenly from one man's estate, and carried to another; and hereby a property is *only* constituted *by acquiescence;* for it belongs to the first owner, unless it shall continue on the other's land for so long a time that it cements and coalesces with the soil.[1] So the Civil Law says, "If the impetuosity of a river should sever a part of your estate, and adjoin it to that of your neighbor, it is certain that such part would still continue yours."[2]

as the established rule. Bac. Ab. tit. Prerogative; Sir John Davies's Rep. 155." And the same rule has been repeatedly declared and adjudged in this Commonwealth. It is derived mainly from the rule, that the riparian proprietor is owner of the soil under the water, and, by the general law of property, becomes entitled as of right to all accessions. The general rule is recognized and established in this Commonwealth, in the leading case of Ingraham *v.* Wilkinson, 4 Pick. 268. It is a case which goes far to settle principles which must govern the present.]

[1] Bract. 221; 2 Bla. Com. 262; Harg. Tracts, De Jure Maris &c.

[2] Coop. Just. lib. 2, tit. 1. [See Trustees of Hopkins Academy *v.* Dickinson, 9 Cush. 544.]

CHAPTER III.

OF THE RIGHT OF FISHERY AS INCIDENT TO THE RIGHT OF PROPERTY IN A WATERCOURSE.

1. Exclusive Right of Fishing in the Riparian Proprietors.
2. Of a Several Fishery.
3. Of a Free Fishery.
4. Of Common of Fishery.
5. Right of Fishery, as derived from Special Grants.
6. User of Private Fisheries.
7. Obstruction of the Passage of Fish.

1. *Exclusive Right of Fishing in the Riparian Proprietors.*

§ 61. It will be seen, by reference to the first chapter, that where a person owns the whole of the soil over which a watercourse runs, in its natural course, he alone is entitled to the use and profits of the water; and that where a person owns only the land upon one side of a watercourse, his interest in the soil, and his right to the water, extend to the middle of the stream. Concomitant with this interest in the soil of the beds of watercourses, is an exclusive right of fishery; so that the riparian proprietor, and he alone, is authorized to take fish from any part of the stream included within his territorial limits.[1]

§ 62. The opinion which has formerly pervaded the minds of many people, that, in this country, the public may fish anywhere, is refuted by a case in the United-States Circuit Court in Rhode Island, at the November Term, 1828. The action was

[1] 2 Bla. Com. 39; Harg. Tracts, De Jure Maris &c. Hale, in the latter work, cites Baker *v.* Hercy, temp. Ed. I.; Owen *v.* Dunch, 2 Jac. B.R.; 3 Kent, 411. And see the opinion of the Court in Gould *v.* James, 5 Cowen, 369; Hart *v.* Hill, 1 Wharton, 124; People *v.* Platt, 17 John. 195; Hooker *v.* Cummings, 20 John. 90; [per Shaw C.J., in McFarlin *v.* Essex Co., 10 Cush. 309; 3 Kent, 411; State *v.* Glen, 7 Jones, Law (N.C.) 321; Ingram *v.* Treadgill, 3 Dev. 59. The right to fisheries in the Susquehanna and Delaware and other large rivers of Pennsylvania, though the tide does not ebb and flow in them, is vested in the State, and open to all. Carson *v.* Blaser, 2 Binn. 475; Shrunk *v.* The Schuylkill Nav. Co., 14 Serg. & R. 71. See Collins *v.* Benbury, 5 Iredell, 118; s.c. 3 Iredell, 277; Ingram *v.* Treadgill, 3 Dev. 59; Cates *v.* Wadlington, 1 McCord, 580; 3 Kent, 417, 418].

trespass, for entering the plaintiff's close, partly covered with water, and taking fish from his mill-pond. The principal question was, whether the plaintiff had any property in the fish. The title of the plaintiff was under a lease of five hundred years, of a certain factory lot, and dam lot, "together with all the land which may be flowed by raising a dam seven feet high from the bed or bottom of the river." The Court said, that the lease having conveyed all the land under the pond, it passed the water and the fish therein to the plaintiff, as incidents to the principal grant.[1]

§ 63. In a case in Massachusetts, the defendant undertook to give evidence of a *custom* for all the inhabitants in the vicinity to take fish in the plaintiff's mill-pond; and that the pond was merely an enlargement of a natural stream. But the Court asserted, that there was no such general right as was suggested; and as to the custom, it might be sufficient to say, that, if it were legal and could be proved to exist, it would not be a defence under the general issue. But the custom proposed to be proved was not one that could be sustained in law, even if specially pleaded; for a custom to take any thing from another's land, or for *profit à prendre*, is not a lawful custom; and if such a right be available at all, it must be set up by prescription, as belonging to some estate, and should be pleaded with a *que estate*.[2]

[1] Smith *v.* Miller, 5 Mason, 191.

[2] Waters *v.* Lilley, 4 Pick. 145; Bland *v.* Lipscombe, 4 Ell. & Bl. 714, note; Race *v.* Ward, 4 Ell. & Bl. 702, 713; 7 Ell. & Bl. 384; Wickham *v.* Walker, 7 M. & W. 63. It was thus decided, the Court said, in Gatewood's case, 6 Co. 60; and Coke says, "Note, reader, the law in this general case well resolved, and no book in the law is adjudged against it." And in the case of Grimstead *v.* Marlowe (4 T.R. 718), Lord Kenyon says, "The law has been so settled ever since the time of Gatewood's case." [In McFarlin *v.* Essex Co., 10 Cush. 310, Shaw C.J. observed, "Whether a party can prescribe for a several fishery in the estate of another, without alleging some estate of freehold, is an important question, which was not discussed in the present case, though very important, should it be tried again. As a general rule, a party cannot allege a custom to claim an interest or *profit à prendre* in the estate of another, without a prescription in a *que estate*, Grimstead *v.* Marlowe, 4 T.R. 717, recognizing the authority of Gatewood's case, 6 Co. 59 b. This rule was applied in this Commonwealth to the case of a fishery, on the soil of a riparian proprietor in a stream not navigable. . . . And yet we believe it has sometimes been said that 'piscary' is a freehold in itself, in which there is no occasion to show to what freehold it is appendant. See a case cited by way of illustration in the *case of the River Banne* Sir John Davies, 151. But we need express no opinion upon this question without the aid of an argument, and need add nothing more than to say, that the cases of Melvin *v.* Whiting, 7 Pick. 79; s.c. 10 Pick. 295; s.c. 13 Pick. 184, afford no

§ 64. The Supreme Court of Massachusetts, upon another occasion, observed, "One of the earliest, and, it seems, the most frequently occurring, subjects of legislation has been that of the fisheries in the numerous streams which communicate with the ocean in this Commonwealth. Though a source of support and profit to multitudes of people, it was found also to be a fruitful source of disorder and contention, growing out of the conflicting rights of individuals, as well as of towns, which, by being owners of land, become owners of the banks of rivers which afforded convenience for fishing. The regulations which have been deemed, from time to time, expedient, qualify and explain private right upon this subject; but beyond these regulations the *right of property according to the principles of the Common Law, is left unaffected*."[1] [And in a still later case,[2] Shaw C.J. remarked, "It is now perfectly well established as the law of this Commonwealth, that in all waters not navigable in the Common-Law sense of the term, that is, in all waters above the flow of the tide, the right of fishery is in the owner of the soil upon which it is carried on, and in such rivers that the right of soil is in the owner of the land bounding upon it. If the same person owns the land on both sides, the property in the soil is wholly in him, subject to certain duties to the public; and if different persons own the land on opposite sides, each is proprietor of the soil under the water, to the middle or thread of the river.[3] This is recognized in many cases as the common right of riparian proprietors, subject, in Massachusetts, to regulation for the common benefit, by the legislature."]

§ 65. The rule, that the right of fishery, within his territorial limits, belongs exclusively to the riparian owner, extends alike to great and to small streams. Thus, the owners of farms adjoining Connecticut River, above the flowing of the tide, have the exclusive right of fishery, opposite their farms, to the middle of the river; though the public have an easement in the river,

authority for claiming such a right by prescription, without reference to an estate, to which it was alleged to be appendant."]

[1] Commonwealth *v.* Chapin, 5 Pick. 199.

[2] [McFarlin *v.* Essex Co., 10 Cush. 309, 310.]

[3] [Case of the River Banne, Sir John Davies, 149; Waters *v.* Lilley, 4 Pick. 145; Commonwealth *v.* Chapin, 5 Pick. 199; Commissioners of Inland Fisheries *v.* Holyoke Water Power Co., 104 Mass. 446, 450; Commonwealth *v.* Vincent, 108 Mass. 446, 447.]

as a highway, for passing and repassing with every kind of water-craft.[1]

[§ 65 *a*. There is no doubt, that, by the Common Law, all persons have a common and general right of fishing in the sea, and in all bays, coves, branches, and arms of the sea, and in all other navigable or tide waters;[2] and the law, in this respect, makes no difference between shell fish and swimming or floating fish.[3] This right, however, like all other rights of fishing, either in the sea or in rivers, is subject to be restrained and regulated by the legislature. The State, as representing the people, have the right to regulate the common rights and privileges of fishing.[4] But no one can maintain an exclusive privi-

[1] Adams *v.* Pease, 2 Conn. 481. [See also, to the same effect, Hooker *v.* Cummings, 20 John. 90, 99; Moulton *v.* Libbey, 37 Maine, 472; Jackson *v.* Keeling, 1 Jones, Law (N.C.) 299. The common right of fishing has always been held and enjoyed in subordination to the right of navigation. Any erection which can be admitted by the latter will not be prevented by the former right. Shepley C.J., in Moulton *v.* Libbey, 37 Maine, 493; Lewis *v.* Keeling, 1 Jones (N.C.) 299.]

[2] [3 Kent, 412, 413; Shaw C.J., in Weston *v.* Sampson, 8 Cush. 351; Shepley J., in Parker *v.* The Cutler Mill-dam Co., 20 Maine, 357; Moulton *v.* Libbey, 37 Maine, 472; Woolrych, Law of Waters, 38; Dunham *v.* Lamphere, 3 Gray, 271; Bickel *v.* Polk, 5 Harring. (Del.) 325; State *v.* Glen, 7 Jones, Law (N.C.) 321.]

[3] [Shaw C.J., in Weston *v.* Sampson, 8 Cush. 355; Lakeman *v.* Burnham, 7 Gray, 437; Porter *v.* Shehan, 7 Gray, 435; Parker *v.* The Cutler Mill-dam Co., 20 Maine, 353; Moulton *v.* Libbey, 37 Maine, 472; Gray J., in Commonwealth *v.* Bailey, 13 Allen, 542; 2 Dane, 690, 700; Martin *v.* Waddell, 16 Peters, 410, 413, 414; Den *v.* Jersey Co., 15 How. (U.S.) 132; Hall *v.* Whillis, 14 Scotch Court of Sess. Cas. (2d series) 324; Gray J., in Proctor *v.* Wells, 103 Mass. 217. Oysters planted by an individual in a bed clearly marked out below low-tide mark, in a bay or arm of the sea, which is a common fishery to all inhabitants of the State, and where there are no oysters growing spontaneously at the time, and where the bed does not interfere with the exercise of the common right of fishing, are the property of the planter, who can maintain trespass for their asportation. Lowndes *v.* Dickerson, 34 Barb. 586. See Fleet *v.* Hegeman, 14 Wend. 42; Decker *v.* Fisher, 4 Barb. 592; Brinckerhoff *v.* Starkins, 11 Barb. 248.]

[4] [Moulton *v.* Libbey, 37 Maine, 472; Dunham *v.* Lamphere, 3 Gray, 268. In Commonwealth *v.* Vincent, 108 Mass. 447, Gray J., said, "The power of the legislature of the Commonwealth over the public rights of navigation and fishing in any waters within its boundaries is unrestricted, provided it does not interfere with the power to regulate commerce, conferred upon the general government by the Constitution of the United States. Cooley *v.* Philadelphia Board of Wardens, 12 How. (U.S.) 299; Gilman *v.* Philadelphia, 3 Wallace, 713. The legislature of a State has power to regulate the time and manner of fishing in the sea within its limits; and, according to the opinions of most respectable judges, may even grant exclusive rights of fishing at particular places in tide water. Burnham *v.* Webster, 5 Mass. 266; Dunham *v.* Lamphere, supra; Smith *v.* Maryland, 18 How. (U.S.) 71; Corfield *v.* Coryell, 4 Wash. C.C. 371, 380; Bennett *v.* Boggs, Baldw. 60. In those waters, whether within or beyond the ebb and flow of the tide, which are not navigable from the sea for any useful purpose, there can be

lege to any part of such waters, unless he has acquired it by grant or by prescription.[1]]

no restriction upon its authority to regulate the public rights of fishing, or to make any grants of exclusive rights which do not impair other private rights already vested. Nickerson *v.* Brackett, 10 Mass. 212; Cleaveland *v.* Norton, 6 Cush. 380; Russell *v.* Russell, 15 Gray, 159, 161.]

1 [Preble *v.* Brown, 47 Maine, 284; 3 Kent, 418; Woolrych, Law of Waters, 80 et seq.; 2 Dane, 690; Mayor of Oxford *v.* Richardson, 4 T.R. 437, 439; Gould *v.* James, 6 Cowen, 369, 376; Day *v.* Day, 4 Md. 262, 270; Carter *v.* Murcot, 4 Burr. 2164; Palmer *v.* Hicks, 6 John. 138; Rogers *v.* Jones, 1 Wend. 237; Delaware & M. R.R. Co. *v.* Stump, 8 Gill & J. 479; Gray J., in Commonwealth *v.* Bailey, 13 Allen, 543; Lakeman *v.* Burnham, 7 Gray, 440; Scratton *v.* Brown, 4 B. & C. 485; Word *v.* Creswell, Willes, 265; Collins *v.* Benbury, 5 Iredell, 118; Lay *v.* King, 5 Day, 72; Peck *v.* Lockwood, 5 Day, 22; Commonwealth *v.* Vincent, 108 Mass. 446, 447; Proctor *v.* Wells, 103 Mass. 216, 218; and cases cited. In Lakeman *v.* Brown, supra, Shaw, C.J., having cited Weston *v.* Sampson and Dunham *v.* Lamphere, supra, and Commonwealth *v.* Alger, 7 Cush. 63, said, "By these cases, we think the following propositions are well established: That by the Revolution, and by the acknowledgment of our independence by the British Government, the State of Massachusetts succeeded to all public rights of British subjects, whether originally belonging by prerogative to the Crown, or exercised and administered by Parliament in due course of law; that, by the charter of the colony of Massachusetts, the people and settlers of the territory acquired not only the right of soil, but a right to the shores and arms of the sea, for all useful purposes of navigation and fishery; that, since that charter, no exclusive right of navigation or fishery, on the sea-shores or in the bays or arms of the sea, could be acquired, except under the authority of the colonial, provincial, or constitutional government, administered by the legislature by act or resolve; that, though perhaps, in the absence of such proof by act or resolve, such grant might be proved by adverse use and enjoyment, it must amount to that degree of exclusive occupation sufficient to raise a belief that such act or resolve had actually been passed, though not now appearing." Chalker *v.* Dickinson, 1 Conn. 382, 383, 384; Collins *v.* Benbury, 5 Iredell, 118; Delaware & M. R.R. Co. *v.* Stump, 8 Gill & J. 479; Gould *v.* James, 6 Cowen, 369, 376. "And in general this can only be done by showing an actual possession of the flats where the tide ebbs and flows, by building thereon or enclosing the same, so as to exclude the access of boats and vessels; that the Common Law, giving the rights of navigation and fishery to the public, remains in force in Massachusetts, except so far as it is qualified and restrained by the Colony ordinance of 1647, giving to the proprietor of the upland the fee in the soil, in flats flowed by tide-water, to the extent of one hundred rods; but by the terms of that ordinance and the construction given to it, the rights of all the members of the community, to navigation and fishery in tide-waters, on the shore and flats below high-water mark, remain until the proprietor elects to build a wharf, or otherwise fill up and enclose such flats." 7 Gray, 440. See Parker *v.* The Cutler Mill-dam Co., 20 Maine, 353; Moulton *v.* Libbey, 37 Maine, 472. Great Ponds, in Massachusetts, containing more than ten acres, which were not, before the year 1647, appropriated to private persons, were by the Colony ordinance of that year made public, to lie in common for public use. Fishing, fowling, boating, bathing, skating, or riding upon the ice, taking water for domestic or agricultural purposes or for use in the arts, and the cutting and taking of ice, are lawful and free upon these ponds, to all persons who own land adjoining them, or can obtain access to them without trespass, so far as they do not interfere with the reasonable use of the ponds by others, or with the public right, unless in cases where the legislature have otherwise directed. West Roxbury *v.* Stoddard, 7 Allen, 158; Ancient Charters, 148, 149; Gray J., in

§ 66. Under the local law of Massachusetts, by which towns may appropriate the fish, in tide-waters, if not appropriated by the legislature, no man, says Parsons C.J., *can lawfully go on the soil of another*, without his leave; and if no such appropriation has been made, any citizen may take the fish, "*so that he does not trespass on the land of others.*"[1] In a very early case in the same State, the defendant claimed the right of going over the plaintiff's land to the river Merrimack, but he relied solely on prescription.[2] In South Carolina, where a person living on an island had a navigable watercourse from his own door to the highway, of no greater distance than to pass through his neighbor's field, the Court held, that it was not such *necessity* as gave him a right of way over the field.[3] In Cortelyou *v.* Van Brundt, in New York,[4] it was held, that the common right of fishing even in *tide-waters*, gives *no* power over the adjoining land. And, though both commerce and fishing, and bathing *in the sea*, are matters favored by the Common Law, by reason of public and national benefits to be derived from them, they do not, because the waters of the sea are open to all persons for all lawful purposes, afford a universal right of access to them over land which is private property.[5]

§ 67. The riparian proprietor has the sole right, unless he has granted it, to fish with *nets* or *seines* in connection with his own land.[6] It was expressly held, also, in Lay *v.* King, in the Supreme Court of Errors of Connecticut,[7] that an adjoining proprietor on the river Connecticut, near its mouth, had an exclusive right to draw a seine on his own land; though the right of fishery in that part of the river was free and common to all the citizens of the State. This exclusive right is considered to give all the owners of land on the margin of the river Schuyl-

Paine *v.* Woods, 108 Mass. 169; Commonwealth *v.* Vincent, 108 Mass. 441, 446, 447. As to ice, see farther, Gray J., in Paine *v.* Woods, 108 Mass. 173; State *v.* Pottmeyer, 33 Ind. 402.]

1 Coolidge *v.* Williams, 4 Mass. 440.

2 White *v.* Whittier, 2 Dane Abr. 702.

3 Lawton *v.* Rivers, 2 McCord (S.C.) 445, cited in 2 Rice Dig. 356.

4 Cortelyou *v.* Van Brundt, 2 John. 357.

5 See Blundell *v.* Catterall, 5 B. & Ald. 268; [Bickel *v.* Polk, 5 Harring. (Del.) 325; 3 Kent, 413; West Roxbury *v.* Stoddard, 7 Allen, 158. The common right of fishery does not authorize the public to fix stakes in flats belonging to the owner of the upland, for the purpose of setting a seine. Locke *v.* Motley, 2 Gray, 267; Duncan *v.* Sylvester, 24 Maine, 486. But below low-water mark one may use a seine. 2 Dane Abr. 692, 693].

6 Hart *v.* Hill, 1 Wharton, 138; Coolidge *v.* Williams, 4 Mass. 140; Brink *v.* Richtmyer, 14 John. 255.

7 Lay *v.* King, 5 Day (Conn.) 72.

kill such great advantages, that it has been hardly worth while for any other persons to attempt to fish with seines. The right of property in front of the river is therefore valuable, and is called a fishery, and one which, in some places is rented for a considerable sum annually.[1] Where certain persons had landed, with their nets, on the bank of a navigable river, and had at various times, dressed and improved the landing place, it was held, that it was properly left to the jury to presume a grant of the right of landing for that purpose, by the owner of the shore. In this case, it was remarked by Burrough J. that every act done by the plaintiffs for *forty-six* years on the *locus in quo*, would have been a trespass, if they had not a right of landing with their nets there; but from 1774, to the present time, all these acts had been done openly; and the only question was whether there were any facts from which a judge could leave it to a jury to presume a grant of the right in question; and, undoubtedly, the circumstances were such as could scarcely have occurred without the knowledge of the owner.[2] The right of landing with and drawing seines upon another's land, is undoubtedly an *easement*,[3] and therefore, as in the case just above referred to, may be acquired by prescription, like a right of way.

§ 68. This right of fishery, growing out of an ownership of the soil, is subject to *dower;* that is, a woman may be endowed of one-third part of the profits.[4] It would seem, however, that dower cannot properly be claimed in a fishery, unless it is attached to, or connected with, *lands*, of which the husband was seised; and, therefore, in a fishery disunited with ownership of the soil, it is doubtful whether dower would arise.

§ 69. Where a fishery belongs to co-heirs, they shall have the

[1] Per Tilghman C.J., in delivering the opinion of the Court in Shrunk *v.* Schuylkill Nav. Co., 14 S. & Rawle, 71.

[2] Gray *v.* Bond, 2 B. & B. 667, and 6 Eng. Common Law, 368. At all the fisheries in the river Tweed, the workmen exercise the right of walking over and along the adjoining shore, while drawing their nets from the river. They also exercise the right of drawing their nets on the adjacent banks, called "a net green." But this right is considered as a mere easement, which may be presumed by twenty years' enjoyment. 28 Lond. Law Mag. 337; and see 3 M. & W. 229; 4 ib. 256, 496; 5 ib. 233; 6 ib. 795. Acts of Parliament have from time to time been passed in England, to give parties engaged in the herring fisheries a right to use the adjoining lands in certain cases. 1 Jac. I. 23; 29 Geo. II. ch. 23, s. 2; 30 Geo. II. ch. 30, s. 7; 11 Geo. III. ch. 31, s. 11.

[3] Hart *v.* Hill, 1 Wharton, 138. A right of way must be by grant or prescription; *mere convenience* gives no right. Seabrook *v.* King, 1 N. & McCord (S.C.) 140; Lawton *v.* Rivers, 2 McCord (S.C.) 445.

[4] Bac. Abr. Dower.

second, third, or fourth fish, according to the number of persons entitled.[1]

§ 70. In one case,[2] it was moved, that ejectment does not lie for a fishery; on which point the Court doubted; but to avoid the question, the plaintiff released his damages, and the question was not agitated. But where a fishery is rented with the soil, it is a tenement within the meaning of the statute of 9 and 10 William III., ch. xi., so as to entitle a person renting it, to a parochial settlement. And, it seems, a fishery, without the soil, would have the same effect. In the case where this point was determined, Mr. J. Ashurst laid it down as law, that a fishery is a tenement; that trespass will lie for an injury to it; and that it may be recovered in ejectment.[3] In this case, Buller J. said, the fact of letting a fishery is sufficient, and we must presume the soil passed along with it; but he was by no means ready to allow that, if it had been any other kind of fishery, it would not have given a settlement.

2. *Of a Several Fishery.*

§ 71. The exclusive right of fishery, we have just considered as being identified with the property in the soil, has been usually denominated a *several* fishery.[4] The town of Dorchester, in Massachusetts, in 1633, made a grant in these words: "It is generally agreed that Israel Stoughton shall build a water mill, if he see cause." Then follows a grant to him of a wear adjoining to his mill; and no person is to cross the river with a net, or otherwise to the prejudice of the said wear; but Stoughton is to sell the alewives at five shillings per thousand, and the other fish at

[1] 3 Bract. 2 b. ch. xxxiv. s. 1.

[2] Cro. Jac. 146.

[3] 1 T.R. 358. That trespass will lie; Hart *v.* Hill, 1 Wharton, 124. The incompetency to bring ejectment respects the incorporeal right, because, where the soil is in question, any fishery incident thereto will pass along with it. But the difficulty arises when the privilege is independent of the land. Ejectment was brought for a lease of a house and lands, and of a *free* fishery in the Trent, and, amongst other things, it was moved that ejectment lay not for a fishery; that it did not appear in what vill the piscary was, and that entire damages had been given. The plaintiff upon this released his damages totally and his action as to the piscary, and then had judgment, the Court being doubtful upon the point of the fishery. Molineux *v.* Molineux, Cro. Jac. 146. The fishery in that case was not one connected with the *soil.*

[4] See the authorities cited, ante, § 61. [A several fishery is an exclusive one. No other person can lawfully fish within its bounds. Per Rice J., in Preble *v.* Brown, 47 Maine, 284; Shepley C.J., in Moulton *v.* Libbey, 37 Maine, 489.]

reasonable rates. The Colony Legislature, in 1634, confirmed the grant to Stoughton and his heirs. It was held, that the wear thus granted and confirmed amounted to the franchise of a *several* fishery at that place.[1]

§ 72. But there seems to have long been a contrariety of opinion, with respect to the point whether the ownership of the soil covered with water be essential to a several fishery. It would be attended with little use, to cite all the various precedents to which this question has given birth. The weight of authority is much in favor of the negative; and two modern writers,[2] who have considered the question with much attention and acuteness, have arrived at the same conclusion, and have expressed decided opinions that a right of several fishery may exist independent of the soil.[3] This is the doctrine of Sir Edward Coke, who observes, that if a man be seised of a river, and by deed do grant a several fishery in the same, and maketh livery of seisin *secundum formam chartæ*, the soil doth not pass, nor the water, for the grantor may take water there, and if the river become dry, he may take the benefit of the soil; for there passed to the grantee but a particular restricted right; namely, a right only to fish, and the livery being made *secundum formam chartæ*, cannot enlarge the grant; but he may exclude the owner from fishing there, for he has departed with his interest therein.[4] For the same reason, he says, if a man grant *aquam suam*, the soil shall not pass, but the piscary within the water passeth therewith.[5] And where, says Mr. Hargrave,[6] is the inconsistency, in

[1] Stoughton *v.* Baker, 4 Mass. 522.

[2] Schultes on Aquatic Rights, and Woolrych on the Law of Waters &c. 111 et seq. The latter published in London as late as 1851.

[3] And see, to the same effect, the authorities cited in Mr. Hargrave's Co. Litt. 122 a. n. 7. Mr. Woolrych (pp. 111 et seq.) cites a case as early as 46 Ed. III.

[4] Co. Litt. 122 a.

[5] Co. Litt. 4 b; and so held in Jackson *v.* Halstead, 5 Cowen, 216; Somerset *v.* Fogwell, 5 B. & C. 875. [In Marshall *v.* Steam Nav. Co., 3 B. & S. 747, Cockburn C.J., having quoted from Lord Coke the passage in the text, added, "Now, independently of the high authority of Lord Coke on such a matter, I must say that this doctrine appears to me the only one which is reconcilable with principle or reason. It is admitted on all hands that a several fishery may exist independently of the ownership of the soil in the bed of the water. Why, then, should such a fishery be considered as carrying with it, in the absence of negative proof, the property in the soil? On the contrary, it seems to me that there is every reason for holding the opposite way. The use of water for the purpose of fishing is, where the fishery is united with the ownership of the soil, a right incidental and accessory

[6] Hargrave's Co. Litt. ut supra.

granting the sole right of fishing with a reservation of the soil and its other profits? Nor do we understand, he adds, why a *several fishery* should not exist without the soil, as well as a *several pasture*.[1] Much confusion, it has been happily suggested by Mr. Woolrych,[2] would be prevented, by calling the sole right of fishery growing out of the property in the soil, a *territorial* fishery; and giving to that the name of several fishery which is enjoyed exclusively by one individual.

§ 73. The exclusive right of fishing being incident to the ownership of the soil, it will be presumed, unless the contrary appear, that such right resides in the owner of the soil;[3] and hence to an action of trespass for an injury to a right of several fishery, it is a good plea that the soil and freehold belong to the defendant. To this, however, the plaintiff may reply title to the several fishery, either by prescription or grant, thereby rebutting the presumption of the right of several fishery being still vested in the owner of the soil.[4] A more modern case is

to the latter. On a grant of the land, the water and the incidental and accessory right of fishing would necessarily pass with it. If, then, the intention be to convey the soil, why not convey the land at once, leaving the accessory to follow? Why grant the accessory, that the principal may pass incidentally? Surely such a proceeding would be at once illogical and unlawyerlike. The greater is justly said to comprehend the less, but this is to make the converse of the proposition hold good. A grant of land carries with it, as we all know, the mineral which may be below the surface. But who ever heard of the grant of the mineral carrying with it the general ownership of the soil? Why should a different principle be applied to the grant of a fishery, which may be said to be a grant of that which is above the surface of the soil, as a grant of the mineral is a grant of that which is below it? Nor should it be forgotten that the opposite doctrine involves the startling and manifest absurdity, that, should the water be diverted by natural causes or become dry, the fishery, which was the primary and principal object of the grant, would be gone, and the property in the soil which only passed incidentally and as accessory to the grant of the fishery, would remain."]

1 [See Melvin *v.* Whiting, 7 Pick. 79; Cortelyou *v.* Van Brundt, 2 John. 357, 362; Ipswich *v.* Browne, Savil. 14.]

2 Woolrych, ut supra.

3 Anon. Loft. 364; Marshall *v.* Steam Nav. Co., 3 Best & S. 732. The owner of a several fishery, in ordinary cases, and where the terms of the grant are unknown, may be presumed to be the owner of the soil. Somerset *v.* Fogwell, 5 B. & C. 875. Trespass lies by owner of several fishery. Hart *v.* Hill, 1 Wharton, 124. [One having a several fishery has a property in the fish, and may maintain trespass for taking them. Collins *v.* Benbury, 5 Iredell, 118; Smith *v.* Kemp, 2 Salk. 637; Holford *v.* Bailey, 13 Q.B. 426, and note, p. 447.] Though there is no reason why a person may not have a several fishery *in alieno solo*, yet *primâ facie*, he is owner of the soil, and that presumption is conclusive, if not opposed. Partheriche *v.* Muser, 2 Chitt. 658.

4 13 Hen. VI. per Paston J.; [Holford *v.* Bailey, 8 Q.B. 1000, 1016; s.c. 13 Q.B. 444, 445; Wightman J., in Marshall *v.* Steam Nav. Co., 3 B. & S. 744. In McFarlin *v.* The Essex Co., 10 Cush. 304, it was held that if a several right of fishery on the land of another can be acquired by prescription, it must be by an actual and exclusive occupation and enjoyment

cited by Mr. Woolrych,[1] as proving no more than what might readily be admitted; namely, that the ownership of a fishery will imply a property in the soil, without further explanation.[2]

§ 74. To constitute a several fishery, it is doubtless requisite that the party claiming it should so far have the right of fishing, independently of all others, as that no person can have a coextensive right with him in the object claimed. But a partial independent right in another, or a limited liberty, does not derogate from the right of the general owner.[3] A several fishery, says Mr. Woolrych, is, as its name imports, an exclusive property. Not but that the territorial owner, or his grantee or lessee, may give permission to another person to fish, and yet preserve the several fishery. An owner of the above description would still remain seised of his original estate or right; and

of the fishery, adverse to the riparian proprietor, and continued for at least twenty years. See ante, § 63, in note; 3 Kent, 418; Melvin *v.* Whiting, 13 Pick. 184].

[1] Woolrych on the Law of Waters &c. 116 et seq.

[2] Rex *v.* Old Arlesford, 1 T.R. 358. A declaration reciting that defendant had been summoned to answer plaintiff in an action of trespass, charged that defendant, with force and arms, broke and entered a fishery of plaintiff, in a certain part of a river then flowing and being over the soil of one F., and then fished for fish in the said fishery of plaintiff, and the fish of the said fishery of plaintiff, there found, and being in said fishery, chased and disturbed: Conclusion, *contra pacem.* Held in arrest of judgment, after verdict for plaintiff, that the declaration was framed in trespass; and that (*semble*) trespass lies for breaking and entering the several fishery of A. on the soil of B.; but the words "sole and exclusive fishery" were not equivalent to "several" fishery; and that no cause for an action of trespass appeared. Holford *v.* Bailey, 8 Ad. & Ell. N.S. 1000. [In Marshall *v.* Steam Nav. Co., 3 B. & S. 749, 750, Cockburn C.J. said, "In Holford *v.* Bailey, 8 Q.B. 1000, Lord Denman, in delivering the considered judgment of this Court, says, p. 1016, 'No doubt the allegation of a several fishery, *primâ facie*, imports ownership of the soil, though they are not necessarily united.' And the same doctrine is enunciated by Parke B., in delivering the judgment of the Court of Exchequer Chamber in the same case, 13 Q.B. 426, 444. And though in both instances, the doctrine may be said to have been extrajudicial, as being unnecessary to the decision, which turned on the question whether trespass would lie for disturbance of a several fishery, the affirmative of which was held on grounds altogether independent of the ownership of the soil, yet it cannot be denied that these *dicta* occurring in the considered judgments of the Courts are entitled to very great weight. And in the learned note to fol. 122 a, of Hargrave and Butler's edition of Coke upon Littleton, the annotator, after passing in review the conflicting authorities on this subject, concludes, 'I cannot but think contrary to the effect of his own reasoning, that the true doctrine on this subject is that a several piscary is presumed to comprehend the soil till the contrary appears. I feel that in disposing of this rule we ought to yield to the authority of these opinions; but entertaining myself individually a very different view, I am desirous to have it known that, while I submit to them, I am far from acquiescing in them.'"]

[3] Seymour *v.* Lord Courtenay, 5 Burr. 2814.

he would be the several proprietor, although he should suffer a stranger to use a co-extensive right with him.[1]

3. *Of a Free Fishery.*

§ 75. A *free* fishery has been defined by Sir William Blackstone to be an exclusive right of fishing in a public river; and he says it is a royal franchise, and is considered as such in all countries where the feudal polity has prevailed; though the making such grants, and by that means, appropriating, what it seems unnatural to restrain, the use of running water, was prohibited for the future by Magna Charta.[2] The same writer distinguishes it from a several fishery, by connecting the latter with the ownership of the soil; and from a *common* of fishery, because it is an exclusive right, while the common is not; and then he adds, that a man has a property in the fish before they are caught, which is not the case in a common of piscary. "To consider such right," he proceeds, "as originally a flower of the prerogative, till restrained by Magna Charta, and derived by royal grant (previous to the reign of Richard I.) to such as now claim it by prescription; and to distinguish it, as we have done, from a several and a common of fishery, — may remove some difficulties, in respect to this matter, with which our books are embarrassed." Upon this illustration, Mr. Hargrave has bestowed the following comment: "Though for the sake of distinction, it might be more convenient to appropriate free fishery to the franchise of fishing in public rivers, by derivation from the crown; and though, in other countries, it may be so considered; yet, from the language of our books, it seems as if our law practice had extended this kind of fishery to all streams, whether public or private; neither the register nor the books professing any discrimination."[3]

§ 76. Blackstone admits, that there are not wanting respectable authorities which maintain that a free fishery implies no exclusive right, but is synonymous with a common of fishery.

[1] Woolrych, ut supra.

[2] 2 Bla. Com. 34. "In this country," says the late C.J. Swift, "any State has the power of granting this right, though it is an abridgment of the common rights of the people. And as it may be granted, it may be prescribed for. In England, such prescription must be founded on immemorial use and occupation, and is not like prescribing for an easement in the freehold of an individual. In this country, there has been no decision as to the length of time." 1 Swift's Dig. 110.

[3] Note to Co. Litt. 122 a.

Mr. Hargrave considers them as convertible terms, and synonymous with each other in regard to their privileges. Mr. Woolrych says, that sometimes a free fishery is confounded with a several, sometimes said to be synonymous with common, sometimes treated as distinct from either; and again, we find it mentioned as a royal franchise. Yet, notwithstanding the diversity of opinions, and the discrepancy of authorities, he thinks that to consider free fishery as the same with common of fishery, will be a reasonable as well as a legal conclusion.[1] We may add, that the doctrine that a free fishery is not an exclusive fishery, has been adopted by the Supreme Court of Massachusetts.[2]

4. *Of Common of Fishery.*

§ 77. To what has been said, in the two preceding sections, there is but little to be added concerning *common of fishery*. We have endeavored to show that it is the same as *free fishery*. On the strength of the various English authorities, according to Mr. Schultes, it must appear plain and unquestionable, that *libera piscaria* and *communia piscaria* are the same; and they are mentioned, he asserts, in the old authors indiscriminately, without signifying any essential difference.[3] All the judges, he says, in the case of Carter *v.* Murcot,[4] were of this opinion. Mr. J. Eyre entertained the like opinion;[5] and in Seymour *v.* Courtenay,[6] it was held, that where one has a co-extensive right of fishing with another (which by legal construction implies a common of fishery), it is a free fishery. In a case in Massachusetts,[7] as lately as the year 1828, the Court adopted the

[1] Woolrych on the Law of Waters &c. 122, 123.

[2] Melvin *v.* Whiting, 7 Pick. 79.

[3] Schultes on Aquatic Rights, 67. Mr. Woolrych is clearly of the same opinion. Woolrych on the Law of Waters &c. 122, 123. [See Carson *v.* Blazer, 2 Binn. 475, 489. "In all the treatises respecting the common right of fishery, the general term '*piscaria*,' or its equivalent, is used as including all fisheries, without any regard to their distinctive character, or to the method of taking the fish. There are many kinds of fishery recognized in them, and in judicial decisions; but the general term is uniformly used not with reference to any one of them, unless that one be particularly named, but as including them all." Shepley C.J., in Moulton *v.* Libbey, 37 Maine, 489, 490.]

[4] Carter *v.* Murcot, 4 Burr. 2162.

[5] Smith *v.* Kemp, 2 Salk. 637.

[6] Seymour *v.* Lord Courtenay, 5 Burr. 2816.

[7] Melvin *v.* Whiting, 7 Pick. 79. This was an action on the case for the destruction of the plaintiff's several fishery. The defendant pleaded the general issue, and soil and freehold in himself. The plaintiff claimed the fishery by prescription. To support his title, he offered in evidence the record of a judgment in a

opinion that a free fishery is only a common of fishery, as most agreeable to authority, and as the most conformable to the popular sense of the term "free fishery" in this country.

§ 78. Mr. Schultes says, in regard to things or liberties mentioned as common, where they relate to or are exercised by a community, that expression applies to the individual use of every person comprising that community; and therefore common use and public use, in this respect, are the same. It is to be observed, however, he adds, that although a public right, namely, the right of fishing in a public water, may be common, yet it does not hold, *e converso*, that a right exercisible in common in a private fishery, is public; because, in the one case, it is unrestrainable and universal; in the other case, it may extend only to a few individuals.[1]

5. *Right of Fishery as derived from Special Grants.*

§ 79. From the foregoing authorities it may be inferred, that property in a watercourse, as derived from the ownership of the land, may be subjected to every kind of restriction by convention and agreement.[2] It has been very properly asserted, that it is agreeable to natural reason, that where a man has an absolute property in a private river, which he necessarily must have if he be owner of the estates on each side, he should have the liberty of using it according to his inclination;[3] and the most ancient Common-Law authorities are cited in support of this position.[4] Hence, he may grant the soil covered with water to one for the purpose of a mill, reserving the right to fish. To another he may grant the entire territorial right of fishing on his own estate, reserving the soil, which would give the grantee

former action between the same parties, respecting the fishery at the same place, in which Melvin was defendant, and Whiting was plaintiff; which was admitted without objection. That was an action of trespass, in which it was alleged that Melvin entered the close of Whiting, covered with water, and there took fish. Melvin pleaded that he was seised in fee of land on the bank of the river, and that he had, by prescription, a free fishery in the fishery mentioned in Whiting's declaration, in which fishery he (Melvin), and all those whose estate he had, fished, and still of right ought to fish, at his or their free will and pleasure. Issue was taken on these allegations; and the jury found that Melvin, and all those whose estate &c. have been used and accustomed to fish in the fishery at their free will and pleasure, and that Melvin still of right might fish in the fishery.

1 Schultes on Aquatic Rights, 68.

2 And such is the conclusion of Mr. Schultes, ut supra, p. 90.

3 Ibid.

4 Bract. lib. 4, c. xxviii.; and ibid. lib. 2, c. xix. s. 4; 46 Ed. III. pl. 21.

an exclusive or several fishery, without ownership of soil. Or, he may grant a privilege to fish to several persons, and then they would have a free fishery with him, and his ownership of the soil would not control their right. Or, he may grant the soil to one of them, having such free fishery in common with others, and yet by this means the fishery of the others would not be destroyed, though the former right of fishing of the grantee might be merged by such acquisition.[1] So one having the absolute property on one side of a river, may grant a free fishing in his own water, to his neighbor on the opposite side,[2] by which means his neighbor would have his own predial or territorial fishing, and a free fishing in the same river; the one being a liberty originally coincident with his estate, and the other a right or service due from another estate. Again, continues Mr. Schultes, a man having one side of the stream, may grant an exclusive right to fish to another, and his opposite neighbor might grant a freedom to fish to the same person; and, by this means, the grantees would have a free fishery and a several fishery in the same river within their respective limits.[3] To illustrate — says the author just referred to — still further, Bracton, in treating of nuisances, says, that if any one shall establish a fishery or a pool, having lands on either side of the water, when his estate is free on every side, and owes no service to the neighboring estate above or below it (although such a thing may be of some damage to his neighbor), yet it shall not be accounted injurious, unless it affect the public utility.[4]

§ 80. It has been held, in one case, that the river and all the profits of it may belong to one person, and the soil and ferry to another.[5] And in a subsequent case, in Great Britain, it was held, that the soil of the river Thames is in the King, and the Mayor is conservator of the river, and it is common to all fishermen; and therefore there is no such contradiction betwixt the soil being in one, and yet the river common for all fishers.[6]

[1] Schultes, ut supra, 91.

[2] Skinner, 667.

[3] Schultes, ut supra. And see ante, ch. II. § 2; and Melvin *v.* Whiting, 7 Pick. 79; and Gould *v.* James, 6 Cowen, 369.

[4] Bract. lib. 4, c. xliv.

[5] Inhabitants of Ipswich *v.* Browne, Savil. case 48.

[6] 1 Mod. 195; and see also Holt, 499. In like manner other territorial rights may exist by grant and constitution. Thus a prescription for sole and several pastures at all times, so as to exclude the lord of the soil from feeding, is good; although an entire exclusion, for all purposes, from the soil, is void; because such prescription does not exclude the

6. *User of Private Fisheries.*

§ 81. The owner of a fishery may lawfully use *nets*, as by setting a *seine*, for the purpose of taking fish,[1] but the nets must be such as will not injure the rights of other persons.[2] Upon most occasions, a man may use any nets, according to his pleasure, in his several fishery; but if he allow another to participate in his property, he cannot be justified in taking the fish with such engines as would leave no fish for his grantee, because the principle is *sic utere tuo ut alienum non lœdas.*[3] With respect to a common of fishery, in England, we are told, the user of nets must be regulated according to the custom of the manor.' In some manors there, the net is employed at certain seasons for the purpose of taking fish; and it would be clearly incompetent for some commoners to drag with instruments of a greater depth than customary, whilst their neighbors were content with the usual manner of obtaining commonable profit.[4]

§ 82. In Massachusetts, the exercise of the right of several fishery in watercourses is regulated by the government, and the right to regulate it has immemorially been granted to towns. Both in that State and in Maine, the rule of the Common Law, that fisheries in streams not navigable belong to the riparian owners, has been modified; it being deemed most conducive to the public good to subject the shad and alewive fisheries to public control, whenever the legislature thought proper to interpose; and the paramount claims of the public have been implied in all grants made by them, and so in all conveyances by individuals.[5] The State of Massachusetts, in a grant of a tract of land, conveyed also the privilege of fishing, to be held in common among the grantees and other settlers. Afterwards the inhabitants of the territory granted became a town, and they were authorized by law

lord of the profits, for he shall have mines, trees, and other things. Bac. Abr. 621. And a service to exclude the lord of the soil from depasturing his own cattle, may be made by specific contract, according to Bracton (lib. 4, c. vi. s. 1)

[1] Commonwealth *v.* Ruggles, 10 Mass. 391; Commonwealth *v.* Chapin, 5 Pick. 199.

[2] Commonwealth *v.* Ruggles, supra.

[3] Woolrych on the Law of Waters &c. 166.

[4] Woolrych on the Law of Waters &c. 166.

[5] Vinton *v.* Welsh, 9 Pick. 87; Cottrill *v.* Myrick, 12 Maine, 222; Commonwealth *v.* Chapin, 5 Pick. 199; Waters *v.* Lilly, 4 Pick. 145; Burnham *v.* Webster, 5 Mass. 266; [Shaw C.J., in McFarlin *v.* Essex Co., 10 Cush. 309, 310.]

to appoint a committee to regulate the fishery within the town; and a penalty was imposed on any person, except such committee, or those authorized by them, who should take any fish. It was held, that the owner of the land adjoining the river was subject to the penalty, notwithstanding he, and those under whom he claimed, had used to take the fish there, before the grant made by the State.[1] The act of the Legislature of Massachusetts of 1807, granting the emoluments arising from the fisheries in the Damariscotta River in the towns of Newcastle and Nobleborough, in Maine, while a part of Massachusetts, and authorizing those towns to choose a committee with power to keep open a sluice or passage-way for the fish, and to go on and over any land or mill, whenever it should be necessary for the purposes of the acts, without being considered as trespassers, was held to be in no violation of the constitution.[2] The legislative right of regulating fisheries, even over those which are private property, having been long exercised in Maine, before its separation from Massachusetts, the constitution of the former does not forbid the exercise of the right.[3]

§ 83. With respect to the quantity of fish which may by the Common Law be taken, it is clear, as will be seen by the first section of this chapter, that where the proprietor has an exclusive right, the number must be unrestricted; but if there be a special grant, by the proprietor, of a right to fish, the extent of such right will depend upon the terms of the grant.[4] As a general principle, the right cannot be so exercised as to injure a similar right belonging to another person. It is, says Mr. Woolrych, most consistent with the origin of the grant, that a commoner should take a reasonable supply only; because it is understood that such a common inures to the sustenance of his family, and that its produce may not be appropriated to any other purpose.[5]

[1] Nickerson *v.* Brackett, 10 Mass. 212.

[2] Cottrill *v.* Myrick, 12 Maine, 222.

[3] Lunt *v.* Hunter, 16 Maine, 9; Pebbles *v.* Hanneford, 18 Maine, 106; Fuller *v.* Spear, 14 Maine, 417; [Parker *v.* Cutler Mill-dam Co., 20 Maine, 353; Moulton *v.* Libbey, 37 Maine, 472, 494.] But whether it is competent for the legislature to provide for the removal of natural obstructions, or for the erection of artificial facilities in the bed of a stream, for the ascent of fish, and the erection of a fishery, where they could not otherwise pass, without the consent of the riparian proprietor, and without making compensation — *quære*. Cottrill *v.* Myrick, 12 Maine, 222.

[4] See ante, § 79.

[5] Woolrych, 166, 167.

7. *Obstruction of the Passage of Fish.*

§ 84. Even the exclusive right of fishery in rivers not navigable, is subject to a reasonable qualification, in order to protect the rights of others, who have a similar interest, but might lose all advantage from it, if their neighbors below them could with impunity wholly impede the passage of fish. The right of several fishery is clearly limited to the right of taking fish, and does not carry with it the right to hinder the passing of them above, and of preventing the supra-riparian proprietors from enjoying a similar privilege. In Rolle's Abridgment, there is cited 17 E. 3, pl. 31, as an authority to show that assize may be maintained against an heir, an alienee, or feoffee, if any one of such refuse to amend the grievance of an obstruction to the privileges of a several fishery.[1] In the modern English case of Weld *v.* Hornby, in the Court of King's Bench,[2] it appeared that the plaintiff, being possessed of a sole and several fishery in a stream of water, undertook to convert a brush wear, through which some of the fish might and did escape, into a solid stone wear, which was entirely impervious. This was determined to be a nuisance, because it obstructed the passage of fish higher up the stream.

§ 85. This private right of fishery, in rivers above tide-water, is, in this country, considered and held to be subject to the qualification of not being used so as to injure the private rights of others; so that it does not extend to impede the passage of fish up the river by means of dams or other obstructions.[3] The above case of Weld *v.* Hornby was recognized by the Supreme Court of Massachusetts as being in conformity with the doctrine of the Common Law, which is thus laid down by Parker C.J.: "It appears that this Common-Law right of several fishery in the owners of land bordering on streams not navigable, is subject to a reasonable qualification, in order to protect the right of others, who, in virtue of owning the soil, have the same right, but might lose all advantage from it, if their neighbors below them on a stream or river might with impunity wholly impede the passage

1 2 Roll. Abr. 142.

2 Weld *v.* Hornby, 7 East, 195.

3 3 Kent, 411; Boatwright *v.* Beekman, 1 Rice (S.C.) Law, 447; Case *v.* Weber, 2 Carter (Ind.) 100.

of fish into the lakes or ponds, where they by instinct repair for the multiplication of their species. This restriction is founded upon that universal principle of every just code of laws, *Sic utere tuo ut alienum non lædas*."[1] And yet (although large rivers, above tide-water, like the Connecticut, extend through several States, and their banks are thickly settled, so that a great population is interested in the preservation of the fish which frequent the river) "manufacturing machinery and steamboats, and the insatiable cupidity and skill of fishermen, have prodigiously diminished the resort of the most valuable fish into the rivers of the northern States."[2]

[1] Commonwealth *v.* Chapin, 5 Pick. 199.

[2] 3 Kent, 411, n. *a*. It appears, by the case of Commonwealth *v.* Chapin, ubi supra, that the Common Law in Massachusetts has been altered by successive legislative acts, from the earliest settlement of the country, as well under the colonial and provincial as under the present form of government. And the rights of the citizens of the Commonwealth, as well as the penalties to which they may be subject, are to be determined by the effect, and according to the form of this legislation, rather than by the ancient Common Law. The Court proceed to say, "By Prov. St. 8 Ann. c. iii., all persons are prohibited from placing in or across rivers or streams, any fixed implement or machine by which the free passage of fish may be obstructed. And by Prov. St. 15 Geo. II. c. vi., it is required of those who build dams across streams or rivers, to keep open, during a certain period, sluiceways or passages for the fish to pass through. These statutes assert the right of the public to regulate the mode of taking fish even in private or several fisheries, and they also, by implication, recognize the right of proprietors to erect dams and other works on rivers or their banks, provided a passage is left through them at certain portions of the year for the escape of the fish. By the St. 8 Ann. above cited, the erection of certain obstructions is declared to be a nuisance, and by a particular process, therein specified, such obstructions are to be abated; but those obstructions are not dams erected for permanent use, but hedges, wears, fishgarths, stakes, and kiddles, which, though not permanent, may occasion an entire interruption of the passage of fish; and there is a special exception of dams erected for the use of mills. But by St. 15 Geo. II. there is an implied grant or recognition of the rights of proprietors to erect and maintain dams, provided they secure a passage for the fish, by sluices &c. during the season when they are accustomed to ascend the streams. This legislative provision, though altering, is not contrary to the Common Law, for by that the proprietors of banks might make such obstructions as were necessary to the taking of fish, leaving room enough for some of them to escape and ascend the streams. The statute only ascertains the mode in which this restriction shall be enforced, and provides the penalty for neglecting or violating it. But it is plain that the mere erecting or continuing a dam whereby fish may be obstructed, is no longer an offence, for that would be committed by any erection, however necessary for any profitable use of the fishery. The offence consists only in having a dam without providing a convenient passage for the fish during two or three months in the year; and the remedy, where this requisition is not observed, is totally different from that which exists at Common Law for a nuisance. Instead of abating a dam which is found to be deficient, the statute provides a pecuniary mulct, and gives power to certain municipal officers to supervise the public interests, and see to the execution of the law. It follows, we think, clearly, that an indictment, as at

§ 86. It appears that statutes of States other than those of Massachusetts and Maine, evince an earnest solicitude in their legislatures to preserve a free passage for fish in rivers; and more especially those which are annually visited by fish from the ocean.[1] In Hooker *v.* Cummings, Spencer C.J. says, that the Legislature of New York "have confessedly the right of regulating the taking of fish in private rivers; and do, every year, pass laws for that purpose, as to rivers not navigable in any sense, and which are unquestionably private property."[2]

§ 87. Causing a superfluity of water to drown or overflow a fishery, is a plain obstruction, and punishable by an action of trespass.[3] An action of trespass was maintained in Ireland, for wrong-

Common Law for a nuisance, cannot be maintained; but that if the dam should be continued without opening through it, at the proper season, a passage-way for the fish, the proprietors will be subject to the penalty provided by statute." See also the following decisions: Stoughton *v.* Baker, 4 Mass. 522; Burnham *v.* Webster, 5 Mass. 266; Nickerson *v.* Bracket, 10 Mass. 212; Commonwealth *v.* M'Curdy, 5 Mass. 324; Vinton *v.* Welsh, 9 Pick. 87. For an act concerning the passage of fish in Mystic River, see Hyde *v.* Russell, 2 Cush. 251.

[1] An old act of Pennsylvania recites in its preamble that large quantities of fry or brood of fish, and young fish, are destroyed by dams, wears, baskets &c. in the rivers Delaware and Schuylkill and Susquehanna, whereby the great quantities of fish that were formerly to be taken in said rivers are greatly diminished; and then prescribes several penalties against persons who violate its provisions by such obstructions. See Hart *v.* Hill, 1 Wharton, 132. In New York, the Revised Statutes regulate the right of fishery in rivers navigable and not navigable. Particularly with regard to certain kinds of fish, and in the waters of the upper Hudson, jurisdiction of the subject is given to the Courts of Common Pleas within their respective counties, in regard to streams, ponds, and lakes. 1 N.Y. Rev. St. 687, 688. In New York, also, salmon cannot be taken between October 20 and February 1; nor between these months, at or below the city of New York, between sunset on Saturday and sunrise on Monday; nor any net used between these hours; nor in the months of March, April, and May, a drift net, at the above places. Ib. In Virginia, a dam shall not be built without an inquiry by jury as to the obstruction of fish. 2 Va. Rev. St. 230, 311, 341. In South Carolina, a statute requires the owners of existing dams to make slopes or openings for the passage of fish, the sufficiency of which is to be determined, as in Massachusetts, by commissioners. When a dam is built for the propelling of machinery, the owner may, at his election, leave sixty feet in width of the river open, or keep open a sluice in February, March, and April. S.C. St. 1827, p. 79. In North Carolina, in the *laying off* of rivers, the commissioners shall allow three-fourths to the owner to erect stops, dams, and stands, and one-quarter, including the deepest part, for the passage of fish. They shall also require a sufficient slope in mill-dams. 1 N.C. Rev. St. 535, 536. In Alabama, where one erects a fish-dam on a watercourse which is a public highway, he shall open in the deepest channel one-third of the stream, including the main channel. Aik. Dig. 442. In Michigan, the diversion from their natural course of *white* fish is forbidden. Mich. Laws, 475. See 2 Hill. Abr. 168 &c.

[2] Hooker *v.* Cummings, 20 John. 90. [See per Shaw C.J., in McFarlin *v.* Essex Co., 10 Cush. 309, 310.]

[3] 1 Ld. Raym. 274.

fully setting up certain wears and traps upon a certain fall of water, in the river Bann, so that salmon, trout, and other fish which would have come from the sea, and that part of the river which lay below the plaintiff's fishery, were hindered from so doing. A writ of error was then brought in the Exchequer Chamber, where the judgment was affirmed; and the case was then carried up to the House of Lords in Ireland, where the judgment was again affirmed.[1] The inquest taken upon a writ of *ad quod damnum,* in Kentucky, for flowing land by means of a dam, must ascertain whether or not fish would be obstructed; and in case they would be, permission to build the dam will be denied.[2]

§ 88. In Shaw *v.* Crawford, in New York,[3] the Court say (*obiter dictum*), "Every owner of a mill-dam or a stream which fish from the ocean annually visit, is bound to provide a convenient passage-way for the fish to ascend;" and they rely expressly on the case of Stoughton *v.* Baker, in Massachusetts.[4] By that case, it appears that an ancient and long-continued usage of the General Court of Massachusetts has been to appoint committees to locate and describe the site and dimensions of passage-ways for fish, and the owner of a mill holds it subject to the limitation that a reasonably sufficient passage-way shall be allowed for the fish. The Court, by Parsons C.J., say, "If the government, in its grant of a mill privilege, expressly or by necessary implication, waive this limitation, it would be bound. But it would be an unreasonable construction of the grant, to admit that by it, all the people were deprived of a free fishery in the river above the dam, to which, until the grant, they were unquestionably entitled." Again, says the learned Judge, "The right to build dams for the use of mills, is, under certain implied limitations, acknowledged; one of these limitations is to protect the enjoyment of a fishery. Every owner of a mill, therefore, holds it subject to the limitation, that a sufficient and reasonable passage-way shall be left for the fish; and, as this limitation is a public benefit, it is not extinguished by any inattention or neglect in compelling the owner to comply with it."

§ 89. But it was decided by the Supreme Court of New York, in the year 1819, that a patent granted by one Z. P., in 1784,

[1] Hamilton *v.* Marquis of Donegal, 3 Ridg. 267, and cited in Woolrych, 189, 190.

[2] Eubank *v.* Pence, 5 Litt. (Ken.) 338.

[3] Shaw *v* Crawford, 10 John. 236.

[4] Stoughton *v.* Baker, 4 Mass. 522.

of a tract of land bounded on the east by Lake Champlain, and extending west on both sides of the river Saranac, seven miles square, the whole river to that distance passed to the patentee; and that, as there was no reservation of the river, nor any restriction in the use of it, the public had no right of fishing in it, within the bounds of the patent; and that, therefore, the erection of a dam by the patentee in 1786, near the mouth of the river, by which salmon were prevented from passing up the river from the lake, was not indictable, as a public nuisance, either at Common Law, nor under the statute, for the preservation of fish in certain waters.[1] The statute, the Court held, ought to be construed with an implied exception of such rivers or streams (not being navigable) as had been fully and absolutely granted by the State, without any reservation; and that so far as it affected the rights of Z. P. and his assigns, it impaired the obligation of a contract, and was unconstitutional and void.[2] In this case the above case of Stoughton *v.* Baker, in Massachusetts, was strongly urged in favor of the plaintiffs, which the Court treated, by Spencer C. J., as follows: "In that case, the Supreme Court of Massachusetts held, that a legislative resolution appointing a committee, who were authorized to require the proprietors of certain dams on Neponset River, to alter them, in such a way as should be sufficient for the passage of shad and alewives, at the dams, was a legal proceeding, not repugnant to the constitution. The opinion is founded on the ancient and long-continued usage of the General Court of Massachusetts, to appoint commissioners to locate and describe the site and dimensions of passage-ways for fish; and, under the circumstances of the case, it was held, that the right of the proprietor of the dam was subject to the limitation that a reasonable and sufficient passage should be allowed for the fish. The Court, however, expressly say, that any prostration of the dam not within the limitation, would be an injury to the owner, for which he might appeal to his country, and have a remedy; and that if the government, in the grant of a mill

[1] Passed in 1800, and enacts, that the owners of mill-dams made across any river running into Lakes Ontario, Erie, or Champlain, so as to prevent the usual course of salmon from going up, shall, within eighteen months from the passage of the act, so alter the dam, by making a slope thereto, that salmon may easily pass up over into the waters above the dam; or by removing the obstruction of such dam in any other manner; and in case such dam shall not be so altered &c. it shall be deemed a public nuisance.

[2] People *v.* Platt, 17 John. 195.

privilege, expressly, or by necessary implication, waive this limitation, it would be bound. In the case then under consideration, the Court said, it would be an unreasonable construction of the grant to admit, that by it all the people were deprived of a free fishery in the river above the dam, to which until the grant, they were unquestionably entitled. Whether, in that case, the Neponset River was navigable above the dam, is nowhere affirmed or denied; but it is perfectly clear that the Court proceeded on local usages and customs, and not upon the general and received doctrines of the Common Law; for not a single case is referred to, nor is it even asserted, that the principles advanced are sanctioned by the English Common Law; whereas, it has been shown that by the Common Law, the property in the river Saranac passed to Zephaniah Platt, and has been transmitted, through him, to the defendants, without any limitation or restriction, and that the fishery itself became vested in the proprietor of the river; it being a conceded fact, that the river is unnavigable for boats of any kind; for there is no weight in the circumstance, that, for a few years past, and since 1810, rafts have occasionally been brought down this river, when connected with the fact that the defendant has received a consideration for that privilege. So far, then, from this being the exercise of a public right, it is a recognition of the defendant's property in the river, and fortifies and supports the defendant's claim to it, as private property. In a case thus circumstanced, the opinion of the Court in Stoughton *v.* Baker, would protect the defendant in the exclusive and undisturbed enjoyment of all the right acquired under the grant, for there is no reservation of the use, by the public, of the river, either for passage or fishing."[1]

[1] [And it has been held in North Carolina, that where one owning the bed of an unnavigable river, under a grant from the State, has erected a dam across the stream, the legislature has not the power to compel him, without indemnity, to take away a part of the dam at his own expense, so as to make an opening for the passage of fish. State *v.* Glen, 7 Jones, Law (N.C.) 321; Cornelius *v.* Glen, 7 Jones, Law (N.C.) 512.]

CHAPTER IV.

OF THE RIGHT OF USE OF THE WATER AS A CORPOREAL HEREDITAMENT.

1. Of the General Right of Use.
2. Of the Injury by Diverting the Water.
3. Surface Water and Drainage.
4. Subterranean Diversion.
5. Easement of Drip.
6. Of the Injury by Obstructing and Detaining the Water.
7. Of the Right of Irrigation.
8. Of the Effect of Prior Occupation, by a Riparian Proprietor.
9. Of the Injury by rendering the Water corrupt and unwholesome.

1. *Of the General Right of Use.*

§ 90. A WATERCOURSE may be either *natural* or *artificial*, and the right of the riparian proprietors to the water thereof, is, in the one case, a *corporeal*, and in the other, an *incorporeal* right.[1] The right to the use of the flow of the water, in its natural course, and to the momentum of its fall on the land of the proprietor, is not what is called an easement, because it is inseparably connected with, and inherent in, the property in the land; it is a parcel of the inheritance, and passes with it.[2] In general,

[1] [Woolrych says, "A watercourse may be either a real or an incorporeal hereditament. If by grant, prescription, or otherwise, one should have an easement of this kind in the land of another person, it would partake of the latter quality; but if the water flow over the party's own land, although indeed it cannot be claimed as *water*, yet it is in effect identified with the realty, because it passes over the soil, and *cujus est solum ejus est usque ad cœlum*. For example, a miller may purchase the water adjoining to his mill, as an easement, the soil being left in the hands of the original proprietor; and in that case he would gain an incorporeal hereditament; but if he was to buy the land itself over which the water flowed, he would then have a corporeal tenement, and the right which he would possess in respect of his watercourse would be real." Law of Waters, 146. Where hydraulic privileges are created by conducting a stream across lands in an artificial channel, the proprietors of lots crossed by the artificial channel, in the absence of any stipulation to the contrary, have the same rights to the use of the water on their respective lots as between themselves, as would exist if the artificial were the natural channel of the stream. Townsend *v.* McDonald, 2 Kernan, 381.]

[2] [Gardner *v.* Newburgh, 2 John. Ch. 166; Holsman *v.* Boiling Spring Bleaching Co., 1 McCarter, 343; Wheatley *v.* Baugh, 25 Penn. St. 528, 531; Shaw C.J., in Johnson *v.* Jordan, 2 Met. 239; Pol-

where a mill site is granted, that is, land on a watercourse on which mills are actually situated, or where it appears by the grant, that the object is to erect mills thereon, the *soil* is the principal subject of the grant; and the right to use it for any and for all mill purposes, at the pleasure of the purchaser, and to change those uses, at pleasure, follows as incident to the ownership.[1] It is in accordance both with common sense and legal interpretation, that, under a grant or a devise of a mill, the soil under it and adjacent thereto will pass by force of the word "mill;" and that the word should be deemed to include the site, dam, and other things annexed to the freehold, and necessary for its beneficial enjoyment.[2]

lock C.B., in Dickinson *v.* Grand Junction Canal Co., 7 Exch. 299, 300; Parke B., in Rawstron *v.* Taylor, 11 Exch. 382; Wood *v.* Waud, 3 Exch. 775; Embrey *v.* Owen, 6 Exch. 353; Evans *v.* Merriweather, 3 Scamm. 492; Wright *v.* Howard, 1 S. & S. 203; Sampson *v.* Hoddinott, 1 C.B. N.S. 590; Shreve *v.* Voorhees, 2 Green Ch. 25; Cary *v.* Daniels, 8 Met. 466; Plumleigh *v.* Dawson, 1 Gilm. 544; Webb *v.* Portland Manuf. Co., 3 Sumner, 189; Tourtellot *v.* Phelps, 4 Gray, 370, 374; M'Coy *v.* Danley, 20 Penn. St. 85; Wheatley *v.* Christman, 24 Penn. St. 298; Hill *v.* Newman, 5 Cal. 445; McCord *v.* High, 24 Iowa, 336; Mayor & City Council of Baltimore *v.* Appold, 42 Md. 442, 456. In Stokoe *v.* Singers, 8 El. & Bl. 36, Erle J. said, "The right to the natural flow of water is not an easement, but a natural right, which is not lost until an adverse easement has been acquired." See per Storrs J., in Wadsworth *v.* Tillotson, 15 Conn. 366, 373: "We consider it as settled law, that the right to have a stream running in its natural course is, not by a presumed grant from long acquiescence on the part of the riparian proprietors above and below, but is *jure naturæ* (Shury *v.* Piggot, 3 Bulst. 339; Tyler *v.* Wilkinson, 4 Mason, 397), and an incident of property, as much as the right to have the soil itself in its natural state, unaltered by the acts of a neighboring proprietor, who cannot dig so as to deprive it of the support of his land." Pollock C.B., in Dickinson *v.* Grand Junction Canal Co., 7 Exch. 299, 300; Wightman J., in Chasemore *v.* Richards, 7 H. L. Cas. 349; 5 H. & N. 984, 985, and Lord Wensleydale in the same case; Parke B., in Rawstron *v.* Taylor, 11 Exch. 382; Wilde J., in Cary *v.* Daniels, 5 Met. 238; Hubbard J., in Crittenton *v.* Alger, 11 Met. 284; ante, §§ 5, 8, and notes.]

[1] Ashley *v.* Pease, 18 Pick. 268; Embrey *v.* Owen, 6 Exch. 353; [Hadley *v.* Hadley Manuf. Co., 4 Gray, 140, 143, stated, post, § 155 *a;* Elliott *v.* Fitchburg R.R. Co., 10 Cush. 193; Pratt *v.* Lamson, 2 Allen, 285.]

[2] Whitney *v.* Olney, 3 Mason, 280; Blaine *v.* Chambers, 1 S. & Rawle, 169; New Ipswich Woollen Factory *v.* Batchelder, 3 N.H. 190; Blake *v.* Clark, 6 Greenl. 436; [Dunklee *v.* The Wilton R.R. Co., 24 N.H. 495, 496, 497, 498, per Bell J.; Selden J., in Lampman *v.* Milks, 21 N.Y. 510; Colt J., in Hapgood *v.* Brown, 102 Mass. 452, 453; Richardson *v.* Bigelow, 15 Gray, 156; post, §§ 156, 157.] Grant of mill conveys the use of the water as a corporeal hereditament. Maddox *v.* Goddard, 15 Maine, 218. It was not unusual in the early history of the country, to find mill privileges conveyed without any exact bounds, and such deeds have been held to convey so much *land* as was necessary and customarily used with the mill. Per Shepley J., in the case just cited. [But a vote passed by a town in 1850, granting to certain persons named "the liberty of erecting a grist-mill on Fort River near Lawrence's Bridge, with the use of said stream," and

§ 91. The following case has been put by a learned judge: "Suppose a man owning land on both sides of a stream (not navigable) should grant to another the land on one side, bounded by the thread of the stream, and should, at the same time, grant a right to erect a mill on his own land, with a dam of sufficient height to raise the water to drive such mill. As such dam could not raise the water, without being extended across the river, and, of course, one-half upon the grantor's own land, such a grant would, by necessary implication, carry the right to build on the grantor's own land, and to occupy it as far as necessary, to maintain the dam, so long as the dam should be kept up." The learned Judge considered it to be not a mere easement, but a *freehold*,[1] determinable upon the cessation of the mills, or as a demise, for the time the mills should continue; and that it carried with it a right of possession, for the violation of which an action of *trespass* would lie.[2]

§ 92. If the owner of a large tract of land through which a watercourse passes should convey parcels above and below his own land, each grantee would take his parcel with a full right, without special words to such effect, to the use of the flowing water on his own land, as parcel, and subject to the right of all other riparian proprietors to have the water flow to and from such parcel. There is, therefore, no occasion for the grantor in such case, to convey the right of water to the grantee, or reserve the right of water to himself, in express words; because being inseparable from the land, and parcel of the estate, such right passes with that which is conveyed, and remains with that which is retained.[3] [In Johnson *v.* Jordan,[4] Shaw C.J. said, "Every

accepted by the grantees, is not to be construed as a grant of land, in the absence of other evidence that the town owned the land on which the mill was erected. Hadley *v.* Hadley Manuf. Co., 4 Gray, 140; post, § 155 *a*. As to what will pass by a conveyance of a "spring," see Woodcock *v.* Estey, 43 Vt. 515, cited ante, § 5, note.]

1 See ante, § 8.

2 Dryden *v.* Jepherson, 18 Pick. 392, per Shaw C.J.

3 See opinion of Shaw C.J., in Cary *v.* Daniels, 8 Met. 466; Hart *v.* Evans, 8 Penn. St. 13. He who purchases land and a watercourse from another, is bound to look at the title before doing so; for his right to dam the water, on investigation, may prove defective. Beidelman *v.* Foulk, 5 Watts, 308. See also Randall *v.* Silverthorn, 4 Penn. St. 173.

4 [Johnson *v.* Jordan, 2 Met. 239. See also Tourtellot *v.* Phelps, 4 Gray, 370, 375, 376; Chasemore *v.* Richards, 5 N. & H. 989; Storrs J., in Wadsworth *v.* Tillotson, 15 Conn. 373; Corning *v.* Troy Iron & Nail Factory, 39 Barb. 311, 322, 323; Holsman *v.* Boiling Spring Bleaching Co., 1 McCarter, 335; Wheatley *v.* Baugh, 25 Penn. St. 528, 531; ante, § 5 and note, § 8; Pollitt *v.* Long, 58 Barb. 20.]

person, through whose land a natural watercourse runs, has a right, *publici juris*, to the benefit of it as it passes through his land, to all the useful purposes to which it may be applied; and no proprietor of land on the same watercourse, either above or below, has a right unreasonably to divert it from flowing into his premises, or obstruct it from passing from them, or to corrupt or destroy it. It is inseparably annexed to the soil, and passes with it, not as an easement, nor as an appurtenance, but as parcel. Use does not create it, and disuse cannot destroy or suspend it. Unity of possession and title in such land with the lands above or below it does not extinguish or suspend it."]

[§ 92 *a*. In Sampson *v.* Hoddinott,[1] Creswell J. said, "It appears to us that all persons having lands on the margin of a flowing stream have, by nature, certain rights to use the water of that stream, whether they exercise those rights or not; and that they may begin to exercise them whenever they will. By usage, they may acquire a right to use the water in a manner not justified by their natural rights; but such acquired right has no operation against the natural rights of a land-owner higher up the stream, unless the user by which it was acquired affects the use that he himself has made of the stream, or his power to use it, so as to raise the presumption of a grant, and so render the tenement above a servient tenement." It matters not how much the owner of land upon a stream has actually used the water or whether he has used it at all, his right to the use of it remains unaffected, during any period of time. A mere non-user of his right raises no presumption against him.[2]]

§ 93. The uses to which the water of a watercourse may be, and has been, applied, are various: but the value of an estate is much enhanced by the existence thereon of what is called a "water privilege."[3] One of the most important uses of it, in many parts of the United States, is its application to working of mills and machinery; a use profitable to the owner, and vastly beneficial to the public.[4] But both his benefit and that of the

[1] [Sampson *v.* Hoddinott, 1 C.B. N.S. 590.]

[2] [Williams J., in Sampson *v.* Hoddinott, 1 C.B. N.S. 608; Buddington *v.* Bradley, 10 Conn. 213; Crossley *v.* Lightowler, L. R. 3 Eq. 296.]

[3] See opinion of Lord Denman, in Mason *v.* Hill, 5 B. & Ad. 1.

[4] See opinion of Shaw C.J., in Cary *v.* Daniels, 8 Met. 466; Blanchard *v.* Baker, 8 Greenl. 253. [But the owner of a mill on a flowing stream is in the same position as a riparian proprietor; he can have no larger right than that which he has by nature against those above or below him, unless it has been acquired by ad-

public would be diminished, just in proportion to the extent which other riparian owners above or below him may deprive him of the water, or use it to his annoyance, and contrary to the established rules of law; contrary to the doctrine which is clearly, though quaintly, stated, in the old books, in which it is said, "A watercourse begins *ex jure naturæ*, and having taken a certain course naturally cannot be diverted." *Aqua currit et debet currere, ut currere solebat*, is also the language of the ancient Common Law.[1] That is, the water runs naturally, and should be permitted thus to run, so that all through whose land it runs may enjoy the privilege of using it.[2] In 32 Ed. III., fol. 8, an assize of nuisance was brought by A. against B., for that B. had made a trench over a river and drew away thereby a part of the water and stream another way from that in which it did formerly use to run; and the assize passed for the plaintiff; and, it was adjudged, that the water should be removed into the ancient channel at the cost of the defendant.[3]

[§ 93 *a*. In Nuttall *v*. Bracewell,[4] Martin B. said, "The application and use of flowing water to work machinery is as old as the law. Corn mills have existed from time immemorial; and it appears, from old legal authorities, that fulling and other mills worked by water for the purpose of manufacture are of very ancient date. Until the last century steam as a power

verse user. A party, whether mill owner or riparian owner, suing for obstruction of water, must establish a right either *jure naturæ* or by user, and in the latter case the user must be such as to establish a servitude affecting the land through which the water flows. Cresswell J., in Chasemore *v*. Richards, 2 H. & N. 181, 182.]

[1] Shury *v*. Piggot, 3 Bulst. 339; s.c. Poph. 166; Countess of Rutland *v*. Bowler, Palm. 290. [Under the maxim referred to in the text, Seymour J., in Keeney & Wood Manuf. Co. *v*. Union Manuf. Co., 39 Conn. 582, said, "Water cannot be detained for the use of mills so as to deprive the proprietors below of what is needed for domestic and agricultural purposes, and under that maxim water cannot be diverted from its natural channel to the prejudice of the lower proprietors upon the stream. But water power is made available mainly by means of dams, by which it is temporarily detained, and its power thereby accumulated and stored up for use, and the maxim of '*debet currere*' is not applicable to such detentions of the current as are convenient and necessary and usual for the purpose of making such accumulations."]

[2] ["This is sustained by numerous judicial decisions and all elementary writers upon the subject." Grover J. in Clinton *v*. Myers, 46 N.Y. 511, 517.]

[3] Callis on Sewers, 268. In the Year Book, 14 Hen. VIII. 31, where an action on the case was brought for diverting a river, it is said by Row, "It seems that here he shall have assize of nuisance, and not action on the case; as if you stop a conduit, I shall have assize of nuisance," Cited by one of the learned counsel in Acton *v*. Blundell, 12 M. & W. 339. Palmes *v*. Heblethwaite, Skinn. 65, 175.

[4] [L. R. 2 Exch. 1.]

was, if known, not much in use; and until it was introduced, water power was very generally used, and it is still the cheapest when available. The mill is sometimes situated upon the bank of the natural stream, but more usually at some little distance from it; the water is conveyed to it by a goit or artificial cut leading from the stream, and then, after turning the wheel of the mill, flows away in what is commonly called the tail-goit. So, also, water was and is very frequently conveyed from the natural stream in the same manner for the purposes of irrigation. And it is not too much to say, that the value of actual or supposed water rights of this character throughout England may be estimated by hundreds of thousands, perhaps millions. The law has been supposed to be well settled, and in my opinion is nowhere more clearly stated than by Lord Kingsdown, in Miner *v.* Gilmour.[1] He says, 'By the general law applicable to running streams, every riparian proprietor has a right to what may be called the ordinary use of water flowing past his land; for instance, to the reasonable use of the water for domestic purposes and for his cattle, and this without regard to the effect which such use may have in case of a deficiency upon proprietors lower down the stream.[2] But, further, he has a right to the use of it for any purpose, or what may be deemed the extraordinary use of it, provided he does not thereby interfere with the rights of other proprietors, either above or below him. Subject to this condition, he may dam up a stream for the purposes of a mill, or divert the water for the purpose of irrigation. But he has no right to intercept the regular flow of the stream, if he thereby interferes with the lawful use of the water by other proprietors, and inflicts upon them a sensible injury.' "[3] The use in all the above cases must be a reasonable one.[4]]

1 [12 Moore P.C. 156.]

2 [Mayor & City Council of Baltimore *v.* Appold, 42 Md. 456, 457; Stein *v.* Burden, 29 Ala. 127.]

3 [Substantially the same general rules of right to the uses of the water of a stream are stated by Rice J. in Davis *v.* Getchell, 50 Maine, 604, 605; Stein *v.* Burden, 29 Ala. 127. In Lord Norbury *v.* Kitchin, 3 Fost. Fin. 292; 9 Jur. N.S. 132, Martin B., in his direction to the jury, quoted the passage which is quoted in the text from Lord Kingsdown as containing the law on this subject, and ruled that the riparian proprietor could only take the water for a purpose of utility, and not to make an ornamental pond. The plaintiff's counsel moved for a new

4 [Davis *v.* Getchell, 50 Maine, 602.]

§ 94. By all the modern as well as by all the ancient authorities, the right of property in the water is *usufructuary*, and consists not so much of the fluid itself, as of the advantage of its *momentum* or *impetus*;[1] and the grant by the legislature of a State of the water-power of a navigable stream, does not pass to the grantee the title to the *corpus* of the water, or prevent its use by others.[2] The owner of the land merely transmits the water over the surface; he receives as much from his higher neighbor as he sends down to his neighbor below; he is neither better nor worse: the level of the water remains the same.[3]

§ 95. In a case in this country of much more than ordinary importance, and one universally and frequently appealed to as of high authority, the general doctrine in relation to the right to apply the water of a watercourse is thus laid down by Mr. Justice Story:[4] "*Primâ facie*, every proprietor on each bank of a river is entitled to the land covered with water, to the middle thread of the stream, or, as is commonly expressed, *usque ad filum aquæ*.[5] In virtue of this ownership, he has a right to the use of the water flowing over it, in its natural current, without diminution or obstruction.[6] But, strictly speaking, he has no property in the water itself; but a simple use of it, while it passes along.[7] The consequence of this principle is,

trial, on the ground that the dictum of Lord Kingsdown stated the right of a riparian proprietor too extensively. The Court did not decide that it was exactly correct, but discharged the rule on the ground that the defendant had not taken an unreasonable quantity of water. The stream sent down 383,000 gallons a day, and the defendant abstracted 8,000 to 9,000.]

[1] Williams *v.* Moreland, 2 B. & C. 510; [Rice J., in Davis *v.* Getchell, 50 Maine, 604; Merrick J., in Pratt *v.* Lamson, 2 Allen, 287; Pollock C.B., in] Dickinson *v.* Canal Co., 7 Exch. 300, 301; [Wood *v.* Waud, 3 Exch. 775; ante, § 8, note; Pixley *v.* Clark, 35 N.Y. 524, 525.] A riparian proprietor acquires no property in *wood* or *timber* floating over his land; but it has been held that he has an exclusive right to seize such wood or timber, and unless claimed within a reasonable time, to convert it to his own use. Rogers *v.* Judd, 5 Vt. 223.

[2] Mayor &c. *v.* Commissioners of Spring Garden, 7 Penn. St. 348. [In Owen *v.* Field, 102 Mass. 104, Ames J. said, "It is to be remembered that running water is not of itself the subject of a grant."]

[3] Per Tindal C.J., in Acton *v.* Blundell, 12 M. & W. 324.

[4] In Tyler *v.* Wilkinson, 4 Mason, 400; and see the opinion of the same learned Judge in Webb *v.* Portland Manuf. Co., 3 Sumner, 189; and the case of Bowman *v.* Latham, 2 McLean, 376.

[5] [Riparian proprietors on opposite sides of a stream are each entitled to use one-half of the water which flows in the stream, without regard to the position and course of its principal channel and current. Pratt *v.* Lamson, 2 Allen, 275.]

[6] [Wadsworth *v.* Tillotson, 15 Conn. 366; Dilling *v.* Murray, 6 Ind. 324.]

[7] [Ante, § 8, note; Agawam Canal Co. *v.* Edwards, 36 Conn. 476, 477; McDonald *v.* Askew, 29 Cal. 207.]

that no proprietor has a right to use the water to the prejudice of another. This," adds the same high authority, "is the necessary result of the perfect equality of right among all the proprietors of that which is common to all."[1] The general right of the riparian proprietors to the use of the water has been defined with ability and clearness by another of our learned judges. "The water-power," says he, "to which the riparian owner is entitled, consists in the fall of the stream, when in its natural state, as it passes through his land, or along the boundary of it; or, in other words, it consists of the difference of level between the surface where the stream first touches his land, and the surface where it leaves it."[2]

[1] [See post, § 101 *a*; Atchison *v.* Peterson, 20 Wallace, 507, 511; Mayor and City Council of Baltimore *v.* Appold, 42 Md. 442, 456; Agawam Canal Co. *v.* Edwards, 36 Conn. 476, 497, 498; Clinton *v.* Myers, 46 N.Y. 511, 516. "The right to the use of flowing water is *publici juris*, and common to all the riparian proprietors; it is not an absolute and exclusive right to all the water flowing past their land, so that any obstruction would give a cause of action; but it is a right to the flow and enjoyment of the water, subject to a similar right in all the proprietors, to the reasonable enjoyment of the same gift of Providence. . . . What is a just and reasonable use of flowing water, may often be a difficult question, depending on various circumstances. To take a quantity of water from a large running stream, for agriculture or manufacturing purposes, would cause no sensible or practicable diminution of the benefit, to the prejudice of a lower proprietor; whereas, taking the same quantity from a small running brook passing through many farms would be of great and manifest injury to those below, who need it for domestic supply or watering cattle; and therefore it would be an unreasonable use of the water, and an action would lie in the latter case and not in the former. It is therefore, to a considerable extent, a question of degree; still the rule is the same, that each proprietor has a right to a reasonable use of it, for his own benefit, for domestic use, and for manufacturing and agricultural purposes." Shaw C.J., in Elliott *v.* Fitchburg R.R. Co., 10 Cush. 193, 194, 196. Subject to the above considerations, the same rules of law apply to a small stream of water as to other watercourses. Elliott *v.* Fitchburg R.R. Co., supra; Gillett *v.* Johnson, 30 Conn. 180, 183. See Van Hoesen *v.* Coventry, 10 Barb. 518; Frazier *v.* Brown, 12 Ohio St. 299, per Brinkerhoff J.; Gerrish *v.* New Market Manuf. Co., 30 N.H. 483; Tourtellot *v.* Phelps, 4 Gray, 370; post, § 136 note.]

[2] Per Chief-Justice Gibson, of Pennsylvania, in M'Calmont *v.* Whitaker, 3 Rawle, 84; per Woodward J., in Brown *v.* Bush, 45 Penn. St. 66; Van Hoesen *v.* Coventry, 10 Barb. 518; Moffett *v.* Brewer, 1 Greene, 348; [Bell J., in Tillotson *v.* Smith, 32 N.H. 94, 95; Townsend *v.* McDonald, 2 Kern. 391; Rhodes *v.* Whitehead, 27 Texas, 310; McDonald *v.* Askew, 29 Cal. 207. As to the mode of ascertaining and proving this natural fall, or difference of level, see per Woodward J., in Brown *v.* Bush, 45 Penn. St. 66, post, § 95 *a*.] It is laid down as the law of Scotland, that although a proprietor may use the water while within his own premises, yet he must allow it to pass on to the inferior heritors; and that he cannot alter its level, either where it enters or where it leaves his property. Bell's Law of Scot. 691. No form of words could express with more exactness the law of England and of the United States upon

[It is also important to observe, that as each proprietor through whose land a watercourse passes has a right to the natural flow and descent of a watercourse, subject to a like reasonable use by all others, he necessarily enjoys the benefits of any improvements made by the proprietors above him. If they increase the head waters, for useful purposes, by flowing increased areas of land, and by making reservoirs to preserve surplus waters for dry seasons, and thus increase the volume of water for hydraulic purposes, every lower proprietor necessarily enjoys the benefit of it.[1]]

the same subject, unless it be the one employed by Lord Ellenborough; viz., "Every man is entitled to a stream of water flowing through his land, without *diminution* or *alteration*." Bealy *v.* Shaw, 6 East, 206. We believe we may with safety state, that nearly all the cases concur in supporting the general proposition of Lord Ellenborough, just mentioned. It is very fully sustained by the late case of Wright *v.* Howard, 1 S. & S. 203, and the still later case of Mason *v.* Hill, in Great Britain, 3 B. & Ad. 304, and 5 ib. 1.

A case in this country many years ago, recognized the same general principles. In Beissell *v.* Scholl, 4 Dallas, 211, the action was a case for diverting a watercourse. The Court left the facts to the jury under this general statement of the law: "That every man in this country has an unquestionable right to erect a mill upon his own land; and to use the water passing through the land, as he pleases; subject only to this limitation, that his mill must not be so constructed and employed as to injure his neighbor's mill; and that, after using the water, he returns the stream to its ancient channel." In the case of Ingraham *v.* Hutchinson, in Connecticut, 2 Conn. 584, the late Chief-Justice Swift laid down the law as follows: "By the common law, every person owning land on the banks of rivers, has a right to the use of the water in its natural stream, without diminution or alteration; that is, he has a right that it should flow *ubi currere solebat;* and if any person on the river above him interrupts or diverts the course of the water to his prejudice, action will lie. This will give to every one all the advantage he can derive from the water, which does not injure the proprietor of lands on the river below him." See also Warring *v.* Martin, Wright's Cond. (Ohio) 380; Arnold *v.* Foot, 12 Wend. 330; Frankum *v.* Earl of Falmouth, 6 C. & P. 529; and 25 Eng. Com. Law, 526; King *v.* Tiffany, 9 Conn. 162; Buddington *v.* Bradley, 10 Conn. 213; M'Calmont *v.* Whitaker, 3 Rawle, 84; Shreve *v.* Voorhees, 2 Green (N.J.) Ch. 25; [Pillsbury *v.* Moore, 44 Maine, 154; Cowles *v.* Kidder, 24 N.H. 365; Tillotson *v.* Smith, 32 N.H. 94, 95; Wadsworth *v.* Tillotson, 15 Conn. 366.] A riparian proprietor, who owns both banks of a stream, has a right to have the water flow in its natural current, without any obstructions, over the whole extent of his land, unless his rights have been impaired by grant, license, or an adverse appropriation for twenty years. Heath *v.* Williams, 25 Maine, 209.

1 [Shaw C.J., in Tourtellot *v.* Phelps, 4 Gray, 376. In this case, it was held, that a grantee of land including the site of a dam, with the privilege of flowing, during the winter only, the meadow of the grantor higher up on the same stream, "for the benefit of carrying on the blacksmith's business," has the right, as against his grantor, or those claiming under him privileges above or below on the same stream, to use at all seasons, for any reasonable purpose, the water of the stream, including any additional power subsequently created by improvements of his grantor. The limitation was only on a use which should cause a flowing of that meadow. Where the

[§ 95 *a.* An owner of land through which a stream of water runs, in the bed of which is an obstruction which he has a right to maintain there, may change that obstruction by clearing it out or otherwise, and erect another on his own land of the same or a different character and purpose, and in the same or some other place, provided that he makes no change in the level or fall of the water entering upon or leaving his territory, to the injury of any other proprietor on the same stream. But great difficulties frequently present themselves in the effort to find some sure test for determining whether such change of level has been made or not. A question of this kind arose in Brown *v.* Bush,[1] where it appeared that a natural or artificial "stone row" had existed in the bed of a stream on the land of the defendant for many years, forming, as alleged, a dam which flooded the plaintiff's land; and it was held that the defendant might clear out the stone row, because it was on his own land, and might raise his dam, so as to cause the same height of water on the plaintiff's land as the stone row caused, "but no more, — not a jot more." The Court say, "The water-power of the defendant consists of the fall of the stream, when in its natural state, as it passes through his land. . . . This natural power is as much the subject of property as land itself." But the Court add, "How is this natural fall to be ascertained? By instrumental levelling, says the plaintiff in error. And his counsel argue, that results so obtained are mathematical demonstrations which cannot be gainsaid. But there was evidence of what the Court call 'actual, visible facts,' to which they led the jury to give preference over the instrumental measurements; and this is the error complained of." The Court then refer to the facts shown; such as the ripples above and below the stone row, and above a bridge which was over the stream; the mudsill under the bridge frequently out of water before the dam was built, but not visible when the

plaintiff had constructed a dam across a certain creek, and the defendant subsequently constructed a dam on another creek, from which the water found its way by natural channels to the plaintiff's dam, and the defendant some time after built another dam on the same creek with the plaintiff's, which stopped the supply of water that usually descended from the defendant's first dam, it was held that the defendant's right to this water was merely usufructuary, and that he was liable to an action Eddy *v.* Simpson, 3 Cal. 249.]

[1] [Brown *v.* Bush, 45 Penn. St. 61.]

dam was full; the rise and fall of the water on the posts and abutments of the bridge; the drowning out of the spring-run, about thirty yards above the bridge. "Witnesses referred themselves to one or more of these circumstances, to establish their opinions, that the dam of the defendant had raised the water higher on the plaintiff's land than the stone row raised it. As there was a struck jury and view in the case, these and similar tests, on the ground, became important evidence; and, when we consider how liable instrumental measurements are to accidents and mistakes, we think the Court gave no undue prominence to the 'actual and visible facts' alluded to. The learned Judge said, with great propriety, 'Water will find its level with more certainty than science can do the same work. The instrumental levelling does show that the defendant has more fall upon his land than he has elevation at his dam; but if that does not tell the height of the water set back as clearly as shown by the water itself, then the fact demonstrated upon the ground must govern.' We cannot see that there was any error in this instruction. We do not undervalue scientific measurements; but the history of all engineering in Pennsylvania has shown that, whenever science has disregarded and set aside the testimony of local experience and observation, it has blundered, and has had to do its work over again. Its conclusions may be fortified by the nicest experiments and the minutest calculations; but there are the fallibility of instruments, the unsteadiness of the hand or eye that uses them, the carelessness of assistants, and other causes which affect the results. And then Nature has her own secrets, which she has not revealed even to science. Who can calculate for what the watermen call 'piling' of water, or for the effect of removing a given obstruction a few rods further down stream, whereby the *velocity* of the current at a particular point is changed; or for atmospheric resistance to water? . . . No doubt, the levelling was well done; but if, in spite of it, the water would make other marks than it did when obstructed only by the stone row, it was a tell-tale that could not be contradicted."]

§ 96. The Supreme Court of Alabama construe the Common Law, in relation to watercourses, as follows: "By the rules of the Common Law, all proprietors of lands have precisely the same rights to waters flowing through their domains, and one can never be permitted so to use the stream, as to injure or annoy those who are situated on the course of it, either above or below him. Should any one interpose an impediment to the flow of the stream to the injury of others, successive actions on the case would in the course of time compel its removal, or induce an accommodation of the injury."[1] The same view of the law is entertained by the Courts of North Carolina[2] and of South Carolina.[3] [So in a late case in New Hampshire,[4] Bell J. said, "Every owner of land situate upon a stream has a right to the natural flow of the stream; a right to insist that the stream shall continue to run *ut currere solebat;* that it shall flow upon his land in the usual quantity, at its natural place, and at its usual height, and that it shall flow off his land upon the land of his neighbor below in its accustomed place, and at its usual level.[5] This right he has as an incident to the property of his land, and he cannot be deprived of it but by grant, actual or presumptive. Whenever, by reason of the interference of the owner above, the water is diverted from his land and made to run elsewhere, or the water of other streams, naturally running elsewhere, is turned upon his land, or the water of the natural stream is made to flow upon his land at a different place from its natural channel, or at a different level, or in an unnatural manner; and so whenever, by the acts of the owner of the land below, the water is obstructed, or drawn down, or made to run off in an unusual place, or in an unusual manner, and actual injury ensues to any material amount, the owner of the land may maintain an action for such injury. These rights are subject to the rights of the owners of the land situate above and below upon the stream, to make a reasonable use of the water upon their own land, while it is passing along the same. . . . It seems very evident that if a man's land is materially damaged by water

1 Hendricks *v.* Johnston, 6 Porter (Ala.) 472.

2 Pugh *v.* Wheeler, 2 Dev. & Bat. (N.C.) 50.

3 The established doctrine in South Carolina is, that every owner of land through which a natural stream runs, has a right to the advantage of the stream as it was wont to flow, and to use it for any purpose of his own *not inconsistent* with a similar right of the owners below. The owner above cannot diminish the quantity of water which would otherwise descend, without grant or license. Omelvansy *v.* Jaggers, 2 Hill (S.C.) 634; Haynes *v.* Gratt, 1 McCord (S.C.) 543.

4 [Tillotson *v.* Smith, 32 N.H. 94.]

5 [See Jones *v.* Stevens, 3 Vt. 308, 316; Pugh *v.* Wheeler, 2 Dev. & B. 50, 53; Martin *v.* Jett, 12 La. 501; Kauffman *v.* Griesemer, 26 Penn. St. 407, 413; Martin *v.* Riddle, 27 Penn. St. 415, note; Overton *v.* Sawyer, 1 Jones (N.C.) 308.]

thrown upon it by reason of the acts of another, it can make no difference what the source of the water may be; whether it be back water, or the flowage of the same, or the water of another stream. The wrong consists in turning any water upon the land which does not naturally flow in that place; and it can make no difference if the water, wrongfully turned upon a man's land against his will, flows in the channel of an ancient stream, or in a course where no water flowed before, if similar damage results."[1]

[§ 96 *a.* In a late English case,[2] a question of some importance was raised and decided in regard to the right of one riparian proprietor to grant rights or privileges in the stream to a mill owner on riparian land, and the extent to which the mill owner could protect himself in the enjoyment thereof as against other riparian proprietors. The plaintiff was the lessee of a mill situated on riparian land. A., through whom he derived title, had, in 1804, under a written agreement with the adjoining higher riparian owner, and subject to an annual payment therefor, constructed a goit or artificial cut on the higher owner's land, intercepting the water of the stream at a wear in that land, and taking it thence to his mill. The flow of the water through this goit had ever since been enjoyed by the mill owner, and used for the purpose of working the mill; and the annual acknowledgment had been paid. The defendant, a riparian owner above the wear, and also a mill owner, intercepted the water of the stream for the purposes of his mill, to the damage of the plaintiff, who was held entitled to recover therefor. Bramwell B. said, "The principle on which it seems to me the plaintiff is entitled to recover is this: as a general rule, when a man has a property, he may grant to others estates in and rights of enjoyment of it, and the grantees may maintain actions against those who disturb them. A man entitled to land may grant leases, may grant the exclusive herbage, a right of depasturing, a right of way, a right to game. He may grant the mines underneath, or the right to get minerals, and other rights in or over the property, or of enjoyment of it. So, if the land is covered with water, he may grant rights of fishing. And in all these cases

[1] [Tillotson *v.* Smith, 32 N.H. 90, 95, 96; Merrill *v.* Parker, Coxe (N.J.) 460; Pardessus on Servitudes, §§ 82, 85–88; Huston J., in Howell *v.* M'Coy, 3 Rawle, 256; King *v.* Tiffany, 9 Conn. 162.]

[2] [Nuttall *v.* Bracewell, L.R. 2 Exch. 1.]

the grantee may maintain actions in respect of the rights granted. Now what is the case here? Mr. Bagshaw, the person with whom the plaintiff made the agreement, is a riparian proprietor, subject to the rights of those opposite and those lower down the stream; he may divert the water where it flows by his land. Why may he not grant this right or mode of enjoyment? I say the burden of proof is on those who say he may not. This right of his, this mode of enjoying his property, is presumably grantable like others. It seems to me that all reason of public convenience, and all other reasons, make this right grantable as much as any other right." Pollock C.B. and Channell B. held, that what was done, in the case above stated, amounted to a division of the stream into two courses; and that the plaintiff was a riparian proprietor in respect of the goit or artificial cut; and in regard to this the latter, speaking for himself and the Lord Chief-Baron Pollock, said, "Since 1804 there has been either an additional supply of water or a substituted one, I am not sure which, through a goit leaving the river higher up on the estate of another proprietor. Now it seems to me that the goit is to all intents and purposes a mere stream, and any person having land upon it would have the rights of a riparian proprietor; viz., to use the water in any way not interfering with others. I see no reason why the law applicable to ordinary running streams should not be applicable to such a stream as this, for it is a natural stream or flow of water, though flowing in an artificial channel. It may be that the case of an entirely artificial stream, as one flowing from a mine, for instance, would be different; but that an artificial stream may be on the same footing as a natural one as regards the rights of riparian proprietors, is held in Sutcliffe *v.* Booth."[1]

[1] [32 L.J. Q.B. 136. A question upon which a considerable diversity of opinion prevails, and it is equally applicable to natural and artificial watercourses, relates to the right of a person, having a mere permission to use the water of a stream, to maintain an action for an injury caused to him in using it. In Whaley *v.* Laing, 2 H. & N. 476. The facts were that the plaintiff, by permission of a canal company, made a communication from the canal to his own premises, by which water got to those premises, and with which water he fed his boilers; that the defendant fouled the water in the canal, whereby the water as it came to the plaintiff's premises was fouled, and by the use of it the plaintiff's boilers were injured. The defendant had no right or permission to do this from the canal owners. Bramwell B. said, "We think these facts establish a cause of action in the plaintiff. The plaintiff had, by permission of the canal owners, got possession of a certain quantity of water, which he was entitled to pump up from his cistern or reservoir, as much as he would have

—"The case where a riparian proprietor makes two streams instead of one, and grants land on the new stream, seems analogous to a grant of a portion of the river bank, but not analogous to a grant of a portion of the riparian estate not abutting on the river. In the case of a grant of land on a new stream, the grantee obtains a right of access to the river, and it is by virtue of that right of access that he obtains his water rights."[1] — "The right to a flow of water in a goit," said Martin B., in Nuttall *v.* Bracewell,[2] "is a well-known easement, and is an incorporeal hereditament, and although it is not competent for an owner of

been entitled to use it if he had taken it in a pail or bucket. The consequence of his doing so, that is, of emptying his cistern or reservoir, is, that other water flows in from the canal to supply its place. This water the defendant has fouled, and consequently by his act foul water flows into the plaintiff's cistern, the plaintiff only contributing thereto by removing the water already there, which, as we have said, he had a clear right to do. This being without justification by the defendant, gives the plaintiff a cause of action. It is true that the great injury the plaintiff sustains, is by his own act in feeding the boilers with the fouled water; but he was not bound to let it remain in his cistern, and we do not know that merely pumping it away would have been less costly than using it as he did." "Our opinion proceeds on the ground that the defendant caused foul water to flow on to the plaintiff's premises without right to do so. And this opinion is warranted by the cases cited, which show that though there may be no right to water, there may be a right, if it comes or is sent, to have it come or sent without pollution." The Court expressly abstained from giving any opinion upon the question, whether an action would have been maintainable against the defendant if the defendant had diverted the water, or if the plaintiff, in order to get the water, had been obliged to go to the canal with a bucket or engine and draw it foul from the canal. In the Exchequer Chamber (3 H. & N. 675, 901), the judgment was reversed, but reversed upon grounds involving no dissent from the judgment below, viz.,—that a man has no right to cause dirty water to flow on to his neighbor's land without some special right to do so; but the judgments in the Exchequer Chamber show that it is very doubtful whether a person, having a mere permission from a riparian owner to take water out of a stream, can maintain an action against a wrong-doer for diverting or fouling the stream higher up. The preponderance of authority appears to be in favor of the negative.]

1 [Stockport Waterworks Co. *v.* Potter, 3 H. & C. 326. In this case, Pollock C.B., said, "There seems to be no authority for contending that a riparian proprietor can keep the land abutting on the river, the possession of which gives him his water rights, and at the same time transfer those rights, or any of them, and thus create a right in gross, by assigning a portion of his rights appurtenant. It seems to us clear that the rights which a riparian proprietor has with respect to the water, are entirely derived from his possession of land abutting on the river. If he grants away any portion of his land so abutting, then the grantee becomes a riparian proprietor and has similar rights. But if he grants away a portion of his estate not abutting on the river, then clearly the grantee of the land would have no water rights by virtue merely of his occupation. Can he have them by express grant? It seems to us that the true answer to this is that he can have them against the grantor, but not so as to sue other persons in his own name for an infringement of them.]

2 [L. R. 2 Exch. 10.]

land to render it subject to a new species of burden at his fancy or caprice, the burden of one man's land being subject to the right of another to have a flow of water running through it to work his mill, is as old as the law itself, and in my opinion is the subject of property and of grant, and not merely of license. It is true that, being an incorporeal hereditament, it cannot be created so as to immediately bind the original grantor except by deed under seal; but I think the actual possession and enjoyment of the goit by the plaintiff gives a good and valid right of action against the defendant, a wrongdoer." [1]]

2. *Of the Injury by Diverting the Water.*

§ 97. Ever since the time of the Year Books, it has invariably been held, that it is illegal *to divert* a watercourse,[2] unless authorized or justified by the particular circumstances of the case.[3] The maxim of the law, which every riparian proprietor is bound to respect, as regards his right to the water, is *sic utere tuo ut alienum non lædas.*[4]

[1] [See Stockport Waterworks Co. *v.* Potter, 3 H. & C. 300; Hill *v.* Tupper, 2 H. & C. 121; Ackroyd *v.* Smith, 10 C. B. 164; Keppel *v.* Bailey, 2 M. & K. 535; post, § 143 and note; Holker *v.* Porritt, L.R. 8 Exch. 107; L.R. 10 Exch. 59. In Hill *v.* Tupper, it was held, that a grant by an incorporated canal company to the plaintiff, of the sole and exclusive right or liberty of putting or using pleasure-boats for hire on their canal, did not create such an interest or estate in the plaintiff, as to enable him to maintain an action in his own name against a person who disturbed his right by putting and using pleasure-boats for hire on the canal. The distinction between Hill *v.* Tupper and Nuttall *v.* Bracewell, is stated by Bramwell B., in the opinion delivered by him in the latter case. L. R. 2 Exch. 11, 12.]

[2] [As to what is meant by diverting a watercourse, see Parker *v.* Griswold, 17 Conn. 299, per Storrs J., post, § 99, note.]

[3] [See Newhall *v.* Ireson, 8 Cush. 595, 599.]

[4] [In reference to this maxim, see Shrewsbury *v.* Smith, 12 Cush. 180, 181; Davis *v.* Winslow, 51 Maine, 291.] Besides the authorities in the two or three preceding sections, see Cottell *v.* Luttrel, 4 Co. 36; Stone *v.* Bromwich, Yelv. 162; Sands *v.* Trefusis, Cro. Car. 573; Brown *v.* Best, 1 Wils. 174; Merritt *v.* Parker, 1 Coxe (N.J.) 460; Hart *v.* Evans, 8 Penn. St. 13. Baron Alderson mentions a case of Dakin *v.* Cornish, tried before him at Leeds, in 1845, where water was taken from the river Ayr to work a steam-engine. There was an artificial course from the river to a reservoir in the yard of a mill; the water was there mixed with other water obtained from the earth, the whole was then used for the steam-engine. What remained was transferred into another tube, and carried back to the river; and the question was, whether this was injury to some other mills lower down the stream. He says, "We took much pains about the case, and I left it to the jury to say if the same quantity of water continued to run in the river." Embrey *v.* Owen, 6 Exch. 353. [A canal company, having under their act power to supply their canal with water from the neighboring streams, bought a mill and turned the mill-stream

§ 98. In an action on the case, in Illinois, for obstructing and diverting a watercourse, in which the plaintiff obtained a verdict, and judgment was rendered thereon, the defendant excepted to the instructions asked for and given, at the instance of the plaintiff. After the cause was brought to the Supreme Court, the parties agreed upon facts as having been proved at the trial, which were, that S. & B., in 1834, bought of T. C. six acres of land, through which a branch run, and erected a steam-mill thereon. They depended upon a *well* and upon the *branch* for water in running their engine. About one or two years afterwards, J. E. bought of T. C. six acres of land in the same branch above, and immediately adjoining the lot of S. & B., and erected thereon a steam-mill, depending upon a *well and the branch* for water in running his engine. Ordinarily there was an abundance of water for both mills; but, in the fall of 1837, there being a drought, the branch failed, so far that it did not afford water sufficient to run the upper mill continually. One of the men employed by J. E. made a dam across the branch, just below J.

into the canal. Many years afterwards a waterworks company diverted part of the mill-stream, and thereby supplied a neighboring town with water; it was determined that the canal company, both under their act and as owners of the mill, were riparian proprietors, and had power to prevent the unlawful use of the water by other riparian proprietors, and that the supply of a neighboring town was such an unlawful use; and that the canal company were entitled to come into equity, and obtain an injunction to restrain this as an unreasonable use of the stream. Wilts and Berks Canal Navigation Company *v.* Swindon Waterworks Company, L.R. 9 Ch. App. 451. Sir W. M. James L.J., in this case said, "The defendants in this case are a waterworks company, who, partly from public motives and partly for private profit, have been minded to supply water to the large town of Swindon," and they "wish to use and divert water for the purpose of supplying that town. That is not a purpose for which a riparian proprietor is entitled to take the water from its natural course; and the defendants are diverting water from the stream for a purpose which is not legal, and in a manner which is not legal." "It has been settled that actual pecuniary damage is not necessary to give a right of action or suit, because it is sufficient to show that the defendants are interfering with that which is a right, and in a mode which may give a future legal right to interfere with the stream when it may be wanted, or may in a pecuniary point of view be useful to the riparian proprietor below." "The canal company, however, only want water legally as a canal company for the purposes of navigation. It is true that, if they have surplus water, there would be great difficulty in saying whether or not they might sell it to other persons. That, however, is a matter as between them and other persons who would be injured by the water being so taken, but, as far as their constitution goes, they are only entitled to take and use the water for the purposes of navigation, and the surplus must be the surplus which arises casually with regard to the water they have so taken." This decision was affirmed on appeal, L. R. 7 H. L. 697. See Owen *v.* Davies, 9 Weekly Notes, 175.]

E.'s mill, and thereby diverted all the water in the branch into J.'s well. After this diversion, the branch went dry below, and the mill below did not run in consequence of it more than one day in a week, and was then supplied with water from the well; for which the suit was brought. The Court held that the diversion, according to all the cases, both English and American, was clearly illegal.[1]

§ 99. In Parker *v.* Griswold, in Connecticut,[2] it appeared that the plaintiff owned land on a natural stream of water, and that the defendant owned land, with a mill thereon, on the opposite side, and bordered by it below the plaintiff's land; and that, under an authority obtained from the proprietors of the land on both sides of the stream above the plaintiff's land, the defendant erected a dam there, and cut a channel therefrom to his mill upon his land, through which a portion of the water was diverted from the stream, producing a considerable diminution thereof; and that the water was not returned until it had passed the plaintiff's land. It was held, that the defendant could not justify such diversion, either by virtue of the authority derived from the proprietors above, or by virtue of his general rights as riparian proprietor below; and that the plaintiff was not precluded from an action for such diversion, because he owned the land only on one side of the stream, and not beyond its centre.[3]

§ 99 *a*. The owners of a mill have not the right, when it becomes necessary for the purpose of repairs, to divert the stream upon which it is situated, to the injury of another proprietor upon the same stream below. If they cannot make their

[1] Evans *v.* Merriweather, 3 Scamm. (Ill.) 492.

[2] Parker *v.* Griswold, 17 Conn. 288.

[3] In this case (Parker *v.* Griswold, 17 Conn. 299), Storrs J. said, "There was not a diversion of the water here, in that loose sense in which that term might be used to denote that incidental obstruction or loss of the water which is necessarily consequent upon the lawful use of it, for which, as was decided in Wadsworth *v.* Tillotson, 15 Conn. 366, an action could not be maintained, by the proprietor below; nor was there a mere interruption of the water, so that it was only delayed in arriving at the plaintiff's land; but it was a *diversion* of the stream from his land, in what may be called the technical sense of that word, which denotes the turning of the stream, or a part of it, as such, from its accustomed direction,— its natural course, — so that the water thus diverted never reached the land of the plaintiff, and therefore could not be used by him, as it might have been, were it not for such diversion." [A mill-owner has no right, as against another mill-owner farther down the stream, to appropriate additional power by lowering or changing the natural bed of the stream, though wholly on his own land. Gleason *v.* Assabet Manuf. Co., 101 Mass. 72.]

repairs without such injurious diversion of the stream, they must obtain the consent of the proprietor below them, for that purpose, or answer to him in damages for the injury he sustains. But if there has been merely a *detention* of the water, then the question arises whether such detention was reasonable.[1]

§ 100. Wherever a watercourse *divides two estates*, the riparian owner of neither can lawfully carry off any part of the water without the consent of the other opposite; and each riparian owner is entitled, not to half, or other proportion of the water, but to the whole bulk of the stream, undivided and indivisible, or *per my et per tout*.[2] To use the language of Platt J. in Vandenburg *v.* Vanbergen, in New York,[3] "The grant of an *undivided share* in a stream of water would not authorize the grantee to appropriate or modify the stream to the injury of others who have a joint interest in it. The property in a stream of water is *indivisible*. The joint proprietors must use it as an entire stream in its natural channel; a severance would destroy the rights of all." In Blanchard *v.* Baker, in Maine,[4] the defendants, who had their dam on the side of the stream opposite to the plaintiff's dam, contended that they had a good and legal right to one-half of the water in the main stream, and to carry it off by deepening an ancient outlet or canal. The diagram on the following page shows the relative positions of the places alluded to in the testimony.

It was held that the defendants had not a right to one-half of the water in the main stream of the river, so as to abstract it by means of the channel in question. The Court said, in reply to the suggestion, that the owners of the dam on the eastern side of the river had a right to half the water, and *to divert to that extent*, "It has been seen, that, if they had been the owners on both sides, they had no right to divert the water, without again returning it to its original channel. Besides, it was impossible, in the nature of things, that they could take it from their side only;

[1] Hoesen *v.* Coventry, 10 Barb. 518; [Davis *v.* Getchell, 50 Maine, 602. The rights of a riparian proprietor are not to be measured by the reasonable demands of his business. His right extends to the use of only so much of the stream as will not materially diminish its quantity or corrupt its quality. Wheatley *v.* Chrisman, 24 Penn. St. 298. The necessity of one man's business is not to be made the standard of another man's rights. Wheatley *v.* Chrisman, supra. See Brace *v.* Yale, 10 Allen, 447; s.c. 4 Allen, 393.] As to *detaining* the water, see post, § 115.

[2] [Pratt *v.* Lamson, 2 Allen, 275.]

[3] Vandenburg *v.* Vanbergen, 13 John. 212.

[4] Blanchard *v.* Baker, 8 Greenl. 253.

an equal portion from the plaintiff's side must have been mingled with all that was diverted."

§ 101. In a case in the Circuit Court of the United States (first circuit),[1] it appeared that at certain falls on the river Presump-

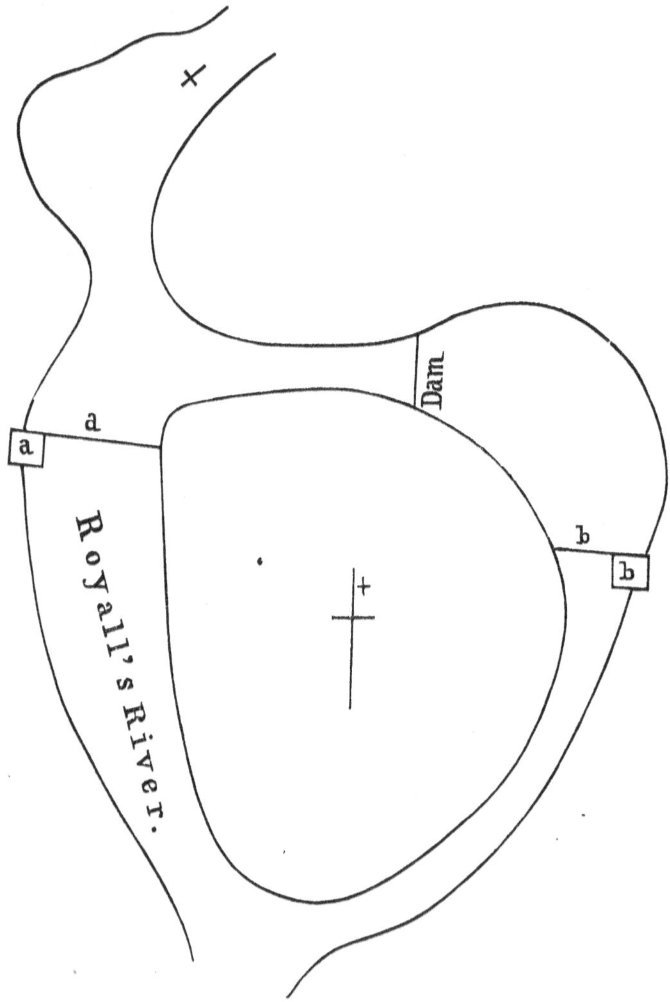

a a Plaintiff's mill and dam. *b b* Defendant's mill and dam.

scut, in Maine, there were two successive falls, upon which there were erected certain mills and mill-dams, being called the upper and lower mill-dams, and the distance between them being about

[1] Webb *v.* Portland Manuf. Co., 3 Sumner, 189.

forty or fifty feet; and the water therein constituted the mill-pond of the lower dam; that the plaintiff was the owner in severalty of certain mills and mill privileges upon the lower dam, and that the defendants were entitled to certain other mills and mill privileges on the *same dam*, also in severalty. The defendants were the owners of a cotton-factory mill near the left bank of the river, and opened a canal, for the supply of the water necessary to work that mill, into the pond immediately below the upper dam; and the water thus withdrawn was returned again into the river immediately below the lower dam. The defendants insisted upon their right so to divert and withdraw the water, by means of their canal, upon the ground, that it was only a small part (about one-fourth) of the water, to which as mill owners on the lower dam, they were entitled. It was held, that both parties were entitled *per my et per tout* to their proportions of the whole stream, on its arrival at the dam; and that neither party could divert any portion of it, though the portion diverted was a less quantity than he would naturally use at his mill on the dam; and that it was no answer to such a violation of right by one party, that the other had increased the quantity of water in the stream by means of a reservoir higher up.[1]

[§ 101 *a*. It is to be observed, also, that the riparian proprietors on opposite shores of a river or stream are each entitled to appropriate to their own use equal parts or quantities of the water passing in the stream, without regard to variations in depth in different parts of its bed, or to the fact that the greater part of it flows nearer to one bank than the other. It is apparent that the rights of riparian proprietors on opposite banks of the stream do not depend upon, and are not affected by, the locality of the channel through or along which the larger, or even the chief and principal, part of the water flows. Wherever this current may be, the central line in the bed of the stream parallel to and equally distant from each shore is the boundary of their lands.[2] And as their respective rights to the use of the water do not result from this line of division, but arise by mere operation of law, as incident to their ownership of the bank, the formation of the bed of the stream, its varying depth, and the consequent course and direction of the

[1] [Harding *v.* Stamford Water Co., 41 Conn. 87.]

[2] [But see Halsey *v.* McCormick, 13 N.Y. 296.]

current, must be circumstances wholly immaterial. The rule that parties so situated are each entitled to the use of an equal share and proportion of the running water, is not only simple, direct, and equitable, but seems to be essential as the only practical rule by which their respective rights can be accurately ascertained or effectually protected. For it must be obvious that the difficulties would often be very great, if not wholly insurmountable, to find the exact course and direction of the channel, or to determine on which side of the boundary line the larger portion of the whole volume of the stream actually flows. But besides this, the constant changes which are taking place in the bed of a river by the operation of natural causes — such as the formation of sand-bars, or excavations caused by accumulation of water in times of flood — would, if any attempt were made to fix and settle the rights of parties according to the quantity of water which flowed nearer towards one shore than to the other, leave them in a state of constant confusion and uncertainty.[1]]

§ 102. The water, a foot or more in depth, that runs over a dam, is not to be considered surplus water, and as of no value; for the head, and of course the water-power, is thereby increased. And, if a right is granted by a riparian proprietor to abut a mill-dam on his land, extending from the opposite side of the river, the grantee has *primâ facie* a right to all the water-power created by the erection of the dam; and the burden of proof is on the grantor to show that the grant was made with restrictions in respect to the use of the water by the grantee.[2]

§ 103. It appeared on the trial, in Curtis *v.* Jackson, in Massachusetts,[3] that the water of Charles River between Newton and Needham, at the place where the plaintiff's mill was situated, was divided by a small island or rock, and that part of the water passed on the Needham side to a certain mill of

[1] [Pratt *v.* Lamson, 2 Allen, 275, 285, 286; Webb *v.* Portland Manuf. Co., 3 Sumner, 189; Trustees &c. *v.* Dickinson, 9 Cush. 544, 552; Schurmeier *v.* St. P. & Par. R.R., 10 Min. 102; Canal Trustees *v.* Haven, 11 Ill. 554; Plumleigh *v.* Dawson, 1 Gilm. 544, 551. And each side owner may restrain the other from diverting the water from the stream to the injury of the former. Corning *v.* Troy Iron &c. Co., 22 How. Pr. Cas. 219; s.c. 39 Barb. 311.]

[2] Bliss *v.* Rice, 17 Pick. 23; Burnham *v.* Kempton, 44 N.H. 90, 91.

[3] Curtis *v.* Jackson, 13 Mass. 507.

the defendant; and the other part passed on the Newton side to the mill of the plaintiff, and to certain other mills on the same side of the river, there being but one dam for all the mills. On the Needham side there was a sand-bank above the defendant's mill; and the defendant having previously dug out a channel between that bank and the Needham shore, down to his mill, placed a dam or pile of stones from the upper end of the said bank to the Newton shore, so as to turn nearly all the water through the above-mentioned new channel to his own mill; and for this injury the action was brought. The defendant justified by endeavoring to prove a right by prescription of using the water of the stream in exclusion of all others, when there was not enough for the mills on both sides. But the Court held, that where there are mills on both sides of a watercourse, if the mill-owner on one side has the exclusive right to use the whole of the water whenever there is not enough for the mills on both sides, he is not authorized to erect a permanent dam to turn the water to his mill; but that he must rely on his legal remedy if his right be infringed by the mill-owners on the other side.[1]

§ 104. In Arthur *v.* Case, in the Court of Chancery of New York,[2] it appeared that the complainants were the owners of certain mills and mill privileges on the *north* side of the outlet of Lake George; and that the defendants owned mills and mill privileges on the *south* side of the same stream or outlet. In the middle of the outlet there was an island, and the main current of the stream ran naturally on the *north* side of the island. A dam extended from the island to the *south* shore on which the mills of the defendants were situate; and a similar dam ran from the island to the *north* shore by means of which the complainants' mills were supplied with water; but in dry seasons there was not water in the stream sufficient to supply all the mills. The defendants, claiming the right to have their mills first supplied, commenced building a dam from the island to strike the *north* shore some distance above the already established dam, the effect of which would be to deprive the mills of the complainants of water in dry seasons, and turn the whole stream to the *south* of the island. The

[1] See Parker *v.* Griswold, 17 Conn. 301.

[2] Arthur *v.* Case, 1 Paige, 447.

complainants, having obtained an injunction to restrain the defendants from building this intended new dam, and, on coming in of the answer, a motion being made to dissolve the injunction, Chancellor Walworth held, that "where hydraulic works are erected on both banks of a private stream, if there is not sufficient water to afford a full supply for all, the owner on each side is entitled to an equal share of the water." Both parties, he said, were entitled to participate equally in the use of the water; and "if either party draws more than a fair proportion, or it is necessary to excavate in the bed of the river to give the defendants a due proportion, the manner of exercising the right, and the nature and extent of the excavation, must be settled under the direction of the Court, on the report of the master."

§ 105. It appeared, in a case in New Hampshire, that a certain deed, under which the defendant claimed, purported to convey "the northerly half of the mill-dam" in dispute, and also the privilege of taking the water from any part of the said "northerly half of the mill-dam," for the use and benefit of the grantee and his heirs and assigns. Under this grant, the defendant contended for a right totally to destroy the north half of the mill-dam, or to draw water from it for his uses in any quantities, in any manner, or at any period of time. The plaintiff, on the contrary, contended, that every thing which passed under the grant was a right to use the north half of the mill-dam for the purposes to which mill-dams are usually devoted, without the legal power either to remove it, or permit decays so as to injure the plaintiff's enjoyment of the other half of the mill-dam. It was held by the Court that the deed passed the right to the use of one-half of the water only, and, therefore, that an action would lie against the grantee for taking more than one-half the water to the injury of the grantor. Mr. J. Woodbury observed, "From the circumstances that when the deed was executed, the mills were situate on *the northerly half* of the dam, as well as on the south half, it is reasonable to presume that the *northerly half* was sold under an expectation it would be used to turn those mills, and not be altogether destroyed, or the gates removed so as to be tantamount to a total destruction of it for the purposes of a mill-dam for the mills situated on both halves." Richardson C.J. construed the law to be, that "a conveyance of one-half of a dam is a conveyance of a right to use one-half of the water; the parties own the dam neither as tenants in common, nor as joint tenants, but each has all the title in his several part. Of the head of water raised by the dam, they are, however, tenants in common;[1] and, in such case, if one draws the water unreasonably to the injury of the other, case may be maintained for the injury.[2]

§ 106. In a case in Massachusetts,[3] it appeared, that the plaintiffs, "and those under whom they claim, owned a stone saw-mill on the east side of Williams River, and had made use of the dam for more than twenty years. The defendant owned a fulling-mill on the west side of the river. On the 11th of July, 1827, the defendant, after making a temporary dam, took away an old flume on the west bank, and dug the dirt away for the purpose of putting in a new flume. This weakened the temporary dam in such a manner that the water pressed through it and undermined it; and to prevent the water from doing damage, the defendant tore off the flash-boards and hoisted the waste-gate of the dam, east of the centre of the river. The effect of this was, to deprive the plaintiffs of the use of their stone saw-mill wholly for two or three days, and partially for ten weeks. On the part of the defendant it was contended, that he had a common right in the dam with the

1 [Water-power, that is, the flow of water in a stream, is of course incapable of practical division, like land, by metes and bounds. Each proprietor of a mill-site may, however, become the owner of any given proportion of the whole power or flow of water. Munroe *v.* Gates, 48 Maine, 466, 467.]

2 Runnels *v.* Bullen, 2 N.H. 532. [See Pratt *v.* Lamson, 2 Allen, 275; Carver *v.* Miller, 4 Mass. 559; Gwinneth *v.* Thompson, 9 Pick. 31.] Where two own severally several parts of the same dam, there is an implied contract or covenant between them, running with the land, that each shall keep in repair his portion of the dam, so long as he uses the water; and that as soon as one ceases to use the water, he shall permit the other to repair the whole. On that implied contract, the statute of New Hampshire of June 16, 1801, entitled "An act relative to the repairs of Mills," &c., is founded. Per Richardson C.J., in Runnels *v.* Bullen, ubi supra. See Lapham *v.* Curtis, 5 Vt. 371, in which it was held, that it was the duty of each owner of a dam to use ordinary care and diligence in making repairs to it, so as to prevent injury being done to the other; and if he does not use ordinary care and diligence, he will be liable for all consequential damages to the other. [Where the owners of land construct an artificial aqueduct, as a substitute for an artificial watercourse passing through their several parcels of land, in the absence of any agreement to the contrary, and as a general rule, there is an implied obligation, as between the several proprietors, that each will make all necessary repairs upon the section of the structure lying within his premises. Winslow *v.* Fuhrman, 25 Ohio St. 639.]

3 Boynton *v.* Rees, 9 Pick. 528.

plaintiff; and that he was not liable for the injury. He proved that, twenty-two years previous to the alleged trespass, one Curtis, under whom he claims, with certain persons under whom the plaintiffs claim, built the dam, and that the plaintiffs and the defendant had repaired it together from time to time, and that, until the time of the trespass, the water privilege had been used in the following manner; viz., the preference in the use of the water had always been claimed by the proprietors of the stone saw-mill, except for the season of fulling cloth for customers, which was stated to be from the 1st of September to the 1st of March, during which period the owners of the fulling-mill claimed the preference for fulling cloth for customers. The defendant contended, that, inasmuch as the injury happened to the plaintiffs when he was in the act of repairing his flume, he ought not to be charged with the damage sustained; but the plaintiffs insisted, that, between the 1st of March and the 1st of September in each year, they had a right to the full use of the water for carrying their mill, and that the defendant had no right, for the purpose of repairing his dam, to do any thing which should injure them in the full use of the water, and that if, from any attempt of the defendant to repair his flume, he had rendered it necessary, in order to prevent greater damage, to hoist their waste-gate and take off their flash-boards, he must be answerable in damages; and that it was his duty, in making his repairs, to have taken such precautions as would have prevented any damage to the plaintiffs. Wilde J. ruled, that the defendant had a right to make repairs upon his flume between the 1st of March and the 1st of September; and that he was not answerable for the damage done to the plaintiffs in taking off their flash-boards and hoisting their waste-gate, provided the jury should be satisfied, that, in making the excavation below the dam for the purpose of repairing his mill, he had used due and ordinary diligence; and the question whether he had used such diligence was submitted to the jury." To this opinion and direction the plaintiffs excepted; and the Court gave their opinion as follows: "The parties were jointly liable to keep the dam in repair, nothing to the contrary appearing, and the flume contiguous to the mill of either was to be supported at his individual expense. It seems clear that this right to repair extends throughout the year. If there was a preference in the use of the water during part of the year, but not an exclusive right, then the defendant was entitled to the surplus water, and he had a right to repair on that account. But besides this, either party had not only a right to keep his flume in repair for his own use, but his duty required him to do so, in order to save the water for the use of the other party. The defendant, then, having had the right to make repairs, the question was, whether he used ordinary diligence. This question was submitted to the jury, with instructions that were correct. If the defendant was bound to keep his flume in repair, he is not answerable for the accidental consequences of repairing, provided he was not guilty of negligence. If any accident happened which rendered extraordinary steps necessary in order to preserve the common property, as lifting the waste-gate or removing the flash-boards of the plaintiffs, he had a right to enter on the plaintiff's land and perform these acts."

§ 107. If two opposite riparian owners upon a watercourse, by an agreement between them, erect mills on the land of one of them, and turn the whole stream to the mills, the water thus becomes appropriated to the mills; so that, if they be held jointly, or in common, a release of the right of one tenant in the mills will pass his right in the water also.[1]

§ 108. Of course, no riparian proprietor opposite to another, without a legal permission, can build a dam which extends beyond the *thread of the river*,[2] without committing a trespass; and, therefore, if, in removing such encroachment, the water is diverted, the law affords no redress. This was expressly held in Wigford *v.* Gill.[3] In that case, the action was trespass, and the facts were, J. S. erected a mill-dam, partly upon his own land and partly upon the adjoining land; the owner of the adjoining land pulled down the part of the dam which was upon his land, by which the whole dam fell down, and consequently the whole water was discharged. The Court held, that the pulling down of the dam, under these circumstances, was entirely justifiable.[4]

[1] Wetmore *v.* White, 2 Caines Ca. in Er. 87.

[2] See ante, ch. 1, § 10.

[3] Wigford *v.* Gill, Cro. Eliz. 269.

[4] [Lindeman *v.* Lindsey, 69 Penn. St. 93. It is not a reasonable use of a river for a riparian proprietor to erect a permanent building in the channel of the stream. The opposite proprietor may maintain an action against him for so doing without proof of actual damage. This was so decided by the House of Lords on a Scotch appeal, and it seems that the law of England is the same. Bickett *v.* Mor-

[3. *Surface Water and Drainage.*

§ 108 *a.* The doctrine prevailing in Massachusetts in reference to this subject as connected with the surface drainage and improvement of lands was very fully developed and clearly stated

ris, L.R. 1 H.L. Sc. 47. Lord Cranworth (p. 58) said, "By the law of Scotland, as by the law of England, where the lands of two conterminous proprietors are separated from each other by a running stream of water, each proprietor is *primâ facie* owner of the soil of the *alveus*, or bed of the river, *ad medium filum aquæ*. The soil of the *alveus* is not the common property of the two proprietors, but the share of each belongs to him in severalty; so that, if from any cause the course of the stream should be permanently diverted, the proprietors on either side of the old channel would have a right to use the soil of the *alveus*, each of them up to what was *medium filum aquæ*, in the same way as they were entitled to the adjoining land. The appellant contended that as a consequence every riparian proprietor is at liberty at his pleasure to erect buildings on his share of the *alveus*, so long as the other proprietor cannot show that damage is thereby occasioned or likely to be occasioned to him. I do not think that this is a true definition of the law." He further says, "If the proprietor on one side can make an erection far into the stream, what is there to prevent his opposite neighbor from doing the same?" "It was said in argument,—'Then if I put a stake in the river, am I interfering with the rights of the riparian proprietors?' To this I should answer, *de minimis non curat prætor*. But further, it might be demonstrated, in such a case, not that there was an extreme improbability, but that there was an impossibility of any damage resulting to any one from the act." Lord Westbury said, "This is a case of very considerable importance, because, as far as I know, it will be the first decision establishing the important principle that an encroachment upon the *alveus* of a running stream may be complained of by an adjacent or an *ex adverso* proprietor, without the necessity of proving either that damage has been sustained, or that it is likely to be sustained, from that cause." "I am convinced that the proposition, as it has been laid down in the court below, and as it has received the sanction of your lordships in your judgments, is one that is founded in good sense, and ought to be established as matter of law." He concludes as follows, "It is wise, therefore, to lay down the general rule, that even though immediate damage cannot be described, even though the actual loss cannot be predicated, yet, if an obstruction be made to the current of the stream, that obstruction is one which constitutes an injury which the courts will take notice of, as an encroachment which adjacent proprietors have a right to have removed." Attorney-General *v.* Earl of Lonsdale, L.R. 7 Eq. Cas. 377; Menzies *v.* Earl of Breadalbane, 3 Bligh N.S. 414. Referring to the language of the Lords in the case of Bickett *v.* Morris, supra, Foster J. in Norway Plains Co. *v.* Bradley, 52 N.H. 108, 109, says, "We find ourselves unable to assent to these doctrines." "A different rule has certainly been applied in this country,—one too universally recognized by this court, as also in our sister States, to be disregarded, the operation of which has not yet been found disadvantageous; namely, that no priority of occupation or use of water by a mill-owner, upon a stream within the limits of his own estate, affects the right of a riparian proprietor above to erect and operate a mill in a suitable and reasonable manner upon his own land, or to cultivate or make improvements thereon, using or diverting the waters of the stream for that purpose, unless he thereby sensibly affects the rights of such mill-owner in the use of the water, and works an injury to his mill. It is competent for a riparian proprietor to change, obstruct, diminish, or deepen the channel of a stream within his own premises, or to change the mode of applying it to use, provided he return the

by Chief-Justice Bigelow in the late case of Gannon *v.* Hargadon,[1] in which he said, "The right of an owner of land to occupy and improve it in such manner and for such purposes as he may see fit, either by changing the surface, or the erection of buildings or other structures thereon, is not restricted or modified by the fact that his own land is so situated with reference to that of adjoining owners that an alteration in the mode of its improvement or occupation in any portion of it will cause water, which may accumulate thereon by rains and snows falling on its surface or flowing on to it over the surface of adjacent lots, either to stand in unusual quantities on other adjacent lands, or pass into and over the same in greater quantities or in other directions than they were accustomed to flow."[2] — "Where there is no watercourse by grant or prescription, and no stipulation exists between conterminous proprietors of land concerning the mode in which their respective parcels shall be occupied and improved, no right to regulate or control the surface drainage of water can be asserted by the owner of one lot over that of his neighbor.

water to its accustomed channel on to the land of the next proprietor at its accustomed point, and do nothing that materially affects the enjoyment of the water by the adjacent proprietors, according to their legal rights. In short every riparian proprietor may make a reasonable use of the stream running over his land." In this case of Norway Plains Co. *v.* Bradley, supra, it was decided that an encroachment, even the erection of a solid building, upon the *alveus* of a stream, thereby diminishing the width of the current, may not be complained of without the necessity of proving that essential damage has been sustained or is likely to be sustained therefrom.]

1 [Gannon *v.* Hargadon, 10 Allen, 106, 109, 110.]

2 [Luther *v.* Winnisimmet Co., 9 Cush. 171; Flagg *v.* Worcester, 13 Gray, 601; Dickinson *v.* Worcester, 7 Allen, 19; Parks *v.* Newburyport, 10 Gray, 28; Gray J. in Emery *v.* Lowell, 104 Mass. 16; Bates *v.* Smith, 100 Mass. 181, 182; Pettigrew *v.* Evansville, 25 Wisc. 223; Hoyt *v.* Hudson, 27 Wisc. 656; Conhocton Stone Road Co. *v.* Buffalo, New York & Erie R.R. Co., 5 N.Y. Sup. Ct. Rep. 651; Wagner *v.* Long Island R.R. Co., 5 N.Y. Sup. Ct. Rep. 163; Greeley *v.* Maine Central Railroad Co., 53 Maine, 200. The owner of land has a legal right to fill it up so as to intercept the flow of surface water over it, whether flowing from a highway or any adjoining land; and it makes no difference in the owner's rights that the land filled up was a swale, provided no watercourse is obstructed. Bangor *v.* Lansil, 51 Maine, 521. A declaration set forth that during the winter season quantities of water flowed from some distance above plaintiff's premises alongside of, and parallel to, a highway, and passed plaintiff's premises without collecting there; that a railroad company, whose lands adjoined plaintiff's, so constructed an embankment as to cause such water to collect on plaintiff's land; it was held that this was not a watercourse, and an action could not be maintained for the obstruction. Wagner *v.* Long Island R.R. Co., 5 Thomp. & C. (N.Y.) 163; 2 Hun, 633. It is only for interfering with and obstructing a defined watercourse, whereby injury is occasioned to another, that a liability for damages arises. Conhocton &c. R.R. Co *v.* Buffalo &c. R.R. Co., 5 Thomp. & C. (N.Y.) 651; 3 Hun, 523.] Eulrich *v.* Richter, 37 Wisc. 226; Barnes *v.* Sabron, 10 Nev. 217.

Cujus est solum, ejus est usque ad cœlum, is a general rule, applicable to the use and enjoyments of real property; and the right of a party to the free and unfettered control of his own land above, upon, and beneath the surface cannot be interfered with or restrained by any considerations of injury to others which may be occasioned by the flow of mere surface water in consequence of the lawful appropriation of land by its owner to a particular use or mode of enjoyment. Nor is it at all material, in the application of this principle of law, whether a party obstructs or changes the direction and flow of surface water by preventing it from coming within the limits of his land, or by erecting barriers or changing the level of the soil, so as to turn it off in a new course after it has come within his boundaries, and cause it to flow in a new direction on land of a conterminous proprietor where it had not previously been accustomed to flow. The obstruction of surface water, or an alteration in the flow of it, affords no cause of action in behalf of a person who may suffer loss or detriment therefrom against one who does no act inconsistent with the due exercise of dominion over his own soil. A party may improve any portion of his land, although he may thereby cause the surface water flowing thereon, whencesoever it may come, to pass off in a different direction and in larger quantities than previously. If such an act causes damages to adjacent land, it is *damnum absque injuria*."[1] It makes no difference in the application of this rule, that land is naturally wet and swampy. A conterminous proprietor may change the situation or surface of his land by raising or filling it to a higher grade, by the construction of dikes, the erection of structures, or by other improvements which cause water to accumulate from natural causes on adjacent land and prevent it from passing off

[1] [See per Colt J., in Wheeler *v.* Worcester, 10 Allen, 591, 602, 603. Bangor *v.* Lansil, 51 Maine, 521; Bowlsby *v* Speer, 31 N.J. Law, 351; Wagner *v.* Long Island R.R. Co., 5 Thomp. & C. (N.Y.) 163; 2 Hun, 633. "No action will lie for the interruption of mere surface drainage." Parks *v.* Newburyport, 10 Gray, 28, 29. "A mere right of drainage over the general surface of land is very different from the right to the flow of a stream or brook across the premises of another." Ashley *v.* Wolcott, 11 Cush. 192, 195; Flagg *v.* Worcester, 13 Gray, 601, 606. See Bassett *v.* Salisbury Manuf. Co., 43 N.H. 569, 573. In Swett *v.* Cutts, 50 N.H. 439, it was held that a land-owner who, in the *reasonable use* of his own land, diverts or obstructs the flow of water not gathered into a stream, but either circulating through the pores of the earth or spreading over the surface in the season of melting snows or heavy rains, is not liable for an injury to his neighbor caused by such diversion or obstruction.]

over the surface. Such consequences are the necessary result of the lawful appropriation of land, whatever may be its nature, and although they may cause detriment and loss to others.[1] And in White *v.* Chapin,[2] Foster J. said in regard to the flow of surface water from upper upon lower land over the natural surface of the earth, "The law is clearly settled that no length of time creates any easement by which the owner of the lower lot is precluded from using his own land as he will, although the natural overflow of water may be thereby stopped and set back upon the upper estate."[3]]

[§ 108 *b*. In accordance with the above views, Denio C.J., in Goodale *v.* Tuttle,[4] said, "In respect to the running off of surface

[1] [Bigelow C.J., in Dickinson *v.* Worcester, 7 Allen, 19, 22; Parks *v.* Newburyport, 10 Gray, 28; Flagg *v.* Worcester, 13 Gray, 601. See Bassett *v.* Salisbury Manuf. Co., 43 N.H. 569. Where land was granted for building subject to a chief rent, and cottages were built upon it, and the owner afterwards granted the adjacent lands to certain trustees for the purpose of erecting a church thereon, and the builder employed by them, by excavations necessary to secure the safety of the church, so far drained the land, which was wet and spongy, on which the cottages stood, that the soil subsided and the cottages were cracked and injured, it was held that he was not liable for the damage done thereby. Popplewell *v.* Hodkinson, L.R. 4 Exch. 248. Cockburn C.J. said, "Although there is no doubt that a man has no right to withdraw from his neighbor the support of adjacent soil, there is nothing at common law to prevent his draining that soil, if, for any reason, it becomes necessary or convenient for him to do so. It may be, indeed, that where one grants land to another for some special purpose, for building purposes, for example, then, since according to the old maxim a man cannot derogate from his own grant, the grantor could not do any thing whatever with his own land which might have the effect of rendering the land granted less fit for the special purpose in question than it otherwise might have been. In the case put by Mr. Holker with regard to Chatmoss, possibly, therefore, his observations might be well founded. If the owners of that moss were to drain it to such an extent as, by the amount of water drawn off, to loosen the foundations of the railway which runs across it, and for the purpose of constructing which they had sold a portion of it to the railway company, that might be an act in derogation of their own grant, and one, therefore, for which they might properly be made responsible." The Court held, however, that there was nothing in the grant to the plaintiff to warrant the inference of an implied condition to prevent the defendant from doing with the adjacent land what was incidental to its ordinary use; viz., draining it in order to render it more capable of being adapted to building purposes.]

[2] [White *v.* Chapin, 12 Allen, 516, 518.]

[3] [Dickinson *v.* Worcester, 7 Allen, 19. The passage of water from rain and melting snow over the surface of land for twenty years gives no right to its continuance. Parks *v.* Newburyport, 10 Gray, 28; Hoyt *v.* Hudson, 27 Wisc. 656. Where the plaintiff and defendant were adjoining owners of land by the side of a highway, in the ditch of which water was accustomed to accumulate, and for many years it found its way off through a depression in the defendant's land, it was held that the plaintiff would acquire no right by prescription to have the water run off over the defendant's land. Swett *v.* Cutts, 50 N.H. 439.]

[4] [Goodale *v.* Tuttle, 29 N.Y. 459; Conhocton Stone Road Co. *v.* Buffalo, New York & Erie R.R. Co., 5 N.Y. Sup. Ct. Rep. 651.]

water caused by rain or snow, I know of no principle which will prevent the owner of land from filling up the wet and marshy places on his own soil for its amelioration and his own advantage, because his neighbor's land is so situated as to be incommoded by it. Such a doctrine would militate against the well-settled rule that the owner of land has full dominion over the whole space above and below the surface." And in a late case[1] in Rhode Island, in which the right of surface drainage for agricultural purposes was a subject of discussion, Ames C.J. said, "Water, whether it has fallen as rain, or has come from the overflow of a pond or swamp, which sinks into the top soil and struggles through it, following no defined channel, is deemed by the law absolutely to belong to the owner of the land upon which it is found, for the avowed purpose of enabling him to cultivate his land by controlling or draining it off in the mode most convenient to him; and is not affected by any right in the owner of an adjoining river, pond, or tank, which it may chance for the time to feed, though that time be ever so long protracted. It is not water in a watercourse, or in an infinitesimal number of minute watercourses, in the sense of being obedient to the law regulating the use of water flowing in such defined natural channels; but is, in the eye of the law, as well as of common sense, the moisture, and a part of the soil with which it intermingles, to be there used by the owner of the soil, if to his advantage, or to be got rid of in any mode he pleases, if to his detriment."[2] In this case there was a grant of "a certain spring or fountain of water" with the privilege of deepening it, and of making other improvements on the land about the fountain for the purpose of obtaining the full use and benefit of the water thereof; but, inasmuch as the fountain appeared to be fed by a spring which issued from beneath a rock at the bottom of the fountain, and the grant contemplated that the land on which the fountain was situated was to be used for agricultural purposes, it was held, that the owner of the land was not thereby deprived of the right of properly draining his land to make it productive, even though the drainage of the land might draw off some of the surface water, which possibly would otherwise have found its way through the soil into the fountain.]

[1] [Buffum *v.* Harris, 5 R.I. 243, 253.]

[2] [See Bassett *v.* Salisbury Manuf. Co., 43 N.H. 569.]

[§ 108 *c*. It is also the doctrine of the English courts, that the owner of land has an unqualified right to drain it for agricultural purposes, in order to get rid of mere surface water, the supply of the water being casual, and its flow following no regular or definite course. In Rawstron *v*. Taylor,[1] Martin B. said, "The proprietor of the soil has *primâ facie* the right to drain his land. He is at liberty to get rid of the surface water in any manner that may appear most convenient to him; and I think no one has a right to interfere with him, and that the object he may have in so doing is quite immaterial." Parke B. said, in the same case, "This is the case of common surface water rising out of springy or boggy ground, although contributing to the supply of the plaintiff's mill. This water having no defined course; and its supply being merely casual, the defendant is entitled to get rid of it in any way he pleases." Platt B.: "This was mere surface water, and the defendant had a right to drain his land, and the plaintiff could not insist upon the defendant maintaining his field as a mere water-table."[2] This was a case in which the plaintiff claimed that by the defendant's mode of draining his land he had lost a portion of the surface water which would have otherwise found its way to the plaintiff's reservoir; presenting a view of the rights and duties of adjoining owners in regard to surface water to be more fully considered hereafter.]

[§ 108 *d*. But it has been held in some cases, that, because water is descendible by nature from an upper to the lower surface, the owner of the upper land has an easement in the land of the proprietor below for the discharge of all waters which by nature rise in or flow or fall upon the land of such upper owner.[3] Several cases maintaining this general doctrine,

[1] [Rawstron *v*. Taylor, 11 Exch. 369.]

[2] [Waffle *v*. New York &c. R.R. Co., 58 Barb. 413; Foot *v*. Bronson, 4 Lansing, 47.]

[3] [Kauffman *v*. Griesemer, 26 Penn. St. 407; Martin *v*. Riddle, 26 Penn. St. 415, note; Laumier *v*. Francis, 23 Mo. 181; Bellows *v*. Sackett, 15 Barb. 96; Lattimore *v*. Davis, 14 La. 161; Adams *v*. Harrison, 4 La. An. 165; Ogburn *v*. Connor, 46 Cal. 346; Hays *v*. Hays, 19 La. 351. In Hooper *v*. Wilkinson, 15 La. An. 497, it was held that an upper estate is entitled to a natural servitude upon the estate situated below it, for purposes of drainage; and levees or dams erected across a bayou, which runs through the two estates, by the proprietor of the lower, to prevent the flow of the waters in this stream, are infringements of the right of servitude appertaining to the upper estate. This is a right of servitude which the proprietor of the upper estate possesses; and in the enjoyment of this right he should not be disturbed or molested, although possibly no actual

and also illustrating the principles of law in reference to the right of drainage in the interest of agriculture and improvements of land, have lately been decided in Pennsylvania, of which Martin *v.* Riddle[1] is worthy of particular consideration. The action was for obstructing a watercourse, and thereby throwing the water back upon the plaintiff's land to his injury. It appeared that there was on the defendant's land a natural channel through which the falling water and some living springs were naturally discharged from the land of the plaintiff and others. The land of both consisted of out lots of the town of Alleghany, and was occupied by them as farming, or rather as gardening land. The land of both was bottom land, and of course subject to the natural flow of the water from the high ground in the rear. There had long been a culvert underneath the road which separated the lands of the plaintiff and defendant, through which the natural flow had been discharged across the road into the said channel. This had become choked up from neglect, and the authorities having care of the road, at the instance of the plaintiff and others, had built a new culvert in its place. After this the amount of water flowing through said channel was greatly increased in time of storms by means of a road cut into the hill by an adjoining proprietor (a cemetery company), which collected into one drain, and thence into this channel, large quantities of water which had been previously discharged in a natural way over a large surface. The defendant, to protect himself from injury by this increase of water, stopped up the culvert, and thus threw the water back upon the road, on the plaintiff's side of it, overflowed his land, and interfered with his garden operations. It appeared also that the plaintiff had constructed several underground drains through his land, which discharged springs and the drainage of his land at the point where the injury occurred. In charging the jury in the above case, Lowrie J., among other things, said, "I shall speak now of the general principles of the law in the matter of rain water and drainage, and of the respective rights and duties of adjoining proprietors in relation thereto. They are in general

injury might result from the interruption of the right. See Delahoussaye *v.* Judice, 13 La. An. 587; Laumier *v.* Francis, 23 Mo. 181. See Bassett *v.* Salisbury Manuf. Co., 43 N.H. 569. Domat (Cushing's ed.) 616; Cresswell J., in Smith *v.* Kenrick, 7 C.B. 566.]

[1] [Martin *v.* Riddle, 26 Penn. St. 415, in note.]

the same as in the case of running water, — they follow nature. Not readily finding the subject treated of in any of our usual books of reference, I venture to extract the law from books of a foreign origin."[1] — "Where two fields adjoin, and one is lower than the other, the lower must necessarily be subject to all the natural flow of water from the upper one. The inconvenience arises from its position, and it is usually more than compensated by other circumstances. Hence the owner of the lower ground has no right to erect embankments whereby the natural flow of the water from the upper ground shall be stopped; nor has the owner of the upper ground a right to make any excavations or drains by which the flow of water is directed from its natural channel, and a new channel made on the lower ground; nor can he collect into one channel waters usually flowing off into his neighbor's fields by several channels, and thus increase the wash upon the lower fields. But he may, and good husbandry sometimes requires that he should, cover up and conceal the drains through his own land, keeping the place of discharge unchanged. And as he may use running streams to irrigate his lands, even though he does thereby, not unreasonably, diminish the supply of his neighbor, so also he may use proper means of draining his ground where it is too moist, and discharge the water according to the natural channel, even though the flow of water upon his neighbor be thereby somewhat increased.[2] If it be difficult to ascertain from the character of the surface what is the natural channel, then the course in which the water has long been peaceably and openly permitted to run will be considered as having had a legitimate origin; for *vetustas vicem legis tenet.* If the owner of the upper ground wrongfully direct an unnatural quantity of water upon the ground of a lower neighbor, by collecting small streams together and discharging them at one place, or by any other means, the neighbor below may have an action against him; but he cannot justify the erection of an embankment to stop the water, if thereby the water is improperly forced upon another owner. So in this case, it is manifest that the cemetery company had no right to collect into one place and discharge upon the defendant's ground, the water falling upon the whole surface of the hill, and which before had

[1] [Corp. Jur. Civ. 39, 3, 1, & 43, 21; Code Nap. § 640; Pothier *du Voisinage.*]

[2] [Woodward J. in Kauffman *v.* Griesemer, 26 Penn. St. 407, 413, 414.]

discharged itself in many directions. If he could stop it without injury to any but the cemetery company, he had a right to do it; but he cannot do it to the injury of the plaintiff. Nor can the defendant justify himself by saying that he only turned the water upon the road, and that it was the duty of the authorities having charge of the road to provide means for carrying it off. A road is a way for travel, not for water; and it would be ruinous to our public roads if each adjoining proprietor could insist upon discharging the drainage of his land upon them, or preventing the roads from being drained upon his land. When there is a natural channel or hollow for discharging the flow of water, it must be suffered to remain until altered by agreement of those concerned, and the water cannot be turned upon the road until the proper authorities have provided the means of carrying it off."[1] This case was reviewed on error by the Supreme Court, and the judgment for the plaintiff was affirmed.]

[§ 108 *e*. The same principles formed the basis of the decision in Kauffman *v.* Griesemer.[2] The facts of this case were substantially these: the plaintiffs and defendant owned adjoining lands, and some thirty rods above the dividing line was a strong spring on the plaintiffs' land, the natural outlet of which was in the direction of the defendant's land, though the water did not appear ever to have reached the defendant's land until the ditch was dug by the plaintiffs, for the obstruction of which the action was brought. This natural outlet, having rising ground on both sides of it, served to carry off not only the water of this spring, but also the water from rain and snow which fell on a large area of land, property of the plaintiffs and others. A public road had been laid out across this outlet, near the spring, with a small bridge, composed of logs and plank, over the outlet, leaving a water-way underneath. The bridge was repaired from time to time, and the passage under it cleared of rubbish, and finally a plank water-way was put in to conduct the water under the bridge. A short time before the action, the public road was vacated, and then the plaintiffs took out the plank water-way, and opened a passage for the water. The defendant alleged that this increased the flow of water upon his land from the plaintiffs' spring, and, to prevent it, he thereupon erected a sod dam across

[1] [Corp. Jur. Civ. Dig. 39, 3, 18, 1.]

[2] [Kauffman *v.* Griesemer, 26 Penn. St. 407.]

the ditch or watercourse on his own land. This obstruction caused the water to flow back on the plaintiffs' land. Hence the action. The Judge who presided at the trial, among other things instructed the jury that "one has no right to alter the natural drainage so as to throw upon his neighbor waters that he had not received before. A familiar illustration of this would be the case of drainage from a roof. One may build his roof as he pleases, but not so as to throw the waters from it upon his neighbor's adjoining lot.[1] And, as it is with a roof, so it is with the drainage of the land itself; one may drain his land as advantageously to himself as possible, but he must not acquire that advantage at the expense of his neighbor. 'Each of the neighbors,' says Pothier, 'may do upon his own heritage what seemeth good to him, in such manner, nevertheless, that he doth not injure the neighboring heritage.'"[2] But one has no "right to cut away or drain natural reservoirs upon his own land, whereby he may reclaim the land occupied by the same, if thereby he causes more water to flow upon his neighbor's land. The reclamation of the land is certainly for the advantage of the common weal, as well as of the person owning it; but such reclamation is not allowed by the law at the expense of a contiguous owner. I have no right to make my property more valuable by making my neighbor's less valuable. Against injuries of this nature one may protect himself by necessary countervailing structures; and if some damage result to the party whose action rendered such structures necessary, not more, however, than may be unavoidable from a judicious and reasonable exercise of a right of self-protection, the party so damnified would have no just ground of complaint. The defendant could have no right to prevent the waters of floods and freshets flowing where they were accustomed to flow. It was the plaintiffs' right

[1] [The owner of land has a right to erect a house thereon, to cover it with a roof which will prevent the rains from falling upon the surface it covers, and to turn the water falling upon such roof upon any portion of his own soil, at any point and in any quantity he may choose. But where the eaves of the defendant's building came within about two feet of a dwelling-house, erected by the plaintiff upon his lot adjacent, and owing to a want of suitable repairs to the gutter of the defendant's building, the water from his roof fell between the buildings, and by percolation found its way into the plaintiff's cellar, through the wall, to the injury of his wall and the lower timbers of his house, it was held, that an action would lie, although it did not appear whether the water from the defendant's roof actually fell upon his own land or not. Bellows *v.* Sackett, 15 Barb. 96.]

[2] [Customs of Orleans, tit. XIII.]

that such water should flow there, and, indeed, all the waters that had been accustomed to flow there."[1] The judgment upon the verdict, which, on these and other instructions, was for the defendant, was affirmed on error by the Supreme Court, who, through Woodward J. said, "Almost the whole law of watercourses is founded on the maxim of the Common Law, *Aqua currit et debet currere.* Because water is descendible by nature, the owner of a dominant or superior heritage has an easement in the servient or inferior tenement for the discharge of all waters which by nature rise in or flow or fall upon the superior. This easement is called a servitude in the Roman law, and consists, says Pardessus, in the subjection of the inferior heritage towards those whose lands are more elevated to receive the waters which flow from them naturally; and, quoting the Code Civil, he adds, 'This obligation applies only to waters which flow naturally, without any act of man;' those which come either from springs, or from rain falling directly on the heritage, or even by the effect of the natural disposition of the places, are the only ones to which this expression of the law can be applied. It is not, however, to be understood," he goes on further to say, "that because the flow of water must not be caused by the act of man, that therefore the proprietor who transmits water to the inferior heritage is not permitted to do any thing on his own land; that he is condemned to abandon it to perpetual sterility, or never vary the course of cultivation, simply because such acts would produce some change in the manner of discharging the water. The law intends not this; it prohibits only the immission into the inferior heritage of the waters which would never have fallen there by the disposition of the places alone. It neither would nor could refuse to the superior proprietor the right to aid and direct the natural flow."—"These cases" (Williams *v.* Gale,[2] and Martin *v.* Riddle[3]) "recognize the principle that the superior owner may improve his lands by throwing increased waters upon his inferior through the natural and customary channels, which is a most important principle in respect not only to agricultural, but to mining operations also. It is not more agreeable to the laws of nature that water should descend, than it is that lands should be farmed and mined; but in many cases they cannot be,

1 [See Bassett *v.* Salisbury Manuf. Co., 43 N.H. 569; post, § 108 *s.*]

2 [3 H. & John. 231.]

3 [26 Penn. St. 415, in note.]

if an increased volume of water may not be discharged through natural channels and outlets. The principle, therefore, is to be maintained; but it should be prudently applied. This Court refused to apply it as among several owners of city lots, each of whom, it was held in Bentz *v.* Armstrong,[1] must so regulate and grade his own lot as that the water which falls or accumulates upon it shall not run upon the lot of his neighbor. It was greatly misapplied by the plaintiffs when they supposed they might not only increase the ordinary flow, but might dig a new channel for it to and into the defendant's land. The construction of the sod dam was not setting up a nuisance against a nuisance, any more than the shutting the door against an unwelcome visitor is a nuisance. The only servitude the plaintiffs could claim in the defendant's land was that it should receive the overflow which was natural and customary, and the Court throughout their charge guarded this right."]

[§ 108 *f*. Similar views of the law were adopted in a late case in Ohio,[2] in which the Court said, "The principle seems to be established and indisputable, that where two parcels of land, belonging to different owners, lie adjacent to each other, and one parcel lies lower than the other, the lower one owes a servitude to the upper, to receive the water which naturally runs from it, provided the industry of man has not been used to create the servitude. Or, in other words more familiar to students of the Common Law, the owner of the upper parcel of land has a natural easement in the lower parcel, to the extent of the natural flow of water from the upper parcel to and upon the lower.[3] But to what extent, if any, the owner of the upper parcel may gather and concentrate, by artificial means, the waters which fall upon or originate on this parcel, and send them upon the lower parcel; and how far a due regard to the great interests of agriculture and the policy of our legislation will authorize the owner of the upper parcel to go in facilitating, hastening, and to some extent temporarily increasing, the flow of water from the upper to the lower estate, — are questions not involved in the record

[1] [Bentz *v.* Armstrong, 8 Watts & S. 40.]

[2] [Butler *v.* Peck, 16 Ohio St. 334.]

[3] [See Martin *v.* Jett, 12 La. 501; Delahoussaye *v.* Judice, 13 La. An. 587; Miller *v.* Laubach, 47 Penn. 154; Kauffman *v.* Griesemer, 26 Penn. St. 407, 413; Tootle *v.* Clifton, 22 Ohio St. 247; Hayes *v.* Hickleman, 68 Penn. St. 324; Bassett *v.* Salisbury Manuf. Co., 43 N.H. 569; post, § 108 *s*, and note.]

under review before us, and which we do not assume to decide." These questions thus left undecided by the Court had been argued with great apparent research and learning by the counsel in the cause, and it is to be regretted that the case did not call for a decision of them by a judge so able and judicious.]

[§ 108 *g*. A late case in Vermont — Beard *v.* Murphy[1] — raised the question whether the defendant had a right to raise and maintain an embankment upon his own land, the effect of which was to flow back, upon the plaintiff's land to the injury of the plaintiff, surface water which fell upon the plaintiff's land and naturally descended upon that of the defendant, when the embankment was raised and maintained only for the purpose of preventing filthy water emptied from the plaintiff's kitchen from descending upon the defendant's land to his injury. The plaintiff, as one point of the case, claimed it to be law that if the surface water naturally falling upon his land would run off upon the defendant's land, the defendant had no right to put up any obstruction to prevent its continuing to do so; and so it was ruled by the Judge sitting at the trial of the cause before the jury. And in the decision of the case by the Court of Law, before which it was taken on exceptions by the plaintiff (the verdict being against him), this ruling was stated to have been made; but, inasmuch as it was favorable to the plaintiff who took the exceptions, no comment upon it was necessary, nor was any assent or dissent required. The Court, however, decided that the defendant had the right by law in a peaceable way, to prevent the plaintiff's turning filthy water on his premises to his injury, and save himself from harm, if he could, and to use the necessary means to that end. If the plaintiff was incidentally injured thereby, it could not be chargeable to the defendant, whose act was rightful. The injury was really caused by the wrongful act of the plaintiff, which made that of the defendant necessary.]

[§ 108 *h*. In Earl *v.* De Hart,[2] it appeared that the plaintiff was the owner of a tract of land on Jersey Street, in the city of Elizabeth. The defendants owned an adjacent lot on the same street. Part of the plaintiff's lot was somewhat elevated, and inclined gradually towards the lot of the defendants. The surface of the plaintiff's land was such as to collect, in wet times,

1 [Beard *v.* Murphy, 37 Vt. 99.]

2 [Earl *v.* De Hart, 1 Beasley Ch. (N.J.) 280.]

and always after heavy rains, a large body of water on her land. This water collected into a narrow but well-defined channel on the same land, and passed off through a like channel over the land of the defendants, and finally emptied itself into a creek. It appeared that the channel was originally made, and was continued, by the natural flow and force of the water, and the same channel had always discharged the water as far back as the memory of the witnesses went. The defendants obstructed this channel, and caused the water to flow back on the plaintiff, to her injury. The chancellor (Williamson) said, "This water having run in the same course for more than twenty years, and the plaintiff, and those under whom she holds, having enjoyed it as a right during that period in its present channel, no one has a right to dam up the channel, or to divert the course of the water, to the injury of the plaintiff's land. It makes no difference whether it is a natural watercourse or an artificial ditch. If it is a mere ditch, and the plaintiff's land has enjoyed the use of it for more than twenty years, and as an adverse right, then it is an easement which the owner of the plaintiff's land has in that of the defendants; it is a privilege without profit, and is as much the subject of protection as a natural watercourse. . . . It is insisted that the law as to running water does not apply to building-lots in a city or large towns. I cannot see why it does not. Here is a body of water which must be discharged either over the building-lot of the plaintiff, or over the building-lot of the defendants. There is a right and an obligation, as between the two lots, which have been acquired and imposed by prescription. To have this water discharged upon the plaintiff's land is as great an injury to her building-lot as it is to the defendants' lot to have it discharged there. There can be no such difference in the application of the law as to building-lots, as will impose a burden upon one which properly and of right belongs to another." It was also insisted in this case that, in consequence of the small quantity of water running, the plaintiff could, at a small expense, cut a drain or outlet for the water before it reached the defendants' premises, and discharge it into Jersey Street. But the Court held that the defendants had no right to require of the plaintiff to make this experiment, or incur its expense. She had a right to have the water discharged on the defendants' land;

when it reached there, they might dispose of it at their pleasure, so that it did not injure the plaintiff.]

[§ 108 *i*. There is no necessary conflict between the above case and that of Bentz *v*. Armstrong, cited above,[1] in which it appeared that several persons united in the purchase of a piece of ground, and divided it into several smaller lots, upon each of which a house was built, and then partition was made between them; upon one of the lots a spring of water rose, and the water from that and from the house on the same lot, in consequence of a natural descent in the ground, ran over another of the lots, and the owner of the latter stopped it, and it ran back into the cellar of the lot from which it started. For this act the action was brought. The Court held, that the plaintiff could not recover, because it was the duty of the owner of each lot so to regulate and grade it as that the water falling and accumulating upon it should not run upon the lot of his neighbor. In this case, the water did not run from the plaintiff's over the defendant's lot in any natural or prescriptive watercourse, as was the case in Earl *v*. De Hart; nor did the water appear to flow in any apparent and continuous gutter or drain at the time of the partition so as to bring the case within any rule of implied grant or reservation; nor did it appear that there was any natural easement or right of drainage of the plaintiff's, as an upper lot, over that of the defendant, as a lower lot; although, in regard to this last point, the Court remarked, "In the argument, something was said about the natural formation of the surface of the ground of the two lots, and that, according to it, the water, as it fell in rain, was naturally inclined to run off from the lot of the plaintiff into that of the defendant below, and the latter was bound to submit to it. This, however, I take to be a *non sequitur;* for in the purchase of lots of ground, laid out and sold for the purpose of building up towns or cities thereon, it has ever been understood, and such has been the practice and usage too, that the natural formation of the surface will, and, indeed, must, necessarily undergo a change in the construction of the buildings and other improvements that are designed and intended to be made; . . . certainly no one ought to be restrained from improving his lot in such a manner as to make it answer the purpose for which it was laid out, sold, and purchased, if prac-

[1] [Ante, § 108 *e*.]

ticable, without overreaching upon his neighbor's lot. He ought to be permitted to form and regulate the surface of it as he pleases, either by excavation or filling up, as may be requisite to the convenient enjoyment of it; taking care, however, not to produce any detriment or injury to his neighbor in the occupation or enjoyment of his adjoining lot. . . . It appears to me to be the duty of the owner of each lot, if he improves it, to do it in such way, if practicable, as to lead and conduct the water that happens to fall or be on it, off" directly to a sewer or other place appropriated for the receipt and discharge of the same, "without regard to the original formation of the surface of the lot. . . . This he ought to do, even if he should be compelled to carry it under or through his house or buildings."]

[§ 108 *j*. But one proprietor of land has no right to cause a flow of the surface water from his own land over that of his neighbor, by collecting it into drains or culverts or artificial channels; he cannot thus, by his own act merely, convert a flow of surface water into a stream, passing from his own over his neighbor's land, with all the legal incidents of a natural water-course.[1] But he may gain a right to such a flow if he maintains it in that manner for a length of time sufficient to acquire the right or easement by adverse user.[2] In Miller *v.* Laubach,[3] it appeared that there was wet or marshy ground on the defendant's land occasioned by what was called winter springs, and which only saturated the earth, without running off by a defined channel. To remedy this, the defendant constructed a drain through the land thus saturated, to the plaintiff's land, and there dis-

[1] [Bigelow C.J., in Dickinson *v.* Worcester, 7 Allen, 19, 22; White *v.* Chapin, 12 Allen, 516, 520; Miller *v.* Laubach, 47 Penn. St. 154; Tillotson *v.* Smith, 32 N.H. 90, 96; Kauffman *v.* Griesemer, 26 Penn. St. 414; Butler *v.* Peck, 16 Ohio St. 334; Foot *v.* Bronson, 4 Lansing, 47. In Curtis *v.* Eastern Railroad, 98 Mass. 428, it was held, that if, without necessity, the water from springs opened by a railroad company in building their road is collected and conducted by them in an artificial trench to a point from which it is discharged upon land of another outside of their location, they are liable in tort therefor, although it reaches such land by trickling from the trench through the soil of the embankment of their road, and mingled with surface drainage.]

[2] [Earl *v.* De Hart, 1 Beasley Ch. (N.J.) 280, 285; White *v.* Chapin, 12 Allen, 516. *A fortiori*, one is not obliged to excavate ditches or construct sewers on his own land for the purpose of draining the low or marshy lands of an adjoining proprietor. Per Denio C.J., in Goodale *v.* Tuttle, 29 N.Y. 466, 467. Nor to suffer the upper owner to construct artificial channels in his ground, and thereby drain the upper land into a canal in the lower one. Minor *v.* Wright, 16 La. An. 151.]

[3] [Miller *v.* Laubach, 47 Penn. St. 154.]

charged the water which had been accustomed to remain on his own until carried off by evaporation, and thereby injured the plaintiff. The Court held, that the plaintiff was entitled to recover on the ground that the defendant had no right in this manner to collect the water from his own land, and turn it in a body upon the lands of the plaintiff, through an artificial channel constructed for the purpose.[1] The Court said, "No doubt the owner of land through which a stream flows may increase the volume of water by draining into it, without any liability to damages by a lower owner.[2] He must abide the contingency of increase or diminution of the flow in the channel of the stream, because the upper owner has the right to all the advantages of drainage or irrigation, reasonably used, which the stream may give him.[3] But that is an entirely different thing from draining the water standing on the lands of one, through artificial channels, on to that of another. That cannot be done without his consent."]

[§ 108 *k*. Butler *v.* Peck[4] is a decision of a similar character. Brinkerhoff J. in this case stated the question to be, "Whether an owner of land having upon it a marshy sink or basin of water, which basin, as to a considerable portion of the water which collects within it, has no natural outlet, may lawfully throw such water by artificial drains, upon the lands of an adjacent proprietor?" And he added, "We are clear that no such right exists. It would sanction the creation, by artificial means, of a servitude which nature has denied. The natural easement arises out of the relative altitudes of adjacent surfaces as nature made them, and these altitudes may not be artificially changed to the damage of an adjacent proprietor. And it makes no difference that, in the hypothetical case on which the charge of the Court below complained of is based, in times of high water, a portion of the waters of the basin would overflow its rim, and find their way along a natural swale to and upon the

[1] [Kauffman *v.* Griesemer, 26 Penn. St. 407; Martin *v.* Riddle, 26 Penn. St. 415, in note; Livingston *v.* McDonald, 21 Iowa, 160, 172.]

[2] [See Williams *v.* Gale, 3 H. & John. 231; Waffle *v.* New York Central R.R. Co., 53 N.Y. 11, 13.]

[3] [Kauffman *v.* Griesemer, 26 Penn. St. 407, 414; Williams *v.* Gale, 3 H. & John. 231; Martin *v.* Jett, 12 La. 501; Lattimore *v.* Davis, 14 La. 161. A riparian proprietor has the right of drainage into the stream opposite his own lands of such of his lands as require it, and has the right to the natural flow of the stream, for that as well as for other purposes. Treat *v.* Bates, 27 Mich. 390.]

[4] [Butler *v.* Peck, 16 Ohio St. 334.]

lands of the plaintiff below; for, as to those waters which naturally could not surmount nor penetrate the rim of the basin, but were compelled to pass off by evaporation, or remain where they were, the case is the same as if the basin had no outlet whatever."]

§ 108 *l*. Town officers in repairing a highway may construct drains and culverts within the limits of a highway; and if the surface water, after flowing in them for some distance, turns upon the land of an adjoining proprietor, no action at law lies for the damage thereby occasioned. Towns are bound to make their highways safe and convenient for travellers; and they and their officers are protected in doing it, so long as they act within the scope of their authority, and execute the work in a reasonably proper and skilful manner,[1] although their operations cause the surface water to flow upon the adjacent proprietors in large quantities to their injury.[2] Their rights are commensurate with their duties. They are not bound to submit the propriety of their judgment or their motives, in making repairs within the scope of their authority, to the supervision of a court or jury.[3] In Turner *v*. Dartmouth,[4] Chapman J. said, "When a highway is laid out, a compensation is allowed to the proprietor of the land for all the damage it will occasion, both direct and incidental. When it exists as an ancient highway; the adjoining proprietors purchase their lands subject to the rights of the public. One of these rights is that of keeping the travelled path free from surface water, in such manner as the officers of the town think proper. . . . If the plaintiff [an adjoining owner] has any remedy for the acts of the town officers in so repairing the highway, and constructing the water bars within its limits, as to cause surface water to flow in large quantities upon his land to his injury, it must be such as the statute gives."]

1 [Flagg *v*. Worcester, 13 Gray, 601; Perry *v*. Worcester, 6 Gray, 546; Sprague *v*. Worcester, 13 Gray, 193; Wheeler *v*. Worcester, 10 Allen, 591, 603; Stone *v*. Augusta, 46 Maine, 127.]

2 [Turner *v*. Dartmouth, 13 Allen, 291; Dickinson *v*. Worcester, 7 Allen, 19; Barry *v*. Lowell, 8 Allen, 127; Wheeler *v*. Worcester, 10 Allen, 591, 603; Morton J., in Brayton *v*. Fall River, 113 Mass. 226; Gray J., in Emery *v*. Lowell, 104 Mass. 16; Hoyt *v*. Hudson, 27 Wis. 656; Phinizy *v*. City Council of Augusta, 47 Geo. 260. See Nevins *v*. Peoria, 41 Ill. 502.]

3 [Benjamin *v*. Wheeler, 8 Gray, 409; Turner *v*. Dartmouth, 13 Allen, 291, 293.]

4 [Turner *v*. Dartmouth, 13 Allen, 293.]

[§ 108 *m*. So, on the other hand, the owner of land which adjoins a highway may lawfully do any acts upon his own land to prevent surface water from coming thereon from the highway; and may stop up the mouth of a culvert built by the selectmen across the highway, for the purpose of conducting such surface water upon his land, providing he can do so without going beyond the limits of his own land. In Franklin *v*. Fisk,[1] Chapman J. said, "As against an adjoining owner of the fee, the defendant [who was the person that stopped the culvert] would have had a right to raise the surface of his land, or build a structure upon it so high, as to prevent any surface water from coming upon it from the adjoining land.[2] The public have no greater right to restrain him in the use of his land than they would have had if they had been absolute owners of the land included in the highway. They may raise the level of their travelled path, and do not violate his rights if the effect of their act is to cause the surface water to flow upon his land. And he may also raise his land, or may erect upon it a building or other structure which shall prevent this effect without violating their rights."[3] — "If by legal acts, done on his own land, the defendant has prevented the water from passing off from the highway through the plaintiff's culvert, their only remedy is to dispose of their surface water in some other way." This seems to produce a conflict of rights; but it is the necessary result of the doctrine adopted and fully stated by Bigelow C.J. in Gannon *v*. Hargadon,[4] referred to above.[5] In Flagg *v*. Worcester,[6] Merrick J. said, "If in consequence of changes" lawfully made by the officers of towns and cities in the natural surface of the soil of a highway, "the water accumulating upon the surface of the way, by the fall of rain or the melting of snow, passes on to adjoining lands in different places, or in somewhat greater quantities in particular places than it otherwise would have done, that is to be considered as one of the natural, probable, or necessary

[1] [Franklin *v*. Fisk, 13 Allen, 211, 212; Bangor *v*. Lansil, 51 Maine, 521.]

[2] [Gannon *v*. Hargadon, 10 Allen, 106; Stone *v*. Augusta, 46 Maine, 127.]

[3] [Parks *v*. Newburyport, 10 Gray, 28; Flagg *v*. Worcester, 13 Gray, 601; Dickinson *v*. Worcester, 7 Allen, 19; Bangor *v*. Lansil, 51 Maine, 525. See Martin *v*. Riddle, 26 Penn. St. 415, in note; ante, § 108 *d*.]

[4] [Gannon *v*. Hargadon, 10 Allen, 106.]

[5] [Ante, § 108 *a*.]

[6] [Flagg *v*. Worcester, 13 Gray, 603.]

consequences resulting from the establishment and maintenance of the way; and, therefore, the damage must be regarded as a matter contemplated in the location of the road, and compensation sought for by the owner of the property in the way pointed out by the statute."[1] And in the same case of Flagg *v.* Worcester, it was decided that the remedy of an owner of land, for injury done to his land by the city by making an excavation in a public street, and thus turning the water accumulated thereon into a private drain running through his land, is, by petition under the statutes, providing compensation for damages caused by raising, lowering, or other act done for the purpose of repairing highways, and not by action of tort.]

[§ 108 *n.* A full discussion of the rights and duties of adjoining owners of land in regard to surface water and drainage requires a more extended treatment of the question already partially considered, which is, how far one owner may detain or use such water upon his land, or turn it by embankments, excavations, ditches, or the like, out of the direction it would naturally take through the soil or over the surface of the earth, and thereby prevent its coming to his neighbor's land or to his profitable use.]

[§ 108 *o.* It is to be observed that it is only when the flow of water on one person's land is identified with that on his neighbor's, by being traceable to it along a distinct and defined course, that the two proprietors can have natural relations with each other in respect of it, considered as the subject of separate existence. If the waters on the two lands do not possess this unity of character, they are in the same category as fish and birds, &c., and are only incident to, and form part of, the produce of, their respective soils, while actually resting upon them; no proprietor can make claim to water in such condition before it arrives within his own borders. Nor can any proprietor claim that another shall receive it within his borders or that he shall not take appropriate measures upon his own land, and in the reasonable use thereof, to prevent its collecting upon his soil.]

[§ 108 *p.* Thus water rising naturally, making land spongy and wet, and squandering itself over the surface, has no public character whatever, although it ultimately finds its way to, and feeds, a stream; and therefore, before it arrives at any defined

[1] [Perry *v.* Worcester, 6 Gray, 546.]

natural channel, it belongs solely to the owner of the land which it covers, and he may deal with it exactly as he thinks fit, while he is making a reasonable use of his own land. Such, also, is the case with water which percolates through the porous basin of a pond, or overflows the edge of a well, or which passes or runs off the surface of the soil, before, in either instance, it makes itself some natural channel. And, clearly, water severed from all other water, as in a pond or tank, and resting solely on the proprietor's own ground, must be in a similar plight.]

[§ 108 *q*. If, however, the natural channel commences at the very source or spring-head, where the water first manifests itself, the two parts are inseparable, and interference with the water thus beginning to form a stream, and a part of it, is no longer a matter of private discretion. The water from a spring flowed in a gully or natural channel to a stream on which was a mill. The spring having been cut off at its source, and the water received into a tank as it rose from the earth, by the license of the owner of the soil on which the spring rose, it was held, that an action lay by the mill-owner against the person so obstructing the water. A river begins at its source, when it comes to the surface; and a stoppage of it at the spring-head is just as much a diversion as if the water had been taken lower down.[1]]

[§ 108 *r*. But, returning to the consideration of the rights of adjoining proprietors in regard to running waters forming no part of a stream or watercourse, it may be stated as a general proposition that every land-owner has a right to appropriate surface water which flows over his land in no definite channel, although the water is thereby prevented from reaching or connecting itself with a watercourse which it had previously supplied. This is the English doctrine, and the same is supported by American authorities. In a late case in the Court of Exchequer,[2] it appeared that the plaintiff's mill, for more than

[1] [Dudden *v*. Guardians of Clutton Union, 1 H. & N. 627; s.c. 26 L.J. (M.R.) 146.]

[2] [Broadbent *v*. Ramsbotham, 11 Exch. 602. This case was cited in Chasemore *v*. Richards, 7 H.L. Cas. 359, 360; and Lord Wensleydale said, "I did not take part in that judgment; I had left the court before it was delivered. I imagined there was a definite stream which fell into the basin, and that an action would lie for interrupting that stream. My learned brothers did not think there was any stream; we differed not on any point of law, but on a point of fact."]

fifty years, had been worked by the stream of a brook, which was supplied by the water of a pond filled by rain, a shallow well supplied by subterraneous water, a swamp, and a well, formed by a stream springing out of the side of a hill; the waters of all which occasionally overflowed and ran down the defendant's land in no definite channel into the brook. The defendant, for agricultural and other useful purposes, had dug a drain in his land, the effect of which was to divert these sources of supply to the brook, the water falling into the drain made by the defendant. The action was for this diversion; and it was held, that the plaintiff had no right, as against the defendant, to the natural flow of any of the waters, and was not entitled to recover. Alderson B., in delivering judgment for the defendant, said, "Now, we think that this water, both that which overflows and that which sinks in, belongs absolutely to the defendant on whose land it arises, and is not affected by any right of the plaintiff. The right to the natural flow of the water in the brook undoubtedly belongs to the plaintiff; but we think this right cannot extend further than a right to the flow in the brook itself, and to the water flowing in some defined natural channel, either subterranean or on the surface, communicating directly with the brook itself. No doubt, all the water falling from heaven and shed upon the surface of a hill, at the foot of which a brook runs, must, by the natural force of gravity, find its way to the bottom, and so into the brook; but this does not prevent the owner of the land on which this water falls from dealing with it as he may please and appropriating it. He cannot, it is true, do so if the water has arrived at and is flowing in some natural channel already formed. But he has a perfect right to appropriate it before it arrives at such a channel. In this case a basin is formed in his land, which belongs to him, and the water from the heavens lodges there. There is here no watercourse at all. If this water exceeds a certain depth, it escapes at the lowest point, and squanders itself (so to speak) over the adjoining surface. The owner of the soil has clearly a right to drain this shallow pond and to get rid of the inconvenience at his own pleasure. . . . The same may be said of the swamp of sixteen perches, which is merely like a sponge fixed (so to speak) on the side of the hill, and full of water. If this overflows it creates a sort of marshy margin adjoining; and there is apparently no course of water, either into or out of it, on the surface of the land. . . . The well at this point is also *in simili casu.* It is not found in the case that it has any subterranean communication with the brook. But no doubt, when this well overflows, the overflow pours itself over and down the declivity towards the brook. But this gives no right to the water." As to the well formed by a stream springing out of the side of a hill, the waters of which occasionally overflowed and ran down the defendant's land in no definite channel into the brook, the Court said, "The water in dispute is only the overflow of a well, and the well is now prevented from overflowing," being drawn off by the drain dug by authority of the defendant. "But when before it did overflow, it ran into a ditch (the lowest adjoining ground) made artificially and for a different purpose, running beside a hedge. This was no natural defined watercourse. After this, it squandered itself over a swamp made by the feet of cattle treading about, and it is not till long after this, that what still remained of it found its way into what may there perhaps be correctly called a definite natural watercourse, receiving this and probably other water from other sources also." But the water in its first origin, and before it had arrived at any definite natural watercourse conveying it onwards towards the brook, had been intercepted by the defendant's drain, and so appropriated by him; and it was held, that the plaintiff, whose mill had, for more than fifty years, been worked by the stream of the brook, had no ground of action against the defendant for the diversion.]

[§ 108 *s.* Another case in the same volume,[1] which has already been referred to, sustains the same doctrine. In this case it appeared that the lands of the plaintiff and of the defendant were contiguous. On the plaintiff's land were certain mills, and also reservoirs which supplied his mills and premises with water. On the outside of the defendant's land, and near to it, was a wet, springy spot, where at most seasons of the year some water rose to the surface, and collected in sufficient quantity to flow down the slope of the land. In wet times a great body of water flowed down, and, after a long drought, there was hardly any, and sometimes no water. There was no regularly formed ditch or channel for the water, the place where it flowed being

1 [Rawstron *v.* Taylor, 11 Exch. 369.]

constantly trodden in by cattle. The water which was not absorbed (and, except in times of drought, all of it was not absorbed) ran into an old watercourse of the plaintiff, which led into the plaintiff's reservoir. The water had so flowed for upwards of twenty years. The defendant, for the purpose of draining his land, and of supplying some part of his property with water, diverted this water from the plaintiff's reservoir. At another spot on the defendant's land, as long ago as any one could recollect, water had always risen to the surface. There had generally been a drinking place for cattle, formed with stones, and the overflow of the water went down a ditch, and thence into a watercourse to the plaintiff's reservoir; and it was held, that the defendant was not liable to the plaintiff for having deprived him of the use of such waters, inasmuch as he had in each instance diverted these waters for the purpose of getting rid of the water by draining his land, and also for the purpose of supplying another part of his property with water for domestic purposes. Parke B. said, "It must be shown that the plaintiff possesses some definite right, in order to deprive the defendant of his general right to cultivate his land in the manner he may think most advantageous to him, with a view to make the most of it. . . . If the plaintiff's argument were correct, the defendant would not be entitled to drain his land for the purpose of building upon it." Platt B.: "This was merely surface water, and the defendant had a right to drain his land, and the plaintiff could not insist upon the defendant maintaining his fields as a mere water-table." Martin B.: "The defendant is at liberty to get rid of the surface water in any manner that may appear most convenient to him; and I think no one has a right to interfere with him, and that the object he may have in so doing is quite immaterial." The above decisions upon this point [1] were followed in a case lately decided in Rhode Island,[2] in which the opinion was delivered by Ames C.J., already quoted upon another branch of this subject.[3] In Bassett *v.* Salisbury Manufacturing Company,[4] it was held, that if the own-

[1] [Broadbent *v.* Ramsbotham, and Rawstron *v.* Taylor.]

[2] [Buffum *v.* Harris, 5 R.I. 243.]

[3] [Ante, § 108 *b.*]

[4] [Bassett *v.* Salisbury Manuf. Co., 43 N.H. 569. In this case, Bartlett J. said, "No land-owner has an absolute and unqualified right to the unaltered natural drainage or percolation to or from his neighbor's land. In general, it would be impossible for a land-owner to avoid disturbing the natural percolation or drain-

ers of a dam on a watercourse, by means of their dam obstruct the natural drainage from the land of another, to his actual injury, they are liable to him therefor, although his land is not situated upon the watercourse, unless such obstruction was caused by them in the reasonable use of their own land or privilege. Any interference by one land-owner with the natural drainage, injurious to the land of another, and not reasonable, is unjustifiable.[1]]

4. *Subterranean Diversion.*

§ 109. We now come to the consideration of the important

age, without a practical abandonment of all improvement or beneficial enjoyment of his land. Any doctrine that would forbid all action of a land-owner, affecting the relations as to percolation or drainage between his own and his neighbors' lands, would in effect deprive him of his property; and, so far from being an application of the maxim, *Cujus est solum*, &c., would work a general denial of effect to it. If A. has the absolute and unqualified right to receive from and discharge into the adjoining land of B. all the drainage and percolation, as they naturally flow between that land and his own, this is substantially a right to the use of B.'s land, practically depriving the latter of all beneficial enjoyment of his property, and in effect amounting to an appropriation of it; and as B. and the other neighboring land-owners must have similar rights, the improvement or beneficial occupation of land becomes in fact impossible, and property in the soil for nearly all useful purposes is annihilated. But we do not think it follows from this, as some recent cases have held, that a land-owner has the full and unlimited ownership, and the absolute and unqualified right of control, of all water in and upon his land not gathered into natural watercourses; for the non-existence of an absolute right does not conclusively disprove the existence of a qualified right."]

1 [Bartlett J. said, "We need not argue that the owner of the land may make some use of the water in it; that he may do some acts that will affect to some extent the drainage; that a well may be dug, under some circumstances, although it will draw water by percolation from a watercourse, from adjoining land, or even from the well of a neighbor. If the views we have expressed are correct, they have already indicated the sole ground of the qualification of the land-owner's right in such cases, and that is, as in certain cases of watercourses, the similar rights of others; and this will of course determine the extent of the qualification, which, as in the analogous cases suggested, and for the same reasons, is the rule of reasonable use, — of a reasonable exercise of one's own right." "As in these cases of the watercourse, so in the drainage, a man may exercise his own right on his own land as he pleases, provided he does not interfere with the rights of others. The rights are correlative, and, from the necessity of the case, the right of each is only to a reasonable user or management, and whatever exercise of one's right or use of one's privilege, in such case, is, such a reasonable user or management is not an infringement of the rights of others; but any interference by one land-owner with the natural drainage, injurious to the land of another, and not reasonable, is unjustifiable. Every interference by one land-owner with the natural drainage, actually injurious to the land of another, would be unreasonable, if not made by the former in the reasonable use of his own property." Bassett *v.* Salisbury Manuf. Co., 43 N.H. 569, 577, 578. See Gerrish *v.* Clough, 48 N.H. 11, 12.]

question which has in several very modern cases been ably discussed; namely, *Whether in the case of two adjoining closes, upon one of which is a spring and watercourse issuing from it, the owner of the other close is liable for sinking a well in it, and thereby cutting off, or diminishing, the water of the spring?* In other words, *whether the same law applicable to the diversion of a watercourse running over the surface of the land, is applicable to springs under ground?* The propounding of such a question at once brings to mind the well-known maxim, that, in contemplation of law, land always extends *downwards* as well as upwards; so that whatever is in a direct line between the surface of any land and the centre of the earth, belongs to the owner of the surface.[1] It would consequently seem to follow, that whether what is *subterranean* be solid rock, mines, or porous soil, or salt springs, or part land and part water, the person who owns the surface may dig therein and apply all that is there found to his own purposes *ad libitum.* The owner of the surface may, by excavating at the extremity, and under the surface of his own land, and so near a newly built house that the house falls down; yet although there is damage, no action is maintainable unless the house had been enjoyed for twenty years; but, if due caution is observed, it is *damnum absque injuria.* In these and similar cases, there is undoubtedly a hardship upon the party injured to be without remedy.[2] But, by that consideration, Courts are not influenced; and as was said by Rolfe J., in Winterbottom *v.* Wright,[3] "hard cases are apt to introduce bad law."[4] But we proceed to what Courts of Justice have said and adjudged upon the subject immediately under consideration.

§ 110. The defendants were the commissioners appointed under an act of Parliament, for paving, cleansing &c., certain squares and streets in London, and were empowered to sink wells and erect pumps, for the purpose of watering those squares and streets. The plaintiffs were trustees, under the same act, for improving and regulating the use and enjoyment of the garden of Queen's Square, London, and repairing the *pump* and *well* in the square. The defendants, having begun to sink a well

[1] [Wheatley *v.* Baugh, 25 Penn. St. 528, 530; Phear on Water, 1, 2.]

[2] See Broom's Legal Maxims, 150, 289.

[3] Winterbottom *v.* Wright, 10 M. & W. 116.

[4] See also Walker *v.* Hatton, 10 M. & W. 259.

at the distance of twenty-three yards from an old well and pump situate within and close to the iron railings round the garden of Queen's Square, a bill was filed in 1840, alleging, that the old well and pump had always been repaired at the expense of the inhabitants of the square, who had at all times been in the habit of having the handle of it locked during the night, in order to prevent the water, with which it was scantily supplied, being exhausted; and that the new well was intended to be sunk deeper than the old one, and would, when completed, draw off the water from it. The bill prayed for an injunction to restrain the defendants from further sinking their well, or doing any other act as tending to diminish the supply of water to the old well. The injunction having been granted *ex parte*, the defendants moved to dissolve it. The Vice-Chancellor (Shadwell) said, that although his opinion was unfavorable to the right claimed by the plaintiffs, yet as the question whether they have that right or not was a legal one, he ought to restrain the defendants from doing the act complained of, until that question had been determined in a Court of Law. He said, however, that there was no evidence at all, that the wells were supplied by a stream of flowing water, or in what other manner they were supplied. The counsel for the defendants contended that the owner of a pump cannot prevent his neighbor from erecting a pump on his land, because it may, *perhaps*, lessen the supply of water to the other pump.[1]

§ 111. In Dexter *v.* The Providence Aqueduct Company, in the Circuit Court of the United States, for the first Circuit,[2] which was a bill in equity, the plaintiff asserted himself to be the owner of a certain meadow, and that *for twenty years* and more, before December, 1832, he and those under whom he claimed and derived his title, were in peaceable possession thereof, with all the rights and privileges, of a certain *spring* and watercourse thereon situated, and passing and flowing upon and over, and extending and running through, a part of the meadow, for the purpose of irrigation, and for drink for his cattle feeding therein; that the defendants, knowing the premises, in December, 1832, dug and sunk a deep well, fountain, and pit, in an adjacent close, and dug a trench therefrom, and

[1] Hammond *v.* Hall, 10 Sim. 552.

[2] Dexter *v.* Providence Aqueduct Company, 1 Story, 387.

laid and placed iron pipes leading from the well or fountain to the city of Providence; whereby they diverted the water from the said spring, and so diverted the natural flow of the spring and watercourse, that they were dry a considerable portion of the year, &c. Mr. J. Story was clearly of opinion that *if the gravamen was made out by sufficient proof*, the plaintiff was entitled to relief under the bill. The case of Balston *v.* Bensted [1] he held to be directly in point. The defence principally turned upon a denial of the *matter of fact*, that the spring and watercourse in question had been diverted at all, or, if diverted at all, that *it had been caused by the digging of the well and fountain and water pipes of the company;* and the company attributed the diminution of the water alleged, to other natural causes wholly independent of their well or fountain. In consideration of the contradictory nature of a great mass of testimony relating merely to the matter of fact, and dependent upon the credibility of witnesses, the Court proposed that the following questions should be submitted to a jury to aid in the decision: 1st, *Whether there was any such diversion of the water as that alleged?* 2d, If so, what damages have been sustained thereby? 3d, What is the permanent diminution or loss in value of the plaintiff's meadow land occasioned thereby? The case of Balston *v.* Bensted, relied on by the Court, was tried at the Summer Assizes, 48 Geo. III. 1808, and it was therein held by Lord Ellenborough, that the owner of a close cannot lawfully cut a drain, whereby the supply of water to the spring of an adjoining close, *after an enjoyment of it for twenty years*, is diminished. Lord Ellenborough held, early in the trial, that the only question was, whether the diminution of the supply of water *had been caused* by the drain dug by the defendant. The *causation* (according to the reporter) being clearly made out, it was agreed, upon the recommendation of the Court, that the water should be conveyed from the defendant's quarry to the plaintiff's works, in the manner that should be directed by an arbitration; and a juror was therefore withdrawn.[2]

[1] Balston *v.* Bensted, 1 Campb. 463.

[2] [As to this case of Balston *v.* Bensted, Lord Chelmsford, in Chasemore *v.* Richards, 5 H. & N. 988, s.c. 7 H.L. Cas. 349, said, "The great distinction between water flowing in a definite stream, and water percolating through the ground, was not presented to the mind of the Judge; and his observation, that twenty years' exclusive enjoyment was decisive as to the presumption in favor of the party, showed that he thought only of

§ 112. In Smith *v.* Adams, in the Court of Chancery of New York,[1] it was held, that where a spring is supplied by a hidden stream passing through the earth, the owner of the land above where the water of the spring issues has no right to divert such water, by an excavation or artificial works upon his own land, to the injury of the riparian proprietors below, who are supplied by the waters of such spring *in their natural course*, or by prescriptive use. The complainant was the owner of a ten-acre lot with a cloth-dressing establishment; and he was also the owner of another lot of one acre adjoining the lands of the defendant, and separated from the ten-acre lot by a turnpike road. Upon the one-acre lot, and only a few feet below the defendant's line, there issued out of the slate rock, from the direction of the defendant's land, a perennial spring; the waters of which, when flowing in their natural course, ran across the one-acre lot, and thence through the defendant's lands situated lower down, into

the rights which arose out of the uninterrupted enjoyment of a right to water flowing in a defined stream on the surface of the ground. The case terminating as it did could hardly be considered as an authority upon the point." In Chasemore *v.* Richards, 2 H. & N. 183, Cresswell J. said, "There are two cases in our books, and I believe two only, which support a claim to water not in a flowing stream, — Balston *v.* Bensted, 1 Campb. 463, and Dickinson *v.* The Grand Junction Canal Company, 7 Exch. 282. In the former of these cases, Lord Ellenborough said, 'that there could be no doubt but that twenty years' exclusive enjoyment of water in any particular manner, affords a conclusive presumption of right in the party so enjoying it.' His lordship is not reported to have explained the nature of the presumption to be made, but at that period it seems to have been supposed that the right of a riparian owner arose out of some presumption of a grant by those higher up the stream. It is therefore probable that in the case then before him, which related to the water springing up in the plaintiff's land, he meant that an enjoyment of it for twenty years raised a presumption of a grant: a presumption not generally made against those who had no knowledge of the existence of that which they are to be presumed to have granted; and I do not understand that any one has insisted in this case upon the doctrine of presumption, which was altogether repudiated in the other case alluded to (Dickinson *v.* The Grand Junction Canal Company), where Lord Chief-Baron Pollock, in giving the judgment of the Court, says, 'We consider it as settled law that the right to have a stream running in its natural course is not by a presumed grant from long acquiescence on the part of the riparian proprietors above and below, but is *ex jure naturæ*, and an incident of property, as much as the right to have the soil itself in its natural state, unaltered by the acts of a neighboring proprietor, who cannot dig so as to deprive it of the support of his land.' It would seem, therefore, that the Court of Exchequer, as instituted when that judgment was given, would not have rested an opinion in favor of the plaintiff, in Balston *v.* Bensted, on the ground stated by Lord Ellenborough." In Frazier *v.* Brown, 12 Ohio St. 300, Brinkerhoff J., alluding to Balston *v.* Bensted, said, "That was a case at *nisi prius*, doubtless hastily decided, and which, in the later cases, has not been followed or regarded as authoritative."]

[1] Smith *v.* Adams, 6 Paige, 435.

a creek which ran through the ten-acre lot, at a point below the complainant's ten-acre lot. In 1804, the then owner of the two lots belonging to the complainant, laid an aqueduct of logs, from the spring, across the turnpike, to the ten-acre lot, for the purpose of carrying water to a distillery which was then in operation there. By this aqueduct the greatest portion of the water of the spring was diverted from its natural course over the defendant's lands below the spring lot, and was discharged upon the ten-acre lot. This change of the natural course of the water had continued by means of the aqueduct, and the waters thus diverted had been used for different purposes upon the ten-acre lot, down to the time of filing of complainant's bill, in 1831. The whole water thus diverted was seldom actually used by the complainant and those under whom he claimed, but a very considerable portion thereof had been suffered to run waste. The defendant, and his father, from whom he derived title to his lands above and below the spring, had for more than thirty years been in the habit of resorting to the spring and taking water therefrom for cattle and for domestic purposes. In 1825, the defendant laid an aqueduct of logs from the spring to his house, and thereby conveyed a small portion of the water in that direction for the use of his family &c.; and he continued to use the water in that manner without objection or molestation for about five years. In 1830, for some unexplained cause, that part of the defendant's aqueduct which was continued for a short distance in the soil of the complainant's lot, to reach the spring, was torn up and destroyed by the plaintiff's direction. The defendant being thus deprived of the power of using a portion of the water in this way, *dug down upon his own land, a short distance above the spring, until he struck the subterranean stream*; and from this point he laid a new aqueduct to his house. The Vice-Chancellor, upon the hearing before him, decided, that the complainant had established a prescriptive right to divert so much of the water of the spring as would pass through an aqueduct of one and a quarter inch in diameter, and to use the same at his discretion; and to have the whole of the residue of the waters to pass over his spring lot *in their natural course.* He therefore decreed accordingly, and granted a perpetual injunction to restrain the defendant from diverting any portion of the waters which supplied the spring, from their natural channel.

From this decree the defendant appealed to the Chancellor, who concurred with the Vice-Chancellor in the conclusion that the evidence established a prescriptive right in the complainant to divert a portion of the waters of the spring across the defendant's land; but as to the *subterranean diversion* he said, "It is necessary, then, to examine whether the diverting the water found in the earth, in the defendant's own land, to the extent to which the water has been diverted by Adams in this case, entitles the complainant to the extraordinary remedy of a perpetual injunction under a decree of this Court; upon principle, I think the rights of the parties must be the same whether the spring issues from the earth upon the land of Adams, or after passing under ground through his land, first makes its appearance upon the surface of the earth upon the lot of Smith, a little farther down. *The only difficulty presented in the latter case is to establish the fact that the water diverted is the same which, in its natural course, issued upon and flowed across the lands below.* And such was the decision of Lord Ellenborough in Balston *v.* Bensted.[1] Here the fact is clearly established, that the stream of water of half an inch in diameter, which the defendant has diverted to his house by means of the aqueduct upon his own land, is a part of the larger stream which naturally issued from the earth upon the spring lot below. The law being well settled, that the owner of the superior heritage has no right to detain or divert the water which passes through his land to the injury of those who were accustomed to receive it upon their lands below, there can be no reasonable doubt of the complainant's right to sustain an action, in the appropriate tribunal for this abstraction of a part of the water of the spring, if he has in fact sustained any damage either directly, or by the prospective diminution of the value of the spring lot."

[§ 112 *a*. Where a subterranean flow of water has become so well defined as to constitute a regular and constant stream, the owner of the land above, through which it flows, may not divert or destroy it to the injury of the owner below, on whose land it issues in the form of a spring. In Wheatley *v.* Baugh,[2] Lewis C.J. says, "It is true that there is a difference between watercourses on the surface and those that run under ground.[3] But

[1] Cited in the preceding section.

[2] [Wheatley *v.* Baugh, 25 Penn. St. 528, 531.]

[3] [See Haldeman *v.* Bruckhardt, 45 Penn. St. 519.]

that distinction does not authorize neighboring proprietors to disregard the necessities of each other's condition in respect to the latter. It is manifest that valuable rights may exist in both; and it is indisputable that whenever they do exist they must be protected by law. In limestone regions, streams of great volume and power pursue their subterranean courses for great distances, and then emerge from their caverns, furnishing power for machinery of every description, or supplying towns and settlements with water for all the purposes of life. To say that these streams might be diverted or obstructed, merely because they run through subterranean channels, is to forget the rights and duties of man in relation to flowing water. But to entitle a stream to the consideration of the law, it is certainly necessary that it be a watercourse in the proper sense of the term. A spring gutter on the surface is none the less a watercourse, although it is not equal in volume to a river. Small as it may be, if it have a clear and well-defined channel, and a regular flow in that channel, it cannot be diverted to the injury of the proprietors below.[1] So a subterranean stream which supplies a spring with water cannot be diverted by the proprietor above, for the mere purpose of appropriating the water to his own use."[2] — "When the filtrations are gathered into sufficient volume to have an appreciable value, and to flow in a clearly defined channel, it is generally possible to see it, and to avoid diverting it without serious detriment to the owner of the land through which it flows. But percolations spread themselves in every direction through the earth, and it is impossible to avoid disturbing them without relinquishing the necessary enjoyment of the land. Accordingly the law has never gone so far as to recognize in one man a right to convert another's farm to his own use, for the purposes of a filter."[3]]

[§ 112 *b*. In conformity with the views of Chief-Justice Lewis, set forth in the preceding section, is the opinion of the Court

1 [Arnold *v.* Foote, 12 Wend. 330. One obstructing a gutter with building materials, is liable for damage caused by the overflow of the water from very heavy rains into another's cellar. Ball *v.* Armstrong, 10 Ind. 181.]

2 [Smith *v.* Adams, 6 Paige, 435.]

3 [See the comments of Strong J. on this case, in Haldeman *v.* Bruckhardt, 45 Penn. St. 518. Where there is nothing to show that the waters of a spring are supplied by any defined, flowing stream, the presumption will be that they have their source in the ordinary percolations of water through the soil. Hanson *v.* McCue, 42 Cal. 303.]

of Exchequer in Dickinson *v.* The Grand Junction Canal Company,[1] which, though generally regarded as erroneous, and, therefore, not to be followed, so far as it undertakes to decide concerning water percolating through the strata of the earth, has been generally approved in subsequent cases in its views of the law respecting water flowing in defined channels beneath the surface.[2] The principle of this case seems to be, that waters flowing in a known and defined stream beneath the earth's surface, are subject to the same rules of treatment as those flowing in a defined channel upon the surface.[3] It was held in it,

[1] [Dickinson *v.* Grand Junction Canal Co., 7 Exch. 282.]

[2] [But these are treated as exceptional cases in Haldeman *v.* Bruckhardt, 45 Penn. St. 514, 518, 519. See Whetstone *v.* Bowser, 29 Penn. St. 59; Wheatley *v.* Baugh, 25 Penn. St. 528.]

[3] [Phear, Rights of Water, 33; Strong J., in Haldeman *v.* Bruckhardt, 45 Penn. St. 518; Wheatley *v.* Baugh, 25 Penn. St. 528; per Wightman J., in Chasemore *v.* Richards, 5 H. & N. 982, 984, 985. In the same case Lord Wensleydale said that the right to a natural stream was not confined to such a stream on the surface, but applied to streams under ground, and was equally an incident to the land itself. If the river Waudle had been supplied by streams above or below ground, flowing in defined channels, the cutting them off would have been a ground of action. If so, there arose the difficulty of distinguishing between them and smaller rivulets; and particles of water percolating the earth, and flowing into them, and supplying the river thereby, were all equally flowing water, and were no more the property of the owner of the soil than water flowing on the surface. . . . Surely the use of the flowing water in each case, and not the property in it, belonged to the proprietors of the surface. . . . There were two distinctions between superficial streams and subterranean waters. *First,* The subterranean waters could not be actually enjoyed without artificial means; the water must be reduced into possession before it could be used, and by such means as the law permitted. Yet, in employing these means, it was almost impossible to avoid occasioning some loss to the subterranean supply of the neighbors, especially as the precise course and direction of such water could seldom be known accurately beforehand. *In the next place,* as the interests of society required that the cultivation of the land should be encouraged, every man had the right to dig in his own soil, which he could hardly do without interfering in some manner with the subterranean waters percolating in his neighbor's land (pp. 989, 990). In the same case, Lord Chelmsford said, that "the law as to water flowing in a certain and definite channel was settled in a variety of decisions, the principle of which seemed to be applicable to all water so flowing, whether under the ground or upon its surface" (p. 986). And in Wheatley *v.* Baugh, Chief-Justice Lewis was evidently of opinion, that subterranean streams, as distinguished from subterranean percolations, are governed by the same rules, and give rise to the same rights and obligations, as flowing surface streams. 25 Penn. St. 528. The case of Acton *v.* Blundell, 12 M. & W. 324, has been unfortunately treated as if an attempt had been made in it to lay down a different rule of law for the enjoyments of waters, according as they are above or below the surface; certainly, the expressions made use of by the Chief-Justice (Tindal) give color to this view; but if the facts are looked at closely, it will be found that he was distinguishing between the case of waters running in defined courses above ground, and waters dispersed over, and percolating through, subterranean strata; and that the real grounds of his antithesis are to be sought in the condition of the

that where water is taken from a river after it has formed part of its stream, not by the reasonable use of it by another riparian proprietor, but by the digging of a well, an action at Common Law will lie by a riparian proprietor for injury to his right, against the party digging the well. Pollock C.B.: "Where the water is on the surface, the right of the owner of the adjoining land to the usufruct of that water is not a doubtful matter of fact. It is public and notorious, and such a right, as a matter of course, is to be respected by every one; and, indeed, if the course of a subterranean stream were well known, — as in the case of many which sink under ground, pursue for a short time a subterranean course, and then emerge again, — it never could be contended that the owner of the soil under which the stream flowed could not maintain an action for the diversion of it, if it took place under such circumstances as would have enabled him to recover, if the stream had been wholly above ground.[1] When, however, the springs come to the surface, and form streams and rivers, the established rules apply, that each riparian owner is entitled, not to the property in the flowing water, but the usufruct of its stream for all reasonable purposes, to drink, to water his cattle, or to turn his mills, according to the nature and situation of the stream. In this case, the water is proved to have been taken from the river after it formed part of its stream, not by the reasonable use of it by another riparian proprietor, but by the digging of a well, which is clearly a diversion; and an action will lie at Common Law against the company, for the injury which has resulted from that unauthorized act to the known right of the mill-owners. If, indeed, it had appeared that the company were ignorant, and could not by any

waters themselves, and not in their local position. Phear, Rights of Water, 34. And Mr. Justice Coleridge, in his dissenting opinion in Chasemore *v.* Richards, 2 H. & N. 186, treats underground waters as if governed by the same rules as those upon the surface.]

1 [Lord Chelmsford quotes this observation of Lord Chief-Baron Pollock, with express approbation, in Chasemore *v.* Richards, 5 H. & N. 986, 987. In New River Company *v.* Johnson, 2 El. & El. 445, Crompton J. said, "Had this been a case of water running in a defined stream, I should have been sorry to give a positive opinion that the obstruction of it might not have afforded the plaintiff a cause of action. There may be some distinction between such a case and the present one, of water merely percolating, as to which Acton *v.* Blundell, 12 M. & W. 324, shows conclusively that no action will lie, and that the only remedy of the owner of a well from which such water has been abstracted is to sink the well deeper." See Arnold *v.* Foot, 12 Wend. 330.]

degree of care have ascertained, before making the well, that it would have the effect of abstracting the water, and when they discovered that it did, could not have repaired the mischief, it might have raised the question, whether the action was maintainable." As to this decision, Parke B. is reported[1] to have said, "That case only decided that, if a person has a right to a stream *jure naturæ*, he has a right to its subterranean course." But in Chasemore *v.* Richards,[2] the same learned Judge, as Lord Wensleydale, said this report attributed to him too limited a view of the decision in Dickinson *v.* The Grand Junction Canal Company. In Dudden *v.* Guardians of Clutton Union,[3] Chief-Baron Pollock, again alluding to this point, said, "If there is a spring, the water from which flows in a natural channel, it cannot be lawfully diverted by any one to the injury of the riparian proprietors. When the stream is above ground, a grant must be presumed, not only of the thing itself, but of all things necessary to the complete enjoyment of it. If the channel or course under ground is known, as in the case of the river Mole,[4] it cannot be interfered with. It is otherwise, where nothing is known as to the source of supply;[5] in that case, as no right can be acquired against the owner of the land under which the spring exists, he may do as he pleases with it, and if, in mining or draining his land, he taps a spring, he cannot be made responsible."[6] It will be observed that the prevailing opinion of the learned Judges, whose decisions have been quoted, is that in order to bring subterranean streams within the rules which govern surface streams, their existence and their course must be, to some extent, known or notorious.[7] And Brinkerhoff J., in Frazier *v.* Brown,[8] said, "It seems to me, that if the question should ever arise, the rights and obligations of adjoining proprietors would have to be subjected to the limitation [above suggested], and this for the reason, that the law cannot properly limit the ordinarily absolute dominion of the owner of the soil, in respect to things concealed

1 [Broadbent *v.* Ramsbotham, 11 Exch. 602, 611.]

2 [Chasemore *v.* Richards, 5 H. & N. 989.]

3 [Dudden *v.* Guardians &c. 1 H. & N. 627, 630.]

4 [The stream at Ingleborough affords another instance. Phear, Rights of Water, 33.]

5 [Haldeman *v.* Bruckhardt, 45 Penn. St. 514.]

6 [Frazier *v.* Brown, 12 Ohio St. 300.]

7 [See Roath *v.* Driscoll, 20 Conn. 533; Brown *v.* Illius, 25 Conn. 594; per Ellsworth J., Haldeman *v.* Bruckhardt, 45 Penn. St. 514.]

8 [Frazier *v.* Brown, 12 Ohio St. 302.]

and hidden in the bowels of the earth, nor recognize an adjoining proprietor as having claims upon, or rights in, a thing passing under the surface of his neighbor's land, the existence of which was first revealed by the very act which would constitute the subject-matter of his complaint. . . . But," he adds, "all of the opinions to which I have adverted under this head of the general subject, are *obiter dicta.*[1] The questions considered did not necessarily arise in any of the cases in which the opinions were expressed,—not even in the case of Smith *v.* Adams; they were there, as they are here, rather matters of curious speculation than otherwise; though the subjects to which they relate must necessarily be noticed, in order to a proper classification of the general subject, and a more ready apprehension of the distinctions which it involves. But the questions remain undecided."[2] In Brown *v.* Illius,[3] Ellsworth J., delivering a dissenting opinion, said, "The distinction is not, as has been intimated, between streams running on the surface and those running below it, but it is whether the waters are streams; i.e., water running in fixed and defined channels, or water in combination with the earth, either in a state of quiescence or percolation, and not under the power of a uniform law, as surface streams under that of gravitation, but moving under influences unknown and unappreciable. If there be a clearly defined continuous stream in the earth which is appreciable, and can be known and is known, I see not why it may not fall within the law of surface streams, as well as any other stream."[4]]

[§ 112 *c.* In Haldeman *v.* Bruckhardt,[5] the question was di-

1 [The same remark applies to all the cases herein referred to in regard to the same point.]

2 [See and consider Roath *v.* Driscoll, 20 Conn. 583.]

3 [Brown *v.* Illius, 25 Conn. 583, 594.]

4 [The plaintiffs, a mining company, in developing their mine, excavated a tunnel into the side of a mountain. In so doing they struck a large and valuable stream of water, which was a source of great revenue to them. The defendants also excavated a tunnel from a point some distance off to a point directly under this stream of water, and the result was that the whole stream of water was diverted into the defendants' tunnel, and by them appropriated to their own use. This was held to be an unlawful diversion by the defendants, which entitled the plaintiffs to an injunction. And it was also held in the case that the preliminary injunction might be granted, although the diversion sought to be restrained had already been effected, and although obedience to the injunction should render necessary the erection by defendants of a bulkhead or a dam across the tunnel. Cole Silver Mining Co. *v.* Virginia &c. Water Co., 1 Sawyer, 470. As to this injunction, see post, § 448.]

5 [Haldeman *v.* Bruckhardt, 45 Penn. St. 514.]

rectly presented, whether a land-owner in the enjoyment of his own land may cut drains, or may mine or quarry, though in so doing he intercepts or interferes with the flowage of water in hidden, unknown, underground channels, to the damage of a neighboring proprietor; and it was answered in the affirmative. The facts of the case were, that the plaintiff in the action owned a large tract of land, on which he and his family resided; on this land, adjacent to his dwelling, there was a large spring of water, sufficient to supply the uses of his family, and never known to be dry, or to be diminished in volume, until the fall of 1860. In 1847, the defendants bought an adjoining tract of land, for the purpose of mining iron ore, about three hundred and thirty feet distant from the spring. Some ten years before the action, the defendants dug a pit to mine iron ore, and then began and continued to mine until the time of the action. At first they employed horse-power in pumping the water from the pit. In 1858 or 1859 they procured an engine with steam-power, and in the fall or spring of 1860 two steam-pumps were put up; and when this steam-power was in full operation, the plaintiff's spring was entirely dried up, the water beginning to diminish in a short time after the pumping commenced. The water was not diminished by the horse-power or the first steam-pump. When the pumping ceased, the spring would fill, and the water in it would be at its natural flow within forty-eight hours. It required from six to eight feet of water in the bank before the spring flowed. There were several distinct streams coming into the pit; and the volume of water pumped out of it largely exceeded the natural flow of the plaintiff's spring. Strong J., delivering the opinion of the Court, said, "A proprietor of land may, in the proper use of his land for mining, quarrying, building, draining, or any other useful purpose, cut off or divert subterraneous water flowing through it to the land of his neighbor, without any responsibility to that neighbor. Some of the grounds for the distinction are clearly pointed out in Acton *v.* Blundell,[1] and others

[1] [Acton *v.* Blundell, 12 M. & W. 324. "Mining must interfere more or less with those subterranean streams and percolations of water which appear upon the surface as springs; to say that the owner of the substrata shall be accountable in damages for their disturbance is to say that he shall have no use whatever of his minerals, for, without interfering to some extent with such waters, mining is impossible." Gordon J., in Coleman *v.* Chadwick, 79 Penn. St. 81, 88.]

may be mentioned. They are, that, in case of an underground supply to a spring or well, or a stream emerging upon land of a lower proprietor, the water does not flow openly in the sight of the owner of the soil under which it passes; that there is, therefore, no reason for implying consent or agreement between the proprietors of the adjoining lands, beneath which underground currents exist, which is one of the foundations upon which the law as to surface streams is supposed to be built; and that, for the same reason, no trace of positive law can be inferred. Again, if the lower proprietor has a right to the undisturbed flowage of water through subterranean passages in his neighbor's land, he has the power of preventing that neighbor from using the water in his own soil; for he cannot use it and return it to its old passage-way, which he may do in the case of a surface stream. Such a right, if it exists, also exposes the upper proprietor to the hazard of incurring fruitless, heavy expenditures in efforts to improve or use his land, since he can have no knowledge, until after his outlay has been made, that his contemplated use will interfere with any rights or interests of an adjoining owner. A surface stream cannot be diverted without knowledge that the diversion will affect a lower proprietor. Not so with an unknown subterraneous percolation or stream." — "The purchaser of lands in which there are unknown subsurface currents must buy in ignorance of any obstacle to the full enjoyment of his purchase indefinitely downwards; and the purchaser of lands on which a spring arises, ignorant whence and how the water comes, cannot bargain for any right to a secret flow of water in another's land. It would seem, therefore, most unreasonable, that the latter should have a right to prevent his neighbor from enjoying his own land in the ordinary way, either by digging wells, cellars, drains, or by quarrying and mining. A further reason for holding that there is no such right, is found in the indefinite nature and great extent of the obligation which would be imposed if the right existed. Instances have occurred where excavations have had the effect of draining land, although at the distance of several miles. Even in the case before us, the mining pit of the defendants is more than three hundred feet distant from the plaintiff's spring. These appear to us sufficient reasons for distinguishing between surface and subterraneous streams, and denying to inferior proprietors any right to control the flow of water in unknown subterranean channels upon an adjoiner's land. They are as appliable to unknown subsurface streams as they are to filtrations and percolations through small interstices. Neither can be defined watercourses, though they may be definable. The distinction thus founded in reason, is recognized by the law. The Civil Law adopted it." — "The Common Law is the same." After citing the cases supporting the above views, he adds, "Nor are there any well-considered decisions which are inconsistent with these. Whetstone *v.* Bowser[1] was a case where the stream diverted was partly on the surface and partly under ground. It was a well-known stream, and the diversion complained of was on the surface. In Smith *v.* Adams,[2] the stream which supplied the spring was known, and the water was taken from a place just above the point where it had emerged, not for the enjoyment of the land where it had flowed, but for the use of another tract at some distance from it." — "The defined watercourses spoken of in Wheatley *v.* Baugh,[3] which a man may not divert to the hurt of an inferior proprietor, are not the hidden streams of which the owner of the soil through which they pass can have no knowledge until they have been discovered by excavations made in the exercise of his rights of property." In this case, the Court carefully guard themselves against being understood to intimate "that an owner may maliciously or negligently divert even an unknown subterranean stream to the damage of a lower proprietor." But the question is yet unsettled whether a land-owner is to be restrained from making a reasonable and profitable use of his land when it appears that he cannot make that use without intercepting or diverting an underground stream of water, which he knows to be flowing through his land and to be feeding a well or spring on the land of an adjoining owner, or otherwise to be beneficial to such owner.]

§ 113. In Greenleaf *v.* Francis, in the Supreme Court of Massachusetts,[4] it was held, that in the absence of all rights acquired by grant or adverse user for twenty years, the owner of land may dig a well on any part of it, notwithstanding he

1 [Whetstone *v.* Bowser, 29 Penn. St. 59.]

2 [Smith *v.* Adams, 6 Paige, 433.]

3 [Wheatley *v.* Baugh, 25 Penn. St. 528.]

4 Greenleaf *v.* Francis, 18 Pick. 117.

thereby diminishes the water in his neighbor's well; unless, in so doing, he is actuated by a mere malicious intent. It appeared that the plaintiff's cellar was dug fourteen years before, and water was then found, and in about two years afterwards an excavation was made in the earth, in the place where the well then stood, about three feet deep, and a barrel was inserted, and the water rose to the surface. Afterwards the defendant dug in his own soil to obtain water, and in a place where it was convenient for him, but near to the well of the plaintiff; and afterwards the water ceased to flow into the plaintiff's well so copiously as it before did. Putnam J., who delivered the judgment of the Court, after stating the case, said, "Then it is to be considered, whether the plaintiff has proved any such easement as she claims to have in the soil of the defendant. She does not pretend that there has been any written grant from the defendant. She relies upon the use, as evidence from which a jury should presume a grant; and there is no other circumstance to be relied upon. But, by our law, the right of the plaintiff to control the operations of the defendant on his own soil must, in the absence of a written agreement, be made out by an adverse possession continued peaceably under a claim of right for twenty years at the least. In the present case such proof is wanting. There is not evidence of any adverse use or possession at all. For the defendant had no means of knowing that the plaintiff's well was supplied by springs in the defendant's soil, until the defendant dug for water there for his own use. He sustained no injury by the use which the plaintiff made of the water she found in her own well; and the use, if it had been adverse, has not been continued for twenty years. Indeed, there is nothing in the case at bar which limits or restrains the owners of these estates, severally, from having the absolute dominion of the soil, extending upwards and below the surface so far as he pleases; each, however, by the law, being held so to operate below the surface as not to cause the soil to fall in from the adjoining estate. These rights should not be exercised for mere malice; and so the Judge ruled at the trial. But the proprietor, in the absence of any agreement subjecting his estate to another, may consult his own convenience in his operations above or below the surface of his ground. He may obstruct the light and air above, and cut off the springs of water below the surface. The proprietor must, at his peril, so place his house and make his excavations below it, as to obtain water, air, and light, even if his neighbor should exercise his full rights of dominion upon his adjoining estate. Now the case finds, that the defendant dug his well in that part of his own ground where it would be most convenient for him. It was a lawful act, and although it may have been prejudicial to the plaintiff, it is *damnum absque injuria*."[1]

§ 114. A very important case upon the subject of subterranean diversion, and one which was considered by the Court by which it was decided, equally novel, is that of Acton *v.* Blundell, in the English Exchequer Chamber, in 1843.[2] The plaintiff below, who was also the plaintiff in error, in his action on the case, declared in the first count for the disturbance of his right to the water of certain *underground springs*, *streams*, and *watercourses*, which, as he alleged, ought of right to run and percolate into the closes of the plaintiff, for supplying certain mills with water; and in the second count, for the draining off the water of a certain *spring* or *well of water* in a certain close of the plaintiff, by reason of the possession of which close, as he alleged, he ought of right to have the use, benefit, and enjoyment of the water of the said *spring* or *well* for the convenient use of his close. The defendants, by their pleas, traversed the rights in the manner alleged in each count. At the trial, it was proved by the plaintiff, that, within twenty years before the commencement of the suit, namely, in the latter end of 1821, a former owner and occupier of certain land and a cotton-mill, now belonging to the plaintiff, had sunk and made in such land a well for raising water for the working of his mill; and that the defendants, in the year 1837, had sunk a coal-pit in the land of one of the defendants at about three-quarters of a mile from the plaintiff's well, and, about three years after, sunk a second

[1] [Delhi *v.* Youmans, 50 Barb. 316; s.c. 45 N.Y. 362; Mosier *v.* Caldwell, 7 Nevada, 363. It was decided in Chase *v.* Silverstone, 62 Maine, 175, that a party who has dug his well on his own land, in good faith, for the purpose of obtaining water for his own domestic uses, is not liable for any damage which may incidentally result to an adjoining proprietor by reason of a consequent diversion of the water which had been accustomed to percolate or flow, in an unknown subterranean current, into the latter's spring. Many of the English and American decisions upon this point were carefully reviewed by Mr. Justice Virgin in the above case of Chase *v.* Silverstone; and it was noticed that a contrary doctrine had been held by the court in New Hampshire. See Basset *v.* Salisbury Manuf. Co., 43 N.H. 569; Swett *v.* Cutts, 50 N.H. 439.]

[2] Acton *v.* Blundell, 12 M. & W. 324.

at a somewhat less distance; the consequence of which sinking was, that, by the first, the supply of water was considerably diminished, and, by the second, was rendered altogether insufficient for the purposes of the mill. The learned Judge before whom the cause was tried, directed the jury, that if the defendants had proceeded and acted in the usual and proper manner on the land, for the purpose of working and winning a coal-mine therein, they might lawfully do so, and that the plaintiff's evidence was not sufficient to support the allegations in his declaration as traversed by the second and third pleas. Against this direction of the Judge the counsel for the plaintiff tendered a bill of exceptions. Upon the argument of the bill of exceptions, on a consideration of the case, in the Exchequer Chamber, it was held that the learned Judge was correct in point of law. The question argued was in substance this: *Whether the right to the enjoyment of an underground spring, or of a well supplied by such underground spring, is governed by the same rule of law as that which applies to and regulates a watercourse flowing on the surface.* The judgment of the Exchequer Chamber was delivered by Tindal C.J., who said, "In the case of the running stream, the owner of the soil merely transmits the water over its surface; he receives as much from his higher neighbor as he sends down to his neighbor below; he is neither better or worse; the level of the water remains the same. But if the man who sinks the well in his own land can acquire by that act an absolute and indefeasible right to the water that collects in it, he has the power of preventing his neighbor from making any use of the spring in his own soil which shall interfere with the enjoyment of the well. He has the power, still further, of debarring the owner of the land in which the spring is first found, or through which it is transmitted, from draining his land for the proper cultivation of the soil; and thus, by an act which is voluntary on his part, and which may be entirely unsuspected by his neighbor, he may impose on such neighbor the necessity of bearing a heavy expense, if the latter has erected machinery for the purposes of mining, and discovers, when too late, that the appropriation of the water has already been made. Further, the advantage on one side, and the detriment to the other, may bear no proportion. The well may be sunk to supply a cottage, or a drinking-place for cattle; whilst the owner of the adjoining land may be prevented from winning metals and minerals of inestimable value. And, lastly, there is no limit of space within which the claim of right to an underground spring can be confined. In the present case, the nearest coal-pit is at the distance of half a mile from the well. It is obvious the law must equally apply if there is an interval of many miles. Considering, therefore, the state of circumstances upon which the law is grounded in the one case to be entirely dissimilar from those which exist in the other; and that the application of the same rule to both would lead, in many cases, to consequences at once unreasonable and unjust; we feel ourselves warranted in holding, upon principle, that the case now under discussion does not fall within the rule which obtains as to surface streams, nor is it to be governed by analogy therewith. No case has been cited on either side bearing directly on the subject in dispute. The case of Cooper *v.* Barber,[1] which approaches the nearest to it, seems to make against the proposition contended for by the plaintiff. In that case the defendant had for many years penned back a stream for the purpose of irrigation, in consequence of which the water had percolated through a porous and gravelly soil into the plaintiff's land; but as this percolation had been insensible, and unknown by the plaintiff until the land was applied for building purposes, the Court held, that the defendant had gained no right thereby, so as to justify its continuance. The case of Patridge *v.* Scott[2] is an authority to show, that a man, by building a house on the extremity of his own land, does not thereby acquire any right of easement, for support or otherwise, over the land of his neighbor. It is said in that case, 'He has no right to load his own soil so as to make it require the support of that of his neighbor, unless he has some grant to that effect.' It must follow, by parity of reason, that if he digs a well in his own land so close to the soil of his neighbor as to require the support of a rib of clay or of stone in his neighbor's land to retain the water in the well, no action would lie against the owner of the adjacent land for digging away such clay or stone, which is his own property, and thereby letting out the water; and it would seem to make no difference as to the legal rights of the parties, if the well stands some distance within the plaintiff's boundary, and

[1] Cooper *v.* Barber, 5 Taunt. 99.

[2] Patridge *v.* Scott, 3 M. & W. 230.

the digging by the defendant, which occasions the water to flow from the well, is some distance within the defendant's boundary; which is, in substance, the very case before us.[1] The Roman law forms no rule, binding in itself, upon the subjects of these realms; but, in deciding a case upon principle, where no direct authority can be cited from our books, it affords no small evidence of the soundness of the conclusion at which we have arrived, if it proves to be supported by that law, the fruit of the researches of the most learned men, the collective wisdom of ages, and the groundwork of the municipal law of most of the countries in Europe. The authority of one, at least, of the learned Roman lawyers appears decisive upon the point in favor of the defendants; of some others, the opinion is expressed with more obscurity. In the Digest, lib. 39, tit. 3, *De æquâ et aquæ pluviæ arcandæ*, § 12, '*Denique Marcellus scribit, Cum eo, qui in suo fodiens, vicini fontem avertit, nihil posse agi: nec ne dolo actionem, et sane non debet habere; si non animo vicini nocendi, sed suum agrum meliorem faciendi, id fecit.*'[2] It is scarcely necessary to say, that we intimate no opinion whatever as to what might be the rule of law if there had been an uninterrupted user of the right for more than the last twenty years; but, confining ourselves strictly to the facts stated in the bill of exceptions, we think the present case, for the reasons above given, is not to be governed by the law which applies to rivers and flowing streams, but that it rather falls within that principle which gives to the owner of the soil all that lies beneath his surface; that the land immediately below is his property; whether it is solid rock or porous ground or venous earth, or part soil, part water; that the person who owns the surface may dig therein, and apply all that is there found to his own purposes at his free

[1] [See remarks of Bartlett J., in Bassett *v.* Salisbury Manuf. Co., 43 N.H. 573–576.]

[2] [See Haldeman *v.* Bruckhardt, 45 Penn. St. 520. In respect to this quotation, Maule J., in Acton *v.* Blundell, said, "The English of it I take to be this: If a man digs a well in his own field, and thereby drains his neighbor's, he may do so, unless he does it maliciously." And in Smith *v.* Kenrick, 7 C.B. 552, Maule J. said, "The Court, in Acton *v.* Blundell, seem to have adopted the doctrine there cited from Marcellus." This rule of the Civil Law is quoted by Lord Wensleydale in Chasemore *v.* Richards, 5 H. & N. 990; s.c. 7 H.L. Cas. 349, with the remark that a very extensive sense was given to these words, "For it was said that the making a work, '*agri colendi causâ*,' and thereby altering the course of the *aquæ pluviæ*, was not actionable. And it would seem by the Roman law, that if the sources of a fountain were cut off by excavation to get minerals, no action would lie."]

will and pleasure; and that if, in the exercise of such right, he intercepts or drains off the water collected from underground springs in his neighbor's well, this inconvenience to his neighbor falls within the description of *damnum absque injuria*, which cannotb ecome the ground of an action. We think, therefore, the direction given by the learned Judge at the trial was correct, and that the judgment already given for the defendants in the court below, must be affirmed."[1]

[§ 114 *a*. It will be observed that the questions before the Court, in the above case of Acton *v.* Blundell, were two; namely, whether a land-owner, by sinking a shaft on his own ground, first, might lawfully intercept water, and prevent it from percolating into another land-owner's well; or, secondly, might actually abstract or withdraw water from the well. The Lord Chief Justice (Tindal), after defining the land-owner's right as set forth in the preceding section, went on to say in the words already quoted, "that if, in the exercise of such right, he intercepts or drains off the water collected from underground springs

[1] [See Pixley *v.* Clark, 35 N.Y. 527. In Dickinson *v.* The Grand Junction Canal Co., 7 Exch. 282, 300, Lord Chief-Baron Pollock refers to the case of Acton *v.* Blundell, as the one in which "a distinction is made for the first time between underground waters and those which flow on the surface." The case of Acton *v.* Blundell is generally cited in subsequent cases where the same points are involved, and with approbation. In New River Company *v.* Johnson, 2 El. & El. 445, Crompton J. said, "There may be some distinction between a case of water running in a defined stream, and the present one of water merely percolating, as to which Acton *v.* Blundell shows conclusively that no action will lie, and that the only remedy of the owner of a well, from which such water has been abstracted, is to sink the well deeper. That is a decision of the Court of Exchequer Chamber of great authority;" and is approved and acted upon by the House of Lords in Chasemore *v.* Richards, 7 H.L. Cas. 349; Wightman J. and Blackburn J. also both refer to it as approved and confirmed by the House of Lords in the same case, 2 El. & El. 444, 447; it is also approved by Lord Campbell in Humphries *v.* Brogden, 12 Q.B. 753; and by Maule J. and Cresswell J. in Smith *v.* Kenrick, 7 C.B. 540, 566; Mellor J. in Regina *v.* Board of Works, 3 B. & S. 727; and by Brinkerhoff J., in Frazier *v.* Brown, 12 Ohio St. 310; by Bennett J., in Chatfield *v.* Wilson, 28 Vt. 55; by Wilson J., in Clark *v.* Conroe, 38 Vt. 473; by Bronson C.J., in Radcliff *v.* Mayor &c. 4 Comst. 195, 200. In Chase *v.* Silverstone, 62 Maine, 175, which is the first case in which the court in Maine has been called upon to declare the law which governs proprietors of adjacent lands in relation to subterranean water not gathered into a fixed, known channel, the doctrine of Acton *v.* Blundell, and of other later cases decided on the same principle, was fully adopted.

But in Bassett *v.* Salisbury Manuf. Co. 43 N.H. 569, 579; Bartlett J. said, "We are not aware that the doctrine of Acton *v.* Blundell, and of the cases which follow it, has been adopted in any decision in this State (New Hampshire); but so far as the subject has been considered at all here we think our decisions have not tended in the direction of that case." See ante, § 108 *s*, note.]

in his neighbor's well, this inconvenience to his neighbor falls within the description of *damnum absque injuria*, which cannot become the ground of an action;" and thus at once he answered both of the questions in the affirmative; and in this he has been very generally sustained by the cases which have since been decided, as to both of the propositions.]

[§ 114 *b*. The authority of the first of the above propositions; viz., that a land-owner, by sinking a shaft on his own ground, might lawfully intercept water, and prevent it from percolating into another land-owner's well, which the Court of Exchequer attempted to depreciate in the case of Dickinson *v*. The Grand Junction Canal Company,[1] has been re-asserted in Chasemore

[1] [7 Exch. 282. The authority of Dickinson *v*. The Grand Junction Canal Company has been very much shaken in subsequent cases, chiefly on the following proposition stated in it; viz., "As to the abstraction of the water, which never did form part of the river, but has been prevented from doing so in its natural course, by the excavation of the well, whether the water was part of an underground watercourse, or percolated through the strata, we are also of opinion that an action would lie. The mill-owners were entitled to the benefit of the stream in its natural course; and they are deprived of a part of that benefit if the natural supply of the stream is taken away." In regard to this statement of the law, Cresswell J., in Chasemore *v*. Richards, 2 H. & N. 186, said, "The subject is dismissed with this simple assertion of the right, and we are not in possession of the reasoning by which the Court arrived at that conclusion. Another point decided in that case; viz., that the company, by sinking a well, had broken their agreement, rendered the rights of the parties at Common Law immaterial to the decision of the case, and which may account for the dismissal of this novel point with so little observation; and in Broadbent *v*. Ramsbotham, the case having been cited in argument, Parke B. observed, 'That case only decided that if a person has a right to a stream *jure naturæ*, he has a right to its subterranean course.' If he went beyond that, it appears to have been repudiated by the same Court in Rawstron *v*. Taylor and Broadbent *v*. Ramsbotham, and I think rightly." Wightman J., in the same case, 5 H. & N. 985, said of Dickinson *v*. The Grand Junction Canal Company, "No remark or comment is made, or reason assigned by the Court for arriving at a conclusion which not only does not seem warranted by the premises previously adopted, but is in effect hardly consistent with them. The plaintiff, in that case, was held to have a cause of action independently of any infringement of a right at Common Law, by reason of the breach of an agreement between the parties and of an act of Parliament; and a decision upon the right at Common Law seems not to have been necessary for determining the suit between the parties." Lord Chelmsford said he agreed with these observations of Cresswell J. and Wightman J., and "could hardly consider that case a satisfactory decision." In New River Company *v*. Johnson, 2 El. & El. 444, Wightman J. said, "It is said that Acton *v*. Blundell has been shaken by Dickinson *v*. The Grand Junction Canal Company. The latter, however, was only a decision of the Court of Exchequer; whereas Acton *v*. Blundell was decided in the Exchequer Chamber. Moreover, in Chasemore *v*. Richards, great doubt is thrown upon Dickinson *v*. The Grand Junction Canal Company; whereas Acton *v*. Blundell is referred to with approbation." Crompton J., in the same case, referring to the case of Acton *v*. Blun-

v. Richards[1] by the Court of Exchequer Chamber, whose judgment has been fully sustained upon a proceeding in error thereon in the House of Lords.[2] The facts in this latter case, as found by an arbitrator, were as follows: The plaintiff was an occupier of an ancient mill on the river Wandle, and, for more than sixty years before the action, he, and all the preceding occupiers of the mill, used and enjoyed, as of right, the flow of the river for the purpose of working their mill. It appeared that the river Wandle is, and always has been, supplied above the plaintiff's mill, in part by the water produced by the rainfall on a district of many thousand acres in extent, comprising the town of Croydon and its vicinity. The water of the rainfall sinks into the ground to various depths, and then flows and percolates through the strata to the river Wandle, part rising to the surface and part finding its way under ground in courses which continually vary. The Local Board of Health of Croydon (represented in the action by Richards, the defendant), for the purpose of supplying the town of Croydon with water, and for other sanitary purposes, sank a well in their own land in the town of Croydon, and about a quarter of a mile from the river Wandle, and pumped up large quantities of water from their well, for the supply of the town of Croydon; and by means of the well and the pumping, the Local Board of Health did divert, abstract, and intercept underground water, but underground water only, that otherwise would have

dell, said, "That is a decision of the Court of Exchequer Chamber, of great authority, and the case of Dickinson *v.* The Grand Junction Canal Company, in the Court of Exchequer, not only does not and could not overrule it, but is itself virtually overruled by the judgment of the House of Lords in Chasemore *v.* Richards, 7 H.L. Cas. 349, in which Acton *v.* Blundell is approved and acted upon." Mr. Justice Brinkerhoff, in Frazier *v.* Brown, 12 Ohio St. 304, said, "On inspection of Dickinson *v.* The Grand Junction Canal Company, it will be seen, that the plaintiff's rights, as there claimed by him, well rested on a basis of express contract, and there was no occasion to pass upon any principle of natural right growing out of the other relations of the parties."]

[1] [Chasemore *v.* Richards, 3 Jur. N.S. Exch. 984; S.C. 2 H. & N. 168.]

[2] [5 H. & N. 982; S.C. 7 H.L. Cas. 349. The percolating water belongs to the owner of the land, as much as the land itself, or the rocks and stones in it. Therefore he may dig a well, and make it very large, and draw up the water by machinery or otherwise, in such quantities as to supply aqueducts for a large neighborhood. He may thus take the water which would otherwise pass by natural percolation into his neighbor's land, and draw off the water which may come by natural percolation from his neighbor's land; and his neighbor may, by a wall or other obstruction, retain the water which is upon his own land, and prevent the water from coming into his soil. Chapman C.J. in Wilson *v.* New Bedford, 108 Mass. 265.]

flowed and found its way into the river Wandle, and so to the plaintiff's mill; and the quantity so diverted, abstracted, and intercepted was sufficient to be of sensible value towards the working of the plaintiff's mill; the arbitrator specially acquitted the Board of having abstracted any water from the river Wandle itself, or from any stream running into it; and also of having been actuated by any malicious motive, or intent to diminish the quantity of water in the river; but the arbitrator did find that the Board had reasonable means of knowing the probable and natural effect of their acts and works during the period of time particularly in question in the cause. The whole Court of Exchequer Chamber, with the exception of Mr. Justice Coleridge, found in favor of the defendant; and the dissentient Judge, seeming to guard himself from being understood to support any natural right on the part of the plaintiff to the percolation of the water, carefully avoided either impeaching the decision in Acton *v.* Blundell, or approving of that in Dickinson *v.* The Grand Junction Canal Company. He rested his judgment entirely upon the fact, that the plaintiff, as a mill-owner, had enjoyed uninterrupted user of the Wandle for upwards of sixty years, by which the learned Judge considered that he had acquired, as against the proprietors of the banks above, a right to such transit of the water under their respective lands as was essential to the proper working of the mill. "This seems, indeed," says Mr. Phear,[1] "to be pushing the doctrine of implied grant so far, as to remove it entirely from the basis[2] upon which it is usually placed, and to a greater distance than it is likely to be followed in any future decisions." This latter point will be noticed more fully hereafter.]

[§ 114 *c.* Upon the hearing of Chasemore *v.* Richards, in the House of Lords, Wightman J. delivered the opinion of the Judges who were summoned to attend their Lordships. Among other things, he said, "The question, then, is, whether the plaintiff has such a right as he claims, *jure naturæ*, to prevent the defendant sinking a well in his own ground at a distance from the mill, and so absorbing the water percolating in and into his own ground beneath the surface, if such absorption has the effect of diminishing the quantity of water which would otherwise find its way into the river Wandle, and by such dimi-

[1] [Rights of Water, 37.]

[2] [Daniel *v* North, 11 East, 374.]

nution affects the working of the plaintiff's mill. It is impossible to reconcile such a right with the natural and ordinary rights of land-owners, or to fix any reasonable limits to the exercise of such a right. Such a right as that contended for by the plaintiff would interfere with, if not prevent, the draining of land by the owners.[1] Suppose, as it was put at the bar in argument, a man sank a well upon his own land, and the amount of percolating water which found its way into it had no sensible effect upon the quantity of water in the river which ran to the plaintiff's mill, no action would be maintainable; but if many land-owners sank wells upon their own lands, and thereby absorbed so much of the percolating water, by the united effect of all the wells, as would sensibly and injuriously diminish the quantity of water in the river, though no one well alone would have that effect, could an action be maintained against any one of them, and if any, which, for it is clear that no action could be maintained against them jointly?" "In the present case, the water which finds its way into the defendant's well is drained from and percolates through an extensive district, but it is impossible to say how much from any part. If the rain which has fallen may not be intercepted whilst it is merely percolating through the soil, no man could safely collect the rain-water as it fell into a pond; nor would he have a right to intercept its fall, before it reached the ground, by extensive roofing, from which it may be conveyed to tanks, to the sensible diminution of water which had, before the erection of such impediments, reached the ground, and flowed to the plaintiff's mill. In the present case, the defendant's well is only a quarter of a mile from the river Wandle; but the question would have been the same if the distance had been ten or twenty or more miles distant,[2] provided the effect had been to prevent underground percolating water from finding its way into the river, and increasing its quantity, to the detriment of the plaintiff's mill. Such a right as that claimed by the plaintiff is so indefinite and unlimited that, unsupported as it is by any weight of author-

[1] [In Regina *v.* Board of Works, 3 B. & S. 726, Mellor J. cites this passage, and says, "We entirely concur in this view of the law."]

[2] [In the course of the argument, Lord Brougham adverted to the French artesian well at the Abattoir de Grenelle, which was said to draw part of its supplies from a distance of forty miles, but underground, and, as far as is known, from percolating water. 7 H.L. Cas. 359.]

ity, we do not think that it can be well founded, or that the present action is maintainable." Lord Chelmsford said, "These principles, applicable to streams whether above or under the ground, did not seem to be applicable to water merely percolating through the ground, which had no certain course or defined limits whatever. The right to water so percolating was of too uncertain a description. When did it commence? If the owner of the land could not intercept it in its course through his land, could he catch it in rain-water tubs, and prevent its reaching the ground at all? Here, the water, the benefit of which the plaintiff claimed, found its way to the river through the soil of several thousand acres. Were the most distant of the land-owners to be subject to this action, or were only the adjoining land-owners liable? This distinction between water flowing in a definite channel, and water percolating through the strata, seemed to have been well settled in some of the previous cases," and he thereupon cites the cases of Rawstron *v.* Taylor, Broadbent *v.* Ramsbotham, and Acton *v.* Blundell, as supporting the principles relied upon by him in deciding against the claim of the plaintiff in the case before their Lordships. Lord Cranworth concurring, among other things, said, that "the argument founded on the use to which the defendant applied this water, did not affect his mind at all, because he thought there was no difference in the case, whether one owner sank a well to supply a thousand other owners, or each of these sank a well to supply himself; indeed, the loss of water in the latter case might be greater than in the former." Lord Wensleydale (late Baron Parke) concurred, but with apparent hesitation, and "not without serious doubts." He said, "Their Lordships had now to decide, for the first time, the question as to the rights of underground water. There were two conflicting authorities on the subject: the case under appeal, and that of Dickinson *v.* The Grand Junction Canal Company, with which the two cases of Rawstron *v.* Taylor, and Broadbent *v.* Ramsbotham are said to be inconsistent. It was a mistake to suppose that these two had overruled the first-named case, as he could assert, from having been a party to pronouncing those decisions. In Broadbent *v.* Ramsbotham, it did not appear that any of the percolating water could have reached the brook, and therefore he considered that the plaintiff could not recover on the ground on which Dickinson *v.* The Grand Junction Canal Company was decided." "The case of Acton *v.* Blundell would be rightly decided on the ground that the injury to the plaintiff's well, in that case, was caused by the lawful exercise of the defendant's right to get the minerals on his own land, and, unless he had that right, the public would have lost the benefit of a valuable gift of Providence. Every man had a right to the natural advantages of his land. It seemed to him, that the question in the case resolved itself into this: Whether the defendant exercised his right of enjoying the subterranean water in a reasonable manner? If he had made the well and used the water for the benefit of those living on his own land, there could have been no question, even though the number of houses upon his own property had been increased to any extent. But he doubted the defendant's right to abstract the water for the purpose of supplying a large district, for the use of persons who would have no right to take it for themselves, and to the injury of those proprietors who had a right to it. On the whole, though he should have wished to give this case further consideration, he acquiesced." [1]]

[§ 114 *d.* As to the decision in Chasemore *v.* Richards, Cockburn C.J. remarked, in Hodgkinson *v.* Ennor,[2] that it was decided in it "that, until water rises to the surface of land, the law gives no right of action to a party who has suffered by its abstraction;" and Blackburn J., in the same case,[3] said, "I admit the distinction between diverting water before it has become the plaintiff's, and after it has become so; that is the intelligible distinction taken in Chasemore *v.* Richards." This leads to the second proposition laid down in Acton *v.* Blundell; viz., that a land-owner, by sinking a shaft on his own ground, might actually withdraw water from another land-owner's well, without rendering himself liable to an action therefor; as to which the case of New River Company *v.* Johnson[4] is an important decision. The same proposition is affirmed in it. In this case, it appeared that the New

[1] [The opinions given in this case illustrate the similarity of the principles which govern waters percolating in undefined courses under ground, and those standing or moving in undefined courses on the surface of the earth.]

[2] [Hodgkinson *v.* Ennor, 4 B. & S. 241.]

[3] [4 B. & S. 242.]

[4] [New River Co. *v.* Johnson, 2 El. & El. 435.]

River Company, under authority of law had executed certain works, by means of which they had intercepted water from percolating under ground into a well belonging to Johnson; and also had abstracted from the well, water which had already so percolated into and was in it. Under the act conferring their authority, they were required to make full compensation to all parties interested for all damages sustained by them through the exercise of their powers. It was decided that a person who sustains injury from the execution of works authorized by a statute, is not, generally speaking, entitled to compensation, under the compensation clauses of the statute, unless the injury sustained is such as, had the works not been authorized by the statute, would have given the claimant a right of action.[1] Proceeding from this proposition, the Court, by Cockburn C.J., said, "In the present case, the respondent complains that the appellants, in interfering with her property under the powers of their act, have injured her in two respects; first, by preventing water from percolating under ground into her well, as, but for the appellants' works, it would have done; secondly, by abstracting from the well, water which had already so percolated into and was in it. Now, as to the first ground of complaint, Chasemore *v.* Richards is an express authority that it would not, irrespectively of the act, have constituted any cause of action; neither, therefore, can it give the respondent any right to compensation under the act. And as to the second ground, Acton *v.* Blundell is as plain an authority that no action would have lain in respect of that cause of complaint had the act never passed. According, therefore, to the principle to which I have adverted, the respondent can have no better claim to compensation on this ground than on the other." Wightman J. said, "Chasemore *v.* Richards decisively establishes that no compensation can be claimed by the respondent for the interception by the appellants of water in course of percolation towards her well. But it is contended on her behalf that, in respect of the abstraction from the well of all such water as had already percolated to and was in it before the appellants commenced their works, she would, but for the act, have had a right of action against them at Common Law. It seems to me that Chasemore *v.* Richards is decisive

[1] [See Regina *v.* Board of Works, 3 B. & S. 710, and the suggestions of Cockburn C.J., on this point, in same case, p. 729.]

against her, on this point also; but it is unnecessary to consider whether that be so, as Acton *v.* Blundell is an express authority that, apart from the act, no such action would have lain." Crompton J. said, that the case of Acton *v.* Blundell shows conclusively that "the only remedy of the owner of a well from which such water has been abstracted is to sink the well deeper." And Blackburn J. referred to the same case as "conclusive against both the heads of claim for compensation relied upon by the respondent's counsel."[1]]

[§ 114 *e.* This subject has been fully discussed in several late American cases, some of which have already been noticed. Thus, in Frazier *v.* Brown,[2] it appeared that a land-owner dug a "hole" on his own land for purposes connected with the use of his own land, thereby cutting off or diverting underground waters which had always been accustomed to percolate and ooze through his land to land of an adjoining proprietor, and there to form the source of a spring and rivulet; it was held, that any damage thereby occasioned to such adjoining proprietor was *damnum absque injuria.* Brinkerhoff J. said, "What was the object for which the 'hole,' of which the plaintiff complains, was designed, we are not fully informed." "The question is, whether, in the absence of all rights derived either from contract or legislation, a land-owner can have any legal claims in respect to subsurface waters which, without any distinct and definite channel, ooze, filter, and percolate from adjoining lands into his own, when such waters are diverted, retained, or abstracted by the owner of such adjoining lands in the use of his property, for any object of either taste or profit, even though the use may be accompanied by a malicious intent to injure his neighbor by means of such use?" "Whatever points of casuistry may arise out of this question, we are of opinion that the law of the land can recognize no such claims; and that subject only to the possible exception of a case of unmixed malice, the maxim, *Cujus est solum ejus est usque ad cœlum et ad inferos*, applies to its full extent; and, whatever damage may result by the exercise of this absolute right of property, to adjoining proprietors, from the loss of such percolating subsurface waters, it is *damnum absque*

[1] [The doctrine of Acton *v.* Blundell, and Chasemore *v.* Richards, was again acted upon in Regina *v.* The Board of Works, 3 B. & S. 710. See the opinion of Cockburn, C.J. in this case, p. 729.]

[2] [Frazier *v.* Brown, 12 Ohio St. 294.]

injuria. The current of decisions to this effect, both in England and the United States, is generally uniform and consistent." "The reasoning on which this current of decision proceeds is entirely satisfactory to us." The learned Judge, after noticing several of the most important cases on this point, proceeds: "From this running abstract of the cases bearing immediately upon the question before us, it will be seen, that though the question is one of no little novelty, niceness, and difficulty, yet the current of decision is singularly uniform and consistent. As I have already said, the reasoning on which this course of decision proceeds is, to our minds, as satisfactory as the cases themselves are uniform and consistent. The reasoning is briefly this: In the absence of express contract and of positive authorized legislation, as between proprietors of adjoining lands, the law recognizes no correlative rights in respect to underground waters percolating, oozing, or filtrating through the earth; and this mainly from considerations of public policy. 1. Because the existence, origin, movement, and course of such waters, and the causes which govern and direct their movements, are so secret, occult, and concealed, that an attempt to administer any set of legal rules in respect to them would be involved in hopeless uncertainty, and would be, therefore, practically impossible. 2. Because any such recognition of correlative rights would interfere, to the material detriment of the common wealth, with drainage and agriculture, mining, the construction of highways and railroads, with sanitary regulations, building, and general progress of improvement in works of embellishment and utility."]

[§ 114 *f.* This subject underwent a careful and elaborate treatment, both on principle and authority, in a late case in Vermont,[1] in which the declaration charged that the defendant had interfered with the natural flow or passage by percolation, of water through the defendant's land, to the plaintiff's, by means of which a reservoir or tub on the plaintiff's land was supplied with water. This tub was sunk by the plaintiff on his own land, a few years previous to the action, as the evidence tended to show, a foot or more below the channel of the brook which ran between the lands of the plaintiff and of the defendant; from this tub the water was taken by artificial means for the use of

[1] [Chatfield *v.* Wilson, 28 Vt. 49.]

the plaintiff. The evidence also tended to show that this tub was supplied with water, which filtrated under ground from the brook, and also from the adjoining land of the defendant. The defendant, in order to prevent the water percolating to the plaintiff's land, dug into his own land and filled in with dry hard earth, and thereby prevented the water from accumulating in the plaintiff's tub, either from the brook directly, or through or under the soil of the defendant's land. The question was on the rights of the plaintiff in underground water percolating through the defendant's lands toward his own. Bennett J. said, "This is the first time, within my knowledge, that the question has ever come before our courts, in relation to the rights of adjoining proprietors of lands to water percolating under the surface, through wet and porous ground;" and the Court held that there are no correlative rights between the proprietors of adjoining lands, in reference to the use of such water. Such water is to be regarded as a part of the land itself, to be enjoyed absolutely by the proprietor within whose territory it is; and to it the law governing the use of running streams is inapplicable. They say, "We think the practical uncertainties which must ever attend subterranean waters is reason enough why it should not be attempted to subject them to certain and fixed rules of law, and that it is better to leave them to be enjoyed absolutely by the owner of the land, as one of its natural advantages, and, in the eye of the law, a part of it; and we think we are warranted in this view by well-considered cases." In a subsequent case, the same Court held that, if a land-owner, by raising the height of water upon his own land, cause subterranean streams to set back and stand upon the land of another, the latter has no ground of action therefor.[1] In Clark *v.* Conroe[2] the same Court again say of underground water percolating naturally through the soil, "Such water is treated as a part of the land, to be enjoyed absolutely by the owner of the soil."[3]]

[1] [Harwood *v.* Benton, 32 Vt. 724.]

[2] [Clark *v.* Conroe, 38 Vt. 469, 473. In this case the defendant conveyed to the plaintiff a piece of land by deed, with covenants of seisin and warranty, the land having thereon a spring of water. Prior to this conveyance the defendant had conveyed to another person the right to the water of the spring, and of drawing it away by aqueduct to his own premises adjoining; and it was held that the deed to such other person conveyed to him a title in the land, and that the title and actual possession of that other person in the spring was a breach of the defendant's covenants of seisin and warranty in his deed to the plaintiff.]

[3] [See Pixley *v.* Clark, 35 N.Y. 527. Ante, § 114 *b*, and note.]

[§ 114 *g*. A case[1] lately arose in Connecticut involving the rights of adjoining owners of land, in regard to waters percolating through the soil; and in the discussion of it the general subject of property in underground waters was treated with great clearness and force. It appeared that the plaintiff, for more than fifteen years before the suit, had on his land a reservoir of water, made by excavating the ground a few feet below the surface, into which the water came, by percolation through the earth, and there it stood, in sufficient quantity for the use of his cattle, but it never rose to a level with the adjoining land; and there never was any stream of water running into or from the reservoir. At a short distance from this reservoir, he made another excavation, which he called a well, and which was at a place higher up the hill. The water stood somewhat higher in the well than it did in the first reservoir, but still never overflowed, nor was any stream known to run into it. By artificial means the plaintiff used and distributed the water at considerable pecuniary profit. The defendant afterwards made an excavation or reservoir in his lot adjoining the plaintiff's, in which the water stood naturally at a level below the water in the plaintiff's well; but the water did not rise to the surface of the land, nor did any stream naturally run into or from the defendant's excavation or reservoir. The defendant acted for his own profit, and without any design unnecessarily to injure the plaintiff. The consequence of the defendant's act was that the water in the plaintiff's well did not rise so high as before, to his injury; but it did not appear how this effect was produced; whether the water was intercepted before reaching, or was abstracted after having reached, the plaintiff's well, did not appear. The plaintiff's well, which caused his first reservoir to become dry, was of less than fifteen years' standing; and the case raised no question of a right acquired by adverse use. The single question made and discussed by the Court was, "Can one of two adjoining proprietors, by first opening a watering-place, prevent other persons from doing the same, on their own land; though by so doing, water is prevented from percolating the land so as to supply the first-made reservoir?" and this question was decided in the negative. Ellsworth J., delivering the opinion of

[1] [Roath *v*. Driscoll, 20 Conn. 533. In this case, Acton *v*. Blundell was quoted and relied upon. Roath *v*. Driscoll was cited and approved in Chatfield *v*. Wilson, 28 Vt. 49, and in Clark *v*. Conroe, 38 Vt. 474.]

the Court, said, "Nothing is gained by a mere continued pre-occupancy of water *under the surface*. Why should any advantage be gained by pre-occupancy? Each owner has an equal and complete right to the use of his land, and to the water which is *in it*. Water, combined with the earth, or passing through it, by percolation, or by filtration, or chemical attraction, has no distinctive character of ownership from the earth itself, not more than the metallic oxides of which the earth is composed. Water, whether moving or motionless *in the earth*, is not, in the eye of the law, distinct from the earth.[1] The laws of its existence and progress, while there, are not uniform, and cannot be known or regulated. It rises to great heights, and moves collaterally, by influences beyond our apprehension. These influences are so secret, changeable, and uncontrollable, we cannot subject them to the regulations of law, nor build upon them a system of rules, as has been done with streams upon the surface. Further, we may say, that, by general consent of mankind, which is to be inferred from the nature of the right itself, each person must be left to enjoy any natural advantage belonging to his own land; and water, appearing and standing, either naturally or by artificial means, but never constituting a running stream, is such a natural advantage; were it otherwise, one man, by sinking a well, though comparatively unimportant, might prevent the sinking of other wells, and the improvement of the neighborhood, by draining marshes, &c., and even the opening of mines of metal or coal; as the water might not percolate with the same freeness or abundance as before. Besides, no man is bound to know that his neighbor's well is supplied by water percolating his own soil; and he ought not, therefore, to be held to lose his rights by such continued enjoyment. He cannot know that the first well requires any other than the natural and common use of water under the surface; nor can he know from whence the water comes; nor by what means it appears in one place or the other; nor which of the persons who first or afterwards opens the earth, encroaches upon the right of the other. The law has not yet extended beyond *open running* streams. Nor can any light be obtained from the law of surface streams. Such streams are recognized as private property; and their use is

[1] [Wilson *v.* New Bedford, 108 Mass. 265.]

regulated by principles of obvious equity and necessity. Their *nature* is defined; their *progress* over the surface *seen*, and *known* and *uniform*. They are not in the secret places of the earth and a part of it; nor is there any secrecy in the influences which move them. As soon as they appear and pass over the surface, they assume a distinct character, and are subject to the law of gravitation. The purchaser of land knows what he purchases, and what control he can exercise over such a stream, and what are the rights of those above or below him."[1]]

[§ 114 *h*. The case next to be considered is that of Ellis *v*. Duncan,[2] which was lately decided in New York, and in which the water affected was that of a natural spring, which was the head and source of a stream of water running upon the surface. The object of the party by whose acts the spring was affected, was in part to cultivate his farm by draining it, and in part to open and work a quarry upon it, and not at all to use the subsurface water upon his farm. The Court held that "the owner of a farm may dig a ditch to drain his land, or open and work a quarry upon it, although by so doing he intercepts one of the underground sources of a *spring* on his neighbor's land, which supplies a small *stream* of water flowing partly through the land of each, and thereby diminishes the natural supply of water, to the injury of the adjoining proprietor." "The rule that a man has a right to the free and absolute use of his property, so long as he does not directly invade that of his neighbor, or consequentially injure his perceptible and clearly defined rights, is applicable to the interruption of the subsurface supplies of a stream, by the owner of the soil; and the damage resulting from such an interruption is not the subject of legal redress." Strong J., delivering the opinion of the Court in the case, says, "There can be no doubt of the correctness of the injunction, *Sic utere tuo ut alienum non lœdas;* but I have frequently had occasion to remark that it refers to such injuries only as the law will redress, and not to the large class which are usually denominated *damnum absque injuria.*"[3]]

[§ 114 *i*. This subject received a very thorough, careful, and

[1] [Similar views were expressed by the same learned Judge, in Brown *v*. Illius, 25 Conn. 593, 594.]

[2] [Ellis *v*. Duncan, 21 Barb. 230.]

[3] [The case of Ellis *v*. Duncan is cited to the same general doctrine by Denio C.J., in Goodale *v*. Tuttle, 29 N.Y. 466.]

clear exposition by the Supreme Court in a late case in Pennsylvania,[1] in which it appeared that a mining company, in the course of necessary operations in mining minerals from their own land, interrupted the percolations which supplied a spring on an adjacent tract, and this was the subject of the action by the owner of the spring. It was maintained, as a general principle, that where a spring of water, issuing from the ground in the land of a lower proprietor, depends for its supply upon percolations through the land of the owner above, and in the use of the land for mining or other lawful purposes, the spring is destroyed, such owner above is not liable for the damages thus done, unless the injury was caused by malice or negligence. The Court, by Lewis C.J., say, that if a claim against the upper owner could be sustained under such circumstances, it "would amount to a total abrogation of the right of property." "Percolations spread in every direction through the earth, and it is impossible to avoid disturbing them without relinquishing the necessary enjoyment of the land. Accordingly the law has never gone so far as to recognize in one man a right to convert another's farm to his own use, for the purpose of a filter. No man could dig a cellar, or a well, or build a house on his own land, because these operations necessarily interrupt the filtrations through the earth. Nor could he cut down the forests and clear his land for the purposes of husbandry, because the evaporation which would be caused by exposing the soil to the sun and air would inevitably diminish, to some extent, the supply of water which would otherwise filter through it. He could not even turn a furrow for agricultural purposes, because this would partially produce the same result. Even if this right were admitted to exist, the difficulty in ascertaining the fact of its violation, as well as the extent of it, would be insurmountable. The Roman law, founded upon an enlightened consideration of the rights of property, declared that a man may dig for water on his own ground, and if he should thereby drain a well or spring in his neighbor's ground, he would be liable to no action for damages on that score.[2] This principle of the Civil

[1] [Wheatley *v.* Baugh, 25 Penn. St. 528, 532.]

[2] [Domat. § 1581; Pardessus, Traité des Servitudes, § 76; Dig. 39, 2, 24, 12; Dig. 39, 3; 1, 12; Dig. 39, 2, 26; Dig. 39, 3, 21.]

Law is also the recognized doctrine of the Common Law."[1] "Neither the Civil Law nor the Common Law permits a man to be deprived of a well or stream of water for the mere gratification of malice.[2] The reason is, that water, like air, is of such a nature that no one can have an exclusive right in it. In the process of evaporation and condensation, it is sent in refreshing showers, all over the earth. In its descent to the ocean, it necessarily passes from one to the other, and is intended for the benefit of all." The owner of land on which a spring issues from the earth, has a perfect right to it against all the world, except those through whose land it comes. He has even a right to it, as against them, until it comes in conflict with the enjoyment of their own property. Strangers cannot destroy it, even though it be derived from lands which do not belong to the owner of the spring. Even a railroad corporation, armed by law with the eminent domain, and having power to take private property for the construction of its road, is answerable to the owner of a spring for destroying it, although its destruction be caused by excavations on the land of an adjacent proprietor.[3] But, while the Court in that case held that the corporation was liable, on the ground that the destruction of the spring was not required for the purposes of the owner of the land through which the excavation was made, the principle was fully recognized that each proprietor has a right to make a proper use of his own land, and that sinking a well upon it is such proper use; and if the water, by its natural current, flows from one to the other, and a loss arises, it is *damnum absque injuria*.[4]]

[[1] Burg *v.* Pope, 1 Cro. Eliz. 118; Parker *v.* Foote, 19 Wend. 309; Hoy *v.* Sterrett, 2 Watts, 331; Greenleaf *v.* Francis, 18 Pick. 121; Acton *v.* Blundell, 12 M. & W. 118.]

[2] [In Haldeman *v.* Bruckhardt, 45 Penn. St. 518, Strong J. said, in regard to the case of Wheatley *v.* Baugh, "In that case it was ruled that where a spring depends for its supply upon filtrations or percolations of water through the land of an owner above, and in the use of the land for mining and other lawful purposes, the spring is destroyed, such owner is not liable for the damages thus caused to the proprietors of the spring, unless the injury was caused by malice or negligence. To such percolations or filtrations, then, the inferior owner has no rights. This was all that was necessary to the decision of the case."]

[3] [Parker *v.* The Boston & Maine R.R. Co., 3 Cush. 107.]

[4] [Parker *v.* The Boston & Maine R.R. Co., 3 Cush. 107. In this case it appeared that, in consequence of the excavation made for a railroad, the water of a well on an estate adjoining, but not crossed by the railroad, was drawn off, and the well thereby rendered dry and useless, and it was held that the owner of such estate was entitled to recover damages therefor, in the same manner as for land, &c., taken for the railroad. But see New Albany Railroad *v.* Peterson, 14 Ind. 112.]

[§ 114 *j*. Cases in which the land-owner, by positive acts, fouls, poisons, or corrupts the waters which percolate from his lands to those of his neighbor, have been supposed to be clearly distinguishable from those we have just been considering, and to depend upon different principles.[1] In a recent English case,[2] it appeared that the plaintiff was the owner of an ancient mill, and lands adjoining, and manufactured paper therein; a business which had been carried on there from time immemorial. The mill and lands were situate in a valley at the foot of a range of hills sloping towards and terminating in a tall precipitous rock abutting upon them. Inside this rock, and at an elevation of a few feet above the lands, was, from time immemorial, a natural cavern, and the water produced by the rain-fall on a portion of the hills ran by underground passages into it, and, after traversing the floor of the cavern in a defined stream, flowed by an underground passage out of the cavern into an open natural basin in the lands of the plaintiff, and from thence in an open and defined stream to the mill in a pure and unpolluted state. Recently the defendant became the possessor and occupier of land and premises on the summit of the hills, at a higher elevation than the cavern, and worked on them a machinery for extracting from the soil minute particles of lead intermixed with it. In working this he constructed "buddles," or circular pits, in the surface of the ground, into which water was brought through artificial cuts. From these buddles polluted water was discharged into drains communicating with two "swallets," or natural rents existing from time immemorial in the limestone rock of the hills, and having an underground passage for water communicating with an outlet, at which the water escaped in an open stream at their foot. The water-passages from these two swallets communicated with the cavern; through which the polluted water flowed, and from thence mingled with the stream flowing through the cavern into the basin, and thence to the plaintiff's lands and mill, whereby the water was fouled. It was held, that the plaintiff was entitled to recover of the defendant for fouling the stream. Cockburn C.J. said, "This case falls under that class of cases

1 [See Frazier *v.* Brown, 12 Ohio St. 294, 312; 3 Am. Law Reg. N.S. 240, in note.]

2 [Hodgkinson *v.* Ennor, 4 B. & S. 229.]

to which the maxim, *Sic utere tuo ut alienum non lædas* is applicable. . . . The right of the plaintiff cannot be disputed, for it is found that he and those whom he represents have always had a right to have the water in question flow in its accustomed course and purity. Then, by the act of the defendant, that water has been polluted and fouled; which being once an ascertained fact, it makes no difference that, by the manner in which the defendant discharges the polluted water from his works, it goes over the surface of the buddles, from whence it flows a certain distance over the limestone formation before it arrives at the plaintiff's watercourse." Blackburn J. said, "Are you not bound, when digging in your own land, to take care not to send, in consequence of it, foul water or bad smells to the land of your neighbor?" The counsel "is correct in saying that the defendant had a right to use the water on his own land, but then in doing so he had to dispose of the poisoned and corrupted water; and I take the law to be as stated in Tenant *v.* Goldwin,[1] that you must not injure the property of your neighbor, and consequently, if filth is created on any man's land, then, in the quaint language of the report in Salk. 361, 'he whose dirt it is, must keep it that it may not trespass.' Now here, by a roundabout course of going through drains and swallets, the foul water was not kept by the defendant so that it should not trespass, in consequence of which the water which the plaintiff had a right to have pure and unpolluted when it came into his possession and on his property, was corrupted. This is both *damnum* and *injuria*." Mellor J.: "There is a great distinction between the abstraction of water before it becomes the property of the plaintiff, and sending polluted water into water to which he is entitled."[2]]

[1] [Tenant *v.* Goldwin, 2 Ld. Ray. 1089; Salk. 21, 360; 6 Mod. 311; Holt, 500.]

[2] [See 3 Am. Law Reg. N.S. 240, in note. The case of Brown *v.* Illius, 25 Conn. 583, seems to conflict. In this case Storrs C.J. remarked, "The Court very properly said to the jury, that if the injury to the well of the plaintiffs was caused by the noxious matter placed by the defendant on his own land, penetrating the earth and corrupting the underground watercourse that supplied the well, and only in that mode, it is difficult to see how the defendant could be guilty of negligence in producing the injury, since he had no means of knowing that the watercourse was there." The verdict was for the plaintiff, and a motion for a new trial was refused by all the Judges; but Ellsworth J., in a dissenting opinion upon the grounds for not allowing the motion, said, "Subterraneous currents, as something different from water mixed with and a part of the earth itself, not passing in currents, but by percolation or chemical attraction, have very little to do with

[§ 114 *k*. Questions have often arisen in regard to the conduct and management of underground waters, collected by

the merits of this case, which is one of filth and poison infused into land and the water in it, through neglect, to the injury of others." See Wood *v.* Waud, 3 Exch. 748; Goodrich *v.* Burbank, 97 Mass. 22. It was held in Ball *v.* Nye, 99 Mass. 582, that one who maintains a vault so that with his knowledge filthy water habitually filters from it, whether above or below the surface of the ground, into land of a neighbor, where it injures a cellar and a well, is liable in damages for the injury, without other proof of negligence. See Baird *v.* Williamson, 15 C.B. N.S. 376; Wormersley *v.* Church, 17 L.T. N.S. 190. In Pixley *v.* Clark, 35 N.Y. 520, the same principle was held in regard to water which percolates through the banks of a reservoir created by erecting a dam across a stream, and damages the plaintiff's land. Rylands *v.* Fletcher, L.R. 3 H.L. 330, affirming the decision of the Exchequer Chamber, states the same principle, in application to a reservoir created artificially, from which the water flowed through some passages apparently filled up, and long disused, into the plaintiff's mine. Lord Cranworth, in delivering his opinion, said, "If a person brings or accumulates on his land any thing which, if it should escape, may cause damage to his neighbor, he does so at his peril. If it does escape and cause damage, he is responsible, however careful he may have been, and whatever precautions he may have taken, to prevent damage." He distinguishes between natural percolation and that which is caused artificially. On this point he says, "If water naturally rising in the defendant's land had by percolation found its way down to the plaintiff's mine through the old workings, and so had impeded his operations, that would not have afforded him any ground of complaint." "But that is not the real state of the case. The defendants, in order to effect an object of their own, brought on to their land, or on to land which for this purpose may be treated as being theirs, a large accumulated mass of water, and stored it up in a reservoir. The consequence of this was damage to the plaintiff; and for that damage, however skilfully and carefully the accumulation was made, the defendants, according to the principles and authorities to which I have adverted, were certainly responsible." Wilson *v.* New Bedford, 108 Mass. 265, 266; Baird *v.* Williamson, 15 C.B. N.S. 376. Rylands *v.* Fletcher, supra, was distinguished in Nichols *v.* Marsland, 23 W. R. (Exch.) 693; 2 Cent. Law Journ. (St. Louis) 523; and see Brown *v.* Collins, 53 N.H. 442. The rule, announced in Rylands *v.* Fletcher, was carried still farther in the late case of Humphries *v.* Cousins, 2 C.P. Div. 239, wherein it appeared that the plaintiff and defendant were respectively tenants and occupiers of adjoining houses. An old drain which commenced on the defendant's premises and received his sewage, ran under and received the sewage of several other houses, turned back through the defendant's premises, ran under the plaintiff's cellar and then away to a public sewer. The fact of the drain turning back through his premises was unknown to the defendant; nor was he aware that it was out of repair; but by reason of the defective state of the return drain under the defendant's premises, from age and want of repair, the water and sewage from it flowed through the party wall into the plaintiff's premises, and caused the damage complained of. The jury found that the defective state of the drain was not attributable to any negligence of the defendant. The Court decided that the defendant was liable for the damage thus done to the plaintiff, on the ground that it was the defendant's duty to keep the sewage which he himself was bound to receive, from passing from his own premises to the plaintiff's premises otherwise than along the old accustomed channel, and that this duty was independent of negligence on his part, and independent of his knowledge or ignorance of the existence of the drain. Denman J. said, "It is to be observed at the outset that the water and sewage which injured the plaintiff came on to

percolation or otherwise, in mining operations. The plaintiff and defendant occupied collieries adjoining to each other. The defendant's predecessor, with whom, however, the defendant had no privity, made holes, called "thyrlings," in a barrier of coal which separated the collieries. This was trespass on the part of the predecessor of the defendant, as the barrier belonged to the plaintiff. The defendant, for the purpose of obtaining the coal, and so working his mine in the manner most advantageous to himself, broke down a seam of coal of his own, in consequence of which the water flowed into the plaintiff's mine through the "thyrlings." The cases of Tenant *v.* Goldwin,[1] Rosewell *v.* Prior,[2] and Haward *v.* Bankes,[3] were cited for the plaintiff, to show that the defendant lay under an obligation of common right to have kept this barrier in so sound a condition as to have prevented the grievances complained of. But Tenant *v.* Goldwin was distinguished, for that was a case in which the defendant's duty to repair a house and office adjoining the premises of the plaintiff came in ques-

the defendant's land by an artificial drain, made for the convenience of the defendant and the other persons whose houses were higher up. Bearing this in mind, it appears to us that it is incumbent on the defendant to show what right he had to allow the filth brought artificially on his land to escape on to the land of the plaintiff. The *primâ facie* right of every occupier of a piece of land is, to enjoy that land free from all invasion of filth or other matter coming from any artificial structure on land adjoining. This right of every occupier of land is an incident of possession, and does not depend on the acts or omissions of other people; it is independent of what they may know or may not know of the state of their own property, and independent of the care or want of care which they may take of it. In the present case the plaintiff was bound to receive sewage from the defendant's land through the old drain, but not otherwise; he was not bound to receive it through the surrounding earth or party-wall, through which in fact it came. Further, as the plaintiff was the occupier of the servient tenement, he was clearly not bound to repair the drain on any of the dominant tenements. The plaintiff's rights, therefore, have been infringed, and the loss he has sustained cannot be said to be *damnum absque injuria*. But the question still remains, has the defendant infringed those rights, and is he the person liable for the infringement? We are of opinion that, as between the plaintiff and the defendant, it was the defendant's duty to keep the sewage which he was himself bound to receive, from passing from his own premises to the plaintiff's premises, otherwise than along the old accustomed channel. That duty, like its correlative right, is independent of negligence on the part of the defendant, and independent of his knowledge or ignorance of the existence of the drain. The duty of the defendant himself to receive the sewage evidently did not depend on such knowledge; and the fact that he unknowingly received it affords no justification for allowing it to escape in a manner in which he had no right to let it pass."]

[1] [2 Ld. Ray. 1089.]

[2] [1 Ld. Ray. 713.]

[3] [2 Burr. 1113.]

tion. Rosewell *v.* Prior was an action on the case for a nuisance, but mines are not a nuisance. Therefore the Court held, that no duty, either special or general, lay on the defendant to do this repair, and judgment was accordingly given in his favor.[1] This is different from wilfully allowing a com-

[1] [Smith *v.* Kenrick, 7 C.B. 515. It seems from this case to be considered that it is the right of each of the owners of adjoining mines, where neither mine is subject to any servitude to the other, to work his own mine in the manner which he deems most convenient and beneficial to himself, although the natural consequence may be that some prejudice will accrue to the owner of the adjoining mine; so long as such prejudice does not arise from the negligent or malicious conduct of his neighbor. Cresswell J. said, "The water is a sort of common enemy, against which each man must defend himself. And this is in accordance with the Civil Law, by which it was considered that land on a lower level owed a natural servitude to that on a higher, in respect of receiving, without claim to compensation, the water naturally flowing down to it." 7 C.B. 566; Dig. lib. 39, tit. III. 1, 22. See Ballacorkish &c. Company *v.* Harrison, L.R. 5 P.C. 49, 63. In Carstairs *v.* Taylor, L.R. 6 Exch. 217, it appeared that the plaintiff hired of the defendant the ground-floor of a warehouse, the upper part of which was occupied by the defendant himself. The water from the roof was collected by gutters into a box, from which it was discharged by a pipe into the drains. A hole was made in the box by a rat, through which the water entered the warehouse and wet the plaintiff's goods. The defendant had used reasonable care in examining and seeing to the security of the gutters and the box. In an action by the plaintiff against the defendant for the damage so caused, it was held that the defendant was not liable either on the ground of an implied contract, or on the ground that he had brought the water to the place from which it entered the warehouse. In the more recent case of Ross *v.* Fedden, L.R. 7 Q.B. 661, it appeared that the plaintiff occupied for business purposes the ground-floor, and the defendants the second floor of the same house, respectively as tenants from year to year. There was a water-closet on the defendant's premises to which they alone had access, and of which they alone had the use. After their respective premises had been closed on a Saturday evening, water percolated from the water-closet through the first floor to the plaintiff's premises and caused damage to his stock in trade. The overflow of the water was owing to the valve of the supply pipe to the pan having got out of order and failed to close, and the waste pipe being choked with paper. The defects could not be detected without examination, and the defendants did not know of them and were guilty of no negligence; it was held that there was no obligation on the defendants to keep in the water at their peril, and that they were not liable to the plaintiff for the damage. These cases were distinguished from that of Fletcher *v.* Rylands, L.R. 1 Exch. 265; 3 H. & C. 774; L.R. 3 H.L. 330, in which it was announced as a general principle that if the owner of land brings upon it any thing which would not usually come upon it, and which is in itself dangerous, and may become mischievous if not kept under proper control, though in so doing he may act without personal wilfulness or negligence, he will be liable for any mischief thereby occasioned. In this case, it appeared that the plaintiff was the lessee of mines, and the defendant was the owner of a mill standing on land adjoining that under which the mines were worked. The defendant employed competent persons, an engineer and a contractor, to construct for himself a reservoir. The plaintiff had worked his mines up to a spot where there were certain old passages of disused mines; these passages were connected with vertical shafts which communicated with the land

munication into an adjoining mine to remain open, so as to suffer water to flow through it, in order to compel other parties

above, and which had also been out of use for years, and were apparently filled with marl and the earth of the surrounding land. No care was taken by the engineer or the contractor to block up these shafts, and shortly after water had been introduced into the reservoir it broke through some of the shafts, flowed through the old passages and flooded the plaintiff's mine; and it was held that the plaintiff was entitled to recover of the defendant for this injury. It was, however, admitted in the case, that where the owner of land, without wilfulness or negligence, uses his land in the ordinary manner of its use, though mischief should thereby be occasioned to his neighbor, he will not be liable in damages. Lord Cairns L.C. said, "The defendants, treating them as the owners or occupiers of the close on which the reservoir was constructed, might lawfully have used that close for any purpose for which it might in the ordinary course of the enjoyment of land be used; and if, in what I may term the natural use of that land, there had been any accumulation of water, either on the surface or underground, and if, by the operation of the laws of nature, that accumulation of water had passed off into the close occupied by the plaintiff, the plaintiff could not have complained that that result had taken place. If he had desired to guard himself against it, it would have lain upon him to have done so, by leaving, or by interposing, some barrier between his close and the close of the defendants in order to have prevented that operation of the laws of nature." "On the other hand, if the defendants, not stopping at the natural use of their close, had desired to use it for any purpose which I may term a non-natural use, for the purpose of introducing into the close that which in its natural condition was not in or upon it, for the purpose of introducing water, either above or below ground, in quantities and in a manner not the result of any work or operation on or under the land; and if in consequence of their doing so, or in consequence of any imperfection in the mode of their doing so, the water came to escape and to pass off into the close of the plaintiff, — then it appears to me that that which the defendants were doing, they were doing at their own peril, and if, in the course of their doing it, the evil arose to which I have referred, the evil, namely, of the escape of the water, and its passing away to the close of the plaintiff and injuring the plaintiff, then for the consequence of that, in my opinion, the defendants would be liable. As the case of Smith *v.* Kenrick, supra, is an illustration of the first principle to which I have referred, so also the second principle to which I have referred is well illustrated by another case in the same court, the case of Baird *v.* Williamson, 15 C.B. N.S. 317." In Baird *v.* Williamson, supra, it was decided that the owner of a mine at a higher level than an adjoining mine has a right to work the whole of his mine in the usual and proper manner for the purpose of getting out the minerals in any part of his mine; and he is not liable for any water which flows by gravitation into such adjoining mine from works so conducted. But he has no right by pumping or otherwise to be an active agent in sending water from his mine into the adjoining mine. Erle C.J. said, "The defendants, as occupiers of the higher mine, have no right to be active agents in sending water into the lower mine. The plaintiffs, as occupiers of the lower mine, are subject to no servitude of receiving water conducted by man from the higher mine. Each mine-owner has all rights of property in his mine, and, among them, the right to get all minerals therefrom, provided he works with skill and in the usual manner. And if, while the occupier of a higher mine exercises that right, nature causes water to flow to a lower mine, he is not responsible for this operation of nature. If the owner of the lower mine intends to guard against this operation, he must leave a barrier at the upper part of his mine, to bay back the water of his higher

to close such communication. A tenant of a mine was restrained on motion from allowing such an opening.[1] So it differs from a case where one for his own purposes brings upon his land, and collects and keeps there, a quantity of water likely to do mischief, if it escapes. The defendants constructed a reservoir on land separated from the plaintiff's colliery by intervening land; mines under the site of the reservoir, and under part of the intervening land, had been formerly worked, and the plaintiff had, by workings lawfully made in his own colliery and in the intervening land, opened an underground communication between his own colliery and the old workings under the reservoir. It was not known to the defendants, nor to any person employed by them in the construction of the reservoir, that such communication existed, or that there were any old workings under the site of the reservoir, and the defendants were not personally guilty of any negligence; but, in fact, the reservoir was constructed over five old shafts, leading down to the workings; and proper care and skill were not used by the persons employed by the defendants to provide for the sufficiency of the reservoir with reference to these shafts. The consequence was, that the

neighbor. The law imposing these regulations for the enjoyment of somewhat conflicting interests, does not authorize the occupier of the higher mine to interfere with the gravitation of the water, so as to make it more injurious to the lower mine or advantageous to himself." In a still later case (Nichols *v.* Marsland, L.R. 10 Exch. 255), it appeared that the defendant's land had upon it artificial pools containing large quantities of water. These pools had been formed by damming up with artificial embankments a natural stream which rose above the defendant's land, and flowed through it, and which was allowed to escape from the pools successively by weirs into its original course. An extraordinary rainfall caused the stream and the water in the pools to swell so that the artificial embankments were carried away by the pressure, and the water in the pools, being thus suddenly loosed, rushed down the course of the stream and injured the plaintiff's adjoining property. The plaintiff having brought an action against the defendant for damages, the jury found that there was no negligence in the construction or maintenance of the works, that the rainfall was most excessive, and amounted to *vis major*. It was held that the action could not be maintained. The principle stated was, that one who stores water on his own land, and uses all reasonable care to keep it safely there, is not liable to an action for an escape of the water which injures his neighbor, if the escape be caused by an agent beyond his control, such as a storm, which amounts to *vis major*, or the act of God, in the sense that it is practically, though not physically, impossible to resist it. Fletcher *v.* Rylands, supra, was distinguished. This case was again noticed and relied upon in Smith *v.* Fletcher, L.R. 7 Exch. 305; and again distinguished in s.c. L.R. 9 Exch. 64.]

[1] [Earl of Mexborough *v.* Bower, 7 Beav. 127.]

reservoir, when filled with water, burst into the shafts, the water flowed down through them into the old workings, and thence into the plaintiff's mine, and there did the mischief complained of. Judgment was rendered for the plaintiff.[1] Blackburn J. said, "We think the true rule of law is, that the person who for his own purposes brings on his lands and collects and keeps there any thing likely to do mischief if it escapes, must keep it in at his peril, and if he does not do so, is *primâ facie* answerable for all the damage which is the natural consequence of its escape. He can excuse himself by showing that the escape was owing to the plaintiff's default; or perhaps that the escape was the consequence of *vis major*, or the act of God. But as nothing of this sort exists here, it is unnecessary to inquire what excuse would be sufficient. The general rule, as above stated, seems on principle just. The person whose grass or corn is eaten down by the escaping cattle of his neighbor, or whose mine is flooded by the water from his neighbor's reservoir, or whose cellar is invaded by the filth of his neighbor's privy, or whose habitation is made unhealthy by the fumes and noisome vapors of his neighbor's alkali works, is damnified without any fault of his own; and it seems but reasonable and just that the neighbor, who has brought something on his own property which was not naturally there, harmless to others so long as it is confined to his own property, but which he knows to be mischievous if it gets on his neighbor's, should be obliged to make good the damage which ensues if he does not succeed in confining it to his own property. But for his act in bringing it there no mischief could have accrued, and it seems but just that he should at his peril keep it there so that no mischief may accrue, or answer for the natural and anticipated consequences. And upon authority, this, we think, is established to be law, whether the things so brought be beasts, or water, or filth, or stenches."[2]]

[1] [Fletcher *v.* Rylands, L.R. 1 Exch. 265; s.c. 3 H.L. 330.]

[2] [An action was brought on the case for damage done to the plaintiff's colliery. The defendant had caused great quantities of water to be conveyed through other collieries into that of the plaintiff, and this he had done in his own colliery within his own soil; and although there was much discussion upon the debated question, whether trespass or case were the proper remedy, it was not doubted but that the action lay for the damage sustained; and, in effect, the plaintiff was permitted to enter up his judgment. Haward *v.* Bankes, 2 Burr. 1113.]

[§ 114 *l*. The question has been raised and discussed in several of the cases cited, whether a land-owner, who, by acts done upon his own ground, has intercepted underground waters, and prevented them from percolating into another land-owner's well, or has actually abstracted water from such well, will be liable therefor, in consequence of being actuated in his operations by *malicious motives*. It will be observed, however, that in no one of these cases has a land-owner been held liable for such acts in any court of last resort, merely upon this ground. In Greenleaf *v*. Francis,[1] the facts of which have already been stated and the opinion quoted,[2] Morton J. instructed the jury that if the defendant dug the well where he did upon his own land, for the purpose of injuring the plaintiff, and not for the purpose of obtaining water for his own use, he was liable in the action; but if he thus dug his well, for the purpose of accommodating himself with water, he was not liable for so doing, even if he at the same time entertained hostility towards the plaintiff and a desire to injure her, and these feelings were thereby gratified. But the verdict was in favor of the defendant; and the full Court, upon the plaintiff's exceptions, were not called upon to determine whether the defendant would have been liable, if he had acted merely from malicious motives. The full Court did, however, say that the rights of the defendant to dig a well on his own land should not be exercised from mere malice. In Wheatley *v*. Baugh,[3] Lewis C.J. cites Greenleaf *v*. Francis to this point, and adds, "Neither the Civil nor the Common Law permits a man to be deprived of a well or spring or stream of water for the mere gratification of malice." "If it could be shown that any distinct watercourse leading to the spring had been cut off or diverted, and it should also appear that it could have been preserved without material detriment to the owner of the land through which it flowed, the destruction of it might be attributed to malice or negligence. In that case the law would furnish redress, because the injury would be unjustifiable." Here it is evident the learned Judge was not referring to mere percolating waters, but to a distinct watercourse. Besides, the determination of the case was in favor of the defendant, and the Court were not required to decide

[1] [Greenleaf *v*. Francis, 18 Pick. 117.]
[2] [Ante, § 113.]
[3] [Wheatley *v*. Baugh, 25 Penn. St. 528.]

the law upon the point. In Haldeman *v.* Bruckhardt[1] the Court advert to the point, but say "we are constrained to say we see no evidence of malice or negligence on the part of the defendants. Mining on their own land, as they did, was no more than the exercise of their legal rights." In Roath *v.* Driscoll,[2] which was a bill in chancery, complaining of injury to the plaintiff, in consequence of a diversion by the defendant of water percolating through the defendant's land so as to prevent its supplying the plaintiff's reservoir, the Court note the fact, which was found in the case, that the defendant was acting with honest motives and without any design unnecessarily to injure the plaintiff; but there is nothing in the opinion of the Court to indicate that this circumstance had any effect on the decision, or that the decision would have been different, if that fact had been otherwise.]

[§ 114 *m.* But it must be admitted that it is the rule of the Civil Law, that the diversion or abstraction must be made in good faith, and not for the mere purpose of doing injury to the adjoining proprietor; and in many of the cases decided under the Common Law, in which the point has been referred to, the good faith of the party causing the diversion or abstraction, though not necessarily controlling the decision, has been treated as an important matter of consideration, and much stress laid upon it. The words of the rule in the Civil Law have already been given.[3] Lord Wensleydale quotes them in Chasemore *v.* Richards,[4] and adds, "Every man, therefore, had a right to the natural advantages of his land; but those advantages were to be obtained subject to the principle, *Sic utere tuo ut alienum non lædas*, and the Civil Law (and the law of Scotland did the same) forbade an act which was otherwise lawful, if done *animo vicini nocendi.*" "It seemed to him that the question was whether the defendant exercised his right of enjoying the subterranean water in a reasonable manner." This language was, however, used by him in the way of partial dissent from the judgment given in that case.]

[§ 114 *n.* But in Chatfield *v.* Wilson[5] the point came up directly for a decision. Poland J. had instructed the jury on

[1] [Haldeman *v.* Bruckhardt, 45 Penn. St. 521.]

[2] [Roath *v.* Driscoll, 20 Conn. 533.]

[3] [Ante, § 114.]

[4] [Chasemore *v.* Richards, 5 H. & N. 990; 7 H.L. Cas. 349.]

[5] [Chatfield *v.* Wilson, 28 Vt. 49.]

the trial of the case that "if they found that the acts of the defendant did prevent the usual and natural flow of the water, in or under the ground, from the defendant's soil to the plaintiff's, and that these acts were done by the defendant solely with the purpose of injuring the plaintiff, and depriving him of water, and not with any purpose of usefulness to himself, then he would be liable to the plaintiff for such damages as he thereby sustained." The jury found a verdict for the plaintiff, and the defendant excepted. Upon argument of the exceptions, the Court ordered a new trial for misdirection, on the ground that the act of the defendant in preventing the flow or escape of water, in or under ground, from his own to the plaintiff's land was legal in itself, and violated no right of the plaintiff, and could not be made actionable on account of the motive which induced it. Bennett J. characterized the remark of Putnam J. in Greenleaf *v.* Francis, that "the rights of the defendant should not be exercised from mere malice," as an *obiter dictum*, no such point being in judgment; "the case found, that the defendant had dug his well in that place on his land where it was most convenient for him; and, we think, as applied to a case like the one then at bar, and the one now before us, the position was unsound, and against principle and authority."[1] The case of Chatfield *v.* Wilson seems to go the full extent of holding that the act of detaining or diverting subsurface percolating waters from an adjoining proprietor, gives no right of action, though the act be one, under the circumstances, of *unmixed* malice.[2] In Frazier *v.* Brown[3] the Court raise, but do not decide, the point, whether an action would lie for such an act done from mere malice, but

[1] [Chatfield *v.* Wilson, 28 Vt. 57, 58. In this case Bennett J. said, "It may be laid down as a position not to be controverted, that an act, legal in itself, violating no right, cannot be made actionable on the ground of the motive which induced it. Such was the case of South Royalton Bank *v.* Suffolk Bank, 27 Vt. 505. If the act is lawful, although it may be prejudicial, it is *damnum absque injuria.* On this point the case of Mahon *v.* Brown, 13 Wend. 261, is a direct authority. There the defendant had built a high fence for the sole purpose of obstructing the lights of his neighbor's house; and it was held, that no action would lie, where the lights were not ancient, and no right had been acquired by grant or user; and that the motive with which the act was done was immaterial. This goes upon the ground that the plaintiff was not injured in a legal right."]

[2] [In Harwood *v.* Benton, 32 Vt. 737, Barrett J., adverting to the case of Chatfield *v.* Wilson, said, "The only criticism that we have heard upon that decision was in respect to excluding the wanton and improper motive as an element in the ground of the defendant's liability."]

[3] [Frazier *v.* Brown, 12 Ohio St. 294, 303.]

reserve it for future consideration, when such a case should arise. This last case arose on demurrer to the plaintiff's declaration, which charged that the defendant being an adjacent owner, and wickedly intending to injure the plaintiff, and to destroy his spring, and the stream of water issuing therefrom, maliciously dug a certain hole on the defendant's own land for that purpose and with that effect. The Court gave judgment for the defendant, on the ground that "for aught that appeared in the declaration, the hole may have been dug for some useful or ornamental purpose, and may also have embraced in its object the malicious design to injure the plaintiff." The Court say, "As an act unlawful in itself, resulting in injury to another, whatever may have been the motive with which it was done, is none the less a subject of legal redress; so the act done, to wit, the *using* of one's own property being lawful in itself, the motive with which it is done, whatever it may be as a matter of conscience, is, in law, a matter of indifference." In Rawstron *v.* Taylor,[1] which involved a question respecting a diversion by the defendant for the purpose of drainage of mere surface waters which would otherwise have come to the land of the plaintiff, Martin B. said, "The proprietor of the soil has, *prima facie*, the right to drain his land; and, unless there is some express authority to show that his motive in so doing affects the question, in my opinion, the motive is altogether immaterial. He is at liberty to get rid of the surface water in any manner that may appear most convenient to him; and I think that no one has a right to interfere with him, and that the object he may have in so doing is quite immaterial." "Unless there is some express authority to show that his motive in so doing affects the question, in my opinion the motive is altogether immaterial."[2]]

[§ 114 *o*. Whichever side the balance of opinion upon the question under consideration may fall, it is quite evident that it is not settled by authority. Whenever settled, it must be upon principles involving the natural rights of property. These rights are based upon two fundamental maxims, one looking to the extent of one's ownership in land, the other to his mode of using it. The time-honored legal maxim, *Cujus est solum, ejus est usque ad cœlum*, has given to the word land, when standing

[1] [Rawstron *v.* Taylor, 11 Exch. 369.] [2] [11 Exch. 378.]

alone, and not otherwise restricted, an extension bringing within its scope every thing which exists naturally, or has been fixed artificially, between the centre of the earth and the confines of the atmosphere; and to this extent the land-owner has an absolute right of property. But inasmuch as every owner or occupier of land may be brought into close proprietary relations with neighbors on all sides of him, it is obvious that he and his neighbors cannot be mutually indifferent to each other's doings. To regulate these relations, the Common Law, otherwise so jealous of interference between the owner and his property, imposes upon him the simple rule, *Sic utere tuo ut alienum non lœdas.* The rights, which spring from the exclusive power, given by Common Law to every possessor of property, of doing what he likes with his own, when modified by the rule last stated, may be conveniently designated *natural rights.* Or, to state the same thing somewhat differently, all which can be enjoyed and practised by neighboring proprietors, each within his own territorial space, without materially affecting the natural state of the other's property, or their respective means of dealing with it, constitutes in the aggregate the *natural rights* of property. Any further restraint, which the owner or occupier may be obliged to put upon the free exercise of his physical power over the land, must rest upon contract either express or implied. Now, it becomes important to know the precise force given by Courts to the maxim, *Sic utere tuo ut alienum non lœdas.* "Confessedly," said Strong J., in Haldeman *v.* Bruckhardt,[1] "the absolute dominion of a proprietor over his land to the centre of the earth is restrained by" it. But what is an injury? The rightful use of one's land may cause damage to another without any legal wrong. An act done, causing damage which the law will redress must not only be hurtful, but wrongful. There must be *damnum et injuria*, an act not merely hurtful, but an infringement of another's right." And in Ellis *v.* Duncan,[2] Strong J. said, "There can be no doubt of the correctness of the injunction, *Sic utere tuo ut alienum non lœdas;* but I have frequently had occasion to remark that it refers to such injuries only as the law will redress, and not to the large class which are usually denominated *damnum absque injuria.*"[3]]

[1] [Haldeman *v.* Bruckhardt, 45 Penn. St. 517.]

[2] [Ellis *v.* Duncan, 21 Barb. 230.]

[3] [Substantially the same is stated in

[§ 114 *p*. To the case of underground waters percolating through the earth, the doctrine of *prescription*, or *presumption of a grant* from lapse of time, can have no application:[1] 1. Because the party against whom the doctrine would have been applied, could not be reasonably required to enter his *caveat* against the appropriation of a thing so hidden and obscure as is percolating underground water; and, 2. Because the appropriation of such waters by an adjoining proprietor is no infringement of his rights, so as to become the subject of legal redress, until such time as he himself has occasion to appropriate them.[2] And in Chasemore *v.* Richards,[3] Lord Wensleydale said "he did not think the principle of prescription could be applied to this case; the true foundation of the right was, that it was an incident to the land *ex jure naturæ*." In Smith *v.* Kenrick,[4] Maule J. said, "As to underground percolations, no rights are gained, because nobody knows any thing about them." In a late case[5] in Connecticut, Ellsworth J. said, "Nothing is gained by a mere continued pre-occupancy of water under the surface." And again, in the case above cited of Chasemore *v.* Richards,[6] Wightman J. said, "There is no case of authority of which I am aware, that can be cited in support of the position contended for by the plaintiff, or in which the right to subterranean percolating water adverse to that of the owner of the soil came in question, except the nisi prius case of Balston *v.* Bensted,[7] and the case of Dickinson *v.* The Grand Junction Canal Company.[8] In the first of these cases, Lord Ellenborough is reported to have expressed an

Chatfield *v.* Wilson, 28 Vt. 57, per Bennett J. See Howell *v.* McCoy, 3 Rawle, 256; Bassett *v.* Salisbury Manufacturing Co., 43 N.H. 569, 577.]

[1] [Wheatley *v.* Baugh, 25 Penn. St. 528. In Swett *v.* Cutts, 50 N.H. 439, 448, Bellows C.J. said, "In respect to water percolating beneath the surface the tendency of the authorities is against acquiring a right by prescription. The use of such water upon one's own land is apparently rightful, and is no such invasion of the rights of the adjoining owner as would enable him to maintain a suit, for it would be impossible to know that he was drawing water from his neighbor's land. In this respect, water that comes to the surface stands on a different footing, and yet in general they are governed by the same rules."]

[2] [Frazier *v.* Brown, 12 Ohio St. 294, 311; Greenleaf *v.* Francis, 18 Pick. 122; Cooper *v.* Barber, 3 Taunt. 99.]

[3] [Chasemore *v.* Richards, 5 H. & N. 982, 990. 7 H.L. Cas. 349.]

[4] [Smith *v.* Kenrick, 7 C.B. 546. See Roath *v.* Driscoll, 20 Conn. 533; Carbrey *v.* Willis, 7 Allen, 367, 368, per Hoar J.]

[5] [Roath *v.* Driscoll, 20 Conn. 541.]

[6] [Chasemore *v.* Richards, 5 H. & N. 984.]

[7] [Balston *v.* Bensted, 1 Campb. 463. See the observations on this case, ante, § 111, note; post, §§ 204, 205, and notes.]

[8] [Dickinson *v.* The Grand Junction Canal Co., 7 Exch. 282.]

opinion that twenty years' enjoyment of the use of water in any manner afforded an exclusive presumption of right. This opinion amounted only to the dictum of an eminent Judge, followed by no decision upon the point, for the case ended in the withdrawal of a juror, and is directly at variance with the judgment of the Court of Exchequer in the other case, upon which the plaintiff relies, of Dickinson *v.* The Grand Junction Canal Company,[1] in which the Court held, 'That the right to have a stream running in its natural course is not by a presumed grant from long acquiescence on the part of the riparian proprietors above and below, but is *ex jure naturæ*, and an incident of the property as much as the right to have the soil itself in its natural state unaltered by the acts of a neighboring proprietor, who cannot dig so as to deprive it of the support of his land.'" — "The case of Dickinson *v.* The Grand Junction Canal Company[2] is an authority to show that a right to water is not by a presumed grant from long acquiescence, but, if it exists at all, is *jure naturæ*, and that the rules of law that regulate the rights of parties to the use of water are hardly, or rather not at all, applicable to the case of waters percolating under ground. In such a case as the present, is any right derived from the use of the water of the river Wandle for upwards of twenty years for working the plaintiff's mill? Any such right against another founded upon length of enjoyment is supposed to have originated in some grant, which is presumed, from the owner of what is sometimes called the servient tenement. But what grant can be presumed in the case of percolating waters, depending upon the quantity of rain falling, or the natural moisture of the soil, and in the absence of any visible means of knowing to what extent, if at all, the enjoyment of the plaintiff's mill would be affected by any water percolating in and out of the defendant's or any other land? The presumption of a grant only arises where the person against whom it is to be raised might have prevented the exercise of the subject of the presumed grant; but how could he prevent or stop the percolation of water? The Court of Exchequer, indeed, in the case of Dickinson *v.* The Grand Junction Canal Company,[3] expressly repudiates the notion that such a right as that in question can be founded on a presumed grant,

[1] [7 Exch. 282.] [2] [7 Exch. 282.] [3] [7 Exch. 282.]

but declares that with respect to running water it is *jure naturæ*. If so, *à fortiori*, the right, if it exists at all, in the case of subterranean percolating water, is *jure naturæ*, and not by presumed grant, and the circumstance of the mill being ancient would, in that case, make no difference."[1] In Wheatley *v.* Baugh,[2] the Court said, "No man by mere prior enjoyment of the advantages of his own land, can establish a servitude upon the land of another." — "No presumption can arise against a party, on the ground of long enjoyment of a privilege by another, until it is shown that the privilege in some measure interfered with the rights of the party whose grant is proposed to be presumed, and that he had a legal right to prevent such enjoyment by proceedings at law. Presumption is when the conduct of the party out of possession cannot be accounted for without presuming a conveyance. Silence or acquiescence, where one is not injured, and has no cause of complaint, can never deprive him of his rights, on the ground of presumption of a grant."[3]]

5. *The Easement of Drip.*

[§ 114 *q*. This subject is sufficiently connected with the running of water to entitle it to be considered in this place. The definition of this servitude given by Kent[4] is that, "by which one man engages to permit the waters flowing from the roof of his neighbor's house to fall on his estate." Though every man is bound so to construct his house as not to overhang his neighbor's property, and construct his roof in such a manner as not to throw the rain-water upon the neighboring land,[5] yet there is authority in our law for the position, that a man may acquire a right by user, to project his wall or eaves over the boundary line of his property, or discharge the rain running from the roof of his house upon the adjoining land. The existence of such a right, both as to the eaves and water droppings, is recognized by the Court of Exchequer in Thomas *v.* Thomas.[6] Where a party builds a house on the line of his lot, with eaves projecting over

1 [See Roath *v.* Driscoll, 20 Conn. 533; Ingraham *v.* Hutchinson, 2 Conn. 584, 597.]

2 [Wheatley *v.* Baugh, 25 Penn. St. 528.]

3 [See Hoy *v.* Sterrett, 2 Watts, 330.]

4 [3 Kent, 436; Burrill Law Dict. verb. Drip.]

5 [11 Hen. VII. *f.* 257; Com. Dig. Action on the Case for a nuisance, A.]

6 [2 Cr. M. & Ros. 34.]

the adjoining lot, so as to throw thereon the water from the roof, it is a manifest encroachment upon, and appropriation of, such lot, to the extent, at least, of the projection; and twenty years' acquiescence, by the owner of the adjacent lot, in this encroachment, is sufficient to lay the foundation for presuming a grant of the right so to use it.[1] So where the eaves of the defendant's building came within about two feet of a dwelling-house, erected by the plaintiff upon his adjacent lot, and owing to a want of suitable repairs to the gutter of the defendant's building, the water from his roof fell between the buildings, and by percolation found its way into the plaintiff's cellar, through the wall, to the injury of his wall and the lower timbers of his house; it was held, that an action would lie, although it did not appear whether the water from the defendant's roof actually fell upon his own roof, or not.[2]]

[§ 114 *r*. There are ancient decisions, recognizing the same easement, in the case of a discharge of water on the neighboring land by means of a gutter or leaden pipe.[3] "If a man hath a sue, that is to say, a spout, above his house, by which the water used to fall from his house, and another levies a house paramount the spout, so that the water cannot fall as it was wont, but falls on the walls of the house, by which the timber of the house perishes, this is a nuisance."[4] Where one had a right to enter the yard of another, and he fixed there a water-spout, by which the rain fell upon the land of the plaintiff, although there was some dispute as to the form of the action, the right to sue was clearly admitted. A man might have a right for the rain-water to fall from the eaves of his house into a yard belonging to another person, and yet cannot justify putting up a spout, and thus collecting the water in a larger body to fall into that yard.[5] But "the discharges of an eave-spout, or the drainage of lands or

[1] [Cherry *v.* Stein, 11 Md. 1; Fay *v.* Prentice, 1 C.B. 828. See Tucker *v.* Newman, 11 Ad. & Ell. 40; Bellows *v.* Sackett, 15 Barb. 96; Carbrey *v.* Willis, 7 Allen, 370; Bloch *v.* Pfaff, 101 Mass. 539; Swett *v.* Cutts, 50 N.H. 439, 448.]

[2] [Bellows *v.* Sackett, 15 Barb. 96.]

[3] [Lady Browne's case, cited in Sury *v.* Pigott, Palm. 446; Comyn's Dig., Action on Case for Nuisance, A. Baten's case, 9 Rep. 50, n. (b).]

[4] [Viner, Abr. Nusance 9, 5, citing 18 Ed. III., 22 b; Rolle, Abr. Nusans, 9. In the case of Pyer *v.* Carter, 1 H. & N. 916, there was an easement of both kinds, one for the defendant to have the rain-water flow from his eaves on to the plaintiff's roof, and another for the plaintiff to have such water, together with the water originally falling on his own roof, carried away together by a drain on the defendant's land.]

[5] [Reynolds *v.* Clarke, 2 Ld. Ray. 1399; Woolrych, Law of Waters, 180.]

mines, or any other temporary flow of water, even where positive and artificial measures are necessary to keep up the stream, if continued the requisite time, may give the right to the dominant owner to flow the water upon the land of the servient owner. For the acquiescence in what would be a nuisance, unless done by permission, will, in law, raise a presumption of a grant."[1]]

[§ 114 *s*. These two classes of easements are distinctly recognized by the Civil Law, under the head of Urban Servitudes, "that a man shall receive upon his house or land the *flumen* or *stillicidium* of his neighbor."[2] "The difference," says Vinnius, in his commentary on this passage, "between the *flumen* and the *stillicidium* is this: the latter is the rain falling from the roof by drops; the *flumen* is when it is poured forth in a continuous stream from the lower part of the building. The servitude of receiving the *stillicidium* exists when my neighbor is compelled to receive upon his house the rain-water running from my roof; the servitude of receiving the *flumen*, when he is compelled to receive the same flowing in a channel or conduit, and falling with force on his house."[3] The Civil as well as the English Law, prohibited a man from projecting the wall or roof of his house over the boundary line of his neighbor's land, even though, by spouts, or other means, the fall of water therefrom might be prevented; but a right to do so might be acquired by user; and where such projection did not, in any manner, rest upon the neighbor's soil, it was called *jus projiciendi;* where the projection was merely intended to protect the wall, either by creating shade against the heat of the sun, or keeping off the rain, it was the *jus protegendi.*[4]]

[§ 114 *t*. Besides the servitude above spoken of, consisting in the right to lead off the water from one's house on to the house or ground of one's neighbor, there was in the Civil Law another, consisting in the right to lead off the water from a neighbor's house on to one's own land for the purpose of cleansing or irrigating the same.[5] This latter seems to have received no recognition in the Common Law. In Arkwright *v*. Gell,[6] which

1 [Norton *v*. Valentine, 14 Vt. 246; White *v*. Chapin, 12 Allen, 520; Carbrey *v*. Willis, 7 Allen, 270.]

2 [Gale & Whatley on Easements (ed. 1876), [176], 273.]

3 [1 Kauff. Mackeldey, § 312; Gale & Whatley on Easements (ed. 1876), [176, 177], 274.]

4 [Gale & Whatley on Easements (ed. 1876), [177], 274.]

5 [1 Kauff. Mackeldey, § 312.]

6 [Arkwright *v*. Gell, 5 M. & W. 203, 233. See post, §§ 206, 206 *a*, and notes.]

involved a similar question, Parke B. said, "Several instances were put, in the course of the argument, of cases analogous to the present, in which it could not be contended, for a moment, that any right was acquired. A steam-engine is used by the owner of a mine to drain it, and the water pumped up flows in a channel to the estate of an adjoining land-owner, and is there used for agricultural purposes for twenty years. Is it possible, from the fact of such a user to presume a grant by the owner of the steam-engine of the right to the water in perpetuity, so as to burden himself and the assigns of his mine with the obligation to keep a steam-engine for ever, for the benefit of the land-owner? Or, if the water from the spout of the eaves of a row of houses was to flow into an adjoining yard, and be there used for twenty years by its occupiers for domestic purposes, could it be successfully contended that the owners of the houses had contracted an obligation, not to alter their construction so as to impair the flow of water? Clearly not. In all, the nature of the case distinctly shows that no right is acquired as against the owner of the property from which the course of water takes its origin; though, as between the first and any subsequent appropriator of the watercourse itself, such a right may be acquired." In Wood *v.* Waud,[1] Pollock C.B. said, "The flow of water for twenty years from the eaves of a house could not give a right to the neighbor to insist that the house should not be pulled down or altered, so as to diminish the quantity of water flowing from the roof. The flow of water from a drain, for the purposes of agricultural improvements, for twenty years, could not give a right to the neighbor so as to preclude the proprietor from altering the level of his drains for the greater improvement of the land. The state of circumstances in such cases shows that one party never intended to give, nor the other to enjoy, the use of the stream as a matter of right."[2]]

6. *Of the Injury by Obstructing and Detaining the Water.*

§ 115. An action for the diversion of a watercourse is grounded on the *deprivation* of the water; and hence, if the party com-

[1] [Wood *v.* Waud, 3 Exch. 778. See post, §§ 206, 206 *a;* Greatrex *v.* Hayward, 8 Exch. 291; Rawstron *v.* Taylor, 11 Exch. 369; White *v.* Chapin, 12 Allen, 520, 521; Swett *v.* Cutts, 50 N.H. 439.]

[2] [See Hanson *v.* McCue, 42 Cal. 303.]

plaining is deprived of the water by any other means, the law will interpose. It is as illegal to *detain* the water unreasonably, as it is to *divert* it; for though all persons have an equal right to erect hydraulic works on their own land, yet they must so construct them, and so use the water, that all persons below may participate, without interruption, in the enjoyment of the same water.[1] A mill-owner, for instance, who shuts down his gate, and detains the water for an unreasonable time, and thus deprives others of a fair participation of the benefits of the stream, is answerable in damages.[2] If the owner of an upper site on a watercourse has obstructed the flowing of the water as accustomed to flow, to the injury of an owner below, it is no defence to an action for the obstruction, that the latter has altered his works so as to require more water than was previously needed,

[1] If a body of water runs out of my pond into another's, I have no right to reclaim it. 2 Bla. Com. 18. See also, Arnold *v.* Foot, 12 Wend. 330; Howell *v.* McCoy, 3 Rawle, 256; Hoy *v.* Sterrett, 2 Watts, 327; Twiss *v.* Baldwin, 9 Conn. 291; Van Hoesen *v.* Coventry, 10 Barb. 518; [Alexander *v.* Kerr, 2 Rawle, 83; Merritt *v.* Parker, Coxe, 460; Tillotson *v.* Smith, 32 N.H. 90, 95.] In Sackrider *v.* Beers, 10 John. 241, the opinion of the Court was as follows: "There is no just objection to the recovery of the plaintiffs below. The defendants were answerable in damages for the injury to the plaintiffs in the enjoyment of their mill, by diverting the natural course of the water. The defendants had, no doubt, a right to build a mill on their land; but they must so construct the dam, and so use the water, as not to injure their neighbors below in the enjoyment of the same water, according to its natural course." In Shears *v.* Wood, 7 Moore, 534, the plaintiffs were owners of copper-mills, and the defendant owner of a silk-mill on the same river, but considerably higher up. The latter caused a dam to be erected, which prevented the water from being supplied as usual to the lower mills. The Court said, "It was in fact stated in the declaration, that the water did not run to the plaintiffs' mills as they were accustomed to have it. That is sufficient to show, that it did not come to them at the proper and usual times, or as it ought to have done; and it was proved, that it did not come to their mills in a sufficient quantity, as it formerly used to do. That fact was sufficient to support the plaintiffs' declaration." See Williams *v.* Morland, 2 B. & C. 910. *Sea* water may occasionally, by some changes proceeding from natural and unknown causes, make gradual inroads on parts of a coast which had been free from its waters for centuries. On such occurrences, it has been justly compared to a common enemy, against which every man may defend himself as he can; but this is different from an occasional course of superabundant inland water flowing in the same direction whenever the occasion happens, and the ordinary channel has become insufficient to carry it off. In the one case, if the works of a riparian proprietor to defend his banks be successful, the water is prevented from coming where, within time of memory at least, it never had come; in the other, it is prevented from passing in the way in which, when the occasion happened, it had been accustomed to pass, and is illegal. Rex *v.* Trafford, 1 B. & Ad. 874.

[2] Merritt *v.* Brinkerhoff et al., 17 John. 306; [Pollitt *v.* Long, 58 Barb. 20. And the damages in such case are to be measured by the value of the use of the water to the parties injured, situated as they were, during the time they were deprived of it. Pollitt *v.* Long, supra.]

and by this means alone the obstruction becomes more injurious to him.[1]

§ 116. But many cases may be supposed where there may be a trivial and temporary diminution of the water, by detention, without amounting to an actionable injury. Property in a water-course, as we have shown, consists in a right to its use; and as it cannot be used in the most beneficial manner (and not at all for hydraulic works), without raising a head of water, there must be incident to the privilege of use, a right to erect a dam, and detain the water long enough to use it to advantage.[2] It was laid down by Ch. J. Kent, that neither the occasional increase of the velocity of the current, and of the *quantum* of water below, nor the insensible evaporation and decrease of water by dams, will amount to an actionable injury. To adopt his own language, "Many such circumstances may be inevitable from the establishment of one dam above another upon the stream; the question in such cases would turn upon the *nature and extent* of the injury."[3] As a general rule, the law, as a practical science, cannot take notice of "melting lines, nice discriminations, and evanescent quantities."[4] In this view, the increased evaporation of water produced by the exposure of a larger surface, by means of the erection of a dam, would not be a *deprivation* of the water in the technical sense in which it is used as denoting a *diversion*; though in a loose and theoretical sense it might be.[5]

§ 117. Upon the subject of the unavoidable inconvenience occasioned by a fair and reasonable use of the water, Mr. J. Story, in giving the opinion of the Court, in Tyler *v.* Wilkinson, observed as follows: "I do not mean to be understood as holding the doctrine, that there can be no diminution whatever, and no obstruction or impediment whatsoever, by a riparian pro-

[1] Johnson *v.* Lewis, 13 Conn. 303.

[2] [Post, § 119 *a*. If one by erecting a mill, and using reasonably the water, leave less for one below him, though the latter be a prior occupant, this is not actionable, for no right of the plaintiff is invaded, and the act is necessary to the defendant's enjoyment of his own rights. 1 Smith Lead. Cas. (5th Am. ed.), 369, in notes to Ashby *v.* White; Palmer *v.* Mulligan, 3 Caines, 307; Platt *v.* Johnson, 15 John. 213; Weston *v.* Alden, 8 Mass. 136; Beissell *v.* Sholl, 4 Dallas, 211; Hartzall *v.* Sill, 12 Penn. St. 248.] A mere theoretical injury to a mill, occasioned by another mill on the same stream, affords no ground for an action. Thompson *v.* Crocker, 9 Pick. 59; and see Boynton *v.* Rees, 9 Pick. 528.

[3] Palmer *v.* Mulligan, 3 Caines, 307. See ante, § 99 *a*.

[4] Jones on Bailm. 9.

[5] See the opinion of Storrs J., in Wadsworth *v.* Tillotson, 15 Conn. 366; [Embrey *v.* Owen, 6 Exch. 353, 371, 372, per Parke B.]

prietor, in the use of the water as it flows; for that would be to deny any valuable use of it. There may be, and there must be allowed of that which is common to all, a reasonable use. The true test of the principle and extent of the use is, whether it is to the injury of the other proprietors or not. There may be a diminution in quantity, or a retardation or acceleration of the natural current indispensable for the general and valuable use of the water, perfectly consistent with the use of the common right. The diminution, retardation, or acceleration, not positively and sensibly injurious, by diminishing the value of the common right, is an implied element in the right of using the stream at all.[1] The law here, as in many other cases, acts with a reasonable reference to public convenience and general good, and is not betrayed into a narrow strictness subversive of common use, nor into an extravagant looseness which would destroy private rights."[2]

[1] [Hayes *v.* Waldron, 44 N.H. 584; Embrey *v.* Owen, 6 Exch. 352; Davis *v.* Getchell, 50 Maine, 602; Wells J., in Bearse *v.* Perry, 117 Mass. 211, 212; and in Hinckley *v.* Nickerson, 117 Mass. 213, 214, 215; and in Merrifield *v.* Worcester, 110 Mass. 219; Mayor and City Council of Baltimore *v.* Appold, 42 Md. 456, 457.]

[2] Tyler *v.* Wilkinson, 4 Mason, 401; [Cummings *v.* Barrett, 10 Cush. 186; Thomas *v.* Brackney, 17 Barb. 654; Parker *v.* Hotchkiss, 25 Conn. 321; Gould *v.* Boston Duck Co., 13 Gray, 442; Drake *v.* Hamilton Woollen Co., 99 Mass. 579, 580; Hendrick *v.* Cook, 4 Geo. 241; Selden *v.* Del. & Hud. Canal, 29 N.Y. 642. In Elliot *v.* Fitchburg R.R. Co., 10 Cush. 195, Shaw C.J. said, "The rule, that no riparian proprietor can wholly abstract or divert a watercourse, by which it would cease to be a running stream, or use it unreasonably in its passage, and thereby deprive a lower proprietor of a quality of his property deemed in law incidental and beneficial, necessarily flows from the principle, that the right to the reasonable and beneficial use of a running stream is common to all the riparian proprietors; and so each is bound so to use his common right as not essentially to prevent or interfere with an equally beneficial enjoyment of the common right by all the proprietors. Were it otherwise, and were it an inflexible rule that each lower proprietor has a right to the full and entire flow of the natural stream, without diminution, acceleration, or retardation of the natural current, it would follow that each lower proprietor would have a right of action against any upper proprietor for taking any portion of the water of the stream for any purpose: such a taking would be a disturbance of his right; and if taken by means of a pump, a pipe, a drain, or otherwise, though causing no substantial damage, it would be a nuisance, and warrant the lower proprietor in entering the close of the upper, to abate it. Colburn *v.* Richards, 13 Mass. 420."—"It would also follow, as the legal and practical result, that no proprietor could have any beneficial use of the stream, without an encroachment on another's right, subjecting him to actions *toties quoties*, as well as to a forcible abatement of the nuisance. If the plaintiff could, in a case like the present, have such an action, then every proprietor on the brook, to its outlet in Nashua River, would have the same; and because the quantity of diminution is not material, every riparian proprietor on the Nashua would have the same right, and so every proprietor on the Merrimac River to the ocean. This is a sort of *reductio ad absurdum*, which shows that

§ 118. The following opinion, on the same nice point, was given by the Supreme Court of New York, and delivered by Wordsworth J.: "The common use of the water of a stream by persons having mills above, is frequently, if not generally, attended with damage and loss to the mills below; but that is incident to that common use, and for the most part unavoidable. If the injury is trivial, the law will not afford redress; because every person who builds a mill, does it subject to this contingency. The person owning an upper mill on the same stream, has a lawful right to use the water, and may apply it in order to work his mills to the best advantage, subject, however, to this limitation, that if in the exercise of this right, and in consequence of it, the mills lower down the stream are rendered useless and unproductive, the law, in that case, will interpose and limit this common right, so that the owners of the lower mills shall enjoy a fair participation; and if, thereby, the owners of the upper mill sustain a partial loss of business and profits, they cannot justly complain, for this rule requires of them no more than to conform to the principle on which their right is founded. It cannot, then, be admitted, that the defendants may use the water as they please, because they have a right to a common use, although their works may require all the water, in order to derive the greatest profit. The plaintiffs' rights must be regarded; they must participate in the benefits of the stream, to a reasonable extent, although the defendants' profits may be thereby lessened. If the defendants insist on the unrestricted use of the water, and appropriate it accordingly, and this proves destructive to the mills below, the law, in that case, allows the

such cannot be the rule, as was claimed by the plaintiff." The diversion of the stream in the above case was made for the purpose of furnishing the defendants' locomotive steam-engines with water, and for other similar purposes; and it was held that no action could be maintained for such diversion, which was of only a part of the water in the stream, unless it caused actual, perceptible damage. See post, § 135 and note, § 124 *a*; Gerrish *v*. New Market Manuf. Co., 30 N.H. 483; Dumont *v*. Kellogg, 29 Mich. 423.

In Davis *v*. Getchell, 50 Maine, 602, it was held, that the equal right of every proprietor of land on the banks of a river or stream to the use of the water, implies a right to control, detain, and even diminish the volume of the water, but only to a reasonable extent; this extent being dependent upon the size of the stream, as well as upon the uses to which it is subservient, as the detention must necessarily be sufficient to accumulate the head of water requisite for practical use. The right of detention is not limited to time necessary for repairs, or to extraordinary occasions; but applies to the ordinary use of such streams, provided it be not an unreasonable use or detention. Merrifield *v*. Worcester, 110 Mass. 219; Cooley J. in Dumont *v*. Kellogg, 29 Mich. 423.]

party injured a compensation in damages, to the extent that, under all the circumstances, shall be considered an equivalent. In that event, the plaintiffs receive no more than they would have realized by their business, had the defendants permitted the water to flow in a reasonable manner." [1]

§ 119. The reasonableness of the detention, by a riparian proprietor *above*, to the injury of a riparian proprietor below, depends much upon the *nature* and *size* of the stream, as well as the employment to which it is subservient.[2] In an action on

[1] Merritt *v.* Brinkerhoff, 17 John. 306; [Hayes *v.* Waldron, 44 N.H. 584; Timm *v.* Bear, 29 Wis. 254; Dumont *v.* Kellogg, 29 Mich. 420. Although the right to have a stream of water flow in its natural state, without diminution or alteration, is an incident to the property in the land through which it passes, still this is not an absolute and exclusive right to the flow of all the water, but only subject to the right of other riparian proprietors to the reasonable enjoyment of it; and consequently, it is only for an unreasonable and unauthorized use of this common benefit that any action will lie. Embrey *v.* Owen, 6 Exch. 353.]

[2] [Hayes *v.* Waldron, 44 N.H. 580, 585; Housee *v.* Hammond, 39 Barb. 95. As to the circumstances to be considered in determining what is a reasonable use of water by the riparian proprietors, see post, § 119 *a;* Elliot *v.* Fitchburg R.R. Co., 10 Cush. 191; Davis *v.* Getchell, 50 Maine, 602; Gillett *v.* Johnson, 30 Conn. 180; ante, § 95, in note; Tourtellot *v.* Phelps, 4 Gray, 375, 376; Norway Plains Co. *v.* Bradley, 52 N.H. 86, 105, 110; Bassett *v.* Salisbury Manuf. Co., 43 N.H. 569; Swett *v.* Cutts, 50 N.H. 439; Timm *v.* Bear, 29 Wis. 254; Mayor and City Council of Baltimore *v.* Appold, 42 Md. 442; Pollitt *v.* Long, 3 N.Y. Sup. Ct. Rep. 232; Keeney & Wood Manuf. Co. *v.* Union Manuf. Co., 39 Conn. 576; Parker *v.* Hotchkiss, 25 Conn. 321; Dilling *v.* Murray, 6 Ind. 324. In Elliot *v.* Fitchburg R.R. Co., supra, Shaw C.J. said, "This appears to have been a small stream of water; but it must, we think, be considered that the same rules of law apply to it, and regulate the rights of riparian proprietors, through and along whose lands it passes, as are held to apply to other watercourses, subject to this consideration, that what would be a reasonable and proper use of a considerable stream, ordinarily carrying a large volume of water, for irrigation or other similar uses, would be an unreasonable and injurious use of a small stream, just sufficient to furnish water for domestic uses, for farm-yards, and watering-places for cattle." In Hinckley *v.* Nickerson, 117 Mass. 213, it was held, in a case where the defendant had a legal right by statute to maintain a dam for the purpose of flowing and irrigating his land for the cultivation of cranberries, that neither a statute provision that "no such dam shall be erected to the injury of any mill lawfully existing, either above or below it, on the same stream;" nor any right which may be acquired for an ancient mill by prescription, prevents the erection of works above, upon the same stream, which are reasonably adapted to the size and character of the stream, although their effect may be to modify or disturb somewhat the regularity of the flow of the current. Wells J. said, "To maintain an action of tort, at Common Law, whether as land-owner or as mill-owner, the plaintiff must show that the defendant's dam is not reasonably adapted to the size and character of the stream, or that the extent of meadow which he undertakes to flow is too great for its capacity, or else that he has so used or managed his gates as to cause an unreasonable detention." One ground on which the plaintiff sought to recover was, that any obstruction to the free passage of water to his ancient mill, whereby its valuable use was diminished, was a violation of his rights as such mill-owner. "But," the Court said, "an ancient mill

the case in Pennsylvania, the plaintiff alleged, that the defendant obstructed and retained the water of a certain stream that flowed through his land, so as to deprive him (the plaintiff) of the use of the water for the purpose of driving his grist-mill. It appeared, that the plaintiff was the owner of a tract of land through which the stream ran, and upon which his grist-mill was; that the defendant was the owner of land above, on the same stream, on which he built a saw-mill, and made a dam across the stream for the purpose of conducting the water to his saw-mill. The plaintiff gave in evidence, that the defendant withheld the water three, four, and five days, and at one time thirteen days; that at times he discharged the water in such quantities as to flood the plaintiff's mill; that when the water was detained in the defendant's dam eight days and longer, it got no higher that when detained three days; that the water sank away in a dam, or dried up when detained so long, as the breast of the dam did not leak; and that the defendant had said that if he let the water run, it would cause his forebay to leak. The defendant, on the other hand, gave evidence to show that when he detained the water, the stream was low, and the season very dry, and that without the detention he could not saw at his mill; that he only used the water for his saw-mill, and for the purpose of watering his meadow; that the water was turned into its natural course before it left his premises; that the stream was a *small one*, and insufficient for both mills; that his dam was a clay bottom, and that the water could not well sink away; that the breast of his dam did leak, and that there were two springs in the dam. In his charge to the jury, the Judge said, " The defendant had a right to use the water as it passed through his land. If he detained it no longer than was necessary for the proper enjoyment of it, the plaintiff cannot recover. Whether, if you believe from the evidence that he did detain the water three days, at times, at other times five days, and at one time

cannot prescribe against the reasonable use of the stream above. Its prescriptive rights are exclusive only so far as its actual appropriation extends."

What is a reasonable use is generally a question for the jury to decide. Wheatley *v.* Baugh, 25 Penn. St. 535; Hetrick *v.* Deachler, 6 Penn. St. 32; Miller *v.* Miller, 9 Penn. St. 74; Davis *v.* Getchell, supra; Hayes *v.* Waldron, 44 N.H. 580; Housee *v.* Hammond, 39 Barb. 95; Snow *v.* Parsons, 28 Vt. 459; Holden *v.* Lake Company, 53 N.H. 552; Phillips *v.* Sherman, 64 Maine, 171; Pollitt *v.* Long, 3 Thomp. & C. (N.Y.) 232; Parker *v.* Hotchkiss, 25 Conn. 321.|

thirteen days, in his own dam, to the injury of the plaintiff's mill, this was longer than was necessary for the defendant's proper enjoyment of the water, at his mill, as it passed through his land, is left to your determination. If you believe it was, you will find for the plaintiff: if you believe it was not, you will find for the defendant, unless you believe that the defendant did vexatiously or wantonly detain the water, or that there was some degree of malevolence in the time or quantity of water discharged, to the injury of the plaintiff's mill; for, if you believe this, your verdict should be for the plaintiff." This charge was objected to; and it was contended, that the Court ought not to have submitted the question of *time* to the jury; that the *time* the water was detained, under the circumstances of the case, was so *long* and *unreasonable* as entitled the plaintiff to recover; and *per Curiam:* "The law of the case is so fully and accurately laid down in the charge, that scarce any thing can be added to it. The reasonableness of the detention, depending as it must, on the nature and size of the stream, as well as the business to which it is subservient, and on the ever-varying circumstances of each particular case, must necessarily be determined by the jury, and not by the Court. It is not many years since the reasonableness of notice of the dishonor of a bill or note, though reducible to rule, was determinable in the same way. But it is impossible to make even a general rule for cases like the present; and the matter was fairly submitted, therefore, to the jury."[1]

[§ 119 *a*. In Thurber *v.* Martin,[2] which was an action of tort for obstructing the natural flow of the water, and diverting it from the plaintiff's mill, Shaw C.J. thus stated the law of the case: "Every man has a right to the reasonable use and enjoyment of a current of running water, as it flows through or along his own land, for mill purposes, having a due regard to the like reasonable use of the stream by all other proprietors above and below him. In determining what is such reasonable use, a just regard must be had to the force and magnitude of the current,

[1] Hetrick *v.* Deachler, 6 Penn. St. 32. [See Davis *v.* Getchell, 50 Maine, 602.] And to the same effect, Hoy *v.* Sterrett, 2 Watts, 327; Hartzall *v.* Sill, 12 Penn. St. 248. See also Miller *v.* Miller, 9 Penn. St. 74; Newhall *v.* Ireson, 8 Cush. 595; Morris Canal & Banking Co. *v.* Society &c., 1 Halst. (N.J.) Ch. 203; [Clinton *v.* Myers, 46 N.Y. 511, 519.]

[2] [Thurber *v.* Martin, 2 Gray, 394. See Tourtellot *v.* Phelps, 4 Gray, 376; Davis *v.* Getchell, 50 Maine, 602, 605.]

its height and velocity, the state of improvement in the country in regard to mills and machinery, and the use of water as a propelling power, the general usage of the country in similar cases, and all other circumstances bearing upon the question of fitness and propriety in the use of the water in the particular case.[1] If any party claims a special right to the use of the water, more beneficial to himself, and more burdensome to the riparian proprietors above or below, than what may be called the natural or general right to the reasonable use of the stream, he must establish such right by grant or prescription." So in Chandler *v.* Howland,[2] the Court say that the owner of the upper mill must "use the water in such manner that every riparian proprietor, at points further down the stream, shall have the enjoyment and use of it substantially according to its natural flow, subject to such interruption as is necessary and unavoidable by the reasonable and proper use of the mill privilege above." And in Davis *v.* Winslow,[3] the Court said, "The detention of water, by a dam for the benefit of a mill, oftentimes results in an injury to the owners of the privilege below. It does not, however, follow that for every such injury there is a remedy. If the detention is indispensable to the owner's reasonable enjoyment of his rights in the common highway, and is continued no longer than is necessary for that purpose, the proprietor below is without remedy for any injury he may have suffered thereby; otherwise, the right of common use is nugatory, and the party requiring such use is himself obstructed in its exercise.[4] It appeared in Pitts *v.* Lancaster Mills,[5] that the defendants were proprietors of land and mills above those of the plaintiffs, on the same stream, and having erected a new dam, which they had a right to do, they detained the water no longer than was necessary to raise their own head of water and fill their own mill-pond. The Court

1 [Ante, § 119, note; and Gould *v.* Boston Duck Co., 13 Gray, 442; Merrifield *v.* Worcester, 110 Mass. 219; Drake *v.* Hamilton Woolen Co., 99 Mass. 579, 580; Pool *v.* Lewis, 41 Geo. 162.]

2 [Chandler *v.* Howland, 7 Gray, 350; Holden *v.* Lake Company, 53 N.H. 552; Appleton C.J. in Phillips *v.* Sherman, 64 Maine, 171, 174; Timm *v.* Bear, 29 Wis. 254.]

3 [Davis *v.* Winslow, 51 Maine, 290.]

4 [See Webb *v.* Portland Manuf. Co., 3 Sumner, 189; Embrey *v.* Owen, 6 Exch. 353; Shrewsbury *v.* Smith, 12 Cush. 181. A mill-owner has no right to unnecessarily and unreasonably detain water from those who have a right to use it subsequent to his own use; and he will be liable in damages for so doing. Phillips *v.* Sherman, 64 Maine, 171; Timm *v.* Bear, 29 Wis. 254.]

5 [Pitts *v.* Lancaster Mills, 13 Met. 156; Brace *v.* Yale, 10 Allen, 444; post, § 219.]

decided "that this was not an unreasonable use of the watercourse by the defendants, and that any loss which the plaintiffs temporarily sustained by it, was *damnum absque injuria*."[1] And in Wood *v.* Edes,[2] Hoar J. said, "We are of opinion that to retain the water by a dam for the purposes of a fish-pond, constantly maintained, and therefore allowing the natural flow of the water to pass unimpeded to the plaintiffs' mill, is a just and reasonable exercise of the defendant's right to use the water as it passes through his land. In the absence of any grant, prescription, or contract, the plaintiffs have no legal right to use the defendant's land as a reservoir, except so far as the erection of their mill-dam may necessarily cause the water to flow back upon it; and the right to cause it thus to flow cannot restrain the defendant from making a reasonable use of the water on his own land, provided he returns it all to its natural channel when it leaves his land, and allows it to flow thence regularly to the plaintiffs' land below."[3]]

7. *Of the Right of Irrigation.*

§ 120. The cases in England in which the controversy has been in respect to the abstraction of water from a watercourse for the purpose of fertilizing land, are few, and generally those in which a right so to abstract it has been claimed on the ground of grant or presciption; but they nevertheless imply, that, as a general rule, the water cannot be so abstracted to the material diminution of the quantity of water which naturally runs in the

[1] [See Hetrick *v.* Deachler, 6 Penn St. 32; Davis *v.* Getchell, 50 Maine, 605; Vliet *v.* Sherwood, 35 Wis. 229.]

[2] [Wood *v.* Edes, 2 Allen, 580.]

[3] [See Springfield *v.* Harris, 4 Allen, 494. A boom company was authorized to erect and maintain a boom, which was done without fault or negligence on the part of the company; it was held that the company was not liable for the flowage of land, taken under its charter, caused by the boom, in co-operation with an unusual accumulation of logs and a large rise of water. Lawler *v.* Baring Boom Company, 56 Maine, 443. See Spring *v.* Russell, 7 Greenl. 273; Rogers *v.* K. & P. Railroad Co., 35 Maine, 319; Whittier *v.* P. & K. Railroad Co., 38 Maine, 27; Cushman *v.* Smith, 34 Maine, 247; Boothby *v.* A. & K. Railroad Co., 51 Maine, 318; Carson *v.* Western Railroad Co., 8 Gray, 423; Pittsburg & Fort Wayne R.R. Co. *v.* Gillieland, 56 Penn St. 445; C & R. Railroad *v.* Speir, 56 Penn. St. 325; Hatch *v.* Vermont Central R.R. Co., 25 Vt. 49; China *v.* Southwick, 8 Fairf. 238; Smith *v.* Agawam Canal Co., 2 Allen, 357; The London & North-Western Railway Co. *v.* Bradley, 3 Mac. & G. (Am. ed.) 336 note (1) and cases cited; Hammersmith &c. R.R. Co. *v.* Brand, L.R. 4 H.L. 197.]

watercourse.[1] But a case is mentioned in a late English publication,[2] of an action brought for the disturbance of a watercourse, where it appeared that the water, after being used for irrigation, was returned to the natural channel; and Wood B. nonsuited the plaintiff. As, however, it was shown that a portion of the water *was lost*, by irrigation and absorption, the Court of King's Bench set aside the nonsuit. The judgment of the King's Bench, in this case, coincides with the law of France, by which, although a riparian proprietor on a brook or river may divert the water for his meadows, "yet every one must use this liberty so as to do no injustice to his neighbors, who have a like want and an equal right." [3]

§ 121. It is very easy to be perceived that judicial tribunals in this country, in a number of instances, in expounding the law of watercourses, and in adjusting the conflicting claims of riparian owners, have had in their minds a distinction between one kind of use of water and another; one of which may be called a use for *natural* purposes, and the other for *artificial* purposes.[4] A distinction of this sort was, for the first time it is believed, expressly laid down in a case before the Supreme Court of Illinois; [5] an entire account of which will be given before the consideration of this branch of the subject of the right to the use of a natural watercourse is concluded. The wants of riparian proprietors on a watercourse, in the opinion of the Supreme

[1] See Greenslade *v.* Haliday, 6 Bing. 379; Strutt *v.* Bovington, 5 Esp. 56; Hall *v.* Swift, 6 Scott, 167. [In Elliot *v.* Fitchburg R.R. Co., 10 Cush. 194, Shaw C.J. said, "It has sometimes been made a question whether a riparian proprietor can divert water from a running stream, for purposes of irrigation. But this, we think, is an abstract question which cannot be answered either in the affirmative or negative, as a rule applicable to all cases. That a portion of the water of a stream may be used for the purpose of irrigating land, we think is well established as one of the rights of the proprietors of the soil along or through which it passes. Yet a proprietor cannot, under color of that right, or for the actual purpose of irrigating his own land, wholly abstract or divert the watercourse, or take such an unreasonable quantity of water, or make such unreasonable use of it, as to deprive other proprietors of the substantial benefits which they might derive from it, if not diverted or used unreasonably." See Ferrea *v.* Knipe, 28 Cal. 343.]

[2] Gale & Whatley on Easements, 284.

[3] Domat, Pub. Law, 1, 8, 2, 11. [See Davis *v.* Getchell, 50 Maine, 604.]

[4] See the opinion of Gibson C.J. in Mayor &c. *v.* Comm. Spring Garden, 7 Penn. St. 328; Pugh *v.* Wheeler, 2 Dev. & Bat. (N.C.) 50; [Union Mill &c. Co. *v.* Ferris, 2 Sawyer, 176.] "The waters made him great, the deep set him up on high with her rivers *running round about his plants*, and sent out her little rivers unto all the trees of the field." Ezekiel xxxi. 4.

[5] Evans *v.* Merriweather, 3 Scam. (Ill.) 496.

Court of Illinois, as expressly declared, may be thus summarily stated: They are either *natural* or *artificial; natural* are such as are absolutely necessary to be supplied, such as *thirst* of people and of cattle, and *household purposes;* and, in *arid* climates, water for *irrigation* is referred to the class of *natural* wants, to which *artificial* wants must ever be legally subservient. So that, whether the want of water for the purpose of irrigation, be a *natural* or an *artificial* want, is dependent upon circumstances. It may be the one or the other. If the want of water is simply for the comfort or convenience or prosperity of a riparian proprietor, it is *artificial;* and under this head is referred the demand for water for manufacturing purposes and for hydraulic purposes in general. These discriminating suggestions are offered *in limine* to prepare the reader for the authorities now to be laid before him.

§ 122. It was decided many years ago in Connecticut, that a riparian proprietor may take advantage of a stream of water running through his land, to fertilize his meadows; provided he does not deprive the adjoining proprietor, below, of a sufficiency of water for kitchen purposes, or for watering cattle; and provided the water, which is diverted for irrigation, shall (unless absorbed on the land) be returned to its natural channel before the stream leaves his land. And if a person, by absorption on his own land, can dispose of the whole of the water, excepting only a bare sufficiency for the purposes before mentioned, he has the prior right, because he is the first on the stream, and has the first opportunity.[1] In another case, in the same State, it appearing that the diversion of the water was for the purpose of irrigation; and that all the water, which was diverted, was absorbed on the land, or returned to the natural channel, before it left the land; the Court held, that no action would lie.[2] In the year 1800, the same doctrine was countenanced in Massachusetts; and the opinion of the Court was then given, that, if the defendant took the water for any other purpose than watering his own meadow, or if he did not return what was not expended in that way, into the usual channel, after using what was necessary, the action might be maintained. The verdict was

[1] Perkins *v.* Dow, 1 Root (Conn.) 535. As to prior occupation, see post, § 130.

[2] Haywood *v.* Mason, 2 Swift's Syst. 87; and 1 Root (Conn.) 537.

accordingly for the defendant.[1] So, in Weston *v.* Alden,[2] the Court gave their opinion as follows: "A man owning a close on an ancient brook, may lawfully use the water thereof for the purposes of husbandry, as watering his cattle, or irrigating his close; and he may do this, either by dipping water from the brook and pouring it upon his land, or by making small sluices for the same purpose; and if the owner of a close below is damaged thereby, it is *damnum absque injuria*." These precedents appear to be much more liberal in favor of upper riparian owners than is warranted by cases of a subsequent date; and with regard to the two which have been cited from the reports of Connecticut, they, in the opinion of the late Chief-Justice Swift, of that State, not only reverse the Common Law, but are repugnant to a statute of that State, in affirmance of the Common Law; which, says he, must remove all doubt upon a question which has been frequently agitated.[3] With respect to the case of Haywood *v.* Mason, the same learned judge has affirmed, that it not only gives to the upper riparian proprietors on rivers the advantages to which the lower are entitled, but denies that even seventy years' exclusive enjoyment, in any particular manner, will confer an absolute right.[4]

§ 123. In the case of Colburn *v.* Richards,[5] in Massachusetts, it was held, that the water could not be taken out for irrigation, to the injury of a mill below. The Court endeavored to reconcile this decision with that in Weston *v.* Alden, as follows: "There is this difference between that case and the one now before us: in that case there was no obstruction to the course of the water; sluices were made for it into the land of the defendant, in that action; and the water, after washing his lands, still passed down the natural channel. Nor does it appear that the plaintiff, in that case, had acquired a right, by prescription, to the use of the stream, to carry works which had been erected and maintained at expense; but he had merely enjoyed the natural benefits of the stream, without any labor or expense of his own. In the case before us, the whole stream was stopped, or at least so much of it as to render the defendant's mill entirely useless. There is no principle

[1] Bent *v.* Wheeler, Sullivan on Land Titles, 273.

[2] Weston *v.* Alden, 8 Mass. 136.

[3] 1 Swift's Dig. 111.

[4] Opinion of Swift C.J., in Ingraham *v.* Hutchinson, 2 Conn. 584.

[5] Colburn *v.* Richards, 13 Mass. 420.

upon which this can be justified." The distinction that would seem to have much force, which is attempted to be shown, between the case of Weston *v.* Alden and this case is, that, in the latter, there was a right in the plaintiff to the use of the water, by *prescription*, for propelling certain works. But the right to use a natural watercourse is not derived from the erection of a mill, nor by *prescription;* but it is a right incident to the ownership of the land.[1]

[1] See ante, § 5 et seq. [§§ 8, 90, 92; post, § 134. In Dickinson *v.* The Grand Junction Canal Co., 7 Exch. 282, 299, 300, Pollock C.B. said, "We consider it as settled law, that the right to have a stream running in its natural course is, not by a presumed grant from long acquiescence on the part of the riparian proprietors above and below, but is *ex jure naturæ*, and an incident of property, as much as the right to have the soil itself in its natural state, unaltered by the acts of a neighboring proprietor, who cannot dig so as to deprive it of the support of his land." In Chasemore *v.* Richards, 7 H.L. Cas. 349; 5 H. & N. 989, Lord Wensleydale said, "It is now settled that the right to the enjoyment of a natural stream on the surface, *ex jure naturæ*, belongs to the proprietor of the adjoining lands, and he is entitled to the benefit of it as of all other natural advantages incident to the land of which he is the owner. He has the right to have it come to him in its natural state in flow, quantity, and quality, and to go from him without obstruction, and this right does not depend upon prescription." See Cary *v.* Daniels, 5 Met. 238; Crittenton *v.* Alger, 11 Met. 284.] All the cases are agreed, that where a natural watercourse is diverted, the plaintiff need not aver that his mill is ancient; in other words, he need not show a prescriptive right. In one of the earliest reported cases, Doddridge J. said, "In this action there was no need that it should be an ancient mill; for if one erects a new mill on his freehold, and another diverts the watercourse of that mill, as it passes by his land, still, if the water used to follow this course, an action on the case lies against him; for he cannot use his land, or the water which passes through his land, to the damage of the other; and that so it had many times been before adjudged." Rutland *v.* Bowler, Palmer 3 Exch. 290, 774. Again, in an [illegible] for diverting a watercourse, running to the plaintiff's mill, the declaration had only a *debet et solet currere;* and it was adjudged to be good, without saying the mill was an ancient mill; for, as the action was against a *wrong-doer*, possession was sufficient; and the Court held, in this case, that an action had lain for diverting a stream, though *no* mill had been erected. Pollexfen, for the plaintiff, went upon the right the owner had in the soil, and said it was lawful for a man to use his own, after what manner he pleased, so as not hurting his neighbor. The defendant, he contended, could no more stop the water, than "where I have a way over several men's land to my land, and I then build my land into tenements, they could stop my way, for that their land is charged with the way." Palmer *v.* Heblethwaite, Skinner, 65, 175. In an action for stopping lights, exception was taken, because the declaration did not state *antiquum messuagium;* but Hale said, "If a man has a watercourse running through his ground, and erects a mill upon it, he may bring his action for diverting the stream, and not say *antiquum molendinum;* and upon the evidence, it will appear if the defendant hath ground through which the stream runs before the plaintiff's; and he *used* to turn the stream as he saw cause; for *otherwise*, he cannot justify it, though the mill be newly erected." 1 Ventr. 237. See also, to the same effect, Sands *v.* Trefusis, Cro. Car. 575; Brown *v.* Best, 1 Wilson, 174; and Twiss *v.* Baldwin, 9 Conn. 291.

§ 124. In the case of Anthony *v.* Lapham,[1] decided by the Supreme Court of Massachusetts, in 1827, reference is again made to the case of Weston *v.* Alden. The defendant contended, that he took no more water than was useful to him for the purpose of irrigating his lands, and that he had a right to all that was necessary for this purpose, although he might thereby deprive the plaintiff of a portion of the water he had before used for the same purpose.[2] It did not appear that the plaintiff had ever appropriated the water in any other way than for irrigating his land. The Court said, if the case was to be supported at all, it was upon the authority of Weston *v.* Alden, the difference being that there the defendant took the water by small sluices over his land and returned it into the natural channel; but, in the case before them, the water was stopped by a dam; a great deal of it absorbed by the land, or lost by evaporation; and the surplus not returned into the natural channel; so that the plaintiff was deprived of the privilege which belonged to him. The Court then proceeded to say, "Every man through whose land water passes, may use it for watering his cattle or irrigating his land; but he must so use it, in this latter way, as to do the least possible injury to his neighbor, who has the same right."[3] The judgment, which had been for the plaintiff, was affirmed.

[§ 124 *a*. In a still later case[4] in Massachusetts, it was held that a diversion of a large portion of the water of a natural watercourse, by a proprietor of land through which the watercourse runs, renders him liable to an action on the case by a proprietor of the land below from which the water is thus diverted; although the latter thereby sustains no present actual damage. Shaw C.J. said, "This was an unwarrantable and injurious use of a common right to a watercourse, running in its natural channel, through the lands of several different proprietors. The rule of law is well settled that each of such proprietors has a right to a reasonable and beneficial use of the current as it passes through his own land; but he has no right to divert or corrupt it, so as to prevent the proprietor below him from having and enjoying the same use, for all usual and

1 Lapham *v.* Anthony, 5 Pick. 175.

2 [See Stein *v.* Burden, 29 Ala. 127.]

3 [Fleming *v.* Davis, 37 Texas, 173.]

4 [Newhall *v.* Ireson, 8 Cush. 595, 599. See Elliot *v.* Fitchburg R.R. Co., 10 Cush. 191.]

beneficial purposes. This substantial diversion of the watercourse, therefore, was unwarranted by any right of the defendants, as proprietors above; was an encroachment on the rights of the plaintiff, and prejudicial to her estate. And although the plaintiff has sustained no present damage, because she has no mill upon it, or otherwise used it for any agricultural or manufacturing purpose, yet such diversion would prevent such beneficial use of it hereafter, and thus impair the value of the estate. It is therefore a case where an action can be maintained to vindicate the plaintiff's right, and to prevent a loss of it by adverse use and lapse of time. Even where it has been considered that a riparian proprietor had authority to make use of the stream for purposes of irrigation, and thus by that use divert a portion of it, it has been held under the condition, that such diversion was, under all circumstances, a reasonable use of the stream, and that the surplus of the water thus used must be returned into its natural channel. These cases carry a strong implication, that a diversion of the entire stream, or of a considerable part of it, is prejudicial to the proprietor below and not justifiable." [1]]

§ 125. The Supreme Court of Maine say, "The proprietor of the watercourse has a right to avail himself of its momentum as a power, which may be turned to beneficial purposes. And he may make a reasonable use of the water itself, for domestic purposes, for watering cattle, or even for irrigation; *provided* it is not unreasonably detained or essentially diminished. For, although by the case of Weston *v.* Alden, the right of irrigation might seem to be general and unlimited; yet subsequent cases [2] have restrained it consistently with the enjoyment of the common bounty of nature, by other proprietors, through whose land a stream had been accustomed to flow; and the qualification of the right by these latter decisions, is in accordance with the Common Law." [3]

§ 126. In a case in the Supreme Court of New York, the parties were owners of adjoining farms. On the farm of the de-

[1] [See Weston *v.* Alden, 8 Mass. 136; Colburn *v.* Richards, 13 Mass. 420; Cook *v.* Hull, 3 Pick. 269; Embrey *v.* Owen, 6 Exch. 353; Gillett *v.* Johnson, 30 Conn. 180, 183; Chasemore *v.* Richards, 2 H. & N. 189, 190, per Coleridge J.; Fleming *v.* Davis, 37 Texas, 173; Dilling *v.* Murray, 6 Ind. 324.]

[2] The Court cite Colburn *v.* Richards; Cook *v.* Hull; and Anthony *v.* Lapham, ut sup.

[3] Blanchard *v.* Baker, 8 Greenl. 253.

fendant, within five or six rods of the land of the plaintiff, there was a living spring, the water from which, in its natural channel, ran over the land of the plaintiff. The defendant diverted the water from his spring and caused it to flow upon his meadow to the extent of three or four acres, for which the plaintiff recovered. The Chief Justice, in giving the opinion of the Court, said, "The defendant has a right to use so much as is necessary for his family and his cattle, but he has no right to use it for irrigating his meadow, if thereby he deprive the plaintiff of the reasonable use of the water in its natural channel."[1]

§ 127. In an action on the case, for the diversion of a watercourse, in Connecticut, as lately as the year 1843, it appeared, that the defendant, who was the owner of the land on which there was a spring, took water from it for his domestic and culinary purposes, and for watering his cattle, by means of an artificial aqueduct from the spring to his house and barn; and after the use of what was necessary for such purpose, the surplus was not returned to the stream before it reached the plaintiff's land below, but was allowed to escape, and either irrigate the defendant's land, or to be lost, by flowing constantly through small apertures in penstocks, at the house and barn, in order to keep the water from freezing in winter, and becoming impure in summer; it being necessary, for these purposes, that it should be kept thus running. It was held, that these acts did not necessarily constitute an infraction of the plaintiff's right; and that the case was not varied by the circumstance, that the water was appropriated by the defendant to his use at a place on his land lower than where the stream, in its natural course, entered the land of the plaintiff. The Court took the ground that the water so used was not used in an unreasonable manner.[2]

[1] Arnold *v.* Foot, 12 Wend. 330; [See Crooker *v.* Bragg, 10 Wend. 264; Fleming *v.* Davis, 37 Texas, 173; Union Mill &c. Co. *v.* Ferris, 2 Sawyer, 176.]

[2] Wadsworth *v.* Tillotson, 15 Conn. 366. [In Gillett *v.* Johnson, 30 Conn. 183, Butler J. said, "The right of the defendant to use the stream for purposes of irrigation cannot be questioned. But it was a limited right, and one which could only be exercised with a reasonable regard to the right of the plaintiff to the use of the water. It was not enough that the defendant applied the water to a useful and proper purpose, and in a prudent and husbandlike manner. She was bound to apply it in such a *reasonable manner and quantity* as not to deprive the plaintiff of a sufficient supply for his cattle." — "The claim of the defendant was that she had a right to divert the whole for the purpose of irrigation, regardless of the rights and necessities of the plaintiff; and she did so divert it. Such diversion, under the circumstances, was clearly unreasonable, and therefore

§ 128. We now proceed to the case which has been already referred to as having been decided by the Supreme Court of Illinois,[1] where the general question was presented, as to what extent riparian proprietors upon a watercourse can use the water, and the Court say, "Each riparian proprietor is bound to make such a use of running water, as to do as little injury to those below him as is consistent with a valuable benefit to himself. The use must be a reasonable one. Now the question fairly arises, is that a reasonable use of running water by the upper proprietor, by which the fluid is entirely consumed? To answer this question satisfactorily, it is proper to consider the wants in regard to the element of water. These wants are either natural or artificial. Natural are such as are absolutely necessary to be supplied in order to his existence. Artificial, such only as, by supplying them, his comfort and prosperity are increased. To quench thirst, and for household purposes, water is absolutely indispensable. In civilized life, water for cattle is also necessary. These wants must be supplied, or both man and beast will perish. The supply of a man's artificial wants is not essential to his existence; it is not indispensable; he could live if water was not employed in *irrigating* lands, or in propelling his machinery. In countries differently situated from ours, with a hot and arid climate, water doubtless is indispensable to the cultivation of the soil, and in them, water for *irrigation* would be a natural want. Here it might increase the products of the soil, but it is by no means essential, and cannot, therefore, be considered a natural want of man. So of manufactures, they promote the prosperity and comfort of mankind, but cannot be considered absolutely necessary to his existence." From these premises, the Court then proceed to state the conclusion resulting; namely, "That an individual owning a spring on his land, from which water flows in a current through his neighbor's land, would have the

illegal, and the Court correctly rendered judgment for the plaintiff." For the facts of this case, see ante, § 4, note. See Fleming *v.* Davis, 37 Texas, 173. If water is diverted for an artificial use, from its natural channel in quantity sufficient to affect injuriously the rights of the proprietor below, and the water is not returned to its channel before it reaches the lands of such proprietor, he may recover damages therefor of the party who caused the injury. And it is no answer that the water would have continued to flow back into the stream, had not a stranger by his unauthorized interference rendered the means provided unavailing for that purpose. Stein *v.* Barden, 29 Ala. 127.]

[1] Evans *v.* Merriweather, 3 Scam. (Ill.) 496; and ante, § 121.

right to use the whole of it, if necessary to satisfy his natural wants.[1] He may consume all the water for his domestic purposes, including water for his stock. If he desires to use it for irrigation or manufactures, and there be a lower proprietor to whom its use is essential to supply his natural wants, or for his stock, he must use the water so as to leave enough for such lower proprietor.[2] Where the stream is small, and does not supply water more than sufficient to answer the natural wants of the different proprietors living on it, none of the proprietors can use the water for either irrigation or manufactures. So far, then, as natural wants are concerned, there is no difficulty in furnishing a rule by which riparian proprietors may use flowing water to supply such natural wants. Each proprietor in his turn may, if necessary, consume all the water for these purposes. But where the water is not wanted to supply natural wants, and there is not sufficient for each proprietor living on the stream to carry on his manufacturing purposes, how shall the water be divided? We have seen, that, without a contract or grant, neither has a right to use all the water; all have a right to participate in its benefits. Where all have a right to participate in a common benefit, and none can have an exclusive enjoyment, no rule, from the very nature of the case, can be laid down, as to how much each may use without infringing upon the rights of others. In such cases, the question must be left to the judgment of the jury, whether the party complained of has used, under all the circumstances, more than his just proportion."[3]

§ 129. It is submitted, whether it may be not fairly deduced from the preceding authorities, that, for any *essential* diminution of the water of a watercourse, which nature has directed to run in a certain and determinate channel, for *any* purpose, the law, in this country, will interpose? Streams of water, says Kent,[4] are intended for the use and comfort of man; and it would be

[1] [Union Mill &c. Co. *v.* Ferris, 2 Sawyer, 176; Ferrea *v.* Knipe, 28 Cal. 343; Tolle *v.* Correth, 31 Texas, 335; Rhodes *v.* Whitehead, 27 Texas, 310.]

[2] [Union Mill &c. Co. *v.* Ferris, 2 Sawyer, 176.]

[3] [See Elliot *v.* Fitchburg R.R. Co., 10 Cush. 197, per Shaw C.J.; Miller *v.* Miller, 9 Penn. St. 74; Arnold *v.* Foot, 12 Wend. 330; Elliot *v.* Fitchburg R.R. Co., 10 Cush. 191, 195; Holden *v.* Lake Company, 53 N.H. 552.]

[4] [3 Com. 439, 440. See Chasemore *v.* Richards, 2 H. & N. 189, 190, per Coleridge J.]

unreasonable and contrary to the universal sense of mankind, to debar every riparian proprietor from the application of water to domestic, agricultural, and manufacturing purposes; *provided*, the use of the water be made under the limitation, that he do no material injury or annoyance to his neighbor below him, who has an *equal* right to the subsequent use of the same water. In a late case in the English Court of Exchequer, the Chief Baron considered, that the rule laid down by Kent is the true rule. In England, says he, it is not very clear, that such a user (*i.e.*, for irrigation) would be permitted as arising out of the right to the use of the water *jure naturæ;* "but no doubt if the stream were only used by the riparian proprietor and his family, by drinking it, or for the supply of domestic purposes, no action would lie for this ordinary use of it; and it may be conceived, that if a field be covered by houses, the ordinary use by the inhabitants might sensibly diminish the stream; yet no action would, we apprehend, lie, any more than if the air was rendered less pure and healthy by the increase of inhabitants in the neighborhood, and by the smoke issuing from the chimneys of an increased number of houses."[1] [In a late case[2] Lord Wensleydale, dur-

[1] Wood *v.* Waud, 3 Exch. 748. The Court below, in Randall *v.* Silverthorn, 4 Penn. St., 173, said as follows: "The plaintiff was entitled to all reasonable use of the water on his land for agricultural and manufacturing purposes, provided he returned it to its channel before leaving his land, without material and unreasonable diminution." So in Miller *v.* Miller, 9 Penn. St. 74. [Under the laws of Texas, a proprietor of a tract of land in which originates a spring, forming a stream, running in a channel through his land and into the land of another person, has a right to divert the stream from its natural channel and cause it to overflow and irrigate the land, provided the stream resumes its original channel before entering the land of the adjacent proprietor, Tolle *v.* Correth, 31 Texas, 362.] The just and equitable principle, Kent says (3 Com. 441), is given in the Roman law: *Sic enim debere quem meliorem agrum suam facere, ne vicini deteriorem faciat.* The Code Napoleon, Nos. 640–645, establishes the same just rules. And see also Dig. 39, 3, 4, 10; Code, lib. 3, tit. 34, 1, 7; Pothier, Traité du Contrat de Société, Second App. Nos. 236, 237. In France, every one may use the water "*en bon père de famille, et pour son plus grand avantage.*" Code Civil, Art. 640, note *a*, by Pailliet. See his *Manuel de Droit Français*, Paris, 1838, cited by Baron Parke, in 20 Law Jour. 212; and s.c. 4 Eng. Law & Eq. on p. 477; 6 Exch. 353.

The case of Embrey *v.* Owen, in the English Court of Exchequer, 6 Exch. 353, was decided in 1851,* and the decision was, that a riparian proprietor has a right to irrigate his land by water from the stream, provided he does not thereby interfere with the rights of others; and whether the use made by him of the stream for this purpose be reasonable

* Embrey *v.* Owen, 20 L.J. N.S. 212, and s.c. 4 Eng. Law & Eq. 466; 6 Exch. 353.

[2] [Chasemore *v.* Richards, 7 H.L. Cas. 349, 362; s.c. 5 H. & N. 982.]

ing the argument of counsel, said, "The English cases have not yet allowed of the use of water for irrigation; the American

and permitted, or not, depends on the *circumstances* of each case: That where an action on the case founded in such an irrigation, is brought against a riparian proprietor by another having a mill lower down on the stream, it appearing that the irrigation does not take place continuously, but only at intermittent periods, when the river is full, and that no damage is done thereby to the working of the mill, and that the diminution of the water is not perceptible to the eye; such is a reasonable use of the water for which no action can be maintained. It was argued by the counsel for the plaintiff, that the plaintiff had a *right* to the full flow of the water in its natural course and *abundance*, as an incident to the property in the land through which it flowed; and that any abstraction of the water, however inconsiderable, by another riparian proprietor, and though productive of no actual damage, would be actionable, because it is an injury *to a right* (see post, 427, et seq.); and if continued would be the foundation of a claim of adverse right in that proprietor. Baron Parke, who delivered the judgment of the Court (the Court consisting of himself, Alderson, Platt, and Martin), said, that he by no means disputed the truth of the counsel's proposition with respect to every description of right. And he added, "Actual perceptible damage is not indispensable as the foundation of an action; it is sufficient to show a violation of a right, in which case the law will presume damage, — *injuria sine damna* is actionable, — as was laid down by Lord Holt in the case of Ashby *v.* White, 2 Ld. Ray. 938, and many subsequent cases. But in applying this admitted rule to the case of rights to running water, and the analogous cases of rights to air and light, it must be considered what the nature of those rights is, and what is a violation of them. The law as to flowing water is now put on its right footing, by a series of cases, and is fully settled in the American courts." (The learned Baron, in the course of his opinion, cited Webb *v.* Portland Manuf. Co., 3 Sumner, 189, and 3 Kent, 439–445.) "The right to have the stream to flow in its natural state without diminution or alteration is an incident to the property in the land through which it passes; but flowing water is *publici juris*, not in the sense that it is *bonum vacans*, to which the first occupant may acquire an exclusive right, but that it is public and common in this sense only, that all may reasonably use it who have a right of access to it; that none can have any property in the water itself, except in the particular portion which he may choose to abstract from the stream and take into his possession, and that during the time of his possession only. But each proprietor of the adjacent land has the right to the usufruct of the stream which flows through it. This right to the benefit and advantage of the water flowing past his land, is not an absolute and exclusive right to the flow of *all* the water in its natural state; if it were, the argument of the learned counsel, that every abstraction of it would give a cause of action, would be irrefragable; but it is a right only to the flow of the water, and the enjoyment of it, subject to the similar rights of all the proprietors of the banks on each side, to the reasonable enjoyment of the same gift of Providence. It is only, therefore, for an unreasonable and unauthorized use of this common benefit that an action will lie; for such a use it will, though there may be no *actual* damage to the plaintiffs. This [a reasonable use] must depend on the circumstances of each case. On the one hand, it would not be permitted that the owner of a tract of many thousand acres of porous soil abutting on one part of the stream, could be permitted to irrigate them continually by canals and drains, and so cause a serious diminution of the quantity of water, though there was no other loss to the natural stream than that arising from the necessary absorption and evaporation of the water employed for that purpose; on the other hand, one's common sense would be shocked by supposing that a

cases do allow it. In Embrey *v.* Owen,[1] an action for using the water for the purposes of irrigation failed, because the evidence showed that no injury had really been occasioned." In Sampson *v.* Hoddinott,[2] it appeared that the plaintiff had immemorially enjoyed the benefit of irrigating certain of his meadows with the water of the river Yeo, subject, however, to the right of the miller at West Mill to detain the water for the use of his mill. Although the natural flow of the river was prevented by the exercise of this right, yet the water was allowed to come down at such times that the plaintiff was enabled to irrigate his meadows effectually. But of late, the defendant, for the purpose of irrigating his own adjacent land, had from time to time diverted the water after it had passed the mill, and before it reached the plaintiff's meadows; and although the facts stated in the special case did not lead to any certain conclusion, that by the mere irrigation on the part of the defendant, the quantity of water which ultimately reached the plaintiff's meadows was sensibly diminished, yet the effect was that the water was detained by the process of irrigation, and did not arrive until so late in the day that the plaintiff was deprived of the power to use it fully. The question was, whether such a diversion and detaining of the water by the defendant was actionable. On the part of the plain-

riparian owner could not dip a watering-pot into the stream in order to water his garden, or allow his family or his cattle to drink it. It is entirely a question of degree, and it is very difficult, indeed impossible, to define precisely the limits which separate the reasonable and permitted use of the stream from its wrongful application; but there is often no difficulty in deciding whether a particular case falls within the permitted limits or not, and in this we think, that as the irrigation took place not continuously, but only at intermittent periods, when the river was full, and no damage was done thereby to the working of the mill, and the diminution of the water was not perceptible to the eye, it was such a reasonable use of the water as not to be prohibited by law. The same law will be found to be applicable to the corresponding rights to air and light. These also are bestowed by Providence for the common benefit of man, and so long as the reasonable use by one man of this common property does not do actual and perceptible damage to the right of another, to a similar use of it, no action will lie. A man cannot occupy a dwelling and consume fuel for domestic purposes, without its in some degree impairing the natural purity of the air; he cannot erect a building, or plant a tree near the house of another, without in some degree diminishing the quantity of light he enjoys; but such small interruptions give no right of action; for they are necessary incidents to the common enjoyment of all." [The decision in this case was recognized and approved in Northam *v.* Hurley, 1 El. & Bl. 665. See per Lord Wensleydale, in Chasemore *v.* Richards, 7 H.L. Cas. 362.]

1 [Embrey *v.* Owen, 6 Exch. 353.]

2 [Sampson *v.* Hoddinott, 1 C. B. N.S. 590. See Crossley *v.* Lightowler, L.R. 3 Eq. 296.]

tiff, it was denied, generally, that a riparian proprietor, as such, had any right to apply the water of the stream to irrigate his adjacent land, although he did so in a careful manner; and it was also contended, that at all events, in this case the plaintiff had gained a title to the uninterrupted flow of the stream by immemorial enjoyment. "As to the latter proposition," the Court said, "it appears to us that all persons, having lands on the margin of a flowing stream, have, by nature, certain rights to use the water of that stream, whether they exercise those rights or not; and that they may begin to exercise them whenever they will. By usage, they may acquire a right to use the water in a manner not justified by their natural rights; but such acquired right has no operation against the natural rights of a land-owner higher up the stream, unless the user by which it was acquired affects the use that he himself has made of the stream, or his power to use it, so as to raise the presumption of a grant, and so render the tenement above a servient tenement. But the mere non-user of the right would not raise a presumption of a grant. If the user of the stream by the plaintiff for irrigation was merely an exercise of his natural right, such user, however long-continued, would not render the defendant's tenement a servient tenement, or in any way affect the natural rights of the defendant to use the water."—"In the present case, it appears to us, on the evidence, that the detention by the defendant, under the circumstances, of the water of the river Yeo, for the purposes of irrigation, was a use of it which, in its character, was necessarily injurious to the natural rights of the plaintiff as the proprietor of land lower down the stream. The effect was obviously the same as if the defendant had placed a bar or wear across the river, and by that means had wholly prevented its natural course for a certain number of hours. And it appears to us that there is neither authority nor principle for contending that such an act can be justified on the ground that it was done for the purpose of improving the adjacent land of the defendant, whether by irrigation or otherwise."[1]]

8. *Of the Effect of Prior Occupation by a Riparian Proprietor.*

§ 130. A question of much importance has been, on several occasions, discussed, whether a title to the use of running water

[1] [See Fleming *v.* Davis, 37 Texas, 173.]

is acquired by mere *occupancy*, so as to authorize any diversion of it from its accustomed course, or any obstruction or detention of it. Blackstone has stated water to be one of those things, the property in which is acquired by occupancy, and that, by first occupancy, a property is acquired in the current;[1] and in Williams *v.* Morland,[2] and in Liggins *v.* Inge,[3] there are dicta to the effect, that, by the law of England, the possessor who first appropriates any part of water flowing through his land to his own use, has a right to the use of so much as he thereby appropriates against any other. The dictum of Lord Chief-Justice Tindal in the case last named, is to this effect: "Water flowing, it is well settled by the law of England, is *publici juris.*[4] By the Roman law, running water, light, and air were considered some of those things which were *res communes*, and which were defined things, the property of which belongs to no person, but the use to all; and by the law of England, the person who first appropriates any part of this water flowing through his land to his own use, has the right to the use of so much as he then appropriates, against any other."[5]

§ 131. The doctrine laid down in Cary *v.* Daniels, in Massachusetts,[6] seems in accordance with that of C.J. Tindal. Shaw C.J., in giving the opinion of the Court in that case, speaks of the right to the use of the water inherent in the land as a right "*publici juris;*"[7] and he considers, that the rule that the limitation of the right to use of the water of a running stream, that the use must not be inconsistent with a like reasonable use by the

[1] 2 Black. Com. 402.

[2] Williams *v.* Morland, 2 B. & C. 913.

[3] Liggins *v.* Inge, 7 Bing. 692.

[4] See ante, § 92.

[5] [Kelly *v.* Natoma Water Co., 6 Cal. 105. A party acquires a right to water flowing in his ditch only from its actual appropriation to some useful purpose, or from an intention, avowed by acts or words and duly followed up, so to appropriate it, and not by using the ditch merely for drainage. Maeris *v.* Bicknell, 7 Cal. 261. Where one has dug a ditch, and appropriated water for the purpose of working certain mining claims, he may use the water at other points and for other purposes than those for which the ditch was constructed, without losing his priority of right as against one who had afterwards tapped the same stream and dug a ditch. Davis *v.* Gale, 32 Cal. 26.]

[6] Cary *v.* Daniels, 8 Met. 466. [In Keeney & Wood Manuf. Co. *v.* The Union Manuf. Co., 39 Conn. 582, it is said by Seymour J., that the doctrine announced by Judge Shaw in the case of Cary *v.* Daniels "appears not now to be the law of Massachusetts. Gould *v.* Boston Duck Co., 13 Gray, 442;" and he adds, "The case of Parker *v.* Hotchkiss, 25 Conn. 321, shows that it is not the law of Connecticut."]

[7] [See Elliot *v.* Fitchburg R.R. Co., 10 Cush. 193, 196; Johnson *v.* Jordan, 2 Met. 239; ante, § 92.]

other riparian proprietors on the same stream, above and below, is to be taken with a *qualification* growing out of the nature of the case, which qualification he thus explains: "The usefulness of water for mill purposes depends as well on its fall as its volume. But the fall depends upon the grade of the land over which it runs. The descent may be rapid, in which case there may be fall enough for mill sites at short distances; or the descent may be so gradual as only to admit of mills at considerable distances. In the latter case, the erection of a mill on one proprietor's land may raise and set the water back to such a distance as to prevent the proprietor above from having sufficient fall to erect a mill on his land. It seems to follow, as a necessary consequence from these principles, that, in such case, the proprietor who first erects his dam for such a purpose has a right to maintain it, as against the proprietors above and below; and to this extent, prior occupancy gives a prior title to such use.[1] It is a profitable, beneficial, and reasonable use, and therefore one which he has a right to make.[2] If it necessarily occupy so much of the fall as to prevent the proprietor above from placing a dam and mill on his land, it is *damnum absque injuria*. For the same reason, the proprietor below cannot erect a dam in such a manner as to raise the water and obstruct the wheels of the first occupant. He had an equal right with the proprietor below to a reasonable use of the stream; he had made only a reasonable use of it; his appropriation to that extent, being justifiable and prior in time, necessarily prevents the proprietor

1 [Pratt *v.* Lamson, 2 Allen, 288; Smith *v.* Agawam Canal Co., 2 Allen, 355, 357; Thurber *v.* Martin, 2 Gray, 394; Gould *v.* Boston Duck Co., 13 Gray, 442. Kelly *v.* Natoma Water Co., 6 Cal. 105; Bigelow C.J., in Fuller *v.* Chicopee Manuf. Co., 16 Gray, 43, 44. It was decided in Lincoln *v.* Chadbourne, 56 Maine, 197, that, as between proprietors of dams on the same stream, he has the better right who was first in point of time. In this case it appeared that of three dams situated within a short distance of each other on the same stream, each erected either by or with the consent of the riparian proprietor on whose land it stands, the middle one belonged to the plaintiff and the lowest to the defendant; and the plaintiff's dam was originally erected before the defendant's. Barrows J. said, "The plaintiff having erected his dam before the defendant had made any movement of the sort, had, so far as the defendant was concerned, a perfect right to maintain it perpetually, and to recover for any injury which the defendant might inflict by means of any subsequent erection below him. Unless he abandoned the right, the temporary destruction of his dam, whether by accident or by design, would not enable the defendant to acquire, as against him, the rights of a prior occupant."]

2 [See Weaver *v.* Eureka &c. Co., 15 Cal. 271.]

below from raising the water, without interfering with a rightful use already made; and it is therefore not an injury to him. Such appears to be the nature and extent of the prior and exclusive right which one proprietor acquires by a prior reasonable appropriation of the use of the water in its fall; and it results, not from any originally superior legal right, but from a legitimate exercise of his own common right, the effect of which is, *de facto*, to supersede and prevent a like use by other proprietors originally having the same common right.[1] It is, in this respect, like the right in common, which any individual has, to use a highway; whilst one is reasonably exercising his own right, by a temporary occupation of a particular part of the street with his carriage or team, another cannot occupy the same place at the same time. But such appropriation of the stream to mill purposes upon the principles stated, gives the proprietor a prior and exclusive right to such use only so far as it is actual.[2] If, therefore, he has erected his dam and mill, with its waste-ways, sluices, and other fixtures necessary to command the use of the water to a certain extent, and there is a surplus remaining, the proprietor below may have the benefit of that surplus.[3] If he erects a dam and mills, for the purpose of using and employing such surplus, he is, as to such part of the stream, the first occupant, and makes the first appropriation. As to that, therefore, his right is prior and exclusive. And although the proprietor above might, in the first instance, have raised his dam higher, keeping within the limits of a reasonable use, yet after such appropriation by the proprietor below, he cannot raise his dam

[1] [But the right which is thus acquired is not so absolute as to give him the control of the whole stream, or to deprive other proprietors of the reasonable enjoyment of the privileges to which they are naturally entitled. They may still construct and maintain dams across the stream at any point either above or below his mill, for the purpose of raising a head of water to propel, operate, and work mills of their own, erected on the adjoining land, provided that their arrangements are so made that they will not unreasonably withhold and detain the water above, nor throw it back from below, so as to affect, impede, delay, or obstruct the movement and operation of the wheels and machinery of his previously existing mill. Thurber *v.* Martin, 2 Gray, 394; Smith *v.* Agawam Canal Co., 2 Allen, 357.]

[2] [See Brook *v.* Winters, 39 Md. 505; Maeris *v.* Bicknell, 7 Cal. 261; Thompson *v.* Lee, 8 Cal. 275; Ophir &c. Co. *v.* Carpenter, 4 Nevada, 534; M'Kinney *v.* Smith, 21 Cal. 381; Ortman *v.* Dixon, 13 Cal. 33.]

[3] [If the first appropriator of the water takes it only for use during certain days of the week, another may afterwards take it during the remaining days of the week. Smith *v.* O'Hara, 43 Cal. 371.]

and take such surplus; because, as to that, the lower proprietor has acquired a prior right."[1]

§ 132. Now the proper construction of the Roman law,[2] as adduced by C.J. Tindal, and referred to by C.J. Shaw, is, that it considered running water, not as a *bonum vacans*, to which the first occupant might acquire an exclusive right; but as public and common *in this sense only*, that all who have a right of access to it might drink it, or apply it to the necessary purpose of supporting life; and that no one had any property in the water itself, except in that particular portion, which he might have abstracted from the stream, and of which he had the possession, and during the time of such possession only. And no other interpretation should be put upon the passage in Blackstone.[3]

§ 133. The case of Mason *v.* Hill, which may be considered as having settled the law on this subject in England, came twice before the Court of King's Bench.[4] Upon the first trial there was a verdict for the defendant; but a new trial was granted, by the unanimous opinion of the Court delivered by Lord Tenterden, upon the ground that the defendant could not, by law, acquire a right to the water by the prior use of it, unless the enjoyment was undisturbed for *twenty years*. Upon the next trial, the question was raised by special verdict, and was elaborately discussed at the bar, and after time taken by the Court,

[1] See post, § 134; [Elliot *v.* Fitchburg R.R. Co., 10 Cush. 198, per Shaw C.J.; Bigelow C.J. in Fuller *v.* Chicopee Manuf. Co., 16 Gray, 44; Gleason *v.* Assabet Manuf. Co., 101 Mass. 72, 77; Dean *v.* Colt, 99 Mass. 486; Knapp *v.* Douglas Axe Co., 13 Allen, 1; Smith *v.* O'Hara, 43 Cal. 371; Lobdell *v.* Simpson, 2 Nevada, 274; Keeney & Wood Manuf. Co. *v.* The Union Manuf. Co., 39 Conn. 576. A fair and reasonable implication from such right is, that he who has it is entitled to a head of water sufficient to enable him to make a practical, beneficial use of the amount to which he is entitled, for the purpose of propelling machinery. This is essential to the enjoyment of the priority of right. Samuels *v.* Blanchard, 25 Wis. 329. Whenever, in such a case, the head of water in the dam becomes so low, that, if parties subsequent in right continue to use the water, they will prevent such a practical beneficial use by the party having the prior right, they are then wrongfully diverting his water, and become liable to an action for the damages. Samuels *v.* Blanchard, 25 Wis. 329. An appropriation for a saw-mill allows the party to use the same amount for a grist-mill instead. McDonald *v.* Bear River &c. Co., 13 Cal. 220.]

[2] See Inst. tit. 1, s. 1; and Vinnius Comm. on the Inst.; Dig. B. 43, tit. 13.

[3] Per Lord Denman C.J., in Mason *v.* Hill, 5 B. & Ad. 1; and per Baron Parke, in Embrey *v.* Owen, 6 Exch. 352, 369; 20 Law. Jour. N.S. Exch. 212, and S.C. 4 Eng. Law. & Eq. 466; [adopted by Cresswell J. in Chasemore *v.* Richards, 2 H. & N. 168, 181; Pratt *v.* Lamson, 2 Allen, 287.] And see ante, § 121 et seq.

[4] Mason *v.* Hill, ub. sup. and 3 B. & Ad. 304.

judgment was pronounced by Lord C.J. Denman. The learned Judge, in giving judgment, said, "The position, that the first occupant of running water for a beneficial purpose, has a good title to it, is perfectly true in this sense, that neither the owner of the land below can pen back the water, nor the owner of the land above divert it to his prejudice. In this, as in other cases of injuries to real property, possession is a good title against a wrong-doer; and the owner of the land who applies the stream that runs through it, to the use of a mill newly erected, or other purposes, if the stream is diverted or obstructed, may recover for the consequential injury to the mill. But it is a very different question, whether he can take away from the owner of the land below, one of its natural advantages which is capable of being applied to profitable purposes, and generally increases the fertility of the soil, even when unapplied, and deprive him of it altogether, by anticipating him in its application to a new purpose. If this be so, a considerable part of the value of an estate, which, in manufacturing districts particularly, is much enhanced by the existence of an unappropriated stream of water with a fall, within its limits, might, at any time, be taken away; and, by parity of reasoning, a valuable mineral or brine spring might be abstracted from the proprietor in whose land it arises, and converted to the profit of another. We think that this proposition has originated in a mistaken view of the principles laid down in the decided cases of Bealy *v.* Shaw,[1] Saunders *v.* Newman,[2] and Williams *v.* Morland.[3] It appears to us also, that the doctrine of Blackstone, and the dicta of learned Judges, both in some of those cases, and in that of Cox *v.* Mathews,[4] have been misconceived." The judgment of Sir John Leach, in Wright *v.* Howard,[5] also settles, that no appropriation of running water, except for such a period as will confer an easement, can diminish the natural rights of other parties possessing lands along the course of the stream.[6]

§ 134. The weight of authority in this country is decidedly

[1] Bealy *v.* Shaw, 6 East, 208.

[2] Saunders *v.* Newman, 2 B. & Ald. 258. [See Heath *v.* Williams, 25 Maine, 209.]

[3] Williams *v.* Morland, 2 B. & C. 915.

[4] Cox *v.* Mathews, 1 Ventr. 137.

[5] Wright *v.* Howard, 1 Sim. & Stu. 190. This accords with the law as laid down by Sergeant Adair, Chief Justice of Chester, in Prescott *v.* Phillips, cited in Bealy *v.* Shaw, 6 East, 208.

[6] [1 Smith, Lead. Cas. (5th Am. ed.) 370, in notes to Ashby *v.* White, 2 Ld. Ray. 938.]

in favor of the doctrine that, if one riparian proprietor upon a natural watercourse, builds a mill, and a supra-riparian proprietor diverts the water, the owner of the mill may recover for the *injury to the mill*, although, before he built, he could only recover for the *natural uses* of the water, as needed for his family and his cattle.[1] But if, instead of building a mill, he had diverted the stream, he cannot justify it against a proprietor below,

[1] [In Holker *v.* Porritt, L.R. 10 Exch. 59, it appeared that a natural stream was divided immemorially, but by artificial means, into two branches: one branch ran down the river Irwell; the other passed into a farm-yard, where it supplied a watering-trough, and the overflow from the trough was formerly diffused over the surface, and discharged itself by percolation. In 1847, W., the owner of the land on which the watering-trough stood, and thence down to the Irwell, connected the watering-trough with reservoirs which he constructed adjacent to, and for the use of, the mill on the Irwell. In 1865, W. became owner of all the rest of the land through which this branch flowed. In 1867, he conveyed the mill, with all water rights, to the plaintiff. In an action brought by the plaintiff against a riparian owner on the stream above the point of division, for obstructing the flow of the water, it was held that the plaintiff was entitled to maintain the action. Lush J. said, "The water which came down to him [W.] at the farm was his own to use it as he pleased. There was no one entitled to share with him in its use, and no one who could call him to account for any use which he chose to make of it there. In this respect his position was different from that of a riparian owner, who only shares the use of the water in common with other riparian owners. In collecting the overflow at the trough and conveying it to the mill, he clearly did nothing in derogation of the rights of any other person, or which he was not entitled to do in the lawful use and enjoyment of his own property. Nor did he thereby lose any right which he then before had. While the water overflowed the trough and ran to waste, he had a right to complain of any undue diversion or obstruction of the stream which diminished the accustomed supply to the trough, and he acquired no greater rights by conveying it to the mill. No doubt the consequences to a wrong-doer became more serious after the drain was made than they were before, because the wrongful act was more injurious, and larger damages would have to be paid for it; but it is a fallacy to say that a man's rights are abridged, if, when he abuses them, he has to make larger compensation. It is the necessary effect of every appropriation of running water to a new and more beneficial use, that a wrongful diversion or abstraction entails a larger measure of responsibility. It is established by many authorities, which are collected in and confirmed by Mason *v.* Hill, 5 B. & Ad. 1, that, as soon as the owner of land on a stream has appropriated the water to a beneficial use, he may sue for the injury done to him in respect of such new use. In that case, the proprietor, having appropriated the stream to the use of a mill newly erected, was held entitled to recover, from a proprietor higher up the stream, damages for the injury to his mill occasioned by the wrongful diversion of the stream, although before the mill was built the wrong-doer would only have been liable to nominal damages. If, therefore, W. had been in possession of the mill in question, it is clear to us that he could have brought this action, not because he happened to be at the same time riparian owner higher up than the mill, and also owner of the mill, but simply as owner of the mill. And there is no conceivable reason why the plaintiff should not have the same right, in as much as he is surrenderee of the mill with all the water rights annexed, and which had become appurtenant to it."]

upon the ground that he had thus made an artificial use of the water, before the other had made any such application of it. Every riparian proprietor, necessarily, and at all times, is using the water running through it, in so far at least as the water imparts fertility to the land, and enhances the value of it.[1] There is, therefore, no prior or posterior in the use, for the land of each enjoyed it alike from the origin of the stream; and the priority of a particular new application, or artificial use of the water, does not, therefore, create a right to that use;[2] but the existence or non-existence of that application, at a particular time, measures the damages incurred by the wrongful act of another, in derogation of the general right to the use of the water, as it passes to, through, or from the land of the party complaining. The right is not founded in user, but is inherent in the ownership of the soil; and when a title by use is set up against another proprietor, there must be an enjoyment for such a length of time as will be evidence of a grant. This is the doctrine expressly laid down by the Supreme Court of North Carolina,[3] who rely for its support upon the above case of Mason *v.* Hill. To give such a construction to the passage from Blackstone above quoted, as that the owner of a mill-site who first occupies it, by the erection of a mill or dam, may use and appropriate the water to the injury of any other riparian proprietor above or below him (unless the use and appropriation has been of so long continuance as to afford the presumption of a grant), would be an extension of the doctrine of occupancy, in the words of Mr. C.J. Thompson, "dangerous and pernicious in its consequences;" and the occupancy, says he, "must be regulated and guarded with a view to the individual rights of all who have an interest in its enjoyment; and the maxim, *Sic utere tuo ut alienum non lœdas*, must be taken and construed with an eye to the natural rights of all."[4]

[1] Pugh *v.* Wheeler, 2 Dev. & Batt. (N.C.) 50. And see ante, §§ 8, 9, 92, 93.

[2] [Bliss *v.* Kennedy, 43 Ill. 67; post, § 352, note.]

[3] See Pugh *v.* Wheeler, ub. sup.

[4] Platt *v.* Johnson, 15 John. 213. See also Palmer *v.* Mulligan, 3 Caines, 397; Merritt *v.* Brinkerhoff, 17 John. 306. [In Keeney & Wood Manuf. Co. *v.* The Union Manuf. Co., 39 Conn. 576, it appeared that the owners of an upper mill, whose business required the running of their mill only by day, detained the water of the stream during the night, such detention and the larger discharge during the day causing serious damage to the owners of the lower mill, whose business required the running of their mill both night and day. The lower privilege was occupied several years

§ 135. By the learned Mr. Justice Story, the right to have a stream flow on in its accustomed course, is laid down to be a right, which can only be interfered with by an easement acquired by grant, or by an adverse enjoyment for the period of time limited by the statute of limitations for entry upon land. "Mere priority of occupation," says he, "of running water, without such consent or grant, confers no exclusive right.[1] It is not like the case of mere occupancy, where the first occupant takes by force of his priority of occupation. That supposes no ownership already existing, and no right to the use already acquired. But our law awards to the riparian proprietors the right to the use in common, as one incident to the land; and

before the upper, and after the upper mill was built the water was for several years allowed to flow during the night, and the lower mill had used it by night and by day. Upon a petition by the lower mill-owners against the upper, for an injunction against the detention of the water by night, it was held: (1) That the petitioners had acquired no superior rights by their earlier occupation, or by their use of the water by night, so long as they had exercised no rights greater than such as belonged to them as riparian proprietors; the full flow of the stream being nothing beyond such right. Seymour J. said, "So long as the defendants had no occasion to detain the water at night, the plaintiffs as riparian owners below were entitled to the uninterrupted flow of the stream by night and by day, and under those circumstances, that being their right, by the exercise of it they could acquire no right to such uninterrupted flow, if afterwards the defendants had occasion to detain more of the water of the stream than they before had done. Nor, on the other hand, do the defendants lose any of their natural proprietary rights by allowing the water to flow past their mill without interruption, or with only a partial interruption. In order to maintain their proprietary rights, they are not obliged to detain more water than they have immediate use for. When the defendants have occasion to detain more water they may do so, keeping within the bounds of reasonable use, and the fact that they have heretofore allowed the water to pass by them without detaining or using it to the full extent of their right, in no manner impairs their present right to its full enjoyment. Parker *v.* Hotchkiss, 25 Conn. 321. The Court in the above case of Keeney & Wood Manuf. Co. *v.* The Union Manuf. Co., farther decided: (2) That all that the petitioners were entitled to, was a reasonable use of the stream against an unreasonable use or detention by the respondents; that the question was whether the respondents had acted unreasonably in detaining the water; and that the burden of proof on this subject was on the petitioners. The right of the proprietor above to make the water useful to him by detaining it long enough to make it useful, is of the same quality as the right of the proprietor below to take the constant course of the current for his use, where both parties are applying the water to the artificial use of propelling machinery. In deciding between these conflicting rights, there are to be considered: (1) The custom of the country as to the running of mills; (2) The local custom, if there be one; (3) The general rule that will best secure the entire stream to useful purposes; (4) Whether the detention of the water is necessarily an injury to the lower mill, and whether the apparent injury is not caused by the insufficiency of its own privilege.]

[1] [See Snow *v.* Parsons, 28 Vt. 463; Ellsworth J., in Roath *v.* Driscoll, 20 Conn. 541.]

whoever seeks to found an exclusive use, must establish a rightful appropriation in some manner known and admitted by the law.[1] Now, this may be by a grant from all the proprietors, whose interest is affected by the particular appropriation, or by a long exclusive enjoyment without interruption, which affords a just presumption of right."[2] In fact, by numerous authorities in this country, the first appropriator of running water has no right to divert or retain the stream to the extent of such appropriation, to the injury of other riparian proprietors, who shall afterwards seek to use the stream;[3] though here, as in England, dicta may be found to the contrary;[4] and that a diversion of a watercourse, without actual injury to a riparian owner lower down the stream, legally imports damage (because it is an in-

[1] [Mere priority of appropriation of the water of a stream confers no exclusive right to the use of it. Heath *v.* Williams, 25 Maine, 209; Ellsworth J., in Roath *v.* Driscoll, 20 Conn. 541.]

[2] Tyler *v.* Wilkinson, 4 Mason, 397. See also the opinion of the same learned Judge in Whipple *v.* Cumberland Manuf. Co., 2 Story, 661. [But an omission by the owner to make use of water rights does not impair his title or confer any right thereto upon another. It is not the non-user by the owner, but the adverse enjoyment by another, which destroys the right. Townsend *v.* McDonald, 2 Kernan, 381, 391, 392; Pillsbury *v.* Morse, 44 Maine, 154, 155.]

[3] Gilman *v.* Tilton, 5 N.H. 231; Martin *v.* Bigelow, 2 Aik. (Vt.) 184; Hoy *v.* Sterrett, 2 Watts, 327; Twiss *v.* Baldwin, 9 Conn. 291; King *v.* Tiffany, 9 Conn. 162; M'Almont *v.* Whitaker, 3 Rawle, 84; Bullen *v.* Runnels, 2 N.H. 257; Buddington *v.* Bradley, 10 Conn. 213; Tucker *v.* Jewett, 11 Conn. 311; Wadsworth *v.* Tillotson, 15 Conn. 366; Plumleigh *v.* Dawson, 1 Gilman, 544; Stout *v.* M'Adams, 2 Scam. (Ill.) 67; Baldwin *v.* Calkins, 10 Wend. 167; Heath *v.* Williams, 25 Maine, 209; Davis *v.* Fuller, 12 Vt. 178; [Gillett *v.* Johnson, 30 Conn. 180, 183; Butman *v.* Hussey, 12 Maine, 410; Cowles *v.* Kidder, 24 N.H. 364, 378.] And as to general rights of riparian proprietors, see ante, § 90, et seq. [In Dumont *v.* Kellogg, 29 Mich. 420, Cooley J. said, "The settled doctrine now is that priority of appropriation gives to one proprietor no superior right to that of the others, unless it has been continued for a period of time, and under such circumstances, as would be requisite to establish rights by prescription." The question, as between riparian proprietors, of the wrongful detention of flowing waters, to the prejudice and injury of proprietors below, was said by the same learned Judge, in the above case, to be essentially different from that of the diversion of the stream from its natural course so as to turn it away from the lower proprietor, or from that of an interference by a stranger in any way to diminish the water; for these acts are wholly wrongful.]

[4] 1 Wm. Saund. 114 a, n. (g). In Strickler *v.* Todd, in Pennsylvania, 10 S. & Rawle, 63, Duncan J., in giving the judgment of the Court, appears to accede to the doctrine that a superior right to the use of a natural watercourse may be acquired by the simple act of prior occupation; but the right of the plaintiff to recover, in that case, was made to rest upon his uninterrupted enjoyment of the water, for a term of time exceeding twenty years. [On the mineral lands of the public domain in the Pacific States and Territories, the doctrines of the Common Law, declaratory of the rights of riparian proprietors respecting the use of running waters, are held to be inapplicable, or applicable only in a very limited extent, to the necessity of miners, and in-

fringement of right), is a doctrine powerfully sustained by American authorities.[1]

adequate to their protection; there prior appropriation gives the better right to running waters to the extent, in quantity and quality, necessary for the uses to which the water is applied. Atchison *v.* Peterson, 20 Wallace, 507; Irwin *v.* Phillips, 5 Cal. 140; Butte Canal and Ditch Co. *v.* Vaughn, 11 Cal. 143; Ortman *v.* Dixon, 13 Cal. 33; Hill *v.* Smith, 27 Cal. 483; Basey *v.* Gallagher, 20 Wallace, 670.]

[1] So laid down by Wilde J., in Bolivar Manuf. Co. *v.* Neponset Manuf. Co., 16 Pick. 241; [Newhall *v.* Ireson, 8 Cush. 595; Cook *v.* Hull, 3 Pick. 269; Stowell *v.* Lincoln, 11 Gray, 434.] Also by the Supreme Court of Maine, Butman *v.* Hussey, 12 Maine, 407; Munroe *v.* Stickney, 48 Maine, 462. And see also Crooker *v.* Bragg, 10 Wend. 260; Baldwin *v.* Calkins, 10 Wend. 167; Heath *v.* Williams, 25 Maine, 209; Whipple *v.* Cumberland Manuf. Co., 2 Story, 661; Branch *v.* Doane, 17 Conn. 402; 18 Conn. 233; Parker *v.* Griswold, 17 Conn. 288; Chapman *v.* Thames Manuf. Co., 13 Conn. 269; Hulme *v.* Shreve, 3 Green (N.J.) 116; Woodman *v.* Tufts, 9 N.H. 88; Bliss *v.* Rice, 17 Pick. 23; Blanchard *v.* Baker, 8 Greenl. 253; Pastorius *v.* Fisher, 1 Rawle, 27; Alexander *v.* Kerr, 2 Rawle, 83; Ripka *v.* Sergeant, 7 Watts & S. 11; Plumleigh *v.* Dawson, 1 Gilman, 551; Webb *v.* Portland Manuf. Co., 3 Sumner, 189; [Harrop *v.* Hirst, L.R. 4 Exch. 43; Cooley J., in Dumont *v.* Kellogg, 29 Mich. 422; Wilts & Berks Canal Navigation Co. *v.* Swindon Waterworks Co., L.R. 9 Ch. 451; S. C. L.R. 7 H.L. 697. See the judgments in Embrey *v.* Owen, 6 Exch. 371–373, in which case the question was, whether the defendant had infringed the plaintiff's right by using the water for irrigation; Sampson *v.* Hoddinott, 1 C.B. N.S. 611, 612, in which the question was as to the right to impede the flow by occasionally shutting sluices; and the case put by Coleridge J., in Chasemore *v.* Richards, 2 H. & N. 190, of a man *exhausting* the running water by irrigation, which would be clearly illegal, though the abstraction of the same amount of water from a large river might have been perfectly legal. The question in each case should seem to be, is the user such as to affect the natural flow of the water of the stream to an extent greater than that which is necessarily incident to the common enjoyment of the stream by all the riparian owners? If it be, then it may be made the subject of an action by any owner whose actual use of, or power to use, the water is affected by it. The question can arise in practice only with reference to some extraordinary use of the water. The result is that no actual damage need be shown if the right to the flow of the stream in its natural state be infringed by a use of it beyond that which every riparian owner is entitled to. The case of Elliot *v.* Fitchburg R.R. Co., 10 Cush. 191, seems to hold a different doctrine. But the difference does not appear to arise so much out of the question whether, on proof of a violation or infringement of the plaintiff's right, a recovery can be had without evidence of actual, perceptible damage, as out of the preliminary question, whether the particular use proved in the case which causes no actual, perceptible damage to the plaintiff is really a violation of the plaintiff's right. This was an action against the defendants, for diverting the water of a small brook, passing through land of the plaintiff in Shirley. The facts were briefly these: The plaintiff was the owner of certain land, and for more than sixty years a small brook, having its sources in several ponds, had, in its natural course, flowed through lands of various persons; viz., of one Clark, of one Furnin, and then through the plaintiff's land, situated about half a mile below said Clark's, and from the plaintiff's land, through various other lands to the Nashua River. Said brook was in part supplied by a never-failing spring, on said Clark's land, near said brook, and having its outlet into it. The defendants — the Fitchburg Railroad Company — pursuant to a warranty deed from said Clark, of a perpetual right to make and maintain a dam and reservoir, and draw and use the

[§ 135 *a*. But if a proprietor of land, which is bounded upon a natural stream, appropriates to his own use so much of the passing water as he is enabled to control, by means of structures

water therefrom, erected such dam across said stream, below said spring, and made said reservoir upon and about the same, and inserted a lead pipe therein, by means of which they have used and constantly taken water, from said reservoir, to their depot in Shirley, and used the same for furnishing their locomotive steam-engines with water, and for other similar purposes. The defendants offered evidence tending to prove that said Clark, where said brook ran through his meadow, which was wet and springy, had cut ditches across the meadow to the brook, thereby increasing the flow of water to the brook; and it was further proved that there was no outlet for the water of said meadow, except into this brook. The meadow was situate below the dam. The plaintiff contended that if the jury were satisfied of the existence of the brook, as alleged, and the diversion of the water therefrom by the defendants, he was entitled to a verdict for nominal damages, without proof of actual damage. But the presiding Judge instructed the jury that unless the plaintiff suffered actual, perceptible damage in consequence of the diversion, the defendants were not liable in the action. In connection with this instruction, the Judge further instructed the jury that if they believed that the defendants, by excavating said reservoir and spring above the dam, or, that said Clark, by digging said ditches, had increased the flow of water in said brook, equal to the quantity of water the defendants had diverted therefrom, then the defendants were not liable in the action. The full Court decided that these instructions, given by the presiding Judge, were correct. Shaw C.J. remarked, "The instruction requested by the plaintiff is, we think, founded on a misconception of the rights of riparian proprietors in water-courses passing through or by their lands. It presupposes that the diversion of any portion of the water of a running stream, without regard to the fitness of the purpose, is a violation of the right of every proprietor of land lying below, on the same stream, so that, without suffering any actual or perceptible damage, he may have an action for the sole purpose of vindicating his legal right." After an elaborate discussion and statement of the rights of riparian proprietors to the water in a running stream, the Chief-Justice proceeds, "We think it was properly left to the jury to find, whether the defendants claiming in the right of Clark, had, by their diversion of the water for a valuable and highly beneficial use, caused any actual or perceptible damage, and, if not, to find for the defendants. It is very clear that here is no complaint of the total diversion of the stream from the plaintiff's land; no such ground of complaint is set forth or relied on. The bed of the stream and the stream itself remain and pass through the plaintiff's land as they did before. The gravamen of the complaint is, not for diverting the stream itself, but for abstracting a part of the water of the stream. This is a right which each proprietor has, if exercised within a reasonable limit. The proper question therefore was, whether, in the mode of taking, in the quantity taken, and the purpose for which it was taken, there was a reasonable and justifiable use of the water by Clark. The use being lawful and beneficial, it must be deemed reasonable, and not an infringement of the right of the plaintiff, if it did no actual and perceptible damage to the plaintiff; and, therefore, we think that question of fact was rightly left to the jury, who must have found that it did him no such damage." See Wadsworth *v*. Tillotson, 15 Conn. 366; Shaw C.J., in Cummings *v*. Barrett, 10 Cush. 189; Norway Plains Co. *v*. Bradley, 52 N.H. 86; Amoskeag Manuf. Co. *v*. Goodale, 46 N.H. 53, 56, and cases; post, § 108, note.

The Court, in the above case of Elliot *v*. Fitchburg R.R. Co., evidently do not mean to state a different doctrine from that laid down in the text. The same question was not before them. The same Court maintain the doctrine of the text in Newhall *v*. Ireson, 8 Cush. 595, 599;

erected upon and within the limits of his own estate, even if it be the whole of it, he can thereby gain no prescriptive right to appropriate and use more than one-half of the same, so long as the opposite proprietor neither uses, nor seeks to use, nor makes any provision, nor has any occasion, for the use of any part of the stream to which he is entitled. The reason for this is, that, in fact, there is, in such a case, no adverse use, occupation, or possession whatever.[1] In Pratt *v.* Lamson,[2] Merrick J. said, "The dam was built and maintained wholly on the land belonging to those by whom it was built and maintained. They owned to the centre of the stream, and the rock upon which the dam abutted was several rods north of that line. As they occupied only their own land, they committed no disseisin, and were guilty of no infringement upon the right, or encroachment upon the property, of any other person. In relation to the stream itself, it is now a well-settled principle, that no one, neither the riparian proprietor, nor the owner of a mill, acquires, or has any property in the water flowing in it, except as to that portion which he actually withdraws and holds in his own possession; but, instead of this, that he has a simple usufruct of it while it passes along. Under this general right, which is incident to the ownership of land bounded by, and therefore extending to the thread of, the stream, no exclusive right is acquired to one-half, or to any definite part, but, as is said by Story J., in Webb *v.* Portland Manuf. Co.,[3] each of them is entitled, *per my et per tout*, to the use of his proportion of the whole bulk and volume of the stream. Such being their relation to each other, it is obvious that the mere use by one of them of all the water,

in Stowell *v.* Lincoln, 11 Gray, 434, and in other cases. See also Tillotson *v.* Smith, 32 N.H. 90; Chatfield *v.* Wilson, 28 Vt. 670; Gerrish *v.* New Market Manuf. Co., 30 N.H. 478; Chasemore *v.* Richards, 5 H. & N. 982, 989; Crossley *v.* Lightowler, L.R. 3 Eq. Cas. 296, 297; Sampson *v.* Hoddinott, 1 C.B. N.S. 590; Embrey *v.* Owen, 6 Exch. 353, 368, 369; Howell *v.* M'Coy, 3 Rawle, 256, 269; Pugh *v.* Wheeler, 5 Dev. & Batt. 50, 59; Van Hoesen *v.* Coventry, 10 Barb. 518; Bower *v.* Hill, 1 Bing. N.C. 549.

Of course no action will lie either in trespass or nuisance, unless a right be infringed; but if the infringement be proved, nominal damages must be awarded, whether actual damage were a consequence or not. Phear on Rights of Water, 107; 1 Smith, Lead. Cas. (5th Am. ed.) 364 et seq. in notes to Ashby *v.* White. In cases where the right alleged to be infringed is merely a right to be protected from *actual damage*, manifestly no action can succeed, unless actual damage be proved. Phear on Rights of Water, 107. And see ante, § 96, in note; post, § 427, et seq.]

[1] [Pratt *v.* Lamson, 2 Allen, 275, 287.]

[2] [Pratt *v.* Lamson, 2 Allen, 287.]

[3] [Webb *v.* Portland Manuf. Co., 3 Sumner, 189.]

unaccompanied by any act of exclusion against the other, or by the assertion of any superior or exclusive claim, is not in its nature adverse, does no injury, and affords no cause of complaint or action. He does nothing for which an action can be maintained against him, or nominal damages recovered in the assertion and vindication of an invaded right. In such circumstances, they stand towards each other in the relation, and with substantially the rights, of tenants in common, where the possession of one is deemed to be the possession and for the benefit of all; and their respective rights will continue to be protected and preserved to them, until some positive act of actual and exclusive adverse possession, by which one of the parties is directly interfered with, and prevented from enjoying his equal privilege in the use of the water." — "The right to an exclusive use of the water may undoubtedly be acquired by adverse possession and enjoyment, where it is real and actual. Thus the proprietor who first lawfully erects his dam across the stream, to create a fall, by means of which he may operate his mill, has a right afterwards to maintain it against all other proprietors, both above and below him; and to this extent priority of occupancy gives priority of title."[1]]

9. *Of the Injury by rendering the Water Corrupt and Unwholesome.*

§ 136. It is clearly the duty of riparian proprietors, upon a watercourse, to refrain from erecting upon its banks any works which render the water unwholesome or offensive.[2] It was long

[1] [Cary *v.* Daniels, 8 Met. 466; Thurber *v.* Martin, 2 Gray, 394; Gould *v.* Boston Duck Co., 13 Gray, 442; Pratt *v.* Lamson, 2 Allen, 288.]

[2] Aldred's case, 9 Co. R. 59; Dictum of Story J., in Tyler *v.* Wilkinson, 4 Mason, 397, of Lord Ellenborough, in Bealy *v.* Shaw, 6 East, 208, and of Lord Denman, in Mason *v.* Hill, 5 B. & Al. 1; 7 Mon. (Ken.) 325; Call *v.* Buttrick, 4 Cush. 345; [Gladfelter *v.* Walker, 40 Md. 1; Attorney-General *v.* Steward, 5 C. E. Green, 416; O'Riley *v.* McChesney, 3 Lansing, 278. The right of every owner of land, through which a stream of water flows, to the use and enjoyment of the water, and to have the same flow in its natural and accustomed course, without obstruction, diversion, or corruption, extends to the *quality* as well as to the quantity of the water. If, therefore, an adjoining proprietor corrupts the water, an action on the case lies for the injury. Holsman *v.* Boiling Spring Bleaching Co., 1 McCarter (14 N.J. Ch.) 335, 342. O'Riley *v.* McChesney, 3 Lansing, 278; Richmond Manuf. Co. *v.* Atlantic De Laine Co., 10 R.I. 106. A riparian proprietor, in the absence of any express grant or prescription, has no right to foul or corrupt the water of a running stream. An injury to the purity or quality of the water, to the detriment of other riparian owners, constitutes, in legal effect, a wrong and invasion of private right in like manner as a permanent obstruction

ago adjudged to be illegal for a glover to set up a lime pit, for calf or sheep skins, so near the water as to corrupt it.[1] Lord Coke says, "If two several owners of houses have a river in common between them, and if one of them corrupt the water, the other shall have an action on the case."[2] Erecting a cesspool near a well, and thereby contaminating the water, has been held to be actionable.[3] The erection of a tan-yard, it has been

or diversion of the water. Dwight Printing Co. *v.* Boston, Suffolk Co. Mass. 1877, 5 Cent. Law Journ. 71. If the water is polluted by a riparian proprietor higher up the stream, so as to occasion damage *in law*, though not *in fact*, to a proprietor lower down the stream, it gives him a good cause of action against the upper proprietor, unless the latter has gained a right by long enjoyment or grant. Wood *v.* Waud, 3 Exch. 748. See Merrifield *v.* Lombard, 13 Allen, 16; Wheatley *v.* Chrisman, 24 Penn. St. 298; Gladfelter *v.* Walker, 40 Md. 1. In Washburn *v.* Gilman, 64 Maine, 163, the plaintiff brought his action to recover for injury to his interval land by the drifting upon it, in consequence of a freshet, of the refuse cast out of the defendant's mill; and it was held, that the defendant, in operating his mill, should have guarded against freshets, which are always liable to occur. See Howell *v.* McCoy, 3 Rawle, 256; Crosby *v.* Bessey, 49 Maine, 539.] Where an action for polluting the water of a watercourse, was referred to an arbitrator, with power to him to regulate the enjoyment of the water; it was held, that an award directing a verdict to be entered for the plaintiff, and that defendant should, at all times, take *all proper and reasonable precautions* for preventing the water from being rendered unfit for plaintiff's use, *and in particular*, should use a process of filtering mentioned in the award, was bad for uncertainty. The direction as to the particular process was, that the water passing from defendant's to plaintiff's premises, should be passed through filtering lodges, made or to be made, by defendant, so as to be thereby purified and cleansed for plaintiff's use, "so far as the same can be purified and cleansed *by the ordinary and most approved process* of filtering." It was held, that the description by reference only to the "ordinary and most approved process," was uncertain, and the award bad in this respect also. Stonehewer *v.* Farrar, 6 Ad. & El. N.S. 730. [In Stockport Waterworks *v.* Potter, 7 H. & N. 160, it appeared that the defendants were calico-printers, and had, for many years, been in the habit of using the water of a certain brook, for the purposes of their works. Arsenite of soda had latterly been used in large quantities in the process of dyeing calico, and arsenic from the defendants' works was traced in the mud of the reservoir of the plaintiffs' (the Stockport Waterworks Co.), which was eleven miles below the defendants' works, and also in the water supplied by them to the town. The plaintiffs gave evidence that the defendants might have prevented the arsenic from escaping, if they had constructed a large settling reservoir below their works. The witnesses were cross-examined, to show that this would have been very expensive, but the defendants gave no evidence as to the mode in which they carried on their works. In answer to a question put by the Judge, the jury found that the defendants' trade was a lawful trade, carried on for purposes necessary or useful to the community, in a reasonable and proper manner, and in a reasonable and proper place; and it was held: *first*, that there was no evidence that the defendants' trade was carried on in a reasonable and proper manner, and in a proper place; and *semble*, that if such evidence had been given, it would have been no answer to an action by the plaintiffs. See Hodgkinson *v.* Ennor, 4 B. & S. 229; Snow *v.* Parsons, 28 Vt. 459.]

[1] Year Book, Hen. 2, b. 6.

[2] Co. Litt. 200; 13 Hen. 7, 26; Crossley *v.* Lightowler, L.R. 3 Eq. Cas. 279.

[3] Norton *v.* Scholefield, 9 M. & W.

held, is illegal, provided it has the effect of rendering the water unwholesome, whether the riparian proprietor below use it for distillation, or for culinary or domestic purposes.[1] So the owner of a tannery situated upon a stream is liable for the injury, if he throws tan-bark and other refuse materials into the stream, so as to clog it and cause damage to the mills of a riparian proprietor lower down the stream, although no injury was intended and the acts were done in a manner usual in tanneries.[2] No user, for a less time than twenty years, will justify the letting off upon the neighboring land, water which has been used for the precipitation of minerals, and which is thereby rendered noxious.[3] In the case of an artificial watercourse, made for the

565. ["A person should not place or negligently allow a deleterious substance to remain, where the useful waters of another may be corrupted either by the ordinary or extraordinary, and yet not very uncommon action of the elements." Shepley C.J. in Woodward *v.* Ahorn, 35 Maine, 271. This was said in an action on the case for placing manure near a well, by which, an extraordinary rain coming on, the water therein was damaged.]

[1] Howell *v.* M'Coy, 3 Rawle, 397.

[2] [Housee *v.* Hammond, 39 Barb. 89. Any use of a stream by a riparian proprietor which defiles and corrupts it to such a degree as essentially to impair its purity, and prevent the use of it for any of the reasonable and proper purposes to which running water is usually applied, such as irrigation, the propulsion of machinery, or consumption for domestic use, is an infringement of the right of other owners of land through which a watercourse runs, and creates a nuisance, for which those thereby injured are entitled to a remedy. Bigelow C.J. in Merrifield *v.* Lombard, 13 Allen, 17; Washburn *v.* Gilman, 64 Maine, 163, 168–171. But the natural right of a riparian proprietor to have the water descend to him in its pure state, fit to be used for the various purposes to which he may have occasion to apply it, must yield to the equal right in those who happen to be above him. Their use of the stream for mill purposes, for irrigation, watering cattle, and the manifold purposes for which they may lawfully use it, will tend to render the water more or less impure. Cultivating and fertilizing the lands bordering on the stream, and in which are its sources, their occupation by farm-houses and other erections, will unavoidably cause impurities to be carried into the stream. As the lands are subdivided and their occupation and uses become multifarious, these causes will be rendered more operative, and their effects more perceptible. The water may thus be rendered unfit for many uses for which it had before been suitable; but so far as that condition results only from reasonable use of the stream in accordance with the common right, the lower riparian proprietor has no remedy. When the population becomes dense, and towns or villages gather along its banks, the stream naturally and necessarily suffers still greater deterioration. Roads and streets crossing it, or running by its side, with their gutters and sluices discharging into it their surface water collected from over large spaces, and carrying with it in suspension the loose and light material that is thus swept off, are abundant sources of impurity, against which the law affords no redress by action. Wells J. in Merrifield *v.* Worcester, 110 Mass. 219, 220. See Pollock C.B. in Cator *v.* Lewisham, 5 B. & S. 115, 143.]

[3] Wright *v.* Williams, 1 M. & W. 77. [But a right to foul or corrupt a stream may be acquired by an adverse user for twenty years. Merrifield *v.* Lombard, 13 Allen, 16; Moore *v.* Webb, 1 C.B. N.S. 673; Carlyon *v.* Lovering, 1 H. & N. 784; Jones *v.* Crow, 32 Penn. St. 398, 406;

purpose of draining mines, if the drainage water has flowed for twenty years, in a pure state, in consequence of the working of the mines having been discontinued, over premises of a person who has used it for that period, the working of the mines cannot be resumed, so as to render the water foul, and thus disturb his enjoyment.[1] [But the mere suspension of the exercise of a prescriptive right to foul a stream is not sufficient to destroy the right, without some evidence of an intention to abandon it; but

Hayes *v.* Waldron, 44 N.H. 585; Murgatroyd *v.* Robinson, 8 El. & Bl. 391. In Carlyon *v.* Lovering, 1 H. & N. 797, the Court of Exchequer decided, that a right to use a natural stream for the purpose of washing ore, and carrying away sand, stones, rubble, and other stuff dislodged and severed from the soil in the working of a mine and winning the ore, and to cause the stream to overflow its banks, might be acquired by custom or prescription at the Common Law, or by user under Lord Tenterden's Act. In Murgatroyd *v.* Robinson, 7 El. & Bl. 391, it was argued that a right to use a natural stream for the purpose of washing away the ashes from a steam engine, and other sweepings of a mill on the bank of the stream, could not be acquired under Lord Tenterden's Act, as being unreasonable and destructive of the property of the owners lower down the stream; the Court pronounced no opinion upon the question, as the case went off on another point, but no valid distinction can be made between this and the case last cited. The owner lower down, clearly might grant the right claimed in one case as well as in the other, and if so, according to the judgment in Carlyon *v.* Lovering, the statute would apply. In Carlyon *v.* Lovering, the Court held that the right being limited by reference to the necessary working of the mine, could not be considered unreasonable, and might be claimed by prescription or custom; although no doubt any objection, on the ground of the claim being unreasonable and destructive, would be equally applicable to it if set up by way of custom, under Lord Tenterden's Act, as if set up by custom at the Common Law, as the second section is confined to such claims as might lawfully have been made at the Common Law. See also Moore *v.* Webb, supra, where a claim of right to foul a stream by using it for the tanning business was set up under the Act, and Stockport Waterworks Company *v.* Potter, 7 H. & N. 160.]

[1] Magor *v.* Chadwick, 11 Ad. & El. 371. [See remark of Parke B. upon this case, in Rawstron *v.* Taylor, 11 Exch. 380. Where a prescriptive right to foul a stream has been acquired, the fouling must not be considerably enlarged to the prejudice of other people. Crossley *v.* Lightowler, L.R. 2 Ch. Ap. 478; s.c. 3 Eq. Cas. 279. But a mere change in the character of a material used in a particular manufacture does not render liable the manufacturer who has acquired a prescriptive right to foul a stream in the business of that manufacture, but who has not by such change increased the amount of pollution. Baxendale *v.* McMurray, L.R. 2 Ch. Ap. 790; post, § 219 *d.*] The act of the State of Tennessee of 1830, ch. 39, directed that the owners of mills should cut down and remove standing or decayed timber in their mill-ponds, west of Tennessee River, and made such owners indictable if they failed. And the act of 1832, ch. 79, authorized one, G. by name, to build a dam without cutting down and removing the timber in his pond; and it was held, that the act of 1832 only exempted the defendant G. from the penalty of the act of 1830, and left him liable as other persons to indictment, if his dam created a nuisance; the Court, in giving judgment, saying, "The legislature should not be readily supposed as meaning to violate that *fundamental principle* of social, natural, and municipal law, which prescribes to every one, in the use and enjoyment of his own property, the necessary limitation, that *he shall not injuriously affect the rights of others.*" State *v.* Gainer, 3 Humph. (Tenn.) 39.

where dye-works had not been used for more than twenty years, and had been allowed to go to ruin, it was held, that any right of fouling a stream attached to them was lost.[1]]

§ 137. Neither can a riparian proprietor use the water in a manner so as to corrupt the *atmosphere*. An action on the case was brought to recover special damages sustained by the plaintiff and his family, in consequence of a mill-dam erected by the defendant; and the plaintiff alleged in his declaration, that the dam, by overflowing the adjacent lands, rendered the atmosphere exceedingly impure and unhealthy, and thereby occasioned the sickness of himself and family, &c. It appeared, on the trial, that not only the plaintiff and his family, but the neighborhood generally, suffered by disease, occasioned by the defendant's dam, and it was insisted, that, as the injury was general, it was a bar to the recovery of individual damages. The Court held, that "every member of society is bound by the principles of natural justice, so to use his own property, as not to injure the rights of others; and if an individual erects a mill-dam which creates disease and sickness, he must be responsible for the consequences." It was also held, that it was no defence to the action, that the injury affected the whole neighborhood, and that the civil remedy was not merged by an indictment and conviction.[2]

§ 138. In Virginia, under the laws of which State, in relation to the erection of mills, the finding of a jury, in a "mill-case," that probably the health of certain families who live near the pond, will be annoyed by the stagnation of the water, is conclusive against a petitioner to erect a dam.[3]

§ 139. An indictment for a nuisance in erecting and main-

[1] [Crossley *v.* Lightowler, L.R. 2 Ch. Ap. 478. This case was very fully discussed by Sir W. Page Wood V.C., L.R. 3 Eq. Cas. 279, where it was held that mere non-user for less than twenty years, of a privilege or easement to discharge foul dye-water into a stream, is not of itself a proof of abandonment, which is a conclusion to be drawn from all the circumstances; amongst which the lying by, and permitting others to incur expense in preparing to do that which, if continued uninterruptedly for twenty years, would destroy the easement, is a fact of great importance. But actual disuser of an easement of the above kind for twenty years, during which others have acquired adverse rights, destroys the right to the easement.]

[2] Story *v.* Hammond, 4 Ohio, 333. [And where in such cases an action at law does not afford an adequate remedy to the land-owner, he is entitled to the aid of a court of equity to have the nuisance abated. Carlisle *v.* Cooper, 21 N.J. Eq. 576.]

[3] Mayo *v.* Turner, 1 Munf. (Va.) 405.

taining a dam, upon the defendant's land, alleged that, by reason of the dam, the animal and vegetable substances brought down the stream, were collected and accumulated in large quantities, and became offensive, and corrupted the water, &c. It was held, that though the proof showed the injury to have resulted from the alternate rise and fall of the water in the pond, or from the action of the sun upon the vegetables growing on the margin, the substance of the issue was maintained; and this, notwithstanding the stream was not a public highway.[1]

§ 140. But to authorize the abatement of a dam, in these cases, on the ground of its being a nuisance, it must, at the time it is abated, be considered as a nuisance. That it had been a nuisance, and was likely to be so again, will not justify the proceeding. The fears of persons, however reasonable, that a thing will become a substantial annoyance, public or private, do not make a nuisance which is actionable, or which may be abated.[2]

§ 140 *a*. The defendant diverted a stream as it passed through his premises, but restored it *undiminished*, as to the quantity of water, to its former channel, before it reached the premises of the plaintiff. The defendant also employed the stream, while on his premises, in a way which rendered the water unfit for ordinary use, but he alleged that the water, by the time it reached the plaintiff's lands, was freed to the utmost possible extent from any noxious ingredients with which it had become impregnated; and it did not appear that any actual damage was sustained by the plaintiff. Under these circumstances, the Lord Chancellor, Cottenham, dissolved an injunction, which had been granted by the Vice-Chancellor, restraining the defendant from diverting or using the water.[3]

§ 140 *b*. In Wood *v*. Sutcliffe,[4] an injunction was asked for to restrain the defendant from pouring into the stream any dye-wares, or dye-liquors, or madder, or indigo, or potash, or matters of that description, which tend to pollute the stream, to the damage of the plaintiff's works. And by the Vice-Chancellor, "I conceive that if the plaintiffs have established such a legal right as that which I have mentioned, and, while they are in the

[1] People *v*. Townsend, 3 Hill, 479.

[2] Gates *v*. Blincoe, 2 Dana (Ken.) 158.

[3] Elmhirst *v*. Spencer, 2 Mac. & G. 45 (1849).

[4] Wood *v*. Sutcliffe, 16 Jur. 75, and S.C. 8 Eng. Law & Eq. 217; 2 Sim. N.S. 163.

enjoyment of that right, another person comes and erects machinery, or any manufacturing works, on that stream above the plaintiffs' works, and by his manufacturing process so fouls the water as that, instead of coming, as before, pure and unsullied to the plaintiffs' works, it arrives at the plaintiffs' works in a less pure and serviceable state than before, so as seriously and continuously to obstruct the effective carrying on of the plaintiffs' manufacture, — if that be the case, and if the restraining of those acts by injunction will restore, or tend to restore, the plaintiffs to the position in which they have a right to stand, and in which they before stood; and if the injury which is occasioned by the works complained of is of such a nature as that the recovery of pecuniary damages would not afford an adequate compensation, that is, such a compensation as would, though not in specie, in effect place the plaintiffs in the same position in which they stood before; and if, moreover (for there were several conditions), the plaintiffs *do not sleep on their rights*, and do not acquiesce, either actively or passively, in the acts which they complain of, but use diligence and vigilance to take such steps as are proper and necessary for the vindication of their rights, — if those conditions occur in such a case as that which is now presented here, the plaintiffs, the parties so injured, have, I conceive, as a general rule, a right to come to the Court of Equity, and say, 'Do not put us to bring action after action for the purpose of recovering damages, but interpose by a strong hand, and prevent the continuance of those acts altogether, in order that our legal rights may be protected and secured to us.' "[1]

[§ 140 c. In Crossley *v.* Lightowler,[2] it appeared that the plaintiffs had a large carpet manufactory at Dean Clough, on the banks of the river Hebble, and had lately purchased of the defendants a piece of land also on the banks of the Hebble and above Dean Clough. The defendants had established large dye-

[1] [When a nuisance operates to destroy health, or to diminish the comfort of a dwelling, an action at law furnishes no adequate remedy, and the party injured is entitled to protection by injunction. Holsman *v.* The Boiling Spring Bleaching Co., 1 McCarter (14 N.J. Ch.) 335. It is a familiar exercise of the power of a Court of Chancery to prevent, by injunction, injury to watercourses by obstruction, diversion, or corruption, on the principle of restraining irreparable mischief. Holsman *v.* The Boiling Spring Bleaching Co., supra; Lewis *v.* Stein, 16 Ala. 214.]

[2] [Crossley *v.* Lightowler, L.R. 3 Eq. Cas. 279; s.c. L.R. 2 Ch. Ap. 478.]

works still higher up the river, and the bill was filed to restrain the defendants from fouling the water of the river, both with respect to the carpet manufactory, and with respect to the piece of land. The plaintiffs had purchased the piece of land, wishing to prevent the water of the river from being fouled by the defendant's dye-works, but did not communicate their object to them. It was held that, in the absence of any express reservation by the defendants — the owners of the dye-works — of the right of fouling the stream, the plaintiffs could maintain this suit to restrain it; although, previously to the sale of the piece of land the defendants had the right to foul the stream in the use of their dye-works; and it was not necessary to show that the fouling had actually injured the plaintiffs. Sir W. Page Wood V.C. said,[1] "I am of opinion that it is not competent for a person to sell property in front of a river, thereby constituting the person to whom he sells it the riparian proprietor, and then so to affect and damage the river as to make it useless for the ordinary and legitimate purposes to which the water may be applied; unless, indeed, there be reserved in the instrument conveying the land an express right to that user." The defendants claimed that the plaintiffs had no right to complain of any pollution of the Hebble occasioned by them, because there were many other manufacturers who poured polluting matters into the stream above the plaintiffs' works, so that they could never have the water in a fit state for use, even if the defendants altogether ceased to foul it. But the Court held that the fact that the stream was fouled by others was not a defence to a suit to restrain the fouling by one.[2] Lord Chelmsford L.C. said,[3] "Where there are many existing nuisances, either to the air or to water, it may be very difficult to trace to its source the injury occasioned by any one of them;[4] but if the defendants

[1] [L.R. 3 Eq. Cas. 287.]

[2] [Gladfelter *v.* Walker, 40 Md. 1; Potter J., in Richmond Manuf. Co. *v.* Atlantic De Laine Co., 10 R.I. 110. The same principle was applied to a case of an action for flowage caused by defendants' dam across one branch of a lake outlet, where the defendants answered that another dam two feet higher than theirs had been erected by another company across the other branch thereof, and that the flowage was caused by the joint action of both dams. Arimond *v.* Green Bay &c. Canal Co., 35 Wis. 41.]

[3] [L.R. 2 Ch. Ap. 481, 482.]

[4] [Still a party cannot be held liable beyond the effect of his own acts in fouling or corrupting a stream; to show this the best proof the nature of the case affords must be produced. Seely *v.* Alden, 61 Penn. St. 302, 306; the Little Schuylkill Nav. & R.R. & Coal Co. *v.* Richards, 57 Penn. St. 142.]

add to the former foul state of the water, and yet are not to be responsible on account of its previous condition, this consequence would follow, that if the plaintiffs were to make terms with the other polluters of the stream so as to have water free from impurities produced by their works, the defendants might say, 'We began to foul the stream at a time when, as against you, it was lawful for us to do so, inasmuch as it was unfit for your use, and you cannot now, by getting rid of the existing pollutions from other sources, prevent our continuing to do what, at the time when we began, you had no right to object to.'"[1]]

[§ 140 *d.* It is not, however, under all circumstances, an unreasonable or unlawful use of a stream to throw or discharge into it waste or impure matter. Whether such a use would be reasonable or not in any given case, would be a question for a jury upon its circumstances. The same circumstances would be open for consideration, and the same rules would govern, in this case, as in respect to the abstraction, detention, diversion, or obstruction of water in a stream. The size and character of the stream, the uses to which it can be or is applied, the nature and importance of the use claimed and exercised by one party, as well as the inconvenience or injury to the other party would be subjects involved in the inquiry. In the construction and repair of mills and dams, in the excavations required for their foundations, and in the frequent removal of the gravel used for tightening such dams, the water must for a time, and necessarily, be rendered so impure as to cause inconvenience occasionally to persons engaged in a kind of manufacture requiring pure water. But if such building and repairs are reasonably conducted, the inconvenience must be borne just the same, and for the same reasons, as the inconvenience caused by the temporary and reasonable detention of the water while filling the dam. So in the uses of a stream for purposes of agriculture, such as washing sheep, crossing it with teams, allowing cattle and swine to traverse it, the same principles will apply. So in the use of many kinds of mills, such as saw-mills, fulling-mills, cotton and woollen factories; there must be thrown into the stream more or less of the waste, such as saw-dust, soap-lees,

[1] [See Tipping *v.* St. Helen's Smelting Co., L.R. 1 Ch. Ap. 66; s.c. 4 B. & S. 608, 616; s.c. 11 H.L. Cas. 642; Wood *v.* Waud, 3 Exch. 772, 773; Attorney-General *v.* Steward, 5 C.E. Green, 415, 419; Hill *v.* Smith, 32 Cal. 166.]

and other impurities, and no ordinary care or prudence could prevent it. In other cases, such disposition of the whole waste, although not absolutely indispensable, would add greatly to the productive value of the mill power. Whether, in either case, it may be rightfully done must depend upon the question whether, under all the circumstances of the case, it is or is not a reasonable use of the stream; and in determining that question the extent of the benefit to the mill-owner, and of inconvenience or injury to others, may very properly be considered. So in respect to the size and character of the stream, it is obvious that an amount of diminution or pollution which would be insignificant in a large stream, might, in a small stream, be wholly destructive of the common right. So also, in determining the reasonableness of suffering the manufacturer's waste to pass off in the current, much must depend upon the use to which the stream below can be or is applied; whether as a mere highway alone, or for purposes of manufacture, requiring pure water, or for the supply of an aqueduct to a large city, as in the case of the Croton River; and in respect to the lands below adjacent to the river, the character of the banks, whether they are usually overflowed, or not, in high-water, should be considered.[1] And in determining the reasonableness of such use, evidence of usage in the deposit of such waste is admissible.[2] Upon this

1 [Hayes *v.* Waldron, 44 N.H. 480; Snow *v.* Parsons, 28 Vt. 459. As to casting waste materials &c. into public rivers, see post, § 554, note.]

2 [Snow *v.* Parsons, 28 Vt. 459. But upon rules of law somewhat peculiar to New Hampshire, the contrary was held in Hayes *v.* Waldron, supra. In this last case the Court rested their decision upon the ground that the jury may be presumed to be already sufficiently informed as to what is a reasonable use of a watercourse, as they are supposed to be as to what shall constitute a reasonable state of repair of a highway (Hubbard *v.* Concord, 35 N.H. 60; Patterson *v.* Colebrook, 29 N.H. 94), or what shall be considered a reasonable use of it by the traveller. But in Snow *v.* Parsons, supra, which was an action for the obstruction of the plaintiff's water-wheel by the tan-bark discharged at the defendants' tannery on the stream above, and suffered to float down to the plaintiff's mill, evidence was offered to prove that it had been the universal and uniform custom in all the counties of Vermont to discharge the spent bark of tanneries into the streams on which they were situated, ever since the country was first settled, and that dam-owners situated below had never until now disputed the right to do so; and that tanneries could not be conducted at any profit without the means of disposing of their spent tan-bark, and that the withholding such use of the streams from tanners, would, in the belief of the witnesses, have excluded that branch of industry from the State; and that the same custom and the same practice had uniformly prevailed in all the States and counties of New England, so far as the witnesses had had opportunity of knowing; and the Court held that this kind of testimony was admissible.]

last point in Snow *v.* Parsons,[1] the Court said, "It is settled law, that every riparian proprietor may use the water for the purposes of manufacture, but so use it as not unnecessarily to abridge the use to others; *i.e.*, every such proprietor may use it with care and prudence. What care and prudence are, in such case, must depend upon the facts of each case, the conclusion to be drawn by the triers of the fact. And to assist them in making this conclusion, if they are not themselves experts in the business, they are entitled to have the experience and wisdom of such as are experts, to enable them to judge of the reasonableness of the particular use. The measure of reasonable care and prudence in such cases, is that which prudent and careful men exercise in the management of their own business. And how are we to know this without proof, in those departments of business with which we are not familiar? Proof that all prudent and careful men, in the management of the business of tanning, pursued a given course of discharging the spent tan into the stream, and that others acquiesced in that course, without objection, would seem to be of the very essence of the inquiry before the jury, in such cases."[2]]

[1] [Snow *v.* Parsons, 28 Vt. 459.]

[2] [In Jacobs *v.* Allard, 42 Vt. 303, it appeared that the plaintiff's starch-mill was on the same stream with the defendant's saw-mill, but a little lower down, and the plaintiff complained that he was disturbed in the use of his starch-mill, by the saw-dust and waste from the defendant's mill. The defendant's right to use his mill was unquestioned; and the plaintiff stood only on the common right of a riparian owner not to be injured in the enjoyment of his water privilege by other riparian proprietors on the same stream. Barrett J. said, "It seems plain that the defendant, in the use of his shingle-mill in a reasonable manner, has the right to discharge the saw-dust, shavings, and waste from it into the stream in the ordinary course of using such mills, and that he is not bound, as matter of law, to prevent them from going into the stream, and have them accumulate or draw them off and deposit them so that they cannot get into the stream. On the other hand he has not a right, wantonly and needlessly, and out of the ordinary course in such cases, and not in the service of his substantial interest and benefit in the use of his mill in a reasonable manner, to throw or permit them to go into the stream, when, by so doing, injury will be caused to the plaintiffs in the use of their starch factory."]

CHAPTER V.

OF THE RIGHT TO THE USE OF WATER, AS DERIVED FROM SPECIAL GRANTS AND RESERVATIONS.

1. Of Natural and Artificial Easements.
2. Extent of the Right Granted or Reserved.
3. Mill and Appurtenances.
4. Secondary Easements.
5. Lex Loci.
6. How Easements in Watercourses are Created.
7. Reservations and Exceptions of Water Rights in Grants of Land.
8. Unity of Possession and Ownership.

1. *Of Natural and Artificial Easements.*

§ 141. THE right to the use of a watercourse *ex jure naturæ*, or as incident to the land, is subject, of course, to be abridged, enlarged, or modified by grant; and, besides the general rights to a natural watercourse, the law recognizes the existence of certain rights accessorial to these general rights.[1] If a miller, or manufacturer, purchases the land itself, over which the water runs, it is evident he would then have a corporeal tenement, and the right which he would possess, in respect to his watercourse, would be real;[2] but if he should purchase a water privilege, or a portion of water power, without any part of the bed of the river, he, in that case, would gain an incorporeal hereditament, or *easement*. The right to a watercourse in its natural course, and derived from the ownership of the land over which it passes, may, it is true, in one sense, be called by that name, that is, a *natural* easement,[3] but the term, as generally used, means an *artificial* easement, as the right to interfere with the accustomed course of running water, by diverting it or keeping

[1] 3 Kent, 441.

[2] See ante, § 90, et seq.

[3] [See ante, §§ 8, 90; Wilde J., in Cary *v.* Daniels, 5 Met. 238; Hubbard J., in Crittenton *v.* Alger, 11 Met. 284; Prescott *v.* Williams, 5 Met. 429; Ashley *v.* Ashley, 6 Cush. 70; Soule *v.* Russell, 13 Met. 436; Johnson *v.* Jordan, 2 Met. 234; Stout *v.* Kindt, 24 Penn. St. 449, 452.]

it back upon the land above, or of transmitting it altered in quality or quantity to the land below.[1] Such artificial easements may be derived from a grant made by the riparian proprietors, whose interests are affected; and, in fact, they may parcel out the water, and combine the water power in any manner they may see fit.[2] Bracton appears to consider the obligation to respect the natural course of a flowing stream, as a duty imposed by law; and that, unless justified by an easement, a man has no more right to divert the course of a stream, than to discharge water on his neighbor's land.[3] An artificial easement is something superadded to the ordinary rights of property; and it may be said to wear a double aspect; first, it destroys, *pro tanto*, the natural easement of the flow of water in its accustomed course; and, secondly, it confers a new right, the disturbance of which gives a good right of action.[4] It may be specially granted, or it may be included in a more general grant, as, for instance, a grant of a privilege of using the water in derogation of the riparian right, would include the secondary easement of *right of way*, or of access to the water, *ex necessitate.*

§ 142. *Easement* is from the French word *aise*, and is defined to be a privilege or convenience which one neighbor has of another *without profit*,[5] as a right of way, a right to bring water

[1] Gale & What. on Easem. 88.

[2] Bardwell *v.* Ames, 22 Pick. 333.

[3] Bract. lib. 4 fol. 221.

[4] Gale & What. on Easem. 89. [Where hydraulic privileges are created by conducting a stream across lands in an artificial channel, the proprietors of lots crossed by the artificial channel, in the absence of any stipulation to the contrary, have the same rights to the use of the water on their respective lots as between themselves, as would exist if the artificial were the natural channel of the stream. Townsend *v.* McDonald, 2 Kernan, 381.]

[5] Easements are specifically distinguished from other incorporeal hereditaments, by the absence of all right to participate in the profits of the soil. A right of way, or the right to receive water, passing across a neighbor's land, may be claimed as an easement; but the right to take something out of the soil, as turf or coal, is a *profit à prendre*, and not an easement. Gale & What. on Easem. 5; 5 Ad. & El. 764; 3 ib. 554; 3 Nev. & Per. 257. [In Race *v.* Ward, 4 El. & Bl. 702, it was held that water, as it issues from a spring or well, is not to be considered as produce of the soil, so as to make the right to take it in *alieno solo*, for domestic purposes, a *profit à prendre.* Owen *v.* Field, 102 Mass. 90, 103. Such right is an easement only, and may be claimed by custom. In Ritger *v.* Parker, 8 Cush. 145, the Court defined an easement or servitude to be "a right which one proprietor has to some profit, benefit, or beneficial use, out of, in, or over the estate of another proprietor." But the use of the word profit in this definition was probably not intended to derogate from the correctness of the definition given in the text. The case did not require it. See Owen *v.* Field, 102 Mass. 90, 103; Bronson *v.* Coffin, 108 Mass. 184; Gale, Easements (5th Eng. ed.) 5, 8; Martin B. in Mounsey *v.* Ismay, 3 H. & C. 497. In Jamaica Pond Aqueduct

through another's land, &c.;[1] and it may properly be called a right of accommodation on another's land, as distinguished from that which is directly *profitable*. Easements are treated of by the civilians, under the name of *services*, some of which they call *real*, and some *personal*. The former is a service which one estate owes to another; or the right of doing something, or of having a privilege in one man's estate, for the advantage and convenience of the owner of another estate. It has the appellation of *prædial*, because it cannot be constituted *sine prædiis*, that is, without lands and tenements. The estate unto which the service is due, is called *prædium dominans*, or the ruling estate, and the other estate which suffers or yields the service, is called *prædium serviens*, or an estate subject to a privilege or service. To constitute such service, it is therefore necessary that there be two estates, the one giving, and the other receiving, the advantage.[2] By a *personal* service, is understood such as has

Corp. *v.* Chandler, 9 Allen, 165, Bigelow C.J. said, "The elementary definition of an easement is 'a liberty, privilege, or advantage in land without profit distinct from an ownership in the soil.'"]

[1] 1 Bl. Comm. 20; Co. Litt. 19, 20; 2 Jac. Law. Dict. 332; Hewlins *v.* Shippam, 5 B. & C. 221; Downing *v.* Baldwin, 1 S. & Rawle, 298; [Mississippi Central Railroad Co. *v.* Mason, 51 Miss. 254.]

[2] Ayl. Civil Law, tit. 5, *Of Services;* Domat, Civil Law, lib. 1, tit. 12; [Seymour *v.* Lewis, 2 Beas. Ch. (N.J.) 439, 449, 450. Lord Cairns L.J. in Rangeley *v.* Midland Railway Co., L.R. 3 Ch. App. 306, 310, 311; Martin B. in Mounsey *v.* Ismay, 3 H. & C. 486, 497; Gale, Easements (5th Eng. ed.) 5, 13 note (d); Shuttleworth *v.* Le Fleming, 19 C.B. N.S. 687, 710.] The Roman Law sets no limits to the number of prædial servitudes; but it prescribes the general conditions that are required to constitute such a servitude (§§ 307, 308). Under these conditions, therefore, all the various rights that one piece of land can enjoy over another, may be granted as prædial servitudes. Accordingly, the prædial servitudes expressly mentioned in the Roman Law, and enumerated in §§ 310–316, are to be regarded only as examples of such servitudes as are of most frequent occurrence. 1 Kauff. Mack. 339. The general principles with regard to prædial servitudes, are as follows: 1. The prædial servitude must have a *causa perpetua*, i.e. the land servient must, from its natural condition, be permanently capable of affording the intended advantage to the land entitled; and that too without any necessity for positive action on the part of the proprietor of the land servient. 2. The servitude is to be regarded as an appurtenance of the land entitled; hence it can be neither alienated, mortgaged, nor leased without the land, nor can it be transferred from the same, to another piece of land. [See Seymour *v.* Lewis, 2 Beas. Ch. (N.J.) 439, 449, 450.] 3. Prædial servitudes are indivisible, and, therefore, cannot be partially acquired, exercised, or lost; yet they may be restricted as to time and place, and also with respect to the mode of their exercise; and their commencement and termination may likewise be made dependent on conditions. 4. When no restriction has been made, a prædial servitude may regularly be exercised over all the land servient; but such exercise must always be confined to the real necessities of the dominant land. See 1 Kauff. Mack. 336, and Heineccius, Diss. *De Causa Servitutum Perpetua* in his works, vol. 3, p. 177. Just. Inst. lib. 2, tit. 3, *De Servitutibus rusticorum et urbanorum prædiorum*.

not been constituted for the benefit of the estate, but which is created for the use of the person merely,[1] and thus differs from an easement which is imposed upon corporeal property, and is attached to the soil of the servient tenement.[2] The utmost extent of the obligation imposed upon the owner of the servient tenement, is not to alter the condition of it, so far as to interfere with the enjoyment of the easement by the dominant.[3] [Applying this to watercourses, every riparian owner is by nature subject to the natural rights of those who are higher up or lower down on the same stream, which are in the nature of a servitude imposed on his land, — a servitude *ne facias*.[4] This obligation, however, applies only to waters which flow naturally without the art of man.[5]]

§ 143. The service of a right of way (*iter*)[6] belongs to the most familiar and important class of easements. It is a comprehensive class, and is susceptible of almost infinite variety. The right may be limited, as to intervals of time, as a way to be used on a certain day in the week; or it may be limited as to the extent of the user authorized, as a foot-way, horse-way, or carraige-way;[7] or to a way for the purpose only of repairing a dam. The right of conducting water through one estate, for the use of an adjoining estate, is an easement, or a prædial service known to the Romans by the name of service *aquæductus*, and is of use, say the civilians, when S. has a scarcity of water, and requires it for his cattle, his lands, or his mills.[8] Distinguished from this, is the personal service, or, at Common Law, the right of *profit*, of taking water out of another's well or pond, which the civilians call service *aquæhaustus;* and to this service is attached the prædial service

[1] See Domat, ut sup., 2 Fred. Code, 81.

[2] [Seymour *v.* Lewis, 2 Beas. Ch. (N.J.) 450. In this case Green Ch. said, "Easements are not rights distinct from the title of the land. They are imposed on corporeal property for the benefit of corporeal property. They pass with the title of the land itself. They cannot exist separate from it. The title to the land could not be in one person, and the easement or right of diversion in another."]

[3] Gale & What. on Easem. 4.

[4] [Cresswell J., in Chasemore *v.* Richards, 2 H. & N. 168, 182. See Martin *v.* Jett, 12 La. 501; Delahoussaye *v.* Judice, 13 La. An. 587; Miller *v.* Laubach, 47 Penn. St. 154.]

[5] [Kauffman *v.* Griesemer, 26 Penn. St. 407, 413; Martin *v.* Jett, 12 La. 501.]

[6] To the rights of way by land and by water, belong the *servitus itineris*, 1 Kauff. Mack. 343; and concerning the Roman rights of way, see Biener, *Diss.*, *De differentiis itineris actus et viæ genuinis*. Leipsic, 1804.

[7] See the examples in Gale & What. on Easem. 138.

[8] Fred. Code, 81.

of a right of way, for going to, or returning from, the well or pond.[1] [It has lately been held in Massachusetts, that a vendor of land may reserve an assignable right of taking water from a spring situated thereon through pipes of certain dimensions, with the right to enter upon the land to make repairs, upon payment of the damages caused thereby; and such right need not be annexed to any particular estate, or be limited as to the place or manner of its enjoyment.[2] Foster J. said, "In the case of rights

[1] Fred. Code. To the servitudes that by the Roman Law relate to the conducting and using of water, belong the *aquæductus* (*servitus aquæ ducendæ*); i.e., the right of leading water to one's premises, from, or at least through, another's land, whether beneath, upon, or above, the surface of the earth. As a general rule, the party entitled can lead the water only through pipes, and not through stone channels, and he must lead it in a certain direction. [See Austin *v.* Cox, 118 Mass. 58.] The servitude, moreover, may refer to *aqua quotidiana*, in which case, the use of the water is not confined to any period of the year; or only to *aqua æstiva*, where it is restricted to the summer. The *aquæhaustus*, or the *servitus aquæ hauriendæ*, i.e., the right of drawing water from another's spring or well, in which the *iter*, as far as it is necessary to the servitude, is tacitly contained. The servitude *pecoris ad aquam appulsus*, or the right of leading one's cattle to water on the servient ground, in which the *actus*, as far as requisite, is tacitly implied. The servitude *aquæ educendæ*, or the right of leading off the water from one's own, on to another's ground. See 1 Kauff. Mack. 345; Hermann, Diss. *De servituto aquæductus.* Leipsic, 1803; Winckler, Diss. *De jure impertratæ aquæ.* Leipsic, 1749.

[2] [Goodrich *v.* Burbank, 12 Allen, 459. In this case a vendor of land reserved to himself, his heirs and assigns, the right of taking, for ever, so much water from a spring situated thereon, from which water was then taken in a pipe to supply the grounds of a neighbor, as then ran in said pipe, so long as the same should last, together with the right to replace the same with a pipe of a certain size, and thereupon to take so much water as would run through the substituted pipe, and to enter and repair the aqueduct at all times, upon payment of the damages caused thereby. The neighbor received the water under a revocable license, and no part of the vendor's remaining land had the use of water from the spring, and the ruling was made as in the text. Where there is a grant of a right to take water from an aqueduct in actual existence and use at the time, the capacity of which is limited to a certain volume, the right of the grantee must be construed with reference to that limit. Within that limit it is to be exercised only as a right in common with the grantor. It is not a general right in the spring; but a right to share in a limited supply of water, brought from the spring by an aqueduct. If the right reaches to the spring itself, it is only through the common aqueduct. The grantee has no right to maintain and keep in repair any other aqueduct than that in which the common right exists. Wells J. in Cheney *v.* Pease, 99 Mass. 448, 452. S., while he was owner of the entire premises now owned by the plaintiff and defendant in severalty, and while he was residing upon that portion thereof now owned by the defendant, conveyed the plaintiff's portion thereof, with "the right to take water at our cistern at or near where it now is, when there is water in said cistern." At the time of said grant, water was supplied to said cistern by means of a pipe laid from a spring, and no other water came to S.'s place, and it was not contemplated that any other would be brought. This cistern was afterwards moved from the back room of the house to the outside of the house, and the plaintiff took water from it as before. The defendant subsequently brought water from another spring into a new cistern that he put into the back room

of *profit à prendre*, it seems to be held uniformly, that, if enjoyed in connection with a certain estate, they are regarded as easements appurtenant thereto; but if granted to one in gross, they are treated as an estate or interest in land, and may be assignable or inheritable.[1] The right to take water from a well or spring is held to be an interest in land, although not a *profit à prendre*, and may be claimed by custom.[2] And we are aware of no case which denies that the right to an aqueduct may be so created as to exist independently of any particular parcel of land owned by the grantee thereof, and be enjoyed by him and his heirs on any estate which he or they may own or acquire, and be capable of assignment or conveyance in gross. The water itself may not be the subject of property, but the right to take it and to have pipes laid in the soil of another for that purpose, and to enter upon the land of another to lay, repair, and renew such pipes, is an interest in the realty, assignable, descendible, and devisable." [3]]

where the old one had stood. Water froze in the pipe that supplied the old cistern, and no water ran therefrom into said cistern; it was held that the grant did not entitle the plaintiff to water from the new cistern. Hoisington *v.* Grimshaw, 48 Vt. 515.]

1 [Post *v.* Pearsall, 22 Wend. 425.]

2 [Race *v.* Ward, 4 El. & Bl. 702.]

3 [The same was held by Curtis J., in Lonsdale Co. *v.* Moies, 21 Law Rep. 664; Owen *v.* Field, 102 Mass. 90, 108; French *v.* Morris, 101 Mass. 68, 71. In Amidon *v.* Harris, 113 Mass. 59, it appeared that A., being tenant by curtesy of a house, entered into an indenture with B., the owner of a spring and of an aqueduct leading therefrom, which, after reciting that A. was desirous of obtaining the right of using the water upon his premises, provided that he, his heirs and assigns, might draw from the aqueduct as much water as might be necessary for the supply of the families resident in the house, as long as water should run from the spring through the aqueduct. After A.'s death his heirs conveyed this right to his widow, who continued to reside in the house. In an action by the widow to enforce the right, it was held, that the indenture conveyed an easement in gross which could be conveyed by the heirs, and enforced by an assignee residing in the house. Endicott J. said, "The indenture conveys an easement in gross to take a certain amount of water from the pipe. It was assignable and inheritable, to him, his heirs and assigns, and the use was restricted to the particular house now occupied by the plaintiff. Such a right may be conveyed without being restricted to a particular locality; and its character is not changed by reason of a restriction in this respect. A man may purchase such right restricted in its use to a particular house, or to a particular purpose, as for running a mill, although he may not own the house or mill; he may do this in contemplation of owning or of building a house or mill, and when he does so, the easement to take the water becomes annexed to the house or mill, or in other words may be availed of to the extent granted." s.c. 113 Mass. 63, 64; Hankey *v.* Clark, 110 Mass. 262. Mr. Gale, in his work on Easements (p. 8, et seq.), says, "An easement, as such, can only be claimed as accessory to a tenement. This position was recognized as law by the judges in a very early case (21 Edw. 3, 2, pl. 5). 'Suppose,' said Shars J., 'I grant to you a way over

2. *Extent of the Right Granted or Reserved.*

§ 144. The accessorial rights or easements in running water, derived from special grants or reservations of riparian proprietors, upon a natural watercourse, are of course to be measured by the nature of the grant or reservation, and the express stipulations

my land to a certain mill, and you are not seised of this mill at the time, but you purchase it afterwards: notwithstanding I disturb you in this way afterwards, you shall not have assize, although you may have a writ of covenant.' To which it was replied, 'In your case it is no marvel to me, although no assize lies, inasmuch as he had not the frank tenement to which he claimed to have (dut avoir) the way, at the time the way was granted to him, and therefore he could not have had assize if he had been disturbed at the time when the grant was made; and as he could not then have assize, the purchase of the frank tenement afterwards would not enable him to maintain this action.'" But the learned author adds, "Probably, however, in the English as in the Civil Law, the grant of an easement in respect of a house about to be purchased, or built, by the grantee, would enure as such. And it would no doubt be held in a case of a grant affecting a tenement with an easement in favor of a tenement, supposed to belong but not really belonging to the grantee at the time of the grant, that upon the grantee subsequently acquiring the tenement this grant would become effectual, but this is more properly a part of the law of estoppel." "Many personal rights, which, in their mode of enjoyment, bear a great resemblance to easements, as, for instance, rights of way, may be conferred by actual grant, independently of the possession of any tenement by the grantee; but such rights, though valid between the contracting parties, do not possess the incidents of an easement. In case of disturbance of a personal right thus given, the remedy would appear to be upon the contract only." Gale, Easements (5th Eng. ed.) 13. This position seems, however, to be controverted by Mr. Willes, the editor, in a note. In Rangeley *v.* Midland Railway Co., L.R. 3 Ch. App. 310, Lord Cairns L.J. said, "There can be no easement properly so called, unless there be both a servient and a dominant tenement. There can be no such thing according to our law, or according to the Civil Law, as what I may term an easement in gross. An easement must be connected with a dominant tenement." An easement, such as a right of way, is never presumed to be personal, when it can fairly be construed to be appurtenant to some other estate. Wells J., in Dennis *v.* Wilson, 107 Mass. 592; Smith *v.* Porter, 10 Gray, 66; Case of a private road, 1 Ash. 417; Stearns *v.* Mullen, 4 Gray, 151; Peck *v.* Conway, 119 Mass. 549. It is to be observed that the law does not favor the annexation to property of incidents of a novel kind at the fancy or caprice of any owner. See Ackroyd *v.* Smith, 10 C.B. 164, 187, 188; Ellis *v.* Mayor of Bridgnorth, 15 C.B. N.S. 78; Bailey *v.* Stephens, 12 C.B. N.S. 91; Keppell *v.* Bailey, 2 My. & K. 517, 535. A grant of a right of way not appurtenant to land is said to operate as a mere personal license, and is not assignable. Ackroyd *v.* Smith, 10 C.B. 164. It confers no right in the land to the grantee, but operates only as a contract between the grantor and grantee. Thus, the grantee of the exclusive privilege of having pleasure-boats on a canal cannot sue a stranger for the infringement of his right. Hill *v.* Tupper, 2 H. & C. 121. A grant exceeding the powers of the grantor is within the same rule. Thus, a waterworks company who claim a right to take water from the river under a grant from a riparian proprietor cannot sue another proprietor for fouling the water of the river. Stockport Waterworks Co. *v.* Potter, 3 H. & C. 300. See White *v.* Crawford, 10 Mass. 188; Bowen *v.* Conner, 6 Cush. 137; De Witt *v.* Harvey, 4 Gray, 486.]

therein contained.[1] The grant may be of a certain quantity of water, as much, for instance, as would pass through a pipe or a flood-gate, or a sluice-way of certain dimensions; or it may be of a certain extent of water power, as much, and no more, as is required to operate certain specified machinery; and there is an obvious and important distinction between a grant of the water itself, and a grant of water power.[2] It has been already stated[3]

[1] [Thus, the owners of a mill-pond executed a deed to the owners of a grist-mill situated below and supplied by a race-way from the pond, in which, after reciting the fact that the grantees and those under whom they held title "had been accustomed to take water from the pond for operating their said grist-mill," conveyed to them, their heirs and assigns "the right at all times hereafter of taking and using the water from said pond for operating any other mill which shall be hereafter erected upon the site of their present grist-mill, to the same extent that they now have a right to do, or have been accustomed to do, for the operating of their grist-mill;" and it was held that the effect of the grant was not merely to extend to the new mill that might be substituted for the grist-mill the rights, already existing as such, with regard to the grist-mill, but to give the grantees a right to all the use of the water to which they and their grantors had been *accustomed*, without reference to the question whether such customary use had ripened into a right; and that parol evidence was admissible to show that the owners of the grist-mill, at and prior to the execution of the deed, had been accustomed to open a certain gate in the dam, at such times as it was necessary, and thus to furnish themselves with water from the pond for their mill, for the purpose of applying the deed to the subject-matter. Avon Manuf. Co. *v.* Andrews, 30 Conn. 476. See Egremont *v.* Williams, 11 Ad. & Ell. N.S. 688, 701. But the use of a mill privilege purchased from the owner of a lower privilege on the same stream, is not regulated by the use made of it before such purchase, but by what is reasonable and proper, conformably to the wants and usages of the community. Haskins *v.* Haskins, 9 Gray, 390.]

[2] See Miller, ex parte, 3 Hill, 418; Bardwell *v.* Ames, 22 Pick. 333; Boston Water Power Co. *v.* Gray, 6 Met. 131; Kennedy *v.* Scovil, 12 Conn. 317. [A privilege in a spring of water was conveyed by G. to B., in the year 1849, in the following terms: "Do lease to the said B. the following right and privilege, the same to be a perpetual privilege to him and his heirs and assigns for ever. Said privilege is, that the said B. shall have the right to lay a pipe one-half inch in diameter from the spring, which is on the lot of said G., and from said spring conduct the same by a pipe, as aforesaid, to the dwelling-house and barn of the said B., and his heirs for ever; and the said B. shall have the right to dig a trench across the lot of said G. from said spring, for the purpose of laying said pipe. From 1849 to 1853, B. made no use of the water of the spring. From 1853 to 1863 he brought the water by an open trench to a tub about thirty rods from his house and barn, where it was used for watering his cattle. In 1863 he put a half-inch pipe into the spring, and brought the water by it to the tub. There was more water thus brought than he needed for his cattle, and a large part of it ran to waste. In a suit brought by B. against G. for disturbing the pipe, it was held. (1) That the easement conveyed by G. to B. was not in gross, but appurtenant to the real estate then owned by B. (2) That B had a right to draw from the spring all the water that would run through a half-inch pipe, and that it was no abuse of the right to permit the water to flow continuously

[3] See ante, § 94.

to have been held, that the grant by a legislature of a State, of an exclusive right to the water power of a river does not pass a title to the *corpus* of the water. In the case referred to, it appeared that the legislature of Pennsylvania granted the privilege of all the water power of the river Schuylkill, and made a subsequent grant to the district of Spring Garden, and Northern Liberties, of the right to erect works, and supply their inhabitants with water from the river; and it was held, that the grant, and the acts done there under it, were not in derogation of the right under the previous grant of the water power. "Now," said Gibson C.J., "a grant of water power is not a grant of the water for any thing else than the propulsion of machinery; and it consequently does not exclude the use of it by any one else, in a way which does not injure or decrease the power. It is not a grant of property in the *corpus* of the water, as a chattel."

§ 144 *a*. "A right may doubtless be granted, if a grant were necessary, to intercept running water, and confine it in reservoirs for separate use; but the grant of such a right would not be the grant of a water power. No two things can be more distinct, and dissimilar."[1] By a deed between A., owner of Greenacre, and B., owner of Blackacre, it was agreed that A. should have, during the first ten days of every month, for the purpose of irrigation, all the water of a stream which flowed through Greenacre into Blackacre, and that at all other times the water should be under the control and at the disposal of B. and his heirs and assigns, and be allowed to flow in a free and uninterrupted manner towards and into Blackacre, through a channel therein particularly described; and that the owner of Greenacre should cleanse and repair the said channel, with liberty to B., his heirs, &c., to do so on his default. It was held, that this deed operated as a grant to B, of an easement of the watercourse therein described at all times, except the first ten days of each month, and that he

from the mouth of the pipe. (3.) That it was no abuse of the right to use the water thirty rods from, instead of at, his house and barn; the owner of an easement, when not limited by words of absolute restraint, having the right to change the mode of using it, if he does not make it more onerous to the servient estate. Bissell *v*. Grant, 35 Conn. 288. B. in the above case, in 1858, conveyed his house and barn, with the land connected with them, to his children, reserving to himself and wife the use of the premises for their lives. The privilege of the spring was not referred to in the deed. Held that the easement was not extinguished, but remained in B., as a part of the life-estate reserved.]

[1] Mayor &c. *v*. Commissioners of Spring Garden, 7 Penn. St. 348.

thereby acquired a right in respect to that channel, and that an alteration of the channel, was an injury to his right, in respect of which B. might maintain an action.[1]

[§ 144 *b*. In Rawstron *v.* Taylor,[2] it appeared, that for upwards of twenty years, water had flowed through an old drain on the defendant's land, and along an ancient watercourse, and thence along a close of the defendant, called G. B., and had thence contributed to supply the plaintiff's mills after their erection in 1845. In that year the defendant by deed conveyed to the plaintiff the close G. B., "together with all ways, watercourses, liberties, privileges, rights, members, and appurtenances to the same close belonging or appertaining," subject to the proviso, that it should be lawful for the defendant to use for any manufacturing, domestic, or agricultural purposes, any water flowing from or through the contiguous lands of the defendant unto and into the close G. B., returning the surplus, or so much as remained, after being used for the aforesaid purposes, into its usual channel at a certain point, so that the water should not be diverted from its then course, but be allowed to flow into the close G. B. The defendant erected a lock-up tank upon his land, and caused the water which arose in his land, near to the close G. B., and which had previously been accustomed to flow along the old drain and ancient watercourse into the close G. B.; and he caused the water to be conveyed from the tank to a lower part of his land, to be used by his tenants. This water was used by them for the purposes mentioned in the proviso to the deed, but the surplus could not be returned to the close G. B. It was held, that by the deed the defendant granted to the plaintiff the use of the water, subject only to the use by himself of it as specified in the proviso, and that by locking it up he had diverted it, and was liable to an action for a breach of his covenant, by reason of such diversion. Parke B.: "The defendant has no right to make any permanent diversion of the water. He may take away the water in buckets, or by any other mode of conveyance, for domestic, agricultural, or manufacturing purposes, but when he has taken what he wants, he is bound to return the surplus into its usual channel at the place mentioned in the plan, for

[1] Northam *v.* Hurley, 22 L.J. 164, and s.c. 18 Eng. Law & Eq. 164; [1 El. & Bl. 665.]

[2] [Rawstron *v.* Taylor, 11 Exch. 369. See Northam *v.* Hurley, 1 El. & Bl. 665.]

the use of the plaintiff, and he cannot divert the water." Martin B.: "The defendant grants all the waters, and cannot derogate from his own grant by cutting off the supply." [1]]

§ 145. Although the words of an instrument of conveyance, taken strictly, import nothing more than a right to erect a dam, the subject of the grant may be the *water power*. A testator being the owner, in whole or in part, of four contiguous tracts of land, which were in part bounded by a watercourse, devised one of them, situated on the west side of the watercourse, to his son B., under whom the plaintiff derived title. To his son H. he devised his "undivided moiety of certain four acres, called the 'saw-mill land,' together with all the rights and privileges thereunto appertaining." This undivided moiety of the four-acre tract had come to the testator, with a privilege appertaining to it, of swelling the water back to the southern boundary of the land devised to his son B. By the same will, the testator gave to his son H., the defendant, the privilege of erecting a dam, at any point between the land devised to his son

1 [A grant of all streams of water that may be found in land, when at the time of the grant there is but one stream and several wells, includes the underground water in the land. The grantor cannot, nor can any one claiming under him, do any thing the effect of which is to drain such underground water from the land. Whitehead *v.* Parks, 2 H. & N. 870. Pollock C.B. said, "In the case of Northam *v.* Hurley, 1 El. & Bl. 665, it was settled that, where rights to water are created under a deed, the Court cannot take into consideration what are the rights which the parties would have had as riparian proprietors or otherwise; but the nature and extent of their interest must be regulated wholly by the deed." Martin B. said, "Lord Derby granted to Woodcock all the water which might be found on the closes in question. Lord Derby cannot derogate from his grant, and the defendant, his lessee, is in the same position." "Now, at the time of the execution of this lease, there was only one stream in the four closes to which I am about to refer. There were several places where water collected, but only one stream in the ordinary acceptation of the term. The Earl demises to Woodcock about fifteen closes of land with 'all streams of water that may be found in the closes of land called the Clough, the Moorin Clough, the Brow, and the Marleds.' Looking at the surrounding circumstances, I should say that the words do not refer to surface streams, because there were none, except Elton Brook, on the property. 'All streams' means, 'all water in the closes in question.' The demise is really a demise of the springs." The following clause was embraced in a warranty deed of land. "Also conveying the right to draw water from any and all the springs on said Clement's [the grantor's] land, easterly, and above the aforesaid described premises, with the right to conduct the same by aqueduct to said premises, for all uses or purposes for ever." It was held that the grantee was entitled to take all the water from the springs, provided the same was in good faith required for use on the granted premises; and it was also held that he was entitled to make such reasonable arrangements about the springs as were reasonably necessary to enable him to use all the water. Stevenson *v.* Wiggin, 56 N.H. 308.]

B. (the plaintiff's land), and the land on the eastern side of the creek devised to another son, J., with a right to dig a race through B.'s land. The defendant erected a dam across the creek, within the limits mentioned in the last devise; and afterwards erected another dam, at a considerable distance below, for the use of "the saw-mill land," where there had many years before been a dam erected, but the use of which had been abandoned at least thirty-eight years. It was held, that the whole of the property in the watercourse, under the testator's control, passed by these devises, to the defendant; that having been used by him in part, by the erection of the first dam, no presumption should arise from lapse of time, of any release or extinguishment of his right to any other part of it, and that consequently he had a right to erect the second dam. It was impossible, said Gibson C.J., not to perceive, that the leading intention of the testator was, to attach to the saw-mill tract, *all the power* which the watercourse afforded, and this with the most extended means of enjoyment which it was in his power to confer; inasmuch as the power being barely sufficient for a mill at the lowest point of the watercourse, within the boundary, would have been altogether worthless, had it been distributed among the different parts of his estate.[1]

§ 146. Water power may be granted without its being necessarily annexed to a mill, or confined to any particular location, if the quantity of water conveyed is not increased. Thus, where several owners of mills and mill privileges, on the same waterfall, apportioned the water among themselves, and a certain part thereof was assigned to W., the owner of a fulling-mill, for the use of that mill, or for other machinery, requiring equal power: it was held, that the right was not inseparably annexed to buildings, or site, at which water was then used; but that it might be used at any convenient site, at which a mill could be so placed as to take an equal quantity of water, without any greater injury to the other mill-owners.[2]

[1] Nitzell *v.* Paschall, 3 Rawle, 76.

[2] Hurd *v.* Curtis, 7 Met. 94; [DeWitt *v.* Harvey, 4 Gray, 486. In an action for flowage brought by the grantor of a water-power, with a license to build a dam and race, against a grantee who had built the dam further down the stream than specified in the deed, and not on the grantor's land, it was held, in the absence of any proof that the flowage extended above the limit fixed in the deed, that the right to flow was not inseparable from the right to build the dam, and that the grantor had no just

[§ 146 *a*. Under a deed of a water privilege, conveying "the right to draw two hundred square inches of water, under fourteen feet head, out of the surplus water from the top of my grist-mill flume, at S.; however, not intending by this deed to convey the water to the injury of the following privileges; viz., to the building now occupied by A. S., as a rake-shop; to the tannery now occupied by A. B.; and the scythe-shop now occupied by J. H. M.; having reference to the deeds of the above-described privileges," the grantee's privilege is subject to the prior use of the quantity of water which, at the time of the conveyance, was reasonably necessary to carry on and operate, at all seasons of the year, and in the state and condition in which they then existed, the mills and works therein of the grantor; and also of the quantity belonging to the three privileges mentioned, reference being had to the deeds thereof for the amount. And the grantee's privilege is not increased by the subsequent removal of the rake-shop, and the erection of a new and larger building on its site, which is used wholly for different purposes, or by the subsequent destruction of the scythe-shop, and discontinuance of the use of water there, although the deed of the privilege for the scythe-shop only conveyed the water to be used at that particular place; nor has he the right to complain of the place where, or the purposes for which, such prior use is made.[1]]

§ 147. A grantee of a water right may unquestionably make as much profit of the privilege granted, as it has capacity to promote; and he doubtless may avail himself of any thing which, in its results, works no alteration in the substance of the contract. An artificer, employed at stipulated wages, may use subsequently invented machinery, though it be to make his wages inordinately high, because the nature of compensation for which his employer bargained, is not disturbed by it; but he may not avail himself of means not in ordinary and familiar use at the time, to the prejudice of another, or to gain a surreptitious advantage.[2]

§ 148. The best judicial construction is that which is made by viewing the subject of the grant, as the mass of mankind

cause of complaint because the grantee had availed himself of only a part of the rights conveyed. Kilgore *v.* Haskell, 21 Mich. 502.]

[1] [Pratt *v.* Lamson, 2 Allen, 275.]

[2] Opinion of the Court, by Gibson C.J., in Schuylkill Nav. Co. *v.* Moore, 2 Wharton, 477.

would view it; as it may be safely assumed, that such is the aspect, in which the parties themselves view it.[1] A result thus obtained is exactly what is obtained from the cardinal rule of *intention*.[2] Such was the doctrine laid down by the Court, in the case of the Schuylkill Navigation Company *v.* Moore, in Pennsylvania,[3] as applicable to hydraulics. In this case it appeared that the plaintiffs, an incorporated company, authorized to use the water of the river Schuylkill, for navigation, and to grant out the water for manufacturing purposes, conveyed to the defendant a certain lot of ground, &c., "together with the privilege of drawing from the canal, through the fore bay or tunnel, from time to time, and at all times hereafter, so much water as can pass through two metallic apertures, one of fifty square inches, and the other of two hundred and fifty square inches, respectively, under a head of three-feet, to be measured from the middle of each of the said apertures, respectively, to the face of the water of said canal, &c.; to have and hold the said described lot, &c., and the right of drawing from the said canal, the quantity of three hundred square inches of water, in manner aforesaid, under a three-feet head," yielding and paying a certain annual rent per inch of water. The defendant applied to the aperture a certain conical tube, called an *adjutage*, by which the flow of water *was enlarged*. It appeared that this invention was known to persons conversant with hydraulics, and to some of the officers of the company, before the making of the contract; and it was held, that the true construction of the contract was, that the water was to be delivered in the ordinary way, and that the defendant had no right to increase the flow by means of an adjutage.[4]

[1] Kennedy *v.* Scovil, 12 Conn. 317; [The Salmon Falls Manuf. Co. *v.* The Portsmouth Co., 46 N.H. 249.]

[2] [Peck *v.* Conway, 119 Mass. 546, 549; Barrows J., in Webster *v.* Holland, 58 Maine, 168, 170.]

[3] Schuylkill Nav. Co. *v.* Moore, 2 Wharton, 477.

[4] And see Vermont Central Railroad Co. *v.* Hills, 23 Vt. 681. "The Society for Establishing Useful Manufactures," in New Jersey, sold a lot in Paterson, "together with the right of taking from their canal twelve inches square of water;" and a mill was shortly after erected on the lot, and water was drawn from the canal for supplying it. The Society gave a notice to the owner of the mill that they had reason to believe he was taking more than the said quantity of water, and requested him to confine the future use of the water to that quantity; but the owner did nothing to limit the flow, and the Society built a stone wall in their canal opposite the head-race leading the water on the lot, and placed in the side of the wall a piece of cast-iron, with an aperture in it of twelve

§ 149. Nor can the grantee of water, to be used by means of a *flume*, make a new one of larger dimensions. Where a grist and saw mill, which were supplied with water by means of a dam and flume, and a clothing-mill and a flume for the supply of that which extended under the other mills, and was connected with and drew water from the flume of the other mills, were all owned by one person; and a conveyance was made of the grist and saw mill, with the land on which they stood, together with the water privilege, "except the clothing-mill and the land sold therewith;" and on the same day, the clothing-mill "and water privilege for said flume, &c., as now enjoyed," were conveyed to another person; and afterwards, the grantee of the grist and saw mill permitted his mills, which were old, to decay, and took them down; and the grantee of the clothing-mill thereupon entered upon the land conveyed with the grist and saw mill, and erected a new flume, for the use of his mill, which was in fact of larger dimensions, and drew more water than his flume drew at the date of the conveyances; it was held, that the grantee of the clothing-mill had not a right to erect, on the land conveyed with the grist and saw mill, a flume larger than the former one, or which drew a greater quantity of water; and that the grantee of the other mills had a right to remove all of said flume which was within the limits of the land conveyed to him. If the conveyance to the owner of the clothing-mill gave him the right to enter upon the land embraced in the deed to the other grantee, it was to repair or rebuild the flume there existing, and not to erect one of different dimensions; nor was he authorized to erect one drawing more water, even if such an one might be more advantageous, and if the grantee of the grist and saw mill, for the time being, forbore to use the water.[1]

§ 149 *a*. Under a reservation in a grant of lands and water privileges of sufficient water to propel certain *specified ma-*

inches square; and thereupon the owner of the mill prostrated the said wall. A motion for a preliminary injunction to restrain the owner from taking more water than would pass through an aperture of twelve inches square, was only denied because the state of affairs had existed for *thirty years*. Society &c. *v.* Holsman, 1 Halst. (N.J.) Ch. 126.

[1] Dewey *v.* Bellows, 9 N.H. 282. The statute of New Hampshire, relative to the repair of mills, dams, &c., owned by tenants in common, does not, on the neglect of one tenant, authorize another to erect a new mill or dam substantially different from the former, and to call on his co-tenant, under an appraisal, for contribution. Bellows *v.* Dewey, 9 N.H. 278.

chinery, the grantor is entitled to the use of the water for any purpose not requiring a *greater power* than is reserved. Thus, where the owner of lands upon a mill-stream granted a portion thereof, together with water sufficient to operate a saw-mill at all times, *when there should be more than enough to drive a grist-mill with three run of stones, and certain other specified machinery;* the Court held that the grantor in the deed and those holding under him were not restricted in the use of the water to the particular objects mentioned in the deed, but might use the quantity reserved, for any other purpose.[1] This construction is supported by Bigelow *v.* Battel,[2] in which case the plaintiffs being the owners of the entire water power of Charles River, at Natick, granted to the defendants the privilege of taking from their dam a specified quantity of water, " except when the quantity of water is so small as not to be sufficient to carry plaintiff's grist-mill, and a cotton factory which may be erected, with no more than five thousand spindles." Although it was no part of the contract that the plaintiffs should have a right to the water for the use of a *paper-mill*, it was held, that the right reserved did not limit the use of the water to a cotton factory; but that the true intent of the reservation was that the water

[1] Cromwell *v.* Selden, 3 Comst. (N.Y.) 253. [See Pratt *v.* Lamson, 2 Allen, 275.] In Luttrell's case, 4 Coke, 86, the plaintiff alleged that he was seised in fee of two old and ruinous fulling-mills, to which from time immemorial, *magna pars aquæ cujusdam rivuli* ran from a place called " Head Wear," that afterwards he had pulled down the fulling-mills and erected two mills to grind corn, and he complained that the defendant had diverted the water from these mills. The plaintiff had judgment, and it was assigned for error, that, by breaking and abating the old fulling-mills, and building new mills of another nature, the plaintiff had destroyed the prescription, and could not prescribe to have any watercourse to grist-mills. If a man grant me a watercourse to my fulling-mills, I cannot, it is said, convert them to corn-mills, *nec e contra.* For prescription in such case shall be intended to commence by grant, and it might be more beneficial to him who made the original grant, and to others who had his estate, to have them fulling-mills rather than corn-mills. Perhaps they have corn mills so near that the building of corn-mills would be prejudicial to them, and it would be against reason to extend a grant or prescription to have a watercourse to fulling-mills to corn-mills, which is not within the purport of the grant or prescription. But it was resolved, that the prescription did extend to the new grist-mills; that the plaintiff might alter the mill into the nature of what mill he pleased, provided always, that no prejudice should thereby arise by diverting or stopping the water, as it was before. And see post, §§ 226, 227. Just so at the present day; lapse of time, increase of population, and improvements in mechanics, must necessarily give rise to changes, and these may occasion a necessity to *change the mode* in which the parties have been accustomed to divide water power to which they are respectively entitled, between them. Cress *v.* Varney, 17 Penn. St. 496.

[2] Bigelow *v.* Battel, 15 Mass. 313.

should, at all times, be left *sufficient* to carry five thousand spindles. [And in Loverin *v.* Walker,[1] where the plaintiff, owning a mill-seat and the land and mills on each side of the stream, conveyed an undivided half of the land and mills on one side to the defendant W., and afterward conveyed the other half of that land, describing it, to another, "with one undivided half of the buildings thereon, with a privilege to draw the water from said saw-mill pond sufficient for one tub-wheel at all seasons of the year," it was held, that the grantee in the last-mentioned deed took only an undivided half of the specified quantity of water; and also, that the quantity must be governed by the amount required to propel the tub-wheel before used to run the mill, although, at the time of the conveyance, the wheel had been carried away by a freshet, and had not then been restored. Bellows J. said, "We are of opinion that the grantee would be limited to the use of so much water as would be sufficient for a tub-wheel of the capacity of the old one, although not restricted in the use of that quantity to this particular kind of wheel."]

§ 149 *b*. Upon the argument in the above case of Cromwell *v.* Selden,[2] the defendant's counsel relied on Ashley *v.* Pease,[3] and Strong *v.* Benedict,[4] as favoring an opposite construction. "It is true," say the Court, "that in both these cases, it was held that the grantee was not only limited in the quantity of water which he had a right to use, but also in the manner of using it. But each of these cases is distinguishable from that of Cromwell *v.* Selden. In Ashley *v.* Pease, the plaintiff being owner of an entire water privilege, granted and conveyed to the defendant's ancestor a fulling-mill, and covenanted with him that when there should be a sufficiency of water to carry and supply the uses of all the mills then standing, or which might thereafter be standing in their place, on the dam, he would suffer and permit him to draw from the flume '*so much water as might be necessary to carry and supply the fulling-mill then standing, or which might thereafter stand upon the lot he had granted;*' but when there was not a sufficiency of water for the purposes and uses aforesaid, then he was to draw water for the use of the said fulling-mill or mills, twelve hours successively in the twenty-four, and no more. The grantee also covenanted in the same instrument,

[1] [Loverin *v.* Walker, 44 N.H. 489.]

[2] Cromwell *v.* Selden, 3 Comst. (N.Y.) 253.

[3] Ashley *v.* Pease, 18 Pick. 268.

[4] Strong *v.* Benedict, 5 Conn. 210.

that he would never use or occupy the fulling-mill, nor any other mill or building which might thereafter stand in the same place, so as to interfere with or obstruct the going or working of the plaintiff's saw-mill, or any other mill or building which the plaintiff might erect in the same place. The defendant erected a carding-machine in the same building occupied as a fulling-mill, and used the water for the purpose of running both, but not both at the same time. The Court held, that it was manifest from the general tenor of the contract, that it was the intention of the parties that the grant should be limited *to the use of* the water for driving the fulling-mill, and that the use of it for a carding-machine was unauthorized. That this is what the parties intended, the Court say is confirmed by the grantee's covenant not to obstruct or interfere with the plaintiff's mills, by using and diminishing the water power except to carry and supply the fulling-mill." [1]

[§ 149 *c*. In Garland *v*. Hodgson,[2] it was held, that where the right to use water from a dam and stream is granted, with a proviso that the grant shall "in no case extend so far as to take water when the same shall be wanted for the grist-mill," which is or may be erected on or near the dam, this is an *exception*, rather than a reservation, and is to be construed most strictly against the grantor; and the grantor and his representatives have no right to use the water so excepted for any but the specified purposes. The Court say this "is not a reservation of 'water sufficient for' a grist-mill, but a limitation of the grant '*when* the water shall be wanted *for the grist-mill*.'"]

§ 149 *d*. In Strong *v*. Benedict,[3] the grant was of four acres of land, "with the privilege of building a mill for the purpose of fulling cloth, together with the privilege of drawing so much water as should be necessary to carry a good well-built overshot fulling-mill, at any time when the grantee *shall have occasion to use the said fulling-mill*." The grantee was to have so much water as was necessary *when he should have occasion to run the fulling-mill*. "It would seem, therefore," say the Court, "as if

[1] [See Sibley *v*. Hoar, 4 Gray, 222; Shaw C.J., in Tourtellot *v*. Phelps, 4 Gray, 374. A grant of "the privilege of drawing water from said canal at all times when it may be done without injury to the forge or to the grist-mill, sufficient for the purposes of a fulling-mill and shearing-machine, but for no other purpose whatever," gives no right to use the privilege for any other purpose. DeWitt *v*. Harvey, 4 Gray, 486.]

[2] [Garland *v*. Hodgson, 46 Maine, 511.]

[3] Strong *v*. Benedict, 5 Conn. 210.

there was a limitation of the use as well as of the quantity. But without expressing a definitive opinion on this subject, it is clear, from the situation and condition of the parties, and other collateral facts known to them at the time, and which may properly be recurred to for the purpose of ascertaining their mutual intentions, that it was intended that the *use* of the water, as well as the *quantity*, should be restricted." — "Thus it will be seen," say the Court, in Cromwell *v.* Selden,[1] "that in the first of these cases (Ashley *v.* Pease) the covenant of the grantee himself amounted to an express prohibition of the use of the water for any other purpose than that specified in the grant; and in the other, although by the terms of the grant the defendant was only entitled to the use of the water, '*when he had occasion to use the fulling-mill*,' the Court refrained from expressing 'a definitive opinion' upon the construction of the terms of the grant, but place their decision upon collateral facts known to the parties at the time, clearly indicating that it was their mutual intention that the water granted should be used for a particular object only."

§ 149 *e*. Lands were conveyed with a reservation in the following words: "The said parties of the first part do hereby reserve *to themselves and to their heirs and assigns*, one acre and a half of land, out of the above-described premises at the south-east corner of lot No. 11, and on which the tannery is erected; and running northwardly with the highway, so as not to exceed twenty-four rods in the rear; and the said parties of the first part as aforesaid, do also reserve to themselves and *their use*, a certain well and waterworks laid down for the purpose of supplying the tannery aforesaid with water." The construction given to this clause by the New York Court of Appeals was, that the reservation of the well and waterworks was *unlimited* in the uses to which the water might be applied, and was not restricted to the purpose of a mere tannery, and that the right would pass to the grantee of the party making the reservation.[2]

1 3 Comst. (N.Y.) 253.

2 Borst *v.* Empie, 1 Selden, 83. [The question whether an easement is a personal right, or is to be construed to be appurtenant to some other estate, must be determined by the fair interpretation of the grant or reservation creating the easement, aided, if necessary, by the situation of the property and the surrounding circumstances. Morton J., in Peck *v.* Conway, 119 Mass. 546, 549; Dennis *v.* Wilson, 107 Mass. 593. In a case where the controversy related to a right of way, Wells J. said, "Such an easement is

§ 149 *f.* The decision in the case of Rogers *v.* Bancroft, in Vermont,[1] shows an inclination on the part of the Court to construe grants of water liberally, so as to impose no unnecessary restriction upon the mode of its use; so that when the words used will admit of one construction which would limit the use to a particular purpose, and another which would allow the use specified to be merely a measure of the quantity to be used, the latter construction is adopted; because it is more favorable to the grantee, and also to progressive improvements.[2] But this rule of construction, the Court were of opinion, had little or no application to the following case: A. and B. were tenants in common of certain land, and of a saw-mill thereon, standing on the north side of a stream passing through the land, and of a bark-mill upon the south side, — both mills being moved by means of the same dam; and they executed at the same time partition deeds, each to the other. A. conveyed to B. all on the north side of the stream, without any mention of the water, or water privilege; and the deed from B. to A. contained this clause: "*Also the tan-yard and bark-mill, with a privilege of water for the said bark-mill, when I the said B., my heirs or assigns, do not want the water for the use of the works now standing on the said dam, or any others to be erected hereafter, that draw no more water than those now standing.*" And it was held, that this gave to the owner of the saw-mill a paramount right to the use of the water for his mill, or for any other works drawing no more water; but that this right was confined to works supplied with water by means of the same dam, then standing, or one substituted for it, in case of its destruction; and that it did not give to B., or his assigns, the right to claim, that an amount of water, equal to what would be required for such works, should be allowed to pass over that dam and be collected in a pond raised

never presumed to be personal, when it can fairly be construed to be appurtenant to some other estate." Dennis *v.* Wilson, 107 Mass. 591, 592. A way may be held to be appurtenant, although there are no words of inheritance in the grant or reservation creating it. Bowen *v.* Conner, 6 Cush. 132; Dennis *v.* Wilson, 107 Mass. 591, 593; Stearns *v.* Mullen, 4 Gray, 151.]

[1] Rogers *v.* Bancroft, 20 Vt. 250.

[2] [Deshon *v.* Porter, 38 Maine, 293, 294; Tourtellot *v.* Phelps, 4 Gray, 374; Ashley *v.* Pease, 18 Pick. 275; Merrick J., in Pratt *v.* Lamson, 2 Allen, 275; Colt J., in Hapgood *v.* Brown, 102 Mass. 454. But this rule has no influence in a question of the construction of a deed, where the intention of the parties is clearly expressed in the written agreement made by themselves. Tenney J., in Deshon *v.* Porter, 38 Maine, 289, 293, 294; Shaw C.J., in Tourtellot *v.* Phelps, 4 Gray, 374.]

by a dam built below, and be there used to supply mills by means of such lower dam.[1]

§ 149 *g*. Reservations of water for a specified use are, of course, as much to be considered a measure of quantity, as grants. In 1824 the defendants' grantors, who were the owners of mills and water power, conveyed to the plaintiffs' grantors the privilege of erecting a suitable building for the use of carding wool and dressing cloth, to be located below the grist-mill which the grantors were about to erect upon the stream, and the privilege of connecting a flume with the flume of the grist-mill, and of drawing water at all times from the flume of the grist-mill, "excepting such quantity of water as is necessary for the use of two runs of stones in the grain or grist mill, and that, in case there is not water in the flume for the use of both carding-machines and clothing-works and the grist-mill, that the grain or grist mill shall at all times have water sufficient for grinding with two runs of stones, in preference to the carding-machines and clothing-works." In 1825 the grantors in that deed erected their grist-mill, with three runs of stones, a corn cracker and smut-mill, which were propelled by four water-wheels; and the

[1] [The owner of land on both sides of a stream, together with the water power created by a dam across it, having a tannery on one side and a saw-mill on the other, conveyed the tannery together with the land connected with it, and also "a right to draw water from the saw-mill flume sufficient to carry on the business of tanning in said yard," the grantee, "his heirs or assigns, to make or pay for one-fourth part of all necessary repairs on the dam;" "to have the right to draw water as aforesaid, sufficient to carry on the tanning in said yard in its various branches in common with" the grantor; "to have the privilege of using more water than aforesaid, when there shall be waste water running over or around the dam;" and the grantor, "his heirs or assigns, is to have the right to increase machinery or mills upon his privilege to any extent that he or they may choose, and to use all the water except what has herein been conveyed for the use of said tan-yard, if he or they shall choose." In an action which required a construction of the provisions relating to the use of the water under this grant, it was held, that by the terms of the deed, the grantee acquired an absolute and prior right to the use of the quantity of water named; that the grant was of a fixed measure of power to be used for any purpose, and not to be confined to that of tanning; and that the measure of power was restricted to that used or required, at or about the date of the grant, "in carrying on tanning in said yard in its various branches." Covel *v.* Grant, 56 Maine, 518. In Griswold *v.* Hodgman, 4 Thomp. & C. (N.Y.) 325, it appeared that a grant was made to the owners of a mill, in 1853, of a right to draw water from a race sufficient to propel four 300-pound (paper) engines, with all the machinery necessary for making paper from the same, and it was held that this was a grant of a quantity of water sufficient to perform the required work with the machinery in use at the mill at the time the grant was made; and the grantees were not restricted to such quantity as with improved machinery and facilities would perform the work. See Miller *v.* Lapham, 46 Vt. 525.]

same season the grantees in that deed erected their clothing-works below the grist-mill, and a flume, to conduct water for the use of the machinery therein, was connected with the flume of the grist-mill. In 1830 the defendants' grantors placed another run of stones in the grist-mill, and erected a machine shop adjoining the grist-mill, and attached the corn cracker and smut-mill to the wheel of the machine shop. In 1831 the defendants' grantors conveyed to the plaintiffs' grantors an additional privilege, which was described as follows: "The farther right and privilege of drawing water from [the] grist-mill flume and pond at all times, for the purpose of manufacturing any and every kind and description of woollen, or cotton, or linen, or hemp, or silk goods, or manufactures; provided, if the said [grantees] shall draw more water from said flume and pond, than they now have a right to draw, they shall not draw such additional quantity of water from said flume and pond, so as to interfere with the privileges now belonging and reserved to the said grist-mill, nor so as to interfere with the privileges belonging to the saw-mill owned by David Stimson." And it was held, that the reservation for the grist-mill, in the first deed, defined the use of water for two runs of stones as a measure of the quantity of water to be used, and not as a restriction to that particular use;[1] and

[1] [J. P., owning a mill-privilege on both sides of the stream, conveyed to the plaintiff the privilege on the east side, "except what may be necessary and sufficient for carrying two run of mill-stones on the west side, and also, when not required for the use of the saw-mills, what may be necessary for such other machinery as may be erected on the west side." In the trial of an action against J. P.'s representatives for an unauthorized use of the water, it appeared that the plaintiff had title to a saw-mill privilege, with a right of water on the east side, and the defendants to a grist-mill privilege with right of water on the west side. At the date of the suit the defendants were using water for five run of stones, two cleansers, and four bolts; they were also using the water to run a carding-machine, and for a cabinet shop. The plaintiff claimed that under the exception of water sufficient to carry two run of mill-stones, the defendants would have no right, as against the saw-mill, to water for operating the carding-machine or cabinet shop; and if the defendants permitted them or either of them to be run when the water was required for the plaintiff's saw-mill, during the time covered by the writ, they were liable in this action. It was held by the Court that the first exception in the deed to the plaintiff was an abstract quantity of water sufficient to carry two run of mill-stones, and its use was not limited to the running of the grist-mill, but it might be applied to a carding-machine and cabinet-shop; and it was further held that upon the true construction of the deed, the rights of the parties to the water of the stream were as follows: (1) The defendants had a right to the use of a quantity of water sufficient to carry two run of mill-stones, operated by the water-wheels in use at the time the deed was made, for the use

that this was the reservation of privileges for the grist-mill which was referred to in the second deed; but that this reservation was to be understood as of the date of the second deed; and that it reserved to the grantors the right to use the quantity of water named, a sufficient portion of the time to do all the business then done in the grist-mill, or which might reasonably be then expected to be done, without essential addition to the machinery, — in no event exceeding an amount of water power that would be given by the constant use of water sufficient to carry two runs of stones. In 1830 the defendants' grantors had also conveyed to one S. the saw-mill upon the same dam, with the privileges belonging to it, but subject to the right of the plaintiffs' grantors, under the deed executed in 1824, to use water for their clothing-works, and also reserving to the grantors in that deed the first privilege of drawing water for the use of the grist-mill. In 1833, subsequent to the grant of the additional manufacturing privilege above mentioned, S. reconveyed to his grantors, by quitclaim deed, the premises and privileges conveyed to him in 1830, and the same grantors, upon the same day, executed to him another deed, conveying the saw-mill, with the privilege of drawing water from the pond for its use, when there should be more water in the pond than was wanted for the use of the grist-mill, and to carry all the machinery therein, as then used, and also making it subject to the clothing-works of the plaintiffs' grantors, or any other machinery that should draw no more water than had been formerly used for the clothing-works, and also imposing certain other restrictions upon its use, and providing, that S. might draw "water for the use of the saw-mill and shingle machinery in manner aforesaid, and no more, nor in any other way, nor for any other purpose whatever." The title acquired by S. under this deed subsequently became vested in the plaintiffs' grantors, and the saw-mill was removed, and the site remained vacant. And it was

of their grist-mill and any other machinery (saw-mills excepted), on the west side of the stream. (2) The plaintiff had the right to use all the rest of the water of the stream, when required for the use of the saw-mills in process of construction when the deed was made, operated by the water-wheels then in use for such purpose. (3) The defendants had the right to the use of the water of the stream for any machinery (saw-mills excepted) on the west side of the stream, subject to the rights of the plaintiff as above defined. Blake *v.* Madigan, 65 Maine, 522.]

held, that the first and second grants to S. were of a *quantity* of water, sufficient to carry the saw-mill, and that the title to it having come to the plaintiffs, they might use that quantity of water to increase their manufacturing privilege, provided they did not encroach upon the rights reserved to the defendants. And it was also held, that although the plaintiffs' grantors, immediately after the execution of the deed of the additional manufacturing privilege in 1831, enlarged the building which they then occupied, and placed in it one set of machinery for manufacturing cassimeres, and continued so to use their privilege until 1836, this was not any such election, or acquiescence in a particular use of the water, as would restrict them, in the exercise of their rights, below the fair construction of their deed. To have this effect, the grant should have been so far general, as to be wholly undefined on the face of the grant, — thus evidently looking to the use, as the grantee's own construction of his grant.

[§ 149 *h*. In Garland *v*. Hodgson,[1] the defendants claimed under a conveyance of a parcel of land situated on a stream, including a part of the dam and mill privilege, with such part of the water power as is embraced in the following clause in the deed: "Together with the right and privilege in the dam and stream, to take and use water sufficient for one fulling-mill, and the necessary machinery for dressing cloth, and, also, for such carding-machines as may be connected with said fulling-mill, not exceeding four single machines, or two double ones." The defendants claimed the right to use the water for any purpose. Davis J. said, "When the intention of the grantor is clearly expressed in the deed either way, courts will always give effect to it. But, if the intention is left doubtful, the tendency of courts is to construe such grants most favorably to the grantee. If one conveys only an incorporeal hereditament, a right to use water for a particular purpose, with no grant of land to which it is appurtenant, the presumption is strong that the right in the water is intended to be restricted to the specified purpose named. But if the grant of water is appurtenant to a parcel of land conveyed by the same deed, the beneficial use of the land, under the changes of business which occur from time to time, may

1 [Garland *v*. Hodgson, 46 Maine, 511.]

require the use of the water for other purposes than those which are specified. And for this reason, unless the contrary intention is clear, the use designated will be taken by the courts merely as the measure of the water granted, which the grantee may use for that or for other purposes. Applying these principles to the case at bar, we are satisfied that the defendants may use the water for other machinery, the quantity not exceeding what would be required for the fulling-mill and carding-machines." In Pratt *v.* Lamson,[1] Merrick J. said, "A difficulty sometimes occurs upon the construction to be given to the language of deeds by which a mere water power is granted, in determining whether it is a grant of water to carry a particular mill, and to be used only for that special and limited purpose, or is a grant of water sufficient to carry a particular mill, making reference to the mill only to indicate and measure the quantity of water power intended to be conveyed. Whenever the description is in such terms as to leave it in doubt which of these two kinds or species of grant was intended, the general rule adopted by the courts appears to be, so to interpret the deed as to make the privilege conveyed a grant of a certain quantity of power, and not of power limited to a specific use." — "When the privilege granted is a given quantity of power, not limited to any specific use, it may be appropriated to any purpose whatever, and by any person to whom it may be transferred or assigned."[2] A grant by the owner of two dams on the same stream, of the lower one, and of "a privilege to draw water sufficient to carry a water-wheel well constructed, with twelve feet head and fall, for two common blacksmith bellows; and, should the head and fall be

[1] [Pratt *v.* Lamson, 2 Allen, 281, 282, 283.]

[2] [Ashley *v.* Pease, 18 Pick. 275; Tourtellot *v.* Phelps, 4 Gray, 374. A construction of a grant of a water-power which will restrict the grantee to the specific use to which the water was applied when the grant was made, will never be adopted unless the language of the grant unmistakably indicates such to have been the intention of the parties. Hines *v.* Robinson, 57 Maine, 324; Miller *v.* Lapham, 46 Vt. 525. Where the owner of a dam and stream of water granted to another, a right to use the water for a mill "to the height that it now is, and, if the parties shall choose, to raise the same, not exceeding six inches, higher," for the use of the mill, it was held to settle and determine the extent of the privilege and the rights of the parties. Nor would the grantee lose or abandon any of these rights by mere non-user for a less period than twenty years. The owner of the water privilege would have the right to grant some part of it to other parties, so that he and his grantees, of smaller portions, could insist upon the full supply of water granted, Leonard J., in Casler *v.* Shipman, 35 N.Y. 533, 541.]

less than twelve feet, sufficient to carry one bellows twelve hours in twenty-four hours, in either case, in the daytime, as near as may be," limits only the extent of the privilege granted, and not the use to which it is to be applied.[1] So where in a deed of a parcel of land connected with a mill-site, there was also a grant of "likewise a water privilege for tanning-purposes in all its various branches, which privilege is to come out of the grist-mill dam," which belonged to the grantor, it was held to be a grant of a water privilege for a specific purpose, restricting the grantee, or those claiming under him, to its use for that purpose alone.[2]]

§ 150. The owner of a mill who is entitled by a grant to the use of the surplus water not required by another mill, and that only, is of course bound to shut his gate when there is not a sufficiency of water for both; and if he omits to do so, the other mill-owner may do it. But if the other mill-owner undertake himself to prevent the passage of water to the mill first mentioned, he will be liable to an action should he not remove the obstruction as soon as the deficiency of water ceases.[3]

§ 150 *a*. If a proprietor of two mills on the same stream, one below the other, directs in his will, providing for the sale and conveyance by his executors, that in times of low water the two mills "should have an equal use of the water alternately; it is not necessary to the ascertainment of the equality of the water that the lower mill should be of the very kind or capacity of the mill existing at the date of the will; and the erection of some new factory by the owner of the lower mill does not prejudice his right to an equal quantity of the water of the stream. Therefore, the owner of the lower mill has the right to recover damages for the undue use and control of the water of the stream by the owners of the upper mill. It is not at all necessary to the ascertainment of this equality, that the lower mill should be of the very kind and capacity of the mill existing at the time of the devise.[4]

§ 151. In England, a local act of parliament authorized a company to enter upon lands within a manor, and to dig and search for any spring of water, and to convey the water from such

[1] [Tourtellot *v.* Phelps, supra; Howe Scale Co. *v.* Terry, 47 Vt. 109.]

[2] [Deshon *v.* Porter, 38 Maine, 289.]

[3] Sumner *v.* Foster, 7 Pick. 32.

[4] Cress *v.* Varney, 17 Penn. St. 496.

springs into the town of South Shields, for the use of the inhabitants of the town, and the shipping in the harbor. It provided, that the company should not take the water from any spring, streams, or ponds, so as to deprive the occupiers of the land of water for their own necessary uses, and for the cattle depasturing therein. The company were empowered to lay down pipes, &c., and the inhabitants, with the consent of the company, might obtain the water by pipes to communicate with the company's pipes, at certain charges, according to the *bore* of the pipes. It was held, that the owners and occupiers of lands within the manor were not prevented by the parliamentary act from sinking wells in such lands, though the effect might be to draw off water from the company's springs.[1]

§ 152. A deed which describes the premises as "a certain part of a stream of water," and mentions the two *termini* of the "part," will pass a right to the whole water which flows within those *termini*. In Bullen *v*. Runnels, in New Hampshire,[2] it appeared on the trial, that the early proprietors of Concord, in that State, in 1732, made a conveyance of the "whole stream of Turkey River;" and that all this stream, from its source to its junction with the Merrimack, was within their boundaries. Under that grant, mills were soon erected upon the margin of the stream, at a place where the plaintiff, at the time of the action brought, owned mills and land, derived by conveyances from the original grantee of "the whole stream of Turkey River." It further appeared, that the defendant owned land and mills situated nearer the source of the river, and to turn his machinery claimed the right to use all the water which flowed in the river. In May, 1780, one F. (under whom the plaintiff held, by a subsequent conveyance) executed a deed to one D., of "a certain part of a stream on Turkey River;" viz., "beginning at the mouth of Great Turkey Pond, and so extending to the head of the lesser pond;" that within those *termini*, D. soon erected mills, where the defendants, at the time of the action, were situated; and for about forty years past, D. and his grantees, including the defendant, had both claimed and used the water in the stream to turn their machinery. The plaintiff objected,

[1] South Shields Waterworks Co. *v*. Cookson, 15 Law J. N.S. Exch. 315; and as to *subterraneous* diversion of water, see ante, §§ 109–115, et seq.

[2] Bullen *v*. Runnels, 2 N.H. 255.

that by the deed to D. nothing passed; or, if any thing, only a fractional portion of the water between the *termini* mentioned. To this objection relating to the uncertainty of the description, Mr. J. Woodbury, who pronounced the opinion of the Court, said, "By 'a certain part of a stream,' we do not apprehend, that the grantor meant some fractional part of the whole water which ran in the stream, and, not having defined the extent of that part, that the deed must be adjudged void for a patent ambiguity. On the contrary, as the grantor owned the whole length of the river, we think, that by 'a certain part,' he intended to convey a part of the whole length; and that this part of the whole length is defined and made 'certain,' by describing it as 'beginning at the mouth of Great Turkey Pond, and so extending to the head of the lesser pond.' All that part of the river which flows between those boundaries, was intended to be conveyed. This construction gives operation to the deed, is consistent with its language, and accords well enough with the nature of the transaction. In A.D. 1780, in a period of perilous war, such a deed would be conveyed with less reluctance, and at a smaller price; the actual use of water was, from thinness of population, and the absence of most manufacturing machinery, very limited; and from physical causes, the quantity of it in this river was then probably much greater. Hence, without any imputation of folly or blindness, the grantor might, for a moderate compensation, convey the use of the whole river at a place some distance above his own mills."[1]

[§ 152 *a*. In a lease of certain premises with their appurtenances, the lessor reserved out of the demise "the free running of water and soil coming from any other buildings and lands contiguous to the premises hereby demised in and through the sewers and watercourses made or to be made within, through,

[1] In the early settlement of Massachusetts, mills were erected over streams of water then sufficient, but which, by the clearing of the country, have so far failed, that the mills could now be wrought but a small part of the year; and the profits would not be a sufficient inducement to keep them in repair. To this discouragement may be added the erection of new mills in the neighborhood in more convenient situations. And as to saw-mills, the consumption of all the timber in their vicinity has rendered many of them useless. Per Parsons C.J., in Carver *v.* Miller, 4 Mass. 558 (1808). The learned Judge added, that as there had been many mills heretofore erected, which could not then be wrought with adequate profit, it would be unreasonable to enable any individual part-owner to compel his partners, in all cases, to keep their mill in repair, under the statute.

or under the said premises," and thereupon it was held, first, that the reservation extended to water and soil coming from contiguous lands and buildings, whether that water or soil in the first instance actually arose on or from such contiguous lands or buildings or not; and secondly, that it did not extend beyond water in its natural condition, and such matters as are the product of the ordinary use of land for habitation, and that therefore it did not give to the occupier of certain tanpits, who claimed under the lessor, a right of passage for the refuse of those pits.[1]]

3. "*Mill and Appurtenances.*"

§ 153. In Nicholas *v.* Chamberlain,[2] it was held, that if the owner of a house builds a conduit thereto through his other land, and conveys the water by pipes to his house, and then sells the house, "with the appurtenances," *excepting the land*, or sells the land to another, reserving to himself the house, the conduits and pipes pass with the house, because it is necessary and *quasi* appendant thereto, together with a right to dig upon the earth for the purpose of repairing the pipes, and laying new ones, when necessary.[3] In Pickering *v.* Staples,[4] a water right, appur-

[1] [Chadwick *v.* Marsden, L.R. 2 Exch. 285.]

[2] Nicholas *v.* Chamberlain, Cro. Jac. 121.

[3] [In Seymour *v.* Lewis, 2 Beas. Ch. (N.J.) 466, it is said that the question in Nicholas *v.* Chamberlain "came up upon demurrer, and it does not appear whether the house or the vacant land had been conveyed. But the Court treat that as a matter of perfect indifference. In either event the conduit and pipes go with the house. This case has never been overruled, but has often been cited with approbation." In Philbrick *v.* Ewing, 97 Mass. 134, Hoar J. said, "It is, indeed, well settled that a conduit or pipe to conduct water to a house will pass as appurtenant to a grant of the house;" and to this he cites Brown *v.* Nichols, Moore, 682; Nicholas *v.* Chamberlain, Cro. Jac. 121; and adds, "But an easement, where it is not expressly described in the conveyance, must actually belong to the estate conveyed, in order to pass by implication. (Spaulding *v.* Abbot, 55 N.H. 423.) The rule is commonly stated to be, that the grantor conveys by his deed, as an appurtenance, whatever he has the power to grant, which is practically annexed to the granted premises at the time of the grant, and is necessary to their enjoyment in the condition of the estate at that time. 'The grant of the principal thing,' says Chief-Justice Shaw, 'carries all things necessary to the use and enjoyment of the thing granted, which the grantor had power to convey.'" Tourtellot *v.* Phelps, 4 Gray, 378; Spaulding *v.* Abbot, 55 N.H. 426; Hammond *v.* Woodman, 41 Maine, 201. See also Johnson *v.* Jordan, 2 Met. 234; Parker *v.* Bennett, 11 Allen, 388. In the above case of Philbrick *v.* Ewing, it appeared that one E. conveyed to P. a house and land by deed of warranty. At the time

[4] Pickering *v.* Staples, 5 S. & Rawle, 107.

tenant to a mill, passed by the word "appurtenances," which was considered as comprehensive of the water right, as if the

of this conveyance the only supply of water to the premises was through a pipe laid across land of a third person to a highway, where it joined a branch leading from the main pipe of an aqueduct company. Under a contract with the aqueduct company, and on payment of an annual compensation therefor, E., at the time of his conveyance to P., had a right to draw water from the main pipe, through this branch, for his own use, and to dispose of it to others. The pipe from the house to the branch was originally laid, for the purpose of bringing water to the house, by a tenant of E., under an oral license from the third person across whose land it passed, and was bought by E. of the tenant at the expiration of his tenancy. No mention of it was made in the deed from E. to P. After executing that deed, E. cut off this pipe at the boundary of the land which he conveyed to P., and dug it up from there to its junction with the branch in the highway, and carried it off. In an action of tort by P. against E., it was held, that the pipe so dug up and carried off was a fixture annexed to the house, and passed by E.'s deed to P., but that the deed conveyed no right of drawing water through that pipe from the branch in the highway. In reference to cutting off the pipe, Hoar J. said, "The defendant owned the whole pipe, from the sink in the house which he sold to the plaintiff, to its junction with the branch in the highway. He undertook to cut it off where it left the plaintiff's land, and claims that only that part of it which was within the premises conveyed passed to the plaintiff by the deed of conveyance. But we see no just ground for this claim. The pipe was put in by his tenant, and afterwards purchased from the tenant by him, as one entire thing. It was designed for the use of the plaintiff's house, and for no other purpose. If it extended into the land of a third person, and into the highway, it does not appear that the owner of that land, objects to its continuance, or authorized or required the defendant to remove it. We are, therefore, of opinion that the whole of it, at the time of his conveyance to the plaintiff, was a fixture annexed to the house, and passed by the deed. He had no more right to cut off a piece of the pipe, because it ran into another's land, than he would have had to cut off a piece of a spout which projected over the adjoining premises. If the owner of that land objected to its continuance, the plaintiff would be obliged to draw her pipe in; but until objection was made, or if she could obtain a license for it to continue, she could let it remain as her predecessor had done. We suppose it is a common thing in cities, for the owner of a house to connect it by a pipe with the pipe in the street belonging to a water company, and that such a pipe would pass by the sale of the house, although the owner of the house did not own the soil of the street. So in the case of a drain-pipe connecting with a common sewer; on a sale of the house the vendor could not take it away." Philbrick *v.* Ewing, 97 Mass. 133; Coolidge *v.* Hager, 43 Vt. 9, involved a similar state of facts and was decided on the same principle. In this case it appeared that the defendant, by a warranty deed in the usual form, conveyed a house and lot supplied with water by an aqueduct running through the land granted from a spring belonging to, and on other land of, the grantor. Upon the principle of the maxim that whoever grants a thing is supposed also, tacitly, to grant that without which the grant itself would be of no effect, the Court held that the grant of the house and land, and that part of the aqueduct in the land, carried with them the running water and the right to have it continue to run as it was then running, because the defendant could grant all these, and without them the rest of the grant could not have been enjoyed in all its material parts. "Since Nicholas *v.* Chamberlain, Cro. Jac. 121," the Court said, "this maxim has in almost all cases that have arisen been applied to grants of land, with water running to buildings upon it, wherever the grantor had a permanent estate that he could convey in

privilege of using the water had been expressly inserted in the conveyance; even though the vendor, when he executed the conveyance, declared that he neither bought nor sold the water right.[1] [A conveyance of one of two ancient mills, which comprise the entire mill privilege of a stream, carries with it such a proportion of the whole right in the stream as the water used to drive the mill conveyed bears to that used by the other mill.[2]]

[§ 153 *a*. But the word "appurtenances" is not necessary to the conveyance of the easement or water right in such cases.[3] The general rule of law is, that when a party grants a thing, he by implication grants whatever is incident to it and necessary to its beneficial enjoyment. The incident goes with the principal thing.[4] This principle is especially applicable to water privileges in grants of mills and factories dependent on a flow of water for motive power. A dam may be distant from a mill, and yet the right to maintain it may pass by a conveyance as incident to the mill. The idea and definition of an easement incident to real estate granted, is a privilege off and beyond the local boundaries of the land or tenement conveyed. Where there is a dominant, there is always a servient, tenement. But it is not necessary they should be contiguous to each other. The proximity of the one to the other is of very little comparative importance in determining the question whether the easement passes by a conveyance of the dominant tenement. It depends rather upon the nature, character, and purpose of the easement, its relation to the subject-matter of the grant, its accustomed use in connection with it, and its necessity to the value, and to the beneficial and convenient use of the premises granted.[5]]

§ 153 *b*. There can be no doubt that a grant in which the simple term "mill-site" is only used, conveys a water power, together with the right to maintain a dam, and wherever such

the water and the aqueduct in which it was running, such as the defendant had in this aqueduct and in this water." See Vermont Central R.R. *v.* Hills, 23 Vt. 681; Swasey *v.* Brooks, 34 Vt. 451; Manning *v.* Smith, 6 Conn. 289.]

1 Whitney *v.* Olney, 3 Mason, 280; and post, § 156.

2 [Crittenden *v.* Field, 8 Gray, 621.]

3 [Post, §§ 158, 159.]

4 [Philbrick *v.* Ewing, 97 Mass. 133. "The general rule of construction is well settled that every thing passes which is necessary to the full enjoyment of the right, title, or estate which is included in the words of a grant; but nothing more." Bigelow C.J. in Jamaica Pond Aqueduct Corp. *v.* Chandler, 9 Allen, 164; Spaulding *v.* Abbot, 55 N.H. 423, 426.]

5 [Perrin *v.* Garfield, 37 Vt. 304, 312; Crittenden *v.* Field, 8 Gray, 621; Brace *v.* Yale, 4 Allen, 393; Colt J. in Hapgood *v.* Brown, 102 Mass. 453.]

dam would be suitable for the convenient and beneficial appropriation of the water power. The word "site" is used in judicial proceedings whenever mills and water rights are spoken of, as comprehending a fall of water suitable for the erection and use of mill-dams. Such a fall of water being denominated a "mill-site," or "mill-seat."[1] [But it has been held, that a deed of a mill-site described by metes and bounds, gives no right to the use of a reservoir dam above, which is owned by the grantor, although the stream is small, and the use of the reservoir dam is necessary to the beneficial use of a mill upon the grantor's premises.[2]]

§ 154. In Farrar *v.* Stackpole, in Maine, it was held, that by the conveyance of a saw-mill, with the appurtenances, the *mill-chain*, clogs, and bars, being in their appropriate places, at the time of the conveyance, passed.[3] In this case, it was not denied, that other parts of the machinery, intended for the operation of the mill, passed with the mill; but it was insisted, that the *chain* was of the nature of personal property, and, therefore, passed not by a deed of the realty, unless specially named. To this the Court answered, "First, that if it be an essential part of the mill, it is included in that term, whether real or personal; secondly, that that which is in its nature personal, may change its character, if fixed, used, and appropriated to that which is real. Is it too much to say, that the mill is incomplete, without a chain, a cable, or other substitute? It may be, that a millwright, who contracts to erect a mill, and to furnish materials, may be deemed to have completed his engagement, without supplying a chain. One millwright, a witness in the case, testified, that such is his impression; and, if this is to be understood generally, his contract might not extend further. But the owner would find that he had yet something more to procure, before he could be in a condition to operate. The chain is the last in the parts of the machinery, to which the impelling power is communicated, to effect

[1] [Stackpole *v.* Curtis, 32 Maine, 383; Tabor *v.* Bradley, 18 N.Y. 113; Le Roy *v.* Platt, 4 Paige, 77. "A mill site comprehends not only the site of the mill building, but also the water power connected therewith for milling purposes." Park J. in Curtiss *v.* Smith, 35 Conn. 156, 158; Pettee *v.* Hawes, 13 Pick. 326. A deed of a tract of land "known by the name of the mill-spot," may be explained by oral evidence of what "the mill-spot" was commonly reputed, at and before the time of the execution of the deed, to include. Woods *v.* Sawin, 4 Gray, 322.]

[2] [Brace *v.* Yale, 4 Allen, 393.]

[3] [See Lampman *v.* Milks, 21 N.Y. 510, per Selden J.]

the object in view. Its actual location in the succession of parts, can make no difference. If it is, in its nature, essential to the mill, it is included in that term; and that, as it has been heretofore remarked, whether it be personal or real property. But, upon consideration, we are of opinion, that it ought to be regarded as appertaining to, and constituting a part of, the realty." [1]

§ 155. By a *devise* of a mill with the appurtenances, it has been held, that a right not only to the building, and use of the water, but also to the *land* which was used with the mill, passed.[2] In

[1] Farrar *v.* Stackpole, 6 Greenl. 154. In giving their opinion in this case, the Court further observed as follows: "There was at Bath, in this State, a saw-mill propelled by steam, generally called the steam saw-mill. Suppose this establishment had been conveyed by the name of the steam saw-mill, without a more particular description. What would pass? There is nothing in the books with respect to this species of property; for it is of quite modern invention; and there is no other mill of the kind in this part of the country. If you exclude such parts of the machinery as may be detached without injury to the other parts or to the building, you leave it mutilated, incomplete, and insufficient to perform its intended operations. The parties, in using the general term, would intend to embrace whatever was essential to it, according to its nature and design; and the law would doubtless so construe the conveyance as to effectuate the lawful intention of the parties. Salt-pans have been held to pass the realty, and to belong to the inheritance; because adapted and designed for, and incident to, an establishment for the manufacture of salt. The principle is, that certain things, personal in their nature, when fitted and prepared to be used with real estate, change their character and appertain to the realty, as an incident or accessory to its principal. Upon this ground we are satisfied that the chain in question, being in the mill at the time, and essential to its beneficial enjoyment, passed by the deed of the defendant to Asa Redington, under whom the plaintiffs claim, independent of any reference to usage. The verdict is therefore sustained, although not upon a ground in accordance with the impressions of the Judge who presided at the trial. This we think, upon the whole, a fair application of the principles of law to the case. Had the term mill, however, by uniform and general usage, been understood not to embrace the chain, a different construction would no doubt have obtained; for it is a term of art, the proper meaning of which would be fixed by the general understanding of those who are skilled and experienced in it. If they were not agreed, the law would adopt that which was most general, and which would best accord with the nature and character of the subject-matter. The jury have found, upon the evidence submitted to them, that by general and uniform usage, the chain passed by a deed of the mill. This finding was somewhat stronger than the evidence warranted. It did appear that there had been exceptions to this usage; but the weight of evidence went to support it. At any rate it is apparent that the usage is rather in favor than against the construction we have adopted. But as we are of opinion that the title of the plaintiffs is well supported by the deed, independent of usage, it becomes unnecessary to decide upon the competency or effect of the testimony adduced upon this point."

[2] Blaine *v.* Chambers, 1 S. & Rawle, 169. [By the demise of a mill, the land on which it stands passes as incident to the demise. Bacon *v.* Bowdoin, 22 Pick. 401. There is a class of implied grants by devise where there is no necessity for the right claimed, but where the

this case, C.J. Tilghman said, "No doubt there must have been also a small parcel of land adjoining. But how much, or how situated, was a fact to be inquired of by the jury. They were to inquire, not what *in their own judgment* was convenient, on a view of the mill, but what was actually used as appurtenant to it by the testator in his lifetime; for that, and that only, would pass by the devise. If no trace of that could be discovered, by evidence of what was occupied by the testator, or by his devisee, soon after his death, then, indeed, the jury could only decide by their own judgment, what was necessary, and this they had a right to presume was intended by the testator."

[§ 155 *a*. A vote passed by a town in 1750, granting to certain persons named "the liberty of erecting a grist-mill on Fort River, near Lawrence's Bridge, with the use of said stream," and accepted by the grantees, is not to be construed as a grant of land, in the absence of other evidence that the town owned the land on which the mill was erected. This does not necessarily imply a conveyance of land. The term "liberty" is commonly used to designate some privilege, license, or authority, and is quite inappropriate to the grant of land. It is not to be doubted that a vote, by owners, of a "liberty" to enter upon and hold such a piece of land, as the grantee's share, would pass the land; but here it is liberty to erect a mill and use the stream. This the town might well do, if they had, or believed they had, a right to the use of the stream, or if they held land which would be flowed by it, or if the mill would necessarily encroach on a highway, or otherwise affect any public right or easement.[1]]

§ 156. Mr. J. Story, in Whitney *v.* Olney,[2] had before him the question upon the very point, whether a devise of a mill and appurtenances, conveyed the land under the mill, and so much adjoining it, as was necessary to its use, and had been actually used with it. In deciding this question, the learned Judge went not upon the ground, that the land was a mere appurtenance to the mill, but that it was a parcel thereof. He admitted it to be

tenement is so constructed as that parts of it involve a *necessary dependence*, in order to its enjoyment in the state it is in when devised, upon the adjoining tenement. Pearson *v.* Spencer, 3 B. & S. 761.]

1 [Hadley *v.* Hadley Manuf. Co., 4 Gray, 140, 143.]

2 Whitney *v.* Olney, 3 Mason, 280.

true, that land cannot strictly be appurtenant to land, so as to pass under the term "appurtenances;" but, said he, *where the intention is clearly expressed*, that the land should pass under that name, the law would give effect to the grant, notwithstanding the misnomer. He then cites Plowden, to show that where it is averred in pleading, that certain land was appertaining to a messuage, although, in point of law it could not be appurtenant to the messuage, was nevertheless well in a grant, because it shall be intended to mean such land as is usually occupied with the messuage; and, therefore, a devise of a messuage, "with the lands to the same appertaining," is good to pass such lands as have been commonly occupied, used, or lying with the messuage. If this be true, continues the learned Judge, in a *grant*, the law will construe the words still more favorably in a *devise*. But in the case before him, he laid no stress upon the words "with the appurtenances," but held, that the land under the mill, and adjacent thereto, passed simply by the force of the word "mill." Both in common sense, and legal interpretation, he observed, a mill does not mean merely the building in which the business is carried on, but includes the site, dam, and other things, connected with the freehold.[1] And so in Lombard *v.* Forbush[2] it was held, that upon the well-established rule of construction, by the grant of a mill, the land under the mill and adjacent thereto, so far as necessary to its use, and commonly used with it, will pass by implication. And the same rule of construction applies to an exception in a grant. But to justify such an implication, it should be made to appear that the land adjacent was necessary for the use of the mill.[3]

[1] *Land appurtenant to land.* In Leonard *v.* White, 7 Mass. 6, the question was, whether under a grant of a mill, with the privileges and appurtenances thereto belonging, the soil in a way passed which had been immemorially used for the purpose of access to the mill from the highway. The Court held, that the soil did not pass, but that the way, as an easement, might be appendant or appurtenant to the mill.

[2] [Forbush *v.* Lombard, 13 Met. 109; Owen *v.* Field, 102 Mass. 102. See Morton *v.* Moore, 15 Gray, 573. "The grant of a mill, *eo nomine*, will carry the head of water by which it is driven, with the building, land, and privileges necessary to its use." Colt J. in Hapgood *v.* Brown, 102 Mass. 453. And in Richardson *v.* Bigelow, 15 Gray, 156, Shaw C.J. said: "It is a well-settled rule of law, that the grant of a mill carries with it, by necessary implication, the right to the use of the watercourse coming to the mill and furnishing power for working it, and also to the canal or race way which carries the water from the mill to the full extent of the grantor's right and power so to grant them." Prescott *v.* White, 21 Pick. 341.]

[3] [By the grant of a mill, the land under it, indispensable to its use, unless

§ 157. The "saw-mill," without any further description, was set off by the commissioners appointed to divide an estate, to one of the claimants. The Court held thus: "Doubtless by this term, the fee of the land upon which the mill stood would pass.[1] Lord Coke enumerates a variety of terms, which, being used in a conveyance, carry lands; and he states to what extent.[2] The land passes, because included in the term used. The word mill, or *molendinum*, is not among those to which he adverts; and probably no authority can be adduced, in which it has been held to convey, *ex vi termini*, any part of the adjoining land. That upon which it stands may be regarded as including land, over and upon which the slip, if it has one, or any other necessary projection from the mill, passes. The term may embrace the free use of the head of water, existing at the time of the conveyance, as also a right of way."

[§ 157 *a*. A deed conveying a mill, "together with the land and privilege where the same is situated, necessary for and attached to said mill, hereby meaning to convey all the land and mill privilege not heretofore sold by us, on the dam connected with said mill and privilege," may be construed to convey not only the land on which the mill stands, but land attached to it necessary for its existence.[3]]

§ 157 *b*. By a testator in his will: "I give and devise to my son W., his heirs and assigns, the houses, mills, and races which he now possesses, together with twenty-four feet from the mill to the dam to enable him to repair the race at pleasure, together with full and free liberty to keep the dam in repair, so as to furnish water to the mill devised to him;" and by a subsequent clause in his will, the testator devised the land through which the race and twenty-four feet were, to his grandson, without

there is in the conveyance language indicating a different intention, passes by implication. The same rule applies to exceptions in a grant. Peters, J., in Moulton *v.* Trafton, 64 Maine, 222.]

[1] Blake *v.* Clark, 6 Greenl. 436; [Esty *v.* Baker, 48 Maine, 495, 500; Farrar *v.* Cooper, 44 Maine, 397; Moore *v.* Fletcher, 16 Maine, 63; Crosby *v.* Bradbury, 20 Maine, 61; Per Bigelow C.J., in Jamaica Pond Aqu. Corp. *v.* Chandler, 9 Allen, 164; Johnson *v.* Rayner, 6 Gray, 110; Smith *v.* Moodus Water Power Co., 36 Conn. 392; Frink *v.* Branch, 16 Conn. 260]

[2] Co. Litt. 4, b.

[3] [Esty *v.* Baker, 48 Maine, 495, 500. The Court say, "There might, from the situation of the mill, be land necessary for its existence, attached to it, and used and occupied with it at the time of the conveyance, which, it would seem, would pass with it. Forbush *v.* Lombard, 13 Met. 109; Moore *v.* Fletcher, 16 Maine, 63."]

reservation. It was held, that the devise to the son of the twenty-four feet along the race, vested in him a fee-simple estate in the soil, and not a mere easement.[1]

[§ 157 *c*. A grant by indenture, in consideration of a fixed sum, of a right to build a dam upon the land of the grantor, the parties agreeing, that the amount of damages thereby done by flowing the grantor's land shall be determined by an arbitrator, and the sum so determined shall be in full satisfaction of such damages, does not authorize the grantee, after building one complete dam, to increase its height so as to flow more land of the grantor. It was claimed on the part of the grantee that the structure originally erected was only the beginning of a higher dam afterwards built, and he offered oral evidence to prove that it was expressly agreed, at the time of making the indenture, that the dam should be raised to the height to which it was ultimately raised, but it was held inadmissible.[2]]

4. *Secondary Easements.*

§ 158. The maxim of the law is, that whoever grants a thing, is supposed also tacitly to grant that without which the grant would be of no effect;[3] and accordingly, whenever any thing is granted, all the means to attain it, and all the fruits and effects of it, are granted also, and will pass inclusive, together with the thing, by the grant of the thing itself, without the words *cum pertinentiis*, or with appurtenances, or any like words.[4] Hence the rule, that by a grant of a piece of ground, there is also granted a right of way to it over the grantor's land, as incident to the grant; and so it has been observed, that, when the use of a thing is granted, every thing is granted by which the grantee may have and enjoy such use; as if a man gives to another a license to lay pipes of lead in his land, to convey water to his

1 Harlan *v*. Moore, 9 Watts, 360.

2 [Goodrich *v*. Longley, 4 Gray, 379.]

3 *Cuicumque aliquis concedit concedere videtur, et id sine quo res ipsa non potuit*, 11 Rep. 52; [Tourtellot *v*. Phelps, 4 Gray, 378, per Shaw C.J.]

4 See Evans *v* Rees, 12 Ad. & Ell. 57; Shep. Touch. 81; Broom's Legal Maxims, 198; and see Co. Litt. 307, a; Hathorn *v*. Stinson, 10 Maine, 224; Oakley *v*. Stanley, 5 Wend. 523; Taylor *v*. Hampton, 4 McCord (S.C.) 96; [Tabor *v*. Bradley, 18 N.Y. 109. "The grant of a principal thing carries all things necessary to the use and enjoyment of the thing granted, *which the grantor had power to convey*." Per Shaw C.J., in Tourtellot *v*. Phelps, 4 Gray, 378. See Hadley *v*. Hadley Manuf. Co., 4 Gray, 148; Virgin J. in Butler *v*. Huse, 63 Maine, 453; Stevenson *v*. Wiggin, 56 N.H. 308, 312, 313.]

cistern, the grantee may afterwards enter, and dig the land, in order to mend the pipes, though the soil is still in the grantor.[1] In a very modern case in England, it was held, that a certain coal-shoot, water, and other pipes, all which were found by special verdict, to be necessary for the convenient and beneficial use and occupation of a certain messuage, did, under the particular circumstances, pass to the lessee, as integral parts of such messuage; and it was further held, that the right of passing and repassing over the soil of a certain passage, for the purpose of using the said coal-shoot, and using, clearing, and repairing the said pipes, likewise passed to the lessee, as a necessary incident to the subject-matter actually demised, although not specially named in the lease.[2] In the case of the United States *v.* Appleton,[3] reliance was placed on the language of the grant, "with all the ways," &c. But this was held by Mr. J. Story, to be wholly unnecessary; for whatever, said he, are properly incidents and appurtenances of the grant, will pass without the word "appurtenances," by mere operation of law.[4] A grant of a right to build a dam, carries with it a right to enter and repair the dam, and cleanse the pond.[5] It was contended in Kent *v.* Waite,[6] that a right of way which had been acquired by prescription, did not pass by a deed of the land, without the words *cum pertinentiis;* but the Court held otherwise.

§ 159. Agreeably to the above doctrine, a water right which has been used with a mill, together with all secondary easements, will pass by a grant of the mill without the words "with the appurtenances."[7] Mr. J. Bayley puts the illustration, "Suppose the owner of two fields sells one, having a stream of water flowing through it, can the vendee stop the watercourse? *Primâ facie* no exception in the conveyance could be presumed."[8]

[1] Per Twysden J., Pomfret *v.* Rycroft, 1 Saund. 323; Hodgson *v.* Field, 7 East, 622.

[2] Hinchcliffe *v.* Earl of Kinnoul, 5 Bing. N.C. 1.

[3] United States *v.* Appleton, 1 Sumner, 491.

[4] See also Grant *v.* Chase, 17 Mass. 443; Hazard *v.* Robinson, 3 Mason, 272, 278; Preble *v.* Reed, 17 Maine, 169.

[5] Fraily *v.* Waters, 7 Barr, 221; ante, § 157 *c.*

[6] Kent *v.* Waite, 10 Pick. 138; [Oliver *v.* Dickinson, 100 Mass. 114, 117; Pettingill *v.* Porter, 8 Allen, 1; Hollenbeck *v.* McDonald, 112 Mass. 247, 250.]

[7] Pickering *v.* Staples, 5 S. & Rawle, 107; Swartz *v.* Swartz, 4 Barr, 353; Vermont Central Railroad Co. *v.* Hills, 23 Vt. 681. [The conveyance of a dam and mills, by necessary implication, carries with it the right to flow the grantor's land then flowed by such dam, and which inevitably must be flowed by a fair and proper use of the dam and mills. Butler *v.* Huse, 63 Maine, 447.]

[8] Canham *v.* Fisk, 2 Tyrw. 155.

[In Dodd *v.* Burchell,[1] Martin B. said, "If the owner of land which has a natural stream flowing through it, grants to one person a part of the land, and the remainder to another person, neither has the right to stop the flow of water through the land of the other."] So in the converse case, the law gives a common-sense construction, and supposes, that each field has the appurtenances thereof in *statu quo*, notwithstanding the grant.[2] A grantor conveyed by deed a tract of land, described by metes and bounds, with a mill upon the same; and, at the time of the conveyance, there was a raceway to conduct the water from the mill, running along the side of the natural stream, beyond the land granted, into other land of the grantor, and there discharging the water into the natural stream. The raceway had been used with the mill several years, and was necessary to the convenience of it. It was held, that a right to have the water flow off through the whole extent of the raceway, passed, as appurtenant to the mill.[3] The "saw-mill," without other description, was assigned to

[1] [1 H. & C. 118.]

[2] Story J. in United States *v.* Appleton, 1 Sumner, 501. A., the owner of a tract through which a stream of water runs, and on which a mill was erected, purchased of the *supra-riparian* owner, the right of diverting the water, by means of a dam, of the height of any former dam. A. then sold part of his land on the stream below the point of division. It was held, that, as against his grantee, A. has the right to divert the whole of the stream, for the use of his mill, and for that purpose to erect a dam higher than that stipulated for in the grant, by the *supra-riparian* owner. Frey *v.* Whitman, 7 Penn. St. 440.

[3] New Ipswich Woollen Factory *v.* Batchelder, 3 N.H. 190; [Perrin *v.* Garfield, 37 Vt. 304, 312; ante, § 153 *a*; Johnson *v.* Jordan, 2 Met. 240. In Hall *v.* Lund, 1 H. & C. 676, it appeared that in 1855, the owner of two mills leased one of them to one P., who carried on therein the business of a bleacher. The refuse from his works was discharged through a drain, partly open and partly covered, into a natural stream or watercourse, three hundred or four hundred yards distant, and upon which the other mill was situate. This discharge of the refuse took place about seven times a fortnight, and polluted the stream. In 1858, P. surrendered his lease, and the lessor granted a new lease to the defendant. In this lease the defendant was described as a "bleacher," and the demise was of the premises "late in the occupation of P." There was a clause that all buildings erected by the defendant for the purpose of bleaching, should, at the end of the term, become the property of the lessor. In 1858, the plaintiff purchased both mills. The defendant discharged the refuse from his works through the drain into the stream in the same manner that P. had formerly done. The plaintiff who carried on in the other mill the business of a paper maker, brought an action against the defendant for polluting the stream. It was held, that the lease might be explained by the state of the premises at the time it was granted, and the mode in which they had been previously enjoyed; and that, thus explained, there was an implied grant by the lessor to the defendant to use the stream for the purpose of his business of bleaching, and therefore the plaintiff, who was in the position of the lessor, could maintain no action against the defendant. But where it appeared that the Holland Land Company

one of the heirs to an estate, and it was decided, that the use of the water, and any easement used with or necessary to its enjoyment, passed.[1] The term "dam," in a grant of land, with a stream of water running through it, and on which there is a dam, flume, and conductor, is construed as including the flume, or as being of equivalent import.[2] In these, and in all cases of a grant of water right, there is implied by the grant, all such use of the land, as is necessary for the enjoyment of the right granted."[3]

§ 160. In Dyer *v.* Depui,[4] in Pennsylvania, the question was, under a grant of water, in respect to the right of entering upon land, as being included in the grant. J. D., who was the owner of a large tract of land, conveyed a part of it to the plaintiff, "together with the privilege of a part of the water flowing along a certain ditch or watercourse, flowing from J. H.'s line, through and across the said J. D.'s other land, on condition that the said M. D. (the plaintiff), his heirs and assigns, will at all times be subject to, and defray one-half the expense of keeping or repairing the dam, and clearing out the said ditch or watercourse." There had existed previously to this deed on the land of J. D. a dam, by which the water was diverted to that part of it sold to the plaintiff. J. D. afterwards died, having by his will devised to S. D. (his son) a tract of land, being between the plaintiff's land, and the defendant's, "together with a drain or watercourse, from J. H.'s line, through and across the lot of land hereinafter devised to my son J. D." (the defendant), "as the same now runs, with a privilege on each side of the drain or watercourse, one perch in width, for the purpose of passing and repassing to mend and repair and clear out the said drain or

conveyed to the defendant, by metes and bounds, without any mention of a mill, dam, or water privilege of any kind, certain land, part of a large tract of wild land, upon which he had previously constructed a mill and a dam, which flowed other land of the company, and there was no evidence that the grantors had notice of the existence of the mill or dam when the deed was executed, it was held, that it did not convey the right of flowing the other land of the grantors. Tabor *v.* Bradley, 18 N.Y. 109.]

[1] Blake *v.* Clark, 6 Greenl. 436.

[2] Kennedy *v.* Scovil, 12 Conn. 317.

[3] Conwell *v.* Brockhart, 4 Mon. (Ken.) 584. The grant of a saw-mill, "with a convenient privilege to pile logs, boards, or other lumber," conveys an easement in the land used for piling. Thompson *v.* Proprs. of Andover Bridge, 5 Greenl. 62. An injury to the raceway is an injury to the mill. Butz *v.* Shrie, 1 Rawle, 281. Wetmore *v.* White, 2 Caines' Ca. 87; Blake *v.* Clark, 6 Greenl. 436; Strickler *v.* Todd, 10 S. & Rawle, 63; Hall *v.* Benner, 1 Penn. 402; Rackley *v.* Sprague, 17 Maine, 281; Maddox *v.* Goddard, 15 Maine, 218; Moore *v.* Fletcher, 16 Maine, 63.

[4] Dyer *v.* Depui, 5 Wharton, 584.

watercourse, as often as the same may be necessary, and without any let or hindrance of him the said J. D., his heirs or assigns," "with the water drain and privilege aforesaid, to him the said S. D., and his heirs and assigns, subject to the water drain now open and running through and across the first-mentioned lot, to M. D.'s line." He then devised to the defendant, J. D., another portion of land, adjoining and "subject to the aforesaid drain or watercourse, from J. H.'s line, through and across the first-mentioned lot of land, with the privilege granted to my son S. D., his heirs and assigns, of a passage or court-way, one perch wide, on each side of said drain, for cleansing or repairing the same." It was held, that the right conveyed to the plaintiff by the deed of J. D. was not restricted to the watering of cattle, but that it was a right to use a portion of the water in the way it was customary and necessary to use it for the benefit of the land conveyed; and that, if to do so, it was necessary to conduct it on or along the defendant's farm by a trench, if that was the only way in which he could beneficially use the privilege, he might cut the trench to conduct the water, and might renew and repair the dam for the purpose. The court considered, that the grants and liabilities evinced the clear understanding and determination of the testator, that the drain was to subsist and remain *in perpetuum* as a matter of importance to the enjoyment of the properties by the respective owners.[1]

§ 161. In a division of real estate, under the statute of descents, if a mill-site is assigned to one of the heirs, he or she takes it with the easements and privileges before attached to it, and with which it had been used. Where A. died intestate and seised of a tract of land on which there was a grist-mill then in

[1] [The owners of a mill-pond executed a deed to the owners of a grist-mill, situated below and supplied by a raceway from the pond, in which, after reciting the fact that the grantees, and those under whom they held title, "had been accustomed to take water from the pond for operating their said grist-mill," conveyed to them, their heirs and assigns, "the right, at all times hereafter, of taking and using the water from said pond for operating any other mill which shall be hereafter erected upon the site of their present grist-mill, to the same extent that they now have a right to do, or have been accustomed to do, for the operating of their said grist-mill." It was held, that the effect of the grant was not merely to extend to the new mill that might be substituted for the grist-mill the rights, already existing as such, with regard to the grist-mill, but to give the grantees a right to all the use of the water to which they and their grantors had been *accustomed*, without reference to the question whether such customary use had ripened into a right. Avon Manuf. Co. *v.* Andrews, 30 Conn. 476.]

operation, and on a division of the land, under the Maryland statute of direct descents, amongst his heirs, the mill was on the part allotted to B., and the dam of which covered a portion of the part allotted to C., it was held, that B. had a right to use the mill and dam in the same way, and to the same extent, as they had been used by A. in his lifetime. The dam, said the Court, was appurtenant to the mill, and if the intestate had conveyed the mill with the appurtenances, it could not be contended that he could have sustained an action against the purchaser for the injury in question; and if he could not, it was difficult to perceive on what principles a suit could be maintained against the assignee of the mill by the other heir; and the assignee of the mill could not be supposed to stand in a worse situation than a purchaser would have done. Besides, it was the duty of the commissioners (and it was to be presumed they did it) in dividing the estate of the intestate, to take into consideration all the advantages and disadvantages attending the respective parts; and it was presumable that they gave to the part allotted to the heir to whom was assigned the land covered by a portion of the dam, an equivalent for the injury and inconvenience occasioned by the mill-dam.[1]

§ 162. The owner of land through which a stream of water passed, had erected thereon a grain-mill, and had raised near it a dam to furnish a water power to drive the mill, and also further up the stream, had erected another dam to preserve water for the use of the mill below, and afterwards had built a shingle-mill on the lower dam near the grist-mill, which was driven by the same

[1] Kilgour *v.* Ashcom, 5 H. & John. 82. [See Pearson *v.* Spencer, 3 B. & S. 761; Elliott *v.* Sallee, 14 Ohio St. 10; Morgan *v.* Mason, 20 Ohio, 401. A brickmaker, who owned and occupied a tract of land for his business, was accustomed to vary the course of a brook across it, from time to time, to suit the convenience of the business, but never varied it so as to prevent its traversing the whole tract. Upon his death, his two heirs, who knew of this custom, divided the tract between themselves by mutual deeds of quitclaim, after which the heir who took the upper portion of it diverted the brook from flowing through the lower portion; it was held, that the first-named heir took no easement in the land quitclaimed to the other heir, and that the latter could maintain an action against him for diverting the course of the brook. Macomber *v.* Godfrey, 108 Mass. 219. Chapman C.J. in this case said, "The use which the ancestor had been accustomed to make of the water would give the defendant no easement in the plaintiffs' lot. The defendant took no grant, and made no reservation of such easement, and therefore obtained no right to the water. However useful or necessary the water might be to his business of brickmaking, neither utility nor necessity would authorize him to take what belonged to the plaintiffs."]

water power. He then, *first* granted to the plaintiff the grain-mill and the land whereon it stood, "with the privilege of drawing water from the mill-pond sufficient for this or any other grist-mill that may be built on the ground that this mill stands on, the grist-mill having the privilege of drawing water over every other machinery on the dam;" *secondly*, he granted to the defendant the shingle-mill and the land whereon it stood, "with the privilege of water sufficient for a shingle saw-mill at all times, except when the water is so low that the grist-mill will require it all, and then the shingle-mill must stop, and not till then." *Thirdly*, he conveyed to the plaintiff the land on which the upper dam had been erected. It was held, that the defendant acquired the right to the use of the water from the upper as well as from the lower dam, when it could be taken without injury to the rights previously granted to the plaintiff for the use of the grist-mill; that the defendant had the right to draw water for the use of his shingle-mill, whenever such drawing did not thereby injure the plaintiff in the use of his grist-mill, although there were "reasonable grounds" to believe the water would be needed for the use of the grist-mill; that when the grant of the right of water for the use of the shingle-mill was made in express terms, there was granted, by operation of law, the right to use the means necessary to the enjoyment of the right, and therefore, by the grant to the defendant, he had the right to enter upon any land then owned by the grantor, when and where necessary, to enable him to obtain his just supply of water. The principal grounds in this case upon which the denial of the right of the defendant to claim water from the upper dam, rested, was that the upper dam was erected to reserve the water for the grain-mill; that it was wholly owned by the owners of that mill; and that the defendant, by the conveyance to him, acquired no interest in it. But the Court considered, that these positions, if admitted, did not authorize the conclusion, and that when the grantor of the land and stream erected the upper dam to preserve the water for his grain-mill, the whole head of water, for whatever purpose created, became "a common fountain of life" to *any* machinery to which it might be his pleasure to impart it.[1]

[1] Elliott *v.* Shepherd, 25 Maine, 371.

§ 163. In Prescott *v.* White, in Massachusetts, it was held, that where one is the owner of an ancient mill, to which there has been attached a raceway, being an artificial canal for conducting off the water, and without the free and unobstructed current of which the mill could not be worked, and such canal has, from time immemorial, passed through the land of another, and there is no grant or contract regulating the rights of the parties, the owner of the mill has a right to enter upon the land, through which the raceway passes, and to clear out the obstructions therefrom in the mode, if any, hitherto practised for clearing out the raceway; otherwise, in the usual and ordinary mode of clearing such canals, doing no unnecessary damage.[1] But there is obviously a material difference between such a case, and that in the same Court, of Prescott *v.* Williams, administrator.[2] The jury in the latter case found, that the stream of water passing through Prescott's land was a *natural* watercourse, and not an artificial raceway or canal, as was assumed in the trial of the former case, which materially changed the features of the case, and presented the inquiry, whether the existence of an easement, in the land conveyed, of a mill-owner above, in a natural stream passing through such land, accompanied by the farther fact, that such mill-owner above had for more than thirty years, as occasion and necessity required, entered upon the land conveyed, to remove obstructions in the stream, — *shows such an incumbrance upon the premises conveyed*, as to subject the grantor of such premises, who conveys them with the usual covenants of warranty and against incumbrances, to an action for a breach of his covenants. It was held, that the existence of the right in the mill-owner to remove the obstructions of the free flow of the water from the mill was not an incumbrance within the meaning of such covenants.[3]

[1] Prescott *v* White, 21 Pick. 431; [White *v.* Chapin, 12 Allen, 521, 522; Daniels *v.* Chaffin, 28 Iowa, 327; Beals *v.* Stewart, 6 Lansing, 408; Roberts *v.* Roberts, 55 N.Y. 275. This is on the principle, that when the use of a thing is granted, every thing essential to that use is granted also. Such right carries with it the implied authority to do all that is necessary to secure the enjoyment of such easement. Tenney C.J. in Hammond *v.* Woodman, 41 Maine, 177, 202, 203.]

[2] Prescott *v.* Williams, 5 Met. 429.

[3] In this case, Dewey J., in giving the judgment of the Court, considered it somewhat remarkable, that there should be found so little direct authority bearing upon the interesting question involved; and he relied upon general principles, as follows: "Now we find it stated in books of authority, that 'the express or implied grant of an easement is accompanied by certain secondary easements necessary for the enjoyment of the principal one.' Gale & What. on Easem. (Am. ed.) 231. So also, 'in the Civil Law, the right to

§ 164. In 1777, A. received a lease of land on a watercourse opposite the site of a saw-mill about to be erected, with the privilege, to him and his heirs, of flowing and building the dam over a part of the lessor's land, during the duration of the saw-mill. In 1809, A. conveyed to his son B. a tract of land on the same watercourse, including a pond, and the saw-mill connected with it, together with a piece of land below, on which a fulling-mill was afterwards erected. In May, 1815, A. conveyed, with covenants of warranty, to C., his heirs and assigns for ever, the

a servitude drew with it a right to such secondary servitudes as were essential for its enjoyment.' Ib. Again, it is said, that 'by the Civil Law, the owner of the dominant tenement had a right to do whatever was requisite to secure to himself the fullest enjoyment of his servitude.' Ib. 232. 'But in entering upon the neighboring soil for the purpose of doing these necessary works, the owner of the dominant tenement was bound not only to exercise ordinary care and skill, but also to repair, as far as he could, whatever damage his labors might have caused to the servient tenement.' Ib. 235. The decision of this Court, in the case of the present plaintiff against White, already referred to (21 Pick. 341), seems to have recognized and adopted fully the principle, that where the use of a thing is granted, every thing is granted essential to such use. Such a right carries with it the implied authority to do all that is necessary to secure the enjoyment of such easement. There are other well-settled legal principles, that have a bearing upon this question. The duty of making repairs, and the labor necessary for keeping the watercourse in a state fit for use, rests wholly upon him who claims an easement on his neighbor's land; and, as a general rule, easements impose no obligation upon those whose lands are thus placed in servitude, to do any thing. Gale & What. on Easem. 215; Taylor *v.* Whitehead, 2 Doug. 745. The owner of the land below, through which the stream passes, being thus free from all *obligation* to cleanse the stream, or remove any obstructions that may arise without fault on his part, and which may impede the free passage of the water; if the right to cleanse such watercourse, or remove such obstructions, rests exclusively with him, the consequence will be, that the same may never be done; and whether done or not, will depend upon the will or caprice of the owner of the land below, who may have no interest in the matter, rather than upon the wishes of the owner of the mill above, whose interests may be deeply affected by it. We are satisfied that in the present case the owner of the mill privilege above, having this natural easement in the land below, would, independently of any right acquired by compact or by prescription, have a right to enter upon the land below, and in a reasonable and proper manner do all acts necessary to secure the enjoyment of his easement. This right to enter upon the land of another, to cleanse a natural stream, or remove any casual obstructions therein, is one doubtless to be held to the strictest and narrowest limits compatible with the enjoyment of the principal easement. It is to be considered as a privilege arising from the necessity of the case, and, like a way of necessity, to be enjoyed only when the party has no other reasonable and suitable mode of effecting this object. It is to be done in such a manner as shall cause no unnecessary damage to the owner of the land below. The incumbrance, occasioned by the easement in the present case, does not appear, by the evidence relied upon to establish the nature and extent of it, to be other and different from the secondary easement embraced within the principles we have stated."

latter piece with the fulling-mill thereon, and the appurtenances thereunto belonging, for carrying on the fulling business; granting also to C. certain privileges reserved by A., to himself and heirs, in a deed of adjoining land previously sold by A. to R.; granting also to C. the privilege of supplying himself with water for the use of the fulling-mill, at all times, from the saw-mill dam, whenever it should be wanted for carrying on his business; C. to have ingress and egress through the road laid across the grantor's land to the public highway; *habendum* to C., his heirs, &c. In June, 1815, B. released to A. his interest in the fulling-mill site, as deeded by A. to C. The water of the saw-mill pond had always been used for the fulling-mill, and was, in fact, essential to its enjoyment. The dam of the saw-mill pond becoming leaky, D., the heir of C., after a fruitless application to B. to repair it, took stones and earth from the bed of such pond, for this purpose, doing no unnecessary damage. In an action of trespass *quare clausum fregit*, brought by B. against D. for such act, it was held, *first*, that the privilege granted to C. was not a mere personal privilege to him, but extended to his heirs and assigns; *secondly*, that the release from B. to A. inured to the benefit of C., not only as to the land and fulling-mill, but also as to the privilege granted by A. to C.; *thirdly*, that the lease to A. in 1777, limiting the privilege therein granted to the duration of the saw-mill, had no effect upon the construction of A.'s deed to C.; *fourthly*, that C., having, by the express terms of A.'s deed to him, the privilege of supplying himself with water, was empowered to do those acts, which were necessary to obtain a supply; and consequently the act complained of was rightfully done.[1]

[§ 164 *a*. A conveyance of one of two ancient mills, which comprise the entire mill privilege of a stream, carries with it such a proportion of the whole right in the stream as the water used to drive the mill conveyed bears to that used by the other mill.[2] "In such a case," said Bigelow J., "where the right of a party is traced back to an ancient privilege, embracing the entire water in a stream, described and designated by the kind of mills to which it was originally appropriated, the conveyance of a grist-mill or a saw-mill, *eo nomine*, passes the entire propor-

[1] Miller *v.* Scholfield, 12 Conn. 335.

[2] [Crittenden *v.* Field, 8 Gray, 621.]

tion or share of the water in the river belonging to such mill." This would be otherwise, if the right of the party rested on a modern grant of a mill, situated on a stream where there were several mills of different kinds, all drawing from the same level, and where there was only sufficient water to supply the power necessary to drive each mill.[1]]

§ 165. In short, under the grant of a thing, whether it be water or any thing else, whatever is parcel of it, or of the essence of it, or necessary to its *beneficial* use, or in common intendment is included in it, passes to the grantee.[2] But the doctrine, in its application to water rights, must be understood as applying to such things only as are incident to the grant, and *directly* necessary for the enjoyment of the thing granted. If, for instance, a person grant to another the fish in his ponds, the grantee cannot cut the banks to lay the ponds dry, for he may take the fish by nets or other engines.[3] Again, if a person, upon a lease for years, reserve a way to himself, through the house of the lessee to a back-house, he cannot use it but at seasonable times, and upon request.[4] A way of necessity to a watercourse would be, therefore, limited to the necessity which created it, and when such necessity ceases, the right of way will also cease; and if at any subsequent period, the party formerly entitled to such way can, by passing over his own land, approach the place to which it led, by as direct a course, as he would have done by using the old way, the way ceases to exist as of necessity.[5]

§ 166. The distinction between what is *necessary*, and what is merely *convenient*, or desirable, in the class of cases above considered, was taken in Howell *v.* M'Coy.[6] In that case, there was

1 [Crittenden *v.* Field, 8 Gray, 627.]

2 Per Story J., in Whitney *v.* Olney, 3 Mason, 272. [But mere convenience and usefulness are not sufficient to establish a way of necessity. In order to establish an implied reservation of such a way, there must be, at the time of the grant, a reasonable necessity for its existence. Chapman C.J., in Oliver *v.* Pitman, 98 Mass. 50; Pettingill *v.* Porter, 8 Allen, 1; Parker *v.* Bennett, 11 Allen, 388; Brigham *v.* Smith, 4 Gray, 297; Leonard *v* Leonard, 2 Allen, 543.]

3 1 Wms. Saund. 282, n. 6; and see Hodgson *v.* Field, 7 East, 613.

4 Tomlin *v.* Fuller, 1 Ventr. 48; and see also Morris *v.* Edginton, 3 Taunt. 24, cited 6 M. & W. 189; Wilson *v.* Bagshaw, 5 Man. & Ry. 448; Osborn *v.* Wise, 7 C. & P. 761; Broom's Legal Maxims, 201.

5 Holmes *v.* Goring, 2 Bing. 76; [Viall *v.* Carpenter, 14 Gray, 126; Collins *v.* Prentice, 15 Conn. 39, 423; Pierce *v.* Selleck, 18 Conn. 321; Nichols *v.* Luce, 24 Pick. 102; White *v.* Leeson, 5 H. & N. 53; Holmes *v.* Seely, 19 Wend. 507; Seeley *v.* Bishop, 19 Conn. 128.]

6 Howell *v.* M'Coy, 3 Rawle, 256. [See per Shepley C.J., in Trask *v.* Patterson, 29 Maine, 503; Pearson *v.* Spencer,

a lease of a piece of ground for a tan-yard, with the use of so much of the water of a stream as might be necessary for conducting the business of tanning; and it was held, that this did not give to the lessee the privilege of emptying the contents of the tan-yard into the stream. The Court in this case were clear that the rule was, that whatever is claimed as passing as an appurtenance must be necessary to the enjoyment of the thing devised, and not merely convenient. It would be extremely convenient if the party possessed the right asserted, of emptying the contents of his tan-yard on the stream below, or disposing of his surplus tan in the land *adjoining his land*, but that this was necessary was a matter of doubt. There were *various ways* of disposing of the matter of the tan-yard, and it was for the grantee to consider of this at the time of the demise. If the grantee did not choose to purchase more land, it was certainly not the fault of the grantor.

[§ 166 *a.* It is to be observed that so long as two estates or the different portions of an entire estate are the property of the same owner, there can be no easement or servitude, technically so considered, annexed to one part or imposed upon another.[1] The owner can make such arrangements and dispositions of the material properties of the whole, for the enjoyment of one part or the other as he pleases, and change them at his pleasure. But the cases already cited and discussed, and those hereafter referred to and considered, go to establish the doctrine, which may be considered the prevailing one, that whenever the owner of an estate divides it into two parts, granting away one of them, he is taken, by implication of law, to include in his grant all those benefits or advantages in the nature of easements over the remaining part, which are practically annexed to the granted premises at the time of the grant, and are *necessary* for the reasonable enjoyment of them in the condition of the estate at that

3 B. & S. 761; Carbrey *v.* Willis, 7 Allen, 369; Nichols *v.* Luce, 24 Pick. 102; Thayer *v.* Payne, 2 Cush. 327. In Dodd *v.* Burchell, 1 H. & C. 113, 122, Wilde B. said, "It is said that the way now claimed is more convenient than the other. Then comes the question whether the plaintiff can claim it as a way of necessity on account of its great superiority over the other way. It seems to me that it would be most dangerous to hold, that where a deed is silent as to any reservation of a way, because it is more convenient to use than another way, it must exist as a way of necessity. There is no foundation whatever for such a doctrine."]

[1] [White *v.* Chapin, 12 Allen, 516, 520 Ritger *v.* Parker, 8 Cush. 145.]

time, and which the grantor has the power to grant.[1] This principle has already been partially discussed, and will be more fully illustrated hereafter.]

[§ 166 *b*. But a much broader doctrine has been stated and earnestly supported by Judges eminent for wisdom and ability; which is, that if the owner of an estate makes or uses upon it artificial arrangements and dispositions of the material properties of the estate in regard to watercourses, drains, gutters, and the like,[2] which are apparent and continuous, i.e., of an open, visible, and permanent character, whereby and in respect of which, one of the parts thereof becomes adapted to another, and dependent upon it for its reasonable enjoyment in the condition into which it has been put or used and enjoyed by the owner; and, in this state of things, such owner sells the dependent part and thereby severs the ownership of the estate, by a conveyance silent as to the continuance of such artificial arrangements and dispositions, the purchaser of the dependent portion will take with it the benefit of them, as easements, by implication of law; and thereafter, to this extent, the two parts of the estate will bear to each other the relation of dominant and servient tenements. If the grantor has already treated this portion as separate property, the mode in which he has enjoyed it, or allowed it to be enjoyed, affords, it is said, a very proper indication of what rights, over the remaining land, he intends to pass as accessory to it.[3] These

[1] [See per Hoar J., in Philbrick *v.* Ewing, 97 Mass. 133, 134, 135; cited ante, § 153, note.]

[2] [This rule has never been applied in England to rights of way. In Pearson *v.* Spencer, 1 B. & S. 571, 583, Blackburn J. said, "We do not think that on a severance of two tenements, any right to use ways which during the unity of possession have been used and enjoyed in fact, passes to the owner of the dissevered tenement, unless there be something in the conveyance to show an intention to create the right to use these ways *de novo*. We agree with what is said in Worthington *v.* Gimson, 29 L.J. Q.B. 116; 6 Jur. N.S. 1053, that in this respect there is a distinction between continuous easements, such as drains &c. and discontinuous easements, such as a right of way; and Pheysey *v.* Vicary, 16 M. & W. 484, is an authority that the same rule in this respect applies to a will as to a deed. But see Pettingill *v.* Porter, 8 Allen, 1, in which this distinction is not noticed. See also other American cases. United States *v.* Appleton, 1 Sumner, 500; Seibert *v.* Levan, 8 Penn. St. 383, per Gibson C.J.; Kieffen *v.* Imhoff, 26 Penn. St. 442; Smyles *v.* Hastings, 22 N.Y. 220. Huttemeier *v.* Albro, 18 N.Y. 48; Carlin *v.* Paul, 11 Mo. 32; Gillis *v.* Nelson, 16 La. An. 275.]

[3] [See Hazard *v.* Robinson, 3 Mason, 272; United States *v.* Appleton, 1 Sumner, 500; New Ipswich Factory *v.* Batchelder, 3 N.H. 190; Dunklee *v.* Wilton Railroad, 24 N.H. 489; Harwood *v.* Benton, 32 Vt. 724; Thayer *v.* Payne, 2 Cush. 327; Kenyon *v.* Nichols, 1 R.I. 427; Huttemeier *v.* Albro, 18 N.Y. 48; Lampman *v.* Milks, 21 N.Y. 506; Smyles

propositions have, of course, no application to watercourses in their natural state, the rights of parties to which depend upon an entirely different principle.]

v. Hastings, 22 N.Y. 220; Brakeley *v.* Sharp, 1 Stockt. (N.J.) 10; Seibert *v.* Levan, 8 Penn. St. 383; McTavish *v.* Carrol, 7 Md. 352; Shaw *v.* Etheridge, 3 Jones (N.C.) 32; Elliott *v.* Rhett, 5 Rich. 415; Curtiss *v.* Ayrault, 47 N.Y. 73.] In an elementary treatise of deservedly high reputation, it is said that the implication of the grant of an easement may arise upon the severance of an heritage by its owner into two or more parts. Upon the severance of an heritage a grant will be implied, — first, of all those *continuous and apparent* easements which have in fact been used by the owner during the unity, though they have had no legal existence as easements; and secondly, of all those easements without which the enjoyment of the several portions could not be fully had. Gale & What. on Easem. 49. The rule of the French Law upon this subject, with the incidents of which the Common Law is said to agree, is thus laid down in the French Civil Code: "If the proprietor of two estates, between which there exists an apparent sign of servitude, disposes of one of these estates without inserting in the contract any stipulation relative to the servitude, it continues to exist actively or passively *in favor* of the land alienated, or *over* the land alienated." Code Napoleon B. 2, tit. 4, § 694. The oldest case upon this point appears to be that of Coppy, 11 Hen. VII. 25 b.; 1 Bro. Abr. 324, which was as follows: A. was the owner of a tenement, to which there was an *ancient gutter* running through an adjoining tenement, and afterwards he bought the adjoining tenement, and then sold the first tenement to the plaintiff, who brought his action for stopping the gutter. It was adjudged, that the easement of the ancient gutter was not extinguished by the unity of ownership, but remained as before; but that it would have been otherwise, if A., during the unity of ownership, had destroyed the gutter, or cut it off. This case shows that if the owner of an entire estate wishes to put an end to a burden, which has been imposed upon one portion for the benefit of another, he must do so before he sells the portion benefited. If he does so, he sells without the burden; if he does not, the burden remains. This supposes that the conveyance is silent in regard to it. But the leading case bearing directly upon watercourses, and the one which has been generally treated as settling the law upon this subject, is Nicholas *v.* Chamberlain, Cro. Jac. 121, which is cited and stated, ante, § 153. In this case the unity of ownership was not admitted to destroy the right to the easement, because it was annexed to the messuage, and in use at the time of the grant. The authority of this case has never been shaken, but, on the contrary, it has generally been referred to with approbation in all the subsequent cases in which the question has been involved. The same doctrine was laid down in Robins *v.* Barnes, Hobart, 131. See Kent J., in Warren *v.* Blake, 54 Maine, 288; Jackson J., in Grant *v.* Chase, 17 Mass. 447, 448; Philbrick *v.* Ewing, 97 Mass. 133, 134. The case of Sury *v.* Pigott, Palm. 444; s.c. Latch. 153; Poph. 166; 3 Bulst. 339, was substantially this: One owned a rectory, a part of which was a close, in which there was a watering-place, supplied by a stream, which flowed from a brook through another parcel of land purchased by him called the hop-yard. He sold the hop-yard, and afterwards the owner of the hop-yard obstructed the stream by erecting a dam across it within the limits of the hop-yard. The Court were unanimously of opinion that the right to the watercourse was not extinguished by the unity of ownership, but that it remained to the owner of the rectory after the sale of the hop-yard. Dodridge, one of the justices, put this case: "A man owns a mill, and afterwards purchases the land upon which the stream goes, which runs the mill, and afterwards alienes the mill, the watercourse remains." This case, Story J. says, in Hazard *v.* Robinson, 3 Mason, 278, "proceeds upon this plain

[§ 166 *c*. As the doctrine, which has been stated in the preceding section, is held to furnish a rule of law governing the operation of all conveyances of property similarly situated, and not merely a rule for the construction of the terms of each particular conveyance, favorable or unfavorable to parties as they are grantors or grantees, if it be a correct doctrine, when applied in favor of a grantee, it has been contended, that there is no good reason, why it should not be reciprocally applied in favor of a grantor in cases where he retains the dependent portion of the estate, and sells that which is burdened for its support; and so it has been laid down in several cases of eminent authority, that the rule is entirely reciprocal, and not for the benefit of purchasers only. Hence, if instead of a benefit conferred, a burden has been imposed upon the portion sold, the purchaser, provided the burden is in its character apparent and continuous,

principle, that a privilege, which was annexed to, and in actual use with, the rectory during the unity of possession, and was not a parcel of the other land or a *profit à prendre* out of that land, was to be considered as still existing as an appurtenance or privilege annexed to the rectory, notwithstanding the unity of possession. The running water over the hop-yard was not a parcel of the hop-yard, or an easement growing out of it. But if, during the unity of possession, the privilege had been disannexed by the owner, as if the owner had during that period stopped the watercourse and thus destroyed the privilege, the case would have been otherwise. A subsequent grant of the rectory would then have conveyed only the privileges actually in existence and use at the time of the conveyance." — "Whatever is actually enjoyed with the thing granted, as a beneficial privilege at the time of the grant, passes as parcel of it." In Pearson *v*. Spencer, 3 B. & S. 761, it was maintained that there is a class of implied grants by devise where there is no necessity for the right claimed, but where the tenement is so constructed as that parts of it involve a *necessary dependence*, in order to its enjoyment in the state it is in when devised, upon the adjoining tenement; and it was decided that, where the owner of a farm divided it by his will into two portions, devising them to A. and B., respectively, and the portion of B. was land-locked, so that in order to reach it, it was necessary that he should have a right of way over the property of A., and the devisor during his life had used a way in a certain direction over that property, a right to use that way passed to B. by the devise. Erle C.J. said, "The testator had a unity of possession of all this property; he intended to create two distinct farms with two distinct dwelling-houses, and to leave one to the plaintiff, and the other to the party under whom the defendant claims. The way claimed by the defendant was the sole approach that was at that time used for the house and farm devised to him. Then the devise of the farm contained, under the circumstances a devise of a way to it, and we think the way in question passed with that devise." The case was held to fall within the class of implied grants stated at the beginning of this note. It is held in Louisiana, that if the proprietor of two estates, between which there exists an apparent sign of servitude, sells one of those estates, and if the deed of sale be silent respecting the servitude, the same shall continue to exist actively or passively in favor or upon the estate which has been sold. Gillis *v*. Nelson, 16 La. An. 275. This is the rule of the French Law. Code Napoleon B. 2, tit. 4, § 694.]

and the marks of it are open and visible, takes the property with the servitude attached. The parties are presumed to contract with reference to the condition of the property at the time of the sale, &c., and to intend that all apparently permanent arrangements then existing and necessary for the reasonable enjoyment of the portion sold or retained, are to remain, unless there is some provision to the contrary; and neither party has a right, by altering such arrangements, to change materially the relative value of the respective parts.]

[§ 166 *d*. It will be convenient to notice, first, the cases which develop or bear upon the doctrine above stated in regard to implied grants of easements; and, second, those which bear peculiarly upon the subject of implied reservations of easements, as connected with running water.]

[§ 166 *e*. New Ipswich Factory *v*. Batchelder,[1] was a case in which the owner of an estate had made a change in the course of a stream in favor of one part of the estate as against the other, the benefit of which was held to remain to the purchaser of the former part, upon the sale thereof to him, as it was used and enjoyed before the sale. It appeared in that case, that a tract of land had been conveyed by metes and bounds, having upon it a mill; and, at the time of the conveyance, there was a raceway to conduct the water from the mill, running along the side of the natural stream beyond the bounds of the land granted, into other lands of the grantor, and then discharging the water into the natural stream. This raceway had been used with the mill several years, and appeared to be necessary to the convenient use of the mill. The Court held, that the right to have the water flow off uninterruptedly, through the whole extent of the raceway, passed as appurtenant to the mill; or "passed with the mill as an incident." The deed, through which the plaintiff claimed the right to the use of the raceway, mentioned "water privileges and all other privileges annexed to or belonging to said premises;" but no stress is laid upon this language by the Court in deciding the case. On the contrary the decision is put expressly upon the principle of Nicholas *v*. Chamberlain, cited and stated in a preceding section.[2] The Chief Justice quotes that case at length, and then remarks

[1] [New Ipswich Factory *v*. Batchelder, 3 N.H. 190.] [2] [Ante, § 153.]

that "the rule here laid down seems to be founded in sound reason and good sense, and to apply in all its force, to the case now before us." He also remarked, "As both the plaintiff and the defendant claim through the same person, it seems to us, that as between them, this raceway is to be considered as the natural channel of the river."[1] Dunklee *v.* The Wilton Railroad Company,[2] decided by the same Court, was another case where water was turned from its natural course into an artificial channel. In this case the plaintiff was the owner of a valuable mill, connected with which was an artificial raceway to conduct the water from the mill in the most direct way to the stream below. This raceway was constructed by the consent of all parties interested, at much expense, because it was regarded as necessary for the operation of the mill in the most advantageous way. The water of the brook or stream was turned from its original channel to the mill, and thence through this new raceway or watercourse, in which the whole water of the brook continued to run until the obstruction complained of in the action. It had been in use for several years, and until the old channel through the plaintiff's land had grown over with bushes and grass, had become filled up, and in many places difficult to trace. The plaintiff became the owner of the land through which both the old channel of the brook and the new raceway passed, from the point where they separated, to the point where they again united. He then conveyed by deed of warranty in the usual form, with covenants against incumbrances, a parcel of the land, through which the lower part of the old and new channels passed till they became united, to one Kidder, who conveyed to the defendants. The defendants obstructed this raceway or watercourse. The Court held that the plaintiff was entitled to recover. Bell J. said, "Property conveyed, passes with all the incidents then rightfully belonging to it, or actually and usually enjoyed with it at the time of the conveyance, so far as they are necessary to the full benefit and perfect enjoyment of the property, without any specification of them, and without the usual phrase, 'with all the privileges and appurtenances to the same belonging.'" The cases which relate to streams and mills, generally

[1] [The above decision seems to be approved by Shaw C.J., in Johnson *v.* Jordan, 2 Met. 240.]

[2] [Dunklee *v.* Wilton Railroad Co., 24 N.H. 489.]

"support the principle that a conveyance of a mill, or of land on which a mill is situated, carries with it, as incidents of the mill, the right to raise the mill-pond, and to flow the lands above as high as the dam has been usually kept up, and to maintain the dam and flume which are necessary to support the water at that height, and to support and use the penstocks, aqueducts, and channels which are necessary to convey the water to the mills, and the channels and raceways which are necessary to conduct the water from the mill to the stream below, in the manner in which they have been kept and used immediately previous to the conveyance, so far at least as the grantor has a right to convey such privileges. The same rule applies in the case of the reservation of a mill or mill privilege in a conveyance of land." The learned Judge cites many cases to these points, and says they are usually supported by the doctrine of implied grant, and may well stand upon that ground. He adds, "The case of ways of necessity are within the same principle. They are burdens of the nature of easements, which are apparent, and which naturally result from the relative situation of different parts of the property. Ways of necessity are usually spoken of as exceptions to the general rule that easements are extinguished by unity of possession. But it seems more correct to regard them as new rights, impliedly granted or reserved by the conveyance. The principle that such ways of necessity are not extinguished by unity of possession affords a clear solution of this class of cases, as far as it applies; but it is by no means broad enough to reach all the cases. It is immaterial, whether there has been an easement of the kind before. The way is implied, not because an easement has previously existed, but because without it the grantee cannot have the enjoyment of the thing granted; or the grantor would be deprived of the enjoyment of the property which he retained." In this case the Court treated the artificial arrangement for the flow of the water of the brook in a new course the same as the natural stream, as between the parties.]

[§ 166 *f*. This same subject has been discussed and similar views taken in the late case[1] in New York, which was an action for changing the course of a stream and flooding the plaintiff's land. It appeared that on the 27th of March, 1850, one Ches-

[1] [Lampman *v.* Milks, 21 N.Y. 505; 202; Roberts *v.* Roberts, 55 N.Y. 275, Hammond *v.* Woodman, 41 Maine, 201, 277.]

bro owned forty acres of land on Elk Creek, through which there was a small brook running. In its natural course it would have run over half an acre of low ground, part of the forty acres, which Chesbro on that day conveyed to the plaintiff for a building-lot, and upon which the plaintiff immediately thereupon erected a house and barn. Several years previously, the owner of the forty acres had diverted the stream through an artificial channel, carrying it into Elk Creek in such a manner as not to flow over land conveyed to the plaintiff. On the 1st of April of the same year, Chesbro conveyed the forty acres to the grantor of the defendant. In 1854 the defendant dammed up the entrance to the artificial channel, so as to cause the stream to run in its original bed, and to overflow the plaintiff's yard. Selden J., in a carefully considered opinion, said, "The owner of real estate has, during his ownership, entire dominion and control over its various natural qualities, and may dispose of and arrange them at will. He may alter the natural distribution of those qualities, so as essentially to change the relative value of the different parts; and may, in a great variety of ways, make one portion of the premises subservient to another. The precise question in this case is, whether an owner, who, by an artificial arrangement of the material properties of his estate, has added to the advantages and enhanced the value of one portion, can, after selling that portion with those advantages openly and visibly attached, voluntarily break up the arrangement, and thus destroy or materially diminish the value of the portion sold. The rule of the Common Law on this subject is well settled. The principle is, that where the owner of two tenements sells one of them, or the owner of an entire estate sells a portion, the purchaser takes the tenement, or portion sold, with all the benefits and burdens which appear, at the time of the sale, to belong to it, as between it and the property which the vendor retains. This is one of the recognized modes by which an easement or servitude is created. No easement exists so long as there is a unity of ownership, because the owner of the whole may, at any time, re-arrange the qualities of the several parts. But the moment a severance occurs, by the sale of a part, the right of the owner to redistribute the properties of the respective portions ceases; and easements or servitudes are created, corresponding to the benefits or burdens mutually existing at the time of the sale." "These principles are obviously just in themselves, and they are also sustained by ample authority." The learned Judge notices, but he does not rely upon, that large class of cases in which various privileges and easements have been held to pass as appurtenances, where the conveyance uses some comprehensive word, such as manor, messuage, farm, mill, and the like, as descriptive of the whole subject of the grant, because those cases are explained upon the ground that all the privileges in use, as parts of the thing conveyed, are virtually included in the general designation of the thing as a whole.]

[§ 166 *g*. The subject under discussion was very fully and elaborately examined by Chancellor Green in a late case in New Jersey,[1] in which it was held, that where the owner of a tract of land with a spring upon it, who was also the owner of another tract, having on it a paper-mill, by an artificial arrangement conducts the water from the spring to the mill, and then sells the spring lot, the purchaser takes it subject to the burden; upon the principle, that where the owner of two tenements sells one of them, the purchaser takes the tenement or portion sold, with all the benefits which appear, at the time of the sale, to belong to it, as between it and the property which the vendor retains. It appeared in the case, that, in 1857, one Gaunt was the owner of two parcels of real estate in Trenton. The first consisted of an extensive and valuable paper-mill, and the second consisted of a lot of land upon which were two brick dwellings. Upon the latter lot there was a valuable spring, which furnished a copious supply of water. The water of the spring was diverted from its natural channel, and was conveyed to the mill, to be used in the manufacture of paper, by a former proprietor of both lots, at least as early as the year 1845. The water was conducted from the spring to the mill, a distance of eight or nine hundred feet, by means of iron pipes or conduits laid under ground. The diversion of the water was effected by the proprietor at great expense, for the exclusive benefit of the mill. It continued to be so used and enjoyed by the successive proprietors of the two lots for several years, and so long as the title to the two lots was united in the same person. It was so used and enjoyed in 1857, when Gaunt conveyed to one Green, the

1 [Seymour *v.* Lewis, 2 Beas. Ch. (N.J.) 439.]

grantor of the defendant, the lot on which was the spring, retaining the paper-mill, which was afterwards conveyed to the plaintiff. The deed from Gaunt to Green, by which the ownership of the two lots was severed, was in the usual form of a deed of bargain and sale, and contained no express reference to the spring, or the water flowing in or from it, either by way of grant or reservation. The suit was brought for the purpose, among other things, of restraining the defendant from diverting or obstructing the flow of water from the spring to the mill; and the material question in the cause was, whether the right to the water flowing from the spring to the mill remained in Gaunt, the grantor, as an appurtenance or parcel of the mill, after his conveyance of the spring lot. The learned Chancellor, after an able discussion of the principles, and a careful examination of the authorities relating to the subject, decided that Gaunt, after the sale of the spring lot, retained the right to take the water from the spring for the benefit of the mill, in the same manner he used and enjoyed it at and before the time of the sale; and a perpetual injunction was granted to restrain the defendant from diverting the water of the spring upon the spring lot from the plaintiff's paper-mill, and from interfering with the flow thereof, as before used. In delivering his opinion in this case, the Chancellor said, "It is admitted that the doctrine adopted in this case applies in its fullest extent in support of all easements claimed by the grantee of that part of the premises first sold by the common owner. Thus it is said, if Gaunt had retained the lot upon which the spring is, and conveyed the mill, the right to use the water would have passed by the conveyance as appurtenant to the mill; but, having retained the mill, and conveyed the lot upon which the spring is, the spring passes by the grant, and the grantor, or those claiming under him, cannot claim the easement of having the water for the use of the mill, for that would be in derogation of the grant. There is no doubt that several of the reported cases are made to rest upon this ground, and the principle may be safely invoked against the grantor in support of the broader right arising from the actual condition of the premises at the time of the severance of the ownership. But there are cases which do not rest upon this principle, nor can it be invoked in their support;" and he instances cases of what are termed easements of necessity, and states the cases of Kilgour *v.* Ashcom, cited in a preceding section,[1] and Brakely *v.* Sharp,[2] and proceeds to say, "These cases show clearly that an easement may be created by the disposition made by the owner of an estate, and that upon the severance of title the owners will take their respective shares as they existed in the hands of the former owner." He then cites and quotes with approbation from the case of Lampman *v.* Milks, the principles above quoted, and adds, "The easement in question, being apparent and continuous in its character, comes within the operation of the principle. The water flows naturally and continuously from the spring to the mill, the fall between the two points being about one foot. Owing to the length of the pipe, and the consequent obstruction to the flow of the water, it was found that the full benefit of the spring was not obtained. The owner, therefore, to overcome the difficulty, applied the pump, driven by machinery, directly to the pipe, and thus obtained the full advantage of the supply of water. It has thus been used nearly from the time that the pipes were first introduced." [3]]

[§ 166 *h*. The same rule holds in cases of partition and simultaneous conveyances of different parts of the same estate.[4] As in the case of Kilgour *v.* Ashcom,[5] which is stated in a preceding section,[6] and in Brakely *v.* Sharp,[7] cited above, in which it appeared that the owner of a farm, upon which there was a spring of water, conveyed the water from the spring to two dwelling-houses upon the premises. The owner died intestate. That part of the land upon which were the spring and one of the dwellings was assigned, by order of the Orphan's Court, to the widow and one of the heirs. The part of the farm on which the other dwelling was, was sold by the commissioners under the order of the Orphan's Court, and came, by sundry mesne conveyances, to the plaintiff. The bill was filed to protect him in the enjoy-

1 [Ante, § 161.]

2 [1 Stockt. 1; s.c. 2 Stockt. 206.]

3 [In Denton *v.* Leddell, 8 C. E. Green, 64, it was decided, that if the owner of a tract of land, of which one part has had the benefit of a drain, waterpipe, water-course, or other artificial advantage in the nature of an easement through or in the other part, sells or devises either part, an easement is created by implication in or to the other part. And this is the case even if it is the servient part that is sold. But the rule is confined to the case of an apparent and continuous easement. See Fetters *v.* Humphreys, 8 C. E. Green, 260; s.c. 4 C. E. Green, 471.]

4 [See Pearson *v.* Spencer, 3 B. & S. 761.]

5 [5 H. & John. 82.]

6 [Ante, § 161.]

7 [Ante, § 166 *g*.]

ment of the water flowing through the pipe to his dwelling. It was held by Chancellor Williamson, that the aqueduct and the right to use the water, as it was held and enjoyed by the former owner, being essential to the beneficial enjoyment of the premises, vested in the plaintiff, and a perpetual injunction was granted to protect him in the enjoyment.]

[§ 166 *i*. Elliott *v*. Sallee[1] was a case in which it appeared that an estate was severed by simultaneous conveyances to different persons, of different parts, some of which, when all were in the possession of the owner of the whole, were burdened for the benefit of other parts. On a natural mill-stream there were three successive dams and mills. E., being the owner of the upper and lower mills only, dug and opened a raceway on his own land from the dam of his lower mill to the stream above the dam of the middle mill, which belonged to another person, so as to tap the stream there, and partially to divert its waters from the middle mill. He afterwards purchased the middle mill, and became the owner of the three mills, and of all the lands affected by them, their dams, races, and appurtenances, and continued to use said raceway as an actual appurtenance to the lower mill, until by deeds of even date, he conveyed said mills with their appurtenances to his three sons, the upper mill to A., the middle mill to B., and the lower mill to C. In an action by the owner of the middle mill, who was the grantee of B., against the owner of the lower mill, who was the grantee of C., to recover damages for the continued partial diversion of the water from the middle mill, by means of said raceway, it was held, that the grantees of E., and those holding under them respectively, each took and was entitled to hold his mill with its appurtenances, as it actually existed in fact and in use at the time of the conveyances from E.[2] Thurman, of counsel for the defendant in error in this case, made the following pertinent statement and inquiry: "Nothing," said he, "is more common than for the owners of land lying on small streams, like White Oak Creek, to straighten the course of such streams through their lands, by means of dams and ditches. Suppose that a proprietor, after thus diverting the stream into a new channel, and thus causing the old channel to become dry land, aliene a portion of his farm embracing the old

[1] [Elliott *v*. Sallee, 14 Ohio St. 10.]

[2] See Morgan *v*. Mason, 20 Ohio, 401, note.

channel, by ordinary deed, — who will pretend that the alienee has any right to require that the stream be restored to its ancient bed? or, which is the same thing, that he can maintain an action for the diversion? Such a claim would be preposterous." The Court, in their decision, say, "On this state of facts, it seems to us clear, on every principle of reason and common sense, that he [E.] must have intended to grant to his sons respectively, and they must have expected to receive, each his mill with its appurtenances as it actually existed in fact and in use at the time of the conveyances — no more, and no less; and this obvious intention on the part of the grantor, and reasonable expectation on the part of the grantees, furnish the exact measure of the rights of the grantees *inter se*, and of all parties holding under them respectively. This seems to us to be the reason of the case, and the authorities bearing upon the question are uniformly accordant to the same effect." He quotes the case of Nicholas *v.* Chamberlain, and says, "It fully justifies the ruling of the Court in this case."]

[§ 166 *j*. The cases thus far considered on this subject, relate chiefly to easements claimed as growing out of changes in the course or current of natural streams; and, to this extent, there seems to be no direct conflict of authority, that, upon the severance of an estate embracing them, those dispositions effected by changes of an apparent and permanent character in the natural flow of the stream, creating a dependence of one part of the estate upon the other for the reasonable enjoyment of the former, which dependence exists at the time of the conveyance, will remain as easements in favor of the dependent estate, the continuance of which, for the use of the purchaser thereof, he will be entitled to claim. But in cases in which, upon the severance of an estate into parts, the grantee of a part claims a right to the use of an artificial drain, constructed through the part retained before the division, for the benefit of the tenement purchased by him, by which a dependence is created of the part purchased on the part retained, the authorities are conflicting, aud cannot well be reconciled.]

[§ 166 *k*. The leading English decision upon this latter point, is Pyer *v.* Carter,[1] in which it was held, that, if the owner of

[1] [Pyer *v.* Carter, 1 H. &. N. 916.]

two or more adjoining houses sells and conveys one of them to a purchaser, such house is entitled to the benefit, and is subject to the burden, of all existing drains communicating with the other house, without any express reservation or grant for that purpose. The necessity for a drain being established, that which was found to exist in the case supplying that necessity was deemed to be the one to the use of which the purchaser was entitled. This case of Pyer *v.* Carter, important and prominent in itself, has been rendered still more so by frequent reference to it, and by criticisms upon it in other cases favorable or unfavorable to its doctrines. The authority of it has never been shaken in the English Courts of Common Law. It has been noticed sometimes to distinguish it, but generally with entire approval, or, at least, without dissent. It was pressed upon the Court in Dodd *v.* Burchell,[1] which was a controversy respecting a right of way to which it was sought to apply the doctrines of Pyer *v.* Carter. Martin B. said it "went to the utmost extent of the law; but, if considered, that decision cannot be complained of; for if a man has two fields, drained by an artificial ditch cut through both, and he grants to another person one of the fields, neither he nor the grantee can stop up the drain, for there would be the same right of drainage as before, since the land was sold with the drain in it. I agree with the law as laid down in that case, and I think it may be supported without extending the doctrine to a right of way." "If the owner of land, which has a natural stream flowing through it, grants to one person a part of the land, and the remainder to another person, neither has a right to stop the flow of water through the land of the other. In fact Pyer *v.* Carter was no more than an implied grant of a right analogous to that of flowing water." And as reported in another work,[2] he said, "In that case the drain was held to be a part of the house." And Pollock C.B. said, "A drain is corporeally attached to a house; it is otherwise with a right of way." "There is a wide difference between that which

[1] [Dodd *v.* Burchell, 8 Jur. N.S. 1180; 1 H. & C. 113. In this case Wilde B. laid down the rule of law upon the subject of implied easements, in these words: "Where a man has used his premises in a certain way for some time, and it can be brought home to the knowledge of the purchaser, the conveyance may be supposed to be made with an intention of reservation on the part of the grantor, and the land passes subject to such a use."]

[2] [25 Law Rep. 302 (March, 1863); 40 Eng. Law & Eq. 413.]

is substantial, as a conduit or watercourse, and that which is of an incorporeal nature, as a right of way." In Pearson *v.* Spencer,[1] Channell B. said, "In Ewart *v.* Cochrane,[2] it was held by the House of Lords, following what is said in Gale on Easements,[3] that the doctrine of Pyer *v.* Carter applies to any drain or easement necessary for the enjoyment of the property." Martin B. said, "I thought that" — Pyer *v.* Carter — "a strange decision; but it has recently been confirmed by the House of Lords." And in Hall *v.* Lund,[4] Channell B. again said, "In Ewart *v.* Cochrane, the House of Lords confirmed the principle of the decision in Pyer *v.* Carter." — "I should have come to the same conclusion independently of authority, but the case of Pyer *v.* Carter, which was confirmed and its principle explained by the House of Lords in Ewart *v.* Cochrane, compels me to come to this conclusion." In the case of Ewart *v.* Cochrane,[5] above referred to, the rule of law is thus stated in the opinion of the Court: "Where two properties are possessed by the same owner, and there has been a severance made of part from the other, any thing which was used, and was necessary for the comfortable enjoyment of that part of the property which was granted, must be considered to follow from the grant." It is said[6] that "the only possible distinction between this proposition and the case of Pyer *v.* Carter, consists in the fact that in one case the implied easement is attached to the portion first conveyed, and in the other it attaches to the portion reserved; in other words the distinction consists in the difference between the construction of a grant and a reservation. This distinction has long since become practically obsolete in the law, except that in a case precisely equally balanced in point of construction, between the grantor and the grantee (a contingency which seldom or never occurs), the equipoise is determined in favor of the grantee. It is idle, at the present day, to claim that any essential distinction between the construction of a grant and a reservation can be maintained."]

§ 166 *l.* But in the English Chancery Courts the doctrine maintained in Pyer *v.* Carter, has met with the most pointed dissent. Lord Westbury refused to accept that case as au-

1 [3 B. & S. 762.]
2 [4 Macq. 117.]
3 [3d ed. 87.]
4 [1 H. & C. 681.]
5 [7 Jur. N.S. 925; 4 Macq. 117.]
6 [4 Am. Law Reg. N.S. 136.]

thority in Suffield *v.* Brown;[1] and in Crossley *v.* Lightowler,[2] Lord Chelmsford quotes with express approval, the remarks in which Lord Westbury expresses his dissent from Pyer *v.* Carter in reference to the implied reservation of an easement to the grantor over property sold by him; and adds, "It appears to me to be an immaterial circumstance that the easement should be apparent and continuous, for *non constat* that the grantor does not intend to relinquish it unless he shows the contrary by expressly reserving it." But in neither of these chancery cases was the easement in controversy apparent or continuous in its character, nor did the facts of either of these cases furnish occasion for overruling Pyer *v.* Carter, or for deciding authoritatively upon the correctness of that decision in reference to the facts involved in it. Suffield *v.* Brown[3] was the case of a dock and wharf owned by the same party, where the bowsprits of vessels in the dock had to project over the corner of the wharf in order to enter the dock, if they were of any considerable size. The wharf was sold to one, without any reservation of the right claimed, and the dock to another. The bowsprits of vessels continued to be run over the edge of the wharf, for a time, after the severance, when the owner of the wharf proposed to make such erections as would interrupt that use, and the question was brought before Sir John Romilly M. R., who decreed in favor of the right to continue such easement, as being necessary to the full and reasonable enjoyment of the dock. The learned Judge said, in giving judgment, "If, therefore, it be true, that the dock can still be used, it is equally true that it cannot be used exactly as it has been heretofore; and my opinion is, that this projection is necessary to the due enjoyment of the dock, in the ordinary sense of that term. What is meant by the use of that word in these and analogous cases is, in my opinion, the full and complete use of the tenement, as it stands, when the joint owner of the two adjoining tenements grants one of them to one person, and the other to another."[4] But when this case came before the Lord Chancellor (Westbury) on appeal,[5] the doctrine of the case of Pyer *v.* Carter was dissented from as stated above, and the decree of

[1] [Suffield *v.* Brown, 10 Jur. N.S. 111; S.C. 4 DeG. J. & S. 185.]

[2] [L.R. 2 Ch. Ap. 486.]

[3] [10 Jur. N.S. 111; S.C. 4 DeG. J. & S. 185.]

[4] [To this he cites Hinchcliffe *v.* The Earl of Kinnoul, 5 Bing. N.C. 1; and Pyer *v.* Carter, 1 H. & N. 916.]

[5] [10 Jur. N.S. 111; S.C. 4 DeG. J. & S. 185.]

the Master of the Rolls reversed, upon the ground that mere knowledge of the manner in which property conveyed was used by the vendor for the convenience of an adjoining tenement, will not affect the purchaser, if the property is conveyed without reservation, and the continuance of the former use is not indispensable.[1]

[§ 166 *m*. The precise degree of favor with which the decision in the case of Pyer *v.* Carter is to be met in this country is quite unsettled.[2] In Leonard *v.* Leonard,[3] Chapman J. cites that case,

[1] [It has been said that the true question upon which all such cases should turn, no doubt, is, whether the continuance of the existing use is indispensable to the future enjoyment of that portion of the premises reserved, so that the purchaser of the portion first conveyed, as a reasonable man, must be presumed to have taken his conveyance with the expectation that such use would be thereafter continued the same as before; if so, the continuance of the use becomes by the assent of the purchaser an implied servitude upon the portion conveyed, which a Court of Equity will enforce by perpetual injunction; otherwise not. The decision of the Lord Chancellor, in Suffield *v.* Brown, and especially in disregarding, and, as far as lay in his power, overruling, the case of Pyer *v.* Carter, has been strenuously dissented from by the bar in England. 4 Am. Law Reg. N.S. 135. In Watts *v.* Kelson, L.R. 6 Ch. App. 166, it appeared that the owner of two closes, having made an artificial watercourse for the supply of cattle-sheds, first conveyed the cattle-sheds to the plaintiff, and afterwards the close through which the watercourse ran to the defendant. The Lords-Justices, after citing the judgment of the Exchequer Chamber in Polden *v.* Bastard, L.R. 1 Q.B. 161, say, "There is a distinction between easements, such as a right of way, or easements used from time to time, and easements of necessity, or continuous easements. The cases recognize this distinction, and it is clear law that, upon a severance of tenements, easements as of necessity, or in their nature continuous, will pass by implication of law without any words of grant; but with regard to easements which are used from time to time, they do not pass, unless the owner, by appropriate language, shows an intention that they should pass." They were clearly of opinion that the easement in the case before them was in its nature continuous. "There was an actual construction on the servient tenement extending to the dominant tenement, by which water was continuously brought through the servient to the dominant tenement for the use of the occupier of the dominant tenement. According to the rule as laid down by Chief-Justice Erle, the right to such an easement as the one in question would pass without any words of grant, and we think that this is the correct rule." The easement was claimed through the land of the grantor. The case, therefore, is the same as Ewart *v.* Cochrane, ante, 166 *k*. In the course of the argument, Mellish L.J. said, "I think that the order of the conveyance in point of date is immaterial, and that Pyer *v.* Carter is good sense and good law. Most of the Common Law Judges have not approved of Lord Westbury's observations on it." James L.J. said, "I also am satisfied with the decision in Pyer *v.* Carter."]

[2] [For American cases which give countenance to the doctrine of Pyer *v.* Carter, see Lampman *v.* Milks, 21 N.Y. 507; Curtiss *v.* Ayrault, 47 N.Y. 73; Roberts *v.* Roberts, 7 Lansing, 55; Simmons *v.* Cloonan, 2 Lansing, 346; Butterworth *v.* Crawford, 3 Daly, 97; Seymour *v.* Lewis, 2 Beas. (N.J.) 437; Fetters

[3] [Leonard *v.* Leonard, 2 Allen, 543.]

with others, to the following statement of the law: "The question whether an easement passes from a grantor to his grantee as appurtenant to the land conveyed is not precisely the same as the question whether a right of way across the land of a stranger is created by necessity. The grantor's deed is to be most strongly construed against him, and if an easement properly belongs to the granted premises, and has been used by him in connection with the premises, it ought to pass as appurtenant to the land granted, though it is not mentioned in the deed, and though it subjects his other land to the servitude. The fact that the easement has been thus used and is merely convenient, is not sufficient. Its use in connection with the land conveyed must be reasonably necessary. And any easement, as, for example, a right of way or of drainage, which can be thus regarded, passes as an appurtenance without being named." This language of the learned Judge goes far to recognize the principle of the decision in Pyer *v.* Carter. In Carbrey *v.* Willis,[1] Hoar J., noticing the case of Pyer *v.* Carter, says of it, that "the terms of the deed are not given in the report of the case, and the decision may perhaps be supported on the ground that the conveyance was of part of a house, having obvious relations to and dependencies upon the other part of the building." And in the later case of Randall *v.* McLaughlin[2] the same learned Judge again notices that case, but only to observe that the authority of it was wholly denied by Lord Westbury in the opinion given in Suffield *v.* Brown.[3] In a late case in Maine,[4] the Court refer to Pyer *v.* Carter, but dissent from the doctrine of it as applicable to rights of way.[5]]

[§ 166 *n*. Several important cases have lately been decided in Massachusetts, having a material bearing upon the doctrine under discussion. The subject received the elaborate considera-

v. Humphreys, 3 C.E. Green, N.J. 260; s.c. 4 C. E. Green, 471; Denton *v.* Leddell, 8 C. E. Green, 64; Coolidge *v.* Hager, 43 Vt. 9. For other cases showing the extent to which the doctrine has been recognized in the American States, see Suffield *v.* Brown, 4 DeG. J. & S. (Am. ed.) 185, note 1.]

1 [7 Allen, 369.]

2 [10 Allen, 366, 368.]

3 [10 Jur. N.S. 111, s.c. 4 DeG. J. & S. 185. See Watts *v.* Kelson, L.R. 6 Ch. App. 166, cited supra 166 *l*, in note.]

4 [Warren *v.* Blake, 54 Maine, 276.]

5 [A way comes within the description of a non-apparent easement. Fetters *v.* Humphreys, 4 C. E. Green, 471. Discontinuous easements not constantly apparent, are continued or created upon a severance only when they are necessary, and that necessity cannot be obviated by a substitute constructed on or over the dominant premises. Fetters *v.* Humphreys, 3 C. E. Green, 260.]

tion of Shaw C.J., in Johnson *v.* Jordan;[1] in which it appeared that the owner of two adjoining messuages and lots of land, one of which he occupied, and the other of which he leased, constructed a drain from the messuage which he leased, through the land which he occupied, into a common sewer, and permitted his tenants to use it for several years, and then sold both messuages and lots, on the same day, to different purchasers, and in his deed to the purchaser of the messuage and lot which he formerly leased, did not mention the drain. The drain was used for the purpose of carrying off the waste water from the sink in the house, the owner of which claimed the benefit of the drain. The learned Chief Justice said, "It is very clear that, whilst both estates were held by the same owner, he had a right to carry his drain as he pleased, through any part of his own grounds; and so long as both tenements were owned and occupied by the same person, no easement was created, or began to be created, in favor of one, and operating as a service or burden upon the other." — "If such an owner will convey one of the tenements and retain the other, he may grant the right of drain, or not, to pass with the estate conveyed, or may reserve such right over the estate conveyed, for the benefit of the one retained, as he pleases. It is matter of contract, and must depend entirely upon the construction of the conveyance. Supposing this to be clear, the question recurs, What construction will the law put upon a conveyance, where the intention of the parties in this respect is not expressed in terms? In the first place it is proper to distinguish an artificial gutter of this description, made for the purpose of draining, from a natural watercourse, the rights of parties to which depend upon a different principle. Every person, through whose land a natural watercourse runs, has a right, *publici juris*, to the benefit of it, as it passes through his land, to all the useful purposes to which it may be applied." "It is inseparably annexed to the soil, and passes with it, not as an easement, nor as appurtenance, but as parcel." "This case is also to be entirely distinguished from one wherein the declivity of the land and the relative position of the tenements are such, that a drain cannot be formed for the benefit of one without passing through the other. Such a case might stand on a different ground." After stating certain of the rules of construction to be adopted, he says, "Another

[1] [2 Met. 234.]

well-settled rule of construction is, that a grant of any principal thing shall be taken to carry with it all which is necessary to the beneficial enjoyment of the thing granted, and which it is in the power of the grantor to convey." — "Under these rules, it might perhaps be held, that if a man owning two tenements, has built a house on one, and annexed thereto a drain, passing through the other, if he sell and convey the house with the appurtenances, such a drain may be construed to be, *de facto*, annexed as an appurtenance, and pass with it; and because such construction would be most beneficial to the grantee." After noticing the fact that the two conveyances from the owner of the whole, under which the parties claimed, were simultaneous, he adds, "It is, therefore, much more like a partition between tenants in common, where each party takes his estate with the rights, privileges, and incidents inherently attached to it,[1] than like the case of grantor and grantee, where the grantor conveys a part of his land, by metes and bounds, and retains another part to his own use, and where the question is, upon the terms of the deed, whether an easement for drainage has been granted with the estate conveyed over that retained, or reserved over that conveyed, for the benefit of that retained." — "The well-known maxim of construction, and a very sound one is, *Expressio unius exclusio est alterius.* Here was a division of these two tenements intimately connected with each other, with detailed provisions in respect of the rights which each should have in the other, and the duties to which should be subject in favor of the other. If it was intended that one should have a perpetual right of drainage through the other, with a right of entry at all times to repair and relay such drain, especially where it is found not to be necessary to the enjoyment of the estate granted, it seems reasonable to suppose it would have been expressed. As no such right was expressed, we are of opinion that it was not intended to be granted; and as it was not necessary to the enjoyment of the estate, and had not been, *de facto*, annexed, so as to pass by general words as parcel of the estate, it did not pass to the defendant's grantor by force of the deed." It was also held, in this and subsequent cases, that the

1 [In Elliott *v.* Sallee, 14 Ohio St. 10, a case of simultaneous conveyance, and Kilgour *v.* Ashcom, 5 H. & John., a case of partition, these circumstances seemed rather to turn the decision in the opposite direction.]

question of necessity for the use of the drain involved the inquiry, whether or not a drain could be conveniently made, with reasonable labor and expense, without going through the plaintiff's land. These extended quotations have been made from the opinion, because every statement of the principles of law coming from Chief-Justice Shaw is worthy of attentive consideration; and this decision is the foundation of several others of a similar character which have followed it. But it will be observed that the easement claimed in the case was not of a watercourse running in its natural, or turned from that into an artificial, channel; but a trench into which water was poured or thrown or collected from sources which would not otherwise have yielded a flow of water in any particular course or direction. It will also be observed that the case was not rested entirely on mere general words of grant common to all conveyances, but chiefly on the construction of certain specific provisions, supposed to show that the easement was not intended to pass. Besides, the "necessity" required is not positive and absolute, but one admitting of degrees. The position is, that if the person claiming the easement could not supply another for a certain sum, then the parties did intend that the easement claimed should pass with the grant; but, if for a certain other less sum, then the easement claimed was not intended to pass. It will also be observed that, in regard to the test of necessity, the case is directly opposed to the decision in Pyer *v.* Carter, in which it was held, that the necessity for the easement is to be considered in reference to the state of things as existing at the time of severance, without alteration.[1]]

[§ 166 *a*. The case of Thayer *v.* Payne,[2] in which the opinion of the Court was given by Mr. Justice Fletcher, is important in this connection, as showing an inclination towards some of the doctrines maintained in Pyer *v.* Carter. It appeared in Thayer *v.* Payne that the plaintiff and defendant were owners and occupiers of adjoining lots of land, the defendant having derived his title from the plaintiff. At the time of the conveyance from the plaintiff to the defendant, there was a drain from

[1] [The rule, for testing the necessity by the amount of expense, even if theoretically wise, has been observed in practice to produce extremely variant results. See the case of Pettingill *v.* Porter, 8 Allen, 1.]

[2] [Thayer *v.* Payne, 2 Cush. 327.]

the defendant's cellar leading through the plaintiff's premises to an outlet beyond. This drain was not mentioned in the deed. The drain being out of repair, the defendant entered upon the premises of the plaintiff for the purpose of opening it; and for this entry the action was brought. It was held, that the defendant had a right to maintain the drain, and to enter upon the plaintiff's premises for the purpose of repairing it, notwithstanding the deed contained the following clause: "To have and to hold the aforegranted premises, with the privileges and appurtenances thereto belonging at the time of the purchase thereof by the said T. & F.," and notwithstanding the drain had no existence at the time referred to in this clause, it having been constructed afterwards, but before the conveyance to the defendant, if the drain appeared to be necessary to the beneficial enjoyment of the defendant's premises. The decision was put upon the ground that, as the plaintiff owned both lots at the time of his conveyance to the defendant, and as the drain was then in existence and use, it passed as an appurtenance without being mentioned, and without even the use of the word "appurtenances;" and hence it could not be affected by the clause in the deed. Fletcher J. said, "What rights, therefore, the defendant acquired under and by virtue of the conveyance of the house and land to him by metes and bounds, must be determined by the general principles of law, as there is nothing in the deed to prevent or restrict the operation of these general principles." "The conveyance by the plaintiff to the defendant of the house and land particularly described in the deed carried with it whatever was necessary to the beneficial enjoyment of the estate granted, which it was in the power of the plaintiff to convey. At the time of this grant, the plaintiff owned the *locus in quo* through which the drain then passed, and, of course, had the power to convey to the defendant the right to use the drain; and it follows, therefore, that if the use of the drain was necessary to the beneficial enjoyment of the premises granted, the right to the use of the drain passed by this conveyance." The same test of necessity was applied as in Johnson *v.* Jordan. But it will be observed that the course of reasoning was not disturbed by any special provisions in the deed showing any intent other than that to be gathered from the general words of the grant. In Carbrey *v.* Willis,[1] the Court manifested much less inclination to adopt the doctrines of Pyer *v.* Carter, which was cited and commented upon by Hoar J., in giving the opinion. The case of Johnson *v.* Jordan was referred to as having reviewed and carefully stated the whole doctrine on this subject. Randall *v.* McLaughlin,[2] another later and similar case in Massachusetts followed in the same direction, apparently with a stronger and more unhesitating inclination against Pyer *v.* Carter, in consequence of the attack on the latter case made by Lord Westbury, in Suffield *v.* Brown,[3] "which," as the Court say, "contains an elaborate view of the whole doctrine, resulting in conclusions substantially like those to which we came in Carbrey *v.* Willis." The case of Suffield *v.* Brown has itself been strengthened by the accession of Lord Chelmsford, in Crossley *v.* Lightowler,[4] as noticed in a preceding section.

[§ 166 *p.* It will be observed that this doctrine of an implied right to drainage in favor of one of two tenements or portions of an estate conveyed, over other land of the grantor, on the ground of necessity, has never gone to the extent of authorizing a purchaser of the tenement or portion in favor of which the right is claimed, to build or construct a new drain through the land of his grantor, but only to use a particular drain already in existence; and to this extent the case differs from a right of way, by necessity, to land purchased, over other land of the grantor, because it does not follow from the fact that the owner of the two estates, when united under one owner, used and enjoyed a particular way across his other land for the benefit of the part sold, that the way so used and enjoyed is to be considered the way of necessity to which the purchaser is entitled.[5] In the one case no particular way passes by force of the necessity; in the other, the particular drain open and in use is the only one impliedly granted. Besides, in the case of the way by necessity, it may be that the grantor never had used any particular way over the premises retained for the benefit of the prem-

[1] [7 Allen, 364.]

[2] [10 Allen, 366. See Philbrick *v.* Ewing, 97 Mass. 183, cited ante, § 153 in note.]

[3] [10 Jur. N.S. 111; 4 DeG. J. & S. 185.]

[4] [L.R. 2 Ch. Ap. 478, 486.]

[5] [See Pearson *v.* Spencer, 3 B. & S. 761; s.c. 1 B. & S. 571, 584, 585; Holmes *v.* Seely, 19 Wend. 510; Smyles *v.* Hastings, 24 Barb. 49; s.c. 22 N.Y. 220; Hart *v.* Cramer, 25 Conn. 331; Russell *v.* Jackson, 2 Pick. 578.]

ises sold, so that an entirely new way must necessarily be adopted.[1]]

[§ 166 *q*. Again, it has been held upon eminent authority that the rule stated in a preceding section[2] does not exist for the benefit of purchasers alone, but is entirely reciprocal, so that, whenever the owner of an estate severs it into two parts, granting away one of them, he is taken by implication of law to reserve out of his grant all such easements connected with the flow of water over the part sold as are necessary for the reasonable enjoyment of the part which he retains, in the form which it assumes at the time of the severance. This rule is deduced from the early case of Nicholas *v*. Chamberlain,[3] which has already been cited and stated;[4] and the same principle was declared by Twisden J., in Palmer *v*. Fletcher,[5] and by Doddridge J., in Sury *v*. Pigott.[6]]

[§ 166 *r*. This point was very elaborately discussed in Dunklee *v*. The Wilton Railroad Company,[7] lately decided in New Hampshire. This case had reference to an easement growing out of a change in the natural stream by turning it into an artificial channel. The facts of the case are stated fully in a former section.[8] Bell J. said, "Our next position is, that property conveyed passes in its existing state, subject to all existing easements and burdens of a similar nature, in favor of other lands of the grantor, which are apparent, and which result naturally from the relative situation of the land, and from the nature, construction, and intended use of the buildings, mills, &c., upon it, and their situation and connection with other property as they were usually enjoyed at the time of the conveyance." — "Every easement connected with the flow of water necessarily implies a duty upon the owner of the servient tenement, and every such duty implies a corresponding right in that owner. Thus the owner of land upon a stream has an easement upon the land above, that the water of the stream shall flow down upon his land at a certain place, at a certain level, and in a certain quantity. This right imposes upon the owner of the land above, the

1 [See Pearson *v*. Spencer, 1 B. & S. 571, 584, 585; Trask *v*. Patterson, 29 Maine, 503; Leonard *v*. Leonard, 2 Allen, 543; Collins *v*. Prentice, 15 Conn. 39; Pierce *v*. Selleck, 18 Conn. 321.]

2 [Ante, § 166 *a*.]

3 [Cro. Jac. 121.]

4 [Ante, § 153.]

5 [1 Lev. 122.]

6 [Palm. 444; s.c. 3 Bulst. 339.]

7 [24 N.H. 489.]

8 [Ante, § 166 *e*.]

duty and obligation of suffering the water to flow agreeably to this privilege of the owner below; and it confers upon the same owner the right to discharge the water in that place and in that way, and imposes upon the owner of the land below the duty and obligation to receive the water in that place and in that manner. These rights and duties are reciprocal, and necessarily co-existent. The creation of one necessarily creates all the others. If one estate has an easement upon that above, to discharge the water in a particular manner, the estate above has a reciprocal easement upon that below, to receive the water in that particular manner. Each estate is in turn the dominant tenement, as to the easement from which it derives a benefit, and the servient tenement, as to the corresponding easement of which the other estate has the advantage. Thus, if a man has a dam extending across a stream, with a mill on each side of it, and he sells to another person one mill, with the land on which it stands, without specifying or reserving any incidental right, the purchaser of the mill has, agreeably to the cases before cited, the right to keep the water raised to its usual height. The grantor is bound to permit the water to flow at the height which is necessary to operate the mill. He cannot build a dam to prevent such flow of the water. He cannot remove his part of the dam, and thus prevent it; but, as a necessary consequence, he has the reciprocal easement upon the land he has conveyed,—the right to require the purchaser to receive the water at the level he is bound to discharge it, and to do no act by which this right may be impaired; which is, in effect, that the purchaser shall maintain the water on his part at the same level his grantor is bound to keep it, of which the mill he has retained will, of course, have the benefit; and, if the purchaser opens his gates or removes his dam, and thus permits the water to flow at a less height, he is answerable to his grantor for diverting the water.[1] The result of this view is, that in every case where there is an implied grant of an easement in favor of the grantee of a mill or water privilege, the same grantee takes the mill or privilege, subject to the corresponding easement in favor of the grantor."[2] —"As the owner of land, having the only interest in the mat-

[1] [Runnels *v.* Bullen, 2 N.H. 532.]

[2] [See Cary *v.* Daniels, 8 Met. 466; Whitney *v.* Eames, 11 Met. 517; Tucker *v.* Jewett, 11 Conn. 311; Seibert *v.* Levan, 8 Penn. St. 383.]

ter, can make no grant to himself, and can execute no instrument in writing, by which a change in the property can be made while he remains owner, and as he has the right, by virtue of his ownership, to make any disposition of the property which he pleases, it seems to follow, that if he does make any change in the property, those who claim under him, and derive their titles from him, must take the property in the state it is in at the time, precisely as if it had been its natural state, and no other had ever existed."]

[§ 166 *s*. Similar views of the law were taken by Selden J., in Lampman *v.* Milks,[1] in which he said, "The principle is, that where the owner of two tenements sells one of them, or the owner of an entire estate sells a portion, the purchaser takes the tenement or portion sold, with all the benefits and burdens which appear, at the time of the sale, to belong to it, as between it and the property which the vendor retains." — "This is not a rule for the benefit of purchasers only, but is entirely reciprocal. Hence, if, instead of a benefit conferred, a burden has been imposed upon the portion sold, the purchaser, provided the marks of this burden are open and visible, takes the property with the burden upon it. The parties are presumed to contract in reference to the condition of the property at the time of the sale, and neither has a right, by altering arrangements then openly existing, to change materially the relative value of the respective parts." These observations were made in a case, where the owner of land, across which a stream flowed, had diverted it through an artificial channel, so as to relieve a portion of it formerly overflowed, which portion he then conveyed; and it was held, that neither he, nor his grantees of the residue, could return the stream to its ancient bed to the damage of the first grantee. Seymour *v.* Lewis[2] is a direct decision upon the point under discussion, and in favor of an implied reservation to a grantor of an easement respecting the flow of water turned from its natural course into an artificial channel, through land conveyed by him, in favor of other contiguous property retained by him, no mention being made of the easement in the conveyance.

[1] 21 N.Y. 507. The facts of this case are stated, ante, § 166 *f*.

[2] [Seymour *v.* Lewis, 2 Beas. (N.J.) Ch. 439. The facts of this case are stated ante, § 166 *g*. See Denton *v.* Leddell, 8 C. E. Green, 64; Fetters *v.* Humphreys, 3 C. E. Green, 260; s.c. 4 C. E. Green, 471.]

It appeared in the case, that the owner of a lot of land with a spring upon it, and of a paper-mill on another tract, by an artificial arrangement conveyed the water from the spring through the spring lot to the mill, and then sold the spring lot, making no mention in the deed of the use of the water from the spring; it was held, that the purchaser took it subject to the burden of the use of the water from the spring in the manner it was used and enjoyed at the time of the conveyance. Green Ch. said, "At the time of the grant of the spring lot, the stream was diverted from its natural course through the land granted by an artificial channel to the mill of the grantor. The grantee took the land as it then stood, with the water diverted from it. Lampman *v.* Milks is an express authority that the grantor could not return the water to its natural channel against the consent of the grantee. The grantee has a right to insist that it shall be continued as it was at the date of the grant; viz., in the artificial channel. He cannot have a right to elect in which channel it shall go. If the grantee have a right to insist upon its being continued in the artificial channel, the grantor must have an equal right to keep it there." The water flowed naturally and continuously from the spring to the mill; but the fall between the two points was so slight that it became necessary to attach an artificial arrangement in order to obtain the full advantage of the supply of water. It was regarded as an important feature in the case, that the easement in question was apparent and continuous. Elliott *v.* Sallee [1] is another case of a similar character, in which the question of reservation by implication arose out of the existence of a stream of water turned from its natural into an artificial channel. It maintains the doctrine of the last preceding cases. The conveyances which caused the severance and raised the question were simultaneous.[2] Pyer *v.* Carter,[3] the facts and authority of which have already been stated and discussed at length,[4] applies the same doctrine to the case of drains, and holds, that where an owner of an estate divides it into two tenements, and constructs a drain from one under the other and thence into a common sewer, and then sells the latter tenement without any express reservation of the use of the drain, he will

[1] [Elliott *v.* Sallee, 14 Ohio N.S. 10.]

[2] [See Johnson *v.* Jordan, 2 Met. 234; Kilgour *v.* Ashcom, 5 H. & John. 62.]

[3] [1 H. & N. 916.]

[4] [Ante, § 166 *k*, et seq.]

still be entitled to the benefit of the drain in favor of the tenement retained by him. The principle as stated in the language of the Court is, "that, where the owner of two or more adjoining houses sells and conveys one of the houses to a purchaser, such house in his hands should be entitled to the benefit of all the drains from his house, and subject to all the drains then necessarily used for the enjoyment of the adjoining house, and that without any express reservation or grant, inasmuch as he purchases the house *such as it is*."[1] It did not appear that there was any descent, either natural or otherwise, from one house to the other; that either was the upper or the lower tenement. The case rather indicates that the flow of water in the direction taken, was caused by the mode of constructing the drain. But it did appear that the water from the eaves of the house under which the right of drainage was claimed fell upon the house claiming the easement, and from thence flowed down a spout into the drain on the tenement embracing the latter house, and so into the common sewer. In Dodd *v.* Burchell,[2] Martin B., said, "In fact, Pyer *v.* Carter was no more than an implied grant of a right analogous to that of flowing water." — "If a man has two fields, drained by an artificial ditch cut through both, and he grants to another person one of the fields, neither he nor the grantee can stop up the drain, for there would be the same right of drainage as before, since the land was sold with the drain in it."]

§ 166 *t.* Before the decision of Pyer *v.* Carter, this same subject had been examined to some extent in Johnson *v.* Jordan,[3] heretofore referred to and stated,[4] in which Shaw C.J., having laid down the rules governing the case said, "Under these rules, it might perhaps be held, that if a man, owning two tenements, has built a house on one, and annexed thereto a drain, passing through the other, if he sell and convey the house with the appurtenances, such a drain may be construed to be *de facto* annexed as an appurtenance, and pass with it; and because such construction would be most beneficial to the grantee; whereas, if he were to sell and convey the lower tenement, still owning the upper, it might reasonably be considered that as the right of

[1] [See Gillis *v.* Nelson, 16 La. An. 275, cited ante, § 166 *b*, note.]

[2] [1 H. & C. 118.]

[3] [2 Met. 234.]

[4] [Ante, § 166 *n*.]

drainage was not reserved in terms, when it naturally would be if so intended, it could not be claimed by the grantor. The grantee of the lower tenement, taking the language of the deed most strongly in his favor and against the grantor, might reasonably claim to hold his granted estate free from incumbrance." The Chief Justice also said, "This case is also to be entirely distinguished from one wherein the declivity of the land and the relative position of the tenements are such, that a drain cannot be formed for the benefit of one, without passing through the other. Such a case might stand upon a different ground. But in the present case it was found by the jury, that a drain could be conveniently made, with reasonable labor and expense, from the defendant's house, without going through the plaintiff's land."[1] But it was added that these rules did not apply to the case then before the Court, which was a severance of two messuages by two simultaneous conveyances to different parties by the owner of the whole. And in Carbrey *v.* Willis,[2] Hoar J. quotes the above extract, and speaks of it as merely an intimation of the opinion of the Court. He however, distinguishes it from the case then before him, on the ground that the grants in Johnson *v.* Jordan were simultaneous, and adds, "But where, as in the case at bar, the grant of the lower estate precedes that of the other, we think the true rule of construction is this, that no easement can be taken as reserved by implication, unless it is *de facto* annexed and in use at the time of the grant, and is necessary to the enjoyment of the estate which the grantor retains."[3] And this necessity cannot be said to exist, if a similar privilege can be secured by reasonable trouble and expense. The learned Judge then refers to "some recent cases in England," in which "a different doctrine seems to have prevailed" from that maintained in Massachusetts, and adds, as showing the tendency of these recent English cases, that "even in the case of the grant of a part of an estate, an easement has been held to be reserved to the grantor as parcel of the remainder, without an express reservation, if it were *de facto* used in connection with it, at the time of the grant, and were necessary to its enjoyment in the condition

[1] [This same consideration was acted on in Carbrey *v.* Willis, 7 Allen, 364; Thayer *v.* Payne, 2 Cush. 327; Randall *v.* McLaughlin, 10 Allen, 366; and in Pettingill *v.* Porter, 8 Gray, 1.]

[2] [7 Allen, 364.]

[3] [Parker *v.* Bennett, 11 Allen, 388, 392.]

in which the estate then was." To this the cases of Pyer *v.* Carter, Ewart *v.* Cochrane, and Hall *v.* Lund are cited. And it is laid down in the same cases as follows: "But where there is a grant of land by metes and bounds, without express reservation, and with full covenants of warranty against incumbrances, we think there is no just reason for holding that there can be any reservation by implication, unless the easement is strictly one of necessity. Where the easement is only one of existing use and great convenience, but for which a substitute can be furnished by reasonable labor and expense, the grantor may certainly cut himself off from it by his deed, if such is the intention of the parties. And it is difficult to see how such an intention could be more clearly and distinctly intimated than by such a deed and warranty." Again in Randall *v.* McLaughlin,[1] it was decided that if the owner of two adjoining estates, through one of which a drain exists for the benefit of the other, conveys them both on the same day to different purchasers, the right to use the drain will not pass as an easement or appurtenance to the purchaser of the upper estate provided that a new drain can be built upon his own land by reasonable labor and expense. In a very recent case in Maine,[2] the Court, referring to the above cases of Carbrey *v.* Willis, and Randall *v.* McLaughlin, say, "We adopt, substantially, the same view of the law, as in accordance with authority, and as sustained by reason and expediency. If we adopt any other rule than that of strict necessity, we open a door to doubt and uncertainty, to the disturbance and questioning of titles, and to controversies as to matter of fact, outside of the language or boundaries of the deed. If an estate, fully granted without exception or reservation, can be incumbered for ever by an easement, or right of use by a third party, by the finding of a jury that such use would be highly convenient, or that it was exercised by a former owner, or was notorious, on any other ground short of strict necessity, the sanctity and security of titles by deeds, exact and precise in their terms, would be seriously shaken and impaired. The record gives no notice of any such right or easement."[3]]

1 [10 Allen, 366.]

2 [Warren *v.* Blake, 54 Maine, 276.]

3 [In Carbrey *v.* Willis, 7 Allen, 369, Hoar J. said, "The rule in respect to easements which pass by implication, has been held with some strictness in this commonwealth, even in the case where a grantee claims them as against his grantor, or where the question arises between grantees under conveyances made at the same time, or in cases of partition." The same seems to be equally true in Maine.]

[§ 166 *u*. The question whether or not the use of the drain claimed in favor of one tenement, through an adjoining tenement, is necessary for the beneficial enjoyment of the former, is one for the jury, under proper instructions from the Court.[1] It has been held, in several cases in Massachusetts, that the proper inquiry for testing the "necessity" in such cases is, whether another drain, equally beneficial with the existing one, through the adjoining tenement, could be constructed on the land of the party claiming the easement with reasonable labor and expense. Because, it is said, if the party claiming the right to the drain, through the adjoining land of another owner could thus furnish his house with a drain upon his own land, it cannot be necessary to the enjoyment of his estate that he should have the drain claimed by him. This rule finds its origin in Johnson *v.* Jordan, and it has since been re-asserted and acted upon in various succeeding cases.[2]]

[§ 166 *v*. But it will be observed that a different test of "necessity" was applied in Pyer *v.* Carter,[3] in which it was said, "We think that the amount to be expended in the alteration of the drainage, or in the constructing a new system of drainage, is not to be taken into consideration, for the meaning of the word 'necessity,' in the cases cited, is to be understood the necessity at the time of the conveyance, and as matters then stood, without alteration;[4] and whether or not at the time of the conveyance, there was any other outlet for the drainage water, and matters as they then stood, must be looked at for the necessity of the drainage." The principle seems to be, that the necessity for a drain appearing, that drain which has been adopted, used, and enjoyed by the grantor before severance, being open and visible, or known to exist, will be taken as granted or reserved, as the case may be, by implication.]

1 [Per Fletcher J., in Thayer *v.* Payne, 2 Cush. 332; and he adds, "The settlement of this question will, of course, involve the inquiry, whether or not a drain could be conveniently made, with reasonable labor and expense, without going through the plaintiff's land. Because, if the defendant could thus furnish his house with a drain, it cannot be necessary to the enjoyment of his estate, that he should have a drain through the land of the plaintiff."]

2 [Thayer *v.* Payne, 2 Cush. 327; Carbrey *v.* Willis, 7 Allen, 364; Randall *v.* McLaughlin, 10 Allen, 366; White *v.* Chapin, 12 Allen, 518. In Pettingill *v.* Porter, 8 Allen, 1, it was applied in the case of a way.]

3 [Pyer *v.* Carter, 1 H. & N. 916.]

4 [See Philbrick *v.* Ewing, 97 Mass. 133, 134, 135, per Hoar J.]

5. *Lex Loci.*

§ 167. If water flows to a mill in another State, and the use *becomes annexed to it*, the use and the title are both governed by the laws of the State in which the mill is situated. In Slack *v.* Walcott,[1] which was a proceeding in equity to establish the title to the use of water for the plaintiff's mill, Story J., in giving judgment, said, "The mill in controversy is situated in Massachusetts; the river, the use of whose waters is claimed as appurtenant to the mill, is the boundary of the two States, and the waters, therefore, partly flow in each State. The right, however, is not a distinct right to the water, as *terra aqua coöperta*, or as a distinct corporeal hereditament, but as an incident to the mill, and attached to the realty. It passes by a grant of the mill, and has no independent existence. It is not real estate situated in Rhode Island. It is an incorporeal hereditament annexed to a freehold in Massachusetts; and a conveyance of the mill, good by the laws of the State, where the mill is situated, conveys all the appurtenances. The wrong done by stopping the flow of the water by any obstruction or drain in Rhode Island is an injury done to the mill itself in Massachusetts. In a just sense, the wrong may be said to be done in both States, like the analogous case of an injury to land lying in one county by an act done in another county. The devisee is entitled to the remedy also by the laws of Massachusetts as the owner of the mill. His title, when unimpeachable by the law of Massachusetts, does not by the general principles of public law require any new probate in Rhode Island. It could receive no new validity from such probate. It could lose none without it. Suppose an ancient house situate on the boundary line of a State, and a person in the adjacent State obstructs its ancient lights, would it be contended, that the right to use such ancient lights, was real estate in the adjacent State? And if the title were derived by grant, or by will, would it be contended, that a registry of the deed or a probate of the will would be necessary in each State before any redress could be obtained by the owner? If necessary at all, it would be equally so, whether the suit were brought in one State or the other. In such a case, if the law respecting grants or wills

[1] Slack *v.* Walcott, 3 Mason, 508.

were different in the different States, a purchaser might rightfully succeed to the propriety of the house, but lose its ancient privileges. The public law, which declares, that the title to real estate can pass only according to the law of the place, where it is situated, supposes the thing to be tangible and fixed, and the *situs* clearly intraterritorial. But where is the *situs* of an incorporeal right? The right to flowing water is no more real estate, than the right to flowing air or light. The very nature of these things forbids durable, fixed, and absolute territorial possession. It is true, that a State has jurisdiction over the waters of the rivers which flow within its boundaries, and may, by its laws, regulate the title, enjoyment, and use of them awhile, and so long as they flow within its boundaries. But its authority stops here; the right to the use of the same waters, when they flow beyond its boundaries, is not within its control. The title is not acquired under the laws of such State. If the waters flow to a mill in another State, and the use becomes annexed to it, the use and the title are exclusively to be governed by the laws of the latter State. What authority has Rhode Island to control the water which flows to a mill in Massachusetts? The right to the use of such water, whether it be deemed real or personal estate, is a right exercised under the jurisdiction of Massachusetts, and is to be governed by its laws. Rhode Island might indeed refuse to recognize in her Courts the title to such property, unless it passed in some special manner prescribed by her laws; and so she might the title to lands in Massachusetts coming incidentally in question in her Courts. But this would not change such title, or give the State a right to annul it. It would be a refusal of that national comity and justice, which the civilized world is accustomed to allow for great public purposes of policy and convenience. Beyond this the authority would have no operation. There is no pretence to say, that Rhode Island has as yet legislated to such an extent. Her laws for the probate of foreign wills go no farther than to provide for such cases, where they affect property lying or being within the State."

6. *How Easements in Watercourses are created.*

§ 168. The ceremony required by law for the creation of easements, and all incorporeal hereditaments, is a *deed*, *devise*, or *record;* and as the same ceremonies are requisite in the transfer of a right as are requisite in its original formation, a water right, as an incorporeal hereditament, can only be assigned by deed, devise, or record. Lord Coke says, "And here is implied a division fee or inheritance; viz., into corporeal, as lands and tenements which lie in livery, comprehended in this word feoffment, and will pass by livery, by deed, or without deed; and incorporeal, which lie in grant, which cannot pass by livery, but by deed, as advowsons, commons, &c.; and the deed of incorporeate inheritance doth equal the livery of corporeate. Grant, *concessio*, is properly of things incorporeate, which, as hath been said, cannot pass without deed."[1] In Gilbert's Law of Evidence,[2] it is laid down, "If a man shows title to a thing lying in grant, *he fails if the seal be torn off from his deed;* for a man cannot show a title to a thing lying in solemn agreement, but by solemn agreement; and there can be no solemn agreement without a seal, so that possession alone is not sufficient, since the thing itself does not lie in possession, but in agreement; therefore, a man cannot claim title to a watercourse *but by deed and under seal.*" With the position of Lord Chief-Baron Gilbert, that the party fails, if the *seal be torn off the deed*, the case of Bolton *v.* The Bishop of Carlisle[3] is at variance; as in that case it was decided, that if the deed be destroyed, other evidence may be given to show that the thing was once granted. The general position, however, that a man cannot claim title to a thing lying in grant, but by deed, was not questioned in the case.

§ 169. The case of Fentinam *v.* Smith,[4] is clear and positive in its language. The plaintiff, in that case, claimed to have a passage for water, by a tunnel, over the defendant's land, and Lord Ellenborough lays it down distinctly: "The title to have the water flowing in the tunnel over defendant's land could not pass by parol license, without deed, and the plaintiff could not be entitled to it as stated in his declaration, by reason of his possession of the mill, but he had it by license of the defendant,

[1] Co. Litt. 9, a. [See Seymour *v.* Lewis, 2 Beasley Ch (N.J.) 451; Morse *v.* Copeland, 2 Gray, 302; Adams *v.* Andrews, 15 Q.B. 284, 296; Selden *v.* Del. & Hud. Canal, 29 N.Y. 639; Fuhr *v.* Dean, 26 Mo. 116; Miller *v.* Auburn & Syr. R.R. Co., 6 Hill, 61; Stevens *v.* Stevens, 11 Met. 251; Foot *v.* The New Haven & Northampton R.R. Co., 23 Conn. 214.]

[2] Page 96, 6th ed.

[3] Bolton *v.* The Bishop of Carlisle, 2 H. Black. 259.

[4] Fentinam *v.* Smith, 4 East, 109.

or by contract with him; and if by license, it was revocable at any time." In Hewlins *v.* Shippam,[1] where the question was whether a right to a drain running through the adjoining land could be conferred by a parol license, and under the Statute of Frauds; in an elaborate judgment delivered by the Court, it was held, that such an interest could only be created by deed. The doctrine laid down in this case was fully recognized in Cocker *v.* Cowper,[2] where an action was brought for stopping up a watercourse. It appeared from the award of the arbitrator, that the channel in question consisted of a drain and tunnel, which had been constructed on the defendant's land by the plaintiff, in the year 1815, with the verbal consent only of the then tenant and of the defendant, and that the water had flowed through it up to the year 1833, when, upon the plaintiff's refusal to pay for the use of the water, the defendant diverted the channel. It appeared perfectly clear to the Court of Exchequer that the plaintiff was not entitled to recover. "With regard to the question of license," said the Court, "the case of Hewlins

[1] Hewlins *v.* Shippam, 5 B. & C. 221.

[2] Cocker *v.* Cowper, 1 Cr., M. & R. 418. And the same has been decided by prior authorities, in reference to different easements, as Monk *v.* Butler, Cro. Jac. 574, where the plaintiff in replevin answered an avowry for *damage feasant* by a plea of license from a commoner who had right for twenty beasts; it was objected, that, if the commoner could license, he could not do so without deed, and of that opinion was the whole Court. So in Hoskins *v.* Robins, 2 Ventr. 123, an objection was taken to such a license on account of its not being stated to be by deed, and although the objection was overruled on the ground, that, after verdict, it must be taken that the license was by deed, yet the Court were unanimous in thinking that such a license could not be granted without deed. So, in Harrison *v.* Parker, 6 East, 154, where liberty and license were given to the plaintiff and his heirs to build a bridge across a river, from the plaintiff's close to the close of A., and liberty and license to plaintiff to lay the foundation of one end on A.'s close, the grant was by deed. The right to be buried in a particular vault, was held in Bryan *v.* Whistler, 8 B. & C. 298, to be an easement which could be created by deed only. A legal right of way cannot pass except by deed. Per Lord Denman C.J., in Tickle *v.* Brown, 4 Ad. & El. 369. The questions as to what are deemed interests in land or otherwise, within the Statute of Frauds, have arisen in England in a variety of cases relating to rates and water-companies. Tolls have not been held ratable as real property (Rex *v.* Eyre, 12 East, 416), unless where connected with some tangible real property, as sluices, engines, or the like. Rex *v.* Cardington, Cowp. 582. So pipes laid in the ground for the conveyance of gas, have been held to come within the denomination of real property. Rex *v.* Brighton Gas Co., 5 B. & C. 466. And on the same principle, pipes for the conveyance of *water* have been held to constitute an interest in land (Rex *v.* Bath, 4 East, 609); and the reservoir with the water would all descend to the heir. Ibid. See Philbrick *v.* Ewing, 97 Mass. 133, 136. Shares in water-companies have also been deemed real estates (2 P. Wms. 127; 1 M. & Sel. 634; 5 B. & Ald. 156; 2 Ves. 182; 2 Dick. 545); unless, as is usually the case, provision is made by act of the legisla-

v. Shippam, is decisive to show that an easement, like this, cannot be conferred unless by deed."[1]

§ 170. Such, it has positively been decided, is the law in this country; and in this country, an owner of land may have granted to his neighbor a right of way by parol, and even on a valuable consideration, and the neighbor may have enjoyed it for a very considerable length of time; and although it may be very unjust for the owner or his assignee, with a knowledge of these facts, to repudiate the grant and cut off the way; yet if he will, he may, because *ita lex scripta est.*[2] Therefore, the claim of a right to enter upon the land of another, to repair a dam and embankment, necessary to the working of a mill, and originally erected with the consent of the owner of the soil, cannot be maintained without deed.[3] And the doctrine has been, in this country, applied directly to water-rights.[4] Thus in Bullen *v.* Runnels, in New Hampshire,[5] the deed described the premises as "a certain part of a stream of water," and it was held, that whether all the interest in the soil beneath the water passed for every purpose, or whether it passed only so far as was necessary for the use and enjoyment of the water, the interest was of such a character, that, under the Statute of Frauds of that State, it could not be conveyed without a deed duly executed and recorded.

§ 171. In Thompson *v.* Gregory,[6] the Court say, "It is not necessary to examine whether the witness was or was not competent, because, assuming him to have been so, his testimony

ture for making the shares personalty. See You. & Coll. 281. And see 1 Crabb, Real Property, § 83.

[1] See also Williams *v.* Morris, 8 M. & W. 488; [Stevens *v.* Dennett, 51 N.H. 331.]

[2] Per Shaw C.J., in Fitch *v.* Seymour, 9 Met. 462. And see Chapin *v.* Noyes, 6 Wend. 461. An instrument was of the following tenure: "I hereby authorize R. to open and continue open a *road* through my field, beginning at, &c., as also to build, keep in repair, and use a bridge over the branch in the field in which the said road will pass; said road and bridge being intended as well for the public use as for the use of R.; and to continue until R. and myself shall agree it shall be shut up or altered." This, executed under the hand and seal of the owner of the land, is a grant of an incorporeal hereditament, and which must be *acknowledged and recorded* agreeably to the acts of registration. Hays *v.* Richardson, 1 G. & John. 366. The same doctrine was maintained in Wright *v.* Freeman, 5 H. & John. 467.

[3] Cook *v.* Stearns, 11 Mass. 533.

[4] Russell *v.* Scott, 9 Cowen, 279; Morse *v.* Copeland, 2 Gray, 302; Houston *v.* Laffee, 46 N.H. 505, 507, 508. See Curtis *v.* Jackson, 13 Mass. 517; Anon. *v.* Deberry, 1 Hayw. (N.C.) 248; Hull *v.* Chaffee, 13 Vt. 150.

[5] Bullen *v.* Runnells, 5 N.H. 255.

[6] Thompson *v.* Gregory, 4 John. 81.

would have been of no avail, since the right in question could not pass by *parol.* The right reserved by the lease to the grantor, and his heirs and assigns, *to erect mills or dams*, was an incorporeal hereditament. It was not the land itself, but a right annexed to it, and it could only pass by grant. The appropriate subject-matter of grants is these incorporeal rights, of which livery cannot be had, and a grant is, in general, good only by deed. This was the rule of the Common Law; and were it otherwise, no such interest could be *assigned* or *granted*, without writing, according to the express provision of the Statute of Frauds." Even a written declaration indorsed on a lease after the date, by the lessor, that he intended to demise a greater interest in the use of the water than the lease expresses, is not operative, it has been held, to convey any interest.[1]

§ 172. A grant of the right of flowing land, without paying damage, as provided by statute, is an easement and an interest in land, and can only be made by deed.[2] In a case in Massachusetts, A. orally requested B. to erect a mill-dam, and orally promised him, that if the dam should flow his land, he would not claim damages for the flowing; and accordingly B. built a dam and mill, and flowed A.'s land; and afterwards conveyed the dam and mill to C., who continued to flow the land. To recover damages from C. for this flowing, A. entered a complaint against him, and it was decided, that he had waived his right to damages by his agreement with B., and could not recover. But A. afterwards conveyed his land to D., with a covenant that it was free from all incumbrances, and D. brought an action against him for a breach of this covenant, alleging the right of C. to flow the land without payment of damages. It was held, that C. had no such right as against D., by virtue of A.'s oral agreement with B.; and that no breach of the covenant was shown. In giving

[1] Russell *v.* Scott, 9 Cowen, 279.

[2] [Morrill *v.* Mackman, 24 Mich. 279, 284. In this case it was decided that an agreement properly evidenced, giving the owner of a mill site the right, for a stipulated annual compensation, to flow the adjoining lands of another for an indefinite period, by the erection of a dam upon his own premises, creates a tenancy in such lands, and such an agreement is within the Statute of Frauds; but that statute permitting leases for a year to be created by parol, and a parol lease for more than a year, under which the lessee has been put in possession, being good as a lease from year to year until terminated by notice, an action cannot be maintained against one in possession under such an agreement, created by parol, except for the agreed compensation, without notice to quit. Morrill *v.* Mackman, supra.

the opinion of the Court, Shaw C.J. said, "The grantee of a right, privilege, or easement in land must secure it in the manner the law provides; otherwise the law will not guaranty it to him.[1] A claim for mere damages caused by flowing land by means of a mill-dam, may undoubtedly be *waived* by parol; inasmuch as it is always a good defence to a claim for a sum of money, that it has been paid, or satisfied by agreement, or waived; and proof of payment, satisfaction, or waiver, may be made by parol." [2] This is, however, different from a permanent right, privilege, or easement in another's land, which is a much more important interest, and which, by the Common Law, and by the Statute of Frauds, cannot pass without writing.

7. *Reservations and Exceptions of Water Rights in Grants of Land.*

§ 173. An easement may also be *reserved* in a deed of conveyance of the land, or *retained* by an exception in such deed; and, as where an easement is granted, whatever is essential to the enjoyment of it passes to the grantee, so in a reservation or exception of an easement, every thing is withheld by the grantor which is essential to its enjoyment; for, notwithstanding a deed contains the words *grant*, &c., such words are to be limited by the general tenor of the context, the subject-matter, and more especially by the express declaration or intent of the grantor contained in the deed itself.[3] A person, may, therefore, accept a deed from a riparian proprietor on a watercourse, in which there is reserved or secured to his grantor an easement, with the

[1] Fitch *v.* Seymour, 9 Met. 462.

[2] Seymour *v.* Carter, 2 Met. 520; [Smith *v.* Goulding, 6 Cush. 154. An agreement to take a certain annual compensation for damages occasioned by flowing land by a mill-dam is not an agreement for the sale of an interest in lands, within the Statute of Frauds. Short *v.* Woodward, 13 Gray, 86.] And see post, Chap. VIII., in which the subject of *parol licenses* is fully considered.

[3] Wade *v.* Howard, 6 Pick. 492; Cocheco Manuf. Co. *v.* Whittier, 10 N.H. 305. ["A right of way may be as well created by a reservation or exception, in the deed of the grantor, reserving or retaining to himself and his heirs a right of way, either in gross, or as annexed to lands owned by him, so as to charge the lands granted with such easement or servitude, as by a deed from the owner of the land to be charged, granting such way, either in gross or as appurtenant to other estate of the grantee." Shaw C.J. in Bowen *v.* Conner, 6 Cush. 132, 137; Peck *v.* Conway, 119 Mass. 546, 549; Barnes *v.* Lloyd, 112 Mass. 224, 232. The grantee, by his acceptance of a deed-poll, becomes bound by all the restrictions, limitations, reservations, and exceptions contained in it. Newell *v.* Hill, 2 Met. 180; Shaw C.J. in Bowen *v.* Conner, 6 Cush. 136, 137; Peck *v.* Conway, 119 Mass. 546.]

privileges secondary thereto, in the premises; and by the use of the words "brook to remain to the use of the proprietor for ever," if the volume of water has been for many years artificially increased for the use of the mills, it is for ever so to remain; the soil passes to the grantee, the grantor reserving the right to the use of the water, as formerly.[1]

§ 174. In order to ascertain what is granted in the case of an *exception* in a deed, it must first be ascertained what is included in the exception; for whatever is included in the exception is excluded from the grant.[2] The words *exception* and *reservation* are often used indiscriminately, though there is a distinction recognized between them. An exception is separating part of that embraced in the description, and already existing in specie; as excepting a particular parcel of land from a

[1] Vickerie *v.* Buswell, 13 Maine, 289. [The grantee in a deed-poll by its acceptance, becomes bound by all its restrictions, limitations, reservations, and exceptions; and the deed may charge with a servitude other lands than those which were the subject of conveyance. Winthrop *v.* Fairbanks, 41 Maine, 307; Vickerie *v.* Buswell, 13 Maine, 289; Newell *v.* Hill, 2 Met. 180. When, in such a deed, it was stipulated that the grantee should guaranty to the grantor a sufficient quantity of water at certain places described, and the deed was accepted by the grantee, it was held that he and his assigns were estopped to deny the grantor's title, although the instrument was a deed-poll and was not signed by the grantee. Emerson *v.* Mooney, 50 N.H. 315.]

[2] Greenleaf *v.* Birth, 6 Peters, 310; Case *v.* Haight, 3 Wend. 632. [Blake *v.* Madigan, 65 Maine, 529. Where the plaintiff by deed conveyed to the grantee a certain well and aqueduct leading therefrom, excepting a certain branch before conveyed, and the plaintiff's right of using all necessary water at certain places which are described, it was held, that the right so excepted always remained in the grantor, and would enure to the benefit of his heirs and assigns, although there were no words of limitation. Emerson *v.* Mooney, 50 N.H. 315. See Wheeler *v.* Brown, 46 Penn. St. 197; Keeler *v.* Wood, 30 Vt. 242; Bowen *v.* Conner, 6 Cush. 132; Winthrop *v.* Fairbanks, 41 Maine, 307. But the contrary doctrine seems to be maintained in Massachusetts. In a case where there was a grant of land, with full covenants of warranty, accompanied with a proviso that, whereas the grantee intends to flow some part of the premises, the grantor shall have the right to improve and cultivate the part of the premises which shall not be so flowed, a life-estate only is excepted. Jamaica Pond Aqueduct Corp. *v.* Chandler, 9 Allen, 159, 170. In this case, Bigelow C.J. said, "On looking at this proviso to ascertain the nature of the incumbrance which is excepted from the warranty, it is plain that it is nothing more than an exception, in favor of the grantor, of a right to improve and cultivate and to take the emoluments to his own use of such part of the granted premises as the corporation did not flow or cover with water. This was a personal right excepted out of the grant in behalf of the grantor only, and not for his heirs or assigns. The same rule of interpretation applies to an exception out of a grant as to a deed, in respect to the limitation of the estate thereby created. If the whole fee is granted, and an exception be made to the grantor himself, without words of inheritance, a life-estate only is excepted. Shep. Touchstone, 100; Curtis *v.* Gardner, 13 Met. 461." See Buffum *v.* Hutchinson, 1 Allen, 58.]

farm granted by general words. A reservation is something newly created, out of the granted premises, by force and effect of the reservation itself, as an easement out of land demised.[1] The effect of the deed, it has been said, does not depend upon the use of the one or the other of these terms, but on the facts which they represent.[2] In Case *v.* Haight,[3] a party who owned land on one side of a stream, and also the bed of a stream, conveyed to another party owning land adjoining the stream on the other side, the land under water to the middle of the stream, reserving to himself the right to butt a dam on both sides of the stream as he should think necessary; it was held, that the reservation had not the effect of an exception, it being indispensable to a good exception, that the thing excepted should be part of the *thing granted*, and not of any other thing; that the parties were entitled to an equal participation of the use of the water, notwithstanding the reservation. The reservation was, however, held to be operative as an *implied covenant*, or by way of *estoppel*, securing the right provided for in the reservation.

§ 175. It is laid down, that an exception must be of a particular thing out of a general one, and must be described with certainty.[4] If the exception be not set down with precision and accuracy, as if one grant a house, excepting one chamber, or grant a manor, excepting one acre, but does not designate what chamber, or which acre, the exceptions are void.[5] A

[1] Per Shaw C.J., in Hurd *v.* Curtis, 7 Met. 94. [Per Davis J., in Garland *v.* Hodsdon, 46 Maine, 515, 516; Winthrop *v.* Fairbanks, 41 Maine, 307; Gray J., in Hill *v.* Cutting, 107 Mass. 597.] An exception is always a part of the thing granted, but a reservation is of a thing not *in esse*, but newly created or reserved. Per Parker C. J., in Cocheco Manuf. Co. *v.* Whittier, 10 N.H. 305, referring to Co. Litt. 47, a; Shep. Touch. 80; Cutler *v.* Tufts, 3 Pick. 272; Jackson *v.* Smith, 9 John. 100. [But in Maine, it was observed, in the case of Winthrop *v.* Fairbanks, 41 Maine, 307, that exception and reservation have often been used indiscriminately, and the difference between them is so obscure in many cases, that it is not regarded; that which in terms is a reservation in a deed is often construed to be a good exception, in order that the object designed to be secured may not be lost. In Bowen *v.* Conner, 6 Cush. 132, 135, Shaw C.J. said, "We know there is much nicety in the technical distinction between an exception and a reservation. In our own conveyancing, this distinction is not so precisely observed, but a clause of reservation is construed to be an exception, if that will best effect the intent of the parties. And so in the English cases, the term reservation is often construed to be a good exception. But the distinction between an exception and a reservation is often very uncertain."]

[2] Per McLean J., in Bowman *v.* Wathen, 2 McLean C.C. 766.

[3] Case *v.* Haight, 3 Wend. 362 (Court of Errors).

[4] See Co. Litt. 142, a.

[5] See Darling *v.* Crowell, 6 N.H. 421, and the authorities there adduced.

description in a deed of a certain tract of land, excepting one acre, which is retained for the use of flowing water, is void for uncertainty.[1]

§ 176. An exception or reservation, of something which the premises granted do not comprise, is void, as having nothing to operate upon.[2] Where the owner of an acre of land adjoining a river, and upon which one end of a dam abutted, conveyed the land by metes and bounds, and the water privilege, reserving to himself the privilege of drawing such a portion of water from the pond, as he might have occasion for, for fulling skins; and it appeared that there was no mill in existence there for such purpose, and that the grantor owned no other land in the vicinity; but there was other land adjacent owned by third persons, upon which a fulling-mill might with convenience be erected, and the water conducted through the premises conveyed; it was held, that a right to erect a mill upon the land conveyed was not included in the reservation. There was nothing about the erection of a building upon the land, or any possession of it except so far as the drawing of water from the pond was concerned. If the party at the time had been the owner of the land adjoining, upon which he had erected, or was then erecting a fulling-mill, there would have been no doubt as to the meaning of the parties. The Court, in fact said, that if the party had been at that time the owner of the land immediately adjoining the acre conveyed, upon which a mill might coveniently have been erected, it could hardly have admitted of a question.[3]

§ 177. In Hurd *v.* Curtis,[4] A. conveyed to B. by deed of release, a parcel of land, " with a paper-mill privilege on the premises, and flumes, watercourses, dams, right of way and passage, with the right of water for one paper-mill with two engines,

[1] Darling *v.* Crowell, supra. In Hull *v.* Leonard, 1 Pick. 31, it is said, if a grant be made to a father and his son, and the father has several sons, it is void; and so if made to a man's cousin. And it was held in the case just cited, that a grant to the heirs of an individual, is void for uncertainty. In a devise of a house, " reserving, however, two rooms of said house, for the use and during the life of W., I desire by this fourth article, that the widow W. may have the choice of those two rooms which shall best suit her, because I desire the said W. should be sure of a shelter during the time she may live." It was held, that this reservation vests in W. an estate in the two rooms for life, of which she may make any disposition. It does not create a mere easement for her personal use. Wasthoff *v.* Dracourt, 3 Watts, 240.

[2] Hurd *v.* Curtis, 7 Met. 94.

[3] Cocheco Manuf. Co. *v.* Whittier, 10 N.H. 305.

[4] Hurd *v.* Curtis, ub. sup.

being one of the six paper-mill rights and privileges established and agreed upon by certain articles of agreement," referred to; said conveyed paper-mill privilege "to be entitled to all the rights, and none other, and subject to all the restrictions, terms, and conditions" in said articles of agreement contained. A. also, in the same deed, granted, assigned, and conveyed to B. "all the rights, privileges, benefits, and interest in and to the exceptions and reservations, which said A. accepted and reserved by his deed to C." of a prior date: By said prior deed of A. to C., A. conveyed to C. a parcel of land, "together with a paper-mill privilege, with the flumes, watercourses, and dam, to the same belonging, with the right of water for one paper-mill with two engines, being one of the six paper-mill rights and privileges established and agreed upon by certain articles of agreement" [the same which were referred to A.'s deed to B.] "*except* the reserve of the right and privilege of conveying water through the premises hereby granted and conveyed, in the channel now open, in which water used to run to a saw-mill; for the purpose of carrying such water works as he (A.) may wish to erect on his premises adjoining the premises hereby conveyed, with the right of widening said channel, not exceeding sixteen feet, and of deepening the same," &c. *Held*, that A.'s grant to B. of the rights, privileges, benefits, and interest, in and to the exceptions and reservations which A. excepted and reserved in and by his deed to C. did not enlarge the water power and privilege released to B. in the former part of A.'s deed to him.

§ 178. Still, as there was occasion in the preceding part of the work to state,[1] if it be the intention of a grantor of land covered by a watercourse, to withhold the water from the grantee, he may easily do so by the use of proper words in the instrument of conveyance to that effect. On the same principle, and by the same means, he may impose in his own favor and for his own purposes, any conditions and limitations, and restrictions in the use of the water by the grantee.[2] Thus, the grantor of a tract of land, without having mentioned a watercourse included within the prescribed limits, declared it to be the understanding

[1] Ante, § 9; Claremont *v.* Carleton, 2 N.H. 371; Hayes *v.* Bowman, 1 Rand. (Va.) 420; note to Jennings, *ex parte*, 6 Cowen, 548; Opinion of Kent C.J., in Palmer *v.* Mulligan, 3 Caines, 319. As to a reservation of the water by bounding in a particular manner on a watercourse, see ante, §§ 17–44.

[2] Pettee *v.* Hawes, 13 Pick. 323.

of the grantor, and the intention of the deed, to convey to the grantee as much of the privilege of the water as should be sufficient for the use of a fulling-mill, whenever there was a sufficiency therefor; and it was held, that this clause was not repugnant to the grant, but was a good reservation of the surplus water.[1] In this case it was urged that the whole of the stream passed by the conveyance of the land, and that the restraining clause, being subsequent, was void for repugnance, whether considered in the light of an exception or reservation, or as an explanation of the preceding words of the conveyance. The Court admitted, that the principle on which the objection rested was correctly stated, but were clear it did not apply to the instrument of conveyance in question. The doctrine advanced by the Court was, that if there be an explicit and unambiguous grant of a thing, any exception or reservation, which is manifestly contradictory, is to be rejected; as if a man conveys twenty acres, excepting one; or where the conveyance is construed to be of a moiety, and in a subsequent clause the grantor said, that he meant to convey a fourth part, which was obviously contradictory and to be rejected.[2]

§ 179. By a grant of a mill, it has been seen,[3] the land under the mill, and adjacent land necessary for its use, passes by the force of the grant; and so it is *eo converso*, if a mill is excepted or reserved in a grant of a tract of land, the land upon which it stands, and adjacent land necessary for its use, will *not* pass. Thus, where land was conveyed, with all the buildings standing thereon, *except* the "brick factory," it was held, that the grantor's title to the land on which the factory stood, and the water privilege appurtenant thereto, did not pass by the deed; for, as the Court say, "when property is granted, all that is necessary for the enjoyment of the grant is impliedly granted, as incident to the express grant; and the same rule of construction applies to an exception in a grant." [4]

[1] Sprague *v.* Snow, 4 Pick. 54.

[2] Cutler *v.* Tufts, 3 Pick. 272; and see Platt on Cov. 313, et seq.; [Denton *v.* Leddell, 8 C. E. Green, 64.]

[3] Ante, § 157.

[4] Allen *v.* Scott, 21 Pick. 25. ["What will pass by words in a grant will be excepted by the same words in an exception." Libbey J., in Blake *v.* Madigan, 65 Maine, 522, 529; Shep. Touchstone, 100; Bowen *v.* Conner, 6 Cush. 132; Hammond *v.* Woodman, 41 Maine, 203. In Moulton *v.* Trafton, 64 Maine, 218, the defendant, being the assignee of Clark Trafton, claimed to hold premises thus described in a deed from another party to the plaintiff: "Excepting by this conveyance a saw-mill and a shingle-machine,

§ 180. So, an exception of a particular mill-site operates as an exception of the soil of the mill-site (just as a grant of a mill-site will convey the soil); and so much land as is necessary for the *mill-pond*, and for erecting and carrying on the business of the mill; and such a reservation is not of a mere easement, but of the soil itself.[1]

§ 181. A general reservation of all watercourses on the demised premises, suitable for the erection of mills, together with the right of erecting mills and other works thereon, with a certain number of acres of land adjoining thereto, will give to the lessor a right to all the mill-sites, whenever he chooses to make a location; it is the same as reserving all the mill-sites on the demised premises, with the number of acres of land specified.[2] But such a reservation or exception extends only to natural mill-sites, and not to artificial ones, such as where water is brought to the land by means of sluices.[3]

§ 182. If two persons, being tenants in common of a lot of land embracing a mill privilege, make partition of the lot by mutual deeds of release, and in each of the deeds make a reservation "of one-half of the mill privileges on said land, with the right of using the same," the effect is to divide the land, but to leave the mill privileges in common as before; and where such owner of half the mill privileges on the whole lot conveys to a third person certain mills not in controversy, and also conveys in the same deed "one-half of all the water for a grist-mill, *on said lot*, below the mills before mentioned," the grantee takes one-half of all the water, if so much be necessary, for the use of a grist-mill to be erected below the mills then existing.[4]

and land enough around said mill to carry on the lumbering business at said mills, and a right of way from said mill to the road leading from Thorndike to Unity Village, conveyed to Clark Trafton, as long as said Trafton occupies said privilege with mills." It was held that these words created an exception, and not a reservation merely; and that the land under the mills was included in the exception; and that the exception constituted a determinable or qualified fee, which could be assigned; and that the duration of the excepted estate was limited by the existence of mills upon the premises, and not by the personal occupancy of Clark Trafton. A grant or reservation of "the whole of the cider-house and cider-mill standing on land" not otherwise included, "so long as the said cider-house shall stand thereon, and no longer," gives a freehold in the land under the building, so long as it stands thereon, even after it has ceased to be used as a cider-house or cider-mill. Esty *v.* Currier, 98 Mass. 500.]

[1] Jackson *v.* Vermilyea, 6 Cowen, 77.

[2] Russell *v.* Scott, 9 Cowen, 299; Butz *v.* Ihrie, 1 Rawle, 281.

[3] Jackson *v.* Lawrence, 11 John. 191.

[4] Bailey *v.* Rust, 15 Maine, 440.

§ 183. If a proprietor of land, on which are a mill and mill privilege, grant to one son the use and benefit of one-half of a saw-mill, and on the same day grants to another son a tract of land, including that whereon the mill stood, "excepting the privilege of one-half of a saw-mill conveyed to the other son, and *his heirs;*" the grant and the reservation are to be considered together, to ascertain the intention of the parties; and one-half of the mill and mill privilege, pass by the grant.[1]

§ 184. Where the premises in a deed were described "a certain grist-mill and bank, wherever the same is situated, with the appurtenances thereof, lying, &c., and adjoining a bridge crossing a river;" it was held, that the bank between such grist-mill and bridge on which a carding-mill stood, was conveyed by such deed; but that a *reservation* in such deed of the "building adjoining on the east end of the mill," wherein the carding machine was then in operation, with the use of water for certain purposes, and on certain conditions, included the mill only, and not the land on which it stood; and that the right so reserved was also restricted to the buildings then existing, and did not extend to any other building subsequently erected on the same site; the Court said, "The intention of the parties is obvious, and the terms of the grant are too plain to admit of a doubt. Were they otherwise, they are to be taken most strongly against the grantors."[2]

§ 185. For the purpose of ascertaining what parties really intend, by a reservation in a grant of a watercourse, it is undoubtedly proper to take into consideration the condition of the property, and the circumstances of the parties. Such was the view taken by the Court in Kennedy *v.* Scovil, in Connecticut.[3] In that case, it appears, that in June, 1822, and before, B. owned two pieces of land with a watercourse running through both of them, and on each side of which he had a mill propelled by the watercourse. On the upper piece he had a dam, mill-pond, flume, and conductor; and the water for the use of both mills passed from the dam through the flume. For the use of the upper mill, the water was taken from the flume by means of two orifices in it; and for the use of the lower mill, the water was taken by the means of a conductor inserted in the flume, and extending from

1 Moore *v.* Fletcher, 16 Maine, 63.
2 Marshall *v.* Niles, 8 Conn. 361.
3 Kennedy *v.* Scovil, 12 Conn. 317.

it to the mill. On the 8th of June, 1832, B. conveyed to S. the upper mill-site, and one-half of the pond flowed by the dam, by a deed containing the following clause: "Always provided, and this deed is given on condition, that the grantor is to have and retain the privilege of conveying water from said dam through a conductor similar to the one now in use, till the same shall arrive at the *east* end of the new shop [the upper mill], and thence, either by a conductor, race, or otherwise, to the shop [lower mill] lying *east* of the new shop." The rights of B. in the lower mill afterwards became vested in K. and S.; K. owning two-thirds, and S. one-third. In November, 1835, S. made a new orifice in the flume, lower than any former one, and thereby drew off so much of the water as not to leave sufficient to keep the lower mill in operation. It was held, that B., at the time of the conveyance from him to S., had a right, and was bound to take the water for the use of the lower mill in the accustomed manner, and that, by such conveyance, B. retained to that mill all the privileges which it then enjoyed; and that the term "dam" in the reservation was to be construed as including the flume, or as being of equivalent import.

§ 186. Where A. let a fulling-mill, together with the watercourse and flood-gates, to a trustee for ninety-nine years, if either his daughter or wife should so long live, for their use, and in order to make provision for them; with an exception of free liberty for the lessor, heirs, &c., his servants, and tenants, at all times, to divert the water from the mill for watering all meadows which they should think proper, and to put up and take down all proper sluices; and part of the profits of the mill consisted of water rents for flooding meadows, with water which was wholly diverted from the mill; it was held, that by the exception, the heir of the lessor was entitled to the water rents, the exception not being repugnant to the grant.[1]

§ 187. An exception in a grant in these words: "excepting and reserving out of the said piece of land so much as is necessary for the use of a grist-mill on the east side of the road, at the west end of the saw-mill dam," is held to be a good exception; although until the grantor or his assigns exercised the right reserved and built the mill, it was inoperative, so that the whole premises so far vested in the grantee as to enable him to

[1] Lambert *v.* Bennet, 3 Smith, 84, in K.B. Geo. III.

maintain trespass against a stranger; or even against the grantor and his assigns, for an entry on the land for any purpose other than that specified in the reservation.[1]

§ 188. An absolute power of revoking the easement of taking and using water for hydraulic purposes *reserved* in a demise thereof, is not invalid as being repugnant to the demise; and the easement may be resumed at any time. The canal commissioners in the State of New York, demised to one M. the right of taking and using, for hydraulic purposes, the water which should flow from a waste wear at a prescribed height, so far as the same might be taken without interfering prejudicially with canal navigation; *reserving* the right to the State *wholly to resume* the subject of the demise at any time the commissioner should think fit, without being liable in damages, or to make compensation for improvements and erections. The lessee transferred all interest in the lease, and the assignee had erected and nearly completed an expensive flour-mill on the premises, when the commissioners caused the waste wear to be raised beyond the height mentioned in the lease. It was held by the Supreme Court of that State, that the power reserved in the lease extended as well to a *partial* as to a *total* resumption of the privilege demised; and that the act of raising the waste wear was, under the terms of the reservation, lawful. Neither was any formal opinion on the part of the commissioners, as to the necessity of resuming the subject of the demise, requisite as a preliminary to the exercise of the right of resumption.[2]

§ 189. An instance of an *implied* reservation was where E. mortgaged a strip of land, including mills thereon, and running a distance along the river; but three years afterwards, having sold a small portion of the mortgaged premises for a hide-mill and lime vats, he obtained a release from the mortgagee for a nominal consideration, of what he had sold, described thus: "Beginning at the end of a dam, running up the river two rods, and so round to the bank of the river." The mortgagee afterwards having foreclosed, one question was, whether the release gave a right to the centre of the river; and it appeared, that

[1] Dygert *v.* Mathews, 11 Wend. 35. The case of Thompson *v.* Gregory, 4 John. 81, was a reservation of a right to flow, but was within the principle of the case just before cited. And see Provost *v.* Calder, 2 Wend. 517.

[2] Miller, *ex parte*, 2 Hill, 418.

if it was to have that effect, it would destroy the value of the mortgagee's mill privileges. The Court held, that it was not to be inferred that the mortgagee intended to release every thing valuable in the mortgaged premises, for which a large consideration had been given; and they considered the release in question, under all the peculiar circumstances, as being no more than a mere exception in the mortgage; and that it excluded any part of the stream.[1]

§ 190. In a case in Pennsylvania, it appeared that W. S., the father of J. S., had purchased a tract of land, and in 1797, or 1798, erected a mill, and diverted a watercourse from its natural channel into the mill-race, by means of a dam erected on that part of the tract which, at the time of the action commenced, was owned by the defendant. This race had been used with the mill, since the time of its erection. In 1813, W. S. made his will, whereby he directed the mill and twelve acres of land to be laid out adjoining for its use, to be sold to pay debts and legacies; "*the right and privilege of the water to remain unmolested and entire for the benefit and use of the mill, whoever may hereafter own said mills.*" The residue of the farm, excepting twenty-eight acres previously "*let*" to his son A. S., he devised to his son J. S., and directed him to pay the purchase-money due on the whole tract. J. S. (the plaintiff) had occupied and used the mill and race, and *cleared* the latter, when necessary, since the death of his father in 1813, and had repaired the dam which diverted the stream when necessary. On the 21st February, 1831, the plaintiff, by a deed recorded, conveyed twenty-eight acres, parcel of the larger tract, with its appurtenances, to A. S., with a covenant of seisin, and that the same was clear of all incumbrance. In 1836, A. S. conveyed to trustees, who, in the same year, conveyed to the defendant. When J. S. conveyed to A. S., without expressly reserving the water right, he left room for a question whether he could show it to have *been impliedly reserved by parol.* It was held, that a purchaser from A. S. had notice of a parol reservation of the right to the race, from the fact of the subsequent occupation of the mill, and user of the race by J. S. It was settled, said Gibson C.J., that a trust was not within the Statute of Frauds of Pennsylvania; and that

[1] Hatch *v.* Dwight, 17 Mass. 289.

the statute was docked of those sections of the English statute which require declarations of trust to be put in writing.[1]

8. *Unity of Possession.*

§ 191. The strong resemblance between the prædial servitudes of the Civil Law, and the easements of the Common Law, has already been pointed out.[2] One other respect in which they are alike, is, they become extinguished by *unity of possession;* or, in other words, the servitude or easement becomes extinguished when the estate to which it is due, and the estate owing it, are united in the same person. The language of the Civil Law is, "Servitutes prædiorum *confunduntur*, si idem utriusque prædii dominus esse cœperit."[3] So it is an established rule

[1] Randall *v.* Silverthorn, in error, 4 Barr, 173. An *implied* reservation: If the owner of land build houses upon it, adjoining each other so as to require mutual support, there is, either by presumed grant or by presumed reservation, a right to such mutual support, and such right is not affected by subsequent subdivision of the property. No man who becomes possessed of one of the houses by any means whatever, can be in a situation to say to his neighbor, "You are not entitled to the protection of my house. I will pull it down, and let the houses on each side collapse and fall into the ruins of my own." Pollock C.B., and the rest of the Court were of this opinion. Richards *v.* Rose, Law Jour. Rep. Vol. XXIII. of the New Series, January, 1854.

[2] See ante, §§ 141–144.

[3] 1 Kauff. Mack. 350. The Civil Code of Louisiana has the following provisions on the subject of the extinction of servitudes:—

ART. 801. Every servitude is extinguished, when the estate to which it is due, and the estate owing it, are united in the same hands. But it is necessary that the whole of the two estates should belong to the same proprietor; for if the owner of one estate only acquires the other in part, or in common with another person, confusion does not take effect.

ART. 802. If the union of the two estates be made only under a condition, or if it cease by legal eviction; if the title be thus destroyed, either by the happening of the condition or by legal eviction, the servitudes revive, which in the mean time will have been rather suspended than extinguished. Thus the exercise of redemption, the happening of the condition on which the estate terminates, the eviction from a succession by a nearer heir, the abandonment or relinquishment of an estate on account of mortgages, will revive all the servitudes, active and passive.

ART. 803. Confusion takes place by the simple acceptance of an inheritance, if there be but one heir. If the heir who has thus accepted an inheritance, disposes of any estate belonging to the succession, which is subject to any servitude towards his estate, without any stipulation for the preservation of his right of servitude, the estate thus alienated, which owed the servitude, remains free from it, in consequence of the confusion which had taken effect while the estate remained in his hands.

ART. 804. But if the heir, under a simple acceptance, sell to a person the whole of his rights in the succession he has received, the sale prevents the confusion, and the estate belonging to the succession will continue to have the rights of servitude previously due to it, or be charged with the servitudes imposed on it, in the same manner as if it had not passed through the hands of the heir; because, in this case, the purchaser is not presumed to have purchased more or less than all the ancestors possessed.

ART. 805. Confusion does not take efof the Common Law, that every easement becomes extinguished when the two estates, the one claiming the easement and the other owning it, are united in the same hands; or when both pieces of ground become the property of one owner.[1] [The law is clear, that if the same person becomes absolute owner of the land from which a stream of water flows, and also of the land into which it flows, the easement which the latter might have claimed, is extinguished.[2]] Then the special kind of property which the right to the easement conferred, so long as the tenements belonged to different owners, are merged (*et tunc moriuntur*)[3] in the general rights of property.[4] This doctrine was discussed as far back as the reign of Henry VII., when it was held that "if a man hath a stream of water which runneth in a leaden pipe, and he buys the land where the pipe is, and *cuts the pipe*, the watercourse is extinct, because he thereby declares his intention and purpose that he does not wish to enjoy them together."[5] In Nicholas *v.* Chamberlain, before cited,[6] it appeared that if a person erect a house, and build a conduit thereto in an-

fect if the heir has only a temporary possession of the estate, subject to the servitude, or enjoying it for the purpose of delivering it to another person to whom it has been bequeathed, or when his right in it terminates at a certain fixed time.

ART. 806. If the heir has accepted the succession under benefit of inventory, the confusion does not take effect; and if the heir is obliged to abandon the succession at the instance of the creditors, the servitudes resume their former state.

ART. 807. The acquets, which the husband and wife make during the marriage, do not become confused with the private property of each; and if these acquets are sold during the marriage, the servitudes, active and passive, which existed previous to their being acquired by the husband and wife, continue to exist, without any stipulation to that effect.

ART. 808. Except in the cases herein mentioned, and similar cases, servitudes extinguished by confusion do not revive, except by a new contract; with the exception of continuous and apparent servitudes, with respect to which the disposition made by the owner of both estates is equivalent to a title.

ART. 809. The renunciation or abandonment of the land extinguishes the servitudes charged on it, of whatever nature they may be, because the owner of the estate to which the servitude is due, is bound to accept the abandonment, which produces in his hand a confusion which puts an end to the servitude.

ART. 810. It is not necessary to produce a discharge of the servitude, that the proprietor of the estate which owes it, should abandon the whole estate; it suffices, if he abandon the part on which the servitude is exercised.

[1] Co. Litt. 313, a; [Ritger *v.* Parker, 8 Cush. 145; Keiffer *v.* Imhoff, 26 Penn. St. 438, 443; Canham *v.* Fisk, 2 Cr. & J. 126; Thomas *v.* Thomas, 2 Cr. M. & R. 34; Pearce *v.* M'Clenaghan, 5 Rich. 178; Atwater *v.* Bodfish, 11 Gray, 152; Stevens *v.* Dennett, 51 N.H. 330.]

[2] [Per Lord Cranworth L.C., in Ivimey *v.* Stocker, L.R. 1 Ch. App. 407.]

[3] Gale & What. on Easem. 553.

[4] 1 Crabb. Real Property, § 425.

[5] Lady Brown's case, cited in Sury *v.* Pigott, Poph. 170, Palm. 446.

[6] Ante, § 153.

other part of his land, and convey water by pipes to the house, and afterwards sell the house with the appurtenances, the conduits and pipes pass with the house.[1] Here it will be observed, the right to the easement was not destroyed by the unity of possession, and for the reason that it was annexed to the messuage, and in use at the time of the grant; and, as in the preceding case, the pipes had not been *cut off*. If the conduit and pipes had been actually severed before the grant, there then could be no pretence for saying that the conduit and pipes passed as appurtenances.[2] The case of Morris *v.* Edginton,[3] though different in its circumstances, has been considered to establish in its reasoning the foregoing conclusion.

§ 192. The above doctrine has been applied in this country in the following case: A. owns an upper mill, and B. a lower mill on the same stream. The lower mill has a dam, which obstructed the free use of the upper mill. B. lowers his dam two feet, and allows it to remain in that state for thirty-eight years; and during that period the upper mill is free from obstruction. B. then sells the lower mill to A., who afterwards sells it to C. The Court decided, that, on the ground of unity of possession, the right of raising the dam two feet was gone, and that the upper mill had acquired a right to use the water without back-flowing.[4] [The use of a mill privilege purchased from the owner of a lower privilege on the same stream, is not regulated by the use made of it before such purchase, but by what is reasonable and proper, conformably to the wants and usages of the community.[5]]

§ 193. The right to a *natural* watercourse, it has been held,[6] is not extinguished by unity of possession in any case, and this

[1] [See Elliott *v.* Sallee, 14 Ohio St. 10, 17; Morgan *v.* Mason, 20 Ohio, 401, cited ante, § 161, note; Pyer *v.* Carter, 1 H. & N. 916; Philbrick *v.* Ewing, 97 Mass. 133. In Dodd *v.* Burchell, 1 H. & C. 117, Pollock C.B. said, "A right to the enjoyment of a conduit is very different from a right of way." Wilde B. said, "A conduit is a thing actually enjoyed with a house, and passes with a grant of the house; but it is not so with a right of way." "There is a wide difference between that which is substantial, as a conduit or watercourse, and that which is of an incorporeal nature, as a right of way." Pollock C.B., p. 120. See Seymour *v.* Lewis, 2 Beasley Ch. (N.J.) 439; Philbrick *v.* Ewing, 97 Mass. 133; ante, § 153.]

[2] Hazard *v.* Robinson, 3 Mason, 278; 11 Hen. VII. 25.

[3] Morris *v.* Edginton, 3 Taunt. 24; and see the opinion of Story J., in Hazard *v.* Robinson, 3 Mason, 172; Perry *v.* Parker, 1 Woodb. & M. 280; Manning *v.* Smith, 6 Conn. 289; Grant *v.* Chase, 17 Mass. 443.

[4] Hazard *v.* Robinson, 3 Mason, 272, 278.

[5] [Haskins *v.* Haskins, 9 Gray, 390; Barrett *v.* Parsons, 10 Cush. 367. See Bruce *v.* Yale, 4 Allen, 393.]

[6] See ante, § 141.]

arises from the necessity of the case and the nature of the subject.[1] This was settled, after a very elaborate discussion, in Sury *v.* Pigott.[2] That was an action for stopping a watercourse which had been used to have its current run into the plaintiff's yard, and fill a pond with water, and it was held, that a unity of possession of the land of the house and place to which, and of the land through which, &c., was no bar; and there is, said Whitelocke J., "a difference between a way or common and a watercourse. These begin by private right, by prescription, by assent, as a way or common, being a particular benefit to take part of the profits of the land; this is extinct by unity, because the greater benefit shall drown the less. A watercourse doth begin *ex jure naturæ;* having taken this course naturally, it cannot be diverted."[3] This case was accurately examined, and deliberately confirmed in all its parts,[4] in Hazard *v.* Robinson;[5] and Mr. Chitty, in considering this subject, remarks, "that there is a peculiarity relating to a claim of this nature; viz., that it never is destroyed by unity of seisin of the land and water, and of the place in respect of which the use of the water was claimed; the law admitting an exception on account of the uncontrollable nature of water; and that the claim to water is not strictly by grant or prescription, but *ex jure naturæ.*"[6]

§ 194. But can any thing of absolute necessity to a building, a *gutter* for example, in the soil of another, to carry off water, be extinguished by unity of ownership?[7] The above case of

[1] 3 Kent, 448; [Shaw C.J., in Johnson *v.* Jordan, 2 Met. 239; Bul. N.P. 74; Hazard *v.* Robinson, 3 Mason, 277. "It will be found upon examination, that some principles of extinguishment which affect other rights, do not apply to watercourses. The latter are incorporeal hereditaments of a very perdurable nature; they survive, notwithstanding alteration or non-user equally with rights of common or rights of way; while, on the other hand, unity of possession, which is fatal to the other privileges, leaves the watercourse subject, upon a division of property, to the same claims as before." Woolrych, Waters, 293, 294.]

[2] Sury *v.* Pigott, ub. sup.

[3] In the report of this case in Latch, 53, is said, "Rent shall be extinguished by unity, and also a way, because it does not exist *durant* the unity; but it is otherwise of a thing which exists notwithstanding the unity;" and a case of warren is cited from Year Book, 35 Hen. VII. f. 55, 56.

[4] 3 Kent, 448.

[5] Hazard *v.* Robinson, ub. sup.

[6] 1 Chit. Gen. Pr. 215. The same law recognized in Tucker *v.* Jewett, 11 Conn. 311, [and in Johnson *v.* Jordan, 2 Met. 239; ante, § 90, notes.]

[7] [Hazard *v.* Robinson, 3 Mason, 278, 279; 11 Hen. VII. 25 b. The case in 11 Hen. VII. 25, was as follows: A. was the owner of a tenement to which there was *an ancient gutter* running through an adjoining tenement, and afterwards he bought the adjoining tenement, and then sold the first tenement to the plaintiff. It was held that the ancient gutter was

Sury *v.* Pigott distinguishes watercourses and ways of necessity from other ways and easements which do not become thus extinguished; "and if," says Parke B., "it is necessary to the safety of a house, that water should flow down a drain, the right of watercourse through it is reserved by implication in every grant of the house;" and many other cases, says he, recognize the distinction taken in Sury *v.* Pigott. In that case, Doddridge J. puts the way of necessity on the same footing as a watercourse or gutter; and, says Mr. B. Alderson, "Its principle seems to be, that nothing of absolute necessity to the tenement is extinguished by unity of possession."[1]

[§ 194 *a.* Two persons had tenements adjoining to each other, the one had an ancient gutter in the land of the other, and both tenements subsequently fell into the same hands. They were then again divided, and the defendant having stopped the gutter, the plaintiff brought the action against him. It was considered that the ancient gutter was not extinguished by the unity of possession, but had revived after the severance, because it was a necessary and subsisting easement; but that it would have been otherwise if, during the unity of possession, the owner had destroyed the gutter, or cut it off.[2] A gutter like this is of

not extinguished by the unity of possession; but that it would have been otherwise if A. during the unity of possession, had destroyed the gutter or cut it off. The reason is, that it was a necessary and subsisting easement. Hazard *v.* Robinson, 3 Mason, 278.]

[1] Pheysey *v.* Vicary, 16 M. & W. 484. In this case, A., being a termor of land, built two houses on it. The whole was then released to him in fee, "with all ways, easements, advantages, and appurtenances thereunto belonging, or therewith usually used, leased, held, occupied, and enjoyed." By his will, he devised one house, and the appurtenances thereunto belonging, to B., and the other to C., in similar terms. During A.'s ownership of both, the entrance from the high-road to the principal door of the house afterwards devised to B., was a set-out carriage drive or sweep, entering from a high-road, passing immediately in front of the house afterwards devised to C., to B.'s door, and then the same point of entrance; B.'s house had a coach-house opening only into the high-road, and a back entrance into the same. After A.'s death, C. made a fence across so much of the carriage drive as passed immediately in front of his house, and across the oval garden, leaving the farther way to B.'s front door by the same carriage drive open; B. brought trespass, claiming the way as appurtenant to his house and garden. It was held, first, that the way as used in A.'s time, *during the unity of ownership* in him, immediately in front of C.'s house, did not pass to B. with the house devised to him, under the word "appurtenances" in A.'s will; and secondly, *comme semble*, that it did not pass as a way of necessity, whether taken in the strict sense, or as a way without which the most convenient and reasonable mode of enjoying every part of B.'s premises could not be had.

[2] [Coppy *v.* I. de B., 11 Hen. VII. 25, pl. 6; Sury *v.* Pigott, Poph. 166; s.c. 3 Bulst. 339; Pyer *v.* Carter, 1 H. & N. 921; Hazard *v.* Robinson, 3 Mason, 278; Robins *v.* Barnes, Hob. 131.]

necessity. Its existence is several, and, like a watercourse, is independent of the soil, and is thus unlike a common way, or rent, which latter perish by the unity of possession. The sheriff cannot give possession of the gutter, nor can ejectment be brought for it,[1] and, although it does not begin like a stream *ex jure naturæ*, it yet partakes of the necessity above mentioned. It can only be extinguished by a manifestation on the part of the owner of the united property, that he will no longer enjoy both together.[2] Things which have an existence during the unity are not extinguished by the unity. And thus a common or a way or a rent become thereby extinct, since their existence ceases upon the union of estates. But this is not so with a watercourse.[3]]

§ 195. It is an expression not uncommon, that ways of *convenience* are extinguished by unity of possession, but *ways of necessity* are not; but, as it has very properly been said, "it appears to be more correct, as well as more in accordance with the general principles of the law of easements, as recognized both by the English and the Civil Law, to consider all easements, whether of convenience or necessity, as extinguished by unity; but, that upon any subsequent severance, easements which previous to such unity were easements of necessity, are granted anew in the same manner as any other easement which would be held by law to pass as incident to the grant."[4] The language of Best C. J. fully supports this view of the law, that all ways are extinguished by unity of ownership; and that ways of necessity are in reality new easements incident to the grant or reservation. "If," says he, "I have four fields, and grant away two of them over which I have been accustomed to pass, the law will presume that I reserve a right of way to those which I retain. But what right? The same as existed before? No; *the old right is extinguished*, and the new way arises out of the necessity of the thing. It has been argued, that the new grant operates as a prevention of the extinguishment of the old right of way, but there is not a single case which bears out that proposition, or which does not imply the contrary. By the grant a new way is created, and that way is limited by necessity."[5] [Blackburn J., in Pearson *v.*

[1] [Challoner *v.* Thomas, Yelv. 143.]

[2] [Woolrych, Waters, 295; Pheysey *v.* Vicary, 16 M. & W. 484, 489, 490. Parke B. and Alderson B.]

[3] [Woolrych, Waters, 295.]

[4] Gale & What. on Easem. (Am. ed.) 60.

[5] Holmes *v.* Goring, 2 Bing. 83; [Viall *v.* Carpenter, 14 Gray, 126, 128; Hazard *v.* Robinson, 3 Mason, 276. Per Bell J.,

Spencer,[1] remarking upon this subject, said, "We do not think that, on a severance of two tenements, any right to use ways which, during the unity of possession, have been used and enjoyed in fact, passes to the owner of the dissevered tenement, unless there be something in the conveyance to show an intention to create a right to use these ways *de novo*. We agree with what is said in Worthington *v.* Gimson,[2] that in this respect there is a distinction between continuous easements, such as drains, &c., and discontinuous easements, such as a right of way."[3] — "It seems to us settled by modern authority, that the ground on which the way of necessity is created is, that a convenient way is impliedly granted as a necessary incident. It is observed by Parke B., in Proctor *v.* Hodgson,[4] that the extent of the authority of Holmes *v.* Goring is that, admitting a grant in general terms, it may be construed to be a grant of such a right of way as from time to time may be necessary. I should have thought it meant as much a grant for ever as if expressly inserted in a deed, and it struck me at the time that the Court was wrong." Alderson B.: "Probably, if this case be taken to a court of error, Holmes *v.* Goring may be reviewed. We certainly do not feel inclined to extend the authority of Holmes *v.* Goring so far as to hold that the person into whose possession the servient tenement comes, may, from time to time, vary the direction of the way of necessity at his pleasure, so long as he substitutes a convenient way. We think we must hold that the way of neces-

in Dunklee *v.* The Wilton Railroad, 24 N.H. 504. Broke, in his Abridgment, says, "The way is revived; *tamen videtur*, that it is a new way (*nouvel chimine*)." Bro. Abr. tit. Extinguishment, fol. 15. And see, to the same effect, Clarke *v.* Cogge, Cro. Jac. 170; Jordan *v.* Atwood, Owen, 121; Morris *v.* Edginton, 3 Taunt. 24; Hazard *v.* Robinson, 3 Mason, 276, per Story J.]

[1] [Pearson *v.* Spencer, 1 B. & S. 583; s.c. 3 B. & S. 767.]

[2] [29 L.J. Q.B. 116; 6 Jur. N.S. 1053; s.c. 2 Ellis & Ellis, 618.]

[3] [In Jamaica Pond Aqu. Corp. *v.* Chandler, 9 Allen, 164, Bigelow C.J. defines a "non-continuous" easement to be one "where the use of the premises by the grantee for the purpose designated in the deed will be only intermittent and occasional, and does not embrace the entire beneficial occupation and improvement of the land." "Among the most prominent of this class of easements is a way." Another definition is, "Continuous easements are those of which the enjoyment is or may be continual, without the necessity of any actual interference by man, as a waterspout, or right to light and air. Discontinuous easements are those the enjoyment of which can only be had by the interference of man, as rights of way, or a right to draw water." Code Civil, Art. 688; Gale & What. on Easem. 17; Lampman *v.* Milks, 21 N.Y. 505; Durel *v.* Boisblanc, 1 La. An. 407.]

[4] [Proctor *v.* Hodgson, 10 Exch. 824, 828.]

sity, once created, must remain the same way as long as it continues at all." "That, however, would not be itself a continuous or permanent easement, but one to be exercised from time to time while the necessity continued to occur."[1]

§ 196. Had there been unity from time immemorial, the law would clearly imply a right of way as incident to a grant, if there existed no other means of such grant taking effect; and it has, therefore, very naturally provoked the question, "Why should this anomaly of non-extinguishment be held to be law, when the same result can be obtained from the ordinary principles regulating other easements of the same class?"[2] Treating the right to a watercourse as a corporeal hereditament, or a right inherent in the land, attaching to each parcel through which the stream, in its natural course, passes; and the right to have the water run to and from each proprietor over that of all others, as a natural easement,[3] each parcel is in turn a dominant tenement and a servient tenement;[4] dominant, to secure the proprietor's own right, and servient, to secure the rights of others. If, therefore, such easement is extinguished by unity of ownership, it is *created anew* by every new division or severance of ownership; and this consequence, it is held, necessarily results from the nature of their rights.[5]

§ 197. In Cary *v.* Daniels,[6] it appeared that certain tenants in common of an ancient mill and water privilege erected, below their mill, a new dam and a smaller mill, on their own land; and while they owned both mills, it was the practice, whenever the lower dam so raised the water as to obstruct the upper mill, for a workman in the upper mill to go down, over the land, owned by the tenants in common, and open the waste-gate of the lower dam, and thus relieve the upper mill from backwater. Afterwards each of the tenants in common, by a separate deed, conveyed his undivided part of the upper mill, and the land near it to W., in these terms: "A certain parcel of land [described], together with an undivided" fractional "part of the privilege of

[1] [Parke B., in Pheysey *v.* Vicary, 16 M. & W. 496. A way of strict necessity ceases with the necessity. Viall *v.* Carpenter, 14 Gray, 126; Collins *v.* Prentice, 15 Conn. 39, 423; Pierce *v.* Selleck, 18 Conn. 321; Seeley *v.* Bishop, 19 Conn. 128.]

[2] Gale & What. on Easem. (Am. ed.) 60.

[3] See ante, § 90, et seq.

[4] See ante, § 141, et seq.

[5] Cary *v.* Daniels, 8 Met. 466.

[6] Ibid.

water creek, factory, saw-mill, dwelling-houses, and other buildings situate on the premises, and of water-wheels, main gear, and main drums connected with the said factory and saw-mill, and of all the privileges and appurtenances thereunto belonging." W. conveyed all the upper land and buildings, with all the privileges and appurtenances, to C., who was one of the tenants in common. W. and D. afterwards became the owners of the lower land, dam, and mill, and W. released all his right therein to D., who abandoned the dam, and erected another for the use of the lower mill, lower down the stream, and by means thereof, threw back the water upon the wheel of C.'s mill, whereby its movements were obstructed. In a suit by C. against D. for this obstruction, it was held, that C. took the upper dam, mill, and privileges, as they existed, and were modified and appropriated by the lower dam, when the conveyance was made to W.; and that he did not acquire a right to the unobstructed flow of the water from his mill; and that D., by removing his dam lower down the stream, exercised his rights justly and without injury to C., if he thereby made only the same appropriation of the stream that was made by his dam and mill as they stood before; but that if B. raised his new dam, higher than his old dam, he was answerable to C. for the consequences. It was argued, that if the proprietors of the lower mill ever had a right to keep up their dam to the height at which it stood at the time of the conveyance, it was an easement; that it became extinct by unity of ownership; that, consequently, when they conveyed the upper mill without reserving an easement anew for their lower mill, the easement was gone. But the Court considered that the water had been used and enjoyed at the lower dam consistently with the general rights of other riparian proprietors, and that it was not used and enjoyed as a mere easement which has been extinguished by unity of ownership, but was parcel of the estate.[1] And for the same reason, the Court held, that there was no breach of the covenant of warranty by the grantors against all incumbrances.

§ 198. Where the tenant holds by a defective title, and an easement in it by a valid title, the easement is not extinguished merely by unity of *possession*, but there must be a unity of *ownership*. In Tyler *v.* Hammond, in Massachusetts,[2] it was argued,

[1] See ante, §§ 8, 90, et seq.

[2] Tyler *v.* Hammond, 11 Pick. 193.

that by the purchase of the tenant, the right of passage merged in the fee. "Such," said the Court, "would have been the legal effect if both rights had been derived from the same title. But the tenant had the fee and the easement by different titles, the one legal and the other defective; and there was, therefore, no merger. Nor can the tortious entry of the tenant under a defective title, claiming the fee, work a forfeiture of his legal rights, nor is he estopped to assert his rights by his having set up this defective title in defence."

[§ 198 *a*. In order to extinguish an easement by the unity of title and possession, both of the dominant and servient tenements, in the same person, he should have a permanent and enduring estate, an estate in fee in both.[1] In the case of a gutter, where a party was seised in fee of the place where the eaves were, and was possessed of a term of five hundred years in another place where the easement was enjoyed, it was held, that this unity of possession did not destroy the privilege, but it was merely suspended, ready to revive upon the severance. And although the plaintiff in this case had raised a wall from whence the water fell upon the defendant's land, it was held to make no difference.[2] "Since the alteration, the drops have to fall from a greater height."[3]]

§ 199. A unity of ownership may be created by act and operation of law.[4] In 1832, the mayor and aldermen of Boston, being duly empowered, caused "Mill Creek" (which was a broad and deep watercourse flowed by the tide) to be filled up and laid out as a highway; and it was held, that the easement was taken away by act of law, and that for the disturbance or destruction of the easement, the tenant was entitled to compensation, in proportion to the injury sustained as the owner of the land.[5]

1 [Ritger *v.* Parker, 8 Cush. 145, 147. Litt. § 561; Co. Litt. 313, a, 313, b; Gale & What. on Easem. 349.]

[2 Thomas *v.* Thomas, 2 Cr., M. & R. 34.]

3 [Alderson B., in Thomas *v.* Thomas, supra, Woolrych, Waters, 295.]

4 Wright *v.* Freeman, 5 H. & John. 467.

5 Hancock *v.* Wentworth, 5 Met. 446.

CHAPTER VI.

OF THE RIGHT TO THE USE OF WATER, AS DERIVED FROM PRESCRIPTION, OR FROM PRESUMED GRANTS.

1. Foundation of Prescriptive Right.
2. Grant as Presumed by Analogy to Act of Limitations.
3. Adverse Enjoyment.
4. Right acquired commensurate with the Extent of Enjoyment.
5. The Presumption as relates to Parties not in Possession.
6. Disabilities.
7. Extinction of Presumed Water Rights.
8. Public Rights.

1. *Foundation of Prescriptive Right.*

§ 200. THE existence of the evidence, which was stated in the preceding chapter[1] to be necessary to prove an actual grant of a special right to a watercourse may be inferred from a long enjoyment without interruption.[2] The foundation of this rule is, that mankind, from the necessity and infirmity of their situation, must, for the preservation of their property and rights, have recourse to some general principle to take the place of individual and specific belief; upon which a conclusion can be formed from particular and individual knowledge.[3] The pre-

[1] See ante, 168, et seq.

[2] A man who has been in possession of a watercourse for sixty years, may bring a bill in equity against a mortgagee, who foreclosed the equity of redemption, to be quieted in his possession, although he had not established his right at law. Bush *v.* Western, Prec. Ch. 530. See Duke of Dorset *v.* Girdler, Prec. Ch. 531; Hillary *v.* Waller, 12 Ves. 261, 266. After a long enjoyment of a watercourse by the plaintiff through the land of another, it was held by the Lord Keeper, that a grant was to be presumed, unless disproved by the other side; and the plaintiff was quieted in his enjoyment by injunction. Finch *v.* Rasbridger, 2 Vern. 390; Per Bell J., in Wallace *v.* Fletcher, 30 N.H. 444–447. So in Massachusetts, in the year 1798, when the evidence was, that at the time the town of Concord was first settled, one hundred and fifty years before the action was brought, a small stream was reserved for the use of the mill there; that its natural course was through the defendant's estate, and that he had diverted and wasted the water; the Court held, that the use of the stream to the plaintiff's mill for sixty years, without interruption, established his right. Sullivan on Land Titles, 273.

[3] Hillary *v.* Waller, 12 Ves. 261, 266.

sumption is made for the purpose, and from a principle of quieting a long possession.[1]

§ 201. It is laid down in Bracton, that all incorporeal rights, or services, may be *acquired* by acquiescence and use, and *lost* by neglect and disuse.[2] Indeed all the writers upon the Common Law of England, as well as the civilians, have recognized the principle that a right to any incorporeal hereditament may be acquired by lapse of time. This mode of acquisition has been by both denominated "prescription," which they say is founded on usage *longa, continua, et pacifica.*[3] They also state, that every prescription supposes a *grant* once made, and afterwards lost;[4] and that therefore nothing can be claimed by prescription, which in its nature could not have been granted.[5] To constitute a prescription, according to the old writers on the Common Law, the enjoyment must have existed *time out of mind;* or, in other words, its commencement must be proved to have been anterior to the reign of Richard I.[6] But in order to make persons on

[1] Eldridge *v.* Knott, Cowp. 215; and see 2 Stark. on Ev. 1023; [Townsend *v.* McDonald, 2 Kernan, 381, 391; Gray J., in Edson *v.* Munsell, 10 Allen, 568; Ricard *v.* Williams, 7 Wheat. 59, 109.]

[2] Bract. lib. 4, c. xxxviii. s. 3; [Hazard *v.* Robinson, 3 Mason, 275, 276; post, § 240; Jennison *v.* Walker, 11 Gray, 423. The term prescription is in strictness applied to incorporeal hereditaments, and not to lands. Ferris *v.* Brown, 3 Barb. 105; Caldwell *v.* Copeland, 37 Penn. St. 431; Carlyon *v.* Lovering, 1 H. & N. 784.]

[3] [Per Bell J., in Wallace *v.* Fletcher, 30 N.H. 444, 449, 450.]

[4] [A right by grant may be increased by twenty years' use in another way. Wheatley *v.* Chrisman, 24 Penn. St. 298.]

[5] [Carlyon *v.* Lovering, 1 H. & N. 784; Rochdale Canal Co. *v.* Radcliffe, 18 Q.B. 287, 314; Davis *v.* Brigham, 29 Maine, 391; Hill *v.* Lord, 48 Maine, 96; Per Bell J., in Wallace *v.* Fletcher, 30 N.H. 450. In Edson *v.* Munsell, 10 Allen, 567, 568, Gray J. said, "The ground on which prescription has generally been put in Massachusetts has been the presumption of a previous grant or agreement, which has been lost by lapse of time. But a grant cannot be presumed against a person legally incapable of making it."]

[6] Bract. lib. 2, c. xxii.; 1 Bla. Com. 75; 2 ib. 263; [Per Bell J., in Wallace *v.* Fletcher, 30 N.H. 445.] By the Common Law, an enjoyment to confer a title to an easement must have continued for a period co-extensive with the memory of man; or, in legal phrase, "during time whereof the memory of man runneth not to the contrary." To this expression a definite meaning was originally attached, as comprising the period elapsed since the year 1189. Now, according to Blackstone, "time of memory," has been used and ascertained by the law to commence from the reign of Richard I., a period adopted by analogy to the stat. 3 Edw. I. c. 29, which fixed that as the date for alleging seisin in a real action. When the shorter time of *sixty* years was filed for a writ of right, and *fifty* for a possessory action, by 38 Hen. VIII., it has been said, that a similar extension of the statute was not made by Courts of Law, and that the time of prescription for incorporeal rights remained as before (1st Report of English Real Property Commissioners, p. 51). It is considered (see Gale & What. on Easem. p. 64) difficult to see upon what ground this distinction is made, as the enacting words of the two statutes are almost identical in expression,

the alert in guarding their rights, and to prevent disputes respecting privileges, that have been long and peaceably enjoyed, the Courts have not required positive testimony that the enjoyment commenced at the remote period we have mentioned, and have even held that *forty* years' enjoyment is presumptive evidence that the right has existed time out of mind, and consequently is a good prescription.[1] By the modern rule, which we shall next proceed to consider, the period has been limited to *twenty years*.

§ 202. The extreme difficulty of giving proof of enjoyment for so long a time as that established in the earlier periods of the English law, was lessened by its being held, that evidence of enjoyment during a shorter time raised a presumption that such enjoyment had existed for the necessary period.[2] In Bury *v.* Pope,[3] "it was agreed, that if two men be owners of two parcels of land adjoining, and one of them doth build a house upon his land and makes windows and lights looking into the other's lands, and his house and lights have continued for the space of thirty or forty years; yet the other may enter upon his own land and soil, and lawfully erect a house or other thing against the said lights or windows, and the other can have no action, for it was his folly to build his house so near the other's lands;" [4] and

and the latter has been considered only as an addition to the former, restricting the period of prescription to sixty years, before action brought, and making no other alteration. The traces of immemorial prescription to be found in the Roman Law are scanty, and the greater part of this doctrine, as now used in Germany, has been introduced by practice. The term *præscriptio immemorialis* (for which *præscriptio indefinata* is now often used) does not appear in the Roman Law, but was first employed by the glossators; the expressions by which it is denoted in the Corpus Juris, are: *vetustas, longævus usus, quod memoriam excedit, cujus origo memoriam excedit, contrarii memoria non extat.* Savigny (System, Vol. 4, Berlin, 1841, p. 481) speaks in favor of the technical expression, *tempus immemoriale;* but learned practitioners have, with more reason, recommended the term, *possessio immemorialis* (1 Kauff. Mack. 300, n.) Every thing sanctioned by long usage was held peculiarly sacred by the Romans; and thus they regarded an old possession as in itself lawful by virtue of its long standing. On the same foundation the modern doctrine is based; viz., on the principle that the uninterrupted exercise of a right beyond the memory of man supplies the want of a legal title, and establishes the right on the part of the possessor. Ibid. [See Wallace *v.* Fletcher, 30 N.H. 444, 445, per Bell J.]

[1] Hill *v.* Smith, 10 East, 476. See also Child *v.* Tilsed, 2 B. & B. 403. From an user of thirty-five years of a ferry, the jury may presume a grant. Trotter *v.* Harris, 2 You. & Jer. 285, Exch. 1828.

[2] Jackson *v.* Harvey, 1 Cr., M. & R. 51.

[3] Bury *v.* Pope, Cro. Eliz. 118.

[4] [The presumption of a grant from long-continued enjoyment only arises where the person against whom the right is claimed might have interrupted or prevented the exercise of the subject of the supposed grant. It was, therefore, held,

this doctrine appears to have been held down to the time of the passing of the Statute of Limitations, 21 Jac. 1, c. xvi.

2. *Grant as presumed by Analogy to Act of Limitations.*

§ 203. The rule now practised upon, is an improvement upon the former rule; because, as it limits the enjoyment to a certain and precise period, viz., to the period limited by the Statute of Limitations for entry upon lands, it leaves less room for dispute. *Certainty* is one of the grand objects of the law; and it is peculiarly important in that branch of the law which concerns the conflicting claims to a watercourse.

§ 204. That a title to any incorporeal hereditament may be supported by an uninterrupted enjoyment for the period limited by statute for the right of entry upon land, was first laid down as law in England by Mr. C. J. Wilmot, in the year 1761. The case we refer to is Lewis *v.* Price, at Nisi Prius.[1] In this case, the rule just mentioned was adopted, in analogy to the Statute of Limitations, 21 Jac. 1, c. xvi. s. 1, which enacts, that no person who has any right or title to entry upon land, shall enter, but within twenty years next after his right or title shall accrue.[2] There is no positive law, however, which says that no ejectment shall be brought, by any person who has not by himself, or by

that a grant of a right to the free and uninterrupted passage of the currents of wind and air to the plaintiff's wind-mill from over the soil of another, cannot be presumed from an uninterrupted user of the mill for twenty years. Webb *v.* Bird, 13 C.B. 841. See Chasemore *v.* Richards, 7 H.L. Cas. 349.]

[1] Lewis *v.* Price, 2 Wm's Saund. 175.

[2] ["The fiction of presuming a grant from twenty years' possession or use was invented by the English Courts in the eighteenth century to avoid the absurdities of their rule of legal memory, and was derived by analogy from the limitation prescribed by the statute of 21 Jac. I. c. 21, for actions of ejectment. It is not founded on a belief that a grant has actually been made in the particular case, but on the general presumption that a man will naturally enjoy what belongs to him, the difficulty of proof after lapse of time, and the policy of not disturbing long-continued possessions. 2 Saund. 175, note; Hillary *v.* Waller, 12 Ves. 239; Coolidge *v.* Learned, 8 Pick. 508." Per Gray J., in Edson *v.* Munsell, 10 Allen, 568. In Tracy *v.* Atherton, 36 Vt. 511, Poland C.J. said, "The general language of the books, found in innumerable cases, is that from such a possession, continued for the period of the statute, the law will presume a grant, or courts will direct juries to presume a grant. But this is purely a legal fiction. The doctrine proceeds wholly upon the ground of presuming a right after such length of possession, and not at all upon the ground that there ever was a grant made, but which has been lost; and though it may be shown ever so clearly that no grant was ever made, the case is not at all varied." The same view of the subject is taken by Wilde J., in Coolidge *v.* Learned, 8 Pick. 504.]

some other under whom he claims, been in possession of the estate for which the ejectment is brought, within twenty years; but as a person cannot enter, he of course cannot maintain an ejectment, which is founded on an entry supposed to have been made by the lessor of the plaintiff. So in an action on the case for the disturbance of an easement appurtenant to the estate, the plaintiff cannot recover if there has been an uninterrupted enjoyment of it for twenty years by another person; and as twenty years' possession of land is considered a bar to an ejectment, so the possession of an easement attached to it for the same period, is by analogy deemed evidence of right in the party possessing it. Indeed, it would seem absurd to acknowledge a right to a greater interest, as having been created by an enjoyment for any given space of time, and to deny it to a lessor, as *omne major continet in se minus.*[1] The doctrine has not only frequently been applied in subsequent cases in England to lights, but frequently also to ways and rights of common, and watercourses, and in fact to all easements and profits arising from or issuing out of land.[2]

[1] The case just referred to, of Lewis *v.* Price, was respecting the obstruction of lights. It was said by Wilmot J., that twenty years is sufficient to give a man title in ejectment, on which he may recover the house itself, and he saw no reason why it should not be sufficient to entitle him to any easement belonging to the house. In the case of Dougal *v.* Wilson, 2 Wm's Saund. 175, which also came before Wilmot, when he was Chief Justice of the Common Pleas, the defendant attempted to show, that the lights did not exist more than sixty years, which would have been sufficient to rebut the evidence of a right by prescription. But it was answered by the Chief Justice, that if a man has been in possession of a house, with lights belonging to it, for fifty or sixty years, no one can stop up those lights. Possession, he said, for such a length of time amounts to a grant of the liberty of making them, and is evidence of an agreement to make them. The possession of an estate, he continued, for so long a period as sixty years, cannot be disturbed even by a writ of right, the highest writ in the law; and as the tenant's possession of the house cannot be disturbed, it would be absurd that he should be disturbed in his lights. [It is said by Gray J., in Brooks *v.* Reynolds, 106 Mass. 32, that "it is now well settled that, by the Common Law of Massachusetts, a deed of land passes no right of light and air over other lands, without express words." And, in Randall *v.* Sanderson, 111 Mass. 119, it is said by Morton J. that it is the established law in Massachusetts that an easement of light and air cannot be acquired by prescription. Rogers *v.* Sawin, 10 Gray, 376; Carrig *v.* Dee, 14 Gray, 583; Richardson *v.* Pond, 15 Gray, 387. For cases showing the extent to which the English law respecting ancient lights has been recognized or repudiated in the American States, see 2 Chitty Pl. (16th Am. ed.) 479, 480; Powell *v.* Sims, 5 W. Va. 1.]

[2] See Darwin *v.* Upton, 2 Wm's Saund. 175 (a.); Holcroft *v.* Heel, 1 B. & P. 400; Campbell *v.* Wilson, 3 East, 294; Daniel *v.* North, 11 East, 371; Bealy *v.* Shaw, 6 East, 208; Balston *v.* Bensted, 1 Campb. 463; Barker *v.* Richardson, 4 B. & Ald. 578; Gray *v.* Bond, 2 Brod. & Bing. 667; Cross *v.* Lewis, 2 B. & C. 686; Wright *v.* Howard, 1 Sim. & Stu. 203; Drewett *v.*

§ 205. The case of Bealy *v.* Shaw[1] has been a leading case in England, on the subject of the acquisition of an adverse right to the use of a natural watercourse; and it was decided in conformity to the doctrine above laid down. It was an action on the case, wherein the plaintiff declared that he was possessed of certain lands, mills, &c., and that a stream of water used to flow out of the river Irwell through his land, and was used to work his said mills; and that the defendants injuriously widened, deepened, and enlarged certain sluices leading out of a part of the river Irwell, higher up than the commencement of the plaintiff's stream, and thereby drew off and diverted from the said river, a greater quantity of water than they had done previously, by which it was prevented from flowing to the premises of the plaintiff. The question presented to the Court was, as to the quantity of water to which the defendant was entitled, by virtue of his uninterrupted enjoyment. Lord Ellenborough C. J.: "The general rule of law, as applied to this subject, is, that independent of any particular enjoyment used to be had by another, every man has a right to have the advantage of a flow of water in his own land without diminution or alteration, but an *adverse* right *may* exist, founded on the occupation of another.[2] And although the stream be either diminished in quantity, or even corrupted in quality, as by means of the exercise of certain trades, yet if the occupation of the party so taking and using it, have existed for so long a time as may raise the presumption of a grant, the other party, whose land is below, must take the stream subject to such adverse right. I take it, that twenty years' exclusive enjoyment of the water, in any particular manner, affords a conclusive presumption of right in the party so enjoying it, derived from grant or act of Parliament." Again, in Balston *v.* Bensted,[3] the defence intended to be set up in that case was, that the plaintiff had no exclusive right to the supply of certain water to which he laid claim, inasmuch as the principle on which twenty years' running water confers a right, appeared from the cases to be, that after an adverse possession for so long

Sheard, 7 C. & P. 465, and 32 Eng. Com. Law Rep. 585; Mason *v.* Hill, 3 B. & Ad. 76, and 23 Eng. Com. Law Rep., and 5 B. & Ad. 1, and 27 Eng. Com. Law Rep. 11; and see for other English authorities, Matthews on Pres. Ev. 296-316; Gale & What. on Easem. 64, et seq. [Phinizy *v.* City Council of Augusta, 47 Geo. 260.]

[1] Bealy *v.* Shaw, 6 East, 208.

[2] [Per Denio J., in Townsend *v.* McDonald, 2 Kernan, 391.]

[3] Balston *v.* Bensted, 1 Campb. 463, and ante, § 111.

a time, a grant was to be presumed from the owners of the land farther up the stream. Such a grant could not here be presumed, as previously to the drain being made, probably no individual knew that the plaintiff's spring was fed by water percolating through the strata in the close [1] now occupied by the defendant. But Lord Ellenborough observed early in the trial, that "the only question was, whether the diminution of the supply of water to the plaintiff's bath had been caused by the drain being dug by the defendant; and that there could be no doubt, but that twenty years' exclusive enjoyment of water, in any particular manner, affords a conclusive presumption of right in the party so enjoying it." [2]

§ 206. In the absence of a special custom, it has been held, that artificial watercourses are not distinguished from natural ones; [3] and that a title may be gained by twenty years' user as well to the former as the latter.[4] The important case of Arkwright *v.* Gell [5] turned upon the right of the party receiving

[1] As to *subterranean* diversion, see ante, §§ 109–115.

[2] [Note the remarks of Wightman J., and of Lord Chelmsford, upon this observation of Lord Ellenborough, in the late case of Chasemore *v.* Richards, 7 H.L. Cas. 349; s.c. 5 H. & N. 982, 984, 988; of Cresswell J., in Chasemore *v.* Richards, 2 H. & N. 183; of Brinkerhoff J., in Frazier *v.* Brown, 12 Ohio St. 300; ante, § 111, note. See per Maule J., in Smith *v.* Kenrick, 7 M., G. & S. 546; Townsend *v.* McDonald, 2 Kernan, 381, 391; Shields *v.* Arndt, 3 Green Ch. (N.J.) 246.]

[3] [See Townsend *v.* McDonald, 2 Kernan, 381; Dunklee *v.* The Wilton R.R. Co., 24 N.H. 506; New Ipswich Factory *v.* Batchelder, 3 N.H. 190.]

[4] Magor *v.* Chadwick, 11 Ad. & El. 571; [Earl *v.* De Hart, 1 Beas. (N.J.) 280, 285; Gaved *v.* Martyn, 19 C.B. N.S. 732; Ivimey *v.* Stocker, L.R. 1 Ch. Ap. 396. A party cannot gain a right to the flow of surface water over his neighbor's land by collecting it in drains or culverts, or artificial channels, unless he maintains them for a length of time sufficient to acquire a right or easement by adverse user. Dickinson *v.* Worcester, 7 Allen, 19, 22; White *v.* Chapin, 12 Allen, 518. But if the face of the country is such that it necessarily collects in one body so large a quantity of water, after heavy rains and the melting of large bodies of snow, as to require an outlet to some common reservoir, and if such water is regularly discharged through a well-defined channel, which the force of the water has made for itself, and which is the accustomed channel through which it flows, and has flowed from time immemorial, such channel is an ancient natural watercourse. Earl *v.* De Hart, 1 Beas. (N.J.) 280, 283, 284.]

[5] Arkwright *v.* Gell, 5 M. & W. 220. See Wood *v.* Waud, 3 Exch. 748, 776, 777. It would appear from the facts of this case, that there was no "*perpetua causa*," the flow of water being of a *temporary* nature only; it also seems by no means clear, that the easement claimed would not have imposed the obligation not only "*pati aut non facere*," but also to do something positive, to continue the mining operations. If this be so, if the flow of water could not have continued in the manner desired by the plaintiff, supposing the mines to be abandoned, it is clear that the obligation thus sought to be imposed was directly opposed to the legal constitution of easements. Gale & What. on Easem. 127. See ante, § 4.

water *drained from a mine*, to compel the owners of the mine to continue such discharge; and the Court decided that in that case no such right existed. The party would only have a right to use the water in question so long as it continued there; and an user for twenty years or longer time, would afford no presumption of a grant of the right to the water in perpetuity; for such a grant would in truth be nothing more nor less than an obligation on the mine owner not to work his mines, by the ordinary mode of getting minerals, below the level drained by that sough, and to keep the mines flooded up to that level, in order to make the flow of the water constant, for the benefit of those who had used it for some profitable purpose. "How can it be supposed," said Parke B., "that the mine owners could have meant to have burdened themselves with such a servitude, so destructive to their interests; and what is there to raise an inference of such an intention? The mine owner could not bring an action against the person using the stream of water, so that the omission to bring an action could afford no argument in favor of the presumption of a grant; nor could he prevent the enjoyment of that stream of water by any act of his, except by at once making a sough at a lower level, and thus taking away the water entirely, — a course so expensive and inconvenient, that it would be very unreasonable, and a very improper extension of the principle which applies to the case of lights — to infer, from the abstinence of such an act, an intent to grant the use of the water in perpetuity, as a matter of right."[1]

[1] [Shields *v.* Arndt, 3 Green Ch. (N.J.) 234, 249; Pollock C.B., in Solomon *v.* Vintners' Co., 4 H. & N. 593; and in Wood *v.* Waud, 3 Exch. 777, 778. See Smith *v.* Miller, 11 Gray, 145, stated post, § 216, note. Where water has flowed, in an artificial and covered watercourse for more than sixty years, from a colliery into an immemorial and natural stream, upon whose banks the plaintiff's mills are situated, the plaintiff, in such case, has no right of action for diversion of the water of such artificial watercourse against a party through whose land it passes, but who does not claim under, or who is unauthorized by, the colliery owners. The case would, however, be different if the waters were polluted. Wood *v.* Waud, 3 Exch. 748. A. had been in possession of land for nearly thirty years, above which on a stream was a dam, by which the water was kept from overflowing A.'s land until it could be carried off by ditches through the same. The owner of the dam cut it through and thereby A.'s land was overflowed as it had been before the dam was constructed. In an action by A. for damages, it was held, that there was here no subject of a grant and no adverse possession by A., and therefore no easement, whose interruption would give a claim for damages. Felton *v.* Simpson, 11 Ired. (N.C.) 84. But see Middleton *v.* Gregorie, 2 Rich. 631, 638.

In Jessup *v.* Laucks, 55 Penn. St. 350,

[§ 206 *a*. In White *v*. Chapin,[1] Foster J., noticing the point stated in the preceding section said, "There is a class of English cases in which it has been held, that where an owner above on his own land has, for his own purposes, collected the water and discharged it upon the land of his neighbor below, the latter does not by length of time acquire an easement entitling him to a continuance of the supply thus created.[2] In the case of Great-

it appeared that a navigation company had a right, under their charter, to build and maintain dams for the purpose of their navigation and to sell surplus water. They granted to a predecessor of the defendants, his heirs and assigns for ever, the full use of the water not wanted for the navigation, with privilege to keep the dam in question in good order. The works fell into entire disuse, the defendants rebuilt the dam and claimed to maintain it under the grant. It was held, that the company had no power to grant the right claimed. Thompson J. said, "The grant under which the defendants claim the right to maintain the dam in its height and efficiency, as it existed when used by the company, fails in effect for two reasons. The first is, that the user by the company having ceased, and the works being abandoned, the authority of the company over them ceased with the user, and the easément acquired, reverted to the owners of the property from whom taken. Secondly, the grant itself, being of an incident connected with or arising out of the principal object in granting the charter to the company, must necessarily expire with the principal, and cease when that ceases. In the nature of things there could be no fee-simple estate in it. The grant might be perpetual if the works continued to be so, but its perpetuity would depend upon that. The company could not be compelled to keep up their works in order to furnish a surplus of water to fill the terms of the grant. This was held, in Cass *v*. Penn. R.R. Co., 51 Penn. St. 351. Such a grant, in its enjoyment, is as permanent only as the creation of which it is an incident, and necessarily as unstable; like the natural phenomenon of the shadow cast by a substance, it vanishes when the substance disappears." In Mason *v*. Shrewsbury & Hereford Railway Co., L.R. 6 Q.B. 578, it appeared that a natural watercourse, called Ashton Brook, flowing through the plaintiff's land, had been diverted for upwards of forty years by a canal company under the powers of their act, and the bed had become silted up, and was no longer adequate to carry off the flood water in its natural state. The canal was discontinued and the waters restored to their former course, and the plaintiff's land was thereby flooded and damaged. The Court held that he had no legal ground of complaint. Blackburn J. said: "He had the ordinary rights and liabilities of a riparian owner on the banks of a natural stream. He was entitled to have the water flow to him in its natural state, so far as it was a benefit, and was bound to submit to receive it so far as it was a nuisance." He held that the enjoyment *de facto* of the relief from the water for more than forty years did not give a right to the continuance of that relief, because no obligation was imposed on the canal company to continue to take the water, and that his enjoyment was not a right, but only so long as the particular purpose for which it was taken was served. Cockburn C.J. gave judgment for the defendants, on the ground that the easement of the watercourse existed for the benefit of the dominant tenement above, and could not operate to make a new right for the benefit of the servient tenement. Like any other easement, it might be discontinued if it became onerous, or ceased to be beneficial to the party entitled.]

[1] [White *v*. Chapin, 12 Allen, 516, 520.]

[2] [Arkwright *v*. Gell, 5 M. & W. 203; Wood *v*. Waud, 3 Exch. 748; Greatrex *v*. Hayward, 8 Exch. 291; Parke B., in Rawstron *v*. Taylor, 11 Exch. 378;

rex *v.* Hayward,[1] it was held, that the flow of water from an agricultural drain for twenty years did not give the adjacent proprietor below such a right to the use of the water as to preclude the owner of the upper lot from cutting off the supply to improve his own land. But these cases have been repeatedly explained. The servitude which subjects the lower land to the continued discharge of water from an artificial cut above may be created under circumstances which do not establish a correlative right to the continuance of the discharge for the benefit of the lower estate. The submission to the exercise of an easement by the owner of the dominant estate, for his own purposes and in his own way, does not necessarily give the servient owner a right to the continuance of the easement imposed, because it is attended with incidental advantages to the latter.[2] The case of Beeston

Alderson B. in Broadbent *v.* Ramsbotham, 11 Exch. 610; Solomon *v.* Vintners' Co., 4 H. & N. 593; Sampson *v.* Hoddinott, 1 C.B. N.S. 590, 606; Yale *v.* Brace, 99 Mass. 488, 492, 493.

The right to artificial watercourses, as against the party creating them, depends upon the character of the watercourse, whether it be of a permanent or temporary nature, and upon the circumstances under which it is created. The flow of water for twenty years from the eaves of a house could not give a right to the neighbor to insist that the house should not be pulled down, or altered so as to diminish the quantity of water flowing from the roof. The flow of water from a drain, for the purposes of agricultural improvements, for twenty years, could not give a right to the neighbor so as to preclude the proprietor from altering the level of his drains for the greater improvement of the land. The state of circumstances in such cases shows that the one party never intended to give, nor the other to enjoy, the use of the stream as a matter of right. Per cur. Wood *v.* Waud, 3 Exch. 779. If a farmer, by some system of drainage, draws off the rain-fall from his lands, and pours it into the plaintiff's ditch, and so creates a new and artificial supply of water, and the latter uses the water for more than twenty years, and after that the farmer adopts a new mode of drainage, and in so doing cuts off the artificial supply of water, the plaintiff has no remedy for the loss of the water, the supply being of a temporary character, and the circumstances showing that the one party never intended to give, nor the other to enjoy, the use of the artificial drainage-water as a matter of right. Greatrex *v.* Hayward, 8 Exch. 291; Bawstron *v.* Taylor, 11 Exch. 369. In cases of this sort no right is acquired as against the owner of the property from which the course of water takes its origin, though as between the first and any subsequent appropriation of the watercourse itself such a right may be acquired. Arkwright *v.* Gell, 5 M. & W. 232; Addison, Wrongs &c., 44, 45.]

[1] [8 Exch. 291.]

[2] [Magor *v.* Chadwick, 11 Ad. & El. 571; North-eastern Railway *v.* Elliot, 1 John. & Hem. 154; Beeston *v.* Weate, 5 El. & Bl. 986. And in Yale *v.* Brace, 99 Mass. 488, it was held, that if the use of the water of a stream, in its natural flow, would be of no value to the owner of a mill situated between the reservoir and the mill of another who has a prescriptive right to draw from the reservoir, for the purpose of working his mill, more or less than such natural flow at his plea ure, the former is not entitled to relief in equity against the latter for making a different use of the water, by raising and tightening his dam and by different machinery at his mill, from that which he made while gaining his prescriptive right. In this case Hoar J. said,

v. Weate[1] recognizes the principle as we have now stated it. And we are aware of no authority, English or American, which gainsays the doctrine that the upper proprietor, by use for a sufficient time, may acquire the right to keep open an ancient agricultural ditch through land below for the purpose of draining his own premises." That there may be a prescriptive easement to enjoy the run of water from the dominant estate through the servient by such an artificial ditch, drain, or watercourse, is well settled in Massachusetts. In relation to a raceway conducting off the water from a mill, Mr. Chief-Justice Shaw said, "It must be taken, according to established rules of the law, that the run of such a canal through the land of another for the time stated is evidence of an antecedent grant."[2] And in another case: "It is immaterial whether the watercourse be natural or artificial."[3] The same doctrine has been applied to an ancient watercourse leading from the meadow of one party through the land of another, in which the water from the meadow, and the rain which fell upon the same, had been wont to run, thereby draining the meadow land, and rendering it arable and of great value.[4] In the recent case of Smith *v.* Miller,[5] where such a right of drainage was claimed, but in the facts as found by the

"The question is raised whether the fact that the defendant by raising and tightening his dam, and putting different machinery into his mill, makes a different use of the water from that which he made while he was gaining his prescriptive right, gives the plaintiff any right to have the flow of the water from the reservoir regulated for his benefit. The acquisition of the prescriptive right to use the reservoir by the defendant certainly gave the plaintiff no right to it. The plaintiff might use it or not at his pleasure." "He is not injured by being deprived of it and is not therefore entitled to any equitable relief. His real ground of complaint is that the defendant does not use the prescriptive right to his advantage, which he is not bound to do. He may omit to exercise it entirely."

[1] [Beeston *v.* Weate, 5 El. & Bl. 986. This case is an instance of a right acquired by the owners of the dominant tenement to go from time to time upon the servient tenement, for the purpose of diverting the water of a natural stream flowing along it, so as to cause it to pass through that tenement by an artificial cut to the dominant tenement, for the purpose of supplying cattle with water. The right claimed was not to a continual flow of the water, and in that respect the case differs from the ordinary one of the owner of a mill not upon the bank of a river, who has acquired by user the right to divert the river to his mill by an artificial cut through a neighbor's land. The use of artificial aids, as mill leats &c., by a riparian owner, does not in any way affect his natural right to the use of the water, if the rights of the other proprietors are not infringed thereby, he may employ such means as he thinks proper.]

[2] [Prescott *v.* White, 21 Pick. 342.]

[3] [Cary *v.* Daniels, 5 Met. 238; Crittenton *v.* Alger, 11 Met. 281.]

[4] [Ashley *v.* Ashley, 6 Cush. 70; s.c. 4 Gray, 197.]

[5] [Smith *v.* Miller, 11 Gray, 145.]

verdict of a jury was decided not to exist, because the use had not been adverse, but permissive and in accordance with the original agreement of the parties, the Court said, "A right to an easement of that kind in the land of another may undoubtedly be acquired by the actual enjoyment of it, provided that the enjoyment is adverse, uninterrupted, and of sufficient continuance and duration."[1]]

§ 207. In Bealy *v.* Shaw,[2] Lord Ellenborough, in giving his opinion, observes, that less than twenty years' enjoyment of the water of a watercourse, may or may not afford a conclusive presumption of right. It is very certain, that an adverse possession for less than twenty years requires *some other* proof in support of the right;[3] but although in general a grant cannot be presumed less than twenty years, yet *a license* may. Thus, an inclosure made from the waste twelve or thirteen years before, and seen by the steward of the same lord from time to time, without objection made, may be presumed by the jury to have been made by the license of the lord; and hence, ejectment cannot be brought against him as a trespasser, without previous notice to throw it up.[4]

§ 208. The doctrine that easements of every sort may be acquired by an adverse user, for the period of time limited by the Statute of Limitations for the right of entry upon land, has been adopted and been very frequently applied by the Courts of the United States.[5] In Ricard *v.* Williams, in the Supreme Court of

1 [Where a riparian proprietor, below a mill upon the stream, changed the flow of the stream into an artificial channel, and it continued to flow there without interruption for fifty years, it was held that the mill-owner had thereby acquired a right to have the channel kept open for the flow of water from his mill. Delaney *v.* Boston, 2 Harr. (Del.) 489.]

2 Bealy *v.* Shaw, 6 East, 215.

3 Rex *v.* Wardroper, 4 Burr. 2024; and see 4 Esp. 69; Ricard *v.* Williams, 7 Wheat. 59. In Haight *v.* Morris Aqueduct, 4 Wash. C.C. 607, it seemed to be considered by the Court, that an enjoyment short of twenty years, under particular circumstances, may create the presumption of a grant.

4 Doe d. Foley *v.* Wilson, 11 East, 56; and see post, Chap. VIII.

5 [The Statute of Limitations does not extend to incorporeal rights, but it has now become universally settled that an uninterrupted use of a way or other easement, under a claim of right, for the period of time fixed by the statute as a bar to the recovery of lands held adversely, gives the person so using it a full and absolute right to such easement, as much as if granted to him. This has been settled by a long course of judicial decisions, and is founded primarily on the ancient doctrine of prescriptions, but has finally by the Court been made to conform, by analogy, to the Statute of Limitations applicable to lands, in all substantial particulars, so far as the difference in the subjects will allow. Per Poland C.J., in Tracy *v* Atherton, 36 Vt. 510, 511; Barnes *v.* Haynes, 13 Gray, 188; Blake *v.* Everett, 1 Allen, 248; Pillsbury *v.* Moore, 44 Maine, 154.]

the United States,[1] that Court declared, that it was the policy of Courts of Law to limit the presumption of grants to periods analogous to those of the Statutes of Limitation, in cases where such statutes did not directly apply; and that there was no difference in the doctrine, whether the grant relates to corporeal or incorporeal hereditaments. Where the right to a ferry was in question, the Court just mentioned considered, that the complainants had so long slept upon their rights, that they were without remedy, whether they knew of an adverse possession, or through negligence, and a failure to look after their interests, permitted the title of another to grow into maturity.[2] In Hill *v.* Crosby, in Massachusetts,[3] the controversy was respecting a *right of way*, the action being for a disturbance of a way over a river, by throwing down the abutment of a bridge which the plaintiff had rebuilt. The counsel for the defendant admitted, that, in England, a grant might be presumed from an adverse enjoyment of twenty years unexplained; but they contended, that, the principle was inapplicable in Massachusetts, in consequence of the statute of 1783, which requires a conveyance of any interest in land to be by deed, and to be recorded; and that the statute of 1786, which provides for laying out private ways, and making them matters of record, negatived the principle, that twenty years' enjoyment shall afford a presumption of a grant. C.J. Parsons, after remarking, that in point of law the facts did not show a title to the way in the plaintiff, observed, "The continued use of the way and bridge by the plaintiff's father and himself, for more than twenty years, the keeping up and repairing the bridge, and the passing the river in the same place in a boat when the bridge was down, show a *continuity of possession* sufficient to warrant the presumption of a grant; and we have no doubt, a right to an easement may be so proved in this country, as well as in England."[4] — "It is a general and highly salutary

[1] Ricard *v.* Williams, 7 Wheat. 59.

[2] Bowman *v.* Wather, 1 How. (U.S.) 189.

[3] Hill *v.* Crosby, 1 Pick. 466.

[4] The question arose in Coolidge *v.* Learned, in Massachusetts, *as to the length of time requisite to create a prescriptive right* to a parcel of land for a landing-place adjoining Charles River. This question was fully considered by Wilde J., who delivered the opinion of the Court. He considered it extraordinary that the time of legal prescription should continue to be reckoned from so distant a period as the reign of Richard I., and it seemed, he said, to the Court, that, for all practical purposes, it might as well be reckoned from the creation. The limitation was founded on the equitable construction of the statute West. 13 Edw. I., c. 39, which

rule of law," says Mr. C.J. Shaw, in a much later case in Massachusetts, "that a right or easement which may be acquired

provided, that no writ of right should be maintained except as a seisin from the time of Richard I. When the limitation of a writ of right was reduced by the statute 32 Hen. VIII., c. 2, to sixty years, a similar reduction should have been made in the limitation of the time of legal memory. This was required not only by public policy, to quiet long-continued possessions, but by a regard to consistency, as it would have been following up the principle upon which the first limitation was founded. No solid and satisfactory reason appeared, why the opinion of Rolle (2 Abr. 269), that an undisturbed enjoyment of an easement for a period of time sufficient to give a title to land by possession, was not adopted by the Courts. But it did appear, that the principle on which his opinion was founded was respected and carried into operation in another form; for although the Courts continued to adhere to the limitation before adopted, yet the long enjoyment of an easement was held to be a sufficient reason, not only to authorize but to require a jury to presume a grant. In the one case, the grant is presumed by the Court, or rather is presumed by the law, and in the other case, it is presumed by the jury under the direction of the Court. As Starkie remarks, "it seems to be very difficult to say, why such presumptions should not at once have been established as mere presumption of law, to be applied to the facts, without the aid of a jury." Coolidge *v.* Learned, 8 Pick. 504. The views of the Court in this case are sanctioned in the subsequent case of Melvin *v.* Whiting, 10 Pick. 297. See ante, § 201, n. 4. [In Wallace *v.* Fletcher, 30 N.H. 446, Bell J., remarking on this subject, said, "The natural, and, indeed, necessary consequence of a rule so absurd (as that of extending the time of prescription back to the reign of Richard I.) and one necessarily productive of so unjust consequences, was that the Courts were driven to evade it by refinements and fictions. It seems by the case of Guernsey *v.* Rodbridge, Gil. Eq. Cas. 4, s.c. 2 Vern. 390, under the name of Finch *v.* Rosbridger, in 1707, that the Court of Chancery first adopted the principle of presuming the former existence and loss of a deed, where a long and uninterrupted possession of an easement was shown. It was not until 1761, that this principle was adopted in the Courts of Common Law in England. Some of the Judges then were, at times, inclined to give to this presumption the effect of a *presumptio juris et de jure*, a legal presumption binding on both Courts and juries, as a rule from which neither had a right to depart, — a presumption of a right constituting a perfect title or bar, as the case might be." — "But the current of English decisions has gone no farther than to hold that long-continued and uninterrupted possession is evidence from which a jury may presume a deed." — "The instruction given to the jury that such proof is competent evidence, from which they may infer the existence and loss of a deed, is understood to be accompanied by a recommendation so to find the fact, whatever may be their individual impressions of its truth, and it seems that verdicts rendered in conflict with such recommendations would be set aside. Bealy *v.* Shaw, 6 East, 214, per Lord Ellenborough C.J.; Bright *v.* Walker, 1 Cr., M. & R. 217, per Parke B.; Jackson *v.* Harvey, 1 Cr., M. & R. 894, per Alderson B. Many cases, in this country, have followed in the track of the English decisions, though it is apparent, that in a newly settled country like ours, where, to a great extent, every thing is of recent date, and the history of our towns, of our roads, farms, mills, and dwellings are known, a rule like that adopted in England is in no respect adapted to our situation. On other subjects, the Common Law has been everywhere modified, to adapt it to the wants of our community. The English decisions on this subject have been but modes of evading the effect of early decisions of their Courts, which have been found inconsistent with the principles of justice, and it is clearly as much within the legitimate sphere and customary action of the Courts to disregard or to overrule such decisions, as it can be to evade them by nice presump-

by grant, may be acquired by long-continued peaceable use and enjoyment, without contest or claim on the part of those who would have an interest in denying or contesting it."[1]

§ 209. The enjoyment and exercise must be adverse in the exact sense that the possession of the land must be so, to warrant the application of the Statute of Limitations, in an action of ejectment.[2] Most of the statutes of limitations in the United States, like the English statute of James I., c. 16, prescribe the period of twenty years for the right of entry upon land held adversely;[3] in Connecticut and Vermont, *fifteen* years;[4] and in

tions, either of fact or of law. It was the wise course, prescribed by principle as well as by public convenience, to overrule the absurd decisions which sanctioned a fixed point in the early history of England, as the limit of legal memory, and at the same time to restore the principle upon which that decision appears to be made, that in cases where the legislature have not fixed a precise rule of limitation, rights shall be acquired and barred by a prescription of such length of time as has been fixed by the legislature as the proper limitation in analogous cases. Ricard *v.* Williams, 7 Wheat. 110; Hunt *v.* Hunt, 3 Met. 185."

And in a late case in Massachusetts, — Edson *v.* Munsell, 10 Allen, 557, 565, — Gray J. said, "The reasons indicated by Bracton, and which controlled the English Courts in the construction of the statute of West. I., and our own in the construction of the statutes of 1786 and 1807, are sufficient to show that since writs of right have been abolished, and writs of entry substituted as the proper form of action to recover the freehold, the limitation of writs of entry should be held the legal limit of prescription of incorporeal rights. And the period of twenty years has been assumed and declared by this Court to be the term of prescription in many recent cases. Ashley *v.* Ashley, 4 Gray, 200; Lawrence *v.* Fairhaven, 5 Gray, 114; Sibley *v.* Ellis, 11 Gray, 417; Currier *v.* Gale, 3 Allen, 330; Leonard *v.* Leonard, 7 Allen, 277."]

[1] Williams *v.* Nelson, 23 Pick. 141; [Bigelow C.J., in Brace *v.* Yale, 10 Allen, 443. For cases showing the effect of contest, denial, or claim on the part of those against whom the easement is claimed, see post, § 215, note.]

[2] Colvin *v.* Burnet, 17 Wend. 562; Hart *v.* Vose, 19 Wend. 365; Dyer *v.* Depui, 5 Wharton, 584.

[3] [So it is in South Carolina, Cuthbert *v.* Lawton, 3 M'Cord, 194; in New Jersey, Campbell *v.* Smith, 3 Halst. 140; in North Carolina, Felton *v.* Simpson, 11 Iredell, 84; Griffin *v.* Foster, 8 Jones (Law), 339; Powell *v.* Lash, 64 N. Car. 456; in Kentucky, Manier *v.* Myers, 4 B. Mon. 514; in Maine, Pierre *v.* Fernald, 26 Maine, 436; in Massachusetts, Sargent *v.* Ballard, 9 Pick. 251; in New York, Parker *v.* Foote, 19 Wend. 309; Miller *v.* Garlock, 8 Barb. 153.] In South Carolina the law on the subject of *prescription* does not seem to take from the Act of Limitations of 1712, for in Sims *v.* Davis, 1 Cheves' Law & Eq. 2, it was assumed as settled law that *twenty* years' enjoyment of a way over another's land, was presumptive evidence of right. In Louisiana, the time of prescription varies according to the subject, from three to thirty years. (Civil Code of La. 3435–3476.) In that State, the right *of drip* is acquired by prescription on an enjoyment of *ten* years without complaint. Vincent *v.* Michel, 7 La. 52.

[4] Ingraham *v.* Hutchinson, 2 Conn. 584; Mitchell *v.* Walker, 2 Aik. (Vt.) 266; Rogers *v.* Page, Brayt. (Vt.) 169; Norton *v.* Valentine, 14 Vt. 239; Rogers *v.* Bancroft, 20 Vt. 250; Parker *v.* Hotchkiss, 25 Conn. 321; Perrin *v.* Garfield, 37 Vt. 308, 309. In Texas it is two years, Haas *v.* Choussard, 17 Texas, 588; so in Louisiana, Delahoussaye *v.* Judice, 13 La. An. 587. In California, it is five years. Campbell *v.* West, 44 Cal. 646.

Pennsylvania *twenty-one* years.[1] Yet, although the periods of limitation be different in different countries or States, as the statutes are drawn with slight variations of phrase, and all being *in pari materia*, the object and intention being the same, they require a uniform construction.[2] The mere change in phraseology in an act of limitations before in force, in a revision of it, will work no alteration in the law previously declared; unless it indisputably appears that such was the intention of the legislature.[3] It is certain, that whatever may be the period of time which the Act of Limitations may prescribe for enforcing a right of entry upon land, an adverse enjoyment of a watercourse, in any particular manner, will, in this country, be presumptive evidence of a grant. For example, the exclusive use of water flowing through an aqueduct by the owners and occupants of a house, for the term of *twenty* years, furnishes, in New Hampshire, evidence of a grant from the owner of the land through which it is brought, of a right to have it flow in the manner it has been accustomed to flow during that time;[4] and in Pennsylvania, no shorter space of time than *twenty-one* years (and that is sufficient) will create a right in one riparian proprietor to the privilege of abutting his dam upon the land of another.[5]

3. *Adverse Enjoyment.*

§ 210. It appears, that, in order to raise the presumption of a grant of an easement in a watercourse, the user or enjoyment must have been *adverse*.[6] The doctrine of the Common Law,

[1] Cooper *v.* Smith, 9 S. & Rawle, 26.

[2] Murray *v.* E. India Co., 5 B. & Ald. 204.

[3] Taylor *v.* Delancey, 2 Caines Ca. in Err. 143; Yates' case, 4 John. 359; Brown (matter of), 21 Wend. 316; Theriat *v.* Hart, 2 Hill, 380.

[4] Watkins *v.* Peck, 13 N.H. 360. [In subsequent cases in New Hampshire it has been held that an adverse, exclusive, and uninterrupted enjoyment for twenty years of an incorporeal hereditament, affords a conclusive presumption of a grant, or right, as the case may be, which is to be applied as a *presumptio juris et de jure*, wherever by possibility a right can be acquired in any manner known to the law. The enjoyment, to have this effect, must be under a claim of right, with the knowledge and acquiescence of the owner, and uninterrupted. Wallace *v.* Fletcher, 30 N.H. 434; Burnham *v.* Kempton, 44 N.H. 88; Bow *v.* Allenstown, 34 N.H. 374; Winnipiseogee Lake Co. *v.* Young, 40 N.H. 433. The presumption of title, or of grant, as the case may be, except so far as time is concerned, is in the nature of a prescription, and is so recognized. Watkins *v.* Peck, 13 N.H. 377; Wallace *v.* Fletcher, 30 N.H. 450.]

[5] Beidelman *v.* Foulke, 5 Watts, 308.

[6] [Trask *v.* Ford, 39 Maine, 437. "The general rule is that the enjoyment of an easement of this character is presumed to be adverse, unless something appears to rebut that presumption. This is the general

as cited by Lord Coke from Bracton, exactly agrees with the Civil Law, which expressed the essential qualities of the user by the clear and concise rule, that it should be "*nec vi, nec clam, nec precario*"[1] — the possession must be peaceable, open, and as of right. When it is said, that the possession must be *long*, it is during the time required by law; when it is said it must be *continuous*, it is meant that it must be uninterrupted by any lawful impediment.[2]

§ 211. As it respects the *pacific* and *uninterrupted* character of the enjoyment or user by the Civil Law, any enjoyment or user was deemed *forcible* to which opposition was offered either by word or deed, by the owner of the servient tenement.[3] Any acts of interruption or opposition, from which a jury might infer that the enjoyment was not rightful, were, at Common Law, sufficient to defeat the effect of the enjoyment; the question being, whether, under all the facts of the case, such enjoyment had been under a concession of right.[4] The principle on which

rule, where there is no express evidence that the user was accompanied by a claim of right, and no express evidence of a disclaimer of the right by the party enjoying the easement. There are some cases where the user is of such a character, and the circumstances attending it are such, as to show that it was a mere privilege enjoyed by leave of the proprietor of the servient tenement, express or implied, and not adverse. These cases are exceptions to the general rule, and peculiar in their character. The fact that the party claiming the easement incurred the expense of erecting a mill, which would be almost worthless without the easement claimed, tends strongly to show that he either had or claimed the right to the easement, or intended to enjoy it in defiance of the owner of the servient tenement." Per Peck J., in Perrin *v.* Garfield, 37 Vt. 310; post, § 221, note. See Brace *v.* Yale, 10 Allen, 441.]

[1] Co. Litt. 113, b; Bracton, lib. 2, f. 51; Co. Litt. 1 ff. de serv. lib. 10, ff. si serv. vind.; Gale & What. on Easem. 83; Wood *v.* Kelley, 30 Maine, 47. In Massachusetts, the term of twenty years is *tempus longum*. Sargent *v.* Ballard, 9 Pick. 251.

[2] Gale & What. on Easem. 84.

[3] Lib. 1, §§ 5, 6, ff. quod vi aut clam; [White *v.* Chapin, 12 Allen, 519; Smith *v.* Miller, 11 Gray, 145; Pollard *v.* Barnes, 2 Cush. 191; Monmouth Canal Co. *v.* Harford, 1 Cr., M. & R. 614. The enjoyment should be exclusive. Davis *v.* Brigham, 29 Maine, 391, 403; Kilburn *v.* Adams, 7 Met. 33; Nash *v.* Peden, 1 Speers, 22.]

[4] See Ang. on Lim. Chap. XXX. §§ 10, 11; [Perrin *v.* Garfield, 37 Vt. 308, 309, per Peck J. An easement in the land of another can be acquired by adverse user only with the acquiescence of the owner of the land in such user under a claim of right, *per patientiam veri domini, qui scivit et non prohibuit, sed permisit de consensu tacito*. Bract. lib. 2, c. 23, § 1; 2 Greenl. Ev. § 539; Sargent *v.* Ballard, 9 Pick. 254; Arnold *v.* Stevens, 24 Pick. 112. From such use of an easement for twenty years, the law will presume a non-appearing grant. But before the lapse of that period, if the owner of land, by a verbal act on the premises in which the easement is claimed, resists the exercise of the right, and denies its existence, the presumption of a grant is rebutted, his acquiescence in the right claimed is disproved, and the essential elements of a title to an easement by adverse use are

the Statute of Limitations is predicated, is, that when an action of ejectment is not brought until after the time limited has expired, it is incumbent on the lessor of the plaintiff to prove an *actual entry*, accompanied with an intention of making claim (*animo clamandi*) within such time; that is, there must be an entry upon the land in question; and if by force or fraud the party is prevented from making such entry upon the land in question, his intent to do so, declared as near the land as possible, is equivalent to an actual entry. The entry must, at all events, be such as to *challenge the right* of the occupant, and such as to amount to unequivocal evidence of an intent to resume possession. The application of this general doctrine to the enjoyment of easements in watercourses, it is presumed, will not be questioned; but still, there may be occasional interruptions of such enjoyment, which under peculiar circumstances, will not be conclusive of a superior right to control and limit the entire use of the water, to suspend it at pleasure, or destroy it at discretion.[1] If the interruption is occasioned by the excessive dryness of seasons, or from some other cause over which the plaintiff has no control, it cannot be held that his right is by such means lost.[2] [So where the easement claimed is a right to flow land, and it appears that during the twenty years of enjoyment claimed, a suspension of the flowing has been rendered necessary for the purpose of making repairs upon the dam which caused the flowing, this has been held not to be such an interruption of the use and enjoyment as to prevent the acquisition of the right.[3] Shepley C.J. said, "When land is not flowed, because the dam occasioning it must be repaired or rebuilt that it may be useful, the very act of rebuilding or repairing, is the exhibition of an intention to maintain and to resume the exercise of the former use of it."[4] In Winnipiseogee Lake Company *v.* Young,[5] which was a bill in equity to protect an easement of flowing land, Bell C.J. said, "It is said the bill does not allege any certain height at which the water was kept

shown not to exist. Per Bigelow J., in Powell *v.* Bagg, 8 Gray, 443; post, § 215, note. The title to an easement by adverse use rests chiefly on the acquiescence of the owner of the land in such use, and evidence which disproves the acquiescence, rebuts the title to the easement. Powell *v.* Bagg, 8 Gray, 443. See the remarks of Poland C.J. upon this case, in Tracy *v.* Atherton, 36 Vt. 503, 514, 515.]

[1] Tyler *v.* Wilkinson, 4 Mason, 397.

[2] Hall *v.* Swift, 6 Scott, 167.

[3] [Wood *v.* Kelley, 30 Maine, 47. See Gerenger *v.* Summers, 2 Ired. (N.C.) 229.]

[4] [Wood *v.* Kelley, 30 Maine, 47.]

[5] [Winnipiseogee Lake Co. *v.* Young, 40 N.H. 420, 436.]

up at any time. It is not, perhaps, necessary to state such a fact. The water may be liable to great fluctuations, and if in substance it is alleged that it was kept up as high as their dam would raise it, when there was water, its being drawn by the plaintiffs for their own purposes would not prevent their acquiring a right to the extent of their claim. There is an easement of drawing water from a well. In the nature of things there cannot ordinarily be any continuous use of such an easement; but if it appeared that a party had claimed the right of drawing water, at all times, at his pleasure, and had exercised the right of drawing, as he had occasion, for twenty years, that would establish his right. Rights of way, and some other easements, are not continuously exercised; but the right is acquired by an uninterrupted use of the right at all times, at the pleasure or convenience of the party claiming the right. On the same principle, if the plaintiffs claimed the right to keep the water in their dam at its full height, whenever they chose, and had water to fill it, and exercised that right for twenty years, agreeably to their claim, it would be conclusive that they possessed the right." [1]]

§ 212. It has been held by Mr. J. Story, that, "the nature, object, and value of the use are very material ingredients to explain and qualify the effect of such interruptions. It is not, for instance, to be presumed that valuable mills will be erected to be fed by an artificial canal from a river, and the stream be indispensable for the support of such mills, and yet that the right to the stream is so completely lodged in another, that it may be cut off, or diminished, or suspended at pleasure; but, if there should not be water enough for the progressive wants of all, the riparian proprietor should reserve to himself the power of future appropriation for his own exclusive use. In such cases, reasonable presumption must be made from acts in their own nature somewhat equivocal and susceptible of different interpretations. The interruptions may arise from resistance to an attempt by the canal owner to extend the reach of his dam further into the river for the purpose of appropriating more water, or from a desire to prevent undue waste, in dry seasons, to the injury of the riparian

[1] [See Carr *v.* Foster, 3 Q.B. 581; Lane *v.* Carpenter, 6 Exch. 825; Winship *v.* Hudspeth, 10 Exch. 5; Esling *v.* Williams, 10 Penn. St. 126; Ingraham *v.* Hough, 1 Jones (N.C.) 39; Battishill *v.* Reed, 18 C.B. 696; Bodfish *v.* Bodfish, 105 Mass. 317; Norway Plains Co. *v.* Bradley, 52 N.H. 103.]

proprietor. But the presumption of an absolute and controlling power over the whole flow, a continuing power of exclusive appropriation from time to time, in the riparian proprietor, as his wants or will may influence his choice, would require the most irresistible facts to support it. Men who build mills, and invest valuable capital in them, cannot be presumed, without the most conclusive evidence, to give their deliberate assent to the acceptance of such ruinous conditions."[1]

§ 213. Where the enjoyment has been under *permission asked* from time to time, this, upon each occasion, amounts to an admission that the asker had then no right.[2] The very mode, indeed, in which this enjoyment, under constantly renewed permission, operates in defeating the previous user, is, that it breaks the continuity of the enjoyment;[3] and it is expressly laid down, that the breaking the continuity is inconsistent with the enjoyment during the period of twenty years, and that, for that very reason, evidence of the breaking of such continuity is admissible on the traverse of the enjoyment.[4] [But where a right has been acquired by adverse enjoyment, it will not be defeated by asking for and obtaining a license for a continued use from the owner of the servient tenement; but this would be evidence tending to prove that the previous user was not adverse, or under a claim of right.[5]]

§ 214. In Sargent *v.* Ballard, in Massachusetts,[6] the plaintiffs claimed a right of *dockage* upon the land of the defendant. It was claimed by what the civilians call a prædial service, due from the estate of the defendant to the estate of the plaintiffs, which is analogous to the right of watering cattle, conducting water, &c.[7] It appeared that a former owner of the land had enjoyed

[1] [Tyler *v.* Wilkinson, 4 Mason, 397. See per Peck J., in Perrin *v.* Garfield, 37 Vt. 310.]

[2] [See Brace *v.* Yale, 10 Allen, 444; Watkins *v.* Peck, 13 N.H. 360; White *v.* Chapin, 12 Allen, 521, 522; Bachelder *v.* Wakefield, 8 Cush. 243; Howard *v.* O'Neill, 2 Allen, 210; Kilburn *v.* Adams, 7 Met. 33; Polly *v.* M'Call, 37 Ala. 20; Pierce *v.* Cloud, 42 Penn. St. 118.]

[3] Gale & What. on Easem. 68, citing 1 Cr., M. & R. 614.

[4] Tickle *v.* Brown, 4 Ad. & El. 383; Beasley *v.* Clark, 2 Bing. N.C. 705; Sargent *v.* Ballard, 9 Pick. 251.

[5] [Perrin *v.* Garfield, 37 Vt. 304; Watkins *v.* Peck, 13 N.H. 360. So in Tracy *v.* Atherton, 36 Vt. 503, it was held, that a right of way, having become established by adverse use, will not be divested by an application for, and obtaining of, a license to use it from the other party. But it would be strong evidence that the previous use had not been under a claim of right.]

[6] 9 Pick. 251.

[7] See ante, §§ 141–144.

the easement in question for less than twenty years, when the land to which it was attached was *confiscated* by the government. The cause was tried before Parker C.J., who instructed the jury, that the plaintiffs, in order to establish their claim to the right they set up, as an easement, it was not requisite for them to produce a deed, or to prove that one ever existed; the rule being, that twenty years' occupation alone is sufficient ground of presumption that the occupation began in virtue of a compact between the parties; but this rule was to be applied only in cases where all the legal qualities of such right are proved to exist.[1] One of these legal qualities, said the learned judge, is, "that the occupation must be *uninterrupted* by the owner of the land." Upon a motion for a new trial, one of the reasons for which was, that the instructions to the jury were erroneous, Putnam J., who delivered the opinion of the court, said, "The Chief Justice instructed the jury, that the plaintiffs could not join the period of the occupation of Governor Hutchinson, before the Revolution, to their own subsequent occupation, because the occupation was interrupted from 1774 to 1780. The objection to this part of the charge has been involved in the consideration of the other. For if it is an essential fact, that the use should be *continued* as well as peaceable for twenty years, the time of the interruption from 1774 to 1780 could not be counted to make out the requisite time of twenty years. Such an interruption would be what the civilians call a usurpation;[2] which is a discontinuance given to prescription, in point of time and possession, 'for upon a commencement of usurpation, prescription is destroyed or annihilated, and must begin again;' which usurpation may be by 'an extrajudicial denunciation or claim of right,' and especially 'by a contestation of suit.' But the time which an ancestor possessed may be extended and allowed to his heirs; and the same rule applies to buyers and sellers, and to devisors and devisees. '*Inter venditorem quoque et emptorem conjungi tempora.*'[3] All that would be

[1] [See Doe *v.* Butler, 3 Wend. 149, 153.]

[2] Ayl. Civ. Law, 321, 324.

[3] Inst. Just. lib. 2, tit. 6, § 8; [Leonard *v.* Leonard, 7 Allen, 277; Kent *v.* Waite, 10 Pick. 138; Hill *v.* Crosby, 2 Pick. 466; Williams *v.* Nelson, 23 Pick. 142; Sawyer *v.* Kendall, 10 Cush. 241. But if there be no such relation or priority between different parties exercising the adverse use or enjoyment for twenty years, no right or easement will be acquired thereby. Sargent *v.* Ballard, 9 Pick. 251; Melvin *v.* Whiting, 13 Pick. 184; M'Farlin *v.* Essex Co., 10 Cush. 304; Okeson *v.* Patterson, 29 Penn. St. 22; Sawyer *v.* Kendall, 10 Cush. 244, 245. Thus in Benson *v.* Soule, 32 Maine, 39, it was held, that

required by the possessor would be, evidence that the possession had been legally continued from one owner to another.[1] It was therefore a correct instruction which was given by the Chief Justice, that the plaintiffs could not *lap on* Governor Hutchinson's time to Parsons's, because of the interruption from 1774 to 1780. But the plaintiffs might avail themselves of the continued possession of their ancestors as well as of their own. And if Governor Hutchinson acquired the right before he went away in 1774, it would have passed with the estate in virtue of the confiscation and the deed of the Commonwealth to Sargent and Parsons."

[§ 214 *a*. So where a plaintiff claimed an easement in land adjoining his mill, on the ground that from the year 1822 to the year 1846, the premises had been used by him as a part of his mill-yard, for the purpose of laying logs, lumber, and boards thereon; and evidence was introduced, on the part of the defendant, tending to show that from the year 1829 to the year 1834, both inclusive, no such use had been made of the premises; it was held, that the omission, if proved, would be such an interruption of the use as would prevent the plaintiff from acquiring a title to the easement by prescription; notwithstanding that the premises had remained unoccupied, during the whole period from 1822 to 1846, except by the plaintiff; that no notice had been given to him to cease occupying; and that no act had been done during that period, by the owner of the land, indicating an intention to interrupt or disturb the plaintiff in his use of the premises.[2] Wilde J. said, "The evidence tended to prove a total cessation of the enjoyment of the easement, and that for a long time; and the owner had good reason to believe, that the claim was abandoned; and, if so, it seems immaterial whether the plaintiff had in fact abandoned his claim or not."—"Whatever breaks the continuity of the possession and enjoyment of an easement, whether by a cessation to enjoy it, or by any act of the owner of the servient tenement, destroys altogether the effect of the previous user."—"And we are all of opinion, both upon principle

although a dam may have flowed land more than twenty years, a prescriptive right is not established unless the adverse enjoyment has been had by the same person all the time, or by different persons having the relation of grantor and grantee, devisor and devisee, or ancestor and heir. See Winship *v.* Hudspeth, 10 Exch. 5; Perrin *v.* Garfield, 37 Vt. 309.]

[1] See Rowland *v.* Wolfe, 1 Bailey, 56.

[2] [Pollard *v.* Barnes, 2 Cush. 191.]

and authority, that the plaintiff cannot entitle himself to the privilege claimed, unless he can prove a continual enjoyment of it for twenty consecutive years, without interruption."[1] So in M'Farlin *v.* Essex Co.,[2] it was held, that an adverse occupation of a fishery by A., for a number of years, which was afterwards interrupted or abandoned, cannot be added to a subsequent occupation by B. to give B. a prescriptive right, although A., after such interruption or abandonment, released all his right in the fishery to B.]

§ 215. The enjoyment must, in the second place, be *nec clam, nec precario*, but open and notorious.[3] By the Civil Law, it was sufficient to do away or vitiate the user, if, from the acts of the party claiming by virtue thereof, an intention of concealment could be inferred;[4] and the user, by the Civil Law, might be secret, either from the mode in which a party enjoys it, or from the nature of the easement itself. Instances of the former kind are where the right is exercised by stealth, or in the night, *Talis usus non valebit, cum sit clandestinus et idem erit si nocturnus;*[5] and instances of the latter occur where a claim is made to an extraordinary degree of support to a house from the neighboring soil, in consequence of an excavation on the party's own land, not visible to the neighbor.[6] The Common Law also proceeds upon the ground that there has been an *acquiescence* on the part of the servient owner;[7] a ground of supposition which can never

1 [This decision is both a declaration of the doctrine of the Common Law, and a construction of the statutes of Massachusetts, in regard to the acquisition of easements. See Monmouth Canal Co. *v.* Harford, 1 Cr., M. & R. 614, 631; Tickle *v.* Brown, 4 Ad. & El. 369, 383; Beasley *v.* Clark, 2 Bing. N.C. 705; Pierre *v.* Fernald, 26 Maine, 436, 442; Edson *v.* Munsell, 10 Allen, 557, 567; Rogers *v.* Sawin, 10 Gray, 379; Stevens *v.* Dennett, 51 N.H. 329; Mansur *v.* Blake, 62 Maine, 38.]

2 M'Farlin *v.* Essex Co., 10 Cush. 304. See Mansur *v.* Blake, 62 Maine, 38.

3 Eaton *v.* Swansea Waterworks Co., 17 Q. B. 267, 269. "An enjoyment must neither be *vi*, *precario* nor *clam:* it must be open." Bramwell B., in Solomon *v.* Vintners' Co., 4 H. & N. 602. See Perrin *v.* Garfield, 37 Vt. 304; Wilde J., in Thomas *v.* Marshfield, 13 Pick. 248; Donnell *v.* Clark, 19 Maine, 174; Morse *v.* Williams, 62 Maine, 445. This rule was applied to the case of a drain running from one house under another, but not known to exist by the owner of either. Carbrey *v.* Willis, 7 Allen, 368.

4 Lib. 3, § 8, ff. quod vi aut clam; Gale & What. on Easem. 85.

5 Bract. lib. 2, f. 52. [See Eaton *v.* Swansea Waterworks Co., 17 Q.B. 267, 269.]

6 Lib. 1, §§ 5, 6, ff.; lib. 6, ff. de adq. vel, amit. poss.

7 [As to the effect of a denial of the right by the person, against whom the easement is claimed, during the twenty years, see Stillman *v.* White Rock Co., 3 Woodb. & M. 549; Smith *v.* Miller, 11 Gray, 148; Nichols *v.* Ayler, 7 Leigh, 546, 565; Powell *v.* Bagg, 8 Gray, 441; Eaton *v.* Swansea Waterworks Co., 17 Q.B. 267, 269.]

exist, if an occupation be so clandestinely taken, as not to afford notice of the same.[1] The same principle will apply, as is applied to the adverse possession of land under the Statute of Limitations, and which has been very clearly and fully expressed by Mr. C.J. Shaw; viz., "One point seems to be well settled, which is, that very strong acts of exclusive possession, such as building, inclosing, and cultivating, and that for a long time, and *openly* and *notoriously*, are necessary, in order to constitute an actual ouster of the true owner, *who has no notice of such acts.*"[2] In the case of uncultivated lands in new settlements, the party claiming title by possession must show an occupation of that nature and notoriety, that the owner may be presumed to know of it; otherwise, length of time would run against a man when he had no ground to believe that his rights had been infringed.[3] Cattle ranging at large, in North Carolina, it has been held, is

[1] [In Perrin *v.* Garfield, 37 Vt. 304, it appeared that, in 1833, F. erected a mill about a mile from the defendants' pond, and entered into the use and occupancy of a dam and flume, previously built by C., at the outlet of the pond, to supply his mill which formerly stood near the site of F.'s mill, and continued so to use it for a period of time sufficient to establish a title by prescription. His mill was almost wholly dependent on the water obtained by means of the dam and flume for its supply; and it was held, that in the absence of proof that F., or C., or his successors, ever procured any license to erect or keep up said dam, or ever acknowledged any title in any one, these circumstances warranted the finding that F.'s use was adverse. Upon the question of notice, Peck J. said, "It is insisted that the case shows no notice to the owners of the servient tenement or lands, and that without proof of such notice no such acquiescence on the part of such owners is shown, as is necessary to the acquirement of an easement. The cases are rare and peculiar where proof of notice has been held necessary. The general current of the authorities is the other way." — "The erection of a structure so obvious and palpable as a dam and flume, and the use of it such length of time by means of a gate at the outlet, to supply the mill, could hardly be otherwise than notorious in the vicinity, and would not be likely long to escape the observation of the proprietor of the lands on which they were situated and which were thereby injuriously affected. It is true the lands about that pond were wild and uncultivated till 1850, but this is not sufficient to rebut the presumption of notice." In a case where the right claimed was the percolating of water under ground, Wightman J. said, "The presumption of a grant only arises where the person against whom it is to be raised might have prevented the exercise of the subject of the presumed grant; but how could he prevent or stop the percolation of water?" Chasemore *v.* Richards, 7 H.L. Cas. 349; 5 H. & N. 985. See Webb *v.* Bird, 13 C.B. N.S. 843.

In Smith *v.* Kenrick, 7 Man., G. & S. 546, Maule J. said, "As to surface flows, parties acquire rights to them because there is the acquiescence of everybody who has any interest in the matter. But, as to underground percolations, no rights are gained, because nobody knows any thing about them." See Cooper *v.* Barber, 3 Taunt. 99.] See Ang. on Lim. Chap. XXX. § 13, et seq., and the authorities there cited in reference to the doctrine of adverse possession of land.

[2] Blood *v.* Wood, 1 Met. 528.

[3] Proprietors of Kennebec Purchase *v.* Skinner, 4 Mass. 416.

not such an occupation, as will give notice to the adverse claimant; and neither, for the same reason, is the overflowing of land remotely situated.[1]

[§ 215 *a*. In Wheatley *v.* Baugh,[2] it appeared that the plaintiff was a tanner, and occupied a tan-yard with its appurtenances from about 1824 to 1853, and carried on his business during the whole of that time. Upon the property, thus occupied by him, there was a spring of water, which he constantly used for the purposes of his business. The spring was fed by subterranean waters, percolating through the strata of the earth, which were diverted by the mining operations of the defendant on his adjacent land. Among other grounds of title, the plaintiff claimed that this use of the spring for his tannery for so many years raised the presumption of a grant of a right to have this subterranean flow or percolation of water through the adjacent land to his spring, continue. The Court decided otherwise. Lewis C.J. said, "The prior occupancy of the spring for the uses of the tannery gave no right of servitude over or through the land of the adjacent proprietor. No man, by mere prior enjoyment of the advantages of his own land, can establish a servitude upon the land of another. This is shown in a satisfactory manner by Mr. Justice Rogers, in Hoy *v.* Sterrett.[3] But it seems to be thought that the enjoyment of the spring by the plaintiff below and those under whom he claims, for the period of twenty-one years, gives him a right to its continued existence, although the neighboring proprietor may thereby be deprived of the chief value of his own land. This depends upon the question whether the enjoyment of the spring was of such a character as to have invaded his neighbor's rights, so as to enable the latter to maintain an action for the injury. No man can be barred by a statute of limitation for not bringing his action within the prescribed period, until it is first shown that he had a cause of action which he could have maintained. In analogy to the statute, no presumption can arise against a party on the ground of long enjoyment of a privilege by another, until it is shown that the privilege, in some measure, interfered with the rights of the party whose grant is proposed to be presumed, and that he had a legal right to prevent such

[1] Andrews *v.* Mulford, Hayw. (N.C.) 311.

[2] [Wheatley *v.* Baugh, 25 Penn. St. 528.]

[3] [2 Watts, 330.]

enjoyment by proceedings at law."[1] — "The owner of the mine had no right to complain of his neighbor below for making use of the spring on his own lands. As long as it flowed there, he had a right to make use of it, and the owner of the land through which the supply of water came, was not in any manner injured by such use of the water. Silence or acquiescence, where one is not injured and has no cause of complaint, can never deprive him of his rights on the ground of presumption of a grant. No man can be said to have granted a right about which it would have been an impertinent interference to utter a complaint.[2] Besides, it was impossible for him to know from whence the supply of water came. He had no knowledge that it was derived from percolations through his own land. In this respect there is a material difference between hidden veins of water under ground and watercourses flowing on the surface. The latter are apparent, and if appropriated in such a way as to injure the rights of the owner through whose land they flow, he can take cognizance of the wrong, and is bound to redress it by action within the period prescribed by law. But the former are not apparent, and the owner of the land is not bound to resort to an action to redress a wrong of which he cannot by any possibility have notice. In a case like the present, therefore, there is no reason whatever for depriving the plaintiff in error of the enjoyment of his rights of property on his own land, on the ground of any servitude established by time, or acquiescence for the benefit of the tannery on the adjacent tract. If it could be shown that any distinct watercourse leading to the spring had been cut off or diverted, and it should also appear that it could have been preserved without material detriment to the owner of the land through which it flowed, the destruction of it might be attributed to malice or negligence. In that case the law would furnish redress, because the injury would be unjustifiable."]

§ 216. Thirdly, and above all, the enjoyment must be *as of right*.[3] The fact of a peaceable and open enjoyment or user,

[1] [Union Mill &c. Co. *v.* Ferris, 2 Sawyer, 176.]

[2] [Hoy *v.* Sterrett, 2 Watts, 331.]

[3] [Per Bigelow C.J., in Brace *v.* Yale, 10 Allen, 444. In Thomas *v.* Marshfield, 13 Pick. 248, Wilde J. said, "As a title by prescription is founded on the presumption of a grant, the possession must be such as to render such a presumption reasonable. It must, therefore, be adverse or under a claim of right, and not by the voluntary permission of the owner of the land. If the use of an easement is under a parol consent given by the

may be said to be *per se* only an introductory fact to a link in the chain of right to an easement, and which will not simply of itself, though long continued, bar the title of him seised of the land in which the easement is claimed. The reason is, the enjoyment or user may not have been originally commenced, or subsequently continued, with an intention to claim the easement; but, on the contrary, may have been, with an entire understanding between the parties, that no such claim is to be set up. The reason, in other words, is that it may have been a *permissive* occupation, which, in the language of the Master of the Rolls, in Cholmondeley *v.* Clinton,[1] "However long it may in point of fact have endured, could never ripen into a title against anybody; for it was not considered as the possession of the precarious occupier, but of him upon whose pleasure its continuance depended." In reference to the effect of possession in questions under the Statute of Limitations (and we have seen that the claim of title to an easement by virtue of twenty years' enjoyment, is analogous to a claim of title to the land itself by virtue of possession for the time prescribed by that statute), Marshall C.J. says that it has not only been recognized in the courts of England, but in all other countries, where the rules in those courts have been adopted, that a possession which was permissive and entirely consistent with the title of another, should not bar that title; and that it would shock the sense of right, which must be felt by all legislators, and all judges, were it otherwise.[2] The enjoyment of an easement had under the license or permission from the owner of the servient tenement, is consistent with the right of the owner of the servient tenement, and consequently confers no right to the easement. Each renewal of the license rebuts the presumption which would otherwise arise, that such enjoyment was had under a claim of right to the easement.[3] The

owner of the servient tenement to use it as if it were legally conveyed, it is a use as of right. Ashley *v.* Ashley, 4 Gray, 197. So an occupation of land under a parol gift from the owner is an occupation as of right. Sumner *v.* Stevens, 6 Met. 337. And in Stearns *v.* Janes, 12 Allen, 582, it was held, that the use of an easement under claim of right, by virtue of a parol contract, is adverse; and if continued for twenty years will create a right. Merely abutting one's mill-dam upon the opposite shore, without claim of right to the land, may create an easement after its continuance for twenty years, but will not divest the owner of the shore of his title. Trask *v.* Ford, 39 Maine, 437.]

[1] Cholmondeley *v.* Clinton, 2 Jac. & W. 1.

[2] United States *v.* Arredendo, 6 Peters, 743. [See Brace *v.* Yale, 10 Allen, 444.]

[3] Monmouth Canal Co. *v.* Harford, 1 Cr., M. & R. 614; ante, § 213; Blaisdell

"precarious enjoyment" of the Civil Law, by which, as has been already seen, no prescriptive right could be acquired, is identical with the permissive enjoyment of the Common Law.[1] If, therefore, the enjoyment is shown to have originated in mistake, license, or favor; or if it was commenced and continued in a manner which has not indicated a *claim of right*, the enjoyment is not adverse.[2] So if within twenty years from the time an adverse user first commenced, the person using it adversely has applied to the owner of the land to purchase the privilege or easement; this, if explained, raises no presumption of a grant.[3] But if such easement has been possessed and used for the term of twenty years, in a manner to furnish evidence of an adverse

v. Portsmouth, Great Falls and Conway Railroad, 51 N.H. 483; Dodge *v.* McClintock, 47 N.H. 383.

[1] Gale & What. on Easem. 85.

[2] Campbell *v.* Wilson, 3 East, 294. [Thus in Smith *v.* Miller, 11 Gray, 145, where it appeared that a land owner, for his own sole benefit, dug a drain or watercourse from a pond on the land of a neighboring proprietor, with the permission of the latter, through his own land to an outlet, and the water afterwards flowed uninterruptedly from the pond through this drain or watercourse, and continued thus to flow more than twenty years after the plaintiff had purchased the land, in which the pond was, from such neighboring proprietor, it was held that the plaintiff had gained no prescriptive right to have his pond drained through this watercourse, in consequence of the use thus made of it, because the enjoyment did not appear to have been had under any claim of right. Merrick J. said, "A right to an easement of this kind in the land of another may undoubtedly be acquired by the actual enjoyment of it, provided that the enjoyment is adverse, uninterrupted, and of sufficient continuance and duration. But the use, the adverse possession, and uninterrupted enjoyment, which are facts necessary to establish the right, must be shown by competent and satisfactory evidence, and are therefore necessarily open to denial, contradiction, and disproof by the party against whom they are asserted. The actual exercise or enjoyment of the right contended for may be *primâ facie* evidence of prescription, and therefore, if uncontrolled, sufficient to show title to the easement which is claimed. Dare *v.* Heathcoate, 36 Eng. Law & Eq. 564. But it is after all only evidence, which may be encountered and controlled by accompanying facts and circumstances, or by proof derived from other and distinct sources." Gray *v.* Bond, 2 B. & B. 667; Livett *v.* Wilson, 3 Bing. 115; Doe *v.* Reed, 5 B. & Ald. 232. "In this commonwealth it has been expressly determined, that in order to make the use of an easement in another's land for twenty years conclusive of the right, it is incumbent upon the party who claims it, to prove that the use was adverse, uninterrupted, and with the knowledge and acquiescence of the owner of the land; and that each of these qualities or ingredients essential to the maintenance of the claim is open to contradiction and liable to be disproved. Sargent *v.* Ballard, 9 Pick. 251; White *v.* Loring, 24 Pick. 319; Stevens *v.* Taft, 11 Gray, 33. In the present case, therefore, the judge who presided at the trial very properly refused to rule, in conformity to the request of the plaintiff's counsel, that the plaintiff had acquired a prescriptive right to the use of the channel dug on the defendant's land, by the mere flowing of the water through it from his own for a period of twenty years, without regard to the accompanying facts and the other evidence in the case."]

[3] Watkins *v.* Peck, 13 N.H. 360.

enjoyment, and raise the presumption of a grant; and the owner, after the expiration of that term of time, denies the right, and there is thereupon a negotiation for a purchase, and an agreement which is not perfected; such attempt to purchase will not preclude the party from relying upon the presumption of grant by reason of the previous adverse possession.[1] The enjoyment without interruption for the length of time for the right of entry upon land, is so strong evidence of a right, that the jury should not be directed to consider small circumstances as founding a presumption, that it arose otherwise than by grant.[2]

§ 217. Lord Ellenborough, in Bealy *v.* Shaw,[3] speaks of twenty years' enjoyment of water, in any particular manner, as affording a "conclusive" presumption of a grant.[4] It has been thought that the word "conclusive" is rather oddly joined to the word presumption, it being of the very essence of presumptive evidence, that it must yield to stronger proof. Lord Ellenborough must undoubtedly be understood as meaning, by a "conclusive" presumption, one, which unexplained or uncontradicted, will conclusively authorize a jury to find the fact. This construction is necessary to reconcile that learned Judge to his own course of decision; for, in Campbell *v.* Wilson,[5] determined only two years before this, he and the whole Court held, that twenty years' enjoyment was merely presumptive evidence to be explained or rebutted like any other presumption.[6] In Livett *v.* Wilson,[7] upon a question of twenty years' possession, Best C.J. says, "I do not dispute, that if there had been uninterrupted usage for twenty years, the jury might be authorized to presume it originated in a deed; but even in such a case, a Judge would not be justified in telling a jury that they *must* presume a deed. If, however, there are circumstances inconsistent with the existence of a deed, the jury should be directed to consider them,

[1] Watkins *v.* Peck, 13 N.H. 360. [See ante, § 213; post, § 252; Perrin *v.* Garfield, 37 Vt. 304; Tracy *v.* Atherton, 36 Vt. 503.]

[2] Campbell *v.* Wilson, ub. sup.

[3] Bealy *v.* Shaw, 6 East, 215, and ante, § 205.

[4] [See per Bigelow C.J., in Brace *v.* Yale, 10 Allen, 445.]

[5] Campbell *v.* Wilson, ub. sup.

[6] Such was the view taken by the Court of Appeals in Virginia, in Nichols *v.* Ayler, 7 Leigh (Va.) 546, and another case in Virginia, therein cited; and by the Supreme Court of Connecticut, in Branch *v.* Doane, 18 Conn. 233.

[7] Livett *v.* Wilson, 3 Bing. 115.

and decide accordingly;" and the rest of the Court were of the like opinion.[1]

§ 218. The words used by Mr. Justice Story, in Tyler *v.* Wilkinson,[2] are, "By our laws, upon principles of public convenience, the term of twenty years' exclusive, uninterrupted enjoyment, has been held a conclusive presumption of a grant or right." But by this language, he is not understood to have intended an enjoyment, which had been by the *favor and at the will* of the owner for twenty years.[3] In two instances, in which the subject of the conclusiveness of the presumption was fully considered by the Court of Appeals of Virginia,[4] it was held, that the presumption of a right or of a grant arises from the long *acquiescence* of the party, and does not arise where the enjoyment is contested; and the Court rely on the authority of Campbell *v.* Wilson.[5]

§ 219. The Supreme Court of Massachusetts hold, that, in order to raise the presumption of a grant, the enjoyment "must

1 [See 2 Greenl. Ev. § 539; Miller *v.* Garlock, 8 Barb. 153; Hoyt *v.* Carter, 6 Barb. 219; Valentine *v.* Piper, 22 Pick. 93; Littlefield *v.* Maxwell, 31 Maine, 140; Gilman *v.* Tilton, 5 N.H. 231, per Richardson J.; Bullen *v.* Runnels, 2 N.H. 255; Wallace *v.* Fletcher, 30 N.H. 434; ante, § 209, note. In Edson *v.* Munsell, 10 Allen, 568, 569, Gray J. said that the fiction of presuming a grant from twenty years' possession or use "is not founded on a belief that a grant has actually been made in the particular case, but on the general presumption that a man will naturally enjoy what belongs to him, the difficulty of proof after lapse of time, and the policy of not disturbing long-continued possessions. In order to require the jury to presume a grant, the possession or use must have all the qualities of a prescription: it must be open, adverse, uninterrupted, and with the acquiescence of the owner. Any fact which directly affects the probability of such acquiescence must be submitted to the jury to assist them in determining whether such a presumption should or should not be made." See post, § 223*a;* Coolidge *v.* Learned, 8 Pick. 509, per Wilde J.; Tracy *v.* Atherton, 36 Vt. 511, per Poland C.J.]

2 Tyler *v.* Wilkinson, 4 Mason, 402.

3 Sargent *v.* Ballard, 9 Pick. 251.

4 See ante, § 217, note.

5 On a stream of water, issuing from a large natural pond, were mills owned respectively by A. & B.; the mill nearest the outlet of the pond being owned by B., and that below by A. Both claimed under C., who, in 1800, owned the land at the outlet of the pond and below, and erected mills on the site of A.'s mill. About the same time, C., in conjunction with other mill-owners below, erected a dam, flume, and gate, at the outlet of the pond, deepening and widening the channel, for the purpose of controlling the water there, for the more advantageous use of it for their mills. B.'s mill was erected in 1834, before which C. and the other mill-owners had claimed and exercised the exclusive right to dam up and control the water at the outlet of the pond, without obstruction. In an action brought by A. against B. for obstructing the water at B.'s mill, it was held, that the acts of C. for such a period, unexplained by any circumstances which deprived them of an adverse possession, constituted a conclusive presumption of a grant. Hickox *v.* Parmelee, 21 Conn. 86.

be under a claim of right, and contrary to the interests of the owner. An enjoyment with the consent of the owner, or consistently with the rights of the true owner, has no tendency to prove a conveyance from him; for the very ground of the presumption is the difficulty or impossibility of accounting for the grant, or some other lawful conveyance. But, if the possession can be accounted for consistently with the title, no presumption arises."[1] A learned Judge of the Supreme Court of the United States, has expressed a like opinion, in which he says, that presumptions (of the nature we are considering) can never arise where all the circumstances are perfectly consistent with the non-existence of a grant.[2]

[§ 219 *a*. It must be some use inconsistent with, and therefore adverse to, the right of others, which can be acquired by prescription, such as diverting the water from its natural course, or fouling the stream to an injurious extent. So far as one riparian proprietor uses the water equally, and in a manner consistent with the equal and common right of others, he makes no adverse use, and acquires no right adverse to theirs. He gives them no right of action against him and his use of the water has no ten-

[1] Arnold *v.* Stevens, 24 Pick. 106; [Bigelow C.J., in Brace *v.* Yale, 10 Allen, 444; Smith *v.* Miller, 11 Gray, 145.]

[2] Ricard *v.* Williams, 7 Wheat. 109. The same doctrine is maintained expressly in Brandt *v.* Ogden, by Mr. J. Spencer, 1 Johns. 156. [" Such a presumption will be made when it is necessary to clothe a rightful possession with a legal title, but the Court must first see that there is nothing but the form of a conveyance wanting." Doe *v.* Butler, 3 Wend. 149, 153. In Nelson *v.* Butterfield, 21 Maine, 220, 234, Shepley J. said, " All presumptions rest upon experience, and are founded upon a knowledge of man and of his motives of conduct. If a person for a long course of years claims the right to possess or enjoy estates or easements, and exercises that right without being molested, it is to be presumed that he has done so lawfully. And if another person permits it, when it would be injurious to him, without interruption, it is to be presumed, that he knows that the person has a legal right to do so. It would be against man's experience, and contrary to his motives of conduct, to account for it so satisfactorily in any other manner. *Omnia rite esse acta* is a maxim of the law; and it also attributes such conduct rather to the exercise of a legal right, than to an encroachment. If this be the true foundation of presumptions, it will follow, that if the continuance of the possession or enjoyment can be accounted for without presuming any thing to favor it, and without imputing a conscious want of right or negligence to him who does not interrupt, the presumption cannot arise. It has no foundation to rest upon; or, in the language of the law, it is rebutted. These positions are not inconsistent with the best administration of justice. They will work no wrong, and will secure to all their rights, unless they have been guilty of negligence in asserting them. And this is believed to be the doctrine relating to presumptions in the decided cases."]

dency to prove a grant from them to him.[1] Thus the erection of a dam across a stream of water to raise a head for the purpose of driving wheels and machinery in a mill, and the cutting of canals, sluices, and water ways to conduct, apply, and discharge the water, although they may change in some degree the natural flow of the stream and cause a temporary obstruction to the passage of the water, yet, if they do not essentially affect the reasonable use of the current by riparian proprietors above and below for similar purposes, would not be inconsistent with the rights of such proprietors in the stream, and could not be deemed to confer any right or to take away any title or privilege. So, too, the erection of a dam, for the purpose of forming a reservoir by flowing a large tract of land, by which the water would be obstructed only until such reservoir should be filled, and would then resume its natural flow, could not be deemed to be adverse or inconsistent with the rights of other proprietors below on the same stream. The obstruction in such case would be only slight and temporary, and would afford no ground for a presumption that any right of others to the use of the stream had been thereby impaired or lost.[2]]

[§ 219 *b*. So, where a proprietor of land upon one shore appropriates and applies to his individual use so much of the passing water as he is enabled to do, even if it be the whole of it, by means of structures erected upon and within the limits of his own estate, and the proprietor of the land on the opposite shore neither uses nor seeks to use, nor makes any provision nor has

[1] [Shaw C.J., in Gould *v.* Boston Duck Co., 13 Gray, 451; Holsman *v.* Boiling Spring Bleaching Co., 1 McCarter (N.J.) 335, 345; Parker *v.* Hotchkiss, 25 Conn. 321; Webb *v.* Bird, 13 C.B. N.S. 838; Chasemore *v.* Richards, 7 H.L. Cas. 349.]

[2] [Bigelow C.J., in Brace *v.* Yale, 10 Allen, 441, 444; Pitts *v.* Lancaster Mills, 13 Met. 156. A dam is an instrument for turning the water of a stream to the use of a mill, as a bulkhead is the means of drawing the water from a dam, but neither may, in fact, have been used for either purpose at all, or if at all, in such a way as to change or affect the original rights of the riparian owners on either hand. Burnham *v.* Kempton, 44 N.H. 78, 89. In Colwell *v.* The May's Landing Water Power Co., 4 C. E. Green, 245, Chancellor Zabriskie said, "The word dam is used in two different senses. It properly means the work or structure, raised to obstruct the flow of the water in a river, but by a well-settled usage it is often applied to designate the pond of water created by this obstruction." And in this case it was held that an act which authorizes the owner of a mill-dam, "to raise the dam and waterworks" to the height of the natural surface of the water at the line of his lands, will be construed to authorize raising the water in the dam to that height, and not to authorize the raising of the structure of the dam, by which the water would be made to flow back upon the lands of the adjoining proprietor.]

any occasion for the use of any part of the stream or proportion of the water to which he is entitled, there is nothing adverse in the action of the former. He does nothing for which an action can be maintained against him, or nominal damages recovered in the assertion and vindication of an invaded right. In such circumstances, they stand towards each other in the relation, and with substantially the rights, of tenants in common, where the possession of one is deemed to be the possession and for the benefit of all; and their respective rights will continue to be protected and preserved to them, until some positive act of actual and exclusive adverse possession by which one of the parties is directly interfered with, and prevented from enjoying his equal privilege in the use of the water.[1]]

[§ 219 *c*. The above cases show clearly that the time of prescription, or that time which is necessary to raise the presumption of a grant or right, does not begin to run until there has been an actionable invasion or infringement of a right, although it is not necessary that actual damages should have been suffered.[2] A late case [3] in New Jersey forcibly illustrates the same doctrine; the plaintiffs alleged that chemicals and other foreign and offensive matters were discharged into the stream at the defendants' bleaching works, of such a character and in such quantities as to render the water of the stream on the lands of the plaintiffs, who were proprietors below, unfit for household use and for other purposes to which it was applied by the plaintiffs. The defendants alleged that the site occupied by them was used and occupied as a mill-site more than twenty years before the plaintiffs purchased; that the business of fulling and dyeing had been carried on for more than twenty years, and that the owners had consequently a right to use the stream for *manufacturing* purposes, although the same might taint and color the

1 [Merrick J., in Pratt *v.* Lamson, 2 Allen, 275, 288, 289. See Corning *v.* Troy Iron &c. Co., 39 Barb. 311; Howe Scale Co. *v.* Terry, 47 Vt. 109, 125, 126.]

2 [See Polly *v.* McCall, 37 Ala. N.S. 20; Holsman *v.* Boiling Spring Bleaching Co., 1 McCarter (N.J.) 335; Cooper *v.* Barker, 3 Taunt. 99; Donnell *v.* Clark, 19 Maine, 174; Crosby *v.* Bessey, 49 Maine, 539; Wood *v.* Waud, 3 Exch. 748, 772, 773; Alexander *v.* Kerr, 2 Rawle, 83; Ripka *v.* Sargeant, 7 Watts & S. 9; ante, §§ 135, 136, and notes; post, § 428. The presumption of a grant from long-continued enjoyment only arises where the person against whom the right is claimed might have interrupted or prevented the exercise of the subject of the supposed grant. Chasemore *v.* Richards, 7 H.L. Cas. 349; Webb *v.* Bird, 13 C.B. N.S. 843.]

3 [Holsman *v.* The Boiling Spring Bleaching Co., 1 McCarter, 335.]

water. The chancellor in discussing the case, said, "The existence of the defendants' mill, or the discharge of dyeing materials or drugs into the stream, *on the defendants' lands*, constitutes no injury to the plaintiffs, if their usufructuary right to the stream is not interfered with. The defendants have a right to use the water upon their own soil in such manner as they may deem for their interest, provided they discharge it upon the soil of the plaintiffs, in its accustomed channel, pure and unpolluted. They can therefore acquire no right by prescription until they show that the acts which are claimed to constitute the adverse user injured the plaintiffs, and gave to them, or to those under whom they claim title, a right of action. The very ground of title by adverse enjoyment, is that the party against whom it is set up has so long permitted the adverse enjoyment, and failed to vindicate his rights, that the presumption of a grant is raised. But there can be no such presumption, and consequently no title by adverse enjoyment, where no violation of a right is shown to exist. Thus where an action is brought for overflowing the plaintiffs' land by backwater from the defendants' mill-dam, it establishes no title by adverse enjoyment to prove that the defendants' mill has been in existence over twenty years, or that the dam has been in existence for that period. The question is not how high the dam is, but how high the water has been held, whether it has been held for twenty years so high as to affect the land of the plaintiffs as injuriously as it did at the time of the action brought. To prove, therefore, that there was a fulling and dyeing mill or other manufactory for twenty years on the defendants' land, and that they discharged drugs and dye-stuffs into the stream during that period, proves nothing, unless it is shown that the materials discharged into the stream were of such character and of such an amount as to pollute the water which flowed upon the plaintiffs' land, and rendered it unfit for use. If the evidence stops short of that, it proves no adverse enjoyment in the defendants or those under whom they claim."[1] Where a tanner has thrown his ground bark into a stream for more than twenty years, he does not thereby acquire a right by prescription to do so, to the injury of an owner of land on the same stream below, on which the natural action of the water deposits the bark, unless it appears that the bark has been depos-

[1] [Holsman *v.* The Boiling Spring Bleaching Co., 1 McCarter (N.J.) 335.]

ited on the same land, and the owner thereof annually injured thereby, for the whole term of twenty years.[1] So where one claimed the right, by twenty years' user, to throw cinders and other refuse into a stream, which injured the occupiers of a mill below, it was held, that until the occupiers of the mill sustained some injury from the user, no right as against them began to be acquired.[2] A similar doctrine has been maintained in other cases.[3]]

[§ 219 *d*. But, on the other hand, if the owner of land on one side of a river erects a mill-dam entirely across it, without obtaining permission from the owner of the land on the opposite shore, this is an adverse and injurious invasion of the rights of the latter, for which he may presently maintain an action, although he has no immediate occasion to make use of the water for any purpose of his own, and suffers no actual loss thereby. And if the dam be continued for a sufficient length of time, this will authorize a jury to presume a grant of the right to abut the dam on such opposite shore, and to use, to the exclusion of all other persons, the whole of the water held back and accumulated by and above it.[4] So, where the owner of a mill, situated upon a small stream, has erected a reservoir dam a short distance above, and exercised control of the water of the stream, under claim of right, by means of gates built in the reservoir dam, drawing sometimes more and at other times less than the natural flow of the stream, as he had occasion, for more than twenty years uninterruptedly, it was held that he might thereby acquire a right so to use the water, as against the intermediate owners of the land over which the stream passes; and might maintain an action to recover damages against any such an intermediate owner, who substantially interferes with this right.[5] Such was the decision

1 [Crosby *v.* Bessey, 49 Maine, 539. See Baxendale *v.* McMurray, L.R. 2 Ch. App. 790; Moore *v.* Webb, 1 C.B. N.S. 673.]

2 [Murgatroyd *v.* Robinson, 7 El. & Bl. 391.]

3 [See Polly *v.* McCall, 37 Ala. N.S. 20; Roundtree *v.* Brantley, 34 Ala. N.S. 544; Cooper *v.* Barber, 3 Taunt. 99; Donnell *v.* Clark, 19 Maine, 174.]

4 [Merrick J., in Pratt *v.* Lamson, 2 Allen, 288; Bliss *v.* Rice, 17 Pick. 23.]

5 [And so it was held in Brace *v.* Yale, 99 Mass. 488, that the owner of a mill on a stream, who has a right to draw down from his reservoir more or less than the natural flow of the stream, at his pleasure, to work his mill, is entitled to relief in equity against the owner of an intermediate dam which delays the passage of the water by the time necessary to fill the defendant's pond, and by its leaky condition allows the water to run so to waste, when the plaintiff's mill is not at work, as to make it necessary to fill the pond from day to day.]

in Brace *v.* Yale,[1] which was an action brought by the plaintiff to recover for an interruption of a prescriptive right to the use of water thus acquired, and in which Bigelow C. J. said, "The reservoir has thus been used to collect water for the immediate purpose of operating the plaintiff's mill, and the water in it has been drawn out, either partly or wholly, whenever it was required for the working of the machinery of the plaintiff. This mode of controlling and regulating the use of the water in the stream, as it essentially interrupted the original and natural flow of the water, and interfered materially with the right of the riparian owners of lands, between the reservoir dam and the plaintiff's mill, to appropriate and use the water, was in its nature adverse, and, having been continued under a claim of right for forty-five years and upwards, affords a conclusive presumption of a grant, from such intermediate owners to the plaintiff and his grantors, of such appropriation and use." "As a riparian proprietor, the defendant has lost the right to use the water in its natural flow or passage through his land, by the long-continued adverse user of the plaintiff and those under whom he claims, not only to control the quantity of water which should be allowed to pass down the natural channel through his land, but also to regulate the time when it should be drawn out of the reservoir, in order to pass down to the plaintiff's mill. He must therefore use the water in subordination to this superior right of the plaintiff." — "If it is asked what is the measure or standard by which the defendant's right is to be regulated and governed, the answer is obvious. He can make a reasonable appropriation of the water as it is let down from the reservoir and passes through his land, having regard to the proper and reasonable use by the plaintiff of the prescriptive right which he has acquired. He can neither retard the water so as to prevent the plaintiff's mill from running for any considerable period of time when the water is let down from the reservoir, nor can he hold it back for the purpose of collecting water which is to be drawn down in such quantities that the plaintiff cannot by the reasonable and ordinary use of his mill properly appropriate and apply it to the driving of his works, and thus cause the water to run to waste." — "It is immaterial that the defendant uses no more water than is advantageous for the working of his mill. He is bound to use the

[1] [10 Allen, 441.]

water with a due regard to the rights of others, and not merely with reference to the profitable employment of his own works."]

§ 220. In delivering the judgment of the Court of Exchequer, in a case in which the qualities of an enjoyment necessary to invest it with right by lapse of time were considered,[1] Mr. Baron Parke said, "In order to establish a right of way, and to bring the case within this section,[2] it must be proved that the claimant has enjoyed it for the full period of twenty years, and that he has done so *as of right;* for that is the form in which, by section 5,[3] such claim must be pleaded; and the like evidence would have been required before the statute, to prove a claim by prescription or non-existing grant. Therefore, if the way shall ap-

[1] Bright *v.* Walker, 1 Cr., M. & R. 219.

[2] Of the Act commonly called the "Prescription" Act of 2 & 3 Will. IV. c. 71, which is as follows: "Sect. 2. And be it further enacted, that no claim which may be lawfully made at the Common Law, by custom, prescription, or grant, to any way or other easement, or to any watercourse, or the use of any water to be enjoyed or derived upon, over, or from any land or water of our said Lord the King, his heirs or successors, or being parcel of the Duchy of Lancaster, or of the Duchy of Cornwall, or being the property of any ecclesiastical or lay person, or body corporate, when such way or other matter as herein last before mentioned shall have been actually enjoyed by any person claiming right thereto, without interruption, for the full period of twenty years, shall be defeated or destroyed by showing only that such way or other matter was first enjoyed at any time prior to such period of twenty years; but nevertheless such claim may be defeated in any other way by which the same is now liable to be defeated; and where such way or other matter as herein last before mentioned shall have been so enjoyed as aforesaid for the full period of forty years, the right thereto shall be deemed absolute and indefeasible, unless it shall appear that the same was enjoyed by some consent or agreement expressly given or made for that purpose by deed or writing."

[3] Of the above act, which is as follows: "And be it further enacted, that in all actions upon the case and other pleadings wherein the party claiming may now by law allege his right generally, without averring the existence of such right from time immemorial, such general allegation shall still be deemed sufficient, and if the same shall be denied, all and every the matters in this act mentioned and provided, which shall be applicable to the case, shall be admissible in evidence to sustain or rebut such allegation; and that in all pleadings to actions of trespass, and in all other pleadings, wherein before the passing of this act it would have been necessary to allege the right to have existed from time immemorial, it shall be sufficient to allege the enjoyment thereof as of right by the occupiers of the tenement in respect whereof the same is claimed for and during such of the periods mentioned in this act as may be applicable to the case, and without claiming in the name or right of the owner of the fee, as is now usually done; and if the other party shall intend to rely on any proviso, exception, incapacity, disability, contract, agreement, or other matter hereinbefore mentioned, or on any cause or matter of fact or of law, not inconsistent with the simple fact of enjoyment, the same shall be specially alleged and set forth in answer to the allegation of the party claiming, and shall not be received in evidence on any general traverse or denial of such allegation."

pear to have been enjoyed by the claimant, not openly and in the manner that a person rightfully entitled would have used it, but by stealth, as a trespasser would have done — if he shall have occasionally asked permission of the occupier of the land — no title would be acquired, *because it was not 'enjoyed as of right.'*"[1] The authority of this case and the doctrines laid down by the Court were fully recognized in the cases of the Monmouth Canal Co. *v.* Harford,[2] and Tickle *v.* Brown.[3]

§ 221. It is clearly, therefore, an enjoyment, *with an intent to claim* against the true owner which renders it adverse to his rights, and upon this the decision in every case is made to depend. The question of adverse enjoyment or not is a question on which the Court may instruct the jury; but the jury must be left to their own view of the effect of the evidence of the intent (*quo animo*) which has attended the enjoyment. That, as Lord Mansfield said of disseisin, "is a fact to be found by a jury."[4] The *burden of proving* the adverse possession is on the party claiming the easement; and *if he leaves it doubtful* whether the enjoyment was adverse, known to the owner, and uninterrupted, *it is not conclusive in his favor.*[5] But if he shows a well-known,

[1] [Smith *v.* Miller, 11 Gray, 145.]

[2] Monmouth Canal Co. *v.* Harford, 1 Cr., M. & R. 614.

[3] Tickle *v.* Brown, 4 Ad. & El. 369.

[4] Taylor *v.* Horde, 1 Burr. 60. That the question of adverse enjoyment should be left to the jury as one of intention, see the following cases: Tyler *v.* Wilkinson, 4 Mason, 397; Haight *v.* Morris Aqueduct, 4 Wash. C.C. 601; Cooper *v.* Smith, 9 S. & Rawle, 26; Strickler *v.* Todd, 10 S. & Rawle, 63; Butz *v.* Ihrie, 1 S. & Rawle, 218; Hepburn *v.* M'Dowell, 17 S. & Rawle, 383; Smith *v.* Smith, 3 Halst. (N.J.) 140; Ingraham *v.* Hutchinson, 2 Conn. 584; Gleason *v.* Gray, 4 Conn. 418; Manning *v.* Smith, 6 Conn. 289; Sherwood *v.* Burr, 4 Day, 244; Curtis *v.* Jackson, 13 Mass. 514; Cook *v.* Hull, 3 Pick. 269; Reid *v.* Gifford, 1 Hopk. Ch. 416; Stiles *v.* Hooker, 7 Cowen, 266; Coalter *v.* Hunter, 4 Rand. 58; Bullen *v.* Runnels, 2 N.H. 255; Mitchell *v.* Walker, 2 Aik. (Vt.) 266; Blanchard *v.* Baker, 6 Greenl. 268; Corning *v.* Gould, 16 Wend. 531; Baldwin *v.* Calkins, 10 Wend. 167; Rogers *v.* Mabe, 4 Dev. (N.C.) 180; Buddington *v.* Bradley, 10 Conn. 213; Tucker *v.* Jewett, 11 Conn. 311; Kennedy *v.* Scovil, 12 Conn. 317; Rogers *v.* Page, Brayt. (Vt.) 169; Norton *v.* Valentine, 14 Vt. 239; Davis *v.* Fuller, 12 Vt. 178; Wilson *v.* Wilson, 4 Dev. (N.C.) 154; Sargent *v.* Gutterson, 13 N.H. 467; Whittier *v.* Cocheco Manuf. Co., 9 N. H. 456; Dyer *v.* Depui, 5 Wharton, 584; Branch *v.* Doane, 18 Conn. 233; Darlington *v.* Painter, 7 Penn. St. 473; Shreve *v.* Voorhees, 2 Green (N.J.) 25; Chapman *v.* Thames Manuf. Co., 13 Conn. 269; Middleton *v.* Gregorie, 2 Rich. (S.C.) 631; Odiorne *v.* Lyford, 9 N.H. 502; Beidelman *v.* Foulke, 5 Watts, 308; Corning *v.* Gould, 16 Wend. 531; Cary *v.* Daniels, 8 Metc. 466; McDougal *v.* Clark, 7 B. Mon. (Ken.) 448; [Edson *v.* Munsell, 10 Allen, 568, 569; Valentine *v.* Piper, 22 Pick. 93; Stevens *v.* Taft, 11 Gray, 33; Smith *v.* Miller, 11 Gray, 145; Biddle *v.* Ash, 2 Ashm. 211, 221.]

[5] 2 Greenl. Ev. § 539; Sargent *v.* Ballard, 9 Pick. 251; Davies *v.* Stephens, 7 C. & P. 570; Jarvis *v.* Dean, 3 Bing.

an open, and uninterrupted enjoyment, proof must come from the other side to show, that it was by license or permission, or that it was to be restrained or limited in point of time.[1] The claim of an easement is in derogation of the ordinary rights of property, and looking at the subject in this view, it appears clearly, that it lies upon the party asserting such claim in opposition to common right, to support his case by evidence. In Cross *v.* Lewis,[2] the absence of any evidence as to the earlier state of the windows was indeed held to operate in favor of the plaintiff, — the party claiming the easement; but the substantial proof (that is, proof of a user for twenty years) had already been given by the claimant; and this, unrebutted by any evidence to take the case out of the ordinary rule, was of course sufficient to establish the easement.[3]

§ 222. A grant *upon condition* may be presumed from the use and enjoyment for twenty years adversely, and also the perform-

447; [Smith *v.* Miller, 11 Gray, 145; White *v.* Loring, 24 Pick. 319; Stevens *v.* Taft, 11 Gray, 33; Polly *v.* McCall, 37 Ala. N.S. 20]

[1] Per Lord Keeper Wright, Finch *v.* Resbridger, 2 Vern. 391; [Per Foster J., in White *v.* Chapin, 12 Allen, 519, 520. In Perrin *v.* Garfield, 37 Vt. 310, Peck J. said, "The general rule is that the enjoyment of an easement of this character," — that of maintaining a dam, and thereby flowing land, — "is presumed to be adverse, unless something appears to rebut that presumption. This is the general rule, when there is no express evidence that the user was accompanied by a claim of right, and no express evidence of a disclaimer of the right by the party enjoying the easement. There are some cases where the user is of such a character, and the circumstances attending it are such, as to show that it was a mere privilege enjoyed by leave of the proprietor of the servient tenement, express or implied, and not adverse. These cases are exceptions to the general rule, and peculiar in their character."]

[2] Cross *v.* Lewis, 2 B. & C. 686, and Gale & What. on Easem. 79, and 1 Crabb, Real Property, § 450.

[3] [See Smith *v.* Miller, 11 Gray, 148, per Merrick J.; Peck J., in Perrin *v.* Garfield, 37 Vt. 310. In White *v.* Chapin, 12 Allen, 519, 520, Foster J. said, "Wherever there has been the use of an easement for twenty years unexplained, it will be presumed to be under a claim of right and adverse, and be sufficient to establish a title by prescription, and to authorize the presumption of a grant; and it is incumbent upon the owner of the land to prove that the use of the easement was under some license, indulgence, or special contract inconsistent with a claim of right by the other party." Miller *v.* Garlock, 8 Barb. 153; Chalk *v.* McAlily, 11 Rich. 153; Williams *v.* Nelson, 23 Pick. 141, 147; Blake *v.* Everett, 1 Allen, 248; Hammond *v.* Zehner, 21 N.Y. 118; Esling *v.* Williams, 10 Penn. St. 126; Steffy *v.* Carpenter, 37 Penn. St. 41; Ingraham *v.* Hough, 1 Jones (N.C.) 39; Polly *v.* McCall, 37 Ala. 30; Garrett *v.* Jackson, 20 Penn. St. 331; Pierce *v.* Cloud, 42 Penn. St. 102; Trask *v.* Ford, 39 Maine, 437. In White *v.* Chapin, supra, it was held, that the right to the use of a ditch through the land of another for the purpose of drainage, may be established by adverse use. An actual use of such a ditch for that purpose for twenty years together, if unexplained, will be sufficient to establish the right.]

ance of the duty connected with the easement.[1] Repairs made upon an aqueduct, which is laid through the land of another, cannot be regarded as in the nature of rent, or as an acknowledgment that the easement is held at the pleasure of the owner of the land, without some other evidence tending to show an agreement to that effect. Nor will the fact, that the owner of the water takes[1] part of the water from the aqueduct, show, that the use by the party who takes the rest, and repairs, is merely permissive; though it may be evidence that the party repairing takes the water, and the privilege of entering and repairing, on the *condition* of furnishing the owner of the land with a portion of the water; and the *performance* of the condition may be essential to the continuance of the right.[2]

§ 223. It has not unfrequently happened in England, that the same presumption has been spoken of by some learned judges as a rule of law, whilst by others it has been treated as above mentioned; that is, merely as proper to be recommended to a jury, or as one which a jury might properly make.[3] The mode of carrying out the policy of the law by the intervention of a jury, has been strongly objected to. A very distinguished writer has objected to it.[4]

[1] Prescriptions may be upon condition. Gray's case, 5 Co. 79; Cro. Eliz. 546; 2 H. Bl. 224. A grant, upon condition that the grantee shall perform certain acts, may be presumed from a usage of more than twenty years to exercise the right adversely, and perform the duty connected with it, as well as an absolute grant may be presumed. Mitchell *v.* Walker, 2 Aik. (Vt.) 270.

[2] Watkins *v.* Peck, 13 N.H. 360.

[3] Phillips & Amos on Evidence, 460 (8th ed.); Gale & What. on Easem. 67; [Keymer *v.* Summers, Bul. N.P. 74; Campbell *v.* Wilson, 3 East, 294; Gray *v.* Bond, 2 B. & B. 627; Cross *v.* Lewis, 2 B. & C. 686; Darwin *v.* Upton, 2 Wms. Saund. 175 *a;* Wallace *v.* Fletcher, 30 N.H. 434.]

[4] Mr. Starkie says, "The practice of requiring juries in any case to be mere passive instruments in finding facts upon their oaths, in the existence of which the Court itself did not believe, although now established, is of singular origin. The effect is indirectly to establish an artificial presumption, which, for want either of inclination or authority, could not be established and applied directly. It seems very difficult to say, why such presumptions should not at once have been established as mere presumptions of law, to be applied to the facts by the Courts, without the aid of a jury. That course would certainly have been more simple; and any objection as to the want of authority would apply with equal, if not superior, force to the establishing such presumptions indirectly through the medium of a jury." 2 Stark. on Ev. 675. Again, "Notwithstanding the admission of the presumptions," says the same learned author, "which appear now to be established and necessary rules of law, this branch of jurisprudence cannot but be considered as imperfect and inartificial, more especially if it be contrasted with the labored distinctions of the Roman Law upon the same subject. The presumption being one of law, arising out of the fact of continued and adverse possession unrebutted, ought, as a rule of

[§ 223 *a*. It was decided in Tracy *v*. Atherton,[1] that the presumption, unrebutted, arising from the adverse possession and enjoyment of an incorporeal right, continued for the length of time fixed by statute as a bar to the recovery of land held adversely, is a presumption of law, and is conclusive evidence, or sufficient evidence to warrant the Court in holding that it confers a right on the possessor to the extent of his use.[2] Poland C. J. observed, "It is said in many of the cases that this length of possession is only evidence to be submitted to the jury. If by this is meant, that where it is conceded or proved that there has been an uninterrupted possession under claim of right for the requisite time, and this is not encountered by any evidence to rebut the legal effect of it, that it is a proper question to be submitted to the jury to say whether this gives a right, or not, it is

law, to be applied whenever the facts to which it is applicable arise; and yet, unless the jury strain their consciences so far as to find a grant, in the actual existence of which the Court itself may not believe, the rule of law is inapplicable; in other words, the rule is useless, unless the jury, upon the recommendation of the Court, find a fact, which, in all human possibility, never existed, and which is perfectly unconnected with the real merits of the case; surely, so heavy a tax upon the consciences and good sense of juries, which they are called on to incur for the sake of administering substantial justice, ought to be removed by the assistance of the legislature." Ibid. 669. The stat. 2 & 3 Will. IV. c. 71 (commonly called the Prescription Act), "was intended," said Mr. Baron Parke, "to accomplish this object, by shortening in effect the period of prescription, and making that possession a bar or title of itself, which was so before only by the intervention of a jury." Bright *v*. Walter, 1 Cr., M. & R. 217. [See Wallace *v*. Fletcher, 30 N.H. 434, 446; Edson *v*. Munsell, 10 Allen, 568, 569.]

[1] [Tracy *v*. Atherton, 36 Vt. 503. Kimball *v*. Ladd, 42 Vt. 747, was a suit between two mill-owners on the same stream, one above the other, in which the lower mill-owner claimed that his grantors had gained the right to draw water from a dam at the upper mill, by fifteen years' adverse use under a claim of right growing out of a parol arrangement between the grantors of the respective parties, by which the then lower mill-owner was to pay the expense of the flowage of lands in consequence of building said dam, and in consideration was to have the right of drawing water therefrom. The ruling in the case, that if the former owners of the lower mill, under claim of right by virtue of that contract, had exercised the right in the manner necessary to gain a right by adverse use, they would not be prevented from acquiring the right, even if the owner of the upper mill did occasionally, while the owners of the lower mill were thus enjoying the right, object or deny the right, if he did not in any way interfere with or interrupt that enjoyment, and they enjoyed it in spite of such objection, as fully as if there had been no objection or denial, was held to be correct; and in the same case it was held, that it was competent to prove that the former lower mill-owner, who was a party to said arrangement, and while he was using the water from said dam, told the witness about the arrangement and what it was, as tending to prove he claimed a right so to draw the water, but not as evidence that such arrangement was made or that any thing was done under it.]

[2] [See Sibley *v*. Ellis, 11 Gray, 417.]

not in our opinion correct. If there be any conflict of evidence as to the length, or character of the use, or any evidence proper to rebut the acquiring the right, it then becomes proper to submit it to the jury.[1] But where it stands solely upon the conceded or proved possession under claim of right for the requisite time, it is never submitted to a jury to find the right established or not, according to their judgments. And whether it is more proper for the Court to tell the jury that it is their duty from this to presume a grant, or to tell the jury that from this the law presumes a grant, is mere idle speculation. In fact, and in substance, it is a verdict directed by the Court, as a matter of law. And if it were submitted to the jury, and they were to return a verdict against the right, no Court would ever accept the verdict."[2]]

1 [See the remarks of Gray J., in Edson *v.* Munsell, 10 Allen, 568, 569; ante, § 217, note; White *v.* Chapin, 12 Allen, 516, 522.]

2 [The same view of the law was taken by the Court in Townsend *v.* Downer, 32 Vt. 183. Aldis J., in giving the judgment of the Court in that case, says, "When from long possession, with or without auxiliary circumstances, a grant is presumed as *matter of law*, and without regard to the fact whether such a grant was really made or not, then it may with the strictest propriety be said that the law presumes a grant. In such a case, under the practice of the Court in Vermont, it would be the duty of the Court to direct a verdict." He then proceeds to speak of the class of cases where lapse of time and long possession are relied upon with other circumstances, as evidence to establish that a grant has been made *in fact*. And thereupon he continues to remark, "We do not understand that there is still a third class of cases in which, although the grant is not presumed by the Court as pure matter of law, and is not found by the jury as a fact, still the Court may direct the jury to presume a grant, and thus by the intervention of the jury, but without the exercise of their judgment upon the evidence, establish the grant as if it were a mere inference of the law. Language may be found in some books and decisions favoring such a view, but the doctrine is clearly against the whole current of English and American decisions, and tends to confound the proper and separate jurisdictions of Court and jury. This erroneous view, we think, has arisen from the want of precision in language, when treating of presumptive evidence and the grants proved by or presumed from it." See the remarks of Bigelow J., in Powell *v.* Bagg, 8 Gray, 443; and of Gray J., in Edson *v.* Munsell, 10 Allen, 568, 569; Wilde J., in Coolidge *v.* Learned, 8 Pick. 504. It is clearly the province of the jury to decide whether the facts which are necessary to constitute the foundation for the presumption of a grant, are fully established; and it is the province of the Court to instruct them that if those facts are satisfactorily proved, or are admitted, by the rules of law a grant is to be presumed, or the right is thereby established; and it is their duty in this, as in other cases, to take the law as it is stated by the Court, so far as the rule of law is one of the elements in the case. If the requisite facts are not admitted, but clearly proved, or if they are admitted, and still the jury should find against the presumption or right, the Court ought to set their verdict aside, as stated by Poland C.J., in the above quotation in the text. If the facts should appear to be really doubtful, but the jury should be controlled in their decision of them by a desire to avoid the result to which the law would lead them, this would constitute a defect in the administration of the law, not chargeable to the law itself, but to a want of intelligence or moral sense in the jury.]

4. *Right acquired commensurate with the Extent of the Enjoyment.*

§ 224. The extent of the presumed right is determined by the user on which is grounded the presumed grant, the right granted being commensurate with the right enjoyed.[1] If one has ancient pits, which are replenished by another, the pits cannot be lawfully enlarged;[2] and if the enjoyment of the water has been limited to certain days in the week, it cannot lawfully be used on any other day.[3] So, a right to a sufficiency of water power to carry a certain number of spindles, cannot be extended to water power sufficient to carry a larger number.[4] In Darlington *v.* Painter, in Pennsylvania,[5] in which it appeared, that the defendant, for more than twenty years, had been in the habit of using a certain ditch to pass off waters running over or accumulating upon his lands, and that in 1844 he built a mill, and at the same time, entered upon the plaintiff's land and cleansed the ditch, saying he intended to use it for a tail-race; but at the time of the action brought, the mill had not commenced working; it was held, that the defendant could not use it for any purpose, that would increase the flow, enlarge the ditch, or affect the water in any way different from that use for which the watercourse was granted.

[1] Bealy *v.* Shaw, 6 East, 208; Alder *v.* Savill, 5 Taunt. 424; Russell *v.* Scott, 9 Cowen, 279; Dyer *v.* Depui, 5 Wharton, 584; Watkins *v.* Peck, 13 N.H. 360; Cowell *v.* Thayer, 5 Met. 253; Chapman *v.* Thames Manuf. Co., 13 Conn. 269; Manier *v.* Myers, 6 B. Mon. (Ken.) 132; Bigelow *v.* Battel, 15 Mass. 313; Strong *v.* Benedict, 5 Conn. 210; Baldwin *v.* Calkins, 10 Wend. 167; Simpson *v.* Seavey, 8 Greenl. 138; Rogers *v.* Bruce, 17 Pick. 184; [Wright *v.* Moore, 38 Ala. N.S. 593; Stein *v.* Burden, 24 Ala. N.S. 130; Morris *v.* Commander, 3 Ired. 510; Whittier *v.* Cocheco Manuf. Co., 9 N.H. 454; Bolivar Manuf. Co. *v.* Neponset Manuf. Co., 16 Pick. 241; Gerenger *v.* Summers, 2 Ired. N.C. 229; Hulme *v.* Shreve, 3 Green Ch. (N.J.) 116; Burnham *v.* Kempton, 44 N.H. 78, 91; Winnipiseogee Lake Co. *v.* Young, 40 N.H. 420; Powers *v.* Osgood, 102 Mass. 454, 457; Powell *v.* Lash, 64 N. Car. 456; Carlisle *v.* Cooper, 6 C. E. Green, 594. The right acquired will be commensurate in *character* and *extent* with the enjoyment. A user of throwing sawdust into a stream cannot establish the right of discharging into it poisonous and noxious drugs. Holsman *v.* Boiling Spring Bleaching Co., 1 McCarter (N.J.), 335, 346. One may have a right for the rain-water to fall from the eaves of his house into a yard belonging to another person, and yet cannot justify putting up a spout, and thus collecting the water in a larger body to fall into that yard. Reynolds *v.* Clarke, 2 Ld. Ray. 1399; S.C. 1 Str. 634; S.C. 8 Mod. 172; Woolrych, Waters, 180.]

[2] Brown *v.* Best, 1 Wils. 174.

[3] Strutt *v.* Bovingdon, 5 Esp. 56.

[4] Bigelow *v.* Battel, 15 Mass. 313. [See Wheatley *v.* Chrisman, 24 Penn. St. 298.]

[5] Darlington *v.* Painter, 7 Penn. St. 473.

[Where one has used a drain from his own land over that of his neighbor for a period of over twenty years, but during those years, the drain has been enlarged, deepened, and varied in its course and termination, no right to the continued use of the drain is thereby acquired. Such right will be acquired only by the use of the drain for twenty years after the enlargement.[1]]

§ 225. The rule that the mode or manner of using the water shall not be materially varied to the prejudice of others, was applied in an important case in the State of New York (an appeal in equity, confirming the decision of the court below), in which it was held, that if the proprietor of land, at the head of a stream, changes the natural flow of the water, and continues such change for twenty years, he cannot afterwards restore the flow of the water to its natural state, when it will have the effect to destroy the mills of other proprietors below, which have been erected in reference to such change in the natural flow of the stream. It appeared, that the complainants were the several owners of different mills situated upon the same stream, which mills depended upon the particular use of the waters of a pond at the head of the stream for the running thereof; and, as such mill-owners, had been in the uninterrupted enjoyment of the water in a particular manner for more than twenty years; it was held, that a Court of Equity had jurisdiction to establish the right of the lower proprietors to the use they had made of the waters of the pond, and to restrain the defendant from disturbing them in the enjoyment thereof, by an alteration made at the outlet of the pond.[2]

[1] [Cotton *v.* Pocasset Manuf. Co., 13 Met. 429; Stein *v.* Burden, 24 Ala. 130.]

[2] Belknap *v.* Trimble, 3 Paige, 577. This case may require a little more explanation. The plaintiffs made out that they were the owners and occupiers of ancient mills on the stream issuing from the pond, and the question was, whether the defendant, by assuming the control of the waters at the pond, to the great and acknowledged damage of the plaintiffs, had not acted in violation of their rights. For more than forty years the plaintiffs and their predecessors were in the habit of constantly resorting to the pond for water when they needed it, and of scouring, altering, and improving the outlet, without the permission of any one, or without the denial of right by any one. The defendant admitted, that at the time, he had no waterworks at the outlet, or on the stream; did not pretend that the pond was of any value to his farm; and it was considered by the Court evident, that in purchasing it, he did it with the view of rendering the property of the plaintiffs useless, until they bought him out, or made terms with him. See Bullen *v.* Runnels, 2 N.H. 255; Whittier *v.* Cocheco Manuf. Co., 9 N.H. 454. In a case in the English Court of Exchequer, in 1846, the substance of the declaration was, that before and at the time of committing the grievances, the plaintiff was, and from hence hitherto had been, possessed of a rolling-mill, with the appur-

§ 226. But although the extent of the right is to be measured and regulated by the enjoyment upon which the right is founded, the party is yet allowed freedom in the manner of exercising it. It was contended in Luttrel's case,[1] that the plaintiff by taking down old fulling-mills, and by erecting new mills of another nature and for another object, had destroyed his prescription, and could not prescribe to have any water to the new mills; and it was said, "If a man grants me a watercourse to my fulling-mills, I cannot convert them to corn-mills, *nec e contra.*" Yet, "forasmuch as in general the mill was the substance, and the addition demonstrates only the quality, and the alteration was not of the substance, but only the quality or name of the mill, and that without any prejudice in the watercourse to the owner thereof; for these reasons it was resolved, that the prescription remained." So, in Saunders *v.* Newman,[2] where the claim in the declaration was for a mill generally, it was held, that the right to the discharge of the water was not lost by an alteration in the dimensions of the mill-wheel. "The owner," said Mr. Justice Abbott, in that case, "is not bound to use the water in the same precise manner, or apply it to the same mill; if he were, that would stop all improvements in machinery." In Hall *v.* Swift,[3] where the plaintiff had a right to water, flowing from the defend-

tenances, and by reason thereof, ought to have had and enjoyed the benefit of the water of a certain watercourse, which until the diversion of the water, had run and flowed by means of a certain wear, therein erected, a little above the said mill, being kept at a certain height, for supplying the same with water. The breach, in substance, was, that the defendant pulled down the said wear, and placed and fixed the same at a much lower height than it ought to have been, and so continued the same. It was pleaded, that the defendant was the occupier of a certain close, next adjoining to the watercourse, and that he and all other occupiers of the same, for the period of twenty years, "*next before the commencement of this suit,*" enjoyed as of right, and without interruption, the right as occasion required, of removing a part of the said wear, and fixing the same at a lower height, and of keeping at such lower height, for the purpose of diverting the water for irrigation, at the times when irrigation was necessary for the close; wherefore, the defendant removed the said part of the wear, and placed and kept it at such lower height, to such an extent, and for such time, and no more or longer than was necessary for diverting the water for the irrigation of the close. It was held, that this plea was good; and that it was not an argumentative traverse of the right alleged in the declaration, inasmuch, as it set up a right, which, under the stat. 2 & 3 Will. IV. c. 71, was not complete, until the commencement of the suit; and, therefore, was not inconsistent with the plaintiffs' right to have the wear at a greater height, at the time of the act complained of. Ward *v.* Robins, 15 M. & W. 237.

[1] Cottel *v.* Luttrel, 4 Co. 87 *a;* and see ante, § 149 *a*, et seq.

[2] Saunders *v.* Newman, 1 B. & Ald. 258.

[3] Hall *v.* Swift, 6 Scott, 167.

ant's land across a lane, to his own land, and it appeared that, "formerly the stream meandered a little down the lane before it flowed into the plaintiff's land; and that, in the year 1835, the plaintiff, in order to render its enjoyment more commodious to himself, a little varied the course, by making a straight cut direct from the opening or spout under the defendant's hedge, across the lane, to his own premises;" and this, it was contended, negatived the right claimed in the declaration. Tindal C.J., in delivering his opinion, said, "If such an objection as this were allowed to prevail, any right, however ancient, might be lost by the most minute alteration in the mode of enjoyment,—the making straight a crooked line or footpath would have this result. No authority has been cited, nor am I aware of any principle of law or common sense upon which such an argument could base itself."[1]

§ 227. In this country the doctrine is as well settled, that where a right has been acquired by virtue of twenty years' enjoyment, to use a certain quantity of water, a change in the mode and objects of use is justifiable; and here, as in England, the only restriction is, that the alterations made from time to time shall not be injurious to those whose interests are involved.[2] It cannot be doubted, says Gibson C.J., that the nature of the user cannot be changed in any case, unless the flow remain the same as to

[1] See also Thomas *v.* Thomas, 2 Cr., M. & R. 34; [Wright *v.* Moore, 38 Ala. N.S. 593; Baxendale *v.* McMurray, L.R. 2 Ch. App. 790.]

[2] Strickler *v.* Todd, 10 S. & Rawle, 63; Blanchard *v.* Baker, 8 Greenl. 253. In Hulme *v.* Shreve, in New Jersey, it was held, that if waste-gates be constructed by the defendants, and used by them for a course of years, with the complainants' assent, the complainants cannot have relief by injunction, so long as the use of the gates is confined to their original purpose; but if an attempt is made to apply them to a different purpose, injurious to the complainants, the Court will, by injunction, prohibit the use of the gates. 3 Green (N.J.) Ch. 116. All that the law requires is, that the mode or manner of using the water should not have been materially varied to the prejudice of others. Per Chancellor Walworth, in Belknap *v.* Trimble, 3 Paige, 605; Johnson *v.* Rand, 6 N.H. 22. [An appropriation of water for a saw-mill allows the party to use the same amount for a grist-mill instead. McDonald *v.* Bear River &c. Co., 13 Cal. 220. See Kaler *v.* Beaman, 49 Maine, 207; Deshon *v.* Porter, 38 Maine, 289; Hynds *v.* Shultz, 39 Barb. 600; Marcly *v.* Shultz, 29 N.Y. 352. Where a prescriptive right to foul a stream has been acquired, the fouling must not be considerably enlarged to the prejudice of other people. Crossley *v.* Lightowler, Law Rep. 2 Ch. App. 478; s.c. Law Rep. 3 Eq. Cas. 279. The right to foul must be measured by the enjoyment; it cannot be used in a different and more extensive manner. McCallum *v.* The Germantown Water Co., 54 Penn. St. 40; Crosby *v.* Bessey, 49 Maine, 207.]

quantity and rapidity.[1] Where the plaintiff erected a dam across the outlet of a pond, and acquired a right by prescription to use the water, it was held, that the erection of a new dam by the defendants higher than the old one, was not, in itself, an infringement of the plaintiff's rights; for the plaintiff had a right to adopt and use the new dam to the height of the old one; but that the defendants were entitled, as against the plaintiff, to use the water when raised by means of the new dam, above the top of the old dam, provided they did not thereby prejudice in any manner the rights of the plaintiff.[2]

§ 228. Where a right exists to use a certain quantity of water for propelling machinery, a change may be made not only in the mode and objects of the use, but in the *place* of using it, if the quantity of water used is not increased, and the change is not to the prejudice of others.[3] Thus, a party had for more than twenty years used a certain quantity of water at a particular dam; it was held, that he might open his gates and draw that quantity, without using it there, in order to use it at other works below on the same stream. And the owner of a mill may even draw a larger quantity of water through his gates than he has been accustomed to use, if he has lawfully provided the surplus, for his own use, by means of a *reservoir* above, and causes no injury thereby to the owner of another mill situated upon the same dam, or to other persons having rights in the stream.[4]

[1] Darlington *v.* Painter, 7 Penn. St. 473.

[2] Rogers *v.* Bruce, 17 Pick. 184. [See Burnham *v.* Kempton, 44 N.H. 90.]

[3] [Carlisle *v.* Cooper, 6 C. E. Green, 595. So a right to an easement of flowing lands may be acquired by prescription, although the flowing was occasioned by different dams, owned by different persons, provided the extent of flowing is, at all times, the same. Davis *v.* Brigham, 29 Maine, 391. So in Stackpole *v.* Curtis, 32 Maine, 383, it was held, that to establish a prescriptive right of flowing water by a dam for the use of a mill, it is not necessary that the dam should have been maintained, for the whole period, upon the same spot; it is sufficient, if shown to have been maintained upon the same mill-site, though removed, from time to time, to different places upon such site. See Whittier *v.* Cocheco Manuf. Co., 9 N.H. 454, 458.]

[4] Whittier *v.* Cocheco Manuf. Co., 9 N.H. 454. And see Bracegirdle *v.* Peacock, 10 Jur. 9; [Baldwin *v.* Calkins, 10 Wend. 167; Morris *v.* Commander, 3 Ired. (N.C.) 510; Gerenger *v.* Summers, 2 Ired. (N.C.) 229; Wright *v.* Moore, 28 Ala. 598; Carlisle *v.* Cooper, 6 C. E. Green, 595. So if a grant is made to a person, owning a dam and mill erected at a particular place, of a right to flow the lands of the grantor, the grantee is not necessarily restricted to the use of the water at the precise place where it was used, when the grant was made. Shepley C.J., in Stackpole *v.* Curtis, 32 Maine, 383. So where the grant of an easement in the use of water is measured by the height in the dam to which the plaintiff is entitled, it is no objection to his assertion of his right that he has increased the capacity of his mill, so long as he demands the use of no more water

§ 229. In a case in the English Court of Exchequer, in 1845,[1] in which the action was for the diversion of water, the plaintiff alleged in his declaration, a reversionary interest in three closes of land, to wit, *three ponds* filled with water, one pond being on each of the said closes, and a right to the flow of the water into the said closes, for supplying the said ponds in the said closes with water for the watering of cattle; and the defendant traversed the right to the flow of the water, as alleged. It appeared in evidence, that the plaintiff had enjoyed an immemorial right to the flow of this water into an *ancient* pond, in one of his closes; but that above thirty years ago, he made a *new* pond in each of the three closes, and turned the water so as to supply them, and thenceforth disused the old pond, which became gradually filled up and overgrown with grass. It was held, that the plaintiff, under his declaration was entitled to recover, in respect to his right to the flow of water to the *old* pond, though it was contended by the defendant's counsel, that the three *new* ponds were alone claimed in the declaration. By Pollock C.B.: "The plaintiff, in bringing his action, and declaring for an infringement of his right to a flow of water to the three ponds, meant, no doubt, to recover, in respect of the three *new* ponds." By Parke B.: "The use of the old pond was discontinued, only because the plaintiff obtained the same or a greater advantage, from the use of the three new ones. *He did not thereby abandon his right, he only exercised it in a different spot;* and a substitution of that nature, is not an abandonment. He has a right, therefore, under this declaration, to recover in respect of the old pond. The right alleged, is a right to have the uninterrupted flow of certain surplus water, into a pond; and that right is equally proved, whether it be by prescription or lost grant, or under Lord Tenterden's Act. The declaration means no more than this, that the plaintiff has a right to the overflow of water, either in one pond or in three ponds."

§ 230. It should, however, be observed, that the fact of how much water has been *actually used*, is not always decisive of the nature and extent of the right; that is, if for the space of twenty years, a certain quantity of water has run uninterruptedly and as

than the limitations of the grant award to him. Carter *v.* Shipman, 35 N.Y. 533.]

[1] Hale *v.* Oldroyd, 14 M. & W. 789: [See Carlisle *v.* Cooper, 6 C. E. Green, 595.]

of right to a certain mill, the right to have that quantity run, becomes an appurtenance to the mill, though the whole of it may not have been necessary for the purposes for which the mill has been employed.[1] In Tyler *v.* Wilkinson,[2] it appeared that a certain quantity of water had been accustomed to run in an artificial canal, called "Sergeant's trench," leading from the main stream; and Mr. J. Story, in giving judgment, said, "The proprietors of Sergeant's trench are entitled to the use of so much of the water of the river, as has been accustomed to flow through that trench, to and from their mills (whether actually used, or necessary for the same mills, or not), during the twenty years last before the institution of this suit, subject only to such qualifications and limitations, as have been acknowledged, or rightfully exercised by the plaintiffs, as riparian proprietors, or as the owners of the lower mill-dam, during that period. But here their right stops; they have no right farther to appropriate any surplus water, not already used by the riparian proprietors, upon the notion that such water is open to the first occupiers. That surplus is the inheritance of the riparian proprietors, and not open to occupancy."[3]

[§ 230 *a.* It has already been stated in a preceding section,[4] and is here again noticed, to illustrate the subject under consideration, that if the owner of the land on one side of a river erects a mill-dam across the river, without obtaining permission from the proprietor of the opposite side, this is an adverse and injurious invasion of the rights of this riparian proprietor, although he may then have no occasion to make use of the water; and if the dam be continued a sufficient length of time, will authorize the jury to presume a grant of the right to abut the dam on such opposite proprietor, and also a grant to have all the benefit, water power, and privileges which would arise from the erection of the same. The extent of this right would be measured by the height and capacity of the dam, and not by the partial use of the water power created by it; unless it be shown that the grant was made with limitations and reservations. And the burden of proof to

[1] See Carlisle *v.* Cooper, 6 C. E. Green, 595.

[2] Tyler *v.* Wilkinson, 4 Mason, 397.

[3] See ante, §§ 130–136. A plea of prescription is supported if the party prove a right more extensive than that pleaded; but the right must be of such a nature that it may comprehend the right pleaded. Per Coleridge J., in Bailey *v.* Appleyard, 8 Ad. & El. 167.

[4] [Ante, § 219 *d.*]

show the limitations and reservations would rest on the party alleging their existence.[1]]

[§ 230 *b*. Where a riparian proprietor has acquired a prescriptive right as against an owner below to pollute a stream in carrying on a particular kind of business, he will not render himself liable to such owner merely in consequence of a change of the material used in that business, which does not increase the amount of pollution. The defendant, the owner of an ancient paper-mill, where the paper had been made from rags, introduced a new vegetable fibre, and carried on the works upon the same scale for making paper from this new material. For more than twenty years before this change, the refuse arising from the paper manufacture had been discharged into a stream which ran past the plaintiff's house; it was held, that the easement to which the defendant had become entitled, was to be presumed to be, not a right to foul the stream by discharging into it the washings produced by the working up of rags, but a right to discharge into it the washings produced by the manufacture of paper in the reasonable and proper course of such manufacture, using any proper materials for that purpose, but not increasing the pollution, and that the burden was on the plaintiff to prove any increase of pollution.[2] In Baxendale *v.* McMurray,[3] in which the above decision was made, Lord Cairns L.J. said, "It is difficult to suppose the existence of an easement founded on, and limited to, the washing of rags. If made specific in this way it would be

[1] [Bliss *v.* Rice, 17 Pick. 23. But in Burnham *v.* Kempton, 44 N.H. 90, the Court, adverting to the propositions laid down in the text, said, "We find ourselves unable to assent to this doctrine. To us it seems that twenty years' maintenance of a dam in a particular mode, is evidence of a grant or right so to maintain it, and twenty years' use of the water in a particular way is evidence of a right thus to use the water. The same proof of user which establishes the right, is equally conclusive in establishing the limitations of that right. Twenty years' accustomed flow and use of a certain stream or pond of water is as good evidence of right to the one party as to the other. Twenty years' support of a mill-dam is evidence of a grant to build and maintain just such a dam, constructed and used substantially in the same manner. Twenty years' use of the water raised by such a dam, to drive a grist, saw, and fulling mill, at all seasons, or at certain seasons, is evidence of a grant to use so much of such water as shall be necessary at those seasons to drive these mills or similar ones. It necessarily implies, also, a grant by the owner of the right to obstruct the stream by the dam, and to force all the water not used by these mills over the dam, and of course necessarily to limit the right of the riparian owner to such use as he may make of the water after it has passed over the dam."]

[2] [Baxendale *v.* McMurray, L.R. 2 Ch. App. 790.]

[3] [L.R. 2 Ch. App. 790.]

confined to rags known and in use at the time the easement was acquired, and the rags of textile fabrics afterwards coming into use must, however valuable for the manufacture of paper, be excluded. Rags, again, would afford no standard by which to test or limit the amount of pollution. Some would be much more dirty than others; the washings from some might be harmless, and from others deleterious."—"I am therefore of opinion that it is not sufficient for the plaintiff to show that the defendant uses in the manufacture of paper a raw material different from that formerly employed. He must show, further, a greater amount of pollution and injury arising from the use of this new material."]

5. *The Presumption as it relates to Parties not in Possession.*

§ 231. In an action for the disturbance of a water privilege, and indeed of any easement, the enjoyment of it may be shown not to have been adverse, by evidence that the plaintiff has not been in possession of the premises, to which the privilege or easement claimed, is attached. Thus, if a tenant for a term of years, permits another to enjoy an easement in his estate for twenty years, and then the particular estate determines, such enjoyment will not, as a general rule, affect the interests of him who has the inheritance in *remainder* or *reversion*. And when the remaining or reversionary interest commences, the party entitled may dispute the right to the easement, and the length of enjoyment will be no bar to his claim; for as the tenant cannot bind the landlord, by his own positive act, so he cannot by his *laches*, or inaction and forbearance.[1]

§ 232. The case of Bradbury *v.* Grinsell, in the King's Bench,[2] was determined according to the rule just mentioned. A., who was a tenant for life, with a power to make a jointure, which he afterwards executed, gave license to B., in 1747, to erect a wear on the river T., in A.'s soil, for the purpose of watering B.'s

[1] Gale & What. on Easem. 75; and see Hale *v.* Oldroyd, 14 M. & W. 789; [Wallace *v.* Fletcher, 30 N.H. 453; Angell, Lim. § 415; Coalter *v.* Hunter, 4 Rand. 58; Nichols *v.* Aylor, 7 Leigh, 546, 565; Biddle *v.* Ash, 2 Ashm. 211, 221; Smith *v.* Miller, 11 Gray, 148; Corning *v.* Troy Iron &c. Co., 39 Barb. 311; s.c. 22 How. P.C. 217; Parker *v.* Framingham, 8 Met. 260; Pierre *v.* Fernald, 26 Maine, 436; Blanchard *v.* Bridges, 4 Ad. & E. 176; Reimer *v.* Stuber, 20 Penn. St. 458; Schenley *v.* Commonwealth, 36 Penn. St. 29.]

[2] Cited in Wms. Saund. 175, n. (d).

meadows; and then A. died, and the jointress entered and continued seised, down to 1799, when the tenant of A.'s farm diverted the water of the river from the wear. Upon which, the tenant of B.'s farm brought an action on the case of diverting the water. It was held, that the uninterrupted possession of the water for so many years, with the acquiescence of the particular tenants for life, did not affect him who had the inheritance in reversion, and the Court were clear upon the point of law as above stated. So in Barker *v.* Richardson,[1] where the plaintiff's windows had existed for more than twenty years. The defendants had erected a building, which occasioned the darkening of the plaintiff's windows, upon their adjoining land, which had been glebe land, belonging to the rectory; but within the last six years, had been conveyed in exchange, by the then rector, with the consent of the bishop and patron, under the authority of 55 Geo. III. and by the grantee conveyed to the defendants. It was objected on the part of the defendants, that although, after uninterrupted possession of an easement for twenty years, the law will, in ordinary cases, presume a grant, yet that rule extended only to those cases where the presumed grantor was capable of making the grant. And that, in this case, the rector, who was a mere tenant for life, had no power to make such a grant, and therefore length of time could not operate against him, who was not seised of any estate of inheritance. Mr. C.J. Abbott admitted, that twenty years' uninterrupted possession of any easement, is generally sufficient to raise the presumption of a grant; but in this case, he thought the grant, if presumed, must have been made by a tenant for life, who had no power to bind his successor; and that the grant, therefore, would be invalid, and consequently the present plaintiff could derive no benefit from it, against those to whom the glebe had been sold; and his opinion was, that the evidence in the case was insufficient to entitle the plaintiff to maintain the action.[2] Lord Ellenborough, on the argument for a new trial, in Daniel *v.* North,[3]

[1] Barker *v.* Richardson, 4 B. & Ald. 578.

[2] [In Wallace *v.* Fletcher, 30 N.H. 434, 453, Bell J. said, "In the case of a reversioner, the time of prescription does not begin to run until his interest becomes vested, so as to give him a right of action. The tenant for life or years may grant easements, or permit them to be acquired by user, and they will be valid against himself or those who hold his estate during its continuance, and perhaps not afterwards, where the reversioner had previously neither cause nor right to complain."]

[3] Daniel *v.* North, 11 East, 372. The action was for obstructing ancient lights, and it appeared that the premises, on

observed, "How can such a presumption be raised against the landlord, without showing that he knew of the fact, when he was not in possession, and received no immediate injury from it at the time?" In delivering his opinion, the learned judge said further, "The foundation of presuming a grant against any party, is, that the exercise of the adverse right on which such presumption is founded, was against a party capable of making the grant;[1] and that cannot be presumed against him, unless there was some probable means of his knowing what was done against him; for it cannot be laid down as a rule of law, that the enjoyment of the plaintiff's windows during the occupation of the opposite premises by a tenant, though for twenty years, without the knowledge of the landlord, will bind the latter, and there is no evidence stated in the report, from which his knowledge should be presumed."

§ 233. It is clearly not incompatible with the above doctrine, and indeed it has so been positively decided, that presumptions may in certain cases be made against the dominant land-owner, during the possession and acquiescence of his tenant. The tenant may suffer a direct and palpable injury to his own enjoyment, and thus fairly be presumed to be on the alert in guarding the rights of his landlord, while guarding his own enjoyment, as in the case, for instance, of the destruction of a way.[2] It is a well-established rule in the construction of the Statute of Limitations, that the rights of persons in remainder and reversion, are not affected by neglect in the tenant for life, or for years, during the continuance of the particular estate, in resisting the acts of wrong-doers; and yet there may be particular cases in which presumptions may exist to the contrary. If a *boundary line* is disputed, and the dispute is adjusted by the agreement of the tenant for life, such agreement is presumptive evidence to bind the remainder-man; for although the remainder-man may assert that his right has been invaded, yet the submission of the tenant for life (if without fraud), will raise a strong presumption against those who succeed him.[3]

which the obstruction was erected, had been occupied, during twenty years, by a tenant at will, and there was no evidence that the owner of those premises was aware of such enjoyment.

[1] See post, §§ 238, 239, and cases in notes; Nelson *v.* Butterfield, 21 Maine, 234, 235; Gray J., in Edson *v.* Munsell, 10 Allen, 568.

[2] Daniel *v.* North, ub. sup. [See Barker *v.* Richardson, 4 B. & Ald. 579; McGregor *v.* Waite, 10 Gray, 75.]

[3] Saunders *v.* Annesley, 2 Sch. & Lef. 101, and cited in Angell, Lim. § 415.

§ 234. There is, says Lord Redesdale,[1] a vast number of cases, in which the act of tenant for life binds the remainder-man as evidence; and he then refers to the enjoyment of easements, in which case, if it can be proved, that the landlord has actual knowledge of a disturbance of the easement, while in the occupation of the tenant, he will be bound. Questions of this sort are undoubtedly proper for the determination of the jury, as depending upon the circumstances proved.[2] In Dawson *v.* The Duke of Norfolk,[3] Mr. J. Bayley, at nisi prius, did not advise the jury to presume a grant, because it did not appear that the turning of the plaintiff's cattle on the common, was generally known to those who had been trespassed upon; and on that ground he left it to the jury, whether it was not an encroachment, negativing the right; and this direction was, by the Court of Exchequer, held proper. In Wood *v.* Veal,[4] it appeared on the part of the plaintiff, that, in the year 1719, a lease for *ninety-nine* years was given of the plaintiff's premises; and it was held by the Court of King's Bench, that, under these circumstances, the jury were well justified in finding that there was no public right of way, inasmuch as there could be no dedication by the tenant, for that term of years, nor by any one except the owner in fee. Therefore, to use the language of Mr. C.J. Dallas, "When lapse of time is said to afford such a presumption, the inference is also drawn from accompanying facts; and here, where there is no direct evidence, whether or not the owner of the land had any knowledge of what passed, the inference to be drawn, must, in a peculiar degree, depend on the nature of the accompanying facts; and the presumption in favor of a grant will be more or less probable, as it may be more or less probable that those facts could not have existed, without the consent of the owner of the land. The circumstances proved in the present case, were sufficient to leave to a jury, as circumstances from which the knowledge of the owner, and his acquiescence, on the supposition of a preceding grant, might fairly be presumed."[5]

§ 235. If the time has once begun to run against the dominant

[1] Saunders *v.* Annesley, 2 Sch. & Lef. 101.

[2] Daniel *v.* North, ub. sup.; Wakeman *v.* West, 8 C. & P. 105.

[3] Dawson *v.* The Duke of Norfolk, 1 Price, 246.

[4] Wood *v.* Veal, 5 B. & Ald. 454.

[5] Gray *v.* Bond, 2 Bro. & Bing. 667. An adverse possession of twenty years, is, in England, not a bar to a rector or vicar, except as against the present incumbent, who submitted to such possession. Runcorn *v.* Doe, 5 B. & C. 696.

land-owner, in consequence of his knowledge of, and acquiescence in, the enjoyment of the easement, the intervention of a particular estate, will not then stop it.[1] From the observations of Bayley J. in Cross *v.* Lewis,[2] it would appear, that provided the existence of the easement prior to the commencement of the tenancy, was shown, and a sufficient length of enjoyment had taken place, to afford evidence of a grant, the burden of proof would be thrown upon the owner of the land sought to be made liable to the easement; and unless he could show such previous user to have taken place, without his knowledge, the right to the easement would be established.[3]

§ 236. The foregoing doctrine, in relation to the enjoyment of easements in estates, during the possession thereof, by tenants for life, or years, will apply to every *temporary interest* in the land;[4] so that time does not begin to run against a privilege reserved in a deed, if by the deed it clearly appears that an immediate occupation and exercise of the privilege was not at the time contemplated by the parties; as where the reservation is to the heirs and assigns of the grantor.[5]

6. *Disabilities.*

§ 237. If the doctrine of adverse possession of an easement, cannot, in general, be applied to reversioners, during the continuance of the particular estate, it would seem *a fortiori* to be inapplicable to persons who are hindered from suing by reason of their *legal disability*. *Contra non valentem agere currit præscriptio*,[6] is a maxim which naturally suggests itself in this place, and which is illustrated by those express provisions in the different Statutes of Limitation, which, in cases of infancy, coverture, and others similar, suspend their operation, until the removal of such disability. As in the case of a debt due, the prescription only begins to run, from the time when the creditor has a right

[1] 2 Greenl. Ev. § 545; Best, Presump. 89; [Cross *v.* Lewis, 2 B. & C. 686. See Pearsall *v.* Post, 20 Wend. 111; Bright *v.* Walker, 1 Cr., M. & R. 211; McGregor *v.* Wait, 10 Gray, 75.]

[2] Cross *v.* Lewis, 2 B. & C. 686; Gale & What. on Easem. 80.

[3] Gale & What. on Easem. 80.

[4] Greenl. Ev. § 545. [Acquiescence in the enjoyment of an easement is not to be presumed against a party who has no choice but to acquiesce, as in the case of private property taken for public use by authority of the State. Jessup *v.* Loucks, 55 Penn. St. 350.]

[5] Butz *v.* Ihrie, 1 Rawle, 281.

[6] Poth. Traité des Obligations, 645; ib. Traité Præscript.; Ayraud *v.* Babin, 19 Mart. (La.) 47; Richards *v.* Maryland Insurance Co., 8 Cranch, 84.

to institute his suit;[1] for in such case to impute *delay* to the creditor, would be contrary to the conclusions of reason.[2]

§ 238. Yet, in commenting on the conclusiveness of the presumption, of which we are treating, Mr. J. Story, in Tyler *v.* Wilkinson,[3] remarked, that its operation had *never yet* been denied in cases where *personal disabilities* of particular proprietors might have intervened, such as infancy, coverture, and insanity: and where, by the ordinary course of proceeding, grants would not be presumed. But Mr. Matthews in his Treatise on Presumptive Evidence, seems to consider, that the right otherwise arising from long enjoyment, may be repelled, by showing, that the parties whose interests have been prejudiced were until lately, incapable, by reason of infancy, coverture, or other legal disability, to give the necessary license. The Supreme Court of New Hampshire have expressly held, that, notwithstanding the remark of Mr. J. Story, in Tyler *v.* Wilkinson,[4] a grant by a *guardian* of an infant, of an easement in the land of his ward, extending beyond the limit of the guardianship, was not to be presumed; inasmuch as a guardian is not authorized to grant incorporeal hereditaments out of the ward's land. "Perhaps," say the Court, "a disability intervening during the lapse of the term, but not extending to the termination of the period of twenty years, might not be sufficient to rebut the presumption; but it would be absurd to presume a grant, where it was clear that no such grant could have existed.[5] And in this case, a

[1] Broom's Legal Max. 700.

[2] It has been the policy of the English legislature, at a modern date, to establish two periods of prescription, except in case of light. By the 7th sect. of the stat. 2 & 3 Will. IV. c. 71 (commonly called the "Prescription Act"), it is enacted as follows: "That the time during which any person, otherwise capable of resisting any claim to any of the matters before mentioned, shall have been, or shall be, an infant, idiot, non compos mentis, feme covert, or tenant for life, or during which any action or suit shall have been pending, and which shall have been diligently prosecuted, until the death of any party or parties thereto, shall be excluded in the periods hereinbefore mentioned, except in cases where the right or claim is hereby declared to be absolute and indefeasible." This has reference to an enjoyment of *twenty years*. The enactment, as to the longer period of *forty* years, materially restricts the Common Law modes of defeating the effect of the user of an easement, declaring that user for *that* time, shall give an *absolute and indefeasible* right, notwithstanding any personal disability on the part of the owner of the servient inheritance, unless it shall appear that the same was enjoyed under some consent or agreement, by deed or writing. See the Act referred to and commented on, in Gale & What. on Easem. 68–75.

[3] Tyler *v.* Wilkinson, 4 Mason, 402.

[4] 4 Mason, 403.

[5] [Edson *v.* Munsell, 10 Allen, 568, per Gray J.; Barker *v.* Richardson, 4 B. & Ald. 579; Erle J., in Rochdale Canal Co. *v.* Radcliffe, 18 Q.B. 287, 315.]

grant by a guardian, of an easement, in the land of his ward, extending beyond the limit of the guardianship, is not to be presumed."[1] [In Edson *v.* Munsell,[2] evidence was offered by the plaintiff to show that an aqueduct had been laid in 1813, from a spring on the land of the defendant, to a tub on the land of the plaintiff, and had been enjoyed from that time by the plaintiff and those under whom he claimed for more than forty years uninterruptedly, and the plaintiff claimed a right to maintain the aqueduct by prescription, or by such and so long an enjoyment as furnished a presumption of a grant. On the other hand, the defendant offered evidence to show that the person owning the land, in which, and at the time, the aqueduct was laid, was then insane, and continued insane and the owner of the land until his death in 1856. The Court held, that under the statutes of Massachusetts, an easement of this character in the land of an insane person, cannot be acquired by prescription, the time of which commences during the insanity, until the expiration of such time after his death or the removal of his disability as would bar an action by him or his legal representatives for the land, no matter how long such disability may continue. In this case Mr. Justice Gray remarked that the dicta of Mr. Justice Story, in Tyler *v.* Wilkinson,[3] if fairly susceptible of a wider interpretation, than that a prescription cannot be interrupted by a disability which does not come into existence until after the time has begun to run, are in conflict with the general current of authority, and can hardly be reconciled with the opinion of the Supreme Court of the United States, as delivered by the same learned Judge, in Ricard *v.* Williams.[4] And Mr. Justice Gray added, "If a person incapable of granting or consenting is to have no longer time to avoid a title by prescription than he would be allowed by the Statute of Limitations to bring an action for the land, he should at least be allowed the benefit of all the time which the statute does give." — "If the time necessary to perfect a title by prescription to an easement in land is measured by any other rule than that derived by analogy from the statutes limiting actions to recover the land itself, it will be quite as difficult to establish such a title by the ordinary period of

1 Watkins *v.* Peck, 13 N.H. 360. The Court cite Gilb. Eq. 3; Guernsey *v.* Rodbridges, cited 2 Cowen's Phil. on Ev. 383.

2 [Edson *v.* Munsell, 10 Allen, 557.]

3 [4 Mason, 402.]

4 [7 Wheat. 109–111.]

prescription against one who has been insane throughout the entire period. It is an essential element of the use necessary to give a title by prescription, as laid down by Bracton, and repeatedly recognized by this Court, that it should be with the acquiescence of the true owner having the power to grant or to interrupt the easement."[1]

§ 239. Where a person claimed title to a several fishery, in the soil of another, on the presumption of a non-existing grant, and relied on the proof of adverse possession, for more than twenty years before the commencement of the action;[2] the jury were instructed, that to raise such presumption of grant, it must appear that such exclusive right as the one claimed, had been used and enjoyed against those, who were *able in law* to assert and defend their rights, and to resist such adverse claim;[3] and, therefore if the persons against whom such right is claimed, were under the disability of infancy, the time during which such disability continued, was to be deducted, in the computation of twenty years. They were further instructed, that if they found that the adverse possession in the lifetime of the person in whose soil the easement in question was claimed, added to that which was held after his heirs became of age (there having been no interruption in the mean time), amounted together to the period of twenty years' adverse possession, then they should find for the plaintiff. This instruction was excepted to and made the ground of a motion for a new trial, at which Wilde J., who delivered the judgment of the Court, said, "These instructions are manifestly correct, and it is not denied, that the evidence was such as would warrant the jury to find a verdict in pursuance thereof, for the plaintiff, provided the use and enjoyment by the plaintiff, and that by those under whom he claims, may be coupled, so as to make up the twenty years, notwithstanding the intervention of the rights of Fletcher's heirs and their disability; and we have no doubt they may. If it were otherwise, it would be difficult to

1 [10 Allen, 567.]

2 [In McFarlin *v.* Essex Co., 10 Cush. 304, it was ruled that, if a several right of fishery on the land of another can be acquired by prescription, it must be by an actual and exclusive occupation and enjoyment of the fishery, adverse to the riparian proprietor, and continued for at least twenty years.]

3 [See Watkins *v.* Peck, 13 N.H. 360; Edson *v.* Munsell, 10 Allen, 568; Erle J., in Rochdale Canal Co. *v.* Radcliffe, 18 Q.B. 287, 315; Nelson *v.* Butterfield, 21 Maine, 234, 235; Melvin *v.* Whiting, 13 Pick. 184; Reimer *v.* Stuber, 20 Penn. St. 458, 463.]

maintain the presumption of a grant, by any lapse of time, and continuance of possession, if death should intervene in every period of twenty years; so that a man and his ancestors, might have the uninterrupted use and enjoyment of an easement, or privilege, for a century, without acquiring any right; which cannot be maintained. It is admitted, that no authority has been found, to sanction such a doctrine, and very clearly it cannot be supported on principle."[1] [So in Lamb *v.* Crossland,[2] it was ruled, that if the ancestors die before the title by prescription is perfected, and the estate descends to minor heirs, the prescription is suspended during the minority.]

[§ 239 *a.* But the present current of authority, and the general force of argument on principle, policy, and convenience, appear to be adverse to the doctrine of a suspension of the time of prescription by the intervention of a disability after that time has once begun to run. In a late case[3] in New Hampshire, Bell J. said, "Under the Statute of Limitations it has always been held, that after the statute has once commenced to run, no intervening disability will defeat the ordinary limitation arising from twenty years' adverse possession.[4] The same rule seems to us proper to be applied in case of disabilities arising to the owners of real estate, after the user and enjoyment of an easement have been commenced under a claim of right, with the knowledge of the owner, and without question or opposition on his part. Such intervening disabilities should not defeat the presumption of title resulting from twenty years' possession."[5] In Tracy *v.* Atherton,[6]

[1] Melvin *v.* Whiting, 13 Pick. 184. [See Watkins *v.* Peck, 13 N.H. 360.]

[2] [4 Rich. 536.]

[3] [Wallace *v.* Fletcher, 30 N.H. 434.]

[4] [Stowell *v.* Zouch, Plowd. 353; Doe *v.* Jesson, 6 East, 80; Eager *v.* Commonwealth, 4 Mass. 182; Jackson *v.* Johnson, 5 Cowen, 74; Griswold *v.* Butler, 3 Conn. 227; McFarland *v.* Stone, 17 Vt. 165; Mercer *v.* Selden, 1 How. (U.S.) 37; Dekay *v.* Darrah, 2 Green (N.J.) 294; Den *v.* Richards, 3 Green (N.J.) 347; Fewell *v.* Collins, 3 Brevard, 286; Allis *v.* Moore, 2 Allen, 306; Angell, Lim. §§ 477–480; Tracy *v.* Atherton, 36 Vt. 503, 515–517.]

[5] [Tyler *v.* Wilkinson, 4 Mason, 402; 2 Greenl. § 545; Cross *v.* Lewis, 2 B. & C. 686; Best, Presump. 89; Reimer *v.* Stuber, 20 Penn. St. 463; Tracy *v.* Atherton, 36 Vt. 503; Mebane *v.* Patrick, 1 Jones (N.C.) 23. The case of Watkins *v.* Peck, 13 N.H. 360, has been supposed to be adverse to the doctrine of the text, and it was so considered in Tracy *v.* Atherton, 36 Vt. 503, 518; but this is denied by Bell J., in Wallace *v.* Fletcher, 30 N.H. 434, 449–451, where he says, "In the present case, the period of twenty years, necessary to give a title by presumption of a grant or title, commenced in 1807,

[6] [Tracy *v.* Atherton, 36 Vt. 503. See per Peck J., in Perrin *v.* Garfield, 37 Vt. 311, 312.]

Poland C.J. said, "In our judgment rights to easements acquired by long possession ought to stand on the same ground as rights by possession in lands. The real principle underlying the right, is the same precisely on which the Statute of Limitations stands. In the first place, it is presumed that one man would not quietly submit to have another use and enjoy his property for so great a length of time unless there existed some good reason for his doing so, and that after allowing it for so long, he should not call upon him to show his right or title, when it may not be in his power to do so; and in the second place, it is a rule of policy, adopted in support of long and uninterrupted possession. It is important, too, in another view, that the doctrine of the law in the two cases should harmonize, that the people may not be misled and perplexed by having the law different ways upon subjects which in reason, and upon principle should be the same. The requisites of a possession by which an easement is acquired, as generally laid down in the books, are, that it should be adverse under a claim of right, exclusive, continuous, and uninterrupted. These are exactly the requisites of a possession of lands to give title under the Statute of Limitations against the proprietor. But it is sometimes said that the possession must be with the acquiescence of the owner. But this is the same as saying that the possession must be *uninterrupted.* If the owner does not interrupt the possession in any way, he does acquiesce as far as is needful in order to make the possession effectual against him."—"We are satisfied, that by the settled construction of the Statute of Limitations, a disability, in order to prevent the operation of the statute must exist when the right *first accrues*, and if the analogy of the statute in this respect is to be followed, it must govern this case;" which was a claim to an incorporeal right on the ground of an adverse use and enjoyment during the period of the Statute of Limitations, although after the time had begun to run the disability of infancy in the owner of the land in which

and ended in 1828, after which time the right was denied, and its exercise interfered with. From 1822 to 1826, the title of the defendant's estate, in which the easement was claimed, was in the minor children of Kelso, the former owner, then deceased, and their interest was sold in 1826, by their guardian, by license from the Court of Probate. The disability of the owners did not extend to the end of the twenty years, but ceased two years previously. That case was not decided in Watkins *v.* Peck, but was in express terms left undecided. The case then before the Court did not require the decision of any question on the subject."]

the right was claimed, had intervened. The learned Judge adds, "We see no reason why the analogy of the statute should not be followed in this particular, if in any, as it stands upon the same reason and is governed by the same policy." And so the Court decided that the adverse use of an incorporeal right, having once commenced, will not be interrupted by the descent of the servient tenement to an infant. The same doctrine is maintained in North Carolina in Mebane *v.* Patrick,[1] which was a claim by the plaintiff that he had acquired a right of way by use. After the use began, the owner of the servient estate became insane. It was decided that as the disability did not exist at the time of the commencement of the plaintiff's adverse use, it did not prevent the use ripening into a right. The Court say, "Such being the law as to the Statute of Limitations, it follows it must be so, in regard to prescriptions also." The same view of the law seems to have been taken by Merrick J., in Currier *v.* Gale.[2] Having in that case stated the principle as established in Massachusetts, that if the owner of an estate is subject to no disability when he is disseised thereof, and, after a lapse of time sufficient to enable him to protect his rights, a disability intervenes, it will not delay or postpone the operation of the Statute of Limitations, the learned Judge adds, "The same rule must for the same reason prevail in relation to easements or other rights acquired by prescription, or to titles established and confirmed by open, adverse possession." This statement of the rule was quoted without disapprobation in Edson *v.* Munsell[3] by Gray J., who added, "Upon the same ground it has been held in other States, that a prescription cannot be interrupted by a disability which does not come into existence until after the time has begun to run."[4]]

[1] [Mebane *v.* Patrick, 1 Jones (N.C.) 23.]

[2] [Currier *v.* Gale, 3 Allen, 328.]

[3] [10 Allen, 566.]

[4] [Neither in Currier *v.* Gale nor in Edson *v.* Munsell is any allusion made by the Court to the case of Melvin *v.* Whiting, 13 Pick. 184, cited and stated in the preceding section. But this latter case is noticed by Poland, C.J. in Tracy *v.* Atherton, 36 Vt. 518, and he says of it, "The case seems to have been very little examined by Court or counsel; no reasons are given, or authorities cited." And he adds, that under the Statute of Limitations of Massachusetts, it is fully settled that no disability avoids its operation, unless it exist at the time the right *first accrues.* The decision of Melvin *v.* Whiting "must therefore have been made in entire disregard of the analogy of the statute, in this respect, and we think it was made by giving undue importance to the fictitious theory of a lost grant." It may be further added, that no allusion whatever is made in that case to the effect of an intervening disability under the Statute of Limitations.]

7. *Extinction of Presumed Water Rights.*

§ 240. First, the loss or extinguishment of a prescriptive or presumed right to a Watercourse, may be inferred from a non-user for such length of time, as that which created it.[1] It is laid down by Bracton, that an incorporeal right may be both acquired by long enjoyment, and lost by disuse and neglect.[2] "Seeing," says Domat, "a service may be acquired by prescription, with *much more* reason may a freedom from a service be acquired in the same way. Thus, he who had a right to water, both by day and night, loses the use of it in the night-time, if he lets it prescribe."[3] This is the well-settled doctrine of the Common Law, and it has been expressly held, that ancient windows, which have been discontinued for twenty years, lose their former right.[4]

[1] 3 Kent, 448; Shields *v.* Arndt, 3 Green (N.J.) Ch. 234; [Prescott *v.* Phillips, 2 Evans's Poth. Obl. 136; Hillary *v.* Walker, 12 Ves. 239, 265; Hazard *v.* Robinson, 3 Mason, 275, 276. In Farrar *v.* Cooper, 34 Maine, 399 Shepley C.J. said, "A right acquired by use may be lost by non-user. Such appears to have been the rule of the Civil Law, which was declared to be the Common Law by Bracton, and it has been repeatedly recognized as such by judicial decisions. A non-user of twenty years is regarded as presumptive evidence of an abandonment and extinction of the right. This presumption may be rebutted by proof of facts inconsistent with such a conclusion;" as that the owner of the easement did not intend to abandon it, but merely suspended the use of it. Pardessus, Traité des Servitudes, 458.]

[2] Bract. lib. 4, c. 38, § 3.

[3] Domat's Civil Law, b. 1, t. 12, s. 1. Libertatem servitutum usu capi posse verius est. Dig. l. 4. Itaque si cum tibi servitutem deberem, ne mihi puta liceret, altius ædificare, et per statutum tempus altius ædificatum habuero sublata erit servitus. Dig. de servit. præd. urb. Si is qui nocturnam aquam habet, interdiu per constitutum ad admissionem tempus usus fuerit, amisit nocturnam servitutem, qua usus non est. Idem est in eo qui certis horis aquæ-ductus habens, aliis usus fuerit, nec ulla parte earum horarum. Dig. l. 10, quemad. servit. amitte. [According to the later Roman law, a continued non-exercise of a servitude does of itself no longer constitute a limitation; so that in all servitudes, personal as well as prædial, the right is not lost by non-user, unless either the proprietor of the servient thing acquires its freedom from the servitude by prescription (*usucapio libertatis*), or a third party acquires the thing as a free property by prescription. 1 Kauff. Mack. 351.]

[4] Lawrence *v.* Obee, 3 Campb. 514, [2 Chitty Pl. (16th Am. ed.) 480. It is said by Chancellor Kent that the mere non-user of an easement, for twenty years, will afford a presumption of a release or extinguishment, but not a very strong one, in a case unaided by circumstances; but if there has been in the mean time, some act done by the owner of the land charged with the easement, inconsistent with or adverse to the existence of the right, a release or extinguishment of the right will be presumed. 3 Kent, 448; 2 Evans's Pothier, 136; Wright *v.* Freeman, 5 H. & John. 477; Knight *v.* Heaton, 22 Vt. 480; Farrar *v.* Cooper, 34 Maine, 394. Very few cases of extinction of water rights will be found to stand upon the mere fact of non-user.]

§ 241. It has been said by a learned Judge (C.J. Abbott), that, "One of the general grounds of presumption, is the existence of a state of things which may be most reasonably accounted for, by supposing the matter presumed. Thus, the long enjoyment of a right of way, by A. to his house or close, over the land of B., which is a prejudice to the land, may most reasonably be accounted for, by supposing a grant of such right, by the owner of the land; *and if such right appear to have existed in ancient times, a long forbearance to exercise it, which must be inconvenient and prejudicial to the owner of the house or close, may most reasonably be accounted for, by supposing a release of the right.* In the first class of cases, therefore, a *grant* of the right, and in the latter, a *release* of it, is presumed."[1] The language of the Court of Appeals, of Maryland, is to the same effect. "If, therefore," say they, "the adverse user of a right of way over the lands of another, for twenty years, shall be a sufficient foundation to presume, that the right originated in a grant, it must follow, upon every principle, that the user of the right may be extinguished, by presuming a release of it, for the purpose of quieting possession." In this case, the presumption of a release was strongly fortified by the circumstance, that the parties to whom the right of way in question was originally granted, and those claiming under them, had used another and distinct route over the defendant's land.[2]

§ 242. By virtue of this doctrine, if an ancient ditch has at one end opened into a watercourse, and the owner of a mill on the stream has kept the opening at the end of the ditch closed, without interruption, for twenty years, the mill-owner will have a right to keep it closed, and the owner of the land on the ditch

[1] Doe *v.* Hilder, 2 B. & Ald. 791.

[2] Wright *v.* Freeman, 5 H. & John. 467. In Hoffman *v.* Savage, 15 Mass. 180, the action was in case for interrupting a right of way, claimed by the plaintiff, which had been assigned to a dowager, over land of her husband; and the interruption complained of, was the erection of a wooden building, upon the soil where the way was before used. The injury complained of, was committed more than twenty years before the commencement of the suit, and the adverse occupation continued from the time of bringing the action. This, the Court held, would be presumptive evidence of an extinguishment, or grant of the privilege to the tenant of the land. The non-user of a highway for twenty years, is *primâ facie* proof of a release of the public, to the owner of the soil; and, therefore, where bars across a highway had been kept up by the owner of the soil about *ninety years*, it was held, that evidence of this fact was admissible to prove an extinguishment of the public right. Beardslee *v.* French, 7 Conn. 125; [Knight *v.* Heaton, 22 Vt. 480.] See also 2 Bay (S.C.) 280.

would not be justified in re-opening the communication; although it might appear, that the communication between the ditch and the watercourse was ancient; and so where the owner of a mill worked by a ground-shot wheel, at a low head of water, altered the wheel to a breast-shot wheel, which required a high head of water; and after that, for twenty years and more, discontinued the use of the breast-shot wheel, and resumed the use of the ground-shot wheel, the discontinuance, it was held, caused the mill-owner to lose his right to the higher head of water.[1]

§ 243. As an enjoyment for the *full period* of twenty years, is necessary to found a presumption of a grant, the general rule is, that there must be a similar non-user, to raise the presumption of a release.[2] In Corning *v.* Gould, in New York,[3] Mr. J. Cowen, in giving the judgment of the Court, considered it perfectly well settled, that in order to make out an effectual answer to a claim upon the ground of a simple non-user of an easement, the enjoyment, and all acts of enjoyment, must have totally ceased for the same length of time, that was necessary to create the original presumption. "We are to inquire first," says he, "was the way used continuously and adversely for twenty years? If so, the presumptive title becomes vested. Secondly, has the use, then, been *altogether discontinued for twenty years?* If not, there is no abandonment."[4] In Massachusetts, a mill privilege cannot be considered as abandoned or extinguished by disuse, until such disuse, entire and complete, has continued for twenty years;[5] and in Pennsylvania, as it takes *twenty-one* years' adverse enjoyment, to acquire a right,[6] so it takes twenty-one years' non-user to extinguish it, and twenty years alone is insufficient.[7]

§ 243 *a*. But it seems now to be well understood, that courts are not to proceed on the ground that as twenty years' user, in the absence of an express grant, is necessary for the acquisition

[1] Drewett *v.* Sheard, 7 C. & P. 465.

[2] 3 Kent, 448; Curtis *v.* Jackson, 13 Mass. 507, 514. [In Curtis *v.* Jackson, Wilde J. said, "But it may be doubted, if such claim and user for twenty years, previous to 1790, be sufficient to support the presumption of a grant, whether the non-claim and non-user since that time [being over twenty years] be not sufficient to rebut such a presumption."]

[3] Corning *v.* Gould, 16 Wend. 531.

[4] Corning *v.* Gould, 16 Wend. 531; [Mississippi Central Railroad Co. *v.* Mason, 51 Miss. 234, 246, et seq.]

[5] Per Shaw C.J., in Hurd *v.* Curtis, 7 Met. 94. [See Pillsbury *v.* Moore, 44 Maine, 155; Williams *v.* Nelson, 23 Pick. 141; Dyer *v.* Depui, 5 Wharton, 584, 597; Mowry *v.* Sheldon, 2 R.I. 369, 378.]

[6] See ante, § 209.

[7] Dyer *v.* Depui, 5 Wharton, 584.

of an easement, so twenty years' *cesser* of the use, in the absence of any express release, is necessary for its loss. But as an express release of the easement would destroy it at any moment, so the *cesser* of use, coupled with *any act clearly indicative of an intention to abandon the right*, would have the same effect without reference to time. It is not so much the duration of the *cesser*, as the nature of the act done by the grantee of the easement, or of the adverse act acquiesced in by him, and the intention in him which either the one or the other indicates, which are material for the consideration of the jury. The period of time is only material as one element from which the grantee's intention to retain or abandon his easement may be inferred against him.[1]

§ 244. The doctrine that the disuse of an easement, acquired by prescription, *must* have continued for the same length of time, which was required for its creation, has been held not to apply to *ancient lights*. In Moore *v.* Rawson,[2] Abbott C.J., in delivering his judgment, said, "It seems to me, that if a person entitled to ancient lights, pulls down his house, and erects a blank wall in the place of a wall, in which there had been windows, and suffers that blank wall to remain for a considerable period of time, it lies upon him, at least to show, that at the time when he so erected the blank wall, and thus apparently abandoned the windows, which gave light and air to the house, that was not a perpetual, but a temporary abandonment of the enjoyment."[3] Littledale J. said, "I think that if a party does any act to show that he abandons his right for the benefit of that light and air,

[1] Per Lord C.J. Denman, in Regina *v.* Chorley, 12 Ad. & E. N.S. 515. [See Dana *v.* Valentine, 5 Met. 8. Any act, which is clearly indicative of the intention to abandon an easement, will be evidence to that effect, and duration of non-user is not a necessary element in the inquiry. Phear on Rights of Water, 109; Co. Litt. 114, b; Liggins *v.* Inge, 7 Bing. 682; Moore *v.* Rawson, 3 B. & C. 332; Wallis *v.* Harrison, 4 M. & W. 538; Regina *v.* Chorley, 12 Q.B. 515; Stokoe *v.* Singers, 8 El. & Bl. 31. Though, from the time of the cessation to use a mill privilege, twenty years may not have elapsed, prior to its being overflowed and destroyed by a dam below, still an abandonment of the privilege may be presumed, if its proprietor, witnessing that erection of the dam and of expensive works upon it, and knowing that it must destroy his privilege above, makes no effort or remonstrance to prevent it, or claim of remuneration for it, within the residue of the twenty years. Farrar *v.* Cooper, 34 Maine, 394.]

[2] Moore *v.* Rawson, 3 B. & C. 332. [See 2 Chitty Pl. (16th Am. ed.) 480; Dyer *v.* Sandford, 9 Met. 395, 402; Taplin *v.* Jones, 8 H.L. Cas. 290; Perkins *v.* Dunham, 3 Strobh. 224.]

[3] [In Stokoe *v.* Singers, 8 El. & Bl. 36, Crompton J. said, "Abbott C.J. seems rather to be making a remark on the effect, as evidence, of erecting the blank wall, than laying down a rule of law."]

which he once had, he may lose his right in a much less period than twenty years;" and Bayley and Holroyd JJ. were of the same opinion. It was, however, urged, in the subsequent case of Bridges *v.* Blanchard,[1] that, as the party could only acquire the right by twenty years' enjoyment, it ought not to be lost, without disuse for the same period; and that, as enjoyment for such length of time is necessary for the presumption of a grant, there must be a similar non-user, to raise a presumption of a release. All this reasoning, said Mr. J. Littledale, might well apply to a right of common, or of a way; but that there was a material difference between the mode of acquiring such rights, and a right to light or air; the latter was acquired by mere *occupancy;* whereas, the former could only be acquired by *user.* A way, said he, over the lands of another, can only be used in the first instance, with the consent, express or implied, of the owner; and a party using the way, without such consent, would be a wrongdoer; but with respect to light, it is otherwise, as every man may erect even on the extremity of his land, a building, with as many windows as he pleases.

[§ 244 *a.* In the case of Stokoe *v.* Singers,[2] windows had been closed for twenty years, and nothing had been done in the mean time on the adjoining land; and then, just as the other owner was thinking of building on the adjoining land, the proprietor re-opened these long-closed windows, and it was left to the jury to say whether or not by the long disuse, the person who owned the windows and who had possessed this easement of light had induced the person who was commencing the building to expend any money, and to place himself in a worse position by reason of such expenditure? That was held to be a right and proper direction. It has been always held to be of considerable importance, that a person in possession of a certain right, and leaving the right wholly unused for a long period of time, and having given so far an encouragement to others to lay out their money, on the assumption of that right not being used, should not be allowed at any period of time to resume his former right, to the damage and injury of those who themselves have acquired a right of user which the recurrence to this long-disused easement will interfere with.[3]]

[1] Bridges *v.* Blanchard, 1 Ad. & Ell. 356.

[2] [8 El. & Bl. 31.]

[3] [Per Sir W. Page Wood V.C., in Crossley *v.* Lightowler, L.R. 3 Eq. Cas. 292, 293.]

§ 245. If the doctrine, that a *prescriptive* right to light may be lost by a non-user, for a period less than twenty years, will not apply to a right of common, or of a way, *a fortiori*, it will not apply to a *natural* watercourse. Yet, Mr. C.J. Tindal, in delivering the judgment, in Liggins *v.* Inge,[1] inquires, "Suppose a person who formerly had a mill upon a stream, should pull it down, and remove the works, with the intention never to return, could it be that the owner of other land adjoining the stream, might not erect a mill, and employ the water so relinquished; or that he should be compellable to pull down his mill, if the former mill-owner should afterwards change his determination, and wish to rebuild his own?" He answers, that, in such a case, "it would, undoubtedly, be a subject of inquiry by a jury, whether he had completely abandoned the use of the stream, or left it for a temporary purpose only." The learned Judge here proceeds upon the assumption, that a right to a particular use of the water, may be acquired by mere *occupancy;* that the riparian proprietor who *first* occupies, gains rights which he would not otherwise have; and then he says "there is nothing unreasonable in holding, that a right which is gained by occupancy, may be lost by abandonment." But we have already had occasion to show it to be clearly settled in England, that no appropriation, except for such a period as will confer an easement (twenty years), can diminish the *natural* rights of the other riparian proprietors, along the course of the stream;[2] and every riparian proprietor, who claims a right, either to throw the water back above his land, or to diminish the quantity of water, which is to descend below, must, in the words of Sir J. Leach,[3] "in order to maintain his claim, either prove an actual grant or license from the proprietors affected by his operations, or must prove an uninterrupted enjoyment of twenty years."[4]

§ 246. It has been considered by Courts in America, that Mr. Justice Littledale, when he says,[5] that when twenty years might be necessary to extinguish the right to a common or way, evidently did not advert to the distinction between a mere non-user, and a *positive obstruction;* and that all the judges lay great stress

[1] Liggins *v.* Inge, 8 Bing. 693.

[2] Ante, §§ 130–136.

[3] In Wright *v.* Howard, 1 Sim. & Stu. 190.

[4] See also Menzies *v.* Breadalbane, 3 Bligh, N.S. 414.

[5] See ante, § 244.

on the possible injury to purchasers of the adjoining premises, who might come in on the faith of an appearance of one. In Corning *v.* Gould,[1] the Court were entirely at a loss to see why Littledale J. should have hinted, in Moore *v.* Rawson, that twenty years' *obstruction* might be necessary to extinguish or bar a way[2] or common, more than a servitude of light to an ancient window. They reason, that both are acquired by the same prescriptive term; and both are, when acquired, equally in the class of incorporeal hereditaments; and the actual deception upon a purchaser, is an important ground of decision.[3]

§ 247. The rule of the Civil Law, most undoubtedly is, that the party himself, to whom *any* sort of servitude is due, may, *short of the period of prescription*, effect its extinguishment, by merely suffering the erection of obstructions of a permanent and solid kind, such as edifices and walls; and *a fortiori*, if the act of obstruction be done by the party to whom the servitude is due.[4] The rule of Common Law, as laid down by Kent, is, "There must be a total cessation of the exercise of the right to the servitude, during the entire time necessary to raise the presumption of extinguishment, or there must have been some permanent obstacle permitted to be raised against it, and which absolutely destroyed its exercise. If the act which prevents the servitude, be incompatible with the nature or exercise of it, and be by the party to whom the servitude is due, it is sufficient to extinguish it; and if it be extinguished for a moment, it is gone for ever."[5] Again,

[1] Corning *v.* Gould, 16 Wend. 531.

[2] [See Bowen *v.* Team, 6 Rich. 298, 305. An interruption of a right of way must have been acquiesced in by the owner of the easement before he can be affected by it. "If the right be once established by clear and distinct evidence of enjoyment, it can be defeated only by distinct evidence of interruptions acquiesced in." Harvie *v.* Rogers, 3 Bligh, N.S. 440, 447; Pillsbury *v.* Moore, 44 Maine, 154; Cuthbert *v.* Lawton, 3 M'Cord, 195.]

[3] [Where the defendants erected, on their own premises, a permanent obstruction to a navigable drain leading from a river through the defendant's premises to the plaintiff's close, it was held, that the plaintiff was entitled to recover in an action for the obstruction, although the portion of the drain which passed through the plaintiff's close had for sixteen years been completely choked up with mud. Bower *v.* Hill, 1 Bing. N.C. 549.]

[4] 3 Kent, 448. When neither a *dies ad quem* nor a *conditio resolutiva* has been specified by agreement, or by law, with respect to the termination of servitudes, they will become extinct by renunciation (*remissio*), on the part of the entitled party, which may be either express or implied. 1 Kauff. Mack. 350. And see Dig. 8, 6, 5; Toullier's Droit, Civil Français, tome iii. n. 673; Répertoire de Jurisprudence par Merlin, tit. "Servitude," in which that article is composed with great care. Civil Code of Louisiana, Art. 815, 816; Haight *v.* Morris Aqueduct (Proprietors of), 4 Wash. C.C. 601.

[5] 3 Kent, 449; Farrar *v.* Cooper, 34 Maine, 394.

says he, "it is a wholesome and wise qualification of the rule, considering the extensive and rapid improvements that are everywhere making upon real property."[1]

§ 248. The great American case on this head, and the one on which the learned author above referred to, founds his doctrine, is that of Taylor *v.* Hampton, in South Carolina.[2] In that case, General Wade Hampton, the defendant, had purchased of Mr. Charles Pinckney, in 1807, 115 acres of land, with a mill-pond, dam, and mill in full operation, which continued till 1814. The pond flowed the land of the plaintiff; and there was no dispute that the defendant had a right to this flow, as a servitude by prescription. In 1814, a new mill was erected by the defendant, above the place where the old mill stood, upon which the water of the old mill flowed; wherefore the lower dam was cut, the water let off, and its use as a mill abandoned. This dam was, however, immediately repaired, and the water raised, occasionally, for the purpose of flowing rice; but in the main, the plaintiff's land was eased of the former flow, from 1814 to 1823, when the upper mill was burned down, and the old mill was rebuilt in the former place; the water being again permanently raised, and the flow resumed over the plaintiff's land. The verdict being for the plaintiff, in a suit for that injury, on a motion for a new trial, Nott J. delivered the opinion of the Court. He stated the main question to be, whether the erection of the upper mill, the existence and enjoyment of that, being incompatible with the use of the other, by means of this pond, did not extinguish the right of flow formerly held by the defendant. After looking extensively into the learning of the Civil and the Common Law, in respect to the extinguishment of servitudes, he comes to the conclusion, that it did. He shows that the act of the party entitled to the servitude, is to be taken strongly against him; and not only by the Civil Law, but by the Common Law, and analogous doctrines of our Courts of Equity, it shall be held to work an extinguishment, where the same circumstances, were they the result of the law, or of inevitable accident, would be a mere suspension. "Where," says the learned Judge, "a right is suspended by the act of God, as by the drying up of the spring, it will revive again, if the spring chance to flow; but if it be

[1] [Mississippi Central Railroad Co. *v.* Mason, 51 Miss. 254, 255.]

[2] Taylor *v.* Hampton, 4 McCord (S.C.) 96.

suspended by the act of the party, as by building a house or wall, it would not be restored, even though the obstacle should be removed by a stroke from heaven." It appears in the course of the opinion, that the plaintiff had purchased the land flowed, intermediate to the erection of the upper mill, and the restoration of the lower pond, perhaps in 1817, though, by the statement of the case (probably a misprint), it seems to have been 1807. On this, the Judge proceeds, "I think it not unimportant, that the present plaintiff was a purchaser for a *bonâ fide* consideration, at the time when the defendant had thus proclaimed to the world, that the privilege which he now claims, was useless, and even incapable of being enjoyed by him."[1]

§ 249. The learned Judge in the above case, adopts as one illustration, the rule as above laid down, in respect to the extinguishment of a prescriptive right to ancient lights, and says, "Suppose a person to be the owner of a house with ancient lights, which no person has a right to obstruct. If he erect a house, or put up a wall, directly covering his windows, has he not extinguished his light, as effectually as if he had blown out his candle? Surely, then, it would amount to a license to his neighbor, to put a similar building on his adjoining lot. Suppose A. to have a right of way over the land of B. If he erect a house on his own land, in such a manner as to obstruct the passage into the lands of B., does he not effectually destroy his right of way? Can he claim a right, the enjoyment of which he has rendered impossible by his own act?" Again "suppose," says he, "in the case before us, the defendant, instead of purchasing a mill-pond, with the right of flowing the plaintiff's land, had purchased arable land, with a right of way to haul away his crop. If he had erected the mill which he now has, and thrown the whole of his land under water, by converting it into a pond, would he not have destroyed his right of way?" The learned Judge considered the question before him one of great public interest, and that it was time it should be settled upon some known and fixed principles.

§ 250. The doctrine, and the reasoning in the above case of Taylor *v.* Hampton, was deliberately considered and adopted by the Supreme Court of New York, in the case of Corning *v.* Gould;[2]

1 [See the discussion of this subject and cases cited, post, § 385; Mississippi Central Railroad Co. *v.* Mason, 51 Miss. 234, 246 et seq., 356.]

2 Corning *v.* Gould, 16 Wend. 531.

a case in which it was expressly held, that the encroachment by one party upon a *way*, held in common, by building part of the wall of a house upon a portion of it, and enclosing another portion, by a fence, work an *extinguishment*, by operation of law; especially where the other party sells his interest after such acts done, and the purchaser, on his part, acquiesces in, and confirms what has been done; that where a party relinquishes the enjoyment of an easement or servitude, it lies with him to show an *intention to resume* the use of it within a *reasonable time;* and where there are no circumstances intimating the suspension to be *temporary only*, a *bona fide* purchaser will be protected in the enjoyment of the property, *as it appeared* at the time of his purchase.

§ 251. The same doctrine was discussed by the Supreme Court of Massachusetts, in Dyer *v.* Sandford,[1] which was an action on the case, for damage alleged to have been done by the defendant, in erecting a house on his own land, in such a manner, as to obstruct the light and air which the plaintiff was entitled to through his staircase window. This was not claimed as a right by prescription for light and air through an ancient window, but as a right reserved in a deed from Nathaniel T. Tilden, administrator of the estate of Christopher Tilden, under which the plaintiff claimed, to Thomas Davis, under whom the defendant claimed. 1. The defendant offered evidence, tending to show that Elizabeth Tilden, the widow of Christopher Tilden, having a right of dower in the estate, and being in the occupation, gave a license, by parol, to Thomas Davis, to erect a building, in such manner as to obstruct the air and light, in whole or in part; also that some obstructions were afterwards erected by persons in the occupation of the defendant's estate, extending to a period of ten or twelve years; and upon these facts, if established, contended that it ought to be submitted to the jury, to prove a license, by the owners of the plaintiff's estate, to the owners of the defendant's estate, to shut out and obstruct the light from entering said window; and that such license was not revocable by the plaintiff. He also contended, that, in fact, the easement in question, if it ever existed, had been lost by non-user, and cessation of enjoyment; and that, if not so extinguished, yet the right to light and air was

[1] Dyer *v.* Sandford, 9 Met. 395.

to such only as could be received, if the estate, derived by Davis from Tilden, and out of which the light was reserved, had been left open and unobstructed; which was the distance of about two feet from the window. Mr. C.J. Shaw, in giving the judgment of the Court, said, "We think there is a distinction between an executed license, to impede or obstruct an easement of this description, and an abandonment of the easement. It may well be maintained, on the authorities, that the owner of a dominant tenement, may make such changes in the use and condition of his own estate as, in fact, to renounce easement itself; and this may be relied on by the owner of the servient tenement as evidence of abandonment. So, if the owner of the dominant, grants a license to the owner of the servient tenement, to erect a wall which necessarily obstructs the enjoyment of the easement, and it is erected accordingly, it may amount to proof of an abandonment of the easement. It is not a release, because it is by parol. But it results from the consideration, that a license, when executed, is not revocable; and if the obstruction be permanent in its nature, it does, *de facto*, terminate the enjoyment of the easement. But the license is for the specific act only; and if, when executed, it is of such a nature, as, *de facto* to destroy the easement, but is only temporary in its nature, or limited in its terms, then, as the easement is not released, when the obstruction erected in pursuance of such specific license, is removed, the owner of the servient tenement cannot erect another obstruction of the same, or of a different kind, without a new license. But as, by the rules of law, an easement is an interest in land, to be acquired and released only by deed, as between the parties respectively, when it is contended, that the owner of the dominant tenement has voluntarily abandoned his right, so as, *de facto*, to withdraw the incumbrance from the servient tenement, without a release to its owner, the proof must go to this extent: *First*, that the acts relied on, were voluntarily done by the owner of the dominant tenement, or by his express authority; *secondly*, that such party was the owner of the inheritance, and had authority to bind the estate by his grant or release; and *thirdly*, that the acts are of so decisive and conclusive a character, as to indicate and prove his intent to abandon the easement.[1] Various illustrations might be given of such conclusive acts of abandon-

[1] Moore *v.* Rawson, 3 B. & C. 332, and 5 Dowl. & Ryl. 234.

ment, as when one takes down the building in which a window was placed, and erects on the site a permanent tenement, so constructed, as not to require, or even permit, a window similarly situated; or when one grants an express license to do acts on his own land, the necessary effect of which is, to take away or impair the easement permanently, and the acts are done accordingly.[1] In the present case, applying these principles to the subject, we are of opinion, that the evidence did not warrant the jury to find an extinguishment of the easement. The license in question, and the acts done under it, could not operate as a release, because not in writing; nor as an abandonment, because Elizabeth Tilden was not the owner of the inheritance, and had, at most, a right of dower in the premises, and the occupation, as guardian of her children, or otherwise; nor could it operate as proof of release, by adverse possession, because it had not continued a sufficient length of time."

§ 252. In the above case of Corning *v.* Gould, the Court consider that *abandonment* is a simple non-user of an easement and that, in order to make out an effectual answer to the claim upon that ground alone, the enjoyment must have actually ceased for the whole period of twenty years.[2] There are two writers, who incline with the Civil Law, to hold, that something beyond mere non-user for the prescriptive term is necessary to work an abandonment;[3] and undoubtedly it is so by the Common Law, where the easement has been created by *deed*. A distinction in this respect is recognized between an easement created by *deed*, and one which is created by *prescription*.[4] An easement to become extinguished by disuse, must have been acquired by use, and the doctrine of extinction by non-user does not apply to servitudes, or easements created by *deed*.[5] In the one case, mere disuse is

[1] Liggins *v.* Inge, 7 Bing. 682, and 5 Moore & P. 712.

[2] [3 Kent, 448, 449; Owen *v.* Field, 102 Mass. 114.]

[3] Evans's Poth. 136; 3 Kent, 448. [And see also Ward *v.* Ward, 7 Exch. 838; Wilder *v.* St. Paul, 12 Minn. 208; Hall *v.* McCaughey, 51 Penn. St. 43.]

[4] [See per Shepley C.J., in Farrar *v.* Cooper, 34 Maine, 400. "Where a grant has been by deed, it will require a clear non-user of the privilege for twenty years at least, to bar the claim on that ground." Leonard J., in Casler *v.* Shipman, 35 N.Y. 542; Hayford *v.* Spokesfield, 100 Mass. 491, 494. "A right acquired by deed is not lost by mere temporary non-user, without any act showing an intention to abandon it. The use of narrow flashboards, or none at all, is not an act showing an intention to surrender all further right." Per Wells J., Knapp *v.* Douglas Axe Co., 13 Allen, 1.]

[5] [Bannon *v.* Angier, 2 Allen, 128, 129; Barnes *v.* Lloyd, 112 Mass. 224, 231, and cases cited. It is difficult to conceive that the distinction stated in the text, which is clearly indicated in the cases, is

sufficient, but in the latter, there must not only be disuse by the owner of the land dominant, but there must be an actual adverse user by the owner of the land servient.[1] In White *v.* Crawford, in Massachusetts,[2] it was directly decided, that an express grant, or reservation of a right of way, was not lost by a non-user for twenty years. And again, in Arnold *v.* Stevens, in the same State,[3] it was held, that in the case of a grant by deed of the right to dig ore in the land of another, the mere neglect of the grantee, for *forty* years, to exercise the right, without any act of adverse enjoyment, on the part of the owner of the land, will not extinguish such right; and moreover, that the occupation and cultivation of the land, by the land-owner, during such period, are not evidence of adverse enjoyment of the right to dig the ore.

founded on any real difference in principle. The lost deed or grant which is presumed from twenty years' enjoyment, must be one that covers the right or privilege enjoyed. Before a deed or grant can be rightfully presumed, the facts must be made out with sufficient clearness to justify the inference or presumption to be made of a formal conveyance. It may well be that, in considering whether a deed or grant shall be presumed from the enjoyment proved, the fact, that the party, claiming that the presumption should be made, has after the period of enjoyment on which his claim is founded, ceased to use the right or privilege in controversy for an equal length of time, would generally have a strong bearing on the question whether the enjoyment had been adverse and under claim of right, and hence whether a case for the presumption had been made out. See Tracy *v.* Atherton, 36 Vt. 503; Perrin *v.* Garfield, 37 Vt. 304; ante, § 213. But unless a title acquired by twenty years' enjoyment, under circumstances from which the Court will infer a lost deed or grant, is to have the force and effect of a title founded on a deed actually produced, the language employed to express the thing presumed is illusory and deceptive. But if a title obtained by sufficient length of enjoyment is of equal force with one obtained by deed, then there seems to be no reason for giving greater effect to non-user in one case than in the other. Suppose, as between two parties, a title to an easement to have been established by the verdict of a jury or decision of the Court, on proof of adverse use and enjoyment, could that be held to be extinguished by a non-user which would not be regarded as sufficient to extinguish a title established on proof by a deed? Veghte *v.* Raritan &c. Co. 4 C. E. Green, 156.

Although it was decided in Massachusetts, in Bannon *v.* Angier, 2 Allen, 129, that a mere non-user of an easement created by deed, without proof of adverse enjoyment by the owner of land, is not sufficient evidence of an abandonment of the right, and the same is intimated in Jennison *v.* Walker, 11 Gray, 425; there is yet no decision in that State that an easement established by proof of long-continued use or enjoyment will be held extinguished on mere proof of disuse during the same length of time.]

1 Nitzell *v.* Paschall, 3 Rawle, 76; [Jewett *v.* Jewett, 16 Barb. 150; Farrar *v.* Cooper, 34 Maine, 394; Smyles *v.* Hastings, 24 Barb. 44; s.c. 22 N.Y. 217. An omission by the owner to make use of his right, does not impair his title or confer any right thereto upon another. It is not the non-user by the owner, but the adverse enjoyment by another, which destroys his right. Townsend *v.* McDonald, 2 Kernan, 381; Pillsbury *v.* Moore, 44 Maine, 155; Ames J. in Owen *v.* Field, 102 Mass. 90, 114.]

2 White *v.* Crawford, 10 Mass. 183.

3 Arnold *v.* Stevens, 24 Pick. 106.

The right to an easement, created by deed, may indeed remain dormant for a long time, and not be lost, and more especially, if from the nature of the right, and the express grant, it is apparent that it was not contemplated, that the owner of the right should exercise it at an early period.[1] In the language of Sutherland J., "The presumption of a grant against written evidence of title can *never* arise from the *mere neglect* of the owner to assert his right."[2]

[§ 252 *a*. Under a grant of a right to lay an aqueduct from a spring on the grantor's land to the grantee's land, together with the privilege of going on the grantor's land to repair the aqueduct, after one aqueduct has been laid, and afterwards taken up by the grantor, and the easement abandoned for thirty years, the grantee cannot lay a new aqueduct in a new direction over the grantor's land, although the construction of a railroad has made it impossible to lay it in the old place.[3] Bigelow J. said, "The evidence at the trial not only proved a non-user of the easement of laying and maintaining an aqueduct through the land now owned by the plaintiff by the owners of the dominant tenement for more than thirty years, but also established a possession and use of the servient estate by the plaintiff and his grantors during the same period, entirely inconsistent with and adverse to the existence of the easement. The right or easement in question having been acquired by grant and not by use, there might have been difficulty in showing a loss or extinguishment of it by proof of a mere omission during twenty years or more to exercise the right by an actual enjoyment of the easement. But the removal

[1] Yeakle *v.* Nace, 2 Wharton, 123; Butz *v.* Ihrie, 1 Rawle, 218.

[2] Doe *v.* Butler, 3 Wend. 149. [An easement passing by implication from a deed, as a necessary right of way, cannot be extinguished by non-user, but only by possession adverse to the easement for twenty years. Smyles *v.* Hastings, 22 N.Y. 217.] When the grantee of a market by *letters-patent* from the crown suffered another to erect a market in his neighborhood, and to use it for the space of twenty-three years, without interruption, it was adjudged, that such user operated as a bar to an action on the case, for a disturbance of his market. Holcroft *v.* Heel, 1 B. & P. 400; and see Yard *v.* Ford, 2 Wms. Saund. 175, and note.

[3] [Jennison *v.* Walker, 11 Gray, 423. The easement of an artificial waterway, which, by the terms of the instrument creating it, is established on a defined line over the servient tenement, cannot, without the consent of the land-owner, be changed in location to his other lands, either for the convenience of the owner of the servitude, or because of disturbance of the easement by the land-owner, or because the particular land subject to it has been taken by the public for a highway. Johnson *v.* Jaqui, 12 C. E. Green, 552, reversing the judgment of the vice-chancellor in the same case, reported 11 C. E. Green, 321. See also s.c. 10 C. E. Green, 210.]

by the plaintiff's grantors of the aqueduct logs which conveyed the water through the land now owned by the plaintiff rendered the enjoyment of the easement impossible. It was an act in its nature essentially adverse. It effectually hindered the exercise of the right, and operated to annihilate it. After this removal took place, no means were adopted to renew the enjoyment of the privilege. It was a continuous disturbance for more than thirty years. There was not only a non-user of the easement by the owners of the dominant estate, but united with it was a use of the servient estate inconsistent with and adverse to the existence of the easement during this period of time. Upon this proof, there was sufficient to justify the inference that the right originally conveyed by grant had been released and extinguished by a subsequent non-appearing deed."[1] In Ward *v.* Ward,[2] it was held, that an immemorial right of way is not lost by non-user for upwards of twenty years, the user having been discontinued merely by reason of the party's having had a more convenient way. Alderson B. in this case said, "The presumption of abandonment cannot be made from the mere fact of non-user. There must be other circumstances in the case to raise that presumption. The right is acquired by adverse enjoyment. The non-user, therefore, must be the consequence of something which is adverse to the user."]

[§ 252 *b*. The mere suspension of the exercise of a right to foul a stream is not sufficient to destroy the right, without some evidence of an intention to abandon it; but where dye-works situated on a stream had not been used for more than twenty years, and had been allowed to go to ruin, it was held, that any right of fouling the stream attached to them was lost.[3]]

§ 253. Secondly, another mode of extinguishment of servitude as incorporeal rights, whether acquired by actual or presumed

[1] [See Arnold *v.* Stevens, 24 Pick. 106.]

[2] [Ward *v.* Ward, 7 Exch. 838.]

[3] [Crossley *v.* Lightowler, L.R. 2 Ch. App. 478. This case was very fully discussed by Sir W. Page Wood V.C., in L. R. 3 Eq. Cas. 279, where it was held by him, that mere non-user, for less than twenty years of a privilege or easement to discharge dye-water into a stream is not of itself proof of abandonment, which is a conclusion to be drawn from all the circumstances; among which the lying by, and permitting others to incur expense in preparing to do that which, if continued uninterruptedly for twenty years, would destroy the easement, is a fact of great importance. But actual disuser of an easement of the above kind for twenty years, during which others have acquired adverse rights, destroys the right to the easement.]

grant, is that of *unity of possession;* the doctrine concerning which has been already considered.[1] With regard to its application to presumed grants, it has been adjudged in Connecticut, that an adverse enjoyment of water of one close, issuing from another, cannot exist where there is an unity of seisin and possession of both; and that, therefore, where A. and B. had adjoining closes, and A., having conducted water from B.'s close to his own, enjoyed it in a particular manner, for a less period than that limited for the right of entry upon land, and then conveyed his close in fee-simple to B.; and B., after a few days' possession, reconveyed it to A.; and after which, A. enjoyed the water, in the same manner he had done before for a period less, but, with the former period, making more than the time limited by the statute; it was held, that A., in consequence of such enjoyment of the water, so interrupted, acquired no right thereto by *user.*[2]

8. *Public Rights.*

§ 254. The doctrine of the acquisition of right to easements, by uninterrupted and adverse enjoyment, is not applicable to rights of a *public* nature; and all encroachments upon privileges, which are open to the whole community, though they may have been uninterruptedly prolonged, for a period exceeding twenty years, are, nevertheless, liable to be suppressed.[3] "No laches," said Ch. J. Parsons, "can be imputed to the Government, and against it no time runs so as to bar its rights."[4] It has been accordingly adjudged, in Great Britain, in Vooght *v.* Winch,[5] that twenty years' exclusive enjoyment of the water of a river, which is a *public highway,*[6] created no title. [A nuisance never can be legitimated.[7] Every continuation of the obstruction is in itself an offence.[8] The same principle applies to rivers which may be used for the floating of logs, rafts, &c., as to rivers which

[1] See ante, §§ 191–200.

[2] Manning *v.* Smith, 6 Conn. 289.

[3] Weld *v.* Hornby, 7 East, 195; Carter *v.* Murcot, 4 Burr. 2163; Thinmo *v.* Commonwealth, 4 H. & M. (Virg.) 57; Johnson *v.* Irwin, 3 S. & Rawle, 292; [Knox *v.* Chaloner, 42 Maine, 156.]

[4] Stoughton (Town of) *v.* Baker, 4 Mass. 522.

[5] Vooght *v.* Winch, 2 B. & Al. 662.

[6] As to what rivers are public highways, see post, Chap. XIII.

[7] [Woolrych's Law of Waters, 270, 271; Knox *v.* Chaloner, 42 Maine, 150, 156; Cowen J. in Renwick *v.* Morris, 3 Hill, 621; Coates *v.* New York, 7 Cowen, 558; People *v.* Cunningham, 1 Denio, 536; Commonwealth *v.* Upton, 6 Gray, 473, 476, 477.]

[8] [Renwick *v.* Morris, 7 Hill, 575.]

are navigable in the strict sense of the term, and for the same reason.[1]] So much regard, indeed, is paid to the interests of the great body politic, that if a river ever has been a public highway (even if it has not been used as such for the period of twenty years, and during the whole time has been in a condition inconsistent with the public use), the right of the public is not extinguished.[2] An act of the legislature is the only means by which the interest, which the public may have in a watercourse, can be transferred;[3] or the proof of such a very great length of enjoyment, as might furnish ground for the presumption of such a mode of transfer.[4]

1 [Knox *v.* Chaloner, 42 Maine, 150, 156. In this case it was held, that the settled doctrine that important individual rights, as against individuals, may be acquired and lost by adverse possession and enjoyment for a period of more than twenty years, does not apply to the rights of the public in a navigable river.]

2 Vooght *v.* Winch, ub. sup.; [Knox *v.* Chaloner, 42 Maine, 150. No accidental or intentional obstruction in a stream, not there in its natural state, will legally take from it its inherent and natural capability as a public highway. Treat *v.* Lord, 42 Maine, 552.]

3 [See Treat *v.* Lord, 42 Maine, 552.]

4 Vooght *v.* Winch, ub. sup.; Chalker *v.* Dickinson, 1 Conn. 382. In an action of trespass, for cutting down and removing a bridge over a navigable arm of the sea, alleged to be the property of the plaintiff, which bridge had been standing upwards of *fifty years*, the Court, in giving their opinion, said, "Public rights cannot be destroyed by long-continued encroachment; at least, the party who claims the exercise of any right, inconsistent with the free enjoyment of a public easement or privilege, must put himself on the ground of *prescription;* unless he has a grant or some valid authority, from the Government; and a right by prescription does not exist in the present case." Inhabitants of Arundel *v.* McCulloch, 10 Mass. 70.

www.ingramcontent.com/pod-product-compliance
Lightning Source LLC
LaVergne TN
LVHW090257210926
848480LV00001B/57